Across the Copperbelt

RELATED JAMES CURREY TITLES ON CENTRAL & SOUTHERN AFRICA

Roots of Rural Poverty in South Central Africa
Robin Palmer & Neil Parsons

Diamonds, Dispossession and Democracy in Botswana
Kenneth Good

Crossing the Zambezi:
The Politics of Landscape on a Central African Frontier
Jo-Ann McGregor

Circular Migration in Zimbabwe and Contemporary Sub-Saharan Africa
Deborah Potts

Remaking Mutirikwi:
Landscape, Water & Belonging in Southern Zimbabwe
Joost Fontein

The War Within:
New Perspectives on the Civil War in Mozambique, 1976-1992
Eric Morier-Genoud et al.

Faith, Power and Family:
Christianity and Social Change in French Cameroon
Charlotte Walker-Said

Manhood, Morality & the Transformation of Angolan Society:
MPLA Veterans & Post-war Dynamics
John Spall

Protestant Missionaries & Humanitarianism in the DRC:
The Politics of Aid in Cold War Africa
Jeremy Rich

The Politics of the Dead in Zimbabwe 2000–2015:
Bones, Rumours & Spirits★
Joost Fontein

Competing Catholicisms:
The Jesuits, the Vatican & the Making of Postcolonial French Africa★
Jean Luc Enyegue, SJ

★ forthcoming

Across the Copperbelt

Urban & Social Change in Central Africa's
Borderland Communities

Edited by
Miles Larmer, Enid Guene, Benoît Henriet,
Iva Peša & Rachel Taylor

 JAMES CURREY

James Currey
is an imprint of
Boydell & Brewer Ltd
PO Box 9, Woodbridge
Suffolk IP12 3DF (GB)
www.jamescurrey.com
and of
Boydell & Brewer Inc.
668 Mt Hope Avenue
Rochester, NY 14620–2731 (US)
www.boydellandbrewer.com

This book is based on research that is part of a project that has received funding from the European Research Council (ERC) under the European Union's Horizon 2020 research and innovation programme (grant agreement no: 681657): 'Comparing the Copperbelt: Political Culture and Knowledge Production in Central Africa'

A catalogue record for this book is available on request from the British Library

ISBN 978-1-84701-266-1 (James Currey paperback)

The publisher has no responsibility for the continued existence or accuracy of URLs for external or third-party internet websites referred to in this book, and does not guarantee that any content on such websites is, or will remain, accurate or appropriate

This publication is printed on acid-free paper

*To Grant Chisapa, Pierrot Monzi Kalonga, and
all the Copperbelt researchers who made this work possible*

Contents

Illustrations

Of Corporate Welfare Buildings and Private Initiative: Post-Paternalist Ruination and Renovation in a Former Zambian Mine Township
Christian Straube

From a Colonial to a Mineral Flow Regime: The Mineral Trade and the Inertia of Global Infrastructures in the Copperbelt
Hélène Blaszkiewicz

Houses Built on Copper: The Environmental Impact of Current Mining Activities on 'Old' and 'New' Zambian Copperbelt Communities
Jennifer Chibamba Chansa

The editors, contributors and publisher are grateful to all the institutions and persons listed in the illustration captions for permission to reproduce the materials in which they hold copyright. Every effort has been made to trace the copyright holders; apologies are offered for any omission, and the publisher will be pleased to add any necessary acknowledgement in subsequent editions.

Notes on Contributors

Hélène Blaszkiewicz holds a doctorate in geography from the University of Lyon. Her research focuses on trade and the differentiated uses of infrastructures networks which enable the circulations of things on the border between Zambia and the DR Congo. Her research interests also include African economic policies and industrialisation. She is currently a postdoctoral researcher at the University of Geneva (Switzerland).

Jennifer Chibamba Chansa holds a doctorate in African Studies and is currently a Postdoctoral Fellow at the University of the Free State in South Africa. She also holds a BA in History and Library and Information Studies from the University of Zambia, and an MA in African Studies from the University of Basel in Switzerland. Jennifer's research interests include mining, labour and environmental history, and African anthropology. Her PhD research focused on environmental pollution, management and regulation within Zambia's 'old' (Copperbelt) and 'new' (North-Western) mining regions. Jennifer's interest in the mining industry stems from her childhood experiences, having been born and raised in Mufulira town.

Hikabwa D. Chipande is Coordinator/Head of the African Union Sports Council at the headquarters in Yaoundé, Cameroon. He is also lecturer of sports studies in the School of Education at the University of Zambia. Chipande has written and published several journal articles and book chapters focusing on the political and social history of sport, particularly football in Africa. He has received several research grants, including the FIFA Joao Havelange Research Scholarship.

Donatien Dibwe dia Mwembu holds a doctorate in History (from the University of Laval in Quebec, Canada). He is Professor of History in the Department of Historical Sciences at the University of Lubumbashi. Since 1990, he has researched the social history of Haut-Katanga, particularly focusing on urban popular culture. In collaboration with Bogumil Jewsiewicki, he initiated the project 'Memories of Lubumbashi' of which he is the president of the local scientific committee. He is also the Director-Coordinator of the 'Observatory of Urban Change', the research centre at the University of Lubumbashi. He has published several important publications on the history of the region and other topics.

David M. Gordon, Professor in the Department of History at Bowdoin College (Brunswick USA), is interested in the history of Southern and Central African encounters with global forces over the last two centuries: Atlantic and Indian Ocean trading networks; British, Portuguese and Belgian colonialism; changing property regimes; and Christianity. His 2012 monograph, *Invisible Agents: Spirits in a Central African History* (Ohio University Press), considers the influence of Christian spirituality on historical agency in Northern Zambia. His recent publications about Central African kingdoms, warlordism, and prophetic movements have appeared in leading journals. Currently he is enriching this research by investigating the diffusion of art and material culture across South-Central Africa during the nineteenth century.

Enid Guene is a Research Associate in Cultural History at the University of Oxford, as part of the Comparing the Copperbelt project. She has a MA in African Studies from the University of Leiden. Her PhD at the University of Cologne focuses on historical processes of cultural and livelihood change among East African hunter-gatherers. Her current research, building on her MA thesis on cross-border migrations in the Copperbelt, focuses on cultural production and exchanges in the mining regions of Zambia and DR Congo.

Benoît Henriet is Assistant Professor in Global History at the Vrije Universiteit in Brussels, Belgium. After completing a doctorate on labour and power relations in a palm oil concession in The Belgian Congo at Université Saint-Louis in Brussels, he was a research associate in the ERC-funded Comparing the Copperbelt project at the University of Oxford, United Kingdom. He is interested in the history of agency, everyday life and local-global connections in (post)colonial Central Africa.

Rita Kesselring is a senior lecturer at the Chair of Social Anthropology, University of Basel, Switzerland. She currently works on new mining towns in Zambia's North-Western Province, making visible the interconnection between global extractivism, commodity trade and urban life at the site of resource extraction. Her monograph, *Bodies of Truth: Law, Memory and Emancipation* (Stanford Universtiy Press, 2017) is an ethnography on apartheid victims in South Africa and its globally entangled system of human rights abuses. She is also co-editor of the journal *Anthropology Southern Africa*.

Stephanie Lämmert is a researcher at the Center for the History of Emotions at the Max Planck Institute for Human Development in Berlin, Germany. Her current research deals with the history of romance and intimacies in twentieth-century Copperbelt towns and urban Tanzania and its implications for broader discourses of nation-building and 'modernity'. Stephanie holds a PhD in History from the European University Institute in Florence, Italy. She studied African Studies and History at Humboldt University Berlin, the University of Dar es Salaam and the University of Wisconsin at Madison. Her research interests include Eastern and Central African history of the twentieth century, the history of emotions, Swahili literature and popular culture, and intellectual histories from below.

Miles Larmer is Professor of African History at the University of Oxford and a Research fellow at the University of Pretoria. He has written extensively on the modern history of Central and Southern Africa. His most recent book, co-authored with Erik Kennes, is *The Katangese Gendarmes and War in Central Africa: Fighting their way home* (2016). He is the Principal Investigator on the ERC-funded project Comparing the Copperbelt: Political Culture and Knowledge Production in Central Africa.

Amandine Lauro is a Senior Research Associate of the Belgian National Fund for Scientific Research (FNRS) at the Free University of Brussels (ULB), where she teaches African, imperial and gender history. Her research focuses on gender, race and security in colonial Africa and more specifically in the Belgian Congo. She has published a book and several contributions on these issues. Her latest research about colonial psychology is part of a new research project on the history of colonial expertise and gender-based violence in the Belgian empire.

Duncan Money is a historian of Central and Southern Africa with a particular interest in the mining industry. He is currently a Researcher at the African Studies Centre Leiden and holds a DPhil in History from the University of Oxford. He is the co-editor of *Rethinking White Societies in Southern Africa* (Routledge, 2020) and is writing a book about white mineworkers on Zambia's Copperbelt provisionally titled *In a Class of their Own* (Brill, forthcoming).

Iva Peša is an Assistant Professor in Contemporary History at the University of Groningen in the Netherlands. Her current research is focused on the environmental and social history of the Zambian and Congolese Copperbelt. In 2014, she completed her PhD at Leiden University on patterns of social change in Mwinilunga District, North-Western Zambia (published as *Roads* *through Mwinilunga,* Brill, 2019). She has published on urban agriculture and environmental thought on the Copperbelt, cassava, labour migration and on the methodological struggles of using oral history.

Christian Straube is a Research Associate at the Max Planck Institute for Social Anthropology in Halle/Saale, Germany. He holds an MA in Chinese Studies, Political Science of South Asia and Macroeconomics from Heidelberg University. He completed his Doctorate in Social Anthropology, at Martin Luther University Halle-Wittenberg, Germany in July 2018. His research engagement has been focused on the Chinese diaspora in South-East Asia, China-Africa relations, the postcolony in Southern Africa and post-industrial ruination on Zambia's Copperbelt.

Rachel Taylor is a postdoctoral research associate at the University of Oxford, working on the Comparing the Copperbelt project, funded by the European Research Council. She has a PhD in African History from North-Western University (Evanston, USA) and an MA in Historical Research Methods from SOAS, University of London. She is particularly interested in how Africans build meaningful lives and communities in times of great social, political and economic change, and her research focuses on gender and labour in nineteenth- and twentieth-century East and Central Africa.

Acknowledgements

The development of this book project over the past five years would not have been possible without the sustained engagement and support of many dozens of researchers and colleagues. The majority of the chapters included in this book have their origins in papers presented at Comparing the Copperbelt project-related events between 2016 and 2019 (full details are available at: http://copperbelt.history.ox.ac.uk/events), as well as seminars held under project auspices at the University of Oxford, and many presentations at universities in Africa, Europe and the United States. These include conferences organised at the Nordic Africa Institute in December 2016; a panel organised at the European Social Science History conference held in Belfast in April 2018; panels in the Congo Research Network conference held in Oxford in April 2018; a major workshop held in Kitwe, Zambia in July 2018; panels organised at the European Conferences on African Studies held in Basel (June 2017) and Edinburgh (June 2019); a major workshop held at the University of Lubumbashi in July 2019; and a panel organised at the African Studies Association US conference held in Boston Mass. in November 2019. The editors and authors are grateful to all participants and audience members at these events, whose comments and questions helped improve both the individual chapters and the book as a whole.

The editors of this volume are, as a result, indebted to so many individuals and organisations that they cannot all be named here without us overstepping our word count beyond the breaking point of our patient publishers. Special mention is therefore necessarily reserved for the following. Dr Patience Mususa kindly hosted an early event for the project in Uppsala in December 2016. That event was co-organised by Prof. Benjamin Rubbers, whose own European Research Council (ERC)-funded 'WORKINMINING' project on the contemporary Copperbelt has run parallel to ours, and who has provided exceptional support and advice for our project researchers. Colleagues at the University of Lubumbashi, particularly Profs Donatien Dibwe dia Mwembu and Germain Ngoie Tshibambe, provided crucial intellectual guidance and practical assistance throughout the entire course of the project. Colleagues in the History Department of the University of

Zambia, particularly Profs Walima Kalusa and Bizeck J. Phiri and (elsewhere at UNZA) Dr Hikabwa Chipande, provided important guidance and played a key role in the 2018 Kitwe conference. At Copperbelt University Zambia (CBU), Profs John Lungu and Owen Sichone and Drs Robby Kapesa and Edna Kabala Litana were equally important in guiding research, helping to organise the Kitwe conference and hosting presentations on the project in 2017 and 2019.

The authors are grateful to the many archivists and librarians who enabled access to their collections. There are too many to mention by name here, but those at the ZCCM-IH archives in Ndola, whose records are cited in many chapters, warrant particular thanks. We are grateful for the permission to reproduce images and figures from the collections of the ZCCM-IH archives; the Royal Museum of Central Africa in Tervuren, Belgium; and Mission Press in Ndola, Zambia.

The editors would also like to thank their all colleagues at the University of Oxford's Faculty of History and African Studies Centre for their unstinting support of the project. Claire Phillips, the Project Administrator, has been central to its activities and achievements throughout. Dr Stephanie Lämmert played a vital role in the project's early development. As well as contributing an important chapter to this collection, she kindly provided our cover image. Drs Thomas Hendriks and Ramon Sarró co-organised the Congo Research Network conference held in Oxford in April 2018.

The editors would like to acknowledge the generous funding by the European Research Council of the project, Comparing the Copperbelt: Political Culture and Knowledge Production in Central Africa (Grant Agreement No. 681657), based at the University of Oxford from 2016 to 2021. European Research Council funding enabled the research carried out by the editors, the organisation of project seminars and conferences, and the Open Access publication of this volume.

Thanks are also due to the following individuals: Mostafa Abdelaal; Wale Adebanwi; Kate Alexander; Miguel Bandeira Jerónimo; Karin Barber; William Beinart; James Belich; Filip de Boeck; Gavin Bridge; Deborah Bryceson; Alexander Caramento; John Darwin; Nicole Eggers; Kristien Geenen; Jan-Bart Gewald; the late Patrick Harries; Marja Hinfelaar; Nancy Rose Hunt; Bogumil Jewsiewicki; Emery Kalema; Sarah Katz-Lavigne; Brian J. Leech; Reuben Loffman; Tom McNamara; Christian Müller; James Musonda; Joël Noret; Margaret O'Callaghan; David Pratten; Francesca Pugliese; Katrien Pype; Corey Ross; Jeff Schauer, Miyanda Simabwachi; Sishuwa Sishuwa; Sarah van Beurden; and Daniela Waldburger.

Finally, and most importantly, particular thanks are due to Grant Chisapa and Pierrot Monzi Kalonga, as well as the many other Congolese and Zambian researchers and translators who were vital to the research carried out by the editors and authors and to whom this book is dedicated. We recognise that, just as the history of the Central African Copperbelt rests on the unjust and unequal exploitation of the region's people, injustice and inequality remains ineluctable to the work of social historians and the production of knowledge about it. We hope that our modest efforts in documenting that history and acknowledging these historical and contemporary inequalities play a small role in addressing it.

Abbreviations

AA	African Archives (Belgium)
AAC	Anglo American Corporation
AGUFI	Association des Agents de l'Union Minière et Filiales
AIDS	Acquired Immunodeficiency Syndrome
BBC	British Broadcasting Corporation
BCK	Chemins de fer du Bas-Congo au Katanga
BEC	Bureau de l'enseignement catholique
BM	British Museum
BSAC	British South Africa Company
CADER	Corps des Activistes pour la Défense de la Révolution
CEDAF	Centre d'études et de documentation africaines
CELTA	Centre for Theoretical and Applied Linguistics
CELRIA	Centre for Studies of African-inspired Romance Literature
CEPAC	Centre for Political Studies in Central Africa
CEPSI	Centre d'étude des problèmes sociaux indigènes
CERDAC	Centre for Studies and Documentary Research on Central Africa
CERPHA	Centre for Research in African Philosophy
CGS	Confédération générale des syndicats du Congo belge
CML	Congo Mining Limited
CSR	Corporate Social Responsibility
CNMC	China Nonferrous Metal Mining (Group) Corporation
DA	Development Agreement
DC	District Commissioner
DO	District Officer
DRC, DR Congo	Democratic Republic of the Congo
ECZ	Environmental Council of Zambia

EPPCA	Environmental Protection and Pollution Control Act
ERC	European Research Council
FC	Football Club
FQM	First Quantum Minerals
Gécamines	Générale des Carrières et des Mines
GIZ	Gesellschaft für Internationale Zusammenarbeit
HIV	Human Immunodeficiency Virus
IFIs	International Financial Institutions
IMF	International Monetary Fund
ISO	International Organization for Standardization
KUL	Katholieke Universiteit Leuven
LCM	Luanshya Copper Mines
LMS	London Missionary Society
MCM	Mopani Copper Mines
MEF	Mindolo Ecumenical Foundation
MP	Member of Parliament
MMD	Movement for Multi-Party Democracy
MPLA	Movimento Popular de Libertação de Angola
MPR	Popular Movement of the Revolution
NAZ	National Archives of Zambia
NCCM	Nchanga Consolidated Copper Mines
NGO	Non-Governmental Organisation
NRMWU	Northern Rhodesia Mine Workers' Union
OCU	Observatoire du Changement Urbain
PPP	Public-Private Partnerships
RACM	Roan Antelope Copper Mines
RAID	Rights and Accountability in Development
RAMCOZ	Roan Antelope Copper Mining Corporation of Zambia
RCM	Roan Consolidated Mines
RLI	Rhodes-Livingstone Institute
RMCA	Royal Museum of Central Africa
RP	Ronald Prain papers

RST	Rhodesian (later Roan) Selection Trust
SNCC	Société Nationale des Chemins de Fer du Congo
SNCZ	Société Nationale des Chemins de Fer du Zaïre
SUBS	Solwezi Urban Baseline Study
TAZAMA	Tanzania-Zambia *Mafuta*
TAZARA	Tanzania-Zambia Railway
TNA	The National Archives (United Kingdom)
UMCB	United Missions to the Copperbelt
UMHK	Union Minière du Haut-Katanga
UNAZA	National University of Zaïre
UNESCO	United Nations Educational, Scientific and Cultural Organization
Unescongo	*Programme d'urgence de l'UNESCO dans le cadre de l'action des Nations Unies pour le maintien des services éducatifs au Congo*
UNILU	University of Lubumbashi
UNIP	United National Independence Party
UOC	Official University of the Congo
WAM	World Apostolate of Mary
ZCCM	Zambia Consolidated Copper Mines
ZCCM-IH	Zambia Consolidated Copper Mines – Investment Holdings
ZDA	Zambian Development Agency
ZEMA	Zambia Environmental Management Agency
ZTRS	Zambia-Tanzania Road Service

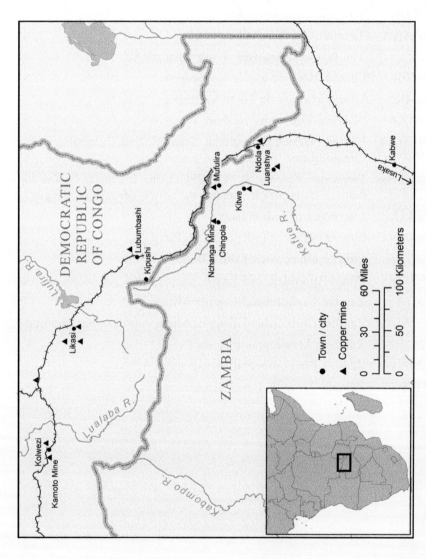

Map 0.1 The Copperbelt region. Map drawn by Rachel Taylor.

Introduction

MILES LARMER, ENID GUENE, BENOÎT HENRIET, IVA PEŠA
& RACHEL TAYLOR

With a roller coaster history of economic boom followed by crushing bust, the Central African Copperbelt has come to epitomise Africa's faltering 'Industrial Revolution'.[1] Throughout the twentieth century, its large-scale industrial copper mines attracted people, capital and power across national and continental boundaries. Following a protracted period of expansion after 1945, which gave rise to what James Ferguson called 'expectations of modernity',[2] the region went through a deep and painful decline in the 1980s and 1990s, when world copper prices collapsed and retrenchment followed. Due to its industrial, economic and geopolitical significance, the Copperbelt has become a key case study from which to theorise about urbanism, development/underdevelopment and modernity in African studies. For a century now, the Copperbelt has been a site of knowledge production on industrialisation, labour relations and urban social change. The mining officials, government agents and social scientists who have studied the Copperbelt have produced cutting-edge and world-renowned studies, on trade unionism, kinship and gender.[3] The current volume seeks to contribute to this long tradition of knowledge production in new and innovative ways, by providing a broader and more diverse account of Copperbelt social change. Our interdisciplinary contributions extend focus beyond male mineworkers,

1   Reginald Moore and A. Sandilands, *These African Copper Mines: A Study of the Industrial Revolution in Northern Rhodesia, With Principal Reference to the Copper Mining Industry* (London: Livingstone Press, 1948).
2   James Ferguson, *Expectations of Modernity: Myths and Meanings of Urban Life on the Zambian Copperbelt* (Berkeley: University of California Press, 1999).
3   See below and for an overview, Miles Larmer, 'At the Crossroads: Mining and Political Change on the Katangese-Zambian Copperbelt', *Oxford Handbooks Online* (2016), DOI: 10.1093/oxfordhb/9780199935369.013.20.

to encompass religion, comics, social work and leisure activities. Together, they show that the Copperbelt has been even more diverse and dynamic than previous studies have suggested.

This book has three distinctive foci. First of all, it understands the Copperbelt as a diverse space of mineworkers, traders, farmers and housewives, paying attention to art and popular culture, in addition to the industrial workplace and trade unionism. Though other studies have certainly looked at the Copperbelt and its population, these works have disproportionately focused on male waged employment and have thereby overlooked other ways to build a meaningful life on the Copperbelt. Second, this book presents an analysis of the entire Central African Copperbelt region, encompassing both sides of the Congo-Zambia border. Although geographically contiguous and shaped by a connected extractive industry, the two sides have been studied as two separate regions, following the divisions and legacies of Belgian and British colonial rule, and subsequent Francophone or Anglophone scholarship. Third, in its attempt to write a more varied account of the Copperbelt region, this book brings together multi- and interdisciplinary perspectives on social and historical change from history, anthropology, human geography and social psychology.

What can the Copperbelt experience contribute to discussions about urban social history more broadly? Jennifer Robinson argues that the Copperbelt is a good example of what comparative urbanism has to offer, illustrating 'diverse urban ways of life in cities across the world'.[4] As eminent social scientists recognised in the 1940s, the Copperbelt population 'was highly mobile as well as diverse, and this made for a fluid, dynamic and very creative form of urban culture'.[5] Scores of analysts have tried to understand Copperbelt residents' uneven and diverse experiences of urbanism and modernity. Max Gluckman of the Rhodes-Livingstone Institute (RLI) maintained that 'Central African towns differ only in degree from any town, anywhere in the world probably'.[6] Within African studies, the Copperbelt has been fundamental to shaping ideas of what urbanism, development/

---

4   Jennifer Robinson, *Ordinary Cities: Between Modernity and Development* (London: Routledge, 2006), p. 41.

5   Ibid., p. 46.

6   Max Gluckman, 'Anthropological Problems arising from the African industrial revolution' in A. Southall (ed.), *Social Change in Modern Africa* (Oxford: Oxford University Press, 1961), pp. 67–82, p. 79.

underdevelopment and modernity look like on the continent.[7] Studying the Copperbelt can thus enrich our understanding of what it means to be urban and modern, in Africa and beyond.[8]

From Boom to Bust: Historical Trends on the Copperbelt

The Central African Copperbelt, encompassing the urban mining towns of Zambia's Copperbelt Province and the Democratic Republic of the Congo's Haut-Katanga region (see Map 0.1), has been a key case study of urban and social change in Africa for a century. The area's mid-twentieth century transformation into an industrial mining region where a new multi-racial working class, equipped with cutting-edge industrial technology, produced minerals that were both highly valuable and of globally strategic importance, attracted the attention of analysts, academics and activists alike.

Copper, mined in this region for centuries by African societies, was – like mineral deposits elsewhere on the continent – an important impetus to the 'scramble for Africa'. In the early twentieth century, surveyors and speculators exploited known and sought out new sources of copper ore in the heart of Central Africa.[9] Turning such deposits into profits required the concentration of capital, the construction of infrastructure and the recruitment of both skilled and unskilled labour. The profitable production of Katangese mines in the 1910s and 1920s by Union Minière du Haut-Katanga (UMHK) fuelled the growth of new urban centres populated by skilled white artisans and thousands of African labour migrants – many from across the border in Northern Rhodesia – segregated by the racial logics of the colonial order. Wartime demands had spurred UMHK production to 14,000 tonnes by 1915, and a decade later this had grown to 90,000 tonnes.[10] From the late 1920s and more particularly after the global depression, Northern Rhodesia's own mines and mine towns grew rapidly. Production more than doubled from 116,600 tons of copper in 1936 to 268,500 tons in 1941, as did the size of its workforce: 7,459 African mineworkers in 1933 rose to 26,023 in 1940. That year the equivalent figure

7   Ferguson, *Expectations of Modernity*; Ulf Hannerz, *Exploring the City: Inquiries toward an Urban Anthropology* (New York: Columbia University Press, 1983).
8   Robinson, *Ordinary Cities*, p. 63.
9   Larry J. Butler, *Copper Empire: Mining and the Colonial State in Northern Rhodesia, c. 1930–64* (Basingstoke: Palgrave Macmillan, 2007).
10   Charles Perrings, *Black Mineworkers in Central Africa: Industrial Strategies and the Evolution of an African Proletariat in the Copperbelt, 1911–41* (London: Heinemann, 1979), p. 247.

for UMHK was 17,074.[11] Central African copper production was vital to the expanding global industrial economy and vital to the allied war effort in the Second World War, comparable in global scale and significance to South Africa's gold mines.[12]

Over time, hastily constructed mine camps became large urban centres, where migrant workers and their families settled in increasing numbers and progressively acquired new skills.[13] Copperbelt residents organised politically and socially, and mine companies, states and their academic advisors were forced to reckon with these new communities, leading to the provision of services such as healthcare, education, housing and social welfare.[14] Mine companies also provided sporting and leisure facilities, while Copperbelt residents produced innovative music, dance and art that articulated their understandings of urban and social change.[15] Racial and economic inequalities fuelled struggles for labour and political rights, influencing the struggle against colonial rule in the Belgian Congo and Northern Rhodesia.[16] Following independence, new one-party state regimes in Zambia and Zaïre (as the Congo was later renamed) nationalised the mine companies and sought to impose authoritarian control over these economically vital

11 Ibid., pp. 117, 247, 253; Ian Henderson, 'Labour and Politics in Northern Rhodesia, 1900–1953: A Study in the Limits of Colonial Power', PhD thesis, University of Edinburgh, 1972, p. 130.
12 Robert E. Baldwin, *Economic Development and Export Growth: A Study of Northern Rhodesia, 1920–1960* (Berkeley: University of California Press, 1966); Jean-Philippe Peemans, 'Capital Accumulation in the Congo under Colonialism: The Role of the State' in P. Duignan and L. H. Gann (eds), *Colonialism in Africa, vol. 5: The Economics of Colonialism, 1870–1960* (Cambridge: Cambridge University Press, 1975), pp. 165–212; René Brion and Jean-Louis Moreau, *De la mine à Mars: La genèse d'Umicore* (Tielt: Lanoo, 2006).
13 Hortense Powdermaker, *Copper Town: Changing Africa – The Human Situation on the Rhodesian Copperbelt* (New York: Harper & Row, 1962).
14 Donatien Dibwe dia Mwembu, *Histoire des conditions de vie des travailleurs de l'Union minière du Haut-Katanga/Gécamines (1910–1999)* (Lubumbashi: Presses Universitaires de Lubumbashi, 2001).
15 J. Clyde Mitchell, *The Kalela Dance: Aspects of Social Relationships among Urban Africans in Northern Rhodesia* (Manchester: Rhodes-Livingstone Institute, 1956); Johannes Fabian, *Remembering the Present: Painting and Popular History in Zaire* (Berkeley: University of California Press, 1996).
16 Henry S. Meebelo, *African Proletarians and Colonial Capitalism: The Origins, Growth and Struggles of the Zambian Labour Movement to 1964* (Lusaka: Kenneth Kaunda Foundation, 1986).

regions.[17] Boom was followed by bust with the global commodities crash of the late 1970s. Both Copperbelt regions experienced economic recession involving the loss of formal employment, privatisation and the collapse of social services provided by mine companies. Many residents endured a drastic decline in living standards and were forced to turn to alternative forms of economic activity. In the twenty-first century new mine investors came to the Copperbelt and to new mining areas in other areas of Zambia and the Democratic Republic of the Congo (henceforth DRC or DR Congo), but they proved unwilling to provide social services, and have provided only a fraction of the jobs of their predecessors.

Studying the Copperbelt

This compelling story, the rise (and later fall) of the globalised Copperbelt, has drawn – like the mineral speculators who sought their fortunes in its rich red seams – generations of external analysts to Central Africa. In the 1950s, social scientists saw the Copperbelt as a test case for rapid modernisation and sought to assess the extent to which Africans could successfully adapt to a 'Western' way of life. Researchers from RLI and the Centre d'Études des Problèmes Sociaux Indigènes (CEPSI) carried out extensive research in the Copperbelt's laboratory of modernity. Researchers from the two institutes disagreed – in ways influenced by the racial thinking of the time – about whether this adaptation was possible, but they agreed that momentous processes of social change were transforming the region and its residents from rural 'backwardness' to an urban industrial society.[18] They also believed this was replicating within a generation a 'modernisation' process that had unfolded over a century or more in Western Europe. Colonial officials and mine company executives, having abandoned their earlier hopes of preventing or delaying urbanisation, aimed to control and/or guide these changes by social intervention, seeking with the help of social science and mission churches to create their ideal of a disciplined urban

17 Wolf Radman, 'The Nationalization of Zaire's Copper: From Union Minière to Gecamines', *Africa Today* 25, 4 (1978), pp. 25–47; Philip Daniel, *Africanisation, Nationalisation and Inequality: Mining Labour and the Copperbelt in Zambian Development* (Cambridge: Cambridge University Press, 1979).

18 For RLI see Lyn Schumaker, *Africanizing Anthropology: Fieldwork, Networks, and the Making of Cultural Knowledge in Central Africa* (Durham NC: Duke University Press, 2001); Ferguson, *Expectations of Modernity*. For CEPSI see Benjamin Rubbers and Marc Poncelet, 'Colonial Sociology in the Belgian Congo: Studies of the Urban Industrial Katanga Province on the Eve of Independence', *Genèses* 99, 2 (2015), pp. 93–112.

working class that would be productive, docile and pious. In doing so, they drew on Western examples of paternalistic company towns such as Saltaire and Bournville in Britain and the Ford company's towns in Michigan and Brazil.[19] Simultaneously, they sought to deny urban residence and rights to those who failed to fit this ideal. On the other hand, the strategic importance of copper for British and Belgian capital and imperialism meant that African nationalists and labour activists sought to mobilise Copperbelt workers as the vanguard of their efforts to redistribute its vast wealth and political power.

Following decolonisation (in Congo in 1960, and in Zambia in 1964), new independent governments saw their respective Copperbelt regions as vital drivers of national economic development, but also as places of social unrest and political opposition – and in the case of Katanga, outright secession. Conversely, local political forces sought to ensure that copper wealth remained in the region and rewarded those who produced it. During this period, development advisors to the Zambian and Congolese states generally shared politicians' view of Copperbelt residents as materialist urbanites, unpatriotic and – precisely because of their urbanism – 'un-African'.[20] Social welfare experts worried about the ability of Copperbelt towns to ensure the stable reproduction of family life and sought to manage 'urban' problems such as divorce and crime. Authoritarian nationalism and nationalisation policies sought to bring these globalised mining regions under one-party state control. However, they struggled to overcome their dependence on global markets and to bring about a balanced form of development. When international mineral prices crashed in the mid-1970s with the onset of the global recession, both countries' dependence on copper and cobalt exports was painfully exposed.

By the late 1980s the Central African Copperbelt, once heralded as the vanguard of modernisation, was characterised by international analysts as an industrial dinosaur, unable or unwilling to adjust to 'market realities'. The indebted Zairian and Zambian governments were 'advised' by international financial institutions to structurally adjust the mining industry, to cut jobs

19 Marcelo J. Borges and Susana B. Torres (eds), *Company Towns: Labor, Space, and Power Relations across Time and Continents* (New York: Palgrave Macmillan, 2012).
20 Robert H. Bates, *Markets and States in Tropical Africa: The Political Basis of Agricultural Policies* (Berkeley: University of California Press, 1981). The assumption that urbanism was un-African was a specifically southern African phenomenon and stands in revealing contrast to for example West Africa, where urban living and large mining towns such as Kumasi had a deep pre-colonial history.

and reduce social services, plans that were resisted by mining unions and communities. The resulting discontent generated criticisms of the corrupt manipulation of the mining industry for personal gain and fuelled demands for political reform. The Copperbelt was again at the forefront of demands for democracy in the early 1990s. In Zaïre/DR Congo, the violent suppression of these demands was followed by the military overthrow of President Mobutu and the devastation caused by 'Africa's world war'.[21] In Zambia, a successful democratic movement was, once in power, unable to prevent continued economic recession. The Copperbelt region suddenly became the focus of academic studies of decline, as retrenched mineworkers and their families pursued 'survival strategies', including out-migration, hazardous artisanal mining and urban agriculture.[22]

In the twenty-first century, the Copperbelt has, in the context of rising mineral prices fuelled by Chinese demand and investment, experienced partial economic recovery but largely without growth in mining employment. Enduring questions regarding the uneven distribution of mineral wealth and Central Africa's place in the global economy have – for Copperbelt residents, academic observers and political activists alike – become enmeshed with concerns regarding, among other things, the environmental impact of current and historical mining. Following the sale of nationalised mine companies in the late 1990s in sometimes corrupt privatisation processes, new private owners have refused to provide the social welfare programmes of their predecessors.[23] Copperbelt communities have, however, continued to demand that new investors address the effects of their extractive activities, often comparing their record to the paternalistic predecessors.[24]

The unique position of the Copperbelt in imagining industrial modernity in Africa has over the last century generated a vast body of Copperbelt

---

21 See Gérard Prunier, *Africa's World War: Congo, the Rwandan Genocide, and the Making of a Continental Catastrophe* (New York: Oxford University Press, 2011).

22 Deborah Potts, 'Counter-Urbanization on the Zambian Copperbelt? Interpretations and Implications', *Urban Studies* 42, 4 (2005), pp. 583–609; Benjamin Rubbers, *Le paternalisme en question: Les anciens ouvriers de la Gécamines face à la libéralisation du secteur minier katangais (RD Congo)* (Paris: L'Harmattan, 2013).

23 John Craig, 'Putting Privatisation into Practice: The Case of Zambia Consolidated Copper Mines Limited', *The Journal of Modern African Studies* 39, 3 (2001), pp. 389–410; Dan Haglund, 'In It for the Long Term? Governance and Learning among Chinese Investors in Zambia's Copper Sector', *China Quarterly* 199 (2009), pp. 627–46; Rubbers, *Le paternalisme en question*, pp. 48–9.

24 Rubbers, *Le paternalisme en question*.

studies, shaped by constant interaction with the changing social, economic and political environment of the region, its nation-states and the wider world. These studies have distorted as much as they have revealed the underlying realities of Copperbelt society, as they have changed and developed from the 1940s to the present day.[25] The simplistic characterisation of the Copperbelt region as a space of inherent urban modernisation, qualitatively distinct from an equally problematic rural 'other', has prevented a clear appreciation of the many ways in which the region and its residents' actual experience of modernity has been uneven, diverse, subject to reversal and constantly contested. While some town dwellers certainly severed ties to their areas of origin, many 'quintessential urbanites' remained closely connected to rural areas via migration and ethnic identities, and the flows of kin, remittances and ideas between town and village – with rural areas themselves experiencing profound social changes as a result. Ethnic identities continued to develop and in new ways remained relevant to urban society, affecting Katangese and Zambian mine towns in very different ways. The rigid rural-urban binary that long dominated academic interpretations of social change was not fully shared by its residents, who made sense of their complex and dynamic social realities in more creative and dynamic ways that reflected the multiple, ambiguous and open-ended forms of modernity that Copperbelt society involved.

While the modernisation narrative surrounding Copperbelt history has been widely critiqued, it has nonetheless continued to pervade political, cultural and intellectual characterisations of social change. When the Copperbelt 'failed' to develop according to conventional models derived from Rostowian 'take-off' theories, World Bank analysts judged this a deviation from normality and in need of explanation in pathological terms.[26] When unionised mineworkers, heralded as a vanguard working class, failed to fulfil the expectations of Marxist sociologists, they were dismissed as a selfish labour aristocracy.[27] When women refused to play their assigned role as housewives and instead engaged in entrepreneurial farming and trading, they were patronisingly dismissed by some colonial and company officials

25 Ferguson, *Expectations of Modernity*.
26 Walt W. Rostow, *The Stages of Economic Growth: A Non-Communist Manifesto* (Cambridge: Cambridge University Press, 1960).
27 Giovanni Arrighi and John S. Saul (eds), *Essays on the Political Economy of Africa* (New York: Monthly Review Press, 1973).

as having brought village practices to town.[28] By unhelpfully comparing the Copperbelt to an idealised version of 'Western' urbanisation, generations of social scientists and international (and many national) observers have problematically distorted the realities of Copperbelt society.

Meanwhile, Copperbelt residents have, in fluctuating and often unpromising structural contexts, gone about the business of making lives and communities for themselves. Copperbelt towns share some of the characteristics of other cities that have developed in Asia, Latin America and elsewhere in sub-Saharan Africa over the past half century. They are places in which manufacturing, trade and farming exist side by side, in which enthusiastic engagement with global socio-cultural phenomena, new technologies and material consumerism are no barrier to widespread millenarian beliefs or an embrace of reconstituted ethnic identities. Yet Copperbelt cities equally display their own specific form of urbanism that can only be explained by close attention to historical developments.[29]

Since the 1980s, historians and anthropologists, building on and engaging with ongoing social scientific research on the Copperbelt region, have made important contributions to our understanding of these changes. Many early studies of the colonial period focused on capital-labour relations, exploring the tensions generated by international businesses and the region's 'working-class in the making'.[30] Following the independence period, the focus shifted to the centrality of the region to African anti-colonial politics and to the economic development of new nation-states. Miles Larmer established the continued prominence of the Zambian Copperbelt and its mine communities in challenging political authoritarianism in the postcolonial period.[31] Over time, and reflecting broader historiographical innovations, analysis shifted to historicising the social development of copper mining towns, particularly gender relations between mineworkers and their wives, who were shown by Jane Parpart (for Zambia) and Donatien Dibwe dia Mwembu (for Katanga) to have played an underappreciated role in shaping

28   Iva Peša, 'Crops and Copper: Agriculture and Urbanism on the Central African Copperbelt, 1950–2000', *Journal of Southern African Studies* 64, 3 (2020), pp. 527–45
29   Robinson, *Ordinary Cities*; Garth Myers, *African Cities: Alternative Visions of Urban Theory and Practice* (London: Zed Books, 2011).
30   John Higginson, *A Working Class in the Making: Belgian Colonial Labor Policy, Private Enterprise, and the African Mineworker, 1907–1951* (Madison: Wisconsin University Press, 1989).
31   Miles Larmer, *Mineworkers in Zambia: Labour and Political Change in Post-Colonial Zambia* (London: I.B. Tauris, 2007).

social relations in mining towns.[32] Charles Ambler studied the social and cultural aspects of Copperbelt society through the lens of alcohol, particularly beer consumption.[33] Haut-Katanga's distinctive cultural and artistic output has been intensively studied by Bogumil Jewsiewicki and Johannes Fabian,[34] while the University of Lubumbashi (UNILU)'s '*Observatoire du Changement Urbain*' has conducted extensive research into the changing societies of Katanga's mining towns as they experienced economic decline and the effects of political and military conflict.[35] In particular, UNILU has been the centre of extraordinarily rich and successful research on the social history of urban Haut-Katanga since the year 2000, in the form of the *Mémoires de Lubumbashi* project implemented by Professors Bogumil Jewsiewicki and Donatien Dibwe dia Mwembu. This project has not only gathered a significant body of invaluable oral histories, it has also helpfully decentred the authority of the academy by treating artists – musicians, theatrical performers and visual artists – as legitimate historians in their own right, bringing such actors together with local residents and university researchers in initiatives to co-create the city's diverse social experiences. This volume is enriched by the contribution of Dibwe dia Mwembu (Chapter 11) in which he locates the *Mémoires de Lubumbashi* in UNILU's history of knowledge production, inextricably bound up as it has been with Katanga's own tumultuous history.

Meanwhile, Patience Mususa, Alice Evans and Jeroen Cuvelier have in different ways revealed the diverse impacts on gender relations of the collapse of company paternalism and its model of 'modern' family life.[36] While

---

32 Jane L. Parpart, 'The Household and the Mine Shaft: Gender and Class Struggles on the Zambian Copperbelt, 1926–1964', *Journal of Southern African Studies* 2, 1 (1986), pp. 36–56; Donatien Dibwe dia Mwembu, *Bana shaba abandonnés par leur père: Structures de l'autorité et histoire sociale de la famille ouvrière au Katanga 1910–1997* (Paris: L'Harmattan, 2001); Dibwe dia Mwembu, *Histoire des conditions de vie*.

33 Charles Ambler, 'Alcohol, Racial Segregation and Popular Politics in Northern Rhodesia', *Journal of African History* 31, 2 (1990), pp. 295–313.

34 Bogumil Jewsiewicki, 'Collective Memory and Its Images: Popular Urban Painting in Zaire – A Source of "Present Past"', *History and Anthropology* 2, 2 (1986), pp. 389–400.

35 Donatien Dibwe dia Mwembu (ed.), *Les identités urbaines en Afrique: le cas de Lubumbashi, R.D. Congo* (Paris: L'Harmattan, 2009).

36 Patience Mususa, 'Contesting Illegality: Women in the Informal Copper Business' in Alistair Fraser and Miles Larmer (eds), *Zambia, Mining, and Neoliberalism: Boom and Bust on the Globalized Copperbelt* (New York: Palgrave Macmillan, 2010), pp. 185–208; Alice Evans, 'Women Can Do What Men Can Do': The Causes and Consequences of Growing Flexibility in Gender Divisions of Labour in Kitwe, Zambia', *Journal of Southern African Studies* 40, 5 (2014), pp. 981–8; Jeroen Cuvelier, 'Men, Mines and Masculinities: The

Walima Kalusa has paid attention to the cultural meanings of death on the Zambian Copperbelt,[37] Naomi Haynes has explored the twenty-first century Pentecostal boom which has provided Copperbelt residents with new ways of dealing with challenging urban realities.[38] Since the 1990s, attention has also focused on the history of knowledge production by social scientists. Lyn Schumaker demonstrated the ways that African researchers – and to a lesser extent, ordinary mine town residents – decisively shaped the work of RLI.[39] James Ferguson's influential *Expectations of Modernity* exposed the modernist assumptions that distorted the findings of both RLI and subsequent researchers, clearing the way for a more open-ended history of Copperbelt society.[40] For Katanga, Marc Poncelet and Benjamin Rubbers have demonstrated how the modernist assumptions of CEPSI and other researchers – as well as their relations with colonial states and mine companies – strongly influenced their understanding of Katangese urbanism.[41]

This volume, and the Comparing the Copperbelt project of which it forms a central part, builds on these historiographical insights, thereby providing a multi-dimensional approach to understand the Central African Copperbelt's history of social change.[42] Relying on a century of studies on the social and urban dynamics of the Copperbelt, it provides both a retrospective account, and a contemporary understanding of, the kinds of knowledge produced on the region. Without claiming to offer a comprehensive analysis of this complex and diverse urban milieu, it proposes a multi-dimensional analysis of Copperbelt society that overcomes some earlier weaknesses and limitations. This book equally provides new insights into social change in urban Africa as it affects a far wider range of actors than have previously received attention from Copperbelt studies. In so doing, the collection offers a critical analysis of existing scholarship, while demonstrating how innovative approaches and new methodologies can be applied.

Lives and Practices of Artisanal Miners in Lwambo (Katanga Province, DR Congo)', PhD Thesis, University of Ghent, 2011.

37 Walima T. Kalusa and Megan Vaughan, *Death, Belief and Politics in Central African History* (Lusaka: Lembani Trust, 2013).

38 Naomi Haynes, *Moving by the Spirit: Pentecostal Social Life on the Zambian Copperbelt* (Berkeley: University of California Press, 2017).

39 Schumaker, *Africanizing Anthropology*.

40 Ferguson, *Expectations of Modernity*; Miles Larmer, 'Permanent Precarity: Capital and Labour in the Central African Copperbelt', *Labor History* 58, 2 (2017), pp. 170–84.

41 Marc Poncelet, *L'invention des sciences coloniales belges* (Paris, Karthala, 2008); Rubbers and Poncelet, 'Colonial Sociology in the Belgian Congo'.

42 For the Comparing the Copperbelt project, see http://copperbelt.history.ox.ac.uk.

While *Across the Copperbelt* is at its core a history of changing urban society, it is equally an interdisciplinary volume. Contributions and approaches drawn from social anthropology, development studies, human geography and cultural studies examine the interchange of past and present in the lived experience and everyday discourse of Copperbelt residents. While in the 1950s and 1960s the rural past served as a negative counter-point to hopes for modernisation and development in the urban Copper-belt, since the 1980s economic decline and political discontent – and in DR Congo, political violence – have fuelled nostalgia for a late-colonial/postcolonial 'golden age' when authoritarian one-party states and pater-nalist mine companies provided stability and social welfare. Analysts of the contemporary Copperbelt are constantly confronted with the potency of this historical memory, while historians must be aware of how this nostalgia, and the current state of the region, shape residents' recall of the past. In bringing together this wide range of disciplinary perspectives, and making use of innovative methodologies and approaches, the book provides a more holistic understanding of the region's historical develop-ment and current situation.

Reassessing the Copperbelt: Approaches and Methods

Shaped by the various iterations of modernity thinking set out above, the existing body of Copperbelt studies has provided both a rich and a distorted picture of the region's societies, political economy, culture and history. This volume builds on this body of work, while simultaneously critiquing and seeking to improve it. Three main issues can be identified.

First, the desire to identify a Western-style Copperbelt working class led to a disproportionate focus on a minority of skilled African male mine-workers, which resulted in the neglect of the lived experience of the vast majority. The scholarship of the 1950s, for example that of RLI scholars such as A. L. Epstein, did so because this 'transitional' class was thought to be a sign of a future in which formal, skilled industrial workers would dominate the urbanised Copperbelt. A similar bias is visible in the works of CEPSI, which aimed to produce knowledge on the 'adaptation' of local communi-ties to urban and industrial modernity.[43] Yet this approach marginalised the diverse experience of most Copperbelt residents: those employed in less skilled or casual labour, itinerant traders, shop owners, domestic workers,

---

[43] Rubbers and Poncelet, 'Colonial Sociology in the Belgian Congo', pp. 98–9.

drivers, bar and sex workers and the tens of thousands of predominantly female farmers whose experiences form a central but neglected part of the Copperbelt story.

The focus on workplace and formal employment certainly reflected a disproportionate interest in the working class as a potential agent of historical change. The facilitation of access and sometimes the direct funding of social scientific research by mine companies, keen to know the ideas and intentions of their employees, equally played a role. For subsequent generations, accessing male mineworkers and union leaders was made easier by the impressive archival practices of mine companies. Zambian mine company records are publicly available at the Zambia Consolidated Copper Mines archives in Ndola. In Haut-Katanga, the records of Générale des Carrières et des Mines (Gécamines) are partially accessible in Lubumbashi and smaller mining towns. These records provide data on mine company townships, where workers and their families resided. These areas were provided not only with housing but with healthcare, schooling and welfare and leisure services, all of which were assiduously documented. But from the 1960s at least, the majority of Copperbelt residents lived in non-mine areas, run by local authorities, that can be understood as symbiotic with – and sometimes parasitic on – the formal mining sector. Non-mine residents had an ambiguous relationship with mines and mineworkers: they recognised that their own fortunes were partly dependent on the fragile prosperity generated by copper mining and they sometimes envied the employment and residential security of mineworkers, but many chafed at their dependency on mine company paternalism and sought a more independent way of life. Many mineworkers' wives equally earned their own income, but their experiences largely went unrecorded in the official record.

Accessing the experiences and attitudes of these multitudes requires both a more critical reading of the official record, and a wider range of research techniques, particularly including oral histories. The Comparing the Copperbelt project conducted significant new interview-based oral histories with long-term residents of the mining towns of Likasi (DR Congo) and Mufulira (Zambia), that are utilised in this volume, particularly in Chapter 1 (Peša and Henriet). Earlier social scientists certainly used interviews, but the data they generated was heavily influenced by the modernist perspective that dominated their research. The researchers contributing to this volume have used a wide range of methods to access their findings: archival and interview-based research, long-term participant observation, as well as a critical re-reading of the data and findings of earlier social scientific research.

Second, the focus on macro-political and socio-economic issues in much of the classic Copperbelt literature meant that the wider social and cultural experiences of Copperbelt life, for example of leisure, literacy and religious belief, were hardly addressed. Although most earlier works focused on political change, industrial disputes and economic development, it was the quotidian, personal experience of change that was often uppermost for those seeking to make a new life for themselves in town. Copperbelt residents, like mine companies and researchers, appreciated that the meaning of 'customs' surrounding initiation into adulthood, courtship and marriage all required reinterpretation in a context in which multi-ethnic residential areas, divorce courts and the cash economy were dominant. Copperbelt residents sought, collectively and individually, to continuously negotiate their 'rights to the city'. Certainly, trade unions, political parties and ethnic associations played an important role in such processes, but equally important were socio-cultural associations and initiatives in which changing gender, generational and other relationships were discussed and re-interpreted. The expression of such debates and ideas can be located in the meetings of groups active in social welfare; in newspapers, magazines and cartoons; in the gendered leisure activities (football teams for men; sewing and handicrafts for women) organised by mine companies and practised by thousands of residents; and the songs and paintings produced by Copperbelt artists. Learning from and studying such commentaries on everyday Copperbelt society enriches our interpretation of the ways in which social change was understood and experienced by its residents.

Third, the two Copperbelt regions were analysed, with only few exceptions, within their colonial or national Zambian or Congolese context.[44] This has meant Copperbelt studies have largely failed to reflect the extent to which capital, people and ideas flowed across the Copperbelt border. The editors of this collection instead argue that the Copperbelt can best be understood as a single mining region, which provides an ideal comparative framework to highlight similarities and differences between the two national settings. This approach illustrates underlying dynamics of social change that might otherwise remain hidden. Although mine towns in Zambia and Congo evolved in ostensibly similar ways, comparative analysis reveals that the experience of these parallel historical changes was significantly different

[44] Exceptions to this general rule include Perrings, *Black Mineworkers in Central Africa*; Mwelwa C. Musambachime, 'The Ubutwa Society in Eastern Shaba and Northeast Zambia to 1920', *International Journal of African Historical Studies* 27, 1 (1994), pp. 77–99; Enid Guene, 'Copper's Corollaries: Trade and Labour Migration in the Copperbelt (1910–1940)', *Zambia Social Science Journal* 1, 4 (2013); and Larmer, 'At the Crossroads'.

in the two regions. As noted, Katanga's mine towns experienced an earlier and more sustained stabilisation from the 1920s than those in colonial Zambia, where permanent African residence was only officially accepted in the 1940s. In Katanga, the provision of comprehensive social services by the triumvirate of the mine company UMHK, the Roman Catholic Church and the Belgian colonial state created a system of paternalism which many mineworkers and their families genuinely regarded as generous. In Northern Rhodesia, similar services were belatedly provided and often only as a result of organised campaigning by African trade unions and nationalist parties. This fuelled a protest-oriented politics that, in overcoming a racial colour bar, created a militant political culture largely absent from Katanga.

The Northern Rhodesian Copperbelt's unified African political activism led it to become the vanguard of Zambian nationalism and a consciously cosmopolitan melting pot. Katanga, in contrast, experienced ethnic conflict during Congo's violent transition to independence, culminating in the Katangese secession and the international diplomatic and military operation that brought it to an end. Consequently, post-independence Congolese rulers, particularly Mobutu Sese Seko, saw the strategic mining region as requiring direct oversight from the capital Kinshasa and they overtly suppressed Katangese political aspirations. As the one-party states of both countries unravelled in the late 1980s and early 1990s, the Zambian Copperbelt's organised labour movement played a leading role in that country's successful transition to democracy. In Katanga, a repressed democratic transition was followed by a new wave of ethnic violence and, following the military overthrow of Mobutu, a devastating civil war and disastrous decline in living standards which has yet to be reversed. The comparative approach applied in this volume enables exploration of the causes and consequences of these similarities and differences, and analyses how they have influenced social change in the cross-border Copperbelt.

Arguments and Structure

The book is divided into three thematic parts, each of which presents a set of chapters that shed new light on the historical and contemporary Copperbelt.

Micro-Studies of Urban Life

The dominant focus on the formal mining sector and male African mineworkers has tended to deflect attention from the experiences of many other Copperbelt residents. As well as the biases of researchers towards issues of capital and labour and macro-political change, the working lives and political organisation of mineworkers meant that they have been relatively easy to find in the scrupulous records kept by mine companies and states. The majority of the Copperbelt population was however never formally employed: the largest group of workers was likely women farmers, and many tens of thousands earned a precarious living from trading or other informal activities. Their activities were, however, barely noticed or were otherwise regarded with disdain and hostility by the authorities. These experiences have required non-traditional methods to access.

In this respect, in Chapter 1, Iva Peša and Benoît Henriet draw on an impressive new body of oral histories conducted with long-term residents of the Copperbelt mine towns of Likasi (DR Congo) and Mufulira (Zambia), to provide a rich history of everyday life that reveals similarities and striking differences. In stepping away from mine work and mineworkers as the assumed norm of Copperbelt life, this study challenges the assumption that mine companies were ever able to dominate or control the lives of Copperbelt residents. This chapter shows the limits of paternalistic order, highlighting how individuals made their own way, economically and culturally. By including the voices of seamstresses, nurses, domestics, as well as doctors, artists and engineers, this chapter provides a wider and more nuanced understanding of Copperbelt modernity, influenced by but not limited to the mining industry.

The lives and outlook of Copperbelt residents were, like urbanites everywhere, shaped by the ideas they found in new publications: books, but also magazines and comics. The mine companies' provision of schooling for mineworkers' children, and the promotion of literacy, helped residents articulate new understandings of their society and lives. Enid Guene examines the experience of growing up on the Copperbelt. On the Katangese side, childhood was experienced in the context of UMHK/Gécamines' cradle-to-grave policies. In this context, the company-sponsored publication of the free monthly magazine *Mwana Shaba Junior* featured the cartoon '*Mayele*', which in humorous ways guided young people in the intricacies of town life. In Zambia, publications produced by the state and by Christian missions included their own cartoon characters. This chapter explores the ways in which companies, governments and missions sought to mould the ideas of the region's inhabitants, but equally argues that such comics provided a venue in which Copperbelt residents created new popular art forms that blended local and global influences.

European mineworkers were of crucial importance to the development of the early Copperbelt. In the colonial period, skilled mineworkers from around the world brought to the booming mines of Central Africa a distinctive globalised perspective that combined radical socialist or communist politics with a strong commitment to racial segregation. In the mid-twentieth century, white mineworkers protected their privileged position against their aspirant African counterparts through a combination of racialised agreements (in Northern Rhodesia this amounted to an explicit colour bar) and periodic industrial action. In the Belgian Congo this cosmopolitan group was rapidly replaced by a largely Belgian group of senior mineworkers, whose numbers and influence were steadily diminished, however, by the advancement of Africans to more senior positions. In Northern Rhodesia, in contrast, settler political power and the colour bar enabled them to protect their privileges and remain an influential workforce up to independence and beyond. In 1945 UMHK employed just 1,100 European mineworkers in the most senior roles, while there were still c. 7,000 whites employed in the Northern Rhodesian mines in 1956. This hugely influential group has however been neglected in recent historical research, arguably because they were regarded – and therefore dismissed – by scholars as motivated solely by a narrow racialised worldview. Duncan Money argues, in contrast, that class and ideological perspectives were equally significant in shaping the outlook and lives of this privileged and little understood community, in a study that for the first time compares and contrasts the lives of white mineworkers in the Belgian Congo and Northern Rhodesia.

The provision of leisure facilities by Copperbelt mine companies extended to the provision of sporting facilities, designed to keep workers fit and distracted from more subversive activities. Drawing on the experience of towns such as Bournville, Saltaire and Port Sunlight in Britain, and Pullman in the United States, companies provided sports and leisure clubs, access to which was strongly determined by race and seniority. In his chapter, Hikabwa Chipande identifies the disciplining intentions behind mine company sponsorship of football teams, which were initially the preserve of European mineworkers. Over time, however, Africans sought and achieved access to – initially segregated – football fields of their own, and Chipande demonstrates how these provided important vehicles for the expression and organisation of collective African urban belonging.

Finally in Part 1, Rita Kesselring challenges many of the established notions that Copperbelt towns are simply the totality of the mine-as-workplace and the mine town-as-residency. She rejects the view that they should be understood as 'enclave' economies that could isolate themselves from wider spatial and political considerations. In the mid-twentieth century, the highly uneven prosperity of Copperbelt mine towns rapidly attracted a much wider urban population, which sought to benefit from the presence of the mine but who advanced the region's urbanisation in new and unexpected ways. At the same time, late-colonial states sought to integrate mine towns politically and to ensure they contributed to the wider socio-economic development of their territories, a process that was rapidly accelerated by postcolonial nation-states that sought to underwrite their development plans with the proceeds of copper and cobalt mining. Demands on mine companies from states and communities shaped the ways in which mines and mine townships were integrated into the wider urbanisation of Central Africa. Focusing on the mine towns of Zambia's North-Western Province, Kesselring demonstrates how the contested growth of Solwezi and Kansanshi's built environment has been shaped over time by the interaction of the global mining economy, national and local political elites, and the urban community itself.

The Local Copperbelt and the Global Economy

The Central African Copperbelt has always been linked to the global economy while being mined for hundreds of years by African societies. Indeed, it provided an important basis for the rise of major centralised societies, most notably the Luba and Lunda kingdoms in the seventeenth and eighteenth centuries, which exported copper ingots, along with other commodities, via African and Portuguese traders to the Atlantic coast. Mineral exports enabled the import of new technologies, which raised population density, expanded the extent of cultivated land, and strengthened central state capacity to enslave subject peoples and extract tribute from areas where copper was mined. Yet this period of precolonial mining, which provided the basis for the region's original integration into global mineral supplies, is normally treated as entirely distinct from the 'modern' exploitation of the region's resources. In this respect, David M. Gordon's chapter, making innovative use of archaeological and documentary evidence, provides an important examination of mineral production, trade and consumption in Southern and Central Africa in the nineteenth century, a period in which the intensification of global and locally linked trade routes spurred technological and cultural innovation in a period of intense conflict.

In the twentieth century, colonially connected companies produced minerals that were essential to Western industrial economies and indeed to militarism and warfare. Copperbelt copper was vital to war economies, and uranium from Shinkolobwe mine was used in the atomic bombs dropped on Hiroshima and Nagasaki in 1945. The region was widely viewed as an island of hyper-modern industrial development in the African 'bush' and optimists believed it would develop into a region of urban industrialisation comparable to those in the Western world. Yet in practice the region's economic development was highly uneven, skewed towards the production of raw minerals with little secondary industrial development. Northern Rhodesia/Zambia remained dependent on its southern neighbours, which provided the lion's share of manufactured imports for the industry and consumer goods for the Copperbelt's residents. Secondary industry was more developed in Katanga, but even here it was largely in the hands of Western companies and small businesses. Compared with West Africa, the development of an indigenous capitalist class was severely restricted. This unevenness was reinforced by economic policies that continued to drain off vast mine revenue away from the mine regions themselves, to the metropole exchequers and to Western-based companies. The region's landlocked position further contributed to its long-term uncompetitiveness.

Similarly, most new urban migrants had little prospect of obtaining the formal employment, education and other markers of modernity that would make them full urban citizens. Most African urbanites scraped out a precarious living through trading, urban farming and other activities deemed unofficial, disreputable and 'un-urban' by most colonial and postcolonial officials. The disjuncture between the vision of the Copperbelt as a place of transformative modernity, and the underlying reality that became increasingly clear during the postcolonial period – of its uneven, unequal and precarious development – has been the dominant motif of Copperbelt society, the lived experience of which has been documented by Ferguson, Mususa and others.[45] A golden age of growth that fuelled unrealistic expectations of modern development was rapidly and brutally displaced by economic stagnation and then decline in the 1980s and 1990s. This fall has created on the Copperbelt a profound sense of nostalgia for a late-colonial/post-colonial 'golden age' that perhaps never really existed. Copperbelt residents today experience a sense of living in a region left behind by a promised modernity that is perpetually out of reach.

Copperbelt residents however continued – and continue – to see the region as one that promised personal and collective advancement through formal employment, but also via the associated provision of social services by mine companies. In the 'golden age' of the 1950s and 1960s, mine

---

45 Ferguson, *Expectations of Modernity*; Patience Mususa, 'Topping Up: Life Amidst Hardship and Death on the Copperbelt', *African Studies* 71, 2 (2012), pp. 304–22; Rubbers, *Le paternalisme en question*.

companies provided housing, social welfare and a host of other extra-economic services that made urban residence possible and desirable. These then became the subject of demands by post-independence labour unions and mine communities. As economic decline led to increasingly savage cuts to the social wage, conflicts sharpened. Following mine privatisation in the late 1990s, new investors in both old and new copper mining regions refused responsibility for social investment, but have found themselves confronted by communities unwilling to accept this divestment. While employment numbers have fallen drastically as a result of technological change and new extractive techniques, international calls for 'corporate social responsibility' have become linked to the enduring belief among Copperbelt communities that investors must take responsibility for the effects of their investment.[46]

This however manifests itself differently on either side of the border. Zambians, notwithstanding the decline in living standards, continue to express expectations of a better life and to assert political claims on mine profits via collective protest and overt political action, characterised by the May 2019 decision by Zambian president Edgar Lungu to cancel the operating licence of Konkola Copper Mines.[47] In contrast, the urban culture of Haut-Katanga appears to divide former mineworkers from other urban groups. Katanga's mineworkers cling to their identity as respectable workers and have protested their redundancy not through political and mass action but via polite entreaties to Belgian and international authorities.[48] More generally, the effects of mine company activity on communities remain both contested and under-researched, as do the ways in which communities organise to insist on the continued social responsibilities of multinational mine corporations to the places and peoples they use to make profits.

For many decades, the considerable negative impact of mining on the environment of Copperbelt communities remained under-researched, an extraordinary absence in the otherwise rich documentation of community organisation and academic research.[49] This has changed since the 1990s as

46 Tomas Frederiksen, 'Political Settlements, the Mining Industry and Corporate Social Responsibility in Developing Countries', *Extractive Industries and Society* 6, 1 (2019), pp. 162–70.

47 'Zambia president vows to wind up copper giant KCM', *News24.com*, 4 June 2019: www.news24.com/Africa/News/zambia-president-vows-to-wind-up-copper-giant-kcm-20190604 (Accessed 19 June 2019).

48 Rubbers, *Le paternalisme en question*.

49 Iva Peša, 'Mining, Waste and Environmental Thought on the Central African Copperbelt, 1950–2000', *Environment and History* (2020), https://doi.org/10.3197/096734 019X15755402985703

new global and national environmental standards have intersected with the increasing expression of local grievances over the long-term effects of mine pollution on lives and wellbeing. Yet, given changes in both mine ownership and in environmental laws, who is responsible for the long-term damage wrought by pollution on, for example, mineworkers' housing? In this regard, Jennifer Chibamba Chansa compares mines in the 'old' and 'new' Zambian Copperbelts to explain the ways in which long-established and more recent mine communities articulate their environmental concerns to mine investors.

For some areas of the Copperbelt, the recent revival of the mining industry has done little or nothing to resuscitate the ghost towns created during the late-twentieth-century decline. In this context, what might be termed post-mine communities have made creative use of the 'ruins' left behind by industry. As Christian Straube demonstrates for Mpatamatu in the mine town of Luanshya, the conversion of mine welfare buildings into a range of new forms – privately run schools, Pentecostal churches, the offices of non-governmental organisations and, representing a degree of continuity, drinking clubs and taverns – represents a collective spirit of creative response. It was also an assertion, Straube argues, of a continuing belief in urban community and belonging, even as their 'town' (once a byword for cosmopolitan connectedness) turned into a disconnected 'village'.

In the contemporary Copperbelt, linkages to the global economy remain as vital as ever to its success. In the twenty-first century, economic globalisation and technological innovation promise to remove the barriers to frictionless trade. Certainly, Hélène Blaszkiewicz demonstrates how infrastructural innovation has enabled the historically rapid transportation of minerals to export markets, making it possible for Copperbelt minerals to remain profitable. However, her analysis equally demonstrates the continuities of recent challenges and changes with the colonial period. Blaszkiewicz makes a convincing argument for a shift of focus away from the study of mine production and towards the infrastructure and transportation companies that make market access and profitability possible.

Producing and Contesting Knowledge of Urban Societies

As noted, the Central African Copperbelt has attracted the attention of generations of social science researchers who, together with mine companies, colonial and postcolonial states and other elite actors, created an image of this region as quintessentially modern and urban, even when this was significantly at odds with reality. It is therefore necessary, while building on the considerable achievements of this body of social science research, to identify and critique the ways it served the interests of colonists, companies and states, all of which sought to control and discipline these new urban societies. Copperbelt communities, it was commonly believed, constituted a threat to the colonial and capitalist order, manifest through riots, industrial action and mass anti-colonial campaigns. While some researchers used their work to challenge the racialised notions inherent to colonial mining societies, others placed themselves, overtly or tacitly, at the service of the mine companies which often funded their research and which enabled them to collect data on their workers, the residents of mine townships or the children educated in mine schools.

This is not to argue, however, that this body of work represents a singular, coherent characterisation of Copperbelt society. Amandine Lauro's critical analysis of intelligence testing in late-colonial Katanga shows how intelligence quotient (IQ) was used to discriminate between Europeans and Africans, and how 'scientific' rationality was for those involved entirely compatible with race thinking. She, however, also demonstrates that Western notions of intelligence, while always problematic, were far from monolithic. Lauro shows how disagreements about cultural and structural influences on performance in IQ testing are revealing of wider debates among Western and/or colonial actors regarding Africans' supposed readiness for 'modernity'.

Elite concern regarding the challenges of urbanisation was equally expressed in relation to familial social change. A central concern of social scientists was that the rapid transition from supposedly paternalistic rural communities to new cosmopolitan urban ones would threaten the reproduction of family life, bringing to the urban Copperbelt the social ills of Western cities, such as marital breakdown and juvenile delinquency. From the 1940s (in Katanga) and 1950s (in Northern Rhodesia) social scientists worked with a growing cadre of trained social workers and community development officers to intervene and manage such cases. Over the coming decades, as Miles Larmer and Rachel Taylor demonstrate, an increasingly Africanised and feminised social welfare community sought to address both the universal concern regarding the dislocating effects of urban development and, with political independence, specifically African concerns regarding rapid social change.

The decolonisation of knowledge production is, as previously noted, considered from a different perspective in Donatien Dibwe dia Mwembu's study of the history department of the region's leading research institution, UNILU. Founded to serve the colonial state's needs for knowledge production, UNILU evolved after independence to become Zaïre/DR

Congo's centre for research into historical and social change. Located in the Katangese capital of Lubumbashi, the region's mine communities provided the ideal subjects for its historical research. Dibwe dia Mwembu's chapter charts the intellectual development of this key centre of Copperbelt knowledge production, but equally demonstrates how it was itself shaped by historical, political, social and economic changes in the region that its researchers sought to understand.

It is a major assertion of the Comparing the Copperbelt project that 'knowledge production' is by no means an activity confined to the academy. New urban communities constantly sought to make sense and to articulate their understanding of the changes they experienced as they moved from village to town, from subsistence to waged employment, from proximate kinship ties to cosmopolitan inter-ethnic relations. While the late-colonial generation of social scientists, along with their political and mine company counterparts, tended to see these processes of change in rigid, binary form, Copperbelt residents, while certainly aware of the rapidity and degree of change, articulated those changes in more dynamic and creative forms, including in popular music and visual art. While social workers sought to manage the effects of dislocation from a supposedly rigid paternalist familial order, many Copperbelt residents engaged in religiously oriented discussions of morality, family and gender, as Stephanie Lämmert shows in the collection's final chapter. Relying on a unique set of archival sources and interviews with key religious actors, Lämmert shows how Copperbelt cosmopolitanism extended beyond rural-urban migration and encompassed denominational flexibility, which she describes as 'surfing'. While many Protestant denominations viewed the urban Copperbelt as a 'threatening' mission field, Catholics and Copperbelt residents themselves stepped in to offer religious comfort to the diverse urban population. Lämmert shows how grassroots interdenominational initiatives arose on the Zambian Copperbelt. She equally demonstrates how concerns over gender transformed into a particular reverence for the Virgin Mary. This final chapter illustrates how intimate considerations were of great concern both to elites and everyday residents, linked as they were to wider processes of social and urban change.

★ ★ ★

Together, these chapters, written by a group of interdisciplinary scholars doing long-term research in and on the Central African Copperbelt, shed new light on the region as a hallmark of urbanism, development and modernity. While it is the aim of the editors and contributors to substantially widen knowledge of under-researched aspects of its historical and contemporary experience, and in doing so draw attention to the knowledge production processes that have privileged some aspects of this experience while neglecting others, its diversity, complexity and richness means that it is not possible in a single study to provide a comprehensive account of the everyday life of Copperbelt society in its entirety. It is nonetheless our assertion that only by understanding its history can contemporary and ongoing processes of social change on the Copperbelt be properly appreciated. This volume provides a multi-faceted, interdisciplinary and cross-border assessment of urban and social dynamics on the Central African Copperbelt.

PART 1

MICRO-STUDIES OF URBAN LIFE

1

Beyond Paternalism: Pluralising Copperbelt Histories

Iva Peša & Benoît Henriet

Introduction

The centrality of copper mining to the social life of Copperbelt communities is the undisputed starting point of the rich Copperbelt historiography.[1] The pervasive influence of colonial/postcolonial paternalism has been a particular focus of such work. Bruce Fetter, for instance, described how the Belgian colonial mining company Union Minière du Haut-Katanga (UMHK) created a 'totalitarian sub-culture', through food supply, housing and welfare services, including schools, hospitals and recreation clubs, which regulated many aspects of employees' lives.[2] Yet the post-independence level of control over workers' lives of the nationalised mining conglomerates Générale des Carrières et des Mines (Gécamines) and Zambia Consolidated Copper Mines (ZCCM) in the 1970s and 1980s was arguably even greater.[3] This latter company operated a 'cradle-to-grave' policy, providing mineworkers' households with light bulbs, window frames and even nappies. The titles of prominent academic works reflect this perceived dominance of mining paternalism to Copperbelt social life. Following severe economic

---

1   Miles Larmer, 'At the Crossroads: Mining and Political Change on the Katangese-Zambian Copperbelt', *Oxford Handbooks Online* (2016), DOI: 10.1093/oxfordhb/9780199935369.013.20.

2   Bruce Fetter, 'L'Union Minière du Haut-Katanga, 1920–1940: La naissance d'une sous-culture totalitaire', *Cahiers du CEDAF* 6 (1973), pp. 1–40.

3   Benjamin Rubbers, 'Mining Towns, Enclaves and Spaces: A Genealogy of Worker Camps in the Congolese Copperbelt', *Geoforum* 98 (2019), pp. 88–96; Miles Larmer, 'Historical Perspectives on Zambia's Mining Booms and Busts' in Alistair Fraser and Miles Larmer (eds), *Zambia, Mining, and Neoliberalism: Boom and Bust on the Globalized Copperbelt* (New York: Palgrave Macmillan, 2010), pp. 31–58.

decline on the Zambian Copperbelt since 1980, James Ferguson speaks of previous 'expectations of modernity' induced by copper mining, while Patience Mususa's ethnography 'There Used to Be Order' juxtaposes ZCCM policies with a neoliberal 'fending for oneself' after privatisation.[4] On the Congolese Copperbelt, similarly, Donatien Dibwe dia Mwembu examines the trajectories of '*Bana Shaba*' (children of copper) who have been 'abandoned by their father' (the mining company), whereas Benjamin Rubbers puts 'paternalism in question', by tracing the consequences of fading mine company welfare policies after 2000.[5]

In contrast, this chapter looks at both the limitations and problems in assuming that mining paternalism was necessarily all encompassing or fundamental to the functioning of Copperbelt communities. Highlighting the diversity of people's responses to paternalism, this chapter explores not only how Copperbelt residents acted within mining's paternalistic framework, but also how they challenged and/or opposed it and how they reacted to its demise in the 1990s. Crucially, paternalism did not affect all Copperbelt residents equally. What can we learn about Copperbelt social dynamics by examining the experience of charcoal burners, market vendors and seamstresses, alongside mineworkers? Based on 100 oral history interviews conducted in Likasi (DR Congo) and Mufulira (Zambia), this chapter focuses on the daily lives of diverse urbanites on both sides of the border. In doing so, it challenges assumptions about the relationship between mining and Copperbelt communities. The persistent image of the Copperbelt as a node of urban 'modernity' has tended to marginalise scholarship on for example female farmers or radio programmes recounting rural marital traditions. Yet this diversity, it is argued, was an integral element of Copperbelt communities. This chapter thus pluralises and challenges notions of what being a 'copper society' entailed.[6]

This chapter also makes several contributions to existing literature. First, it jointly examines the Zambian and the Congolese Copperbelt, which

4   James Ferguson, *Expectations of Modernity: Myths and Meanings of Urban Life on the Zambian Copperbelt* (Berkeley: University of California Press, 1999); Patience N. Mususa, 'There Used to Be Order: Life on the Copperbelt after the Privatisation of the Zambia Consolidated Copper Mines', PhD Thesis, University of Cape Town, 2014.
5   Donatien Dibwe dia Mwembu, *Bana Shaba abandonnés par leur père: Structures de l'autorité et histoire sociale de la famille ouvrière au Katanga, 1910–1997* (Paris: L'Harmattan, 2001); Benjamin Rubbers, *Le paternalisme en question: Les anciens ouvriers de la Gécamines face à la libéralisation du secteur minier katangais (RD Congo)* (Paris: L'Harmattan, 2013).
6   Timothy J. LeCain, *The Matter of History: How Things Create the Past* (Cambridge: Cambridge University Press, 2017).

the historiography has predominantly treated as separate entities.[7] Second, it provides a history of everyday experiences among a broad segment of Copperbelt communities. Third, it uses oral history as a lens to write a social history not dominated by the institutional views of governments, mining companies or trade unions.[8] Taken together, these approaches challenge assumptions about the role of mining and paternalism in Copperbelt social history by exploring leisure activities and social relationships beyond the workplace.[9] After a brief historiographical background, which situates the case studies of Mufulira and Likasi and explains the methodology, the chapter is organised in thematic sections on mining and work ethic; leisure and culture; non-mining occupations; and gender on the Copperbelt.

Social History through Oral Sources in Likasi and Mufulira

The towns of Likasi and Mufulira have both depended heavily on copper and cobalt mining and processing industries. Likasi, once described as 'Congo's prettiest town', is a mid-sized agglomeration famed for the tropical mansions built for UMHK's European workforce. Established as an urban community in 1931 under the name Jadotville – which changed to Likasi in 1965 – it remains the second most important urban and industrial centre of Haut-Katanga after Lubumbashi.[10] Apart from the city's economic prominence, it has played a key role in the complex history of colonial/postcolonial Katanga. Jadotville was a laboratory of political participation, one of only three towns in the Belgian Congo where the first local elections were organised in 1957.[11] It was a theatre of war during the Katangese secession (1960–63), where Katangese *gendarmes* defeated UN soldiers after

7   Enid Guene, *Copper, Borders and Nation-Building: The Katangese Factor in Zambian Political and Economic History* (Leiden: African Studies Collection, 2017).
8   Patience Mususa, 'Mining, Welfare and Urbanisation: The Wavering Urban Character of Zambia's Copperbelt', *Journal of Contemporary African Studies* 30, 4 (2012), pp. 571–87; Iva Peša, 'From Life Histories to Social History: Narrating Social Change through Multiple Biographies' in Klaas van Walraven (ed.), *The Individual in African History: The Importance of Biography in African Historical Studies* (Leiden: Brill, 2020), pp. 89–113.
9   Dibwe dia Mwembu, *Bana Shaba*.
10 Jean Omasombo (ed.), *Haut-Katanga: Lorsque richesses économiques et pouvoirs politiques forcent une identité régionale*, Monographies des provinces de la RD Congo, Tome 1 (Tervuren: Royal Museum of Central Africa, 2018), p. 148.
11 Isidore Ndaywel è Nziem, *Nouvelle histoire du Congo: Des origines à la République démocratique* (Brussels: Le Cri, 2012), pp. 428–9.

a prolonged siege in September 1961.[12] Decades later, the mining industry's decline fuelled long-standing internecine tensions between purportedly 'Katangese' city dwellers and 'migrant communities' from neighbouring Kasaï, resulting in periodic violence in 1992–93.[13]

Correspondingly in then Northern Rhodesia, Mufulira town, the 'place of abundance', was established in 1937 following the discovery of copper deposits in 1923. Mufulira mine has consistently been one of the largest copper producers in the Zambian industry.[14] The town's 1967 development report attributed 'its origins, expansion and viability to the copper mine'.[15] The report noted that 50% of those employed in Mufulira worked for the mine or ancillary services, or depended on commerce with the mining population.[16] Mufulira relied on mining not only for economic activities, but also for its administrative, social and cultural life, as mine taxes funded local government services and the mines sponsored sports teams. The town struggled after the 1970 disaster, a massive tailings inrush that caused temporary mine closure and 89 deaths. Mufulira only recovered from the protracted economic crisis with the development of deep-level mining in the 1980s, which boosted production.[17] The choice of Likasi and Mufulira, both secondary towns built around the mining industry, provides a cross-border perspective on Copperbelt social dynamics. This chapter considers the Copperbelt as 'a single region, officially divided by a colonial/postcolonial border, across which flowed minerals and peoples', creating striking differences and commonalities.[18]

Copperbelt historiography has hitherto focused on mineral production, mineworkers and politics. The Rhodes–Livingstone Institute (RLI) in Northern Rhodesia and the *Centre d'Études des Problèmes Sociaux Indigènes* (CEPSI) in the Belgian Congo set the scene with studies of urban social life,

---

12 Erik Kennes and Miles Larmer, *The Katangese Gendarmes and War in Central Africa: Fighting Their Way Home* (Bloomington: Indiana University Press, 2016), pp. 61–77.

13 Donatien Dibwe dia Mwembu, 'La réharmonisation des rapports entre les Katangais et les Kasaïens dans la province du Katanga (1991–2005)', *Anthropologie et Sociétés* 30, 1 (2006), p. 127.

14 Miles Larmer, *Mineworkers in Zambia: Labour and Political Change in Post-Colonial Africa* (London: I.B. Tauris, 2006).

15 National Archives of Zambia, Mufulira Review of Development Plan, 1967, p. 3.

16 Ibid., p. 16.

17 See: Zambia Consolidated Copper Mines archives (hereafter ZCCM-IH), 15.3.7D, 'The Mufulira Mine Disaster', 1970; ZCCM-IH, 18.7.4C, 'An Interim Report of Mining at Depth, Mufulira', 1987.

18 Larmer, 'At the Crossroads'; Rubbers, 'Mining Towns, Enclaves and Spaces'.

kinship and political organisation.[19] These institutes aimed to identify and help solve the 'issues' arising from the 'modernisation' of Copperbelt urban communities. Authors such as J. Clyde Mitchell and Ferdinand Grévisse in the 1950s assumed a clear rural–urban dichotomy, asserting that 'towns and cities everywhere stand out as distinct social phenomena.'[20] Although these researchers did pay attention to the socio-cultural life of mineworkers and their families, notably in Hortense Powdermaker's *Copper Town*, they rarely focused on non-mineworkers.[21] In the 1970s and 1980s John Higginson, Bruce Fetter, Charles Perrings, Jane Parpart and George Chauncey produced detailed Copperbelt studies.[22] In this same period, the University of Lubumbashi became a source of knowledge production on Katanga's colonial and contemporary social fabric. Researchers such as Bogumil Jewsiewicki, Johannes Fabian and Augustin Mwabila Malela studied the socio-economic and political dynamics, and leisure practices of mining communities.[23] To them, the study of the Copperbelt highlighted that industrial communities across the world were subject to comparable structures and faced similar

19 Lyn Schumaker, *Africanizing Anthropology: Fieldwork, Networks, and the Making of Cultural Knowledge in Central Africa* (Durham NC: Duke University Press, 2001); Benjamin Rubbers and Marc Poncelet, 'Sociologie coloniale au Congo Belge: Les études sur le Katanga industriel et urbain à la veille de l'Indépendance', *Genèses* 2, 99 (2015), pp. 93–112.

20 J. Clyde Mitchell, 'Theoretical Orientations in African Urban Studies' in Michael Banton (ed.), *The Social Anthropology of Complex Societies* (London: Routledge, 1966), p. 37; Ferdinand Grévisse, *Le centre extra-coutumier d'Élisabethville: Quelques aspects de la politique indigène du Haut-Katanga industriel* (Brussels: CEPSI, 1951).

21 Hortense Powdermaker, *Copper Town: Changing Africa – The Human Situation on the Rhodesian Copperbelt* (New York: Harper & Row, 1962).

22 John Higginson, *A Working Class in the Making: Belgian Colonial Labor Policy, Private Enterprise, and the African Mineworker, 1907–1951* (Madison: University of Wisconsin Press, 1989); Bruce Fetter, *Colonial Rule and Regional Imbalance in Central Africa* (Boulder: Westview Press, 1983); Charles Perrings, *Black Mineworkers in Central Africa: Industrial Strategies and the Evolution of an African Proletariat in the Copperbelt, 1911–41* (New York: Africana Publishing, 1979); Jane L. Parpart, *Labor and Capital on the African Copperbelt* (Philadelphia: Temple University Press, 1983); George Chauncey Jr., 'The Locus of Reproduction: Women's Labour in the Zambian Copperbelt', 1927–1953', *Journal of Southern African Studies* 7, 2 (1981), pp. 135–64.

23 Augustin Mwabila Malela, *Travail et travailleurs au Zaïre: Essai sur la conscience ouvrière du proletariat urbain de Lubumbashi* (Kinshasa: Presses universitaires du Zaïre, 1979); Bogumil Jewsiewicki, 'Collective Memory and Its Image: Popular Urban Painting in Zaire – A Source of "Present Past"', *History and Anthropology* 2, 2 (1986), pp. 389–400; Johannes Fabian, *History from Below: The 'Vocabulary of Elisabethville' by André Yav. Text, Translations, and Interpretive Essay* (Amsterdam: John Benjamins Publishing, 1990).

challenges. Although scholars paid some attention to women or manual labourers, they still centred their analysis on mineworkers, framing Copperbelt communities as part of the global dynamics of class struggle.[24] The 1990s saw a new wave of scholarship by Ferguson and Dibwe dia Mwembu, who studied social change on the Zambian and Congolese Copperbelt in a context of decline.[25] Such works clearly showed awareness of non-mineworkers and broader social dynamics. Recent studies by Rubbers, Mususa and Miles Larmer have further highlighted the precariousness of mining and the resilience of Copperbelt communities.[26] This chapter contributes to this reframing of the historical study of the Copperbelt, by pursuing a bottom-up approach to the social history of these dynamic communities. It foregrounds the experiences of those urbanites that did not directly depend on mining. Always a numerically significant group, their role became all the more important in the wake of the mining industry's economic decline from the mid-1970s onward.

By drawing on oral history with a more diverse range of Copperbelt residents than previous research, we challenge the established historiographical focus on mining companies and political and economic change on the Copperbelt. Oral sources can provide a more diverse picture of Copperbelt historical trajectories, especially as mining and government archives are so rarely concerned with individuals not employed by the mines. Oral sources 'help us to understand relationships between structure and agency, revealing how individual lives, social processes, institutions, and contexts affect one another'.[27] However, previous oral history research in the region has tended to reinforce the emphasis on mineworkers and to a lesser extent their wives. We therefore include more varied and contrasting individual stories, while asking how these 'fit into, challenge or alter dominant theories of social change.'[28] This chapter argues that mineworkers should not be understood as a separate group, different from the rest of Copperbelt urban society, as the experiences of both mineworkers and non-mineworkers were influenced but not determined by mining. All our informants were long-term residents

---

24 Bogumil Jewsiewicki, 'Anthropologie marxiste et recherche empirique', *Cahiers d'études africaines* 26, 101/102 (1986), pp. 265–9.
25 Ferguson, *Expectations of Modernity*; Dibwe dia Mwembu, *Bana Shaba*.
26 Rubbers, *Paternalisme en question*; Mususa, 'Mining, Welfare and Urbanisation'; Miles Larmer, 'Permanent Precarity: Capital and Labour in the Central African Copperbelt', *Labor History* 58, 2 (2017), pp. 170–84.
27 Lisa A. Lindsay, 'Biography in African History', *History in Africa* 44 (2017), p. 23.
28 Peša, 'From Life Histories to Social History', p. 89.

of the Copperbelt, having lived there since at least the 1970s. (We interviewed 50 people in Likasi and 50 in Mufulira; 30 people had an in-depth
follow-up interview.) To reflect population diversity in Likasi and Mufulira,
we sought a range of informants in terms of occupation (mineworkers,
council employees, farmers, traders, teachers, artists and 'housewives'), gender
(we interviewed 34 women and 66 men) and residential area (mine townships, city council areas and informal settlements). An open-ended ques-
tionnaire served as a guideline to these interviews, covering topics such as
education and upbringing, work life and marriage, as well as leisure activities and religion. Most of these interviews took place in people's residential
homes, though some preferred to be interviewed in their workplace.[29] The
next sections draw extensively on this interview material.

A Culture of Mining: Work Ethic, Welfare and Paternalism

Copperbelt historiography has usefully explored how mining companies
sought to develop a specific work ethic among their labour force. Mineworkers were supposed to be punctual, hardworking and disciplined –
qualities inculcated through schooling, on-the-job training and social
services. In addition, paternalistic policies, in the form of food rations,
housing, medical care and welfare provisions served to 'stabilise' the
workforce and distinguish it both from rural dwellers and other urban
residents.[30] In the 1940s, UMHK's Doctor Motoulle remarked that the
company wanted workers to 'love their work and stay attached to it as long
as possible.'[31] Recent authors have similarly argued that mining companies
on the Copperbelt were much more than employers, as '*kazi*' (salaried
employment) structured the everyday lives of workers and their families,
not only in the workplace but also through company provision of beer

29 Interviews were conducted between May and August 2018. Special thanks go to
Pierrot Monzi Kalonga in Likasi and Grant Chisapa in Mufulira. They proved indis-
pensable in contacting interviewees, facilitation and translation of interviews.
30 Jane L. Parpart, '"Where Is Your Mother?": Gender, Urban Marriage, and Colonial
Discourse on the Zambian Copperbelt, 1924–1945', *The International Journal of African
Historical Studies* 27, 2 (1994), pp. 241–71; Timothy Makori, 'Abjects retraité, jeunesse
piégée: Récits du déclin et d'une temporalité multiple parmi les générations de la
"Copperbelt" congolaise', *Politique africaine* 3, 131 (2013), pp. 51–73.
31 L. Motoulle, *Politique sociale de l'Union Minière du Haut Katanga pour sa main-d'œuvre
indigène et ses résultats au cours de vingt années d'application* (Brussels: Institut Royal Colonial
Belge, 1946), pp. 11–12.

halls, music and sports.[32] A focus on mining, work culture and paternalism still dominates historical understandings of Copperbelt social life. Such a focus problematically obscures the experiences of non-mineworkers and it does not help explain opposition to paternalism, which became particularly pronounced once economic decline set in from the mid-1970s. While our interviews clearly bring out the importance of mining companies on the Copperbelt, they also highlight a paternalistic dependency that many resented. This section, on the one hand, highlights Copperbelt residents' critiques of paternalism and its overwhelming social control, criticism which became particularly pronounced in the context of economic decline since the 1980s. On the other hand, our interviews give clues that people resisted or evaded mining companies' paternalistic controls, even in the 1960s and 1970s.

The promotion of a work ethic among mining communities started in schools, as personnel managers from the mines would visit schoolchildren to recruit potential workers.[33] By various means, including apprenticeships, mine companies sought to direct the modes of thought and behaviour of their prospective and existing workforce. Senior ZCCM employee Patson Katwisi therefore remembers the mines as 'very disciplined'.[34] Not only in the workplace, but also at home, employees and their families were subject to the control of the mining company.[35] Gécamines officials, for instance, represented the town of Likasi as an embodiment of modernity, an aesthetic which was proudly internalised by certain workers. Jacques Magenda, a Gécamines chemist, asserted: 'We had a good house in those days, it was 'modernised' ... Likasi was called Congo's prettiest town.'[36] Yet these ideals of 'cleanliness' and 'beauty' were maintained through pervasive social control. Valérienne Ngoye, a welfare worker, recalls how until the 1970s, 'inspectors would come to sensitise us about cleanliness. If we did not keep our house clean, we would be sanctioned. They would confiscate our ration tickets. ... It was a good system.'[37] Although some welcomed this control as contributing to order, Euphrasie Joa, married to a mineworker, grudgingly

32 Dibwe dia Mwembu, *Bana Shaba*; Johannes Fabian, '*Kazi*: Conceptualizations of Labor in a Charismatic Movement among Swahili-Speaking Workers', *Cahiers d'Études africaines* 50 (1973), pp. 293–325; Rubbers, 'Mining Towns, Enclaves and Spaces'.
33 Higginson, *A Working Class in the Making*.
34 Interview, Patson Katwisi, Mufulira, 1 August 2018.
35 Marcelo J. Borges and Susana B. Torres (eds), *Company Towns: Labor, Space, and Power Relations across Time and Continents* (New York: Palgrave Macmillan, 2012).
36 Interview, Jacques Magenda, Likasi, 7 June 2018.
37 Interview, Valérienne Ngoye Mudimbi, Likasi, 9 June 2018.

recounted that 'agents would perform unannounced visits to check if the houses were clean'.[38] This attempt to police public space also becomes evident in the account of Jérôme Kipili, who was councillor (*chef de cité*) of a Gécamines neighbourhood in Likasi in the 1970s: 'Gécamines was very rigorous … I had to know every family personally, to help bereaved families, to take charge of the relatives of Gécamines workers.'[39] A further expression of Gécamines' ubiquitous social control of Likasi was Trabesha, a peripheral neighbourhood where 'deviant' workers and their families were relegated. Councillor Jacques Kibombo explained that 'if you behaved badly, they would move you to Trabesha, the neighbourhood of the unruly (*la cité des indisciplinés*)'.[40] Through such measures, Gécamines discouraged drunkenness, quarrelling, theft and violence and encouraged punctuality, cleanliness, discipline and order. Though seemingly hegemonic, interviews evidence that mining communities could evade and subvert these measures of social control, as the following examples will show.

In Mufulira, many mineworkers and their families fondly remember the welfare provisions that mining companies provided until the 1980s. Tamarizika Nguni, a mineworker's wife, praised the mine as 'a source of livelihood', claiming that 'when you were working for the mine, you would enjoy, as you would get free electricity, water and housing'.[41] Yet paternalistic policies were never universally accepted as beneficial. As early as the 1960s and 1970s, some members of mining communities critiqued social welfare provision for generating overdependence on the mines, referring to it as 'spoon-feeding.'[42] Mine nurse Gertrude Dhaka explains:

> There was a dependency syndrome on the mines. The mines did all maintenance. You could not buy a light bulb without calling maintenance. Simple skills like fixing a light bulb became hard due to such dependency. Because of this … many of our young people still cannot develop skills to earn a living.[43]

Council employee William Chinda likewise suggested that because 'everything was given' to mineworkers, they tended to become lazy, while their wives 'just stayed at home'. After privatisation, however, this situation has

---

38 Interview, Euphrasie Joa, Likasi, 14 June 2018.
39 Interview, Jérôme Kipili Mulunga, Likasi, 4 June 2018.
40 Interview, Jacques Kibombo, Likasi, 11 June 2018.
41 Interview, Tamarizika Nguni, Mufulira, 3 July 2018.
42 Interview, William Bwalya Chinda, Mufulira, 8 August 2018.
43 Interview, Gertrude Kabwita Kabinda Dhaka, Mufulira, 2 August 2018.

reversed and now 'everybody must fend for themselves'.[44] Rather than simply a fond memory, nostalgia for paternalistic welfare provisions provides a way to criticise present hardships.[45]

Likasi's residents similarly resented the city's dependence on Gécamines' paternalism. When comparing Likasi to Lubumbashi, 'a big city with a lot of opportunities', trade unionist Ilunga wa Kumanza lamented Likasi's reliance on Gécamines which 'did not make our lives any better'.[46] Critiques also revolved around the inability to maintain the city's beauty after Gécamines' economic collapse. Kibombo regrets: 'everything changed in 1990 ... nobody cared for the roads or public lighting anymore ... Likasi was built by Gécamines. When Gécamines experienced hardship, so did Likasi.'[47] Still, the ubiquity and numbing effects of mining pater-nalism, especially between the 1940s and the 1970s, undermined the extent of nostalgia for a *belle époque*. In the 1990s, when the disappearance of social welfare services left many members of mining communities feeling unprepared for a life outside of the mines, such criticism of Gécamines and ZCCM paternalism endured.

Existing scholarship has tended to reinforce the idea that an all-encom-passing mining sub-culture, accompanied by benevolent paternalism, char-acterised the Copperbelt's historical experience until the 1980s.[48] This section has nuanced such claims by demonstrating that, even if residents of Mufulira and Likasi welcomed the wealth, jobs and urban development industry had brought, they remained critical of the more negative effects of mining on social life. The memories of mining communities across the Copperbelt recorded here bring out striking similarities. On both sides of the border, Gécamines and ZCCM's 'cradle-to-grave' policies evoked a mix of nostalgia and resentment. Whereas pervasive social control had perhaps brought certainty to everyday life, it left mining communities unable to fend for themselves once companies collapsed. The next section demonstrates that a vibrant social life took place outside of the orbit of mining companies.

---

44 Interview, William Bwalya Chinda, Mufulira, 8 August 2018.
45 William Cunningham Bissel, 'Engaging Colonial Nostalgia', *Cultural Anthropology* 20, 2 (2005), pp. 215–48.
46 Interview, Ilunga wa Kumanza, Likasi, 8 June 2018.
47 Interview, Jacques Kibombo, Likasi, 11 June 2018.
48 Fetter, 'L'Union Minière'.

Leisure, Culture and Social Life

Throughout the colonial and postcolonial period, Copperbelt towns were important centres of leisure activity. In the 1950s, Powdermaker portrayed the rich cultural life on the Northern Rhodesian Copperbelt, suggesting that forms of entertainment such as cinema, radio and religion were enthusiastically embraced by residents as part of their distinct urban identity.[49] Mining company paternalism sought to dominate the cultural lives and leisure activities of Copperbelt communities. Congolese mines organised leisure centres (*cercles*) where workers could come to drink, watch theatre performances, play chess or read books. Mineworkers' wives attended the sewing and knitting classes organised in welfare centres (*foyers sociaux*).[50] In Zambia, beer halls were a popular form of entertainment, generating revenue for mining companies and municipal governance, but they were also important places of social exchange.[51] Sports, football in particular, helped workers to relax after their shifts (see Chipande, Chapter 4). Such forms of entertainment created 'new urban social networks, communities, and identities'.[52] Our oral histories however demonstrate that Copperbelt residents developed their own cultural pursuits and perspectives, in relation to but not determined by company provisions. Some Congolese mineworkers for example deliberately chose not to patronise mine-sponsored social facilities. Instead, they would go and drink in the *cité* (public neighbourhood) to escape the mines' control. A focus on such assertion and cultural creativity puts mining paternalism into perspective.

In Mufulira the mines and the municipality organised a range of social clubs. These included sports (tennis, football, golf and draughts), theatre and cinema, as well as women's clubs for tailoring, cooking and housekeeping. Teacher Fridah Mwale explained how these provided complementary forms of knowledge, necessary to cope with urban life: 'At the club, we learnt how to sew and cook, at school we learnt how to write and read, and from the radio I learnt what was happening.'[53] Mufulira's workers generally praised the mine's social facilities as a form of 'caring' for

---

49 Powdermaker, *Copper Town*.
50 Dibwe dia Mwembu, *Bana Shaba*; Nancy Rose Hunt, 'Domesticity and Colonialism in Belgian Africa: Usumbura's *Foyer Social*, 1946–1960', *Signs* 15, 3 (1990), pp. 447–74.
51 Charles Ambler, 'Alcohol, Racial Segregation and Popular Politics in Northern Rhodesia', *Journal of African History* 31, 2 (1990), pp. 295–313.
52 Hikabwa D. Chipande, 'Mining for Goals: Football and Social Change on the Zambian Copperbelt', *Radical History Review* 125 (2016), pp. 55–73.
53 Interview, Fridah Mwale, Mufulira, 6 July 2018.

employees. Samson Chama, councillor for Zambia's ruling United National Independence Party (UNIP) in the 1970s and 1980s, attested that 'clubs were very popular; nearly everybody wanted to go there to pass time'.[54] Simon Bwalya, a ZCCM employee, explains how 'Chawama Hall was a socialising place and it provided recreation for miners. After going home, we would go there and ... discuss work. It kept miners busy and relaxed.' Even non-mineworkers could attend, Bwalya describes: 'we would offer a bottle of beer and share ideas'.[55] Although the mines utilised leisure activities as a form of social control, individuals commonly circumvented this. Mine-worker Nathan Mwamba patronised an independent beer hall, rather than the mine beer hall.[56] Not only were closing times more flexible there, but mineworkers could also enjoy a drink outside the purview of their fellow workmates and supervisors. Occupational and class boundaries prevented certain forms of socialisation. Mine captain Kathbert Nchema recalled: 'I was never mixing carelessly. I chose whom to go about with, who to speak to, what sort of issues I could talk about.' He added, 'as we were getting higher in the ranks, we were advised [by management] not to drink with our subordinates'.[57] Personnel manager Katwisi concurred: 'the mines knew that somehow we would not mix. For example, you would not find a sweeper with a manager drinking in the same place.'[58]

Mining companies thus used recreation as a means of control, to discipline and segregate the workforce. Katwisi recognised that the mines had leisure activities

> to keep us busy. They say an idle mind is the devil's temple. After work we wanted to put work aside, have a good time and go home. Because we were kept busy, we had no time to engage in bad habits.[59]

Owess Sinkamba, ZCCM club organiser in the 1960s and 1970s, argued that 'it was important for the mines to invest in clubs', including sports, because 'this taught the boys and girls discipline'.[60] Clubs were designed to make youths amenable to social control, although youth read their own meanings into club messages. Councillor Chama remembers that in the 1970s social clubs were meant 'to solve unemployment among young men'.

54 Interview, Samson Chama, Mufulira, 27 July 2018.
55 Interview, Simon Bwalya, Mufulira, 1 August 2018.
56 Interview, Nathan Mwamba, Mufulira, 6 July 2018.
57 Interview, Kathbert Nchema, Mufulira, 7 July 2018.
58 Interview, Patson Katwisi, Mufulira, 3 July 2018.
59 Interview, Patson Katwisi, Mufulira, 1 August 2018.
60 Interview, Owess Sinkamba, Mufulira, 8 August 2018.

According to him, the mines 'knew that if they kept people busy, they would produce better results'.[61] This applied to women as well, and in this respect ZCCM employee Boniface Lupale recalls that 'mine management encouraged attendance of sewing and knitting clubs among women'[62] (see Larmer and Taylor, Chapter 12). Nonetheless, the available forms of leisure were multiple and Copperbelt urbanites attended cinema shows, theatre performances and drinking venues in areas beyond mine control.

Apart from mine company leisure provisions, Likasi's residents highlighted other social networks, independent from or only loosely connected to Gécamines. Faith and ethnicity-based associations were particularly important in making Haut-Katanga's urban culture. The Catholic Church, a pillar of the Belgian colonial order, continued to play a central role in the everyday life of Katangese residents after independence.[63] Jacques Magenda alludes to the support the church provided him: 'it stabilised me, it made me more responsible ... the church adopts you, it supported me spiritually during the Gécamines crisis'.[64] Catholicism helped councillor Kibombo integrate when he first moved to Likasi in the 1970s, providing social support: 'I was a member of a liturgical group. The members advised me about the people and places I should avoid.'[65] Sculptor and painter Ferdinand Kakompe underlined the role the church played in his artistic training: 'Everything I learned came from the church.'[66] Social activities, thus, did not merely centre on mine welfare provision. Independent leisure activities and alternative social networks were just as important in defining Copperbelt urbanism.

Art and media were, for instance, means through which the Copperbelt population discussed and redefined the boundaries between rural and urban spheres. Radio programmes such as '*Kabusha*', a question and answer call-in show in Zambia aired between 1964 and 1990, proved extremely popular.[67] According to Bobby Kabamba, *Kabusha* was very educational because it 'gave you wide experience of how to live and cope with different problems',

61 Interview, Samson Chama, Mufulira, 27 July 2018.
62 Interview, Boniface Lupale, Mufulira, 12 July 2018.
63 Reuben Loffman, *Church, State and Colonialism in Southeastern Congo, 1890–1962* (New York: Palgrave Macmillan, 2019).
64 Interview, Jacques Magenda, Likasi, 7 June 2018.
65 Interview, Jacques Kibombo, Likasi, 11 June 2018.
66 Interview, Ferdinand Kakompe, Likasi, 19 June 2018.
67 '*Kabusha Takolelwe Bowa*' ('the one who asks questions never goes wrong'), presented by David Yumba; Debra Spitulnik, 'The Language of the City: Town Bemba as Urban Hybridity', *Journal of Linguistic Anthropology* 8, 1 (1999), pp. 42–5.

including workplace issues and those specific to urban life.[68] Mineworker Henry Longwane explains how through '*Kabusha* we used to learn about customs, traditions and ways of life, about how people should be living'. Importantly, such cultural expressions were in no way determined by the mining company. Longwane continued:

> Being on the Copperbelt and coming from different areas with different customs, traditions and beliefs, it was very important to know about others. For instance, if a Bemba wants to marry a Luvale, they need to know what those people believe in, what they stand for.[69]

Likewise, Likasi residents enjoyed adorning their walls with paintings of village scenes.[70] For Kibombo, such paintings were informative: 'I enjoy looking at how our ancestors lived. I have always lived in town and I do not know much about village life.'[71] Far from the rural–urban dichotomy suggested in much Copperbelt research, connections to rural areas remained important even among 'permanent urbanites'. Rather than being either 'cosmopolitan' or 'localist', the Copperbelt urban population tapped into various social networks.[72] In Mufulira, Tamarizika Nguni was member of a Nsenga social group, 'so that if there was any problem, suffering or death then all the Nsenga people would come together and assist.'[73] Similar forms of identity-based solidarity (socio–cultural associations) prevailed in Likasi.[74] Solidarity networks complemented and provided alternatives to mine welfare provision. After the collapse of Gécamines, these associations played an increasing role in their members' lives. Former councillor Kipili underlined how members of his association 'facilitated the recruitment [to Gécamines] of the children of their … brothers.'[75] For councillor Kibombo these associations provided a safety net in times of hardship: 'we help each other at funerals, in case of illness, or when somebody is looking for a job'.[76] Paradoxically, identity-based

---

68 Interview, Bobby Jackson Kabamba, Mufulira, 10 July 2018.
69 Interview, Henry Longwane, Mufulira, 7 July 2018.
70 Interview, Jacques Magenda, Likasi, 7 June 2018; Interview, Valérienne Ngoye, Likasi, 9 June 2018; Interview, Thérèse Kyola, Likasi, 7 June 2018; Jewsiewicki, 'Collective Memory and its Images'.
71 Interview, Jacques Kibombo, Likasi, 11 June 2018.
72 Ferguson, *Expectations of Modernity.*
73 Interview, Tamarizika Nguni, Mufulira, 3 July 2018.
74 Sandrine Vinckel, 'La violence et le silence: Politiques de réconciliation, relations interpersonnelles et pratiques sociales de coexistence au Katanga, RDC', PhD Thesis, Université Paris I, 2016, pp. 68–79.
75 Interview, Jérôme Kipili, Likasi, 4 June 2018.
76 Interview, Jacques Kibombo, Likasi, 11 June 2018.

associations fed into ethnic conflicts between 'Katangese' and 'Kasaïens' in Haut-Katanga in the 1990s, causing hundreds of casualties in Likasi.[77] More generally however, such associations provided the Copperbelt population with a social network independent from mining companies.

By paying attention to art, leisure and socialisation, it becomes evident that mining companies on the Copperbelt influenced the social lives of mining communities in multiple ways. In Likasi and Mufulira, mineworkers and their wives, children and friends attended mine-sponsored dancing, football matches and household classes. Yet these social facilities did not serve as simple instruments of control. Copperbelt communities appropriated the classes offered at welfare centres for their own purposes, to earn an income or to expand social networks. Moreover, numerous forms of leisure took place beyond the grasp of mining companies.[78] Identity-based associations or rural connections informed urbanism on the Copperbelt, just as much as beer halls and guitar music did.

Agriculture, Trade and Non-Mining Occupations

Historical studies of the Copperbelt have documented in great detail the emergence of an industrialised working class, as part of a modern urbanised society.[79] However, it is fallacious to assert that the majority of the Copperbelt's population was ever employed by the mining industry – or indeed formally employed at all (see Tables 1.1 and 1.2). Since the first emergence of Copperbelt towns, activities such as trading dried fish or second-hand clothes and piecework have been widespread.[80] Larmer explains that

> both Copperbelts did develop a large population of women and men
> … engaged in economic activities both symbiotic with and parasitic
> on the mine economy – charcoal burning, growing food (illegally)
> on mine-owned land, beer brewing, and so on. This was an essential
> but still neglected element of their actually existing modernization.[81]

---

77 Donatien Dibwe dia Mwembu, 'L'épuration ethnique au Katanga et l'éthique du redressement des torts du passé', *Canadian Journal of African Studies* 33, 2/3 (1999), pp. 483–99.

78 See: Parpart, '"Where Is Your Mother?"'; Dibwe dia Mwembu, *Bana Shaba*.

79 Ferguson, *Expectations of Modernity*; Dibwe dia Mwembu, *Bana Shaba*.

80 Deborah Potts, 'Debates About African Urbanisation, Migration and Economic Growth: What Can We Learn from Zimbabwe and Zambia?' *Geographical Journal* 182, 3 (2016), pp. 251–64.

81 Larmer, 'At the Crossroads'.

The historiographical neglect of non-mining occupations has caused a skewed image of Copperbelt communities as wholly or largely focused on formal mine employment. A more balanced view of Copperbelt social life needs to consider other livelihood activities. It was not only those labelled 'squatters' who engaged in informal employment; even senior mine employees often had subsidiary businesses to earn extra income.[82] Moreover, the importance of non-mining occupations changed over time. As opportunities for formal employment contracted in the 1980s and 1990s, informal economic activities became an even more central element of Copperbelt urbanism.

Agricultural production has always been a very common economic activity on the Copperbelt.[83] Mineworker Dennis Tembo and his wife Iness Zulu in Mufulira explained: 'We grew up as farmers. If you do not cultivate, what is it that you can eat?'[84] Beyond being a rural practice transmitted to the urban Copperbelt, agricultural production could stabilise and/or supplement urban wages. Victoria Mwewa grew crops to earn extra income, to cope with her husband's erratic salary.[85] In Likasi, Valérienne Ngoye's family had a small field to complement the food ration provided by Gécamines: 'we were well served, but we still needed fresh vegetables'.[86] To some, Foster Kunda explains, farming symbolised the economic downturn since the 1990s: 'Way back there was nothing like farming in town, we relied on jobs, but now here in town we are also farming.'[87] Yet in fact, agriculture on the Copperbelt long predated economic decline and was a distinct adaptation to urban life. To senior ZCCM employee Levi Chushi, farming was a 'training ground' for his children and wife who had grown up in town.[88] Even if some wage earners had comfortable salaries, Elizabeth Malokotela explained: 'When it comes to expenditure, you cannot be buying everything. So the garden reduces some expenses.'[89] In Likasi in the 1970s, councillor Kipili's wife cultivated crops and had a few chickens: 'she did not do it out of necessity, but it provided something to eat and it allowed us to save

82   B. A. Kasongo and A. G. Tipple, 'An Analysis of Policy towards Squatters in Kitwe, Zambia', *Third World Planning Review* 12, 2 (1990), pp. 147–65.
83   Iva Peša, 'Crops and Copper: Agriculture and Urbanism on the Central African Copperbelt, 1950–2000', *Journal of Southern African Studies*, 69:3 (2020), pp. 527–45.
84   Interview, Dennis Tembo and Iness Zulu, Mufulira, 6 July 2018.
85   Interview, Victoria Mwewa, Mufulira, 17 July 2018.
86   Interview, Valérienne Ngoye Mudimbi, Likasi, 9 June 2018.
87   Interview, Foster Chimfutumba Kunda, Mufulira, 20 July 2018.
88   Interview, Levi Aaron Chushi, Mufulira, 11 July 2018.
89   Interview, Elizabeth Malokotela, Mufulira, 2 August 2018.

some money'.[90] These accounts make it clear that urban agriculture on the Copperbelt had many functions and was not merely an activity driven by economic necessity. Instead, farming stabilised urban residence and diversified income sources, among the wealthy and among the poor. There were, however, many other ways to earn additional income.

Respondents' reasons to engage in piecework or trade were manifold. Trader Tamarizika Nguni explained: 'I did not want to be admiring things from other people and I wanted my children to live and feed well.'[91] When he first arrived in Mufulira in the 1950s, Nathan Mwamba joined a club, which gave him access to piecework. He would line up in the morning to see which jobs were available and work until the contract was finished.[92] After he finished school in 1969, Chrispin Chani worked for various private companies and in civil service. He explained that 'the differences in salary scales made me move from one job to another'. The conditions of service in government attracted him: 'There was no strict schedule, you could even come to work late.'[93] To improve food security, people engaged in all kinds of activities. While working for Gécamines in Likasi in the 1970s, Gaston Mutiti set up a small business, buying salt in a neighbouring village to resell it in town: 'It went very well, but maintaining the truck cost a lot of money. You earn a bit of cash, but then you have to use everything to replace broken parts.'[94] Boston Mwenya, ZCCM employee, bought fishing nets to take to Luapula Province, repurposing rural ties to engage in urban business.[95] Many women sold clothes, shoes or foodstuffs in the market to supplement household incomes. In order to sustain her family in Likasi in the 1980s and 1990s, Pauline Kingombe sold doughnuts, opened a beer parlour and traded second-hand clothes from Tanzania.[96] Through sewing skills acquired in a Gécamines welfare centre, Euphrasie Joa boosted her household income: 'when I could not make ends meet, my sewing activities would put some money on the table'.[97] William Chinda started trading from a young age, selling mangoes to contribute to his school fees. Later, he acquired a wheelbarrow to deliver maize flour to households. Chinda

90 Interview, Jérôme Kipili Mulunga, Likasi, 4 June 2018.
91 Interview, Tamarizika Nguni, Mufulira, 3 July 2018.
92 Interview, Nathan Mwamba, Mufulira, 6 July 2018.
93 Interview, Chrispin Chani, Mufulira, 16 July 2018.
94 Interview, Gaston Mutiti, Likasi, 4 June 2018.
95 Interview, Boston Mwenya, Mufulira, 10 July 2018.
96 Interview, Pauline Kingombe, Likasi, 12 June 2018.
97 Interview, Euphrasie Joa, Likasi, 14 June 2018.

attributed such 'entrepreneurship' to economic downturn and the discontinuation of paternalistic welfare policies in the 1990s:

> Initially, most people did not think of businesses like trading, we relied on people from Congo to bring *salaula* [second-hand clothes]. Later on, when there was unemployment, we took over and we are making our own things now. In the 1970s, my uncle would put everything on the table, so I would go to the stadium for a show, and there was no need to start a business.[98]

Such depictions romanticise a golden age that probably never existed. Trade, tailoring and agriculture were in reality part of Copperbelt life and urban identity from the very beginning. Furthermore, such activities, rather than being supplementary, were often central to household budgets.[99]

Even senior mineworkers and civil servants engaged in activities to earn additional income. In Mufulira, Patson Katwisi explained:

> My wife … used to say that employment would end. … She had seen some of our friends leave employment, retire and become destitute. So she asked: 'Don't you think we should do something so that we have something to fall back on if anything happens?'[100]

Given their capital, skills and knowledge, senior mineworkers were more likely to have commercial farms in peri-urban areas, to run a transport business or to engage in profitable trade. Affluent Copperbelt residents practised agriculture to strengthen their socio-economic position. Jacques Magenda, a Gécamines manager, explained: 'I cultivated … to strengthen my home. I was a senior employee (*cadre*) and although the wages were good, you had to maintain your status.'[101] These accounts, on the one hand, illustrate the blurred boundaries and interconnections between formal and informal employment: mineworkers used their salaries to set up farming or trading businesses, whereas second-hand clothes sellers relied on mineworkers as their clientele. On the other hand, these recollections show the inadequacy of considering formal mine employment as the quintessential expression of urbanism. Formal employment was a privilege restricted to

98 Interview, William Bwalya Chinda, Mufulira, 8 August 2018.
99 Patience Mususa, '"Getting By": Life on the Copperbelt after the Privatisation of the Zambia Consolidated Copper Mines', *Social Dynamics* 36, 2 (2010), pp. 380–94; Alex Nyumbaiza Tambwe, Kasongo Nkulu, Kitaba Kya Ghoanys, Kunkuzya Mwanachilongwe, Kaimbi Mpyana and Kayiba Bukasa (eds), *Le développement du Katanga méridional* (Paris: L'Harmattan, 2015).
100 Interview, Patson Katwisi, Mufulira, 1 August 2018.
101 Interview, Jacques Magenda, Likasi, 7 June 2018.

a small proportion of the Copperbelt urban population. More importantly, activities such as urban agriculture or trade did not merely serve livelihood purposes. Instead, growing vegetables or working as a tailor was central to establishing a place for oneself on the Copperbelt. Through these activities, individuals asserted a specific form of urbanism. Focusing only on formal employment neglects such creative and valuable ways of making a living on the Copperbelt.[102]

Gender on the Copperbelt

Due to its history of industrial mining activity, the Copperbelt has long been imagined as a male-dominated environment. Evans explains how copper deposits 'were mined, managed and administered by men – as wage labourers, breadwinners, trade union officials, civil servants and politicians'.[103] Women, in this context, have often been portrayed as and assumed to be docile housewives, enabling the male breadwinner model. Yet Parpart equally provided examples of independent women on the Copperbelt, who did not follow the directives of their 'husbands'.[104] Female beer brewing, prostitution and trade on the Zambian and Congolese Copperbelt have been amply documented.[105] The economic crisis of the 1980s and 1990s turned gender stereotypes and inequalities on their head, due to 'the declining economy, which has turned many women into important contributors to household welfare in the face of men's shrinking incomes from wage employment'.[106] The Copperbelt thus provides a good test case to examine the changing nature and contestation of gender relations and roles. By centring analysis on women, this section reassesses the role of elder male mineworkers on the Copperbelt.

102 Peša, 'Crops and Copper'.
103 Alice Evans, '"Women Can Do What Men Can Do": The Causes and Consequences of Growing Flexibility in Gender Divisions of Labour in Kitwe, Zambia', *Journal of Southern African Studies* 40, 5 (2014), pp. 981–98, p. 981.
104 Parpart, '"Where Is Your Mother?"'
105 Benjamin Rubbers, 'When Women Support the Patriarchal Family: The Dynamics of Marriage in a Gécamines Mining Camp (Katanga Province, DR Congo)', *Journal of Historical Sociology* 28, 2 (2015), pp. 213–34; Donatien Dibwe dia Mwembu, 'Les fonctions des femmes africaines dans les camps de l'Union Minière du Haut-Katanga (1925–1960)', *Zaïre-Afrique*, 272 (1993), pp. 105–18.
106 Karen Tranberg Hansen, *Keeping House in Lusaka* (New York: Columbia University Press, 1997), p. 103.

Historical accounts assume that men were primarily attracted to the Copperbelt because of employment opportunities. In Mufulira, mine-worker John Mule recalls: 'There was no job for young men in the village, so we came to the Copperbelt looking for employment.'[107] Unsurprisingly, in oral histories men tend to assert an idealised image of 'masculinity', promoted through education, formal employment and social activities. Council employee Chinda explains that young men were 'trained to be strong and find solutions'.[108]

Some accounts suggest a clear-cut gender division of labour in the household, whereby a male breadwinner would cater for his wife and educate and discipline his children. In Mufulira, mineworker Nathan Mwamba attested that 'in those days women were not working'.[109] Yet what being a 'housewife' involved depended on definitions of work. Indeed, few women were formally employed, yet many earned a considerable income through trade or agriculture. Boston Mwenya declared that 'my wife was just a housewife', but went on to explain that 'she used to sell items at the market such as vegetables and other things'.[110] Boniface Lupale's wife worked as a tailor and social welfare instructor for mineworkers' wives. Mine management encouraged the attendance of women at welfare clubs and in doing so inculcated specific gender norms and expectations.[111] Simon Bwalya recalls that 'women were supposed to keep the home together, they watched over the household'.[112] Yet trader Annie Lukwasa attested that stereotypical gender roles were far from universal. She recalls drinking beer with friends in front of her house, an activity which her husband condoned and to which the mine company turned a blind eye.[113] Emeria Mweupe sold vegetables, fish and groundnuts in the market. Together with other female traders, she would go to distant cities, such as Lusaka or even Johannesburg, to order goods.[114] Such examples show that some Copperbelt women have long enjoyed considerable physical and social mobility.

107 Interview, John Mule, Mufulira, 12 July 2018.
108 Interview, William Bwalya Chinda, Mufulira, 8 August 2018.
109 Interview, Nathan Mwamba, Mufulira, 7 July 2018.
110 Interview, Boston Mwenya, Mufulira, 10 July 2018.
111 Interview, Boniface Lupale, Mufulira, 12 July 2018.
112 Interview, Simon Bwalya, Mufulira, 1 August 2018.
113 Interview, Annie Lukwasa, Mufulira, 18 July 2018.
114 Interview, Emeria Mweupe, Mufulira, 19 July 2018.

The economic recession of the 1980s and 1990s further challenged and sometimes reversed gender roles. Bobby Kabamba, an engineer with ZCCM, explained: 'Women are looking after men now. They are paying for schoolchildren through their businesses and marketing.'[115] In practice however, gender roles on the Copperbelt probably always deviated from the male breadwinner model.[116]

In Likasi, Gécamines provided significant professional opportunities for women, occasionally even in management positions. Although she did not graduate from secondary school, Sarah Léontine Bulanda enrolled in typist training in a company school. Upon completion in 1968, she became a Gécamines secretary and eventually a mess manager.[117] Valérienne Ngoye took courses in a UMHK household school, where she received instruction in sewing, cleaning and cooking. She became instructor (*monitrice*) in a Gécamines welfare centre, where she taught workers' daughters and wives household skills. Ngoye acquired further responsibilities and started advising the wives of managers, crossing class lines: 'They were under my care … I visited them at home … We sat together at the table and taught the children how to behave.'[118] Beyond her advisory role, Ngoye could act on behalf of women with marital problems and sanction male workers:

> It was called *action sociale*. For instance, if a man came home drunk … I would give him two warnings and sanction him by withholding a part of his salary … The women would come to me to complain, I had to take initiative.[119]

Stéphanie Mumba was the manager of Likasi's mine hospital launderette, supervising fifteen employees, including men demoted from higher positions. She recalls: 'Despite their age, they obeyed me. … I learnt what it meant to be a manager: not being pushed around by employees, having authority, how to talk to a subordinate, how to give orders, punish the rebels.'[120] Gécamines thus offered these women employment opportunities that put them on par with – or even in charge of – men. This further challenged the position of men as household heads.

---

115 Interview, Bobby Jackson Kabamba, Mufulira, 10 July 2018.
116 Francesca Pugliese, 'Mining Companies and Gender(ed) Policies: The Women of the Congolese Copperbelt, Past and Present', *Extractive Industries and Society* (2020), https:// doi.org/10.1016/j.exis.2020.08.006.
117 Interview, Sarah Léontine Bulanda, Likasi, 6 June 2018.
118 Interview, Valérienne Ngoye Mudimbi, Likasi, 9 June 2018.
119 Ibid.
120 Interview, Stéphanie Mumba, Likasi, 6 June 2018.

Gender relations were a continuous topic of debate within households and among groups of women. Spouses discussed or argued about the sharing of household income and economic responsibilities. Numerous people recalled a play by Likasi's popular theatre group Mufwankolo (see Dibwe dia Mwembu, Chapter 11).[121] The play depicts a greedy husband, who hides his income from his wife and always keeps his money in his pocket.[122] One day he drops an entire monthly salary into the toilet. Ngoye recalled: 'The message is that a husband should not keep the money to himself, but share it with his wife.'[123] Theatre thus offered an effective way to discuss and reconfigure gender roles. Yet households approached the pooling of resources in different ways. Bulanda testified that 'my husband allowed me to manage the household budget'.[124] On the other hand, Euphrasie Joa's husband never showed her his payslip: 'I did not know how much he earned, he just came home with an amount of money that I had to manage, he kept a share to himself, to enjoy himself.'[125] Yet the different income patterns of men and women were often symbiotic. In Mufulira, William Chinda's wife was a trader. He would give her some money from his salary and she would order goods and prepare beer for sale.[126] Even if men were historically more often wage earners, this does not mean that women simply followed their lead.

The changing nature of life on the Copperbelt continually challenged and redefined gender relationships. Although government and mine company officials, through employment, schooling, church and social work, asserted certain ideals of masculinity and femininity, these rarely went undisputed. Men's salaries were too precarious and seldom sufficient to uphold a 'housewife' and the idealised family, particularly after the 1980s. Women earned an income and had much freedom to socialise and drink with neighbours while their husbands were at work. Nonetheless, some women voluntarily asserted an image of 'propriety', especially through church involvement or household classes. By upholding an idealised image of an elder male mineworker as household head, Copperbelt

---

121 Johannes Fabian, *Power and Performance: Ethnographic Explorations through Proverbial Wisdom and Theater in Shaba, Zaire* (Madison: University of Wisconsin Press, 1990).
122 Interview, Valérienne Ngoye Mudimbi, Likasi, 9 June 2018; Interview, Pauline Kibombe, Likasi, 12 June 2018; Interview, Jacques Kibombo, Likasi, 11 June 2018.
123 Interview, Valérienne Ngoye Mudimbi, Likasi, 9 June 2018.
124 Interview, Sarah Léontine Bulanda, Likasi, 6 June 2018.
125 Interview, Euphrasie Joa, Likasi, 14 June 2018.
126 Interview, William Bwalya Chinda, Mufulira, 8 August 2018.

historiography has glossed over its changing gender dynamics.[127] Female-headed households are no exception on the Copperbelt today and children rarely grow up in a nuclear family. Acknowledging such diversity is crucial to understanding historical and contemporary Copperbelt communities.

Conclusion

In 2009, Rubbers depicted memories of the past among Haut-Katanga's residents as 'the story of a tragedy'. Facing economic hardship and an uncertain future, Copperbelt urbanites made sense of their current suffering by invoking their 'abandonment' by the Belgians, or their subjection to diverse powerful actors, ranging from global capitalist companies to supernatural forces.[128] Although such pessimism towards history was present in some of our respondents' accounts of Likasi and Mufulira, most offered a more nuanced assessment of their personal trajectories and current predicament. The heyday of ZCCM and Gécamines paternalism was, for example, fondly remembered for the security it provided, but simultaneously resented for the dependency it created. More positively, many informants proudly spoke of their own agency when confronted with hardships, by relying on non-mining economic activities or religious and identity-based solidarity networks. The experiences of women particularly highlighted the adaptability of Copperbelt residents in a shifting socio-economic context. Some supported their households through informal activities. Others made money by working as tailors, relying on 'housewife skills' acquired in the patriarchal education system. A few actively pursued a career in mine companies, still too often perceived as an exclusively masculine sphere.

While the Copperbelt has been depicted as the spearhead of urban-industrial 'modernity' in Central Africa, oral history accounts suggest a more complex understanding of what 'modernity' meant in daily life.[129] Rather than revolving solely around mining, agriculture, either

127 Arnold L. Epstein, *Urbanization and Kinship: The Domestic Domain on the Copperbelt of Zambia, 1950–1956* (London: Academic Press, 1981).

128 Benjamin Rubbers, 'The Story of a Tragedy: How People in Haut-Katanga Interpret the Post-Colonial History of Congo', *Journal of Modern African Studies* 42, 2 (2009), pp. 267–89.

129 See the Introduction to this volume; Jennifer Robinson, *Ordinary Cities: Between Modernity and Development* (London: Routledge, 2006); Garth Myers, *African Cities: Alternative Visions of Urban Theory and Practice* (London: Zed Books, 2011).

as a subsistence activity or as a means of entrepreneurship, was omni-present on the Copperbelt. Radio shows and popular paintings brought depictions of village 'tradition' into urban living rooms. 'Ethnic' identi-ties – connecting urban dwellers to their 'ancestral' roots – supported people when the state and mining companies collapsed, but could also be the cause of conflict. Most importantly, oral histories suggest that mining paternalism – though irrefutably important – did not dominate Copperbelt social life. Even when Gécamines and ZCCM provided schooling, food rations, housing and leisure to their employees, the mining companies never controlled Copperbelt communities. In order to understand Copperbelt social history, equal attention needs to be paid to independent bars as to mine-run beer halls and to petty tomato vending in addition to underground mining.

When analysed from a cross-border perspective, Copperbelt residents' historical experiences are characterised by striking similarities. Although divided by a political border, Copperbelt oral histories bring out compa-rable challenges and opportunities. Accounts highlight how, on both sides, boundaries between formal and informal activities, gender roles, urban and rural, 'tradition' and 'modernity' or past security and present uncertainty were and remain fundamentally blurred. The oral history approach thus shows that Copperbelt social life was even more vibrant and creative than has hitherto been assumed.

Table 1.1: Mufulira mine employees and total urban population[130]

Year	Mine employees	Urban population
1956	8,572	50,000
1961	9,472	80,600
1969	N/A	107,802

130 We are grateful to Duncan Money for providing us with these figures. These come from the following sources: Federation of Rhodesia and Nyasaland, Census of Popula-tion 1956, pp. 4, 76–78; Federation of Rhodesia and Nyasaland, Final Report on 1961 Census, p. 25; George Kay, *Social Geography of Zambia* (London: Hodder & Stoughton, 1967), p. 95; Government of Zambia, Census of Population 1969, A7; Central Statistical Office, Monthly Digest of Statistics, Jan–Mar 1981, p. 2; ZCCM-IH, Zambianisation Report – Mufulira Division, December 1981–September 1985, p. 1; ZCCM-IH 5.5.1D, Actual Labour Strengths by Grade as at 31 January 2000; Government of Zambia, Summary Report for 2000 Census, p. 12.

Table 1.1 continued

Year	Mine employees	Urban population
1980	N/A	149,778
1985	8,355	N/A
1990	N/A	152,069
2000	4,554	143,930

Table 1.2: Likasi mine employees and total urban population[131]

Year	Mine employees	Urban population
1950	13,339	48,000
1955	17,892	64,000
1960	22,692	87,000
1965	27,103	99,000
1970	29,650	150,000
1975	32,840 (Total Gécamines)	170,000
1980	35,149 (Total Gécamines)	193,000
1985	33,045 (Total Gécamines)	220,000
1990	32,992 (Total Gécamines)	252,000
1995	22,257 (Total Gécamines)	288,000
2000	21,704 (Total Gécamines)	330,000

131 Until 1970, Quinquennial average for the Panda headquarters, Donatien Dibwe dia Mwembu, 'Industrialisation et santé: Transformation de la morbidité et de la mortalité à l'Union Minière du Haut-Katanga', PhD Thesis, University of Laval, Quebec, 1990, p. 122. After 1970 we only have numbers for Gécamines as a whole (including Lubumbashi and Kolwezi); these numbers are derived from Gécamines Annual Reports. Urban population figures come from https://populationstat.com/democratic-republic-of-the-congo/likasi, n.d. (accessed 14 October 2020).

2

Being a Child of the Mines: Youth Magazines and Comics in the Copperbelt

ENID GUENE

Introduction

The Copperbelt has many claims to fame, not least among them the various forms of popular art that developed there over the course of the past century. As it grew in scale, the mining industry threw up a spattering of new urban centres to which large numbers of people from myriad cultural and linguistic backgrounds flocked, thus providing ample fertile ground for new creative endeavours. Perhaps best known among such endeavours is what has become known as 'Congolese Popular Painting': a new approach to figurative painting which gained prominence in the mid-twentieth century and is known for its brightly coloured depictions of the daily lives and struggles of the Congolese people. Yet, there existed another type of popular art which, though it did not achieve quite the same level of international recognition, was no less prevalent on the Copperbelt: comics (*bandes dessinées* in French). Not only were comics of all kinds widely read on the Copperbelt, but Katanga and Zambia have also seen the creation of several widely available and influential youth magazines that published popular comic strips. In September 1964, Katanga's all-powerful mining company, the *Union Minière du Haut-Katanga* (known as Gécamines after independence), launched *Mwana Shaba Junior*, its very own magazine for the youth. The magazine, which had a peak print run of 41,500 copies in the 1980s, was distributed monthly to the families of every Gécamines employee for free.

Meanwhile, from 1971, Zambian children had access to *Orbit* ('The magazine for young Zambians'), a magazine with an initial print run of over 65,000 copies,[1] which was commissioned by the Zambian Ministry of Education to be circulated in schools across the country. This was followed in 1984 by *Speak Out!* – a bimonthly produced by the Franciscan Mission Press in Ndola with a distribution of 40,000.[2] Not only are these magazines some of the longest-lasting comic magazines on the continent, thus allowing large numbers of children to engage with the medium of comics over an extended period of time, but they also provided local talents with the chance to produce their own. Yet Zambia is not known for its comics at all, while the Katangese Copperbelt continues to be much better known for its popular paintings.

As will be shown in this chapter, comics were a key component of a childhood spent on both sides of the Copperbelt's border. They had played an important role in the imaginative development of the Copperbelt youth even before any of these magazines were published, which, in time, allowed key institutions – in this case, a powerful mining company, the Zambian State and the Catholic Church – to use the medium for their own purposes: as a tool to convey specific messages and values. At the same time, while comics were originally an imported medium to the Copperbelt, and were usually produced to 'educate' or 'steer' their African audience in a certain direction, their target populations were by no means passive consumers. In fact, *Mwana Shaba Junior*, *Orbit* and *Speak Out!* availed the primary space for comics in the region and provided aspiring Copperbelt cartoonists with the opportunity to 're-appropriate' and transform the medium. Crucially, this reappropriation took place against the backdrop of the fast economic, political and social changes that followed the dramatic downturn in copper prices of 1974–75. In this context, comics became an avenue through which to have 'conversations' about these changes. In this way, as will be argued, a medium which had previously been actively deployed to promote a vision for an industrial and 'modern' future became a tool to critique the failures of modernity and the corrosive effects of economic decline.

1 According to the *The Europa World Year*, it was published about nine times a year.
2 Yvonne Malambo Kabombwe, 'A History of the Mission Press in Zambia, 1970–2011', MA Thesis, University of Zambia, 2015, p. 25.

The Comic Cultures of the Zambian and Congolese Copperbelt

At first glance, there appears to be a clear 'comics division' between the Democratic Republic of the Congo and Zambia. Nancy Rose Hunt argued, based on a meticulous study of magazines and newspapers from colonial Congo, that 'comic imagery flourished in Congo in the 1930s, not only in cities but wherever newspapers travelled'.[3] Similarly, according to Andreas Knigge, Congo was the only African country to have started to develop its own comic culture as early as the 1940s.[4] Independent Congo, for its part, has been associated with an explosion of comic forms, ranging from development comics, to Mobutu's life story, and to ephemeral street comics, and has produced some of the continent's best-known comic artists including the man whom the British Broadcasting Corporation (BBC) described as 'the Congolese author best known outside his country', Barly Baruti.[5] In contrast, English-speaking Southern Africa, excepting South Africa, has produced few prominent comic artists.[6] Congo's early start in comic-making has been linked to both the popularity of comics in Belgium and their resulting availability in the Belgian Congo,[7] and the fact that they were quickly identified as a useful teaching tool in colonising educational projects. Semi-didactic comics for Congolese audiences proliferated in the post-war period, especially in Catholic (or Catholic-influenced) newspapers

3   Nancy R. Hunt, 'Tintin and the Interruptions of Congolese Comics' in Paul Landau and Deborah S. Griffin (eds), *Images and Empires: Visuality in Colonial and Postcolonial Africa* (Berkeley: University of California Press, 2002), pp. 90–133, p. 97.
4   Andreas C. Knigge, *Vom Massenblatt ins multimedia Abenteuer* (Hamburg: Rowohlt, 1996), p. 238.
5   Thomas Hubert, 'Capturing Kinshasa through Comics', BBC, 2011, www.bbc.co.uk/news/world-africa-11996279 (accessed 19 July 2020).
6   According to comic scholar John A. Lent, as far as the Southern African region is concerned, South Africa and Tanzania 'stand alone in all aspects of comic art'. See John A. Lent, 'Southern Africa: Hardly a Cartoonist's Eden' in John A. Lent (ed.), *Cartooning in Africa* (New York: Hampton Press, 2009), pp. 219–46, p. 223. South Africa has spawned some of the continent's best-known comics, including Zapiro's political cartoons, comic strip *Madam and Eve*, and the underground-style *Bitterkomix*. Tanzania is known for its Swahili comics and cartoons, some early examples of which may have been influenced by Congolese magazines. See Jigal Beez, 'Stupid Hares and Margarine: Early Swahili Comics' in John A. Lent (ed.), *Cartooning in Africa* (New York: Hampton Press, 2009), pp. 137–57.
7   Hunt, 'Tintin', p. 96, p. 111; Christophe Cassiau-Haurie, *Histoire de la BD congolaise* (Paris: Harmattan, 2010), p. 150.

and magazines. Perhaps the most striking example of this didactic brand of comics was *Les aventures de Mbumbulu*, a series created in 1946 for the state-published – though missionary influenced – magazine *Nos Images*. Each Mbumbulu 'story' ended with a moralising sentence, such as 'on reflection, he understood that in order to be able to complete a job successfully, one must be prepared for it',[8] or 'beware of magicians and witch doctors, they make a living at your expense'.[9] Nothing of the kind is known to have existed in colonial Zambia, though this may in part be due to lack of research on the topic.[10] Yet, oral evidence collected on both sides of the border suggested that by the 1960s and 1970s, the inhabitants of the Copperbelt had access to the full range of whatever comics were available in the British and Belgo-French markets at the time, and more besides.

Jacky Mulenda, for example, who worked for *Mwana Shaba Junior* in the 1980s, remembers from his childhood in the 1960s and 1970s that 'everything was there: *Bécassine*, *Spirou* and *Tintin* [comic strips], *Tintin* and *Spirou* magazines as well'.[11] Other comics which informants recalled reading in the same period included *Lucky Luke*, *Ric Hochet*, *Buck Danny*, *La patrouille des Castors*, *The Smurfs*, *Alix*, *Gaston Lagaffe* and *Bob et Bobette*, the latter a French translation of the Flemish series *Suske en Wiske*. In other words, Katangese readers were familiar with the full range of mainstream comics published in Belgium in the middle decades of the twentieth century. As Jacky Mulenda recalled,

> You know when we read *Lucky Luke*, my older brothers always sat down on the ground to read them. Then, we would hear a burst of laughter. It was because of the tomfoolery of the Dalton brothers [characters in Lucky Luke]. You would hear several waves of laughter as the jokes came in the story. They were in stitches.[12]

Similarly, British comics loom large in the memory of Zambian informants who grew up on the Copperbelt prior to the 1990s. Most read *Andy Capp*, a funny strip centred on a wife-beating figure who never works, and

---

8   *Nos Images*, Issue 30, 15 December 1950.
9   *Nos Images*, Issue 6, 15 December 1948.
10 Several magazines and newspapers published for Africans were circulating on the Zambian Copperbelt in the early 1960s, some produced locally, others imported. It may be that closer examination of this literature would reveal cartoons and comics. See Hortense Powdermaker, *Copper Town: Changing Africa* (New York and Evanston: Harper & Row, 1962), pp. 281–2, p. 340, p. 367.
11 Interview, Jacky Mpungu Mulenda, Lubumbashi, 14 August 2019.
12 Ibid.

Garth, an immensely strong hero who battles various villains across time and space. Both were originally published in the British Newspaper *Daily Mirror*, from 1957 and 1943 respectively, but also appeared in the *Times of Zambia*. Their presence in a national newspaper made them eminently accessible, and several informants remembered having kept a scrapbook. As one recalled, 'I never wanted to miss those ... I actually used to cut them out and paste them into an old phone book.'[13] In addition, when prompted about the comics they read as children, informants on the Zambian Copperbelt almost invariably first cited *Dandy* and *Beano*, two children's comics published by the Scottish publisher D.C. Thomson since 1937 and 1938 respectively. Angel Phiri, a comic enthusiast who now works in the televisual field, noted that *Dandy* and *Beano* 'were the go-to magazines for children. If you were bringing anything for the kids, it would have been those.'[14] D.C. Thomson's main rival in the world of British comics, Amalgamated Press (renamed Fleetway Publications in 1959), appears to have been popular in the Copperbelt too. In the 1950s, Amalgamated Press had introduced the 'Picture Library' format, which consisted in one long complete story set in one of several set genres: westerns, detective/thriller stories, sport, science fiction, and war.[15] Peter Kapenda, a cartoonist who later contributed many drawings to *Orbit*, was very fond of 'Fleet Street comics', particularly 'Second World War and detective comics', which, he says, inspired the development of his own style:

> I had a lot of influence from the British comics, the Fleet Street comics ... [what inspired me was] the way they told the stories, especially the war comics [and] the artwork. There were some artists who were very good at line drawings. Just black ink on white.[16]

Access to such literature must, in part, have been facilitated by the presence of libraries and bookshops across the mining towns. Even Gécamines' social centres (known as '*cercles*') and youth centres had their own little libraries. Dominique Ilunga, who worked as a librarian for one of Gécamines' *cercles* in the 1960s and early 1970s, recalled that comics such as *Bob et Bobette* and *Tintin* were his library's most popular items, among adults and youths alike. Gécamines did not pay for these books however. Instead, 'we would

---

13 Interview, Henry Chitaika, Ndola, 18 July 2019.
14 Interview, Angel Phiri, Lusaka, 7 July 2019.
15 For more on British comics, see James Chapman, *British Comics: A Cultural History* (London: Reaktion Books, 2011).
16 Interview, Peter Kapenda, Ndola, 18 July 2019.

go to houses of the Europeans, or of the Congolese who liked to read. [We would collect] the books they had already read to add them to our library collection.'[17] On the Zambian side, while council and mine libraries reportedly prioritised novels over comics, one significant exception was the Hammarskjöld Memorial Library, which is attached to the Mindolo Ecumenical Foundation in Kitwe. This was a well-equipped library, which had opened in 1963 with funds from Sweden, and which, crucially, children could access for free.[18] As Angel Phiri recalled, 'almost half of Kitwe used to borrow books there':

> For me, [the Hammarskjöld library] was like a paradise. Almost half the time, as long as you are out of school, you would go to the library. If you are not playing soccer, you would go to the library. If it's a holiday, the first thing you'll think about is the library.[19]

It is, however, a bookstore which seems to have played the most crucial role in disseminating comics on the Zambian Copperbelt: Kingstons Ltd. The successor to Herald Stationery and Book Store which had established bookstores in Kitwe and Ndola by the 1930s,[20] Kingstons was Zambia's main source of newspapers, records, books, magazines, and comics, and was probably the main route via which D.C. Thomson and Fleetway Publications were distributed in Zambia. This is borne out by the fact that Fleetway comic magazines were published with a note stating that their 'sole agent' for 'Rhodesia and Zambia' was 'Kingstons Ltd'. This also chimes with informants' recollections that 'Kingston was … the source of everything' and 'the sole supplier and distributor of all books from abroad'.[21] Cartoonist Peter Kapenda recalled:

> When magazines came from the UK, they were supposed to sell them for a certain period. If they didn't sell all of them, they used to tear them so that people would not be able to read them and then throw them in the rubbish dump. That's where the boys used to go and pick them up.[22]

17 Interview, Dominique Ilunga, Likasi, 10 August 2019.
18 *Orbit*, 1, 6 (1971), p. 12.
19 Angel Phiri interview.
20 William D. Gale, *The Rhodesian Press: The History of the Rhodesian Printing and Publishing Company Ltd* (Salisbury: Rhodesian Printing & Publishing Company, 1962).
21 Interview, Ben Phiri, Ndola, 15 July 2019.
22 Peter Kapenda interview.

In this way, via bookshops and libraries, and as children shared their comics with each other, comics circulated widely on the Copperbelt, reaching even children who did not necessarily have the means to buy books first-hand.

In addition, when asked about what imported comics he read, Angel Phiri immediately came up with a list which suggested horizons going beyond what the former colonial powers produced:

> If you are going to talk about imported comics we had a lot of them. You had *Beano, Dandy, Asterix, Tintin, Apache, Archie* and *Sabrina* … We had Marvel and DC comics. All those things used to be around and used to have a lot of influence.[23]

This short list is enough to give an idea of the breadth of material on offer: *Beano* and *Dandy* are from the United Kingdom; *Archie* and *Sabrina* and Marvel and DC Universe are from the United States. *Tintin* is from Belgium, *Asterix* from France, and *Apache* is a photocomic from South Africa. It is perhaps significant that the informants who grew up before the 1960s do not remember seeing any translated Belgo-French comics, as this more or less corresponds to the period when these comics were first translated into English.[24] According to Austin Kaluba, a cultural journalist at the *Times of Zambia, Asterix* and *Tintin* were easily obtainable from Kingstons, circulated in schools and were 'massively popular'. He went as far as saying that 'you have not lived in Zambia if you have not read *Asterix* and *Tintin*'.[25]. Similarly, American comics were, by all accounts, largely available on both sides of the border. Even the oldest Zambian informant, who grew up in the 1950s, remembers reading *Popeye*, as well as Disney and superheroes comics (Marvel and DC universe) such as *Batman, Superman* and *Spiderman*. In Katanga, Jacky Mulenda recalled that,

> [Superheroes comics] were always in the A5 format and every other page was printed in colour and the others in black and white. I did not know their origin … But they did not interest us much … We were used to comics published in colour and we preferred humorous characters.[26]

---

23 Angel Phiri interview.
24 The full process of translating *Tintin* into English was commissioned in 1958 by Methuen, Hergé's British publishers, while the first translated album of *Asterix* was published in 1969 by Brockhampton Press. Other comics of Belgian origins which Zambian informants cited were *Lucky Luke* and *The Smurfs*.
25 Interview, Austin Kaluba, Lusaka, 1 July 2019.
26 Jacky Mpungu Mulenda interview.

In turn, South Africa's main contribution to the Copperbelt's comic culture, at least that of the Zambian Copperbelt, came in the form of photocomics. These enjoyed enormous popularity in South Africa in the 1960s, 1970s and 1980s.[27] In Zambia, according to informants' recollections, the most popular ones were: *Lance Spearman* (aka 'The Spear'), a super-spy character, created in 1968 by Drum Publications; *Chunky Charlie*, a funny inspector character who carried fancy gadgets in his huge coat; and *She*, described as a 'kickass character' who 'was always in a miniskirt with an afro and very high boots'.[28]

From the mid-twentieth century, and especially from the early years of independence, comics circulated on the Copperbelt in many forms. The breadth and diversity of comics in circulation meant that the cultural trends that influenced Copperbelt children were equally wide. They consumed swashbucklers from the United Kingdom, and glossy adventure or humorous *bande dessinée* albums from France and Belgium, sword-and-sandals stories of ancient Rome and cowboy tales of the American West, photocomics from South Africa, and superheroes from America. Although comics appeared in Congo earlier than in Zambia, by the 1960s, they were a key part of the experience of growing up on both sides of the Copperbelt. Many children cut and pasted comic strips, redrew them, played games involving comic book characters, discussed them at school, and lent each other comic books. The fact that Copperbelt children were not passive readers of comics, but instead, played around with them, is an indication of how popular the medium was and how important a part it played in a Copperbelt childhood. In turn, the fact that a certain number of prerequisites were needed for comics to circulate, such as a knowledge of French or English or the presence of specific bookstores, made sure that comics would be, if not necessarily a Copperbelt-only phenomenon, then at least a mostly urban, and fairly middle-class, one. Henry Chitaika recalled that when he lived in Ndola with his parents,

> [I would] buy comics from Kingstons and start drawing with my friends. Even in class sometimes we'd exchange drawings – *Doctor Strange*, *Captain America*, *Spiderman*. But when we moved from Kansenshi [an affluent neighbourhood] to Chifubu [a poorer township] I noticed that it was a bit different. My friends, when they saw me do this ... it was like magic to them. Even the books when I took them out they

---

27 See Lily Saint, 'Not Western: Race, Reading, and the South African Photocomic', *Journal of Southern African Studies* 36, 4 (2010), pp. 939–58, p. 939.
28 Angel Phiri interview.

couldn't even say, 'Oh, can I read your comic for a few days, I'll bring it back.' No. They would just look at them. The interest wasn't there.[29]

Still, in the 1960s and the early 1970s, a time when both Copperbelts were experiencing a period of economic boom and its populations enjoyed a comparatively high quality of life, the situation was ripe for various institutions to use this very popular medium for their own purposes, as the Catholic Church had already been doing for decades in the Congo. By this point, the youth of the Copperbelt had been exposed to a large variety of comics from various horizons while at the same time a large pool of disparate tastes had developed. This, therefore, is the background against which Gécamines and the Zambian State launched their respective youth magazines: *Mwana Shaba Junior* and *Orbit*.

Mwana Shaba Junior and *Orbit*: Science, Paternalism and Expectations of Modernity

In September 1964, UMHK, soon to be renamed Gécamines, became the first Katangese company to produce its own youth magazine, *Mwana Shaba Junior*. Some seven years later, in January 1971, *Orbit* was born in Zambia. Though it was originally developed in 1970 under the aegis of Valentine Musakanya, then Minister of State for Technical Advocational Education, *Orbit* quickly received its own Civil Service department under the Ministry of Education. Despite their different origins, there were significant similarities between the two magazines. Both were educational and sought to ignite interest in science and technology, and both therefore dedicated a significant amount of space to illustrated articles on these subjects as well as history, geography and sport. Yet there were also important differences in tone. When it was first conceived, *Orbit*'s main intended purpose was, in the words of Wendy Bond, one of the creators of the magazine, to 'lay a really secure technical foundation for every child'.[30] This was a very important cause to Valentine Musakanya, who, unlike most prominent members of the Zambian Government at the time, including President Kenneth Kaunda, was known as an opponent to Africanist models and insisted that the future

---

29 Henry Chitaika interview.
30 Wendy Bond, 'Mporokoso, Chinsali, Bancroft, Mongu, Lusaka, Kitwe' in Tony Schur (ed.), *From the Cam to the Zambezi: Colonial Service and the Path to the New Zambia* (London: Bloomsbury, 2014), pp. 195–212, p. 209.

of Zambia lay in the use of Western technology.[31] Mick Bond, Wendy Bond's husband, recalls Musakanya saying: 'When science and technology replace witchcraft, as they must, here, everyone should have the knowledge to understand them and not blindly believe, changing one superstition for another.'[32] There was also a certain emphasis on agriculture. Wendy Bond was expressly asked to include a permanent 'Young Farmers' Club' section by the Ministry of Agriculture,[33] as it was keen to reduce the country's dependence on imported food. The section offered practical agricultural advice and featured many variations on statements such as 'whatever you do in the future, you will be a richer man if you can grow food. ... it is useful not just for you – but also for Zambia'.[34] Created as it was at a time of economic expansion, when the future was envisaged as prosperous and technologically advanced, *Orbit* was designed to steer the youth towards the advanced employment opportunities which the Zambian Government expected would soon need filling.

While *Mwana Shaba Junior* similarly sought to steer the eyes of the youth towards science, technology and, by extension, the mining industry, it went further. *Mwana Shaba Junior* was published as a supplement to *Mwana Shaba* ('Child of Copper'), a free monthly magazine created in 1957 by UMHK for its employees. Both magazines were part and parcel of the distinctive brand of corporate paternalism which the *Union Minière* had pursued since the 1930s but which, with the looming prospect of Congolese independence, was going through a new phase of intensification in the late 1950s. While *Mwana Shaba*'s role was to give company-related news, it also took pains to paternalistically emphasise topics such as the importance of discipline at work, a stable family life, and good behaviour. In other words, it played the role of 'moralizer of the population', as Donatien Dibwe dia Mwembu put it.[35] *Mwana Shaba Junior* was intended to play much the same role for the next generation of Gécamines employees. Every issue was introduced by an editorial, which, in the magazine's own words, intended to give young

31 Miles Larmer, *Rethinking African Politics: A History of Opposition in Zambia* (Farnham: Routledge, 2011), pp. 40–41, p. 163.
32 Mick Bond, *From Northern Rhodesia to Zambia: Recollections of a DO/DC 1962–73* (Lusaka: Gadsden Publishers, 2014), p. 187.
33 Bond, 'Mporokoso', p. 210.
34 *Orbit*, 4, 3, 1975, p. 22.
35 Donatien Dibwe dia Mwembu, *Bana Shaba abandonnés par leur père: Structures de l'autorité et histoire sociale de la famille ouvrière au Katanga 1910–1997* (Paris: Harmattan, 2001), p. 86.

people 'moral, cultural and scientific' advice.[36] These editorials cover a wide range of topics but it is the related themes of the importance of education and discipline which come through the most frequently and the most clearly. One editorial entitled 'La réussite' ('How to achieve success') stressed that 'the path to success necessarily involves regular effort', and with 'effort' comes 'suffering, pain and sacrifice'.[37] Even articles on sport were turned into another opportunity to draw an analogy between discipline and success: 'What matters if you want to achieve anything is discipline: to love making effort, work with perseverance, respect the property of others, observe the rules which are necessary for society to function properly'.[38] *Mwana Shaba Junior* thus displayed a rather explicit brand of didacticism, the aim of which was to produce the hard-working employees of tomorrow while encouraging the Gécamines population to think of itself as a community with common interests.

These divergences in tone and choice of emphasis were reflected in the comics *Junior* and *Orbit* chose to publish. Comic strips published in *Junior* were fully incorporated into the magazine's overall didactic mission: they were to serve, as the editorial team of the March/April 1988 issue revealingly put it, 'as a support for the instruction and moral education of the young honest citizens of tomorrow'.[39] In this, they recycled the paternalistic and moralistic qualities typical of colonial comics but also of the mid-twentieth-century Belgian comic tradition as whole. Partly because of the influence of the Catholic Church and partly as a reaction to France's very strict 1949 censorship law which closely regulated depictions of sex and violence,[40] Belgian comic artists carefully policed their work, producing comics intended to entertain the youth, but also to educate it, and to offer it good role models. Accordingly, the first comic strips published in *Junior* were realistically drawn stories set in antiquity, such as *L'histoire merveilleuse*, which depicted the lives of various Biblical characters, and *Ben Hur* (1965–67), which broadly told the same story of revenge, redemption and

---

36 *Mwana Shaba Junior*, 349–50, March–April 1988, p. 2.
37 *Mwana Shaba Junior*, 327, May 1986, p. 2.
38 *Mwana Shaba Junior*, 178, 1 December 1974, p. 3.
39 *Mwana Shaba Junior*, 349–350, March–April 1988, p. 2.
40 This had been enforced in response to the post-liberation influx of American comics, as a thinly veiled measure to protect the domestic comic market. It also came in handy to regulate the availability of Belgian comic magazines in France. See Philippe Delisle, *Bande dessinée franco-belge et imaginaire colonial, des années 1930 aux années 1980* (Paris: Karthala, 2008), p. 6.

Christian awakening as the 1959 Hollywood film of the same name.[41] Along with these, *Junior* introduced in September 1965 a humorous series called *Les aventures de Mayele*, which quickly became the magazine's flagship series. Mayele (meaning 'clever' in Swahili) was originally invented by two Belgian *Union Minière* engineers called Theo Roosen and Paul Baeke. That the makers of Mayele were influenced by the Franco-Belgian tradition is obvious. Mayele is friends with two young adolescents, a boy and a girl, who are dressed just like the two heroes of the Flemish comic *Suske en Wiske*. His 'adventures' consist of one-page gags, with many of the jokes drawing on slapstick-type humour and the main character's clumsiness, just like *Gaston Lagaffe*, a lazy and accident-prone character from the *Journal de Spirou*. Mayele is an urban young man who owns a dog, and whose 'adventures' take place in the realistic setting of a person's 'normal' everyday life, as they do in the series *Boule et Bill*. For example, in 'Pas de chance!', Mayele finds himself stuck between his garage door and ceiling in an attempt to show off his new electric garage door to his neighbour [42] Mayele lives in a big suburban house, owns a car and various technological items, which provide the basis for much of the hilarity (as they malfunction).[43] He lives in a city, where he has arguments with friends in cafes,[44] clashes with policemen,[45] and goes to football matches.[46] Mayele's stories, in other words, are largely aspirational aimed at an (aspiring) African middle class in the purest tradition of both Gécamines' and mid-twentieth-century Belgian comic paternalism.

The first comic strips published in *Orbit* were more graphically sophisticated than what appeared in *Mwana Shaba Junior*, despite Congo's supposed head start in comic-making, because they were produced by professional cartoonists. Wanting the magazine to be professionally produced, Valentine Musakanya had elicited the help of Peter Clarke, then Managing Director of the London-based news service GeminiScan Ltd. As a result, though the

41 *Mwana Shaba Junior*, 14 February 1966, p. 7.
42 *Mwana Shaba Junior*, 126, 15 May 1972, p. 1.
43 E.g. in 'Mayele tond sa pelouse' (*Mwana Shaba Junior*, 82, 15 April 1970, p. 1), Mayele gets angry because he thinks the lawnmower his neighbour lent him is faulty when the issue is that he did not pay his electricity bill.
44 E.g. in 'Elles existent' (*Mwana Shaba Junior*, 178, December 1974), Mayele argues with a friend about whether 'flying saucers' exist, irritating another customer who throws his saucer, a 'flying saucer', at them.
45 E.g. in 'Une bonne occasion' (*Mwana Shaba Junior*, 57, 15 February 1969, p. 1), Mayele is persuaded to buy a beautiful car for 6 Zaïres. He is then fined 6 Zaïres by a policeman because most of the car's appliances do not function properly.
46 e.g. 'Mayele Supporter' (*Mwana Shaba Junior*, 21, 15 July 1966, p. 1).

editorial copy was provided by the Zambia-based team and the magazine was printed in Zambia,[47] all the artwork and editing were done in Britain by British artists commissioned or employed by GeminiScan. That this was the case was kept as discreet as possible. 'One of the many things Peter insisted on was that there should be no indication to the young reader that *Orbit* was being produced in the UK', John Egglesfield who was art editor for GeminiScan, recalled. 'We wanted all the focus to be on Zambia.'[48] Thus, though John Egglesfield elicited the services of some of Fleet Street's finest cartoonists and illustrators to produce the comics, their names never appeared in the magazine. 'Space Safari', *Orbit*'s flagship series which featured two Zambian heroes named Marion and Robert, was a space adventure written by Sydney Jordan with art by Martin Ashbury, both well-established British cartoonists known for their science fiction comics. In turn, *Orbit*'s emphasis on space is not random. *Orbit* had been conceived in an era marked by the moon landing (1969), the success of cult phenomenon series *Star Trek* (1966–69) and the release of two major science fiction films which revolutionised mainstream pop culture: *Planet of the Apes* (1968) and *2001: A Space Odyssey* (1968). In fact, the very title 'A Space Safari' is a clear reference to Stanley Kubrick's film. Science fiction's appeal thus provided a convenient hook to attract children's attention and ignite their interest in science.

In this way, not only were comic strips given pride of place in *Orbit* but, like their counterparts in *Mwana Shaba Junior*, they had a clear role to play, designed as they were to reinforce the specific message outlined by the magazine as a whole. Neither were they devoid of moralising contemplations. Tellingly, Marion and Robert's mini-adventures combine science fiction with agricultural concerns. Marion and Roberts are plant experts who work for the 'Pan-African Survey System'. In their first adventure, which ran over the first four issues of the magazine, they are called to help over mysterious meteor showers which have caused crops to die all across Africa. These showers are identified as missiles or 'sand-bombs' and traced back to one of Mars' moons, to which Robert and Marion duly travel on an international space mission. In their second adventure entitled 'Trojan Horse',[49] a mysterious spaceship shows up in African cities and offers all sort of expensive gifts: cars, tractors, etc. Robert and Marion are sent in a

47   Bond, 'Mporokoso', p. 209.
48   John Freeman, 'Discovering "Orbit" – Zambia's Unique Science and Comic Magazine', 6 February 2020, https://downthetubes.net/?p=114717 (accessed 21 June 2020).
49   *Orbit*, 1, 5, 6 and 7, 1971, pp. 1–2.

special plane to negotiate with the ship's commander and are informed that offering worthless gifts had been used as a way to test people's spirit 'to see if you understand the supreme law of survival': 'to help one another – to work for the creation of the good life – to scorn the ready-made Baubles of the Gift-horse'. Robert is sent back with a spade and ears of corn which he describes as the 'greatest gift'.[50] In this way, science fiction is harnessed to disseminate the government's agricultural agenda. In addition, accompanying Marion and Robert in every issue were two pages of an adventure story drawn in realistic black-and-white style, stylistically similar to Amalgamated comics. These alternated between the aerial adventures of 'Mike Chanda, Charter Pilot' who works for an air company based in Ndola, the investigative adventures of Inspector Mark Phiri, and the sanitary adventures of 'Jenny Moonga, Health Inspector'. These adventure stories must have given their young Zambian audience a sense of possibilities for what the future might hold: all characters have typical Zambian names and all have 'cool' modern jobs.

Early issues of *Orbit* and *Mwana Shaba Junior* followed the comic canons of the former colonial powers. This is not surprising; not only were the artists who produced the comic strips European, but, as demonstrated above, literature of this type had been circulating on both sides of the Copperbelt for at least a couple of decades. As a result, its graphic and storytelling codes would have already been familiar to at least a part of Katanga and Zambia's population, thus making it easier to re-purpose them for these publications' new aims. Gécamines used Belgian-style one-gag-in-a-page and realistically drawn moralising adventures to reinforce its paternalistic vision. *Orbit*, meanwhile, used UK-type space and adventure stories to reinforce the state's belief in a flourishing industrial future. These early comics, particularly *Orbit*'s, are emblematic of an era when, as James Ferguson put it, 'Africa was "emerging"' and 'no place was emerging faster or more hopefully than Zambia'.[51] This was a time when, as Wendy Bond recalled, Zambia was 'buzzing with optimism and opportunity':

> It was all very exciting because everyone was determined to make a success of the new nation … and to do it fast! Doors were opening for everyone. … Zambia became international … there were new projects and new cars and new buildings going up and new roads.[52]

50 *Orbit*, 1, 7, pp. 1–2.
51 James Ferguson, *Expectations of Modernity: Myths and Meanings of Urban Life on the Zambian Copperbelt* (Berkeley: University of California Press, 1999), p. 1.
52 Bond, 'Mporokoso', p. 208.

Thus, while *Orbit* was not a Copperbelt production, nor was it solely aimed at a Copperbelt audience, it is likely that this is where it was most widely read, along with Lusaka. It is also where it found its most fervent fans, as is suggested by the fact that many of those who later contributed comics to the magazines were Copperbelt natives. Besides, the aim was to inspire the country's youth to aspire to live in a 'Copperbelt-like' society, one characterised by well-organised cities, state-of-the-art infrastructures, an educated labour force and – cherry on the cake – a self-sustained agricultural system.

The script of the Copperbelt's 'emergence' via industrialisation and urbanisation was later confounded by the decades of steep economic decline which followed the fall in copper prices of the mid-1970s.[53] By the early 1990s, *Mwana Shaba Junior* had disappeared and *Orbit* had so severely declined in popularity that it was supplanted, at least on the Copperbelt, by a newcomer youth magazine produced by Mission Press in Ndola: *Speak Out!* Yet, until then, they had become the main vehicles through which the youth of the Copperbelt produced and consumed comics. For one thing, these magazines' longevity and accessibility gave them enormous reach, allowing them to become an 'official space for comics', as Katangese cartoonist Tetshim put it.[54] For another, from the early 1970s, when Congo and Zambia went through a period of 'Africanisation' and 'nationalisation', it was Zambian and Congolese artists who became the sole producers of comic art for the magazines. In fact, for a time, comics became one of the most lucrative activities available to visual artists in Katanga. Cartoonist Kika recalled that in the 1980s, while he and other artists continued to work on painting and metal work, comics were 'what paid best'.[55] Similarly, Kinshasa-born artist Michel Bongo-Liz 'got stuck' in Lubumbashi in the mid-1980s when he was on his way to Southern Africa because 'Gécamines paid good money for the comics which we were producing'.[56] As a result, these magazines provided local artists with the opportunity to 're-appropriate' the medium and say with it what they wanted. Fatefully, they did so in a context of fast economic, political and social change.

53   Ferguson, *Expectations of Modernity*, p. 6.
54   Interview, Tetshim, Lubumbashi, 14 August 2019.
55   Interview, Kika, Lubumbashi, 21 August 2019.
56   Interview, Michel Bongo-Liz, Lubumbashi, 30 July 2019.

Re-Appropriation of the Medium in a Changing Socio-Economic Context

A few years into the 1970s, as the two magazines started using homegrown African talents rather than exported ones, there started to be important shifts in the tone and content of the comic strips published in both *Mwana Shaba Junior* and *Orbit*. Though Mayele survived unscathed because of its popularity with the readers,[57] comic strips published in *Junior* from 1972 showed an increasing 're-appropriation' of Belgo-French narrative and graphic codes in ways that subverted or reversed them. An early example of this are the adventures of 'Mwana' and 'Shaba', two new characters which first appeared in the *Mwana Shaba Junior* in the summer of 1972.[58] The first two of these, *Echec aux Espions* (1972–74) and *Le Trésor de Targaz* (1975–77), follow a fairly similar template in which its two young journalist heroes travel to exotic locales – New York and 'Tibera', a fictional North African country – and are confronted with gangs of villains, whose plans they thwart. These two stories still have many characteristics that connect them to the Franco-Belgian comic tradition. Both are high-adventure stories set in exotic locations and broadly follow the aesthetics of mid-twentieth-century Belgian comics, being reminiscent of Franquin's *Spirou et Fantasio*. Both are full of slapstick humour – Mwana falls down the stairs of his hotel twice in high comical fashion yet never seems to get physically injured – and present Mwana and Shaba as moral paragons. For example, a new character introduced in *Le trésor de Targaz*, a spoiled princess, who is used to her every whim being catered for, progressively learns to emulate the behaviour of Mwana and Shaba who are selfless and help others without expectation of rewards. Yet, on the whole, the usual template is here reversed. While Mwana and Shaba's country of origin has featured in more than one European comic as the exotic destination, in this case, it is the two heroes who are doing the travelling, visiting such exotic locales as the United States, and they are the ones who are greeted as heroes by the 'natives'. Elements of *Authenticité*-era Zaïre,

---

57 Paul Baeke continued the series from Belgium until 1987, when he was replaced by Gécamines employee Mukiny Nkemba.
58 In total six 'Mwana and Shaba' adventures were published between 1972 and 1989. Cassiau-Haurie suspects that the first two adventures were produced by the Chenge brothers, who ran an influential artistic workshop in Lubumbashi. Cassiau-Haurie, *Histoire de la BD congolaise*, p. 39.

as Congo was known from 1971, are also visible throughout.[59] Characters refer to each other as 'citoyen' or 'citoyenne', Mwana and Shaba conspicuously use 'Air Zaïre' to fly everywhere, and Zaïre is constantly implicitly being presented as a modern nation, a member of the United Nations on par with any other player on the international chessboard. In this way, European codes of comic-making were here used in a way that updated them for a contemporary 'Zairian' audience.

From around the mid-1970s, *Orbit* and its comic strips started to change too, both in outlook and in subjects. These changes were claimed by the editorial team of 1977 to have been inspired by readers' letters,[60] yet this was a period when Zambia too was experiencing important political changes. In 1973, Zambia had become a one-party state, and, as economic decline started to bite, its politics became increasingly centred around the person of the President and the ideologies of the nationalist struggle.[61] This new party line was openly advertised in the *Orbit* of October 1974 which celebrated Zambia's tenth anniversary of independence. For the occasion President Kenneth Kaunda penned a letter for *Orbit*'s young readers in which he grandly stated that 'we older ones fought and won a battle for political freedom' but this, he continued 'was just the beginning – Not the end!'[62] This was accompanied by a 'special insert', a comic advertised as an 'exciting picture-story' depicting

> how the Zambian people became united by the belief that every man or woman has the right to help decide the kind of life they live … to choose their own government! Orbit tells you how the people of Zambia gave voice to that idea through the leadership of Kenneth Kaunda. And how the people, the idea and the man became one nation on October 24 1964.[63]

Soon thereafter, Marion and Robert were taken down from their pedestal as *Orbit*'s star cartoon to be replaced by *Fwanya*, a young Zambian schoolboy whose two-pages-long stories were meant to be amusing and to educate

---

59 '*Authenticité*', or 'Zairianisation', was an official state ideology implemented by the Mobutu regime in the late 1960s and early 1970s. In an effort to rid the country of the lingering vestiges of Western influence, the country was renamed Zaïre, and Zaïriens had to adopt new 'authentic' names, and change their ways of dressing and addressing each other. See Crawford Young and Thomas E. Turner, *The Rise and Decline of the Zairian State* (Madison: University of Wisconsin Press, 1985).

60 *Orbit*, 6, 6, October 1977, p. 1.

61 Larmer, *Rethinking African Politics*, p. 167.

62 *Orbit*, 3, 7, p. 5.

63 *Orbit*, 3, 7.

children on good behaviour. In 'Fwanya learns that laziness does not pay', for example, Fwanya collects copies of *Orbit* which he is supposed to bring to his teacher so they can be sold. He stops to rest and to read them, allowing the wind to blow all the copies away.[64] Just as Mwana and Shaba had stuck close aesthetically to earlier Belgian and Congolese comics, Fwanya's realistic black-and-white aesthetics are only a stone's throw away from the Fleetway-style comic strips which had previously been the norm in *Orbit*. Similarly, despite this aesthetic continuity, there is a change in content, in this case towards a new brand of moralistic didacticism.

The content of these comics also differed at times from their predecessors in being located in a more distinctly Zambian or Katangese context and making references to events and societal change experienced by Copperbelt society. For example, in January 1975, a new comic in *Junior* entitled *Un espion à Lusaka* featured a young girl foiling a bomb attack at a summit held in Lusaka, where delegations of all 'African copper-producing countries' met to discuss the impact of the fall in copper prices.[65] In fact, from the mid-1970s onwards, *Junior*'s adventure and detective stories took a darker turn and, by the 1980s, stories depicting a character struggling against crime and corruption grew increasingly common. Similarly, comic strips in *Orbit* had become much less 'European-looking' by the late 1970s and, apart from *Fwanya*, all now touched upon topics relating to the realities of contemporary Zambian life. The stories of *Constable Mulenga*, for example, highlighted urban dangers, such as going home alone from the cinema after dark.[66] In a story entitled *Choose a Husband* published in 1977, it was the tricky topic of marriage and the rift between cities and villages that was explored. Tisa, a chief's daughter, decides to marry 'a successful young man from the city who has come back to the land', who, unfortunately, turns out to be a goat transformed into a man. 'You had a lot of handsome young men to choose from', the goat–husband teases Tisa. 'You just wanted my money and my car and a goat for a husband Ha! Ha! Ha!'[67] This is consistent with the evolution of the depiction of the village-town relationship in twentieth-century Zambian literature identified by Giacomo Macola. Whereas there had previously been a tendency to assign moral superiority 'either to the urban or to the rural space as a whole', he argued, 'the demise of social expectations of urban permanence led to both spheres of social

64   *Orbit*, 4, 3, p. 10.
65   *Mwana Shaba Junior*, 180, January 1975, p. 8.
66   *Orbit*, 6, 6, October 1977, p. 3.
67   Ibid., pp. 22–3.

relationships' and was increasingly 'perceived as fundamentally deficient and unappealing'.[68] Similarly, the story here serves as a cautionary tale for young women who get dazzled by the lures of the city, while it also criticises both city dwellers for their empty promises and villagers for their naivety and longing for material wealth.

Similar changes in perception were expressed in *Junior's Le Masque de la Tortue* (1989–90), in which a young village man named Sadiki travels to the city to help his cousin, only to be disabused by the reality of crime and squalor he finds there. However, instead of going home as the heroes of such stories often do, Sadiki stays, and the message seems to be that people from the village and the city should help each other and are stronger if they do so. City life was further de-idealised with the arrival, in 1987, of a new comic character named Mafuta. As with Mayele, Mafuta's comic strips are one page long, and consist of jokes derived from the frustrations of daily and domestic life. Yet this comic strip differs from Mayele in fundamental ways. Whereas Mayele's jokes are slapstick-based, Mafuta's play on (changing) societal mores and situations that Katangese readers may actually have encountered in real life. Mafuta jokes cover a large number of topics such as gender relationships, superstition, insecurity, and religion, and a great number find humour in family and social obligations. In *L'heureux papa*, for example, two drunk men come to Mafuta's house and demand he offers them a drink since a child was born in his family. They pester him until Mafuta buys them one glass of beer, and when they complain, Mafuta protests, 'what are you complaining about? I bought you "a" drink, didn't I?'[69] In *Les visiteurs*, Mafuta receives the visit of his uncle, aunt and children from the village. While his uncle is busy listing all the items he requires from Mafuta (a sewing machine, a bicycle, a suit, a hoe, clothes for his wife and children), Mafuta thinks: 'what a disaster! Now I have five additional mouths to feed ... life has become too expensive ... I will get rid of them, and quickly.' In order to do so, he gives them a bad supper, leading the unwanted guests to decide to leave of their own accord.[70] Mayele and Mafuta's jokes have in common that they take place in urban settings, mostly in and around the home. Yet, whereas Mayele's jokes show a life of abundance and middle-class aspirations, Mafuta's highlight all that is lacking.

68   Giacomo Macola, 'Imagining Village Life in Zambian Fiction', *Cambridge Anthropology* 25, 1 (2005), pp. 1–10, pp. 6–7.
69   *Mwana Shaba Junior*, 366, August 1989, p. 5.
70   *Mwana Shaba Junior*, 372, March 1990, p. 5.

From 1989, the year that the Kamoto mine collapsed, causing Gécamines' total production to drop by 90% between 1989 and 1993, the implicit social and political commentary of *Junior's* comic strips became distinctly more explicit. *Les tribulations de Mashaka*, published between 1990 and 1991, for example, straightforwardly dealt with the effects of poverty. Mashaka is a perennially unemployed character whose wife urges to go out and find work. Yet everything goes wrong for Mashaka. He loses the little money he had earned, breaks his leg yet continues looking for work, finds a job then gets fired, gets evicted from his house, and even tries to commit suicide. He is only saved when a rich uncle comes back from America and offers him a job on no other basis than the fact that he is family. The suggestion is that the only remaining way to get out of one's situation is through a wealthy relative or going abroad. Similarly, *Msumbuko Le syndicaliste, les victimes de la tentation* (1989–90, by Mukiny Nkemba and Nansong Yav), deals with the effects of economic collapse. In this story, the protagonist is Masumbuko, the chief trade unionist for the textile company, I.T.M., which acts as a stand-in for Gécamines. The company originally does well but the salaries are too low and as one employee comments, 'it's impossible to make ends meet'.[71] As time goes by, an increasing quantity of goods goes missing from the company as employees help themselves to them to compensate for their low salaries. Masumbuko then summons all of his fellow employees and lectures them on having endangered the company's survival and by extension the ability of all workers to feed their families. Another worker then takes the stand and expresses what must have a widely shared opinion among Gécamines' employees: that the directors of the company shared a part of the blame since they had sold out to 'the capitalist system of exploiting Man to extract as much profit out of him as possible' and neglected their 'obligation to think about improving the living conditions of workers'.[72] In that way, I.T.M.'s story is a thinly veiled reference to Gécamines' contemporary struggle with debilitating thefts and underpaid employees.

On the Zambian side, meanwhile, *Orbit* had been largely been supplanted by *Speak Out! A Christian Magazine for Youth*, created by the Franciscan Mission press in 1984. It too contained comic strips, though fewer in number and of a very different kind than those contained in *Orbit*, having been conceived in a very different political context. Whereas there had hitherto been no significant challenge to the party and its government, by

---

71 *Mwana Shaba Junior*, 364, June 1989, p. 9.
72 *Mwana Shaba Junior*, 376, June 1990, p. 9.

the late 1970s and early 1980s, the unprofitability of the mining industry, rising foreign debt and periodic harvest failures finally led to rising discontent.[73] In this context, Zambia's Catholic Church found itself in the position of mouthpiece for the opposition to the one-party state. This it was largely able to do because of its ownership of independent media including magazines such as *Icengelo* (1971-present) and *Speak Out!* (1984-present).[74] Like *Orbit* and *Mwana Shaba Junior*, *Speak Out!* had games, a questions-and-answers section ('Dear Kabilo'), and competitions. The overall tone however was very different. Whereas *Orbit* was resolutely turned towards a vision of Zambia as a nation at the cutting edge of technology and fully incorporated in a global (or at least Pan-African) world, *Speak Out!* was very Copperbelt-focused, and resolutely turned towards questions of politics and morality. The educational articles on science, technology or history which were *Orbit*'s hallmark, were gone. Instead, the bulk of the articles consisted of thinking pieces, fictional and real-life stories often contributed by readers, and scripted conversations in which two friends debated a topic of interest. While political critiques were present in the magazine, with discussions about the education system[75] or the extent of individual responsibility in the quest of employment,[76] these were now approached through the prism of topics that concerned the youth of the Copperbelt. As Danny Chiyesu, who has been producing comics for Mission Press since 1991, explained, *Speak Out!* stood for 'speaking out on all the issues about youth: smoking, sex, marriage, romance, jobs ... anything to do with the youth'.[77] It is thus meant to be educational, but in a very different way to *Orbit*. Much in *Speak Out!* was to do with life in the city, changing social mores, and surviving in a world marked by economic hardship. These, accordingly, were the topics which the comic strips published in *Speak Out!* also tackled.

Whereas *Icengelo*, the 'adult' magazine, had a recurring comic character called Katona, whose jokes were written in Bemba and poked fun at daily life in a Zambian urban environment, the 'comic' strips that appeared in *Speak Out!* were not based around jokes. Most were produced by the same person, Ndola

---

73 Larmer, *Rethinking African Politics*, p. 82.
74 Marja Hinfelaar, 'Legitimizing Powers: The Political Role of the Roman Catholic Church, 1972–1991' in Jan-Bart Gewald, Marja Hinfelaar and Giacomo Macola (eds), *One Zambia, Many Histories: Towards a History of Post-Colonial Zambia* (Leiden: Brill, 2008), pp. 127–43, p. 141.
75 *Speak Out!* March–April 1984, p. 10.
76 E.g. *Speak Out!* January–February, p. 2, pp. 3–4.
77 Interview, Danny Chiyesu, Ndola, 15 July 2019.

resident Michael M. Nkaka, and usually involved two characters, often a man
and a woman named Friday and Frida, discussing an issue of political or societal
relevance. Some of Friday and Frida's comic strips were more on the straightforwardly moralising side. Nkaka, for example, chose to portray the dangers
of drunkenness by having a drunken Friday slip on a banana peel and break
his leg.[78] Similarly, exhortations to avoid sex outside of marriage would be
accompanied by warnings that it leads to abortion and AIDS.[79] Yet, in most
cases, the dialogue format enabled the expression of critical opinions on debates
which do not have easy answers, and were sometimes used to air controversial
points without appearing to do so. Some comic strips, for example, tackled
the question of the legacy of colonialism. In that of March–April 1984, Friday
comments to Frida that he does not like going to church as he dislikes the
noise of the drums, and considers 'Gregorian chant' to be 'the only suitable
music for church'. In this case, it is Frida who was given the last word, arguing
that 'it seems you're another one of those old colonials who can't sever their
ties with Europe. It's about time you became an African!'[80] By far the most
covered topics, however, were those of love, sex and changing gender relations.
The May–June 1984 issue, for example, had Friday and Frida entangled in a
debate about men and women's role in society in which Friday argued that
without a man, a woman is 'a lonely old spinster' while Frida exclaimed that
'you men have ruled us like servants for far too long'.[81]

The village-town relationship is yet another topic which recurs regularly
(see Figure 2.1). In the very first issue, Friday complained that he is forced
to do manual labour whenever he returns to the village, feeling that, as
the best student in his class, he is above such work. Frida responded: 'you
should be clever enough to see that manual work will make a man out of
you. There are more ways of learning than out of books!'[82] These are but
a few examples in a long list of such discussions published in comic form
Speak Out! in the 1980s. The comic strips themselves had a simple graphic
style and were drawn in black and white. Similarly, while Friday and Frida
share space in *Speak Out!* with a series of other characters, they are all inter-
changeable: all serve as vehicles through which to discuss societal questions.
In this sense, *Speak Out!*'s strips were an illustration of the extent to which
comics, had, by this point, been fully 'weaponised'.

---

78 *Speak Out!* January–February 1985, p. 20.
79 *Speak Out!* May–June 1987, p. 20.
80 *Speak Out!* March–April 1984, pp. 12–13.
81 *Speak Out!* May–June 1984, pp. 12–13.
82 *Speak Out!* January–February 1984, pp. 12–13.

Figure 2.1 'Frida and Friday', *Speak Out!*, May–June 1986, back cover. Reproduced by permission, Mission Press, Ndola.

In her 2016 article 'Belgo-Congolese Transnational Comics Esthetics', Véronique Bragard argued that post-independence Congolese *bandes dessinées* displayed what she calls 'a re-fashioning of the genre's form and themes, leading to new engaged postcolonial aesthetics.'[83] She cites the work of Mongo Awai Sisé, one of the first major comic artists who emerged in Congo in the second half of the twentieth century, as establishing the tradition of 'the same but not quite'. By this she means that he borrowed a series of codes and aesthetics from the Belgo-French comic traditions but subverted these codes and aesthetics to tell his own story.[84] Sisé's Bingo series, for example bore some resemblance to *Tintin*, but in a reverse paradigm. In contrast to Tintin, Bingo does not serve as a spokesperson of any civilising mission but instead suffers the consequences of the colonial inheritance, for example when he migrates to the city to find work, only to be confronted with fraud, corruption and general inefficiency (*Bingo en ville*, 1981) or when a trip to Belgium confronts him with the North-South wealth gap (*Bingo en Belgique*, 1982). In that sense, Sisé used some of the codes of the Belgo-French comic traditions to highlight some of the grim realities which Congolese citizens faced.[85] Similarly, the period of nationalisation and Africanisation, coinciding with a fast-changing economic and political environment, marks the beginning of a process of 're-appropriation' of the medium by Copperbelt artists as they sought to distance it from its Western roots. The manner in which this reappropriation took place, along with the themes and stories tackled by the authors, evolved and varied over time, influenced by the intentions of the institutions for whom the comics were produced and also by the socio-political context in which they were produced. The faith in a future that would be urban, prosperous and technologically advanced, and the subsequent gradual deterioration of that faith, have been key features of contemporary Zambian and Katangese literature.[86] It is not surprising therefore that they should also be central to contemporary Zambian and Katangese comics. *Speak Out!*'s comic strips represent the ultimate point at which, in a context of fast-changing societal and economic realities, comics become a means through which to have a conversation about these changes.

---

83 Véronique Bragard, 'Belgo-Congolese Transnational Comics Esthetics: Transcolonial Labor from Mongo Sisse's *Bingo en Belgique* to Cassiau-Haurie and Baruti's *Madame Livingstone: Congo, la Grande Guerre* (2014)', *Literature Compass* 13, 5 (2016), pp. 332–40, p. 332.
84 Bragard, 'Belgo-Congolese Transnational Comics Esthetics', p. 334.
85 Ibid., p. 339.
86 Macola, 'Imagining Village Life', p. 23.

Conclusion

Much like other forms of popular culture, comics constitute complex and ambiguous historical material. In recent comics scholarship, they have been increasingly thought of as cultural forms existing in relation to the social/ popular context in which they are produced.[87] On the one hand popular culture has been seen as instrument of social control: it is one of the means through which members of society are instructed in appropriate values, attitudes and behaviour. On the other hand, popular culture responds to the cultural tastes and social values of its consumers and, in this sense, can be seen as a 'mirror' to society. In other words, comics are both a product of social processes and a medium through which social values are constructed and conveyed, particularly because it is usually aimed at the youth. This tension is visible in the way that comics were produced and consumed on the Copperbelt. Comics were originally an imported form of popular art and, when first embraced by local institutions, it was largely for instrumental reasons, to influence or even manipulate the readers, to inculcate in them carefully chosen values and ideas. At the same time, they had to do so in a way that would 'speak' to its audience. Thus, they not only had to tackle subjects of relevance to Zambian and Katangese society but also had to rely and play on aesthetics already known and appreciated by them. In this sense, the range of comics influences to which the Copperbelt youth was exposed and the extent to which these influences were recycled or updated in comics produced for and by them, is testament to how much of an intercultural crossroads the Copperbelt was, with networks of cultural influences connecting it to several continents. Once Copperbelt cartoonists started publishing, they were able to pick from a wide range of existing codes and themes, and soon adapted them in the way they wished. In the early years, comics in *Mwana Shaba Junior* mirrored Belgo-French albums both in their graphic and didactic style. Similarly, early comics in *Orbit* were influenced both by Fleetway comics and the science fiction craze of the late 1960s and 1970s. Yet, as the political horizon shifted, these styles were increasingly subverted and adapted in order to address aspects of the massive societal changes that the communities who read the magazines were experiencing. As a result, though the medium was introduced in a time when there was little doubt that the future would be industrial and prosperous, it became an important avenue through which the effects of the failure of this future to materialise can be observed.

[87] See for example Jean-Paul Gabilliet's *Of Comics and Men: A Cultural History of American Comic Books* (Jackson: University Press of Mississippi, 2010).

3

Divergence and Convergence on the Copperbelt: White Mineworkers in Comparative Perspective, 1911–1963[1]

Duncan Money

Introduction

The first rumours of impending unrest in Elisabethville (Lubumbashi) reached the Kasumbalesa border post between Northern Rhodesia and newly independent Congo on 7 July 1960 – though the first carloads of whites did not begin arriving until two days later. Rapidly, the numbers trying to cross the border became overwhelming and immigration officials abandoned formalities and opened the barriers. Over a four-day period approximately 7,500 whites from Katanga passed through Kasumbalesa into the safety of the Northern Rhodesian Copperbelt, still firmly under colonial rule. Kasumbalesa border crossing now marked the northern edge of the bloc of white-ruled states in Southern Africa.

The *Force Publique* – Congo's military – had mutinied, first in Léopoldville (Kinshasa) on 5 July, and then across the country. Troops in Elisabethville mutinied on 9 July, prompting the exodus of some 13,000 whites across various parts of the border into Northern Rhodesia. Rumours abounded that dozens of whites had been massacred in Elisabethville and immigration officers reported that 'fear and despair' predominated among the whites passing through Kasumbalesa; by the third day, these included Belgian policemen, military officers and all sections of white society in Katanga.

1   Earlier versions of this chapter were presented to conferences at the Nordic Africa Institute in December 2016 and the University of Lubumbashi in July 2019. I am very grateful to Iva Peša and to Lazlo Passemiers for their generosity in sharing archival documents with me.

Many of the refugees were heavily armed and five troop carriers were filled with the firearms and ammunition taken from them at the border.[2]

Whites in the Northern Rhodesian towns of Chingola, Kitwe, Luanshya and Mufulira rallied round. Space was made in mine clubs, sports halls and people's homes to accommodate new arrivals. White civil society – the Women's Institute, ex-servicemen's associations, and the white mineworkers' union – mobilised to distribute food and drink, while local colonial officials dipped into the budget to provide subsistence money and coupons to obtain petrol.[3] They recognised in the refugees from Katanga a people like themselves, both in great need, and – in their eyes – deserving of assistance and kindness that they would never have offered to Africans.

This incident is a powerful example of white solidarity, in which whites offered help and assistance to those seemingly displaced by the collapse of colonial rule. Yet this incident also shows how far the historical experiences of white communities on the Copperbelt had diverged, and why it is pertinent to talk of two communities with different though at times entangled histories. These have seldom attracted the attention of scholars, aside from some discussion of the ostentatious social life enjoyed by whites, which is however not the focus of this chapter.[4] References to whites are scattered across works that deal primarily with other subjects – though both Charles Perrings and John Higginson pay attention to the actions of white mineworkers, and their consequences[5] – and there is relatively little on the topic aside from my earlier work, which focuses almost entirely on Zambia, and Benjamin Rubbers' study of whites in contemporary Katanga.[6]

2   National Archives of Zambia, Lusaka (hereafter NAZ), WP 1/14/58, The Battle of Kasumbalesa. See also Lazlo Passemiers, 'Racial Solidarity in Africa: Apartheid South Africa's Reaction to Congo's White Refuge-Seekers' (unpublished conference paper).
3   'The Copperbelt Opened its Doors', *Horizon*, August 1960.
4   Ian Phimister, 'Proletarians In Paradise: The Historiography and Historical Sociology of White Miners on the Copperbelt' in Jan-Bart Gewald, Marja Hinfelaar, and Giacomo Macola (eds), *Living the End of Empire: Politics and Society in Late Colonial Zambia* (Leiden: Brill, 2011), pp. 139–60.
5   Charles Perrings, *Black Mineworkers in Central Africa: Industrial Strategies and the Evolution of an African Proletariat in the Copperbelt 1911–41* (London: Heinemann, 1979); John Higginson, *A Working Class in the Making: Belgian Colonial Labor Policy, Private Enterprise, and the African Mineworkers, 1907–1951* (Madison: University of Wisconsin Press, 1989).
6   Benjamin Rubbers, *Faire fortune en Afrique: Anthropologie des derniers colons du Katanga* (Paris: Karthala, 2013).

This chapter traces broad similarities and contrasts in the migration of whites to the Copperbelt, their relationships with the state and mining companies, and the organisations and movements they established. The Copperbelt can usefully be considered as one continuous region, as other chapters in this volume argue, but examining the history of whites shows us how the border dividing the region was one which came to structure the experiences of whites who came to live there. Focusing on white mineworkers, with occasional references to other sections of the white population, I argue that despite initial similarities, the histories of white communities on different sides of the border diverged considerably, and this divergence was influenced by colonial and corporate policies as well as the actions of white mineworkers themselves. Determined and persistent action by the colonial state and *Union Minière du Haut-Katanga* severed earlier links between whites in Katanga and white societies to the south.

The category of 'white' is not a stable one.[7] The people who left Katanga in 1960, described as 'white' or 'European' refugees in contemporary sources, included people who were listed by British colonial officers on arrival as Egyptians, Indians, Lebanese and Turks. At its broadest, the term could include virtually anyone on the Copperbelt who was not a black African. In other instances, a much narrower definition was deployed as some European nationals found their status as 'white' to be tenuous and people who regarded themselves as 'white' could be removed as undesirable troublemakers. 'White' status was no guarantee of permanency on the Copperbelt.

Mining, the Colonial State and White Migration

The presence of what was, relative to other parts of colonial Africa, a substantial white population was directly related to the development of industrial mining in the early twentieth century. Prior to this, there was only a handful of whites in the region and, without copper, it would likely have stayed that way. Few substantial white urban settlements were formed in either the Belgian Congo or Northern Rhodesia. In a taxonomy of white settlement in Africa, the Central African Copperbelt had a more substantial and enduring white presence then the flurry of white itinerants who descended on gold rushes in Tanganyika or the Gold Coast, but was on a smaller scale than the permanent urban white population implanted on South Africa's Witwatersrand by the gold industry.

---

7 For an overview of whiteness studies and how this relates to African Studies, see Danelle van Zyl-Hermann and Jacob Boersma, 'Introduction: The Politics of Whiteness in Africa', *Africa* 87, 4 (2017), pp. 651–61.

The threadbare administration on either side of the border did little to encourage white settlement and more commonly sought to discourage it. Indeed, across the colonial period, the colonial authorities had an ambivalent attitude towards white settlement as something that both demonstrated the apparent transformation of 'backward' regions by European enterprise and represented a potentially destabilising force to colonial rule. Authorities and large employers therefore carefully surveilled and policed the white population and usually dealt with perceived recalcitrants by physically removing them.

The first whites who came to live on the Copperbelt were missionaries from the Plymouth Brethren — a conservative British Protestant sect — who arrived in the late 1880s, although their presence in Bunkeya had little impact.[8] Colonial occupation initially changed little and between 1892 and 1900 there were never more than six Belgians in the whole of Katanga.[9] Similarly, in 1910 there were only 64 whites in Ndola District in Northern Rhodesia, almost all of them men, and this figure had only increased to 50 white men and 25 women by 1921.[10] Most were traders, hunters or prospectors, who drifted across the region in search of fortune.

Belgium pursued an elitist vision of colonisation that discouraged mass emigration.[11] The colony's white population — especially non-Belgian whites — was therefore monitored, and potential new arrivals closely scrutinised. The British South Africa Company (BSAC), the first rulers, or, more accurately, proprietors, of Northern Rhodesia had a more practical than ideological orientation, but the effect was the same. The Company saw the territory as a labour reserve for industries to the south and sought to deter white settlement as it would interfere with that goal. In 1909, one BSAC board member declared 'the policy of the Board' to be that 'the resident white population' should not increase 'beyond just what will supply the wants of the mining population', i.e. the whites operating small-scale mining and prospecting operations dotted across the territory.[12]

8   Robert Rotberg, 'Plymouth Brethren and the Occupation of Katanga, 1886–1907', *Journal of African History* 5, 2 (1964), pp. 285–97.
9   Bruce Fetter, *The Creation of Elisabethville* (Stanford: Hoover Institution Press, 1976), p. 18.
10 Brian Siegel, 'Bomas, Missions, and Mines: The Making of Centers on the Zambian Copperbelt', *African Studies Review* 31, 3 (1988), pp. 61–84, p. 73.
11 Guy Vanthemsche, *Belgium and the Congo, 1885–1980* (Cambridge: Cambridge University Press, 2012), pp. 61–2.
12 Peter Slinn, 'Commercial Concessions and Politics during the Colonial Period: The Role of the British South Africa Company in Northern Rhodesia 1890–1964', *African*

White settlement schemes of the kind implemented in the early 1920s in Kenya and Southern Rhodesia or, later, in Angola and Mozambique were not emulated in the Belgian Congo or Northern Rhodesia, aside from a brief, and very expensive, attempt to settle poorer Belgian farmers in Katanga by the Ministry of Colonies.[13] Early accounts were optimistic – one 1912 article claimed 'colonists were prospering' in Katanga with many families settled on small plots of land[14] – and the Ministry of Colonies even published a guide for emigrant farmers, but the scheme soon collapsed due to the vast costs and the disinclination of would-be farmers to remain on the land.[15] Between 1910 and 1920, 755 Belgian agricultural settlers were sent to Katanga with assistance from the Ministry of Colonies, but in 1920 there were only 129 still living in Katanga, and only 32 of these continued to farm.[16]

There was to be little place for white farmers on the Copperbelt and, in fact, relatively little land was alienated across the whole of the Belgian Congo or Northern Rhodesia. Only 3.29% of the total area of Katanga was alienated for whites by the end of the colonial period.[17] The future of the region, and of its white presence, was instead bound up with mining. The white population of Ndola District had risen to a few hundred in the mid-1920s, and then jumped to 6,873 by 1931 following the onset of industrial mining.[18] Katanga had experienced a similar leap in its white population when the railway arrived, connecting Elisabethville to areas of white settlement further south. As in Northern Rhodesia, there was a small, predominately male, influx, and Elisabethville's white population reached over 1,000 by the end of 1911.[19]

Affairs 70, 281 (1971), pp. 365–84, p. 370.

13   Charlotte Vekemans and Yves Segers, 'Settler Farming, Agriculture and Development in Katanga (Belgian Congo), 1910–1920', *Historia Agraria* 81 (2020), pp. 195–226. For subsequent debates in Belgium on the viability of white settlement schemes, see Jacques Legouis, 'The Problem of European Settlement in the Belgian Congo', *International Labour Review* 34, 4 (1936), pp. 483–9.

14   *La Revue Congolaise*, 14 July 1912, p. 206.

15   Ministère des Colonies, *Guide pour les Emigrants Agricoles Belges au Katanga* (Brussels: Imprimerie Industrielle et Financière, 1912).

16   Bogumil Jewsiewicki, 'Le colonat agricole européen au Congo-Belge, 1910–1960: Questions politiques et économiques', *Journal of African History* 20 (1979), pp. 559–71, pp. 561, 564.

17   Georges Brausch, *Belgian Administration in the Congo* (Oxford: Oxford University Press, 1961), p. 20.

18   'Report of the Director of Census Regarding the Census taken on the 5th May 1931' (London: Government of Northern Rhodesia, 1931), pp. 46–7.

19   Fetter, *Creation of Elisabethville*, p. 33.

Colonial borders at this time were relatively porous. Whites could cross easily and transport connections to the south meant that Elisabethville's white population had a strongly Anglophone element. The city had an English Club and the first newspapers, *Etoile du Congo* and *Journal du Katanga*, both established in 1911, published articles in English and French.[20] Katanga's new white population was the latest extension of a white population expanding and moving across Southern Africa. It even included a handful of Afrikaners who had come from Southern Angola, making Elisabethville the northern-most extremity of the Treks.[21]

Most new arrivals did not hang around for long. This was a transient population, and many of the whites in Elisabethville in 1912 had left the following year.[22] 'No-one could be called a permanent resident' of Elisabethville in the mid-1910s, concluded Bruce Fetter.[23] High death rates caused by disease drove most whites away, and 43 whites died in Elisabethville during 1911.[24] The same subsequently occurred in Northern Rhodesia, where malaria, dysentery and typhoid caused a mortality crisis at the new mines, and encouraged the swift departure of many whites.[25] Stories of deadly conditions spread across the region and railway staff in Cape Town reportedly delighted in telling those heading to the Copperbelt that it was a waste of money buying a return ticket, as they would never make it back alive![26]

Labour Migration and Industrial Unrest

The changes wrought by large-scale mining represented a serious challenge to vision of the colonial authorities in both the Belgian Congo and Northern Rhodesia. Despite the turnover in population, the expansion of

20 *Etoile du Congo* also published articles in Flemish. Johannes Fabian, *Language and Colonial Power: The Appropriation of Swahili in the Former Belgian Congo 1880–1938* (Cambridge: Cambridge University Press, 1986), fn. 3 p. 176.

21 Lindie Koorts, *DF Malan and the Rise of Afrikaner Nationalism* (Cape Town: Tafelberg, 2014), p. 84.

22 Fabian, *Language and Colonial Power*, p. 94.

23 Fetter, *Creation of Elisabethville*, p. 53.

24 Ibid., p. 32.

25 Lyn Schumaker, 'Slimes and Death-Dealing Dambos: Water, Industry and the Garden City on Zambia's Copperbelt', *Journal of Southern African Studies* 34, 4 (2008), pp. 823–40.

26 Malcolm Watson, *African Highway: The Battle for Health in Central Africa* (London: John Murray, 1953), p. 4.

mining operations in Katanga in the 1910s and 1920s, and then in Northern Rhodesia from the mid-1920s, drew in more and more white mineworkers, and other white migrants followed in their wake. The mechanisation of mining operations required skilled workers and connected the Copperbelt to the world of white labour, a transnational network of white workers extending across Southern Africa and beyond. White workers brought with them not only particular industrial skills, but also the knowledge and traditions of the international labour movement. These ideas helped spark waves of industrial unrest from the late 1910s, and again the 1940s, and helped persuade *Union Minière* to decisively alter its labour policies. White industrial unrest across the Copperbelt is thus comparable, but was mostly not concurrent, for reasons that will be explored below.

Union Minière's operations were mechanised in response to persistent shortages of African labour, and Rhodesian Anglo American (RAA) and the Rhodesian Selection Trust mechanised their mines from the outset for the same reason. Accordingly, *Union Minière*'s workforce swelled from 175 whites and 3,868 Africans in 1914 to 2,261 whites and 20,915 Africans in 1929. By 1930, the company could boast that 'operations were mechanised to the greatest extent, so as to reduce the workforce to a minimum.'[27] In Northern Rhodesia, both companies collectively employed some 2,221 white workers in 1931, alongside 13,948 African workers.[28] White labour was recruited from mining and industrial centres elsewhere in the world. In 1929, RAA forecast that the problem of attracting 'trained white labour will no doubt solve itself... Men will come from South Africa, from Britain, Australia, New Zealand, Canada, the United States and the Continent of Europe.'[29] *Union Minière* had followed the same policy and in 1920 43% of their white workforce was from Belgium, 23% from Britain, 16% from South Africa, 5% from the United States and 13% from elsewhere.[30]

These whites disrupted the smooth running of colonial rule, both as individuals and collectively. *Union Minière* advertised to potential recruits that 'a sober and dutiful worker is able to save' at least 1,000 francs each

27   Union Minière du Haut-Katanga, *Le Katanga: Pays du Cuivre* (Liège: Maison Desoer, 1930), p. 10.
28   Perrings, *Black Mineworkers in Central Africa*, p. 252.
29   Rhodesian Anglo American, *Mining Developments in Northern Rhodesia* (Johannesburg: Radford Cadlington Ltd, 1929), p. 63.
30   Perrings, *Black Mineworkers in Central Africa*, p. 51.

month, but not all were sober.[31] In Katanga, 'White industrial workers', according to John Higginson, 'frequently amused themselves with alcohol and firearms', and regularly appeared before the courts on charges relating to this.[32] The same was true in Northern Rhodesia, and visitors frequently commented on the vast quantities of alcohol consumed by white mineworkers. One senior colonial official in Northern Rhodesia referred to the Copperbelt's white population as 'a sort of human Whipsnade containing some fine specimens of rogues', Whipsnade being what was then Britain's largest zoo.[33]

Collective action by white mineworkers, however, presented the greatest threat. At the outbreak of the First World War, many Belgian nationals left *Union Minière* to join the armed forces and their proportion among the white workforce fell sharply from 53% in August 1914 to 22.5% in June 1917.[34] The gap was filled by new white recruits from Southern Africa and, to a lesser extent, the United States. This brought the new mines and railways of Katanga into closer connection with a white labour movement whose politics were a volatile mixture of industrial militancy, political radicalism and segregationist ideas. White male workers with a transnational work experience, one that closely informed their demands, were at the centre of unrest on both sides of the border.

One key figure in the unrest in Katanga was E. J. Brown, who came from the Rand to work for *Union Minière*. Brown had arrived on the Rand from Australia and was one of the leaders of the 1913 South African white mineworkers' strike, which culminated in a general strike and unrest that left twenty people dead. When further strikes in 1914 were suppressed by the imposition of martial law, Brown came to work for *Union Minière*, and tried to organise the white workforce. For this, he was swiftly sacked and deported to South Africa in 1920. He last appears in the historical record in a letter from the Communist Party of South Africa to Comintern providing a list of their leading militants.[35]

31　Union Minière du Haut-Katanga, *Le Katanga*, p. 45.
32　Higginson, *A Working Class*, pp. 67–8.
33　Ian Henderson, 'Labour and Politics in Northern Rhodesia, 1900–53: A Study in the Limits of Colonial Power', PhD thesis, Edinburgh University, 1972, p. 104.
34　Union Minière du Haut-Katanga, *Union Minière du Haut-Katanga: 1906–56* (Brussels: L. Cuypers, 1956), p. 124.
35　Jonathan Hyslop, 'Workers Called White and Classes Called Poor: The 'White Working Class' and 'Poor Whites' in Southern Africa 1910–1994' in Duncan Money and Danelle van-Zyl Hermann (eds), *Rethinking White Societies in Southern Africa, 1930s–1990s* (London, Routledge, 2020), pp. 23–41, p. 25.

Brown's experience in the more radical end of the labour movement was mirrored by the men who established the whites-only Northern Rhodesia Mine Workers' Union (NRMWU) in 1936. These included Tommy Graves, a veteran of the 'labor wars' in the American copper industry who had been deported from the United States, and Jim Purvis, who had been jailed in Australia after a strike and had worked in Britain and South Africa. In the 1940s, as will be discussed below, two white mineworkers were deported from Northern Rhodesia for instigating strikes: Frank Maybank, who had worked as a miner in New Zealand and Australia and had spent time in the Soviet Union, and Chris Meyer, a South African mineworker who had been a prominent member of the white miners' union on the Rand.[36]

Katanga was hit by the wave of industrial unrest that engulfed Southern Africa in the period after the First World War, but the specific trigger for action was the devaluation of the Congolese Franc in 1919, which cut the value of salaries for white workers in sterling terms. White mineworkers took wildcat strike action in response in May 1919, and some militants tried to blow up the offices of the Attorney General.[37] This was followed by a strike of white railway and government workers and the formation of a new trade union in May 1920, *L'Union Générale des Ouvriers du Congo*. This was a whites-only union, just as were the trade unions formed on the mines in Northern Rhodesia. The following month, this new union demanded a salary increase compensating for the devaluation of the franc – as they saw themselves as workers in an international labour market – and a bar on African workers performing jobs done by whites.[38]

Gains won by white workers on Rhodesia Railways after a major strike in 1920, whose effect would soon have been felt in Katanga, triggered further action by white workers in Katanga, who embarked on a five-week strike in September. This dispute was also marked by militancy and violence, with white strikers trying to halt railway traffic by dynamiting a bridge at Sakania, derailing an approaching freight train. White workers won a pay increase but not their wider demands, and *Union Minière* and the colonial authorities cracked down decisively on the union in the aftermath.[39] Strike

36 Duncan Money, 'The World of European Labour on the Northern Rhodesian Copperbelt, 1940–1945', *International Review of Social History* 60, 2 (2015), pp. 225–55.
37 Perrings, *Black Mineworkers in Central Africa*, pp. 50–51.
38 Jean Ryckbost, *Essai Sur les Origines et le Développement des Premières Associations Professionnelles Au Congo* (Léopoldville: Universiteum Lovanium, 1962), pp. 8–9.
39 Perrings, *Black Mineworkers in Central Africa*, p. 54.

leaders were sacked and then expelled from the colony.

Although Belgian workers had participated in the strikes, both *Union Minière* and the colonial administration were convinced that the strikes had been instigated by British and South African white workers to undermine Belgian rule.[40] This reflected persistent Belgian fears that Britain would attempt to bring Katanga into the orbit of its colonies in Southern Africa and annex the territory.[41] There is no evidence of British, or South African, strategic intrigue behind these strikes, but this provided a convenient excuse for *Union Minière* to change its labour policy, so that the structure of the mining workforce in Katanga was noticeably different than the one in Northern Rhodesia by the 1930s.

Union Minière made a determined effort to sever links with the trans-national world of white labour, and redirected recruitment efforts towards Belgium, specifically the Hainaut region (where coal mining was prominent), and the proportion of white employees hired in Europe rose from 37% in 1919 to 89% by 1929.[42] These white workers were recruited on fixed-term contracts and repatriated to Belgium on completion, and could thus be controlled more closely. White militants had been removed from the workforce by the mid-1920s and the white mineworkers' union crushed. It took twenty years and the circumstances of another world war for trade unionism to revive on the Katanga mines.

Changes in the Racial Division of Labour

The brief recession in the global copper industry in the early 1920s soon gave way to a boom period. Copper production in Katanga rose sharply – from 18,962 tonnes in 1920 to 138,949 in 1930 – while over the border prospecting efforts discovered vast copper ore bodies, triggering a rush to bring new mines into production.[43] Soon, there were more white mine-workers in Northern Rhodesia than in Katanga, and many of these had previously worked for *Union Minière*. More and more whites flocked to the region, and one American mining engineer confidently forecast in 1931 that

---

40   Fabian, *Language and Colonial Power*, pp. 105–6.
41   Vanthemsche, *Belgium and the Congo*, p. 118.
42   Perrings, *Black Mineworkers in Central Africa*, p. 251.
43   Simon Katzenellenbogen, 'The Miner's Frontier, Transport and General Economic Development' in Peter Duignan and L. H. Gann (eds), *Colonialism in Africa 1870–1960*, vol. 4, *The Economics of Colonialism* (Cambridge: Cambridge University Press, 1975), pp. 360–426, p. 377.

'this region will… support and require a half a million whites in the very near future'.[44] Yet as this prediction was being made, developments on the Copperbelt would reveal how tenuous white settlement was, as the Great Depression struck and *Union Minière* implemented its new labour policy.

Modest white urban centres developed in this period. Elisabethville's white population rose from 1,476 in 1920 to 4,168 in 1930, while Kitwe became the largest town in Northern Rhodesia, with a white population of 1,762 in 1931.[45] Racial segregation was inscribed on the landscape of these new urban spaces through physical separation. European and African areas of Elisabethville were purposively constructed with a 170-metre wide strip – later widened to 500m – between them.[46] New mining towns in Northern Rhodesia used the mine itself to segregate the African and white workforces, with townships for each built on opposite sides of the mine. Virtually all the inhabitants of Northern Rhodesia's new mining towns worked for the mines, but the same was not true in Katanga. In the early 1920s, white *Union Minière* employees in the mining camps were given the option of moving into the main towns, and almost all of them did.[47] In Northern Rhodesia, the mining companies housed almost their entire white workforces throughout this period.

Insofar as spatial segregation in new urban areas reflected divisions *within* the white population, in Northern Rhodesia it was an occupational division separating mining and non-mining populations. Katanga's white population, however, had a broader occupational profile and was more cosmopolitan. Elisabethville was not 'just another Belgian colonial city', and had substantial Italian, Greek and Portuguese communities, the latter bolstered by the Benguela Railway that linked the city to Angola from 1929.[48] The

44   Ronald Prain Papers, American Heritage Center, University of Wyoming (hereafter RP), Box 1, File 2, Letter from Fred Searls Jnr to Vivian Smith, London, 24 February 1931.
45   Rubbers, *Faire fortune en Afrique*, p. 35. 'Report of the Director of Census…1931', p. 46.
46   Sofie Boonen and Johan Lagae, 'A City Constructed by "des gens d'ailleurs"': Urban Development and Migration Policies in Colonial Lubumbashi, 1910–1930', *Comparativ: Zeitschrift für Globalgeschichte und Vergleichende Gesellschaftsforschung* 4, 25 (2015), pp. 51–69, pp. 56–7.
47   Sean Hanretta, 'Space in the Discourse on the Elisabethville Mining Camps: 1923 to 1938' in Florence Bernault (ed.), *Enfermement, prison et châtiments en Afrique: du 19e siècle à nos jours* (Paris, Karthala, 1999), pp. 305–35, p. 324.
48   Johan Lagae, 'From "Patrimoine partagé" to "whose heritage"? Critical Reflections on Colonial Built Heritage in the City of Lubumbashi, Democratic Republic of the

respective status of these groups was reflected in their physical location; Italian, Greek and Portuguese traders– termed '*gens de couleur*' in colonial legislation and often referred to as 'second class whites' –primarily catered for African customers and were pushed to the edge of the European city in the buffer zone between the European and African areas.[49] Katanga also had a sizeable Jewish community which supported an array of communal institutions, 'including a Jewish scout troop, youth movement, women's group, and a range of Zionist organisations'.[50]

Katanga's white population still included some 2,500 white mineworkers in 1930, and more were sought:

> In the category of specialist workers, the company is looking among others for mechanics, fitters, turners, machine operators, boilermakers, electricians, power shovel operators, overhead crane drivers, locomotive drivers, power station operators, miners and woodworkers, masons, concrete workers, etc.[51]

Such people would soon no longer be required. The sharp fall in copper prices in the Great Depression almost throttled the new copper industry in Central Africa. Most mines in Northern Rhodesia shut down and across the Copperbelt the white population fell precipitously. In Katanga, almost 2,000 white mineworkers were sent back to Europe, and others followed in their wake.[52] Elisabethville's white population plummeted to 548 in 1932 and in Jadotville (Likasi) more than half the houses were unoccupied.[53] Similarly, the white workforce on Northern Rhodesia's mines fell from

Congo', *Afrika Focus* 21, 1 (2008), pp. 11–30, p. 25; Jean-Luc Vellut, 'La communauté portugaise du Congo belge (1885–1940)', in John Everaert and Eddy Stols (eds), *Flandre et Portugal: Au confluent de deux cultures* (Anvers: Fonds Mercator, 1991), pp. 315–45, pp. 339–40.

49 Boonen and Lagae, 'A City Constructed', pp. 59–61.

50 Guy Bud, 'Belgian Africa at War. Europeans in the Belgian Congo and Ruanda-Urundi, 1940–1945', MPhil thesis, University of Oxford, 2017, p. 28. There was a Jewish community on the Northern Rhodesian Copperbelt but it was smaller, see Hugh Macmillan and Frank Shapiro, *Zion in Africa: The Jews of Zambia* (London: I.B. Tauris, 1999).

51 Union Minière du Haut-Katanga, *Le Katanga*, p. 41.

52 Bogumil Jewsiewicki, 'The Great Depression and the Making of the Colonial Economic System in the Belgian Congo', *African Economic History* 4 (1977), pp. 153–76, p. 158.

53 Union Minière du Haut-Katanga, *Union Minière 1906–1956*, p. 173.

3,456 in January 1931 to a low of 995 in October 1932.[54]

Unemployed and impoverished whites posed a severe threat to colonial rule, and across the Copperbelt the respective colony authorities deported thousands of whites to prevent the emergence of a class of 'poor whites' – a category much feared elsewhere in the sub-continent for the threat it posed to racial hierarchies.[55] In total, the authorities in the Belgian Congo used an *arrêté d'expulsion* to deport whites from the colony at least 1,450 times, ostensibly because the individual in question was bankrupt.[56] Northern Rhodesia's Governor James Maxwell gravely warned in 1930 that the 'growing population' of 'poor whites' was 'the greatest danger to the existence of white civilisation in tropical Africa'.[57] His counterpart in the Belgian Congo, Pierre Ryckmans, justified the exclusion of some whites from the colony in the mid-1930s in the same way, stating that 'the "poor whites" are pariahs' condemned to 'the destiny of the natives'.[58] In 1929, entry requirements for whites had been tightened for this reason, and potential white immigrants had to deposit a substantial sum of money to guarantee they would not become a burden on the public purse.[59]

The copper industry gradually revived through the 1930s but when it did the composition of the workforce was altered, especially in Katanga. White industrial unrest in 1919–20 and the costs of continually recruiting African labour prompted serious changes to labour policy by *Union Minière*. Having curtailed the prospect of resistance from white workers, the company now embarked on a policy of training African workers to replace them.[60] Between 1933 and 1935, *Union Minière's* workforce doubled in size and output increased by almost a third, but total labour costs remained static, as

---

54 Robert Kuczynski, *Demographic Survey of the British Colonial Empire* Vol. II (London: Oxford University Press, 1949), p. 422.
55 Tiffany Willoughby-Herard, 'South Africa's Poor Whites and Whiteness Studies: Afrikaner Ethnicity, Scientific Racism, and White Misery', *New Political Science* 29, 4 (2007), pp. 479–500, p. 492.
56 Matthew Stanard, 'Revisiting Bula Matari and the Congo Crisis: Successes and Anxieties in Belgium's Late Colonial State', *The Journal of Imperial and Commonwealth History* 46, 1 (2018), pp. 144–68, p. 154.
57 James Maxwell, 'Some Aspects of Native Policy in Northern Rhodesia', *Journal of the Royal African Society* 29, 117 (1930), pp. 471–7, p. 477.
58 Boonen and Lagae, 'A City Constructed', p. 55. See also Amandine Lauro, 'Maintenir l'ordre dans la colonie-modèle: notes sur les désordres urbains et la police des frontières raciales au Congo Belge (1918–1945)', *Crime, Histoire & Sociétés*, 15, 2 (2011), pp. 97–121, pp. 103–4.
59 In 1957, the sum was 50,000 Belgian Francs. Rubbers, *Faire fortune en Afrique*, p. 46.
60 Perrings, *Black Mineworkers in Central Africa*, pp. 54–61.

the replacement of white workers with Africans allowed the company to effectively implement a huge wage reduction for certain jobs.[61]

Rhodesian Anglo American and Rhodesian Selection Trust tried to follow the same policies, though with greater hesitation. Underground mining was more complex than open-pit mining, the demand for skilled labour was consequently greater and white mineworkers had a stronger position. Both companies were well aware of *Union Minière*'s labour policy and company representatives told the British Government in 1938 that they intended to follow the same policy, but 'we have been very careful not to go too fast', lest they provoke resistance.[62] White workers in Katanga offered no resistance to these policies, and did not engage in any collective organising, as those recruited in these years 'were paralyzed with fear of losing their jobs and of being repatriated'.[63] African workers in Northern Rhodesia did progressively undertake more skilled work, and the composition of the workforce did change, but there were far more whites at work on the mines of Northern Rhodesia: 2,609 in 1939 compared with 870 in Katanga.[64]

While Anglo American and Rhodesian Selection Trust saw *Union Minière* as a model to emulate, for their white workforces Katanga was a possible future to be feared and avoided. The cross-border proximity of two different racialised labour structures made it a constant reference point. Harold Hochshild, chair of the American Metal Company, the parent company of Rhodesian Selection Trust, visited the Copperbelt in 1949 and was very impressed with *Union Minière*'s operations, where 'in their mines and plants one rarely sees a white man unless one searches for him'. He regarded the extension of this system to Northern Rhodesia as 'inevitable'.[65] Senior figures at Anglo American reached the same conclusion, and one posed the question: 'Is it possible to have different lines of development in adjacent territories without creating some degree of unrest as progress is made towards different ends?'[66]

61 John Higginson, 'Bringing the Workers Back in: Worker Protest and Popular Intervention in Katanga, 1931–1941', *Canadian Journal of African Studies* 22, 2 (1988), pp. 199–223, pp. 205–6.
62 Zambia Consolidated Copper Mines archives (hereafter ZCCM-IH), 18.4.3E, Meeting at the Dominion Office, 14 April 1938.
63 Jewsiewicki, 'Great Depression', p. 167.
64 Elena Berger, *Labour, Race, and Colonial Rule: The Copperbelt from 1924 to Independence* (Oxford: Oxford University Press, 1974), p. 218. Perrings, *Black Mineworkers in Central Africa*, p. 251.
65 RP, Box 1, Unnumbered File, 'Visit to the Rhodesias', 22 October 1949.
66 A. Royden Harrison, 'African Skill in Darkest Africa', *Optima* (June 1951), p. 17.

It is important to note that all three mining companies were careful to maintain a racial division of labour, and that *Union Minière* did not abolish the racial division of labour. Instead, the colour bar was moved up the occupational hierarchy of the mines. Although Africans performed skilled work in Katangese mines, factories and railways, the lines of authority were clear: no African held a position of power over any white. In 1959, almost 40 years after *Union Minière*'s training and stabilisation labour policy was introduced, there were no African engineers, and only eighteen Africans were employed in *contremaitre* (foreman) positions otherwise occupied by whites.[67] African workers could not be trusted in positions of authority, as one *Union Minière* director explained: 'the indigenous worker… has one failing which distinguishes him clearly from the European worker… his will-power is always unreliable and he remains a creature of impulse.'[68] A clear racial division of labour therefore had to be maintained. During the Second World War, for instance, *Union Minière* tried to overcome white labour shortages by recruiting in Mauritius, until it became obvious that many of the men recruited from there were mixed-race. Recruitment efforts were swiftly redirected to the more distant, though racially more secure, Portugal.[69]

Connections and Attempted Convergence in the Second World War

Circumstances brought about by the Second World War forged closer connections across the Copperbelt and allowed white mineworkers to attempt a convergence across the border. For a brief period, many white mineworkers imagined that their struggles were linked, and Katanga was re-integrated into the world of white labour. White mineworkers in Northern Rhodesia saw what had happened in Katanga as a future to be avoided, while their counterparts in Katanga viewed what was happening on the mines in Northern Rhodesia as something to be emulated. Many among the white workforce saw the war as an opportunity to permanently improve their position, and their demands were shaped by what was happening in other mining and industrial regions.

67 Brausch, *Belgian Administration*, p. 32.
68 Leopold Mottoulle, 'Medical Aspects of the Protection of Indigenous Workers in Colonies', *International Labour Review* 41, 4 (1940), pp. 361–70, p. 364.
69 Bakajika Banjikila, 'Les ouvriers du Haut-Katanga pendant la Deuxième Guerre mondiale', *Revue d'histoire de la Deuxième Guerre mondiale et des conflits contemporains*, 33, 130 (1983), pp. 91–108, pp. 95–6.

The Second World War temporarily severed the Belgian Congo's connection with the metropole following the occupation of Belgium by Nazi Germany in May 1940. The British Government was already purchasing all copper produced in Northern Rhodesia and now extended this scheme to cover the Katanga mines, and the Congolese Franc was pegged to the Pound Sterling in June 1941.[70] Across the Copperbelt, white mineworkers were now producing copper for the same ends and their wages were directly comparable. Wartime need for copper also placed these whites in a strong negotiating position.

White mineworkers in Northern Rhodesia were the first to strike. Wildcat strikes in March 1940 quickly secured an array of concessions, including wage increases, followed by a closed shop for their union and a colour bar in 1941, safeguarding them from the fate that had befallen their counterparts in Katanga.[71] Soon after, whites struck on Katanga's mines in October 1941, initially over the employment of an Italian national at the UMHK plant in Jadotville, but the strike soon spread to other UMHK operations and demands broadened to cover pension rights and wage increases.[72] Immediately after this strike, a whites-only trade union was formed clandestinely with the assistance of NRMWU militants: the Association des Agents de l'Union Minière et Filiales (AGUFI), which soon had 850 members.[73]

This was a boom period for white trade unionism. The closed shop gave NRMWU an unprecedented degree of control over the mines, and white mineworkers in Katanga forced *Union Minière* to engage in collective bargaining. In April 1942, the colonial authorities in the Belgian Congo were forced to grant legal recognition to white trade unions, followed in June 1944 by a decree guaranteeing freedom of association for whites.[74] Dozens of white trade unions were formed, including four others in Elisabethville, and together they established a colony-wide white labour body at a congress held in Elisabethville: the Confédération générale des syndicats du Congo belge (CGS).[75] White labour organisations soon established links with their counterparts elsewhere in the region. In 1943, white trade unionists from the across the Copperbelt attended the Southern Africa

70 Ryckbost, *Premières Associations*, p. 18.
71 Money, 'World of European Labour', pp. 234–41.
72 Banjikila, 'Les ouvriers du Haut-Katanga', pp. 96–7.
73 Ryckbost, *Premières Associations*, pp. 22–3.
74 George Martens, 'Congolese Trade Unionism: The Colonial Heritage', *Brood en Rozen* 4, 2 (1999), pp. 128–49, p. 134.
75 Ryckbost, *Premières Associations*, pp. 29–30.

Labour Congress in Johannesburg, a gathering of representatives of the white labour movement that established a short-lived organisation to coordinate a region-wide movement.[76]

In the Belgian Congo and Northern Rhodesia, the mining companies acted in concert with the state to crack down on white industrial unrest. The problem, the British Consul in Elisabethville observed, was that 'the distance is so small' between the mines 'and the frontier so difficult to control', so preventing liaison between their respective white workforces seemed impossible.[77] In June 1942, another wildcat strike by white mineworkers in Jadotville resulted in the arrest and prosecution of two AGUFI leaders, Joseph Heynen and Jean Dutron, for voicing defeatist sentiments; the two men were removed to Ruanda-Urundi. The authorities suppressed further wildcat strikes in August and September, and 'a virtual state of siege was declared in Jadotville', according to the British Consul. Telephone services were suspended, a curfew imposed, road and rail traffic curtailed and troops patrolled the streets.[78]

Katanga's white mineworkers had sent urgent requests for help to their counterparts across the border, and the NRMWU leadership, having met secretly with AGUFI representatives inside Katanga in early August, now attempted to launch sympathy strikes in Northern Rhodesia to demand the return of Heynen and Dutron to Katanga. Northern Rhodesia's colonial administration panicked. The Governor pleaded with the British Government to send troops after the NRMWU General Secretary Frank Maybank tried to organise a sympathy strike and warned the Governor that white mineworkers were armed. As in Katanga, troops were rapidly deployed from East Africa, and two of the union's leaders, Maybank and Chris Meyer, were arrested and deported.[79] The prospect of united strike action by whites across the Copperbelt was firmly extinguished.

There were, however, limits to the power of the colonial state, both practical and ideological. Embarrassingly, Heynen and Dutron escaped twice from Ruanda-Urundi and made their way back to Katanga. On the second occasion, in September 1944, they arrived during a CGS conference, where

---

76 Duncan Money, 'Race and Class in the Postwar World: The Southern Africa Labour Congress', *International Labor and Working-Class History* 94 (2018), pp. 133–55.

77 The National Archives UK (hereafter TNA), CO 795/123/7, Letter from T. R. Shaw to F. M. Shepherd, 5 September 1942.

78 TNA, CO 795/123/7, Letter from T. R. Shaw to F. M. Shepherd, 28 September 1942.

79 Money, 'World of European Labour', pp. 242–6.

they were elected to that body's leadership.[80] In Northern Rhodesia, wildcat strikes by whites continued to disrupt production during 1944, and the colonial state was unable to prevent the return of Maybank to the Copperbelt in 1945.

The response by the colonial states to strikes by white mineworkers was very different to the response to strikes by African mineworkers: there were some forms of repression that the state would not enact against whites. White strikers could have their movements restricted and be subject to sudden arrest and deportation. African strikers could be massacred, as happened at Nkana in April 1940, and at Panda and Lubumbashi in December 1941. It was inconceivable that African troops, who made up the large bulk of colonial armed forces, could be used against whites. In Katanga, the *Corps des Volontaires Européens* had been formed in 1920 to deal with unrest by whites because, as the Colonial Minister explained, 'the use of black troops is not desirable for the repression of European riots'.[81] In Northern Rhodesia, the colonial authorities relied on guarantees of troops from Britain to deal with white unrest.

On both sides of the border, white mineworkers stood aloof during strikes by African mineworkers. Still, white mineworkers were often blamed by their employers and the colonial state for instigating or inspiring strikes by African workers.[82] It is true that strikes by African mineworkers directly followed strikes by white mineworkers in 1940 in Northern Rhodesia and 1941 in Katanga, but there is no evidence that white trade unions encouraged this, even if some individual white mineworkers were sympathetic. In any case, open expressions of sympathy for African workers tended to attract swift censure and action from the state.[83]

Attempts by white mineworkers to bring the two workforces together failed, and their histories diverged. By 1949, CGS had split and then disintegrated, while AGUFI lapsed into inactivity, but NRMWU went from strength to strength.[84] Further strikes in 1946 preserved Northern Rhodesia's industrial colour bar and secured a copper bonus that would be the source of immense affluence in the post-war period. White mineworkers

80 TNA, CO 795/128/5, Note on M. Heynen and M. Dutron.
81 Lauro, 'Maintenir l'ordre dans la colonie-modèle', pp. 107–8.
82 Banjikila, 'Les ouvriers du Haut-Katanga', p. 96.
83 One white trade unionist, George Lievens, who contradicted the official account of the African strike at Lubumbashi, was imprisoned and then deported: Higginson, *A Working Class*, pp. 193–4.
84 Bud, 'Belgian Africa at War', p. 46.

in Katanga failed both to improve their position in wartime or to change *Union Minière*'s labour policy. Their numbers increased only marginally, from 923 in 1940 to 1,075 in late 1944.[85]

The Boom Years

Many similarities existed between the white communities on the Copperbelt in the post-Second World War period, but there were few direct connections. Both became substantially larger as the mining industry expanded and the white population across most of Southern Africa rose markedly. By 1960, there were around 35,000 whites on Northern Rhodesia's Copperbelt and almost 32,000 white residents in Katanga.[86] More white women arrived and the gender imbalance in the white population, marked in the early mining camps, disappeared. Recruitment material for the mining companies began to emphasise education facilities for children and the ease of life for housewives, as mining work continued to be restricted to men.

These white communities also became wealthier, benefitting handsomely from the post-war boom that saw copper production in Northern Rhodesia rise from 192,000 tons in 1947 to 559,000 tons by 1960.[87] Increases in *Union Minière*'s operations were more modest, though production still doubled from 151,000 tons in 1947 to 301,000 tons in 1960.[88] Expanding production and further mechanisation meant that additional white skilled workers and mining professionals were needed. The number of white mineworkers employed by *Union Minière* increased by 48% between 1942 and 1958, while the number of African mineworkers decreased by 50% as production required less labour.[89] In Northern Rhodesia, where a colour bar remained, white employment on the copper mines more than doubled in the same period, and reached a peak of almost 8,000 in 1962.[90]

The composition and structure of the white mining workforce was quite different on different sides of the border, however, and this had consequences

85 Union Minière du Haut-Katanga, *Union Minière 1906–1956*, p. 189.
86 Government of Zambia, 'Final report of the September 1961 censuses of non-Africans and employees' (Lusaka, Government Printer, 1965), pp. 43–4; Jules Gérard-Libois, *Secession au Katanga* (Léopoldville: INEP, 1964), p. 3.
87 Berger, *Labour, Race, and Colonial Rule*, p. 238–39.
88 Katzenellenbogen, 'Miner's Frontier', p. 337.
89 Jean-Luc Vellut, 'Mining in the Belgian Congo', in David Birmingham and Phyllis Martin (eds), *History of Central Africa*, vol 2 (London: Longman, 1983), pp. 126–62, p. 138.
90 Berger, *Labour, Race, and Colonial Rule*, p. 239.

for life on the mines for whites. In 1942, NRMWU had justified intervention in disputes in Katanga by claiming that, with the British Government
purchasing all copper produced in the region, soon 'someone would want
to know why our wages were much higher for the same work'.[91] Whites
on both sides of the border were not doing 'the same work', however.
Membership of AGUFI encompassed all whites employed by *Union Minière*;
Heynen, for instance, had been employed as a secretary to a manager. Few
whites in Katanga were directly involved in production and this is one reason
why, along with swift repression, strikes by white mineworkers there failed.
Mining operations did not cease when whites ceased work in Katanga,
whereas strikes by white mineworkers were able to shut down operations
in Zambia well into the 1960s.

The 1956 recognition agreement between NRMWU and the Northern
Rhodesian companies stipulated that the workers represented by the union
included miners, timbermen, semi-skilled operators, banksmen, brick-
layers, locomotive drivers, crane drivers, carpenters and electricians, all jobs
performed in Katanga by African mineworkers.[92] As a case in point, only
one of the ten white *Union Minière* employees interviewed by the company
magazine in 1957, a plumber, was employed in such a job. The other nine
were mining professionals (geologists, mining or chemical engineers) or
administrative personnel.[93] When the International Labour Organisation
compiled a comparison of European and African wage rates across the
continent it concluded: 'There can be few, if any miners in the world with
a higher standard of living than that of the Europeans in the Northern
Rhodesian Copperbelt', but the Belgian Congo was excluded from this
analysis because 'the number of European wage earners is insignificant'.[94]

One consequence of this was very different levels of conflict within white
society during the 1950s. As *Union Minière* explained to new white recruits
in the mid-1950s, 'as a general rule, the European staff of the company
is a managerial staff whose main task is to direct the work of Congolese
workers'.[95] The company emphasised racial solidarity among the whites

[91] Money, 'World of Labour', p. 243.
[92] International Institute for Social History, Miners' International Federation, Box 360,
'Recognition Agreement between the NRMWU and Rhokana Corporation, 1956'.
[93] 'Tableau d'Honneur', *Haut-Katanga*, April 1957.
[94] International Labour Organisation, 'Interracial Wage Structure in Certain Parts of
Africa', *International Labour Review* 68, 1 (1958), pp. 20–55, p. 24.
[95] Union Minière du Haut-Katanga, *L'Union Minière et la vie au Katanga* (Brussels:
Union Minière du Haut-Katanga, 1954), p. 18.

they employed, pointing out to potential new arrivals that white employees worked, lived and socialised together so that, in contrast to Belgium, 'relations are more direct and almost constant, with both your bosses and your colleagues'.[96] The same was not true in Northern Rhodesia, where there were sharp and sometimes hostile divisions between white mineworkers and mine management, and industrial conflict persisted until the mid-1960s.

There were during this period intermittent contacts between the white workforces across the border. In 1958, a delegation of white mineworkers from Katanga attended the NRMWU annual conference, whom the NRMWU General Secretary claimed arrived 'quite unexpectedly'. One colonial official however drily noted 'the remarkable coincidence of the arrival of the Belgian delegates precisely at the time when the Union was holding its Annual Conference'.[97] Dissimilarities between the position and experiences of the white workforces may explain why nothing came of this meeting, though it's possible language barriers also played a role.

Still, despite regular industrial upheaval, there was no difficulty attracting white mineworkers to Northern Rhodesia as the high standards of living, common across the Copperbelt, proved an excellent advert. Recruitment material from all three companies emphasised both the quality of life and, as Roan Antelope put it, that 'earnings, job for job, are on a much more generous scale than in the United Kingdom or the Union [of South Africa]'.[98] Moreover, white employees and their families could enjoy a remarkable range of leisure activities, all subsidised by the companies. By the 1950s, the mines were accompanied with swimming pools, football and rugby pitches, tennis courts and golf courses at a minimum, along with evening entertainment in the form of theatres, dances, concerts and, above all, bars.[99] Corporate magazines from the 1950s – *Haut-Katanga*, *Rhokana Review*, etc. – contain virtually identical pictures and descriptions of their white workers' vibrant social life. This was partly a shared culture, as whites across the Copperbelt largely played the same sports, and teams regularly played their counterparts across the border (see Chipande, Chapter 4), or participated jointly in more

96 Ibid., p. 18.
97 ZCCM-IH, 10.5.8D, Notes of a conversation between Mr F. B. Canning-Cooke and Mr J. F. Purvis, 31 December 1958.
98 Roan Antelope Mines, *Information Book for European Employees*, p. 13 (in author's possession).
99 For instance, see the wide variety of events organised for white employees at UMHK for the feast of St Barbara (patron saint of miners) in December 1957, 'Fêtes de Ste Barbe', *Haut-Katanga*, February 1958.

ostentatious pursuits. In mid-1959, for instance, a speedboat club from Elisabethville took part in a regatta at the dam in Luanshya, having been invited after three speedboat clubs from the Northern Rhodesian Copperbelt had visited Elisabethville.[100] The creation of industrial towns with modern recreational facilities was heralded in company publications as the embodiment of modernity, making the Copperbelt 'not Central Africa at all, but Pittsburgh or Wigan or Johannesburg', a place where the 'mere list of the amenities must read like a guide-book or even an advertisement'.[101]

Union Minière did try and impress on its white workforce the importance of their role as colonisers in the Belgian Congo, stressing to new recruits that 'you will contribute to the work of civilisation that Belgium tirelessly pursues in Congo'.[102] The policy of training African workers was articulated in these terms, as *Union Minière*'s director of labour policy, Léopold Mottoulle, wrote in 1946: 'the colonizer must never lose sight that the blacks have the spirits of children, spirits which mould themselves to the methods of the teacher'.[103] The extent to which white mineworkers in Katanga internalised this message is not clear, but it is noteworthy that the equivalent material provided to new white employees arriving in Northern Rhodesia contained nothing about the colonial project, and only mentioned the existence of the African workforce briefly.

White society on the Northern Rhodesian Copperbelt was much more uniform in terms of occupation, nationality and language than in Katanga, though more sharply divided along lines of class. Indeed, a snapshot of Katanga's comparatively cosmopolitan white society is offered by the exodus of refugees who passed into Northern Rhodesia in July 1960. Among the 7,530 people who were temporarily housed on the Copperbelt, only 5,564 (74%) were Belgian nationals. The remainder included 690 Italians, 556 Greeks, 160 British, 154 Portuguese, 116 French, 53 Dutch, 45 Americans, only 25 South Africans, and then a smattering of other mostly European nationalities.[104] The white population on the Northern Rhodesia Copperbelt were almost uniformly English-speaking. The 1961 census found that 94% of the 74,549 whites living in Northern Rhodesia had citizenship of

---

100 'Round the Group', *Horizon*, August 1959.
101 Kenneth Bradley, *Copper Venture: The Discovery and Development of Roan Antelope and Mufulira* (London: Roan Antelope Copper Mines, 1952), pp. 21–2.
102 Union Minière du Haut-Katanga, *La vie au Katanga*, p. 25.
103 Hanretta, 'Elisabethville Mining Camps', p. 306.
104 NAZ, WP 1/14/58, Nationality List. Only 79% of Belgian Congo's total white population held Belgian nationality in 1959: Vanthemsche, *Belgium and the Congo*, p. 280.

a state in the British Empire or Commonwealth.[105] There was a noticeable presence of Afrikaners in Northern Rhodesia's mining towns, but a study commissioned by the Chamber of Mines found that only 9% of their white workforce spoke Afrikaans as a first language.[106]

Conclusion

Several weeks after Katanga's secession, some whites in Katanga proposed constructing a monument in Kitwe 'to thank our Rhodesian friends for their magnificent welcome', and as a lasting symbol of the ties between whites across the border.[107] It was never built, perhaps a fitting conclusion to the way that deep and enduring connections between the two white communities had been repeatedly thwarted. Many whites who left Katanga with the exodus in July 1960 did not return. In the National Archives of Zambia, there are many letters on file from white former Katanga residents requesting the return of their firearms from the authorities in Northern Rhodesia and asking them to be sent to their new addresses in Belgium, South Africa or elsewhere since, as one man bluntly put it, 'I am no more interested in going back there [sic]'.[108] Some did return, and white *Union Minière* employees were escorted back in a column guarded by Belgian paratroopers; but things would never be the same.

In contrast, life for whites in Zambia was much the same as it had been before independence in 1964. The historical experience of whites on the Zambian Copperbelt after 1960 was very different to their counterparts in Katanga who remained amid war and secession. White society on the Zambian Copperbelt also came to an end, though in a less dramatic fashion, when the deep recession in the global copper industry in the mid-1970s, alongside steady efforts towards Zambianisation, encouraged their departure.

The Copperbelt's population of white mineworkers was never a stable one, and this was by design. Even in 1930, *Union Minière* asserted that 'the worker... generally returns to Europe with better skills than when he left', the assumption being that these white workers would naturally return to

---

105 Government of Zambia, 'Final report of the 1961 censuses', pp. 53–4.
106 J.F. Holleman and Simon Biesheuvel, *White Mine Workers in Northern Rhodesia 1959–60* (Leiden: Afrika-Studiecentrum, 1973), p. 109.
107 'Problèmes Européens', *Essor du Congo*, 26 July 1960.
108 NAZ, WP 1/14/58, Letter from Raoul Goutiere to District Commission, Bancroft, 2 September 1960.

Europe at the end of their contracts.[109] Almost all members of this workforce were employed on fixed-term contracts and repatriated to Europe, from where they had been recruited, at the end of those contracts. In Northern Rhodesia, most of the white workforce were employed on contracts with a 24-hour notice period, until Zambian independence when all white mineworkers were put on fixed-term contracts with repatriation clauses, contracts that were partly modelled on those in Katanga.

This is a curious inversion of what is generally understood as the model of migrant labour in Southern Africa, with Africans as short-term labour migrants in industrial centres and whites as permanent settlers. On the Copperbelt, Africans were semi-permanent urban residents with lengthening careers on the mines, while whites were effectively long-distance labour migrants who usually left after relatively short periods at the mines. The presence of most whites on the Copperbelt, and virtually all white mine-workers, was ultimately temporary and tied to the mining industry and its needs. Without copper, very few would have migrated there.

Ultimately then, the histories of whites on the Copperbelt did converge, in the sense that white communities have disappeared and only a scattered white presence remains today, much smaller and more temporary than previously.[110] For much of the colonial period, however, it makes sense to think of two histories, as life and work on the mines in Katanga was in many ways quite different to that on the Northern Rhodesian Copperbelt. The kind of militant strikes by white mineworkers that unsettled Katanga in the early 1920s were still going on in an independent Zambia some 40 years later. Nonetheless, their proximity meant that both white communities had close knowledge of the other and, at different times, each white commu-nity was imagined by the other as representing a possible future for itself.

109 Union Minière du Haut-Katanga, *Le Katanga*, p. 41.
110 Rubbers, *Faire fortune en Afrique*, pp. 38–9.

4

Football on the Zambian and Katangese Copperbelts: Leisure and Fan Culture from the 1930s to the Present

HIKABWA D. CHIPANDE

Introduction

European mineworkers, railway workers, and missionaries introduced football (soccer) to the Central African Copperbelt region, made up of the Copperbelt Province in Northern Rhodesia (later Zambia) and Katanga in the Belgian Congo (later Zaïre/Democratic Republic of the Congo) following the colonisation and industrialisation of the region in the late nineteenth and early twentieth centuries.[1] The emergence of the Northern Rhodesian and Katangese mining and industrial centres created a foundation for the diffusion of modern sports such as football.[2]

To placate and discipline their new workforce, colonial and mining authorities in Katanga and Northern Rhodesia adopted welfare schemes. They were concerned by urbanising African mineworkers' leisure activities that focused on beer drinking, traditional dances and visiting neighbours, which authorities considered as increasing misconduct, criminality and other disruptive behaviours.[3] A central aspect of these welfare schemes was the provision of recreational and sporting amenities in new mine townships, and

---

[1] Hikabwa D. Chipande, 'Mining for Goals: Football and Social Change on the Zambian Copperbelt, 1940s–1960s', *Radical History Review* 125 (2016), pp. 55–73; Peter Alegi, 'Katanga vs Johannesburg: A History of the First Sub-Saharan African Football Championship, 1949–50', *Kleio*, 3 (1999), pp. 55–74; Hikabwa D. Chipande, 'Copper Mining and Football: Comparing the Game in the Katangese and Rhodesian Copperbelts c. 1930–1980', *Zambia Social Science Journal* 6 (2016), pp. 28–46.

[2] Chipande, 'Mining for Goals', p. 57.

[3] Ibid., p. 59.

football was identified as one of the leading leisure activities.[4] In Katanga, a combination of the Roman Catholic Church, Belgian colonial authorities and the Anglo-Belgian copper mining giant Union Minière du Haut-Katanga (UMHK) used sport to create 'a disciplined, efficient, moral and healthy African working class'.[5] Similar welfare schemes were developed across the border in Northern Rhodesia after the 1940 Copperbelt strike, with sports as one of the main activities.[6] Hortense Powdermaker reveals how welfare centres in the Roan Antelope African mine compounds in Luanshya offered a variety of activities such as literacy classes, knitting, nutrition, cinema, dancing, with sports, and particularly football, being the most popular of these.[7]

In the minds of colonial and mining authorities, sports such as football were important aspects of colonial domination because they inculcated discipline, consciousness, endurance and courage in African mineworkers.[8] They believed that vigorous sports activities provided a cheap and effective means of social control.[9] The British imperial notion of a 'games ethic' was centred on ethnocentrism, hegemony and patronage.[10] As elsewhere in Africa and other parts of the world, local mineworkers in the Copperbelt abandoned their traditional leisure activities, appropriating and adopting football as a part of their popular culture in the mining towns. Crowds of fans flocked to open grounds and new stadiums in the mining compounds every weekend to watch their favourite teams.[11]

4   Alegi, 'Katanga vs Johannesburg'; Patience N. Mususa, 'There Used to Be Order: Life on the Copperbelt After the Privatisation of the Zambia Consolidated Copper Mines', PhD thesis, University of Cape Town, 2014, p. 26; Chipande, 'Mining for Goals, p. 59.
5   Ibid.
6   Patience Mususa, 'Mining, Welfare and Urbanisation: The Wavering Urban Character of Zambia's Copperbelt', *Journal of Contemporary African Studies*. 30, 4 (2012), pp. 571–87.
7   Hortense Powdermaker, *Copper Town: Changing Africa – The human situation of the Rhodesian Copperbelt* (New York: Harper & Row, 1965), p. 107.
8   Emmanuel Akyeampong and Charles Ambler, 'Leisure in Africa: An Introduction', *International Journal of African Historical Studies*, 31, 1 (2002) pp. 1–16, p. 11.
9   Chipande, 'Mining for Goals', p. 59.
10   J.A. Mangan, *The Games Ethic and Imperialism Aspects of the Diffusion of an Ideal* (New York: Viking, 1985), p. 17.
11   Gerard Akindes and Peter Alegi, 'From Leopoldville to Liège: A Conversation with Paul Bonga Bonga' in Chuka Onwumechili and Gerard Akindes (eds), *Identity and Nation in African Football: Fans, Community and Clubs* (London: Palgrave Macmillan, 2014), pp. 254–68; Akyeampong and Ambler, 'Leisure in Africa'; Peter Alegi, *African Soccerscapes: How a Continent Changed the World's Game* (Athens: Ohio University Press, 2010); Chipande, 'Mining for Goals', p. 57.

While leisure on both Katanga's and Northern Rhodesia's mine towns has attracted extensive attention from scholars, there appears to be none that have explored how football became a popular leisure activity, playing an essential role in the lives of African mineworkers and their families.[12] There is however a growing body of historical and anthropological literature on football fandom in Africa in general. This work has explored practices and rituals of spectatorship, rivalries, violence, how the game constitutes fans' social identities, and the role of media and migration in the increasing identification of African fans with European teams.[13] Nevertheless, apart from the South African mines, little historical analysis has been carried out on how the game played a role in building colonial and postcolonial African urban mine communities.[14] Drawing on archival documents, press articles and oral interviews, this chapter explores how playing and supporting football became a popular leisure activity for black mineworkers in Katanga and the Rhodesian Copperbelt from the 1930s to present. It also shows how looking at football closely can shed some light on colonial and post-colonial politics in the region and formation of collective urban identities.

---

12 See for example J. Clyde Mitchell, *The Kalela Dance: Aspects of Social Relationships Among Urban Africans in Northern Rhodesia* (Manchester: Manchester University Press, 1956); Powdermaker, *Copper Town*, p. 107; Albert B. K. Matongo, 'Popular Culture in a Colonial Society: Another Look at Mbeni and Kalela Dances on the Copperbelt', in Samuel N. Chipungu (ed.), *Guardians in Their Time: Experiences of Zambians Under Colonial Rule, 1890–1964* (London and New York: Macmillan, 1992), pp. 180–217; Charles Ambler, 'Alcohol, Racial Segregation and Popular Politics in Northern Rhodesia', *Journal of African History* 31 (1990), pp. 295–313; Charles Ambler, 'Popular Film and Colonial Audiences: The Movies in Northern Rhodesia', *American Historical Review* 106 (2001), pp. 81–105; Mususa, 'There Used to Be Order'; Chipande, 'Mining for Goals, pp. 55–73; Johannes Fabian, *Jamaa; A Charismatic Movement in Katanga* (Evanston, Northwestern University Press, 1971); S. E. Katzenellenbogen, *Railways and the Copper Mines of Katanga* (Oxford: Clarendon Press, 1973).

13 See Peter Alegi, *Laduma! Soccer, Politics, and Society in South Africa, From its Origins to 2010* (Scottsville, University of KwaZulu-Natal Press, 2010), p. 51; Gerard Akindes, 'Football Bars: Urban Sub-Saharan Africa's Trans-local "Stadiums"', *International Journal of the History of Sport* 28, 15 (2011), pp. 2176–90; Chuka Onwumechili, 'Nigeria, Football, and the Return of Lord Lugard', *International Journal of Sport Communication* 2 4 (2009), pp. 451–65; Onwumechili and Akindes, *Identity and Nation*, p. 96; Tafadzwa Choto, Manase Kudzai Chiweshe and Nelson Muparamoto, 'Football Fandom, Ethno-Regionalism and Rivalry in Post-Colonial Zimbabwe: Case Study of Highlanders and Dynamos', *Soccer and Society* 20, 1 (2017), pp. 153–67; Manase Kudzai Cheweshe, 'Till Death do us Part: Football as Part of Everyday Life amongst Dynamos Football Club Fans in Zimbabwe', *African Identities* 14, 2 (2016), pp. 101–13.

14 Alegi, *Laduma!*; Alegi, 'Katanga vs Johannesburg'.

Early Football Development in the Northern Rhodesian and Katangese Copperbelt

As already noted, Europeans played a central role in the diffusion of football in the Copperbelt region. As the game became popular among African mineworkers, it generated increasing interest from white colonial and mining authorities, leading to the sponsorship of competitions in order to provide symbolic control over the mineworkers. According to Peter Alegi, the popularisation of football in the Belgian Congo in the 1930s and 1940s can be linked to the notion of muscular Christianity drawn from a Latin expression '*mens sana in corpore sano* (a healthy mind in a healthy body)' that was popularised by Catholic missionaries and accepted by colonial and mining authorities.[15] This went together with the ideology of political athleticism, the belief that, as Alegi argues, football could be a means to educate 'civilised' black youth physically and morally in such important habits as discipline and endurance.[16] This belief in the importance of workers being healthy and happy was captured by the UMHK motto, 'good health, good spirit and high productivity.'[17] Football was used by UMHK to direct African labour in Katanga's mining communities to what they perceived as 'healthy' leisure activities, while missionaries such as Father Gregoire Coussement used sport and other activities in Benedictine schools to develop Catholic elites. The Belgian colonial government heavily depended on the Catholic Church and companies such as UMHK to establish and maintain education and control systems because it did not have sufficient resources to support these activities directly.[18]

As Belgian colonial racism permeated all areas of Congolese society, early football in Katanga was played on segregated lines, leading to the formation of the Europeans-only *Ligue de Football du Katanga* in 1911 in the provincial capital Elisabethville.[19] In 1925, four teams competed in the European-only B. Smith Cup.[20] African football, on the other hand, only took off with the support of Father Coussement, who organised a football

15 Alegi, *African Soccerscapes*, p. 4.
16 Ibid.
17 Alegi, 'Katanga vs Johannesburg'.
18 Bruce Fetter, The Luluabourg Revolt at Elisabethville', *African Historical Studies* 2, 2 (1969), pp 269–77.
19 Akindes and Alegi, 'From Leopoldville to Liege'; Alegi, *African Soccerscapes*, 4.
20 Alegi, *African Soccerscapes*, p. 3.

league for Africans in Elisabethville in 1925. [21] It was only after the Second World War that the Elisabethville Football Association (EFA) was formed to govern black football.[22]

Similar activities were happening across the border in British-colonised Northern Rhodesia. The birth of its Copperbelt in the early 1920s led to an influx of European mineworkers that introduced modern sports such as football in the area.[23] The first form of organised football started with the formation of a whites-only Rhodesia Congo Border Football Association in 1927 that administered both football and rugby until 1930, when the Rhodesia Congo Border Rugby Union separated from it.[24] When the authorities first introduced football to African mineworkers however, some were unenthusiastic about playing the game, regarding its introduction as part of their mine work, and therefore believed it would require payment, as revealed in the Roan Antelope mines compound manager's report of January 1932:

> We have to meet the needs of a more primitive type [of natives compared to those in South African mines] who as yet have not felt the necessity for passing the time, during their recreation hours, in playing games instituted by the Europeans. They have the idea that whatever is required of them, whether it be an exhibition of Physical Drill or game of football, it is solely for the amusement of the Bwanas [bosses]. We have several instances of natives having failed to turn up for a game of physical drill and putting forth the excuse that they did not get any overtime pay for doing the 'work'.[25]

This reveals the efforts that mining authorities were making to introduce 'modern' sports to African mineworkers on the Copperbelt and the resulting differences between Africans and the European employers regarding the conceptualisation of leisure. Scholars such as Phyllis Martin, Emmanuel Akyeampong and Charles Ambler have revealed the divisions that emerged between Europeans and Africans in the early colonial period over the

21 Ibid.
22 Akindes and Alegi, 'Leopoldville to Liege'.
23 Chipande, 'Mining for Goals', p. 57.
24 Hikabwa D. Chipande, 'Introduction and Development of Competitive Football in Zambia (1930–1969): A Historical Perspective', Master's Thesis, Norwegian School of Sport Science, 2009, p. 62.
25 Zambia Consolidated Copper Mines archives (hereafter ZCCM-IH), 10.7.10, Ndola Roan Antelope mine Compound Manager's monthly report, January 1932.

conceptualisation of leisure time and space.[26] In her work on leisure in colonial Brazzaville, Martin convincingly argues that studying sport sheds light on 'the multi-faceted colonial experience', showing how cultural and political life were interconnected.[27] Looking at sport can reveal both everyday colonial experiences and the underlying struggles of definition between coloniser and colonised. Similarly, Laura Fair's work on football and politics in colonial Zanzibar reveals how, despite Europeans' hope that football would inculcate values of discipline and colonial order, it became an arena of daily struggles between colonialists and the colonised. The locals used football to challenge colonial hegemony by defeating their supposed European superiors in front of thousands of fans, publicly defying European referees, and using the game to define the shape of life in their communities.[28]

The Africanisation of Copperbelt Football

Despite their initial resistance, as the number of Africans migrating from rural areas to work in the mines increased, they appropriated and began playing the game in their residential compounds outside direct European supervision.[29] Europeans, particularly those of British origin, firmly believed that physical activities in general and sport in particular, provided a civilised and cheap way of controlling potentially violent new African mine-workers.[30] The use of football to control African labour in the mines was also seen in South Africa and Katanga where authorities supported the game based on their belief that it increased workers' morale and productivity levels in the mines.[31] Despite this 'hidden' agenda and African miners' initial lack of enthusiasm, over time they appropriated football from the Europeans and indigenised it into the popular culture of the Copperbelt mining communities.[32]

---

26 Akyeampong and Ambler, 'Leisure in African History'; Phyllis Martin, *Leisure and Society in Colonial Brazzaville* (Cambridge and New York: Cambridge University Press, 1995), p. 99.

27 Martin, *Leisure and Society in Colonial Brazzaville*, p. 99.

28 Laura Fair, 'Kickin' It: Leisure, Politics and Football in Colonial Zanzibar, 1900s–1950s'. *Africa* 67, 2 (1997), pp. 224–51.

29 Hikabwa D. Chipande, 'Chipolopolo: A Social and Political History of Football (Soccer) in Zambia', PhD thesis, Michigan State University, 2015, Ch. 1.

30 Chipande, 'Mining for Goals', p. 60.

31 Alegi, *Laduma!* p. 41; Akindes and Alegi, 'Leopoldville to Liège'.

32 Chipande, 'Chipolopolo', Introduction. This was similar to how Africans in other territories such as Congo-Brazzaville, Zanzibar, the Belgian Congo and South Africa

As the game established roots in African mine compounds, the Governor of Northern Rhodesia offered to sponsor a competition in 1936 that came to be called the Governor's Cup. Qualifying matches for the Governor's Cup involved African teams from all the main mining towns such as Luanshya, Nkana (Kitwe), Mufulira, Nchanga (Chingola) and Bancroft (Chililabombwe). The inaugural final of the competition took place between Nkana and Luanshya on 4 October 1936 at the Rugby Football Club in Ndola, with Nkana beating Luanshya 2–1. The significance of this event can be seen in the presence of the Governor, Sir Hubert Winthrop Young who, accompanied by the Senior Provincial Commissioner, District Commissioner, and other colonial and mining officials, attended the final match and presented the Cup to the winning team.[33] While the Governor's Cup gave colonial and mining authorities' symbolic control over the game, it also played a vital role in the development of organised football and raised enthusiasm among Africans in the mining towns. This can be seen in the presence of what the *Mutende* newspaper described as large numbers of fans.[34] The successful organisation of the Governor's Cup also led to the creation of an (all-white) Native Football Committee made up of mine compound managers and charged with the responsibility of controlling African football on the Northern Rhodesian Copperbelt in 1937. As Africans began to enjoy the game, Europeans feared that its popularity in black mine communities could serve as an avenue for anti-colonial rebellion. This was not unique to Northern Rhodesia; French colonialists imposed strict control on football in colonial Brazzaville's black townships of Bacongo and Poto-poto fearing that the game might be used as an opportunity for political agitation.[35] The Native Football Committee evolved in the 1940s into the Copperbelt African Football Associations that managed football in the region.[36]

Parallel to these processes in Northern Rhodesia, the growing popularity of football among Africans in the Katangese mining towns led the President of UMHK, M. Gillet, to introduce a football competition in 1956 for what came to be known as the Gillet Cup.[37] Significantly, the competition

---

appropriated the game: see Martin, *Leisure and Society in Colonial Brazzaville*, p. 110; Laura Fair, *Pastimes and Politics: Culture, Community, and Identity in Post-colonial Zanzibar, 1890–1945* (Athens: Ohio University Press, 2001), p. 247; Akindes and Alegi, 'Leopoldville to Liège'.

33 'Climax of the Copperbelt Football Season', *Mutende,* November 1936.
34 Ibid.
35 Martin, *Leisure and Society in Colonial Brazzaville*, p. 43.
36 Chipande, 'Mining for Goals', pp. 57, 62.
37 'Trophée President Gillet', *Mwana Shaba,* May 1957.

involved both African and European teams from across the mining towns of Katanga: Elisabethville, Jadotville, Kolwezi and Shinkolobwe. The white football governing body *Ligue Royale de Football du Katanga* managed the Gillet Cup, but as well as featuring African and European teams, the football matches drew what *Mwana Shaba* magazine describes as large crowds of both African and European spectators.[38] Like the Governor's Cup in Northern Rhodesia, the Gillet Cup became the biggest football competition in Katanga in the 1950s.[39] Following the successful introduction of the Gillet Cup, Henry Buttgenbach, the administrator of UMHK, introduced another football competition for Katangese teams that came to be known as Buttgenbach Cup in 1957.[40] The Buttgenbach Cup was played in the same way as the Gillet Cup involving African and European teams in Katanga. The introduction of these competitions popularised the game in the Katangese mines: the Panda mine (white) team from Jadotville (today Likasi) was the most successful in 1957, winning the Gillet Cup, the Fiftieth Challenge Cup and the newly introduced Buttgenbach Cup.[41] Leagues were still racially segregated in Katanga throughout the 1950s, but competitions like the Gillet Cup and Buttgenbach Cup began to break down the football colour bar. In contrast, in Northern Rhodesia racial segregation in football continued until 1962.

The interest that both colonial and mining authorities across the Copperbelt region showed in sponsoring African football would not have been possible if Africans had not themselves engaged with the sport, both as players and spectators. This mass popularity, however, could be viewed as a danger as well as an opportunity. This necessitated efforts to direct its development and project symbolic control over it by organising competitions named after colonial and mine company officials, as detailed above.[42] On the other hand, African mine communities enjoyed football, and the game generated a lot of fun and excitement among mass gatherings in mining towns in both parts of the Copperbelt region.[43] Phyllis Martin argues that, in Brazzaville, '[n]o other form of popular culture could rival the excitement generated by football matches. To be part of the crowd was to be at

38 Ibid.
39 Chipande, 'Chipolopolo', Ch. 1.
40 'Trophée Buttgenbach', *Mwana Shaba*, 1957.
41 Ibid.
42 Chipande, Mining for Goals', p. 57.
43 'Climax of the Copperbelt Football Season', *Mutende*, 1936; 'Trophée President Gillet', *Mwana Shaba*, May 1957.

the heart of a city experience.'[44] Similarly, people in Northern Rhodesia and Katanga found football to be fun and exhilarating, and being part of the crowed during matches meant being part of the urban excitement. Competitions in open township grounds and newly constructed stadiums usually brought communities to a standstill as hundreds of people assembled to cheer on their local teams.[45] The game's sociability also helped African miners to build new urban social networks, bonds and neighbourhoods.[46] These networks and bonds extended across the colonial border separating Katanga from Northern Rhodesia.

Football Excursions between Katanga and Northern Rhodesia

Although divided by a colonial border, connections between the mines of Katanga and Northern Rhodesia existed from the start of colonial mine exploration. In 1899 Cecil Rhodes's company Tanganyika Concessions Ltd and the Belgian *Comité Spécial du Katanga* shared mineral rights in Katanga – 40% and 60% shares respectively.[47] The establishment of UMHK in 1906 was itself a collaborative venture between British and Belgian investors. This history intricately tied the two companies that shared a lot, including reports, communication, leaders and shares.[48] This cross-border collaboration later extended to leisure activities such as football. Following the formation of the *League de Football du Katanga* in 1911 and the Rhodesia Congo Border Football Association in 1927, that – as noted above – governed whites' only football in the two regions, matches were organised between their member teams from the 1930s to the 1950s.[49]

The Copperbelt African Football Association and the Elisabethville Football Association also began organising cross-border football competitions for Africans in the 1940s.[50] The number of such competitions increased

---

44 Martin, *Leisure and Society in Colonial Brazzaville*, p. 118.
45 Chipande, 'Mining for Goals', p. 62.
46 Fair, *Pastimes and Politics*, p. 247; Alegi, *Laduma!* pp. 54–5; Chipande, 'Copper Mining and Football', p. 29.
47 Matthew Hughes, 'Fighting for White Rule in Africa: The Central African Federation, Katanga, and the Congo Crisis, 1958–1965', *International History Review*, 25, 3 (2003), pp. 592–615.
48 Hughes, 'Fighting for White Rule in Africa', p. 595.
49 Alegi, *African Soccerscapes,* p. 3; Sundowner, 'Copperbelt Soccer', *Horizon*, May 1959.
50 'Copperbelt Outclassed Congo in a Big Soccer Tussle', *The African Eagle,* 22 October 1957.

in the late 1940s, leading to Elisabethville hosting what was characterised as the 'first sub–Saharan African football championship' in 1950.[51] This football contest involved select teams from Johannesburg and other areas of South Africa; the Northern Rhodesian mining towns of the Copperbelt and Broken Hill, and those in Katanga. The final of the tournament was played between teams representing Katanga and South Africa in the Léopold II Stadium. Katanga beat South Africa 8–0 to win the championship.[52] Elisabethville subsequently hosted other regional soccer competitions that involved select teams from Northern Rhodesia, Katanga and Congo Brazzaville, making it the centre of regional football competitions in the 1950s.[53]

As these football tours became increasingly fashionable in the 1950s, a Northern Rhodesian Copperbelt select team even travelled as far as the Belgian Congo capital Léopoldville (Kinshasa) in 1951 on invitation of the Congo Football Association. In Léopoldville, this team was given an excellent reception by the Congo Football Association, the British Consul and Belgian colonial officials. Exciting football matches were all won by the Léopoldville select team.[54] The long distances that teams covered to these competitions, and the prestige with which their visits were marked, demonstrates both their significance to the authorities and also how African communities perceived the importance of the game. It became an avenue through which local people aspired to another material and symbolic existence, as it was one of the few areas where Africans could stand out in the setting of colonial and mining society.[55] John Ginger Pensulo who played for the Copperbelt African Football Association in the 1950s in Northern Rhodesia, emphasised during an interview that sharing cultural experiences, and playing the game with fellow Africans in Katanga, was an exciting experience.[56] The cross–border football events, and the fanfare associated with the visits and tournaments of African football teams, provided a space where Africans could compete for prestige and success on an 'equal' playing field.

51 Alegi, 'Katanga vs Johannesburg', p. 58
52 Ibid.
53 'Brilliant Victory by Brazzaville in the Elizabethville Tournament', *Mwana Shaba*, August 1958.
54 National Archives of Zambia (hereafter NAZ), WP 1/5/1, Luanshya African Welfare 2nd Quarterly Report, Luanshya, June 1951.
55 Nuno Domingos, *Football and Colonialism: Body and Popular Culture in Urban Mozambique* (Athens: Ohio University Press, 2017), p. 4
56 Interview, Pensulo, Luanshya, 7 March 2014.

Even after the Congo gained independence in 1960, football exchanges between the two regions continued. In 1962, a racially integrated team from Luanshya called Roan Antelope United FC, under the leadership of former Portuguese international Tony Castela who acted as both captain and coach, made a tour of Katanga and played a select team in Jadotville (today's Likasi). The thrilling match was played at Panda Stadium, in which Jadotville led Roan 2–0 in the first half, while Roan managed to equalise in the second half, with the match ending 2–2.[57]

Although there are no exact figures for attendance at these competitions, such matches are widely reported to have drawn thousands of spectators from their host cities. For example, a match organised by the Northern Rhodesia Football Association between teams from Elisabethville and Northern Rhodesia, held at the Nchanga Sports Club in 1962, attracted about 3,000 spectators.[58] In the context of mine town populations in the 1960s, this was a huge number of fans and it reveals how the game had become a central part of leisure practices in the mines. It is also important to note that these matches (and their crowds) were widely reported upon in newspapers and magazines. This means that they had an afterlife in newspapers, which memorialised star players, and the excitement of the events. The match reports inspired people to read the newspapers so they also helped to broaden the audience and increase followers. The matches themselves, and the matches as memoralised through newspapers, therefore, became unmistakable communitarian spectacles in the African mining towns of both Northern Rhodesia and Katanga.[59] The popularity of football, as Chiweshe demonstrates for Zimbabwe, also shows how the locals used the sport to create their own spaces under colonialism, limiting colonial and mining authorities' control over their lives.[60] Football would continue to be a popular activity in the changed circumstances of the postcolonial period.

Social Welfare and Football Development after Independence

The Belgian Congo gained independence in 1960 with Patrice Lumumba as Prime Minister. Within a few months, Lumumba faced an army mutiny and Moïse Tshombe's secessionist movement of the copper-rich Katanga region,

57 'Roan Antelope United... a Panda' *Mwana Shaba,* December 1962.
58 'Nchanga Incident: N.R.'s Soccer Prestige will Suffer', *Inshila,* 19 June 1962.
59 Domingos, 'Football and Colonialism', p. 2.
60 Kudzai Chiweshe, 'Till Death do us Part'.

led by his *Confédération des Associations Tribales du Katanga*. Lumumba was eventually detained and murdered, with the collusion of Western intelligence agencies.[61] Despite the political turbulence that engulfed the Congo, leading to Joseph Mobutu becoming president in 1965, UMHK (and its successor company Gécamines) continued to provide the welfare programmes started in the colonial era, offering various leisure activities to mineworkers and their families.

Each mining town – such as Elisabethville (later Lubumbashi) or Jadotville (later Likasi) – had a social services division overseen by the personnel manager, whose primary role was to provide and promote leisure activities.[62] Welfare committees coordinated different activities, each with a president, vice-president, secretary and a treasurer. Social welfare centres provided libraries to encourage a reading culture, and other amenities such as musical and cinema shows and occasionally art exhibitions. Katangese social centres, like those in Northern Rhodesia/Zambia, provided a wide range of sporting amenities that included football, volleyball, basketball, swimming, tennis, boxing, rugby, chess, darts and many others.[63] These facilities were however only available to the employees of companies and their families, who had to accept the strict regulations that governed the centres.

Following Zambia's independence in 1964, its booming copper-dependent economy made it possible for President Kenneth Kaunda's socialist-leaning government to continue with Copperbelt social welfare schemes that Europeans started in the colonial era. The mine companies, with support from government, provided mineworkers with housing and recreational facilities that included well-managed football grounds and stadiums, in line with Kaunda's policy of redistributing copper wealth to build a prosperous Zambia.[64] This policy was further reinforced by the nationalisation of major companies, including the copper mines, in the late 1960s and early 1970s. With government encouragement, these nationalised corporations, particularly Zambia Consolidated Copper Mines (ZCCM), increased support of football.[65] In his

---

61 Chipande, 'Copper Mining and Football', p. 39; David Goldblatt, *The Ball is Round: A Global History of Football* (New York: Riverhead Books, 2008), p. 506.
62 'The Sports and Entertainment Circles', *Mwana Shaba*, 244, 15 December 1975.
63 Ibid.
64 Alastair Fraser, 'Introduction' in Alastair Fraser and Miles Larmer (eds), *Zambia, Mining, and Neoliberalism: Boom and Bust on the Globalized Copperbelt* (New York: Palgrave Macmillan, 2010), p. 6.
65 The first stage of nationalisation resulted in the creation of Roan Consolidated Mines (RCM) and Nchanga Consolidated Copper Mines (NCCM) in 1969. These structures were merged into ZCCM in 1982.

speech at the United National Independence Party (UNIP) 3rd National Convention in 1984, President Kaunda stated 'the party and its government should continue to encourage sport and recreation, especially among young people in order to get them off the streets. … parastatals and other working places should endeavour to provide these recreational facilities'.[66]

Following these directives, ZCCM developed a comprehensive football programme in the early 1980s that involved the recruitment of sports advisers and employment of full-time mine divisional coaches by its Department of Community Services.[67] They hired experienced British football coach Jeff Butler as a Sports Adviser with the responsibility of offering guidance on effective planning and successful implementation of mine sports programmes.[68] The company also employed eight full-time experienced local football coaches, one for each of the ZCCM mine districts.[69] Apart from being provided with the best available advisers and coaches, ZCCM supplied its sports clubs with equipment and necessities on an annual basis even when the company was not making profits, following the fall of the copper prices on the international market from the late 1970s. In 1989 ZCCM was financing five professional football clubs, namely Nkana Red Devils, Power Dynamos, Roan United, Mufulira Wanderers and Nchanga Rangers, at a time when the company was making a loss.[70]

With such plentiful and powerful sponsorship, it is no surprise that mine-sponsored football clubs continued to dominate competition, making the Copperbelt the hub of football in both Congo/Zaïre and Zambia. On the other hand, the continuation of mine social welfare structures to support soccer can be understood as a continued use of colonial-era methods to control African labour in the mines.[71] It also suggests that postcolonial African states and nationalised enterprises had simply substituted for colonial structures that had socially and economically exploited the local population, which resonates with Frederick Cooper's argument that the end of colonialism in many African states involved 'a mere change of personnel within

---

66 NAZ, Kenneth Kaunda speech at United National Independence Party (UNIP) 3rd National Convention, 23–25 July 1984,

67 ZCCM-IH, Minutes of Divisional Coaches meeting held on 5 September 1984.

68 Ibid.

69 The eight divisions referred to are: Nchanga, Mufulira, Nkana, Luanshya, Kalulushi, Konkola, Kabwe and Ndola Lime Company.

70 Hikabwa D. Chipande, 'The Structural Adjustment of Football in Zambia: Politics, Decline and Dispersal, 1991–1994', *International Journal of the History of Sport*, 33, 15 (2016), pp. 1847–65.

71 Alegi, 'Katanga vs Johannesburg', p. 58; Chipande, 'Mining for Goals', p. 57, p. 61.

structure[s] that remain[ed] colonial'.[72] On the other hand, it is difficult for one not to see how much the local people in the mining towns enjoyed and participated in football, creating their own fan culture that owed little or nothing to the demands of company or state patronage.

Soccer, Rhumba and Patronage in Katanga

In the 1960s and 1970s, thriving Katangese football teams included clubs such as Kipushi, Saint-Éloi Lupopo, Tout Puissant Englebert, Lubumbashi Sports, Union Sportive Panda and Vaticano.[73] Saint-Éloi Lupopo dominated the Katangese league by winning the Elisabethville Championship from 1954 to 1964, when Lubumbashi Sports took the championship from them.[74] In addition to competitive local football matches, regional competitions continued to be organised in Lubumbashi. In 1963, a regional competition was held in Lubumbashi stadium involving teams from Northern Rhodesia, Katanga and Brazzaville. The matches attracted crowds of fans that filled Lubumbashi stadium to watch local and visiting teams. In addition to the matches, François Luambo, popularly known as Franco and his O.K. Jazz Band, entertained fans in the stadium with live rhumba music.[75] Phyllis Martin reveals how 'Congolese music' popularly known as rhumba developed in the 1950s as a result of a mixture of assorted 'rhythms, instruments and lyrics from the whole of central Africa'.[76] For Congolese football fans, rhumba went together with the popularisation of the game and fashion in imported clothes that became markers of power and prominence in urban Congo in the 1960s and 1970s.[77] Evidence of this kind may suggest how rhumba, dancing and football became part of Congolese urban popular culture.[78]

Towards the end of the 1960s, Tout Puissant Englebert became the most successful club not only in Katanga and Congo but the African continent as a whole. The club had been formed in 1939 and was initially called Saint Georges Elisabethville. A few years later; a tyre manufacturing company Englebert began sponsoring the club, leading to the change of name to

---

72 Fredrick Cooper, *Africa Since 1940: The Past and Present* (Cambridge: Cambridge University Press, 2002), p. 4.

73 '*Lubumbashi Sports … Une Euipe A Suivre*', *Mwana Shaba*, 8, August 1963.

74 'Lubumbashi Sports Champion', *Mwana Shaba*, 13 December 1964.

75 *Mwana Shaba*, 9, September 1963.

76 Martin, *Leisure and Society in Colonial Brazzaville*, p. 127.

77 Ibid., p. 155.

78 Goldblatt, *The Ball is Round*, p. 507.

Englebert. The club started performing well and earned itself the label *Tout Puissant* (meaning 'all powerful' in French), and changed its name to Tout Puissant Englebert.[79] After Congo's independence in 1960, it was renamed Tout Puissant Mazembe (meaning 'Crows' in Swahili) under the influence of President Joseph Mobutu's Africanisation policy.[80] 'TP Mazembe', as the club came to be popularly known, won both the Katangese and Congolese football league championships and the African Champions Cup for two consecutive years in 1967 and 1968, and reached the finals of the latter competition for four successive years from 1967 to 1970.[81]

With this success, TP Mazembe attracted a large army of fans that could be seen and heard during matches through its impressive display of traditional regalia, dancing, singing and beating drums throughout matches. According to Brian Mulenga, who watched TP Mazembe play against Mufulira Wanderers in 1979 in Zambia, the organisation of their fans was far ahead of any Zambian team: they came to Mufulira with marching majorettes and a band all dressed in black and white, the team's official colours.[82] In the early 1980s, the fans became even more organised and were then known as '*Les cent pour cent*' meaning 'The 100 percenters'. The 100 percenters created a lively and festive atmosphere during matches regardless of the score.[83] The great atmosphere they consistently created during matches shows how TP Mazembe's fans' singing and dancing is deep rooted in the club's culture, and survived despite the team's decline in the 1980s and early 1990s.[84]

The emergence of TP Mazembe's 100 percenters is today associated with financial support from Moïse Katumbi Chapwe, who later became chairperson of the club and Governor of Katanga Province. Katumbi started supporting TP Mazembe when he was nine years old when his older brother was chairperson of the club. His brother banned him from watching matches for misbehaving, but he would sneak out and climb trees to watch games.

---

79 'The Secrets of TP Mazembe's Success', FIFA Club World Cup UAE 2010, 18 December 2010: www.fifa.com/clubworldcup/news/the-secrets-mazembe-success-1353395 (accessed 25 November 2019).

80 Goldblatt, *The Ball is Round*.

81 Chipande, 'Copper Mining and Football', p. 39.

82 Interview, Brian Mulenga, Lusaka, 25 November 2019.

83 'TP Mazembe's Tales of the Unexpected', *FIFA Club World Cup* 2015, 12 December 2015: www.fifa.com/clubworldcup/news/tp-mazembe-s-tales-of-the-unexpected-2743835-x3734 (accessed 25 November 2019.

84 Manase Kudzai Chiweshe, 'Online Football Fan Identities and Cyber-fandoms in Zimbabwe' in Onwumechili and Akindes, *Identity and Nation*, pp. 236–53, p. 236.

Katumbi subsequently made his fortune from the mining, transport and fishing businesses that he ran in both Zambia and the Democratic Republic of the Congo.[85] In 1997, he was elected president of TP Mazembe and immediately embarked on the vigorous transformation of the club in order to regain its lost glory. In 2007, building on the high profile achieved by his association with the club, Katumbi was elected Governor of Katanga. Meanwhile his investment in TP Mazembe started producing results: the club won five Congolese club championships, as well as the Confederation of African Football (CAF) Champions League title in both 2009 and 2010.[86] Katumbi invested about $12 million in the club, enabling the renovation of the Stade TP Mazembe in the Kamalondo area of Lubumbashi and realising his goal of making TP Mazembe one of the largest football clubs on the continent. While Katumbi denied the connection between investment in TP Mazembe and his political ambitions, anthropologist Arnold Pannenborg argues that, 'Katumbi understands the political ramifications of the club's massive following, having stated that "TP Mazembe is the hope of the Congolese people"'.[87] Katumbi's profile was such that he declared his aim of standing for the Congolese presidency in 2018, although he was prevented from doing so by the government of the day.

The presence of famous musicians such as Franco during soccer matches in Lubumbashi stadium, and the drumming, singing and theatrical performances by TP Mazembe's fans, suggests not only the Africanisation of Katangese football, but also the prominence of football in the formation of fans' identities as Katangese, mineworkers and urbanites. As Katumbi himself pointed out, the club symbolised hope for many Congolese people following a period of economic and political crisis and military conflict, and has become central to the identity of Congolese football. [88] Football has generated a lot of fun, excitement and an urban popular culture and experience for many people. It has also played an essential role in strengthening individuals and groups' existential attachments and community identities in Katanga's copper mining towns.[89] The game constructed similar identities across the border in Zambia's mining towns.

85   Arnold Pannenborg, *Big Men Playing Football: Money, Politics and Foul Play in the African Game* (Leiden: African Studies Centre, 2012), p. 1.
86   Ibid.; Ossu Obayiuwana, 'TP Mazembe the Building of a Giant: After Conquering the African Summit, Does TP Mazembe Possess a Sustainable Plan to Stay at the Top', *New Africa,* November 2012.
87   Pannenborg, *Big Men Playing Football*, p. 1.
88   Ibid.
89   Chiweshe, 'Till Death do us Part', p. 105.

Fandom and Rivalries on the Zambian Copperbelt

In late-colonial Zambia, football took on a national form with the formation of the non-racial Northern Rhodesia National Football League (NFL) in 1962. Of thirteen clubs that played in the NFL in 1962, the mine companies sponsored ten of them.[90] By the time Zambia gained independence in 1964, football team loyalties on the Copperbelt were deep rooted in mine townships. The dual administrative system that colonial authorities established, in which each Copperbelt town was divided between the mine area and municipal council area, meant that there were football teams in both mine and council townships.[91] While the mines had more resources and dominated with their remarkable recreational facilities, councils also supported football clubs that drew large numbers of fans from municipal townships.[92] As football fandom is both a public and private experience, fans identified themselves with teams from their residential areas to create and maintain both their teams and community identities.[93]

In Mufulira for example, there were three major football clubs in the 1970s and 1980s: Mufulira Wanderers FC located in Kantanshi mine compound, Butondo Western Tigers FC in Butondo mine compound (both sponsored by the mines), and Mufulira Blackpool FC, located in Kamuchanga township and sponsored by the municipal council. The three clubs competed for Mufulira's football fans and players. Mufulira Wanderers emerged as the town's leading and famous club. During their home matches at Shinde Stadium, passionate fans who could not afford tickets climbed rooftops, electric poles and trees around the stadium to get a glimpse of their favourite team. In March 1976, following an accident in which two fans fell from the roof of a shelter they had climbed to watch a match, Mufulira Wanderers management warned that they would not accept responsibility for any deaths or injury of fans as a result of such undertakings during games.[94] The large numbers of fans and their

90 Mining companies associated football with motivating miners to increase production, see Chipande, 'Chipolopolo', Ch. 1.
91 Mususa, 'There Used to Be Order', p. 25; A. L. Epstein, *Politics in an Urban African Community* (Manchester: Manchester University Press, 1958), pp. 5–30.
92 On Copperbelt colonial social welfare schemes, see Powdermaker, *Copper Town*, p. 112 and Chipande, 'Mining for Goals'.
93 Beth Jacobson, 'The Social Identity of the Creation of a Sports Fan Identity: A Theoretical Review of the Literature', *Athletic Insight: The Online Journal of Sport Psychology*, 5, 2 (2003), pp. 1–13.
94 'Club warns soccer fans', *Mining Mirror*, 5 March 1976.

desperation to watch matches shows how popular the game had become in the mining towns.

In Kitwe, the arch-rivals in the 1980s and 1990s were Nkana FC, located in Wusakile mine township inhabited mainly by underground mineworkers, and Power Dynamos FC located in Ndeke village where Copperbelt Energy Corporation employees resided.[95] Those who watched these matches argue that, whatever the result on the pitch, Nkana fans dominated their Power Dynamos neighbours. Former Football Association of Zambia (FAZ) chairperson Simataa Simataa, himself a staunch Nkana FC supporter, explained in an interview that the combative mentality of Wusakile mine compound residents made Nkana FC fans notoriously boisterous. This conduct was in turn reflected in the club's 1982 change of name to become Nkana Red Devils FC.[96] Nkana FC fans were known for their dominant presence in the stadium and for being well organised.

Like TP Mazembe fans, Nkana Red Devils fans developed well-rehearsed and entertaining chants and drumming during matches in the 1970s, 1980s and 1990s. Their success inspired the fans of other clubs, transforming football fandom in Zambia. Their fan base included such well-known individuals as Malama, who was a dancer, singer and composer. Malama could spend the entire match singing, during which he danced facing fans and away from the match. When the Nkana team scored, he would always ask the nearby fans in Chibemba (the Zambian Copperbelt lingua franca) '*ninani aingisha?*' meaning 'who has scored?' After that, he continued singing and dancing in the same way until the final whistle.[97] Popular songs were adapted to acclaim the club and they engaged the famous Serenje Kalindula Band to play live music during home matches. This fan culture led the band to compose the famous song '*Ba Nkana ba wina*' meaning 'Nkana has won', that was regularly played on the radio. The song calls upon everyone to support Nkana while praising football players and administrators for the success of the club.[98]

Although anyone could become a member of the fans' club, most members of Nkana FC from the 1960s to the 1990s were mineworkers and their families, reflecting the strong integration between mine company sponsorship, place of employment, area of residence and club affiliation. For

95 Chipande, 'Mining for Goals', p. 63.
96 Interview, Simataa Simataa, Lusaka, 3 July 2014.
97 Interview, Simon Stone Chibwe, Kitwe, 18 July 2018; interview, Leonard Koloko, Kitwe, 19 January 2014.
98 Interview, Leonard Koloko, Kitwe, 19 January 2014

Nkana FC and other mine-sponsored supporters' clubs, the mines deducted monthly subscriptions from the salaries of fan club members, showing close integration of football participation and fandom with mine companies. The money was used to buy regalia, food and transport during games.[99] For example, Moses Chabala Mandona migrated from Kawambwa in Luapula Province in the 1950s to work in the mines in Kitwe in the Personnel Department, where he became an Nkana FC fan. His son Edward Chabala was born in 1964 in Kitwe and grew up in Mindolo mine compound, where his father introduced him to Nkana FC at a young age. Edward grew up as a supporter and became a member of the Nkana FC football fans community. Towards the end of the 1980s, he joined the leadership of Nkana Football fan club and later became chairperson of one of the sub-groups of the club.[100] Chabala's family history shows how football fan culture can illuminate the broader history of migration and urbanisation on the Copperbelt.

The close relationship between the mining sector and football fandom also helped to structure the gendered nature of football fandom. Until recently, the vast majority of copper mineworkers were men, and playing and watching football were important elements of mineworker sociability. Football fandom was associated with mining, miners' shifts and cohorts that excluded women.[101] However, the picture slowly started changing in the post-independence period with the emergence of vibrant supporters' clubs in which specific women were important organisers and singers.

While men dominated the game in the mines, the Copperbelt also contributed to the development of women's football. A Zambia national women football team was organised in 1983 and played a curtain raiser match for the men's African Nations Cup qualifier between Zambia and Uganda at Dag Hammarskjöld Stadium in Ndola.[102] This match raised enthusiasm about the women's game, leading to the formation of the Zambia Women Football League in February 1984.[103] Just like men's football league, the Copperbelt provided the best teams in the league that included teams such as Kitwe Flying Angels from Kitwe with fullback Victoria Mutondo as one of the best players. Other good Copperbelt women football clubs

---

99 Interview, Simon Stone Chibwe, Kitwe, 18 July 2018.
100 Telephone interview, Edward Chabala, 17 July 2018.
101 Chipande, 'Mining for Goals', p. 66.
102 'Women Soccer is a non-starter', *Mining Mirror*, 30 September 1983.
103 'Lumbuka Retained To Steer Women's Soccer League', *Times of Zambia*, 6 February 1984.

included Mufulira Flying Queens from Mufulira and Konkola Blades from Chililabombwe.[104] Most of the Copperbelt women football teams disbanded in the 1990s because of the collapse of the copper mines that sponsored them. However, these teams sowed the seeds that popularised women's football in Zambia, leading to the Zambia national women's team qualifying for the Tokyo 2021 Olympic Games in Japan.

Apart from having fun supporting one's favourite football club, the benefits of being a member of the fan club (and other similar fans' groups) went beyond the football stadium. Simon Chibwe was born in Wusakile mine compound in 1948, played for Nkana FC from 1966 to 1977 and later became an assistant coach and team manager of the club. Chibwe recalls that the benefits of being a member of Nkana Football fan club were numerous. When a member of the club was in distress or financial difficulty, such as a family funeral, other club members came to their aid by providing support in the form of money or provisions.[105] According to Chibwe, 'it was a community that supported each other as a family'.[106] As other scholars have pointed out, football played a role in forging new loyalties, urban networks, social identities, neighbourhoods and communities for Africans who had migrated to the mining towns.[107] In this way, fan clubs replaced the role that neighbourhoods and clans played in rural areas and provided support as mutual aid societies. Mutual aid practice shows that football fan club activities in the mining towns went beyond the playing fields. In this respect it can be compared with the mutual aid role played by dance societies such as those who – as anthropologist James Clyde Mitchell explored – danced Kalela in the 1950s and subsequently.[108]

Conclusion

The emergence of the copper mines in the Copperbelt region led to an influx of European mineworkers that introduced football in Katanga and Northern Rhodesia's mining areas. Catholic missionary activities and social welfare schemes, that were intended to be used as tools for modernising and controlling the new African urban population, played a central role in popularising the game in African mine compounds. Football asserted

---

104 'Women's Soccer Final On', *Times of Zambia*, 31 October 1984.
105 Interview, Simon Stone Chibwe, Kitwe, 18 July 2018.
106 Ibid.
107 Fair, *Pastimes and Politics*, p. 247; Alegi, *Laduma!* p. 100.
108 Clyde Mitchell, *Kalela Dance*, p. 20.

itself as a communitarian spectacle in the mining towns to an extent that few activities, if any, can be compared with football in terms of triggering mass excitement and shared urban experience. The growing popularity of the game among African mineworkers prompted the colonial authorities to sponsor competitions named after themselves, such as the Governors' Cup and the Gillet Cup, in order to control and prevent the game from being used as an avenue for political rebellion. Through the sponsorship of competitions, social welfare schemes and clubs, the mine companies on both sides of the border played an essential role in turning the Copperbelt into a leading football hub on the African continent.

Following independence, powerful groups of football supporters emerged and developed different forms of fan culture. In Katanga, football fandom sometimes went together with Congolese rhumba music played by stars such as Franco and his O.K. Jazz Band. This helped to underpin the transformation of the identities of African mineworkers from rural dwellers into urbanites with a shared culture. With their theatrical fans, the 100 percenters, and support from influential businessman Moïse Katumbi, TP Mazembe became one of the most successful clubs on the continent. In Zambia, teams like Nkana Red Devils FC also developed similar fans clubs. These organised football followers not only cheered on their teams but also provided mutual aid to their members in times of distress, helping to generate new urban social identities, networks and communities.[109] This shows how the study of football in Africa can reveal ordinary people's experiences and how the game shaped their urban culture, in ways that could never have been imagined by its first colonial sponsors.[110]

109 Alegi, *Laduma!* p. 126.
110 Marc Fletcher, 'Reinforcing Divisions and Blurring Boundaries in Johannesburg Football Fandom' in Onwumechili and Akindes, *Identity and Nation*, pp. 133–51, p. 134.

5

Beware the Mineral Narrative: The Histories of Solwezi Town and Kansanshi Mine, North-Western Zambia, c. 1899–2020

RITA KESSELRING

Introduction

The most recent global commodity boom starting in the mid-2000s came a few years after the reprivatisation of Zambia's mining industry. Through massive foreign investment, Kansanshi mine in Zambia's North-Western Province outpaced the mines in DR Congo and Zambia and quickly grew into the largest copper mine by output in Africa. Kansanshi mine lies ten kilometres north of Solwezi, the administrative centre, known as the *boma* (see Map 5.2). Solwezi town is the provincial capital and host to approximately 266,000 residents.[1] Shaped by cycles of global metal prices and the evolution of mining techniques over the past 120 years, Kansanshi mine – contrary to the often-used description of it as a 'dormant mine' – was almost continuously developed and invested in throughout the twentieth century. However, it only took off as a reliably productive mine since 2005. As a result, Kansanshi mine is rarely considered in histories of the Zambian and Katangese Copperbelts. If at all, it is mentioned as the first mine in Northern Rhodesia that started commercial production in 1905. The history of Kansanshi and the adjacent town of Solwezi from the 1920s, when the Katangese mines took off, or the 1930s, when the Zambian Copperbelt started industrialising and urbanising, and the mine's redevelopment in 2005, is not widely known.

---

1 Lena Preuss and Daniel Schmidt-Eisenlohr, 'Final Report Solwezi Urban Baseline Study' (Lusaka: GIZ, 2016).

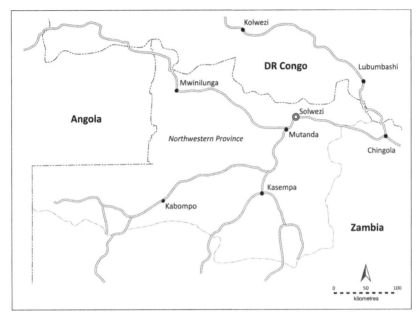

Map 5.1   Zambia's North-Western Province. Map drawn by the author.

Solwezi town has not gained much attention either. Starting as a small administrative centre overseeing mining activity, the town never stopped growing throughout the twentieth century. While the most impressive spike in demographic development happened in the past fifteen years, Solwezi had continuously grown throughout the twentieth century due to regional, inter-regional and rural-urban migration to this easternmost urban centre of the North-Western Province and its proximity to the Zambian and Congolese Copperbelts (see Map 5.1).

In this chapter, which is based on archival and published sources and on 18 months of ethnographic and oral history research between 2013 and 2018, I present the history of Solwezi and the history of Kansanshi mine as clearly interconnected, but still as separate in principle and shaped by sometimes overlapping, sometimes diverging forces. Solwezi town and Kansanshi mine have always been seen as peripheral in terms of geographic location, with no connection via 'line-of-rail',[2] in geological terms (relatively low-grade copper), politically (as an opposition region) and scholarly

2   The line-of-rail is the region along Zambia's railway linking the Copperbelt with Lusaka and Livingstone.

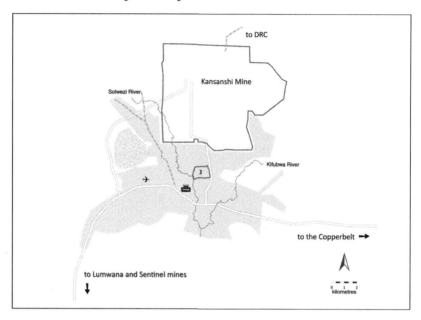

Map 5.2   Solwezi Town and Kansanshi Mine today. Grey areas indicate populated area. Map drawn by author.

(the Copperbelt towns have received the bulk of scholarly attention since the 1940s). Writing their history seems particularly important against a renewed interest in the province's mining industry, which increases the risk of ignoring the area's particular history and imposing a historical narrative on it that is shaped both by the dominant, mine-centred history of the Copperbelts and by the latest resource boom of the early 2000s.

My contribution presents an analysis along the nexus of mining, urban development and demography over 120 years. It responds to a renewal and reinforcement of a narrative that has been prevalent since the Rhodes-Livingstone Institute's scholars focused on the interrelation between mining and urbanisation processes. In this narrative, towns and urban life developing close to a mine appear as strictly dominated by the mine, and they are described and analysed as mining towns alone. Facets of their urban life not dominated by mining tend to disappear from view. Examining the current impact of global mineral production cycles and commodity chains on urbanisation processes, Deborah Bryceson and

Danny MacKinnon for example use the term 'mineralised urbanisation'.[3] They observe a new wave where urban growth and settlement coalesce and where mining has direct catalytic and fluctuating effects on migration and urban growth.

Some scholars of the Central African mining towns have tended to be more careful in this regard. For Kolwezi, for example, Kristien Geenen[4] does not see such a correlation. Kolwezi town, an urban centre across the border from Solwezi into DR Congo, was founded in the 1930s. Between 1965 and the post-2000 commodity boom, Kamoto mine and the nearby Mutanda mine lay dormant. Geenen argues that 'regardless of the rhythm of production by UMHK/Gécamines, the city has always continued to grow at steady pace'. Even if urban growth in demographic terms happens more or less independently from the mineral world, Geenen relates urban development to mining cycles. For instance, the fact that the town literally sits on minerals has resulted in a situation where profits are put above human presence whenever commodity prices are high; a situation she calls 'urbanised minerals'. Making a similar point albeit for housing compounds, a typical mining infrastructure, Benjamin Rubbers shows how mining companies in Katangese towns responded to local constraints and historical changes in their spatial governance.[5]

My contribution pushes in a similar direction, seeking to differentiate the two – population growth and urban development – more explicitly. I start on the premise that we must leave open the possibility that urban centres even in mining areas grow, change and develop independently from global mining cycles. Local agency does not only show at moments of mining booms and busts. If we ignore that fact, we have succumbed to the grand mineral narrative. With a few exceptions, notably Emmanuel Mutale[6] and this volume, the Copperbelt towns on either side of the border have mostly been viewed through the 'mining lens' where changes of demographic, political, infrastructural and economic nature have hardly been looked at in their own right. To a certain extent, Kansanshi mine

3   Deborah Bryceson and Danny MacKinnon, 'Eureka and beyond: Mining's Impact on African Urbanisation', *Journal of Contemporary African Studies* 30, 4 (2012), pp. 513–37.
4   Kristien Geenen, 'Dealing with Urbanised Mineral Deposits in DR Congo: The City of Kolwezi and its Pending Removal', unpublished paper presented at the 2018 European Social Science History Conference conference in Belfast.
5   Benjamin Rubbers, 'Mining Towns, Enclaves and Spaces: A Genealogy of Worker Camps in the Congolese Copperbelt', *Geoforum* 98 (2019), pp. 88–96.
6   Emmanuel Mutale, *The Management of Urban Development in Zambia* (Burlington: Ashgate, 2004).

and Solwezi town have already fallen victim to this 'mineral narrative' in scholarly work. The region is typically described as the 'New Copperbelt' or as 'an extension of the Copperbelt'.[7] Yet Solwezi, throughout much of the twentieth century, has shown little infrastructure development directly linked to the mining industry and, due to its intermittent productivity, the mine plays a less dominant role for Solwezi's urban development. This opens up a space for us to ask 'what happened in town?' in times when the mine was not producing. Migrants have partly been attracted by the mine's presence, but most of them have contributed to ordinary urbanisation processes, developing a specific form of urbanism as does every city across the globe.[8] The urbanisation process of Solwezi town shows how a mining town is much more than a mine's compounds: it is the outcome of the interaction of the global mining economy, national politics of rent distribution, regional histories and the urban communities living in it. While my analysis is restricted to Solwezi, I suspect that these dynamics can also be found in other towns in the Copperbelts, where they are easily hidden from view by the overpowering presence of the mines.

My aim here is threefold. First, by decentring the mine, I will show that mining towns have always been more than simply a workplace or a town of residence for mineworkers. Second, examining demographic and infrastructural developments across the town's 120-year history, I aim to show that urban centres portray regional trajectories which are only indirectly related to the mining industry. Finally, narrating the increasingly entangled histories of Kansanshi mine and Solwezi town will enable me to lay out the impact on urban communities of the mine's recent formidable rise and thereby suggest a nuanced conceptualisation of the currently dominant form of resource extraction in the Central African region.

---

7   Hugh Macmillan, 'Mining, Housing and Welfare in South Africa and Zambia: An Historical Perspective', *Journal of Contemporary African Studies* 30, 4 (2012), pp. 539–50, p. 545. For this reason, I do not use the term the 'New Copperbelt' extensively.

8   Jennifer Robinson, *Ordinary Cities: Between Modernity and Development* (London: Routledge, 2006). Independently of recruited labour, migration from the North-Western Province to the Copperbelt may have been underrated, see Iva Peša, *Roads Through Mwinilunga: A History of Social Change in Northwest Zambia* (Leiden: Brill, 2019), p. 217, fn. 355.

Early Mining at Kansanshi and the Beginnings of Solwezi Town

Most of the mining sites that were pegged in Southern and Central Africa from the late nineteenth century onwards by European prospectors had been exploited by local miners long before. Excavations revealed that exploitation and smelting at the Kansanshi site and its associated smelting area were carried out at different times from the fourth to the nineteenth century.[9] Sir Robert Williams, a friend and associate of Cecil Rhodes, founded the London-based Tanganyika Concessions Limited (Tanks) in 1899, obtained concessions from the British South Africa Company (BSAC) and King Léopold in Katanga, and charged his friend George Grey to lead a party to today's Kansanshi mine.[10] There are at least two different explanations for how he found the Kansanshi deposits: he either relied on the help of the Kaonde Chief Kapijimpanga, or his group noticed the ancient workings of the Kansanshi copper mine with pits over a hundred feet deep.[11] Either way, the commercial exploration of the Kansanshi deposits depended on local actors rather than on Grey's own mineralogical acumen.

With the railway running as far as Broken Hill (today Kabwe) in 1906, Grey had transported a small blast furnace by steam traction engine to start smelting high-grade oxide ores on the spot. In December 1908, the traction engine took back the first 50 tons of copper to Broken Hill. The ore's high grade soon decreased, though. Nevertheless, by 1914, about 3,256 tons of high-grade copper had been produced at Kansanshi.[12] Under poor working conditions and with short contracts, Africans did the hard work, like shaft

9   Michael Bisson, 'Pre-Historic Archeology of North-Western Province, Zambia' in David S. Johnson (ed.), *North-Western Province,* Regional Handbook Series No. 8 (Lusaka: Zambia Geographical Association, 1980), pp. 61–3; Mwelwa C. Musambachime, *Wealth from the Rocks: Mining and Smelting of Metals in Pre-Colonial Zambia* (Bloomington: Xlibris Corporation, 2016), ch. 3.

10   Francis L. Coleman, *The Northern Rhodesia Copperbelt, 1899–1962: Technological Development up to the End of the Central African Federation* (Manchester: University of Manchester, 1971), pp. 7–8, 11–15; Lewis H. Gann, *A History of Northern Rhodesia; Early Days to 1953* (London: Chatto & Windus, 1964), pp. 121–2.

11   J. Austen Bancroft, *Mining in Northern Rhodesia: A Chronicle of Mineral Exploration and Mining Development* (Salisbury: British South Africa Company, 1961), p. 106; Timo Särkkä, 'The Lure of Katanga Copper: Tanganyika Concessions Limited and the Anatomy of Mining and Mine Exploration 1899–1906', *South African Historical Journal* 68, 3 (2016), p. 325.

12   Bancroft, *Mining in Northern Rhodesia*, pp. 107–8; Jan-Bart Gewald, *The Speed of Change: Motor Vehicles and People in Africa, 1890–2000* (Leiden: Brill, 2009), p. 32.

sinking, clearing vegetation and wood-cutting, building bridges and anti-malaria drainage projects. Taxation, which was introduced in 1907, was one attempt to secure a steady flow of labour.[13] In 1913, Kansanshi employed 85 so-called 'local' Kaonde and 788 so-called 'imported' labourers, who were originally Ndebele, a fact indicating early labour migration between mining areas within the territory.[14] At Kansanshi, the problem of 'desertion' persisted during these early years and at least one case of an 'anti-European movement' was recorded.[15]

While Kansanshi's deposits had been interesting, they were soon overshadowed by the discovery of deposits in Congo's Katanga, for whose exploitation the Union Minière du Haut-Katanga (UMHK) was formed in 1906. A combination of reasons led Tanks to focus on the Katanga deposits rather than Kansanshi's: few and poor roads and high costs of steam-powered traction engines[16] (meaning that transport had to be done by human porters), tsetse flies, the lack of food supply for African workers,[17] the failure to negotiate the quick advance of the railway to Kansanshi, BSAC's high interest in any profits coming from the Kansanshi concession, the outbreak of war, the low value of Kansanshi's ore, and the high costs of treating oxide ores in general.

To transport copper to the harbours, the Rhodesian Railway was extended from Bulawayo to the Congo border, for whose construction Tanks formed a new company, the Rhodesia-Katanga Junction Railway and Mineral Company. The latter took control of Kansanshi mine in 1909, which relieved Tanks from major interests in Northern Rhodesia and allowed it to fully concentrate on the Katanga deposits.[18] Kansanshi remained a base for subsequent exploration into the Congo. Against a shortage of porters and labour for construction and development work at the Katanga mines, Kansanshi also served as a 'minor collection and distribution point of Kaonde workers' for UMHK's Katangese mines in which Tanks held a

13 P. G. D. Clark, 'Kasempa: 1901–1951', *The Northern Rhodesia Journal* 2, 5 (1954), p. 64.
14 Gann, *A History of Northern Rhodesia*, pp. 123–4; Brian Siegel, 'Bomas, Missions, and Mines: The Making of Centers on the Zambian Copperbelt', *African Studies Review* 31, 3 (1988), pp. 61–84, p. 70.
15 Gann, *A History of Northern Rhodesia*, p. 124.
16 Gewald, *The Speed of Change*.
17 Tomas Frederiksen, 'Unearthing Rule: Mining, Power and Political Ecology of Extraction in Colonial Zambia' (PhD dissertation, University of Manchester, 2010), pp. 95–7.
18 Bancroft, *Mining in Northern Rhodesia*, p. 108.

40% share between 1911 and 1931.[19] Kansanshi mine's closure during the Second World War is counter-intuitive given the rise of the London Metal Exchange copper price from a low of £52 in 1914 to a high of £171 in 1916. Williams was, however, focused on the Katangese mines, 'determined to go for a quick return on capital, abandoning all exploratory work on unknown deposits and going instead for the rapid extraction of known high-grade deposits'.[20] The mine was left abandoned until 1927.

While Kansanshi's deposits started to be explored and mined, ten kilometres south of Kansanshi mine, Solwezi was established as an administrative centre overseeing mining activities in what was then Kasempa District. Its history differs from the concurrent establishment of administrative and police camps in Kasempa and Mwinilunga. In Solwezi, prospectors, miners and administrators settled, and men in charge of the mine simultaneously served as representatives of BSAC. In 1905, a police post was opened in Shilenda, west of Solwezi.[21] By 1908, Kansanshi was the base for sixteen white miners and four labour recruiters, a medical doctor, a shopkeeper and three white farmers.[22] The number of farmers was reported at eighteen in 1910, but two years later, their cattle succumbed to tsetse flies and the farms were abandoned.[23]

The arrival of Western missionaries in the province followed rather than preceded urban development.[24] The interdenominational group South African General Missionaries, later renamed the Africa Evangelical Fellowship, opened Chisalala mission in 1910, a day's walk south-west of Kansanshi mine, 'in Kaondeland, where it would also have a captive audience of mine laborers'.[25] In 1929, the thinly staffed mission moved to where it still is today,

19 Charles Perrings, *Black Mineworkers in Central Africa: Industrial Strategies and the Evolution of an African Proletariat in the Copperbelt, 1911–41* (London: Heinemann, 1979), pp. 14, 34, 55, 72.
20 Ibid., p. 33.
21 Clark, 'Kasempa: 1901–1951', p. 63.
22 Siegel, 'Bomas, Missions, and Mines', p. 70.
23 Frank H. Melland, *In Witch-Bound Africa: An Account of the Primitive Kaonde Tribe and Their Beliefs* (New York: Barnes & Noble, 1967), p. 23.
24 M.M. Maimbolwa, 'Urban Growth in North-Western Province' in David S. Johnson (ed.), *North-Western Province*, Regional Handbook Series No. 8 (Lusaka: Zambia Geographical Association, 1980), p. 175.
25 Robert I. Rotberg, *Christian Missionaries and the Creation of Northern Rhodesia 1880–1924* (Princeton: Princeton University Press, 1965), p. 77.

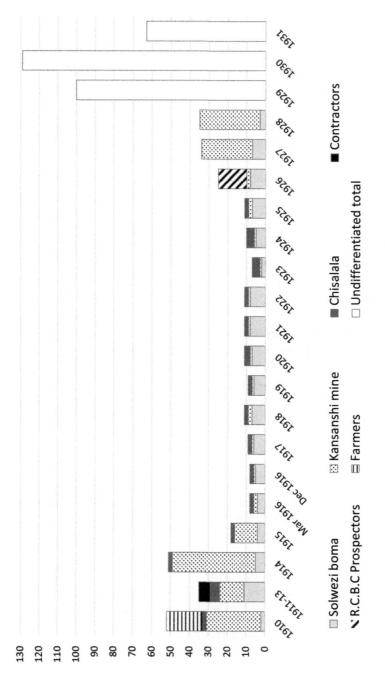

Figure 5.1 European residents in Solwezi Boma and Kansanshi Mine 1910–1931

to Mutanda, and the mission started to offer an educational programme.[26] Until the beginning of the First World War, Wilhelm Frykberg, a Swedish former sergeant-major turned trader, operated a store (shop) at Kansanshi.[27]

Figure 5.1 shows the number of European residents living either at Kansanshi mine or in the Solwezi area. Unsurprisingly, the number of those Europeans connected to the mining operations immediately declined with the closure of the mine in 1914, leaving less than eleven colonial officers and missionaries and their families (including children, both in Solwezi and Kansanshi), and a few individuals presumably charged with minimal maintenance of the mine. The only constant European presence was the colonial administration. The officials, often only two or three men, were in charge of the entire district.

Indeed, the administration only gradually developed a presence in the region. From 1909, Kansanshi was a sub-district of Kasempa District and was renamed Solwezi Sub-District in 1912, when officials moved from the Shilenda post to present-day Solwezi.[28] In 1912, Solwezi *boma* was small. It comprised the houses and compounds of the District Commissioner, the Native Commissioner and Assistant Native Commissioner, government offices and a store, the Native Clerk's, Messengers' and 'Visiting Natives" compounds, the Medical Officer's house and office, the Gaol (jail) and a Native Hospital.[29] Most of the time, government did not directly interfere with the running of the privately owned mine.[30]

The numbers of Africans living in the district are more difficult to ascertain. Figure 5.2 shows a steady increase in Solwezi (Sub-)District between 1916 and 1929. The trend is clear: a move to the district and an increase of the African population, despite the mine's inactivity throughout. The majority did not live in the *boma* but spread across the district, with likely some increased density in peri-urban areas.

Kansanshi's and Solwezi's early development shows that commercial exploration and mining were dependent on local labour and expertise, making

26 Paul David Wilkin, *To the Bottom of the Heap: Educational Deprivation and Its Social Implications in the Northwestern Province of Zambia, 1906–1945* (PhD thesis, Syracuse University, 1983), pp. 112–19, 137, 222.

27 S. Grimstvedt, 'The "Swedish Settlement" in the Kasempa District', *The Northern Rhodesia Journal* 3, 1 (1956), pp. 34–43, pp. 34–5.

28 African Affairs Northern Rhodesia, 'Annual Report for the Year 1952' (Lusaka: Government Printer, 1953), p. 17.

29 NAZ KTB 3/1, Solwezi District Notebooks.

30 Gann, *A History of Northern Rhodesia*, p. 124; Maimbolwa, 'Urban Growth in North-Western Province', p. 178.

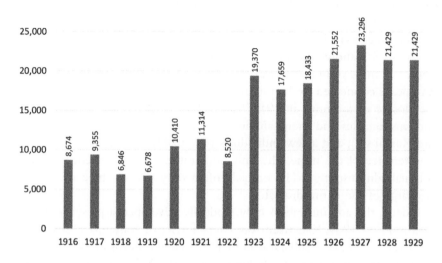

Figure 5.2   Number of African residents, Solwezi, 1916–1929

mining locally embedded rather than exogenous. The first phase of mining at Kansanshi (1905–14) – albeit brief and minimal compared with the subsequent developments in the Katangese Copperbelt – did have a political and demographic impact in the region.[31] Apart from the fact that territorial European control of this part of Northern Rhodesia began to be established through the combat of slave raiding[32] and the introduction of taxation, Kansanshi contributed to the beginning of a regional African labour regime. Solwezi town was first founded due to the minerals at Kansanshi but it soon began to grow more or less independently from the mine's status, by attracting Africans from the province, missionaries, traders and shop owners.

A Slumbering Town and Mine

Between the world wars, there was some limited activity at Kansanshi, such as underground development and exploration and the sinking of the north and south shafts.[33] Nevertheless, for the year 1930, the considerable

31 Jan-Bart Gewald, *Forged in the Great War: People, Transport, and Labour, the Establishment of Colonial Rule in Zambia, 1890–1920* (Leiden: African Studies Centre, 2015).
32 Frederiksen, 'Unearthing Rule', pp. 204–10.
33 A. Findlay, 'Kansanshi Mine', in David S. Johnson (ed.), *North-Western Province*, Regional Handbook Series No. 8 (Lusaka: Zambia Geographical Association, 1980), p. 192.

workforce of 1,925 'Africans' and 96 'Europeans' was recorded, and included prospectors working for the Rhodesian Congo Border Concession Limited at the mine and across the province.[34] The Depression forced the mine to close down again in 1932.[35] In 1937 and 1938, prospectors tried to understand the complex structure of the ore bodies through drilling. The outbreak of the Second World War created an unprecedented demand for copper by the British Government, and companies in Northern Rhodesia responded to this. Kansanshi, however, was once more not part of this development, only reopening after its acquisition by Anglo American in 1951.

During these inter-war years, Solwezi *boma* became increasingly attractive for shop owners and traders, among others serving the many prospectors. The Robinson family opened a shop between Solwezi *boma* and Kansanshi mine[36] and in 1921, Solwezi *boma* was expanded to include the Mailmen's, the Warders and Witnesses' and the Medical Patient's compounds.[37] Solwezi lost regional importance when, between 1936 and 1947, the government's regional office was moved back to Kasempa. Solwezi Sub-District was incorporated into Kasempa District and Solwezi *boma* was closed down. Through the auspices of an African clerk, the District Commissioner of Kasempa was the local authority for Solwezi. The Kasempa District formed part of the newly created Kaonde-Lunda Province, which only existed between 1939 and 1946. Solwezi's offices were reported to be maintained, but the houses for Europeans fell into 'despair'.[38] In 1947, the district boundaries were once again reconstructed and Solwezi Sub-District was reactivated.[39] However, between 1946 and 1952, the Kaonde-Lunda Province, together with today's Copperbelt Province, was incorporated into the vast Western Province, which focused administrative development elsewhere and indicated the marginal interest in the area.

34   Bancroft, *Mining in Northern Rhodesia*, p. 109.
35   J. W. Brigden, 'Trade and Economic Conditions in Southern Rhodesia, Northern Rhodesia and Nyasaland' (London: Department of Overseas Trade, 1933), p. 40.
36   Wilkin, *To the Bottom of the Heap*, p. 70.
37   NAZ KTB 3/1, Solwezi District Notebooks, p. 200.
38   Ibid., p. 201.
39   J. C. Stone, 'Some Reflections on the History of Administrative Division in Northwest Zambia', in David S. Johnson (ed.), *North-Western Province*, Regional Handbook Series No. 8 (Lusaka: Zambia Geographical Association, 1980), p. 70.

Urban Development and a Mine
'Springing Out of the Bush'

Economic growth in the Copperbelt was rapid in the post-war years and the creation of a separate province for the Copperbelt towns and its environs came to be seen as a necessity. Subsequently, a number of administrative and economic changes pulled Solwezi out of its slumber. In 1951 and 1952, the north-western region was first run under the name of North-Western 'Area' and eventually reorganised as North-Western Province, with provincial status in 1953. The Solwezi Native Authority was officially established in 1952,[40] and Solwezi town finally became the province's headquarters. It was now relatively easily accessible by road from the line-of-rail as the province's most eastern urban centre and promised to be increasingly important economically with Kansanshi mine nearby.

Solwezi's ascension to provincial headquarters and the acquisition of Kansanshi mine by Anglo American (see below) resulted in a construction boom by the administration. Key infrastructure was completed in 1955, namely the aerodrome and police station.[41] In the *boma*, the decaying old offices were replaced in 1948. A new African dispensary and an education office were built, and by 1949 a number of additional segregated structures were completed: the African latrines at the offices, a carpenter's shop, the African recreation hall, permanent African staff quarters and some public works buildings. In 1950, fourteen messengers' houses and one clerk's house were finished and in 1951, the already existing rest house received an extension in the form of a dining-room block.[42] Additional African staff houses were built in 1955 and six new houses for Europeans were completed in 1957. In the early 1960s, more residential houses and the new *boma* block were finished.[43] All these structures first and foremost served the governance of the province; they did not provide housing for African labour at the mine.

The mine's acquisition by Anglo American Corporation through its subsidiary Kansanshi Copper Mining Company Ltd in 1951 surely boosted

---

40 Northern Rhodesia, 'Annual Report for the Year 1952', pp. 17–18.
41 Colonial Office, *Annual Report on Northern Rhodesia for the Year 1955* (London: Her Majesty's Stationery Office, 1956), pp. 44, 51.
42 African Affairs Northern Rhodesia, 'Annual Report for the Year 1951' (Lusaka: Government Printer, 1952), p. 98.
43 NAZ, KTB 3/1, Solwezi District Notebooks, pp. 201–4.

the importance of the urban centre.[44] The mine was placed under the direction and guidance of Rhokana Corporation.[45] The following year, a number of drill holes were put down, hitting veins of sulphide ores.[46] Exploratory work was however soon suspended due to a large inflow of water, and again had to be stopped in 1954 due to a shortage of funds.[47] When exploratory and development work was resumed during the first half of 1955, substantial veins of sulphide ore were found. Encouraged by these finds, a power plant was set up and a concentrator constructed. Apart from the high water levels, one of the ongoing difficulties remained the treating of the low-grade oxide ores.[48] The skilled underground workers mainly came from the Copperbelt: 'the local Kaonde are not considered to be well adapted to underground work, and the other tribes of the Province have not offered themselves'.[49] There was, allegedly, no 'friction' due to the 'influx of alien tribes' reported.[50]

The Provincial Commissioner was greatly impressed by the progress at Kansanshi where 'a new copper mine with its attendant townships was visibly springing out to the bush.'[51] Indeed, Anglo American also invested in solid housing structures which are still in use today, the 'Kansanshi village'. Between 1952 and 1957, 23 houses for mine officials were built about one kilometre west of the mine. A recreational club provided amenities for 54 (1956) or 62 (1957) Europeans.[52] The Provincial Commissioner was convinced that the mine 'will be a considerable pocket of industrialism'.[53]

44　Minority owners of Kansanshi Copper Mining Company Ltd were the AAC Group, the RTS Group (10%), the Tanganyika Concessions Group and the British South African Company. Richard L. Sklar, *Corporate Power in an African State: The Political Impact of Multinational Mining Companies in Zambia* (Berkeley: University of California Press, 1975), p. 30.

45　Rhodesian Congo Border Corporation, N'Changa and Bwana M'Kubwa merged into the Rhokana Corporation in 1931, majority owned by Rhodesian Anglo American Corporation, the Rhodesian branch of Anglo American.

46　Bancroft, *Mining in Northern Rhodesia*, pp. 110–11.

47　African Affairs Northern Rhodesia, 'Annual Report for the Year 1954' (Lusaka: Government Printer, 1955), p. 17.

48　Coleman, *The Northern Rhodesia Copperbelt*, p. 148.

49　In the years 1955, 1956 and 1957, 500, 567 and 540 Africans, respectively, were employed. Findlay, 'Kansanshi Mine', p. 195; African Affairs Northern Rhodesia, 'Annual Report for the Year 1955' (Lusaka: Government Printer, 1956), p. 18.

50　Northern Rhodesia, 'Annual Report for the Year 1955', p. 18.

51　Ibid., p. 9.

52　Findlay, 'Kansanshi Mine', p. 195.

53　Northern Rhodesia, 'Annual Report for the Year 1955', p. 9.

In those years, employees at the mine and BSAC officials would meet at the *muzungu* (white person) club or at one of the two trading stores in town[54] and purchase general merchandise. If one continued westwards from Andrew Sardanis' *Mwaiseni* store,[55] the government buildings housed the offices of the District Commissioner, the Provincial Commissioner and the Education officer. Further west, 'it was nothing more but bush'.[56] Visitors stayed at the European Rest House close to Solwezi river. Solwezi *boma* in the 1950s was a separate entity from Kansanshi whose labour force was housed at Kansanshi mine in a temporary compound.[57]

The heavy investment in housing and mining infrastructure testifies to Anglo American's optimism when taking over Kansanshi mine. But then, on 1 November 1957, an ingress of water overwhelmed the pumping station and the mine was put on care and maintenance.[58]

Independence, Optimism and Nationalisation

While Kansanshi mine remained under care and maintenance in the 1960s, some infrastructural development took place in Solwezi town. In 1960, the Solwezi Secondary School was opened.[59] Shortly after independence in 1964, two rural electricity generating units were installed in Solwezi[60] and the telephone lines reached the town. Traffic increased to the extent that national representatives complained in parliament about the little funds allocated in the national budget for their upgrade.[61]

This increase in activity in Solwezi needs to be explained at the provincial level. North-Western Province is the third largest province by surface in Zambia, but had (until the creation of the new Muchinga Province in 2011)

---

54   Northern Rhodesia, 'Annual Report for the Year 1952', p. 25.
55   Andrew Sardanis, *Africa, Another Side of the Coin: Northern Rhodesia's Final Years and Zambia's Nationhood* (London: I.B. Tauris, 2011), pp. 71–4.
56   Interview, Andrew Sardanis, Lusaka, 16 September 2017.
57   Northern Rhodesia, 'Annual Report for the Year 1955', p. 20.
58   Chamber of Mines Northern Rhodesia, *Chamber of Mines Yearbook Northern Rhodesia 1957* (Kitwe: Parow Works 1958), p. 89.
59   Wilkin, *To the Bottom of the Heap.*
60   Republic of Zambia, *An Outline of the Transitional Development Plan* (Lusaka: Government Printer, 1965).
61   Republic of Zambia, 'Official Verbatim Report of the Parliamentary Debates of the National Assembly' (Lusaka: Government Printer, 1967).

the smallest population.[62] Starting at independence, though, population growth increased more rapidly than in other provinces not served by the line-of-rail. To understand population increase in Solwezi District, migration patterns within and out of the province need to be considered. Residents from the province's districts have migrated to the Katangese or the Rhodesian mining hubs, the latter competing with the former throughout the century. Work seekers from Mwinilunga District in the west, for instance, 'weigh[ed] working conditions on both sides of the border, choosing those that seemed most favourable to their specific aims and aspirations'.[63] Similarly to other districts, the percentage of tax-paying males 'away at work' were reported in Solwezi District as 45% (3,950 out of 8,799) in 1951[64] and at 50% in 1952.[65] These figures must of course be questioned,[66] but they show that there was temporary or permanent out-migration from the province. This out-migration from areas such as Mwinilunga also resulted in an increase of population in Solwezi District. Migrants first settled in what Johnson calls 'nucleations' across the province, moving from villages to small urban centres, 'before making the much more ambitious and formidable move east to Solwezi or the Copperbelt.'[67] Solwezi District, situated at the eastern end of the province, acted 'as a buffer between the more rural parts of the Province and the Copperbelt' and thereby tended 'to receive migrants from the western districts of the Province en route to the Copperbelt.'[68] The fact that Solwezi attracted this population was due to its urban and administrative status, not primarily to the mine.

The post-independence years saw massive reforms, among them the nationalisation of the mining sector. The state's Nchanga Consolidated Copper Mines (NCCM) acquired a 51% interest in Kansanshi Copper Mining Company and had it managed by NCCM's Konkola Division.[69] The mine was turned into an opencast mine in 1973 and a leach-solvent plant was constructed

62   David S. Johnson, 'A Note on the Population of North-Western Province', in Ibid. (ed.), *North-Western Province*, Regional Handbook Series No. 8 (Lusaka: Zambia Geographical Association, 1980), p. 73.

63   Peša, *Roads Through Mwinilunga*, p. 219.

64   Northern Rhodesia, 'Annual Report for the Year 1951', p. 102.

65   Ibid., p. 21.

66   Peša, *Roads Through Mwinilunga*, p. 243.

67   Johnson, 'A Note on the Population of North-Western Province', p. 81.

68   Ibid., p. 75.

69   Zambia Copper Investments Ltd (ZCI), incorporated in Bermuda and controlled by Anglo American (27.3%), Roan Selection Trust (6.9%) and public shareholders in the United States and the United Kingdom acquired the remaining 49%. Sklar, *Corporate Power in an African State*, p. 42.

in 1974. It produced 16,000 tonnes of copper per annum out of 700,000 tonnes in total in Zambia. The following year, due to the slump in global copper prices in the context of the global economic recession, production at Kansanshi was halted again. Nevertheless, NCCM kept to its plans, invested heavily in the mine and continued with the construction of 120 houses for workers as part of 'Kansanshi Township', a small residential area five kilometres south-west of the pit. The township had a population of 500, and included a government primary school, a mine clinic, a United National Independence Party (UNIP) office, a social centre and two temporary churches, football, netball and volleyball clubs, and a small market.[70]

Between the two oil crises of 1974 and 1979, Zambia's copper production peaked in 1976 with a total output of 712,000 tonnes, which represented about 11% of the world's total copper production. At Kansanshi, limited mining – now opencast – was resumed in 1977. The workforce was small: 13 white supervisors and 95 Zambians. The latter were divided into 'skilled Zambians' with Copperbelt mining experience and 'labourers' from 'local rural origin'.[71] As later in the revamped mine in the 2000s, skilled labour came from the Copperbelt and unskilled labour from the region. With no processing facility on-site, ore was treated in Chingola at Konkola mine.[72]

After the merger of NCCM and Roan Consolidated Mines (RCM) into Zambia Consolidated Copper Mines (ZCCM) in 1982, the government remained Kansanshi's majority shareholder with a 60.3% share. Zambia's copper production continuously declined in the 1980s and 1990s. Between 1986 and 1988, Kansanshi mine closed due to economic conditions. In 1988, ZCCM resumed mining operations and constructed a small sulphide flotation plant for the supply of concentrate to an offsite smelter (Mufulira). Ten years later, in 1998, ZCCM formally ceased operations at the mine site and initiated closure and reclamation activities.[73] At the turn of the millennium, copper production in Zambia hit an all-time low of 250,000 tonnes per annum.

[70] Findlay, 'Kansanshi Mine', p. 195.
[71] Ibid., p. 194.
[72] Roan Consolidated Mines, *Zambia's Mining Industry: The First 50 Years* (Ndola: Roan Consolidated Mines Ltd, 1978), pp. 65–6.
[73] First Quantum Minerals Ltd, 'Kansanshi Operations: North West Province, Zambia, NI 43-101 Technical Report' (West Perth, Australia: First Quantum Minerals Ltd, 2015), p. 34.

Solwezi, the Neglected Town

In the 1970s, Zambia felt the closure of the southern transport route due to the sanctions against Southern Rhodesia, and it was difficult to get basic supplies into the stores. The town's elite would nevertheless find entertainment at the Kansanshi Mine Social Club at Kansanshi village, dancing with the mine's management. To get there one needed a car and quite likely an invitation. Movies were shown and the club had the only swimming pool in the district.[74]

Many local residents of the North-Western Province felt neglected or ignored by the UNIP government.[75] The so-called Mushala Rebellion, an internal armed rebellion against the postcolonial Zambian state led by Adamson Mushala between the mid-1970s and the early 1980s which put the North-Western Province on the map of national politics, is surely an expression of this shared sentiment. The rebellion pressed for a revived Lunda polity across national borders, 'fired by the increasingly manifest failure of the independent Zambian state to fulfil its people's expectations of national social and economic development', a feeling which is still expressed today.[76] The rebellion explicitly criticised unequal rent distribution when the profits from the province's mine industry were flowing out elsewhere: although the province was earning money, the population did not benefit from the taxes it was paying. As one of Mushala's lieutenants expressed it:

> God help us to topple the UNIP government. Money from Kansanshi and Kalengwa mines is not spent on tarring Mutanda–Chavuma road. Instead the money has been used to build a railway line from Dar-es-Salaam to Kapiri Mposhi. All the revenue from these mines goes somewhere else. Why are we neglected?[77]

Until the early 2000s, copper prices never really recovered from the global recession of the 1970s, nor did Zambia's mining industry or Kansanshi mine. In the 1970s, the independent Zambian state still used the revenue from the nationalised mines to provide public services across the country and to invest

---

74 https://davidwilkinnwpzambia.com/davids-story-photographs/unza-in-nwp-1975-79 [n.d.] (accessed 10 May 2020)

75 Peša, *Roads Through Mwinilunga*, pp. 194–9.

76 Miles Larmer and Giacomo Macola, 'The Origins, Context, and Political Significance of the Mushala Rebellion Against the Zambian One-Party State', *International Journal of African Historical Studies* 40, 3 (2007), pp. 471–96, p. 472.

77 Patrick Wele, *Kaunda and Mushala Rebellion: The Untold Story* (Lusaka: Multimedia, 1987), p. 92.

in large infrastructure such as schools, hospitals and roads. Although these years are often referred to as a time of massive development, for Solwezi this did not materialise in substantial infrastructure with a few exceptions: the tarring of the road from Chingola to Solwezi and from Solwezi to Kansanshi finally took place in 1971,[78] and Solwezi General Hospital, which in a parliamentary debate in 1967 was described as 'rotten',[79] was upgraded to a 120-bed hospital in 1975,[80] including a nurses' hostel, staff housing and three ward blocks. The latter additions were only possible due to private financial support of Anglo American.[81]

The University of Zambia's Extra-Mural Department opened a centre for the North-Western Province in Solwezi in 1975. Other projects were started in the 1970s but, due to lack of funds, rarely completed. A building for the regional radio transmitter station was constructed. In 1975, the construction of the Solwezi Sports Stadium started, but by 1983 the stadium was still 'far from being completed'.[82] A Zambia News Agency branch was established in 1976[83] and banking service became available in 1980.[84] In 1979, the first intake at Solwezi Teachers' College graduated[85] and, despite financial restrictions, Solwezi Day Secondary School opened in 1981, heavily relying on volunteer work. In addition to Solwezi Main Market, Kyawama (or Chawama) market, initially known as Mwinilunga market and today

78   Findlay, 'Kansanshi Mine', p. 196.
79   Republic of Zambia, 'Official Verbatim Report of the Parliamentary Debates of the National Assembly'.
80   Republic of Zambia, 'North-Western Province Annual Report 1975' (Lusaka: Office of the Cabinet Minister for the North-Western Province, 1977).
81   Margaret O'Callaghan, 'Copperfields: A History of the Impact of the First Decade of a Mining Boom in North Western Province, Zambia, circa 2002–2015' (Canberra, 2019), p. 46: https://margocall.wordpress.com/2020/03/28/copperfields-a-history-of-the-impact-of-the-first-decade-of-a-mining-boom-in-north-western-province-zambia-circa-2002-2015 (accessed 14 October 2020).
82   Republic of Zambia, 'Annual Report of the Provincial and Local Government Administration Division North-Western Province 1983' (Lusaka: Office of the Prime Minister, 1987), p. 7.
83   Republic of Zambia, 'North-Western Province Annual Report 1980' (Lusaka: Office of the Member of the Central Comittee for North-Western Province, 1982), p. 4.
84   Maimbolwa, 'Urban Growth in North-Western Province', pp. 185–86.
85   Republic of Zambia, 'Provincial and Local Government Administration Division, North-Western Province Annual Report 1979' (Lusaka: Office of the Prime Minister, 1980), p. 7.

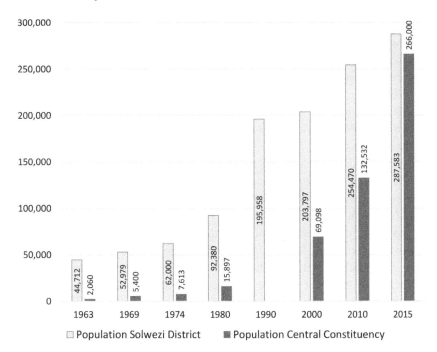

Figure 5.3   Population growth Solwezi District and Solwezi Central
Constituency

the largest open-air market in the district, was built in 1983.[86] These investments could however not do justice to the rapid growth of the urban
centre attracting the province's rural population, which resulted in 'urban
unemployment, poverty and the expansion of shanty towns'.[87]

Faced with increasing demand, the state, the largest employer, continued
to have massive financial challenges in the 1980s. The fact that the library
reported 8,458 books gone missing in 1981 alone, leaving 9,417 books
only, is maybe a good indicator of the continuous downturn of Zambia's
formal economy.[88] Informal economic practices thrived and 'the shortage of

86 Mbaraka Matitu, 'Women and the Retailing of Secondhand Clothing in Urban
Zambia: A Case Study of Kyawama Market, Solwezi', MA Thesis, University of Basel,
2018, pp. 25–6.

87 Maimbolwa, 'Urban Growth in North-Western Province', p. 186.

88 Republic of Zambia, 'Annual Report of the Office of the Cabinet Minister for the
North-Western Province 1981' (Lusaka: Office of the Prime Minister, 1981), p. 4.

essential commodities continued to put people in hardships'.[89] The growth of Solwezi town's population has been subject of much guesswork, and figures 'are very hard to come by'.[90] Among the province's districts, Solwezi District did not always have the largest share of residents. By the time of the 1980 census it accounted for 30% of the provincial population, with 92,380 residents. This trend persists until today: in 2010, Solwezi District was host to 35% of the provincial population, followed by Mwinilunga and Kabompo.

Figure 5.3 differentiates the population growth of Solwezi District and Solwezi town (or Solwezi Central Constituency) from the 1960s until today, showing that the district's population has grown steadily over the past 50 years.[91] Apart from the above-mentioned general trend of Solwezi 'catching' the province's urbanising population, the increase in population numbers in the 1970s and the 1980s points to the influx of people from Zaïre – where thousands fled the conflict in Shaba Province (now Katanga) – and specifically to Meheba refugee settlement in Solwezi West Constituency, rather than the growth of Solwezi town.[92] The refugee settlement, about 70 kilometres west from Solwezi town, was founded in 1971 and has been extended five times since.

The figure suggests that, as a proportion of the district's residents, Solwezi town's population was comparatively small until the 1970s (approximately 9% in 1974). Despite continued, albeit fluctuating, activity at Kansanshi mine, Solwezi was not the drawing force of migration into the district until 1980, but it rapidly became so during the following decade. This new in-migration was not centred on Kansanshi mine and it no longer simply used Solwezi as a step to further destinations, given the difficulties of finding mine-related jobs in the Copperbelts. Instead, it is the expression of growing mobility and multilocality within households and extended families. In a situation in which lifestyles, consumption patterns and integration into social institutions increasingly necessitated access to cash income and urban infrastructure, while

[89] Ibid., p. 6.
[90] Johnson, 'A Note on the Population of North-Western Province', p. 83.
[91] The numbers are taken from a variety of sources, mainly provincial and district government reports, reconciled in the figure. Apart from incorrect citations, revised census methods and very poor data, authors typically conflate numbers for the district and the town. The District was, until recently, made up of three constituencies: East, Central and West. The town's boundaries roughly run along the boundaries of Solwezi Central Constituency. In some publications, this urban part is described as a 'township'.
[92] Republic of Zambia, 'North-Western Province Statistical Handbook' (Lusaka: Provincial Planning Unit Solwezi, 1985).

economic decline and job scarcity made full-scale urban life more difficult to sustain, many families had members spread across different economic and social spheres. Relatives living in urbanised areas enabled rural family members access to urban infrastructure (from jobs and cash income, to schools and hospitals, to shops or churches) and sometimes provided access to markets for agricultural products, while agricultural production of rural relatives was an important source of food and security for urban dwellers. In this regard, as well, Solwezi does not stand alone. Urbanisation in Zambian mining towns has never been solely centred on mining, even though the mine's presence often hid other dynamics from view.[93]

Urban Growth Despite Economic Downturn

In the 1990s, Solwezi's residents saw even less formal infrastructural development than before, and the fact that Zambia had a multi-party system since 1991 did not change residents' perception of a province neglected by national government. The Province and Solwezi District continued voting for the opposition, be it for the Movement for Multi-Party Democracy (MMD) in the 1990s and 2000s or, more recently, the United Party for National Development (UPND). Although the council received some revenue from renting out its remaining assets, local taxes, or charges, most of the administration's plans were thwarted by the lack of funds, transport and fuel, as evidenced in the council's minutes. The growth of the district's population was such, though, that already in 1994, the Ministry of Local Government and Housing 'seriously' considered granting municipal status to Solwezi District Council, something which was again discussed twenty years later.[94]

Here, Deborah Potts' argument that the Copperbelt's urban residents started to ruralise for the first time in history in the 1990s – due to the impact of International Monetary Fund (IMF) structural adjustment programmes and massive decline in real income for public sector workers –

[93] Kate Crehan, *The Fractured Community: Landscapes of Power and Gender in Rural Zambia* (Berkeley: University of California Press, 1997); Henrietta Moore and Megan Vaughan, *Cutting Down Trees: Gender, Nutrition, and Agricultural Change in the Northern Province of Zambia, 1890–1990* (London: Heinemann, 1993); Johan Pottier, *Migrants No More: Settlement and Survival in Mambwe District, Zambia*, International African Library (Manchester: Manchester University Press, 1988).

[94] Minutes of the Proceedings of the Council and its Committees, Solwezi Municipal Council, 31 March 1995.

must also be considered for Solwezi.[95] Numbers are not precise enough to make a definitive case, but most likely Solwezi did not experience net out-migration and instead continued to grow, much like Lusaka.[96] Residents of urban centres in North-Western Province in general and in Solwezi in particular never had the kind of welfare capitalism that was established in the Copperbelt towns in the 1950s and collapsed in the late 1990s.[97] Similar to what Iva Peša shows for the Copperbelt towns from the 1950s until 2000 and Patience Mususa for the 2000s, food gardening has been part of urban life in Solwezi since the economic downturn of the 1970s (and before).[98] What is more, many Solwezi residents held farming land outside the urban boundaries with the consent of respective chiefs. This land only became scarce, overused and commercialised after the reopening of Kansanshi mine and the more rapid increase in population since 2005.

Kansanshi's Re-Privatisation, Mechanisation and Expansion

Zambia, like many countries in the Global South, has gone through, and suffered from, IMF-imposed structural adjustment programmes. The state was unfortunate enough to majority-own the mining industry in economically depressed years, and to be forced to sell its assets shortly before the next global metal boom. Soon after the lengthy process of privatisation of Zambia's mining sector was completed, global copper prices started to rise and Zambia experienced a revival of the mining sector and a construction boom.

In 1997 and in 1999, Cyprus Amax Minerals Corporations undertook some diamond drilling at the Kansanshi mine site. In 1998, Cyprus Amax acquired majority ownership of surface leases and selected assets at Kansanshi

95 Deborah Potts, 'Counter-Urbanisation on the Zambian Copperbelt? Interpretations and Implications', *Urban Studies* 42, 4 (2005), pp. 583–609.
96 Macmillan, 'Mining, Housing and Welfare'.
97 Benjamin Rubbers, *Le paternalisme en question: Les anciens ouvriers de la Gécamines face à la libéralisation du secteur minier katangais* (Paris: L'Harmattan, 2013); Benjamin Rubbers, 'Towards a Life of Poverty and Uncertainty? The Livelihood Strategies of Gécamines Workers after Retrenchment in the DRC', *Review of African Political Economy* 44, 152 (2017), pp. 189–203.
98 Patience Mususa, 'Mining, Welfare and Urbanisation: The Wavering Urban Character of Zambia's Copperbelt', *Journal of Contemporary African Studies* 30, 4 (2012), pp. 571–87; Iva Peša, 'Crops and Copper: Agriculture and Urbanism on the Central African Copperbelt, 1950–2000', *Journal of Southern African Studies* 46, 3 (2020), pp. 527–45.

mine and the mine was thus re-privatised.[99] In 2001, the current owner of Kansanshi mine, Canada-based First Quantum Minerals (FQM) acquired Cyprus's 80% share in Kansanshi and ZCCM (now ZCCM Investment Holdings) retained its 20% share. The mine was reopened in 2005 with unprecedented, massive foreign investment – such as the construction of a new power line, the upgrading of the access road, the road between Chingola and Solwezi and the airport – and the mechanisation and expansion of the opencast mine. With new technology, low-grade ore ceased to be an unsurmountable obstacle; the ore structure merely posed a challenge (and sometimes a puzzle) to geologists. Kansanshi quickly grew into the largest copper mine by output in Africa. It employs a small operations workforce of 2,705 and a further 4,874 contract workers[100] and processes large quantities of low-grade copper ores at very low cost. The mine contributed 23.6% to total Zambian Government revenues in 2015.[101] The FQM mine complex is registered in Canada but operates from Perth (Australia) and London (UK). In 2019, there were talks of a looming Chinese takeover after Jiangxi Mining's purchase of 9.9% of FQM. According to analysts, Western interest in the Copperbelt area was fading due to changing political conditions and growing scrutiny of international oil and mining companies. China in contrast would buy up assets in the Copperbelts to extend its control of supply chains in the high-tech sector.[102]

Since FQM's purchase of the mining rights, Kansanshi has been continuously expanding. In 2014, the license area increased considerably with an expansion to the east. Kansanshi also occupies large pieces of land for its 'golf estate', housing approximately 200 expatriate employees and their families, a game reserve and corporate social responsibility offices close to Solwezi's *boma*. These infrastructures which primarily serve the management and senior and junior employees resulted in the resettlement of urban and peri-urban residents and the closure of commons on customary land.

With the reopening of Kansanshi mine and the continued growth of the urban population, Kansanshi mine and Solwezi town moved closer than they ever were, socially, economically, politically and geographically; a relationship that, notably, goes both ways. Residents started to build right up to the mine fence, on what was (and often still officially is) land under

99   In 1999, Cyprus Amax was taken over by Phelps Dodge Corporations.
100 First Quantum Minerals Ltd, 'Annual Information Form 2016' (Vancouver, 2017).
101 Zambia EITI, 'Extractive Industries Transparency Initiative (EITI) Eighth Report for the Fiscal Year Ended 31 December 2015' (Lusaka: EITI, 2017), p. 18.
102 Africa Confidential, 'The China Price', *Africa Confidential*, 13 September 2019.

customary tenure. The compounds became more populated through the selling and sub-division of plots. Mine employees and contract workers live spread out in compounds, a majority of them in the densely popu-lated western compounds. Workers from the Copperbelt usually maintain a home in a Copperbelt town and share a house (and sometimes a bed) in Solwezi's compounds. As it is for other mines which are close to urban areas, such as Mutanda and Kamoto mines near Kolwezi in the DR Congo,[103] the mine management relies on this housing infrastructure and the entre-preneurship of landowners to build cheap housing for migrant workers. In an attempt to counter criticism from the central government for not contributing to housing projects, to encourage miners to move and live with their families, and to remain attractive for Zambian members at the rank of junior management, the company built a suburb outside town and the first families moved there in 2014. The housing project Kabitaka never completely took off as a project. Houses are far away from the town centre and the shops, stand on land with tenure insecurity, are offered for rental only and considered substandard by potential tenants. Nevertheless, some one hundred houses are occupied. Most Kansanshi and contractors' employees prefer to live in town, share a house and commute to work.[104] The mine also heavily relies on workers' families, in Solwezi town or in the Copperbelt towns, to bolster the many externalities of mining and pay the daily costs of labour reproduction. It does not offer a social welfare system for workers' families, nor housing, schooling or other social services. Its contributions to the communities are voluntary through its social corporate responsibility programmes.

During the construction phase, some labourers, referred to as 'locals' (typically unskilled Kaonde, Lunda and Luvale people), were recruited from the area, in addition to Filipinos and Indonesians who were brought in on short-term contracts in 2013 and 2014 to build the smelter.[105] Once the mine operated, most Zambian workers came from the Copperbelt Province, equipped with grades and experience in mining, thereby 'dashing' expecta-tions of local residents, producing collective grievances and ethnic tensions

103 Rubbers, 'Mining Towns, Enclaves and Spaces', p. 93.
104 Rita Kesselring, 'Disenclaving the Planners' Enclave: The Housing Project Kabitaka in Solwezi, Northwestern Zambia', *Comparing the Copperbelt* (blog), 21 August 2017, http://copperbelt.history.ox.ac.uk/2017/08/21/disenclaving-the-planners-enclave-the-housing-project-kabitaka-in-solwezi-northwestern-zambia-rita-kesselring (accessed 14 October 2020).
105 O'Callaghan, 'Copperfields', p. 45.

and preventing strong unionisation and furthering intra-union accusations of tribalism.[106] Managerial and supervisory positions are mostly occupied by South Africans, Britons and Australians.

In addition to Kansanshi mine, Lumwana Mine in 2008, owned by Barrick Gold (acquired from Equinox in 2011), and Sentinel/Kalumbila Mine, fully owned by FQM, in 2015 opened further west. Unlike Kansanshi, Kalumbila and Lumwana were constructed as 'greenfield' projects in rural areas.[107] The reopening of Kansanshi mine and these two mines attracted tens of thousands of temporary and permanent migrants looking for opportunities. Again, Solwezi acts as a buffer, this time catching work and opportunity seekers from the Copperbelt, and areas to the east, rather than out-migrating north-westerners from the west as during the twentieth century. Importantly, Solwezi can only have this function due to its character as a long-established urban centre.

The new clientele, the miners and the mine, attracted suppliers and private investors in banking and retail services, and three malls sprung up in the course of ten years (Shoprite,[108] Solwezi City Mall and Kapiji Mall). Two high-end hotels (Kansanshi Hotel and Royal Solwezi) initially made up for the lack of housing before the construction of the golf estate. Although plans for new rail links between the Copperbelt, Angola and Solwezi, through Lubumbashi were discussed – in fact, have been discussed since 1913 – they never materialised.[109] Copper cathodes, anodes and concentrate leave Solwezi on trucks to ports in South Africa, Namibia, Mozambique or Tanzania.[110]

[106] Robby Kapesa, Jacob Mwitwa, and D. C. Chikumbi, 'Social Conflict in the Context of Development of New Mining in Zambia 2014', *Southern African Peace and Security Studies* 4, 2 (2014), pp. 41–62; Robby Kapesa and Thomas McNamara, '"We Are Not Just a Union, We Are a Family": Class, Kinship and Tribe in Zambia's Mining Unions', *Dialectical Anthropology* (2020), https://doi.org/10.1007/s10624-019-09578-x; Rohit Negi, 'The Mining Boom, Capital and Chiefs in the "New Copperbelt"' in Alastair Fraser and Miles Larmer (eds), *Zambia, Mining, and Neoliberalism: Boom and Bust on the Globalized Copperbelt* (New York: Palgrave Macmillan, 2010), pp. 209–36.

[107] Rita Kesselring, 'The Electricity Crisis in Zambia: Blackouts and Social Stratification in New Mining Towns', *Energy Research & Social Science*, 30 (2017), pp. 94–102, pp. 98–9.

[108] Rohit Negi, '"Solwezi Mabanga": Ambivalent Developments on Zambia's New Mining Frontier', *Journal of Southern African Studies* 40, 5 (2014), pp. 999–1013.

[109] Peša, *Roads Through Mwinilunga*, pp. 1–2.

[110] Gregor Dobler and Rita Kesselring, 'Swiss Extractivism: Switzerland's Role in Zambia's Copper Sector', *The Journal of Modern African Studies* 57, 2 (2019), pp. 223–45.

At Kansanshi, as in the Copperbelt, foreign-owned suppliers and service providers primarily benefitted from the investments with little impact on local value addition.[111] Despite the disconnect between foreign-driven investment and local elites, some families who are either part of the traditional authorities or have held political (opposition) positions in the provincial and local government managed to appropriate land and business opportunities and make the boom profitable for themselves. With direct access to state resources and information or, in the case of the traditional leadership, entry points for negotiations with the mine for land, they could seize the opportunities, offer their services and monopolise information and bids, and thereby help drive land commercialisation and elite land capture.[112]

Solwezi Today

Solwezi residents experience the direct consequences of mining through the mine's physical expansion and heavy vehicle frequency, and the indirect consequences through land encroachment, the increase of costs for goods and services and the impact of the municipality's lack of planning capacity.[113] The local state's urban governance is often indirectly undermined by the mine's strong capacities to change the infrastructural situation according to its needs. The municipality sometimes hands over state functions to the mine in exchange for tax relief and it has become heavily dependent on the mine's local revenue, emanating primarily from land rates.[114] In 2016, Solwezi District was subdivided into three districts – Mushindamo District, Solwezi District and Kalumbila District; leaving the urban and peri-urban areas and Kansanshi mine to the now much shrunk – in terms of area and local revenue (as Kalumbila and Lumwana mines now fell under Kalumbila District) – Solwezi District.

---

111 Alexander Caramento, 'Cultivating Backward Linkages to Zambia's Copper Mines: Debating the Design of, and Obstacles to, Local Content', *The Extractive Industries and Society* 7, 2 (2020), pp. 310–20.
112 Nicholas J. Sitko and T. S. Jayne, 'Structural Transformation or Elite Land Capture? The Growth of "Emergent" Farmers in Zambia', *Food Policy*, 48 (2014), pp. 194–202.
113 Kesselring, 'The Electricity Crisis in Zambia'; Rita Kesselring, 'At an Extractive Pace: Conflicting Temporalities in a Resettlement Process in Solwezi, Zambia', *The Extractive Industries and Society* 5, 2 (2018), pp. 237–44; Rita Kesselring, 'The Local State in a New Mining Area in Zambia's North-Western Province' in Jon Schubert, Ulf Engel and Elisio Macamo (eds), *Extractive Industries and Changing State Dynamics in Africa: Beyond the Resource Curse* (London: Routledge, 2018), pp. 129–47.
114 Kesselring, 'The Local State'.

The Solwezi Urban Baseline Study (SUBS), a comprehensive household survey conducted in 2015 with the financial and operational help of the German organisation Gesellschaft für Internationale Zusammenarbeit (GIZ), estimated about 266,000 residents in urban Solwezi in 2015.[115] Despite the availability of this exceptionally thorough on-the-ground study, most government reports (and scholarly publications) still work with outdated numbers; the SUBS data has not yet penetrated planning processes. This undercounting contributes to even poorer service provision and the municipality's incapacity to plan ahead.

Today, Solwezi town's population is very young. What is maybe more surprising is the fact that in the past 50 years, all available official data show that gender ratios were more or less on par. The 2010 census even shows a slight skew towards females for Solwezi District (as for all districts in the province).[116] This speaks to the fact that Solwezi has had a history independent of the mining industry. For much of the twentieth century, Zambian Copperbelt towns have had a skewed gender ratio due to male-dominated in-migration attracted by the mining industry. Because Copperbelt mines allowed miners to bring dependents to live in company compounds from the industry's inception in 1926, though, the gender ratios were less unbalanced than for instance in the South African mining centres.[117]

Certainly, many male employment seekers, mine employees and contractors move to Solwezi while leaving their families in the Copperbelt towns. They then straddle two households. These Solwezi male households are found in clusters in the densely populated western compounds. Kabitaka, the mine's housing rental scheme, is exclusively occupied by 'non-local' families.[118] Today, all in all, Solwezi town is an ordinary town, in which mineworkers only make up a small percentage of the overall population. Skilled mineworkers have never constituted a permanent constituency in Solwezi; they continue to move between Solwezi and their (Copperbelt) homes depending on employment opportunities.

---

115 I participated in the study both as an observer and as an advisor to the interviewees.
116 Central Statistical Office Zambia, 'Zambia 2010 Census of Population and Housing: Report on Characteristics of Households and Housing' (Lusaka: Central Statistical Office, 2013), p. 40.
117 Jane L. Parpart, 'The Household and the Mine Shaft: Gender and Class Struggles on the Zambian Copperbelt, 1926–64', *Journal of Southern African Studies* 13, 1 (1986), pp. 36–56, p. 53; Hugh Macmillan, 'The Historiography of Transition on the Zambian Copperbelt – Another View', *Journal of Southern African Studies* 19, 4 (1993), pp. 686–7.
118 Kesselring, 'Disenclaving the Planners' Enclave'.

As throughout the twentieth century, boom and bust are never far away from each other. In 2015, and again in 2020, the Zambian economy felt the consequences of China's slowing demand. The slump in global copper prices triggered the closure of some mines (e.g. Luanshya) and the decision to put others on maintenance (e.g. Mopani Copper Mines). Against the trend, the three new mines in the North-Western Province remained open, not least due to the pressure to recover recent massive investments, and Kansanshi continued with the construction of a smelter, which started to process concentrate in 2015. Kansanshi mine also remained open when other mines were put on care and maintenance during the global Covid-19 pandemic which started in 2020.

Conclusion

Activity at Kansanshi mine has often been described as 'intermittent' over the twentieth century. I tried to draw a more nuanced picture of its history. There was hardly any year when there was no activity at all, such as processing or exploration. Interest in Kansanshi mine never vanished, and the ore bodies were always considered as potential, which, for a number of reasons could not be fulfilled: low-grade ore and harder access compared with the exceptionally high-grade ore at the Katangan and later Zambian mines, world wars, recessions, flooding, too little processing capacity, difficult connections to the line-of-rail, remoteness of the area as seen from the Copperbelt and so forth. In spite of all these challenges, though, investment never ceased. Solwezi has remained an entry point to a region interesting in terms of minerals. The mine has always been there, be it for planners on a global level or in the self-understanding of the town and its residents.

Looking at Solwezi town in relation to the mine's trajectory shows that, in terms of population numbers, the town has developed more or less independently from the mine. While the increase of residents since the mid-2000s is clearly noteworthy and extraordinary, it has to be seen in a historical context. Since its inception in the early twentieth century, the town has never stopped to grow, with higher growth rates since independence. The dynamics fostering this population increase cannot be understood as simply mirroring the development of the mine. Three factors were decisive: Solwezi's geographical location at the eastern boundary of a large province, turning it into a hub for people migrating to the Copperbelt and beyond; 'ordinary' urbanisation processes of secondary urban centres since Zambia's independence; and rural-urban migration within the province.

Solwezi's history shows what should be self-evident: mining towns have never been isolated from wider spatial and political processes. Since the mid-twentieth century, the Copperbelt mining towns, too, rapidly attracted a much wider urban population that cannot be explained by the mines alone – a population which certainly sought to benefit from the presence of the mine, but which also advanced the region's urbanisation in new ways. Towns were a space of relative autonomy and freedom from societal control by elders and 'tribal' hierarchies[119]; they were places of access to cash markets, both production and consumption, and they offered a number of informal economic opportunities; they were social and cultural hubs, as this volume shows, in which people could experiment with new forms of sociality. *Pace* Ferguson,[120] the 'modernity' of mining towns has never been restricted to the mining world, and it did not cease when mines stopped providing mass employment.

Unlike in the Copperbelt towns, throughout the twentieth century, the mining industry in Solwezi contributed very little to the town's development and its infrastructure; its main investments were undertaken on the mining license area. In many aspects, life in Solwezi is and has been like life in other secondary cities in Southern Africa. Since the 1980s, the majority of Solwezi residents are engaged in informal business activities, straddle rural connections – through ethnic affiliations, extended household integration and agricultural practices as a backup in economically harsh times – and integrate family and work life in one or two urban areas, continuously contributing to the growth of a secondary city through formal and informal planning and building processes. Most of the (residential) infrastructure in today's Solwezi has been built by residents or 'Copperbelt landlords', not by town authorities or the mine.

This context, however, has helped to produce a particularly uneven distribution of the benefits and externalities of the most recent mining boom. Solwezi continues to develop independent from the mine, and that allows the mine to feed on the town. The company, in line with global practices of neoliberalised extractivism, reopened the mine without the requirement of integrating urban communities. In fact, instead of providing for it, it heavily relies on urban infrastructure, most of all on housing and care structures. It is built on reproductive work done by the town's residents, the

119 Gregor Dobler, 'Umkämpfter Freiraum: Die Erfindung des Städtischen im Norden Namibias, 1950–1980', *Peripherie* 36, 141 (2016).
120 James Ferguson, *Expectations of Modernity: Myths and Meanings of Urban Life on the Zambian Copperbelt* (Berkeley: University of California Press, 1999).

majority of which happens in the informal realm. It is only through this informal work of Solwezi's residents that the formal economy of extraction can exist and extract more or less unhindered. Unlike throughout the twentieth century, the mine cannot today untangle itself from urban life in its courtyard. This reliance results in a high degree of interference in residents' everyday lives – through infrastructure overuse, rising land and housing prices, often unchecked planning of the mine's own infrastructure resulting in resettlements and land loss. The unequal distribution of benefits is even more clearly visible in Solwezi than in the Copperbelt with its old, underground mines, where the required workforce is small and mostly comes in from outside the region.

Kansanshi's ebb and flow throughout the last century thus points to what we increasingly see elsewhere today: large-scale mining relies on competitive global investment and generates investment decisions informed by that point of view. Companies are quick in reacting to global changes, often leaving employees and contractors destitute (see Mopani's recent closure during the Covid-19 crisis). In such years or decades, urban life necessarily goes on. Booms and busts do exist and have huge consequences, but they happen against a continuity of urban life.

Finally, Solwezi's infrastructural and demographic history foreshadow the current form of resource extraction in the whole Central African region, where infrastructural and other benefits for the urban communities, if they exist, are limited and precarious. Investors do not feel historically responsible for the towns, nor are they held to account. The different phases of extraction and finance throughout the twentieth century have left traces in the urban environments across the Copperbelts (e.g. Mususa[121] and Straube, Chapter 7 this volume) and, to a lesser degree, in Solwezi. Today, urban communities invariably bear the brunt of the externalities of the mining industry: they are exposed both to its environmental, societal and infrastructural legacies and the contemporary logics of disengaged capital.

---

121 Patience Mususa, '"Getting by": Life on the Copperbelt after the Privatisation of the Zambia Consolidated Copper Mines', *Social Dynamics* 36, 2 (2010), pp. 380–94.

PART 2

THE LOCAL COPPERBELT
AND THE GLOBAL ECONOMY

6

Kingdoms and Associations: Copper's Changing Political Economy during the Nineteenth Century

DAVID M. GORDON

Introduction

Historians of Africa associate copper with wealth and political power, the 'red gold of Africa', as the title of one of the most influential books on the subject puts it.[1] Copper in African history evokes a celebration of the glories of precolonial African kingdoms, the palatial copper alloy castings of Benin and the Ife sculptural heads. For South-Central Africa, Katanga copper crosses are symbolic remnants of wealth and power prior to European conquest and colonisation. In part, copper's reputation contrasts with iron, viewed as essential for tools and weaponry rather than the decoration of elites. Current historiography continues to evoke such narratives, relating copper mining, artisanship, and trade in early modern South-Central Africa to the accumulation of wealth and the centralisation of political power, culminating in the rise of kingship. The measured and empirically thorough analysis by Nicolas Nikis and Alexandre Livingstone Smith concludes that 'evidence exists of a relationship between copper production and important centres of political power.'[2]

Historians should move beyond the gleam of 'red gold', however. For one, in the Copperbelt region at least, copper ore was relatively abundant, like iron, and not rare and precious, like gold and ivory. And, although a

---

1 Eugenia Herbert, *Red Gold of Africa: Copper in Precolonial Culture and History* (Madison: University of Wisconsin Press, 2003).
2 Nicolas Nikis and Alexandre L. Smith, 'Copper, Trade and Polities: Exchange Networks in Southern Central Africa in the 2nd Millenium CE', *Journal of Southern African Studies* 43, 5. (2017) pp. 895–911, p. 906.

relationship between copper and power clearly existed, copper not only supported centralised, sedentary political authority, but also encouraged other forms of associational life, sometimes offering alternatives to elite accumulation. 'With ivory, wealth only belongs to the chief', Nkuba, the titleholder of a copper-producing polity remembered, '[but] with copper foundries, everyone was wealthy.'[3] Copper could cut against the power of wealthy elites, contributing to uneven processes: political centralisation and decentralisation; the wealth of elites and the well-being of the poor; the establishment of sedentary political hierarchies and movements of people. This chapter seeks to disentangle how copper produced and traded in South-Central Africa inspired novel political formations, networks of wealth and opportunity, vertical hierarchies and horizontal associations during the era of the caravan trade (1750–1900) and across what would become the modern Copperbelt.

The history of the nineteenth-century Copperbelt is of interest to historians of later periods, since, similar to the colonial and postcolonial Copperbelt, South-Central Africa in the nineteenth century witnessed complex and non-linear political and economic dynamics. When European colonial exploitation of copper began, colonial powers imagined they were replacing the traditional and artisanal production of copper with a modern, industrial one. This chapter demonstrates that copper was involved in the formation of wealth and communities well before colonial rule, encouraging distinctive political, economic and social changes imbricated in international trading networks. In the 150 years prior to colonialism, the exploitation of copper involved periods of intensification, the recruitment of free and forced labour from far away, connections to regional and even global economies, and also the decline of copper production. As in the experiences of the late-colonial and postcolonial Copperbelts, the exploitation of copper did not always provide a stable foundation for the consolidation of political power, and contributed to a waxing and waning of forms of associational life.

The Copperbelt prior to colonialism also provides comparative perspectives to gauge the distinctiveness of the 'modern' Copperbelt political economy. An instructive example from this chapter concerns alternative patterns of labour exploitation in the context of the expansion and contraction of copper production. As with the decline of the Copperbelt in the

---

3 '*Chez les chasseurs d'ivoire, la richesse appartient seulement au chef et à quelques hommes de métier; chez les fondeurs de cuivre, tout le monde est riche.*' Cited in Jean-Félix de Hemptinne, 'Les "Mangeurs de Cuivre" du Katanga', *Bulletin de la Societé Belge d'Études Coloniales*, 1, 3 (1926), pp. 371–403, p. 400.

1970s and 1980s, copper production appears to have decreased in the latter half of the nineteenth century alongside the declining value of copper. Just prior to colonialism, however, this decline in copper production occurred in the context of an increased demand for labour for the exploitation of other exports, in particular ivory, rubber and beeswax. On the other hand, the decline of copper production in the postcolonial period was not accompanied by the rise of other forms of export-oriented production. In this sense, this longer-duration temporal comparison allows for a reformulation, or even rejection, of ideas of modernisation catalysing the exploitation of underutilised labour. To be sure, the effects of technology and productivity on such labour arrangements need to be fully appreciated. Still, the experience of the Copperbelt prior to colonialism challenges certain assumptions of modernisation theory, even before modernisation supposedly began! At the very least, the chapter shows that the history of the nineteenth century needs to be part of the history of the modern Copperbelt.

The key historiographic problem explored in this chapter concerns the relationship of commodities to the connections that constituted societies and polities.[4] Copper as a commodity was tied to various levels of production and trade – each constituting distinctive political, economic and social relationships, and leaving different evidentiary traces. During the nineteenth century, copper was first mined, then smelted, and then smithed and moulded into artifact, tool and weapon. Copper was traded, used as a form of currency, as status item, and as a form of tribute. It thus connected individuals in associations that combined different skills, concerns, and socio-economic positions. These connections, changing over time, constituted a copper network, a 'chain of associations among actors', as Nancy Jacobs puts it in her study of African knowledge production about birds. This chapter pivots away from a view of copper against the backdrop of kingship, detailing instead the changing associations of copper's historical actors, including miners, smelters, coppersmiths, traders, and political titleholders.[5]

---

4 Inspired by Arjun Appadurai (ed.), *The Social Life of Things: Commodities in a Cultural Perspective* (Cambridge: Cambridge University Press, 1988), this chapter seeks to orient copper around its broader social life.
5 Building and borrowing on the notion of network developed with respect to copper by borrowing from Nikis and Smith, used effectively in Nancy Jacobs, *Birders of Africa: History of a Network* (New Haven and London: Yale University Press, 2016), p. 14.

Evidence

A study of Katangese copper in this early modern period requires evidentiary innovation. Archaeological evidence indicates thriving industries of mining and smelting of South-Central African copper that date to the ninth century, if not earlier. Such archaeological evidence, based principally on the excavation of gravesites, postulates a periodisation of copper ingots according to their size, shape, and distribution, reconstructs possible trade routes, and speculates on corresponding forms of political power.[6] The excavation of gravesites yields uneven information, biased towards the use of copper as regalia by elites who chose to be buried with it. (Oral testimony referring to the nineteenth century suggests that there may have been religious sanctions against burial with copper).[7] This evidence is best oriented towards a history of the last millennium. Copper ingots and status items in gravesites favour analyses of elite and longue durée uses of copper.

An additional limitation is that few archaeological sites relate to the mining and smelting of copper itself since the richest deposits of copper ore were exploited by colonial copper mines that destroyed archaeological evidence.[8] The best archaeological reconstruction of a mine in Kansanshi, in North-Western Zambia, gives some indications of mining communities and techniques from the fourth to the nineteenth centuries; however, broad generalisations from this single site are difficult to make.[9] Ethnographic upstreaming instead forms a key element of historical reconstruction, particularly early- or mid-twentieth-century re-enactments by elders who remembered aspects of the process, a ritual of historical invention of tradition that continues on

---

6   Based especially on the work of Pierre de Maret, *Fouilles Archéologiques dans la vallée du Haut-Lualaba, Zaïre. II: Sanga et Katongo, 1974* (Tervuren, Musée royal de l'Afrique centrale, 1985); Pierre de Maret, *Fouilles archéologiques dans la vallée du Haut-Lualaba, Zaïre. III: Kamilamba, Kikulu, et Malemba Nkulu, 1975* (Tervuren, Musée royal de l'Afrique centrale, 1992); see also more recent synthesis by Nikis and Smith, 'Copper, Trade, and Polities'.

7   For comment that copper was not a grave item due to religious sanctions as if a chief was buried with copper, knowledge of copper production would be lost, see Royal Museum of Central Africa archives (henceforth RMCA), Verbeken Papers, 'Procès-Verbal d'Enquete de la Commission Locale, Prévue par l'Ordonance du Gouverneur Général du 6 Octobre 1930, au Sujet de la Détermination des Droits des Indigènes sur les Mines de KASONKA, de l'ETOILE, de RUASHI, de LUKO et de KIBUTU en vue de leur Abandon au Profit du Comité Spécial du Katanga, p. 17.

8   Ibid., p. 17

9   Michael Bisson, 'Prehistoric Copper Mining in Northwestern Zambia', *Archaeology* 27, 4 (1974), pp. 242–7.

the Katangese Copperbelt.[10] Such sources leave the unfortunate impression of mining as traditional, with only some 'tribal', not temporal, variations in techniques, leaving scant indication of historical change.

From the eighteenth century, documentary evidence of traders, travellers and missionaries, originating from Angola, Mozambican Zambezi and Zanzibar provides additional historical details. Such European and Swahili (but not colonial) documentary evidence demonstrates the use of Katangese copper in ordinary items and as elite fashion through the Zambezi basin, Angola, and even the Great Lakes; copper trade through this region; and, in the first half of the nineteenth century, the use of copper as a regional currency. The richest early to mid-twentieth-century colonial documentary sources are historical investigations into precolonial copper mining. These investigations sought to exculpate colonial copper mining companies from remunerating Katangese for mineral production. Still, read with a critical eye and against the grain, they provide valuable historical details, including the recording of oral traditions, oral testimony about forms of production, and details of titleholders who held rights over copper.

This chapter also introduces early twentieth-century ethnographic collections of copper and copper alloy material artifacts held in museums with rich Central African collections and accompanied by provenance records of late nineteenth and early twentieth-century acquisitions. Largely unused by previous scholarship, with careful attention to when and where objects were collected, and positioned alongside other evidence, use of this material culture as historical evidence reinforces certain historical interpretations, and leads to some novel clues about widespread copper artisanry as well as trade and use of copper across the Copperbelt and its neighbouring commercial partners.

Booming Copper Production to the Mid-Nineteenth Century: Katanga and Kazembe

In the century prior to European colonialism, African societies and economies had begun rapidly and sometimes violently changing.[11] In South-Central Africa, from the late eighteenth century, caravan traders, by

10 The best known is de Hemptinne, who witnessed them in 1911 and 1924, described in de Hemptinne 'Les 'Mangeurs', and for summary description in English, see Herbert, *Red Gold of Africa*, pp. 51–6.

11 A vast literature, but best presented in the nineteenth-century military revolution illustrated in Richard J. Reid, *Warfare in African History* (Cambridge: Cambridge University Press, 2012).

importing foreign cloth and guns from the Eastern Swahili and Western Angolan ports, intensified the production and trade of international exports, first slaves and then ivory. A range of local manufactures, destined for regional and not global markets, were also increasingly commercialised as part of this economic process, namely raffia cloth, salt and, most of all, copper. Not only did Katangese copper ingots function as a type of regional currency, as they had for some centuries prior, but copper was manufactured into everyday items, weapons, bullets, decorative arts, and status objects, all of which could be traded regionally for international exports and imports.

Caravan traders from the west, east and north of Katanga contributed to the expansion of copper production in the early nineteenth century. From the east, the Nyamwezi of present-day central Tanzania pioneered the nineteenth-century copper trade, using copper for regalia, status items, and exchanging it for ivory destined for the east coast.[12] From the west, the Chokwe (and perhaps Lunda), as well the Ovimbundu began to seek trading opportunities in the interior.[13] From the north, Luba traded salt and hoes for copper from Katanga.[14] Within Katanga, local polities, the Sanga in particular, responded to the increase in long-distance trade by producing large copper ingots.[15]

The Eastern Lunda Kazembe kingdom centred on the Luapula River and Lake Mweru was at the nexus of these early nineteenth-century trade routes. A series of Portuguese expeditions describe the Kazembe polity in the late eighteenth and early nineteenth centuries organised around a wealthy, apparently all-powerful, and sometimes despotic Mwata Kazembe

---

12 Andrew Roberts, 'Nyamwezi Trade', in Richard Gray and David Birmingham (eds), *Pre-colonial African Trade: Essays on Trade in Central and Eastern Africa before 1900* (London: Oxford University Press, 1970), pp. 54–7.

13 Chokwe and Ovimbundu trade with Katanga is well documented. John Thornton has recently argued that eighteenth and nineteenth centuries encompassed a period of Lunda expansion northwards and eastwards, instead of the usual assumption of a westward expansion towards Angola: John K. Thornton, 'Rethinking Lunda's Expansion: 1720–1800 from Within', paper presented to 'Angola in the Era of the Slave Trade', London, 19–20 June 2019.

14 Anne Wilson, 'Long Distance Trade and the Luba Lomami Empire', *Journal of African History* 13, 4 (1972), pp. 575–89, p. 580.

15 Wilson, 'Long Distance Trade', pp. 579–80, citing Jacques Nenquin, *Excavations at Sanga, 1957: The Protohistoric Necropolis* (Tervuren: RMCA, 1963), pp. 194, 198, 200.

titleholder.[16] This description of the Kazembe polity obfuscates the range of reciprocal relationships that underpinned its political and economic structure. The diversity of its local sources of wealth, including salt, fish, copper and the fertile Luapula Valley, entwined the polity in an array of local political structures difficult to discern in Portuguese accounts focused on powerful kings and lucrative ivory exports.[17] Instead, oral traditions, including those emanating from copper-producing elites, indicate webs of reciprocation.[18] For example, the oral traditions that refer to the earliest chiefs who controlled the copper production of Katanga, notably, the Kipimpi, Kibuye and Kasongo titleholders, relate their settlement to that of the migration story in the Eastern Lunda oral tradition of Mwata Kazembe. They, in turn, tell how they formed alliances, through marriage, with local owners of the land and copper-producing artisans. This may or may not mean that the ancestors of these titleholders migrated from Lunda with Kazembe in the eighteenth century; they do reveal the early nineteenth-century ties of trade and clientage that came to be expressed in terms of these narratives.[19] Copper was one way that reciprocal forms of tribute incorporated the diverse autonomous polities of Katanga into the titleholders that underpinned the Eastern Lunda Kazembe political structure, expressed in terms of relationships of fictive and perpetual kin.[20]

---

16 F. J. M. de Lacerda e Almeida, 'Explorações dos Portuguezes no Sertão da África Meridional', *Annaes Maritimos e Coloniaes* 4, 7–11 (1844); 5, 1–3 (1845); F.J. Pinto, 'Explorações dos Portuguezes no Sertão da África Meridional', *Annaes Maritimos e Coloniaes* 5, 4,5,7,9,10,11,12 (1845); P. J. Baptista, 'Explorações dos Portuguezes no Sertão da África Meridional', *Annaes Maritimos e Coloniaes* III, 5–7, 9–10 (1843); Antonio C. P. Gamitto *King Kazembe* (2 Vols., Lisbon: Junta de Investigaç es do Ultramar, 1960), trans. Ian Cunnison, orig. A. C. P Gamitto *O Muata Cazembe* (2 Vols. Lisbon, 1937; 1st edn., 1854); J. R. Graça, 'Expidicão ao Muatayanvua: Diaro de Joaquim Rodrigues Graça', *Boletim da Sociedade de Geographia* 9, 8/9 (1890).

17 For agriculture and salt, Giacomo Macola, *The Kingdom of Kazembe: History and Politics in North-Eastern Zambia and Katanga to 1950* (Hamburg, LIT, 2002), 44–54; for long-distance trade, Macola, *Kazembe*, pp. 128–35. For fish and agriculture, David Gordon, *Nachituti's Gift: Economy, Society and Environment in Central Africa* (Madison: University of Wisconsin Press, 2006), pp. 50–59.

18 For an example of political reciprocation related to dishing resources, see the role of narrative in defining relationships between Lunda aristocrats and owners of the lagoon, discussed in Gordon, *Nachituti's Gift*, pp. 36–50.

19 Oral traditions 'Procès-Verbal'. Also see R. Marchal, 'Renseignements historiques relatifs à l'exploitation des mines de cuivre par les indigènes de la région de Luishia', *Bulletin des juridictions indigènes et du droit coutumier congolais BJIDCC* (1936), p. 10.

20 For perpetual kinship, see Ian Cunnison, 'Perpetual Kinship: A Political Institution of the Luapula Peoples', *Rhodes-Livingstone Journal*, 20 (1956), 28–48; Gordon, *Nachituti's*

Such interpretations of oral traditions are further supported by a close examination of oral testimony about production found in colonial documentary sources. These sources suggest that mining copper was labour intensive, even as it involved an extensive division of labour based in a differentiation of expertise, especially compared with other high risk or hyper-exploitative activities linked to the consolidation of polities, such as hunting elephants, trading slaves or collecting wild produce like rubber or wax. Copper production instead seemed akin to activities like the production and processing of fish, salt and raffia cloth, all of which were traded over long distances but involved local and rooted forms of production and expertise. Elites profited little from the production of copper in Katanga itself; instead, copper production distributed wealth across society, constituting cross-gender sodalities that included individuals of different expertise, such as miners, smelters, and those who produced energy inputs, food and other commodities essential to copper production. Different skills encouraged salaried labour, along with a relatively egalitarian form of copper rent: the final product belonged to many workers, including those who dug the mineral, who were involved in smelting, smithing, provision of wood and charcoal, and even those who fed the workers.

The most prominent position associated with copper production was a spiritual expert, a titled position that could be occupied by a man or a woman, termed *fondeur* in the colonial sources, or *sendwe*. This titled *sendwe* position was a mediator, an owner of the copper mine, who gave permission for others to work the mine.[21] Nineteenth-century traveller's accounts indicates that the *sendwe* owner of the mines were frequently women. In other regards, however, oral testimony suggests that a gendered division of labour was evident. Teams of men extracted the copper-bearing rocks with hoes and axes, while women and children washed and dried it. Nonetheless, the distinctive masculine culture found in the blacksmithing traditions of West-Central Africa does not seem prevalent.[22]

Work began after harvest and at the commencement of the dry season. When enough mineral was acquired, the *sendwe* titleholder chose an appropriate termite hill for a smelting site. Malachite ore was transported for

---

Gift, 27–50.

21 See for example the Inamfumo of Kalabi discussed by Hermenegildo Capelo and Roberto Ivens, *De Angola á contra-costa: Descripcão de uma viagem através do continente africano* (Lisbon: Impresa Naçional, 1886), p. 70.

22 Coleen E. Kriger, *Pride of Men: Ironworking in Nineteenth-Century West-Central Africa* (Portsmouth NH: Heinemann, 1999).

several kilometres from the site of initial processing to the smelting furnace in special baskets made out of strong and fibrous wood. Near the furnace, charcoal was produced out of hardwood, and transported to the foundry furnace. The process took several months – during which time food had to be supplied to workers.[23]

Oral evidence collected by the colonial District Administrator, R. Marchal, indicates that by the 1850s or even prior, the exploitation of these deposits had reached a veritable boom, attracting labour from across the region. Even as the sources do not indicate the exact nature of servitude, they claim that 'slaves' could purchase their freedom after three to four seasons of copper mining.[24] Testimonies indicate that migrant (or foreign) workers outnumbered original inhabitants. This was a cosmopolitan copper rush, with people arriving to make their fortune. The Kapururu titleholder ensured they were fed, which created the need for a food service, with those who provided food also paid in copper.

This form of labour differentiation suggests a degree of permanent settle-ment and political organisation linked to the production of copper. The mining camp of Lubushia (present-day Luishia), only one of several pros-perous Katangese mining centres, was, according to informants in the 1930s, 'aussi important que celui de l'Union Minière.' An uninterrupted line of carriers transported the mineral from the mine to the foundry four kilo-metres away. In fact, informants remembered it being so busy that there had to be a two-way road. At the foundry, workers supplied charcoal, and they were also paid in copper. Even given potential exaggeration, these were years of prosperity. Marchal estimated that the number of miners at Lubushia mine surpassed 900, with approximately one-third migrants. According to his estimates, to feed these miners, Lubushia would need to have had four to five thousand inhabitants, an expansive economic endeavour for this region and this time period.[25]

---

23 For wood, food, termite hills, religious and technical expertise, see 'Procès-Verbale', p. 14. For description of process, see de Hemptinne, 'Les "Mangeurs"', 380–82.

24 For forms of slavery and manumission in this region during the nineteenth century based mostly on oral testimony, see David M. Gordon, 'The Abolition of the Slave Trade and the Transformation of the South-Central African Interior', *William and Mary Quarterly* 66, 4 (2009), pp. 915–38. An example of Catholic Missionary sources on slavery and manumission, in David M. Gordon, 'Slavery and Redemption in the Catholic Missions of the Upper Congo, 1878–1909', *Slavery and Abolition*, 38, 3 (2017), pp. 577–600.

25 Marchal, 'Renseignements historiques', p. 15.

Mining was also undertaken in a decentralised fashion, perhaps typical of older mines and foundries. In the area of a chief, called Kiembe, each village had one or two copper mining teams, consisting of ten to fifteen men, producing around 1,000 kg in a season. In these areas, migrants who had an agreement with the *sendwe* titleholder could as well be part of teams, or form their own teams, which seems to have been the general preference. Kiembe claimed some twenty villages of his chieftaincy were involved in copper mining, with around 300 local workers and 200 migrants working on the copper fields.[26]

Worker remuneration, according to Marchal's informants, was fairly standard, and rendered in the form of the famous 20 kg Katanga copper crosses (*fishinkoro*).[27] All the families from the titleholder Katanga's area where men mined copper and the women and children furnished food, received three crosses or about 60 kg of copper for one season's work (up to five months), or equivalent trade items, including cloth, tools and arms. Two crosses were received immediately after work and another one or two months later, when the Katanga titleholder called all chiefs and distributed refined copper and trade items. Those from away, migrant workers who received food from Katanga as part of their payment, were paid from 30 to 50 kg of copper for a complete season. Workers used the copper to purchase cloth and slaves in addition to local manufactures. Thus, copper production multiplied into other economic activities.

In terms of political structure and authority, copper tribute reinforced the titleholding system found across this region (represented in the oral traditions discussed above). At the base of a triangle, independent teams of about fifteen men producing around 1,000 kg per season, gathered around lesser titleholders. In addition to each member of the team receiving three crosses (60 kg) as payment, each team gave a tribute (*mulambo*) to the lesser titleholder of 100 kg. Moving up the triangle, lesser titleholders gave 60 kg as tribute to the chief *sendwe* titleholder. Each *sendwe* titleholder sent tribute to political titleholders, such as the Katanga titleholder, who in turn sent an annual tribute to regional political authorities at the apex of the triangle, such as the Kazembe titleholder. Katanga sent Kazembe around 450 kg annually, which had to be carried by 20 to 25 men. Marchal estimated that about 115,000 kg was distributed from workers through these titleholders yearly.[28] The Kazembe apex of this copper production was so well known

---

26 Ibid.
27 De Hemptinne describes these as *milopolo*.
28 Marchal, 'Renseignements historiques', p. 17.

in the 1860s, prior to the consolidation of Msiri's polity, that copper was known to come from 'Kazembe's country', not Katanga.[29]

That this oral testimony makes such a clear distinction between a local, ancestral community on the one hand and new migrants on the other suggests that migration in response to copper production had increased through the nineteenth century. By the middle of the century this was an expanding industry, spurred on by greater trade opportunities and the emergence of commodities that entered central Africa via Eastern African trade routes, in particular cloth. These imported commodities, in turn, inspired the need for local manufactures, copper in particular, that could be traded regionally for commodities, chiefly ivory, that underpinned international trade. By the middle of the century, the Nyamwezi (from present-day Tanzania) were the brokers of this regional-global trade.[30] They dealt directly with the titleholders who sat at the apex of tribute triangles, and accumulated quantities of copper to exchange. One such title-holder who worked closely with the Eastern African traders was Nsama, who, at the time of his defeat by Hamed ben Muhammed (Tippu Tip), had some 700 *frasilahs* (24,500 lb.) of copper stored in his village (alongside 68,250 lb of ivory), which he was then trading with the Nyamwezi.[31]

Beyond mining and trade, copper items were produced for various uses during this period. Here, the archaeological record, in particular De Maret's informative work, needs to be supplemented by additional sources, including documentary sources and ethnographic collections. De Maret identified a gradual move towards the proliferation of small crosses and the production of larger copper ingots, probably due to inflationary pressures on copper (see Figures 6.1–6.3).[32] The point to appreciate, however, is also that due

---

29 As evidenced in collections made in by David Livingstone along the Shire in 1861 of copper wire from 'Bazembe's country' (presumably Kazembe). National Museum of Scotland (henceforth NMS), Museum Reference A.762.4. Presumably the labeller used the common prefix "Ba" instead of the correct "Ka". Personal communications, Sarah Warden and Lawrence Dritsas.

30 Roberts, 'Nyamwezi Trade', p. 57. The best contemporary documentary record of Zanzibari and Nyamwezi copper traders in this period is from David Livingstone, *The Last Journals of David Livingstone in Central Africa* (London: John Murray, 1874), pp. 291, 298, 301, 310, 331–3, 337, 358–9.

31 François Bontinck (trans. and ed.), *L'autobiographie de Hamed ben Mohammed el-Murjebi Tippo Tip, ca. 1840–1905* (Brussels: Académie Royale des Sciences d'Outre-Mer, 1974), pp. 56, 202–3, fn. 103.

32 Pierre de Maret, 'L'évolution monetaire du Shaba Centrale entre le 7e et le 18e siecle', *African Economic History* 10 (1981), pp. 117–49. Pierre de Maret, 'Histoires de croisettes' in Luc de Heusch (ed.), *Objets-signes d'Afrique* (Tervuren, Musée royal de l'Afrique centrale, 1995), pp. 133–45.

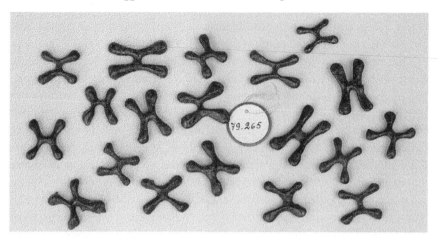

Figure 6.1   Copper ingots from Sanga, Haut-Lomami, Katanga. From thirteenth to fifteenth century, 4cm in length (PO.0.0.79265, collection RMCA Tervuren; photo J.-M.Vandyck, RMCA Tervuren ©)

to the increasing availability of copper within expanding economies, finer amounts of copper were generally traded in the form of copper wire (or strips and nails) instead of crosses. (Dating the introduction of techniques of producing Katangese copper wire still requires investigation). In 1861, during his Zambezi Expedition (1858–64), David Livingstone acquired a finely smithed coil of copper wire in the Shire River (Manganja), identified as being from the country of Kazembe.[33] Henry Stanley collected a very similar copper wire coil, as illustrated below. In 1884–85, Capelo and Ivens detail a well-established technique of wire manufacture and use:

> The people of Katanga ... reduce it [copper] to long and fine bars, which after spinning, reduce to wires the size of chords of European musical instruments, which they adorn on handles of axes, of weapons, and above all bundles of buffalo or gnu hair, to make the celebrated manillas and bracelets that today are fashionable across the countryside.[34]

33 NMS, A.762.4. The label identifies the object as .Manganja from the country of Bazembe'.
34 'A gente da Katanga ... reduzem-no a longas e finas barras, que depois por fieiras sucessivas elles adelgaçam até ao ponto de fazerem fios da grossura de qualquer das cordas dos instrumentos musicaes da Europa, com que guarnecem cabos de machadas, canos de armas, e sobretudo feixes de pelo da cauda do búfalo ou gnú, para confeccionar as celebradas manilhas e braceletes, que têem hoje voga por todo o sertão.' Capelo and Ivens, De Angola á Contra-costa, pp. 70–71.

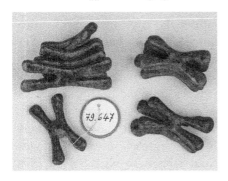

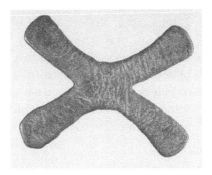

Figure 6.2   Copper ingots from Sanga, Haut-Lomami, Katanga. Likely sixteenth to eighteenth century, 6cm in length (PO.0.0.79647, collection RMCA Tervuren; photo J.-M. Vandyck, RMCA Tervuren ©)

Figure 6.3   Copper ingots from Sanga, Haut-Lomami, Katanga. 24.2cm x 18.3cm *fishinkoro* cross, likely nineteenth century (EO.1954.57.137, collection RMCA Tervuren; RMCA Tervuren ©)

Figure 6.4   *Mitako* wire coil collected by Henry M. Stanley, in the style collected by Livingstone and described by Capelo and Ivens (HO.1954.72.82, collection RMCA Tervuren; photo J.-M. Vandyck, RMCA Tervuren ©)

Copper wire could be fashioned into many items and used for a range of decorative purposes, along with other manufactures such as hoes, axes, and knives. The currency function of copper crosses began to decline, as trade items began to be measured in terms of imported beads and cloth. These imports nonetheless spurred copper production, particularly wire (see Figure 6.4).

Production of copper and use of wire also observed by David Livingstone, *Last Journals*, 265. Livingstone collected a fine example of copper wire from the 'Manganja' to the east of the Copperbelt, and now in the National Museum of Scotland (NMS), Museum Reference A.762.4.

Ethnographic collections of objects from the late nineteenth century also indicate that artifacts, many of them made with copper wire, strips or nails, proliferated through this period. Around the Kazembe kingdom, copper was used as a form of status, decorating weaponry as well as adorning bodies of men and women. Artifacts collected near Lake Mweru by Emil Torday in 1904, but which appear to have been used for decades before that, include status items: a snuff box inlaid with copper and brass strips and a large knife, engraved with two triangles on each side, with a handle of wood inlaid with copper and brass wire, with copper/brass studs and a conical copper cap. A third object collected by Torday in the same Lake Mweru area, identified as a 'Luba Charm', is a remarkable small figure of hard black wood studded with copper nails, probably indicating the status of the spiritual figure or ancestor depicted.[35]

By the middle of the century, Katanga, then referred to as the land of Kazembe, was known across Central Africa as the place of copper and associated opportunities. Leaders like Katanga Kapururu encouraged in-migration, benefitting from their labour and exploitation of copper, and facilitating relationships from migrants and local masters of country. They also served as intermediaries between migrants, autochthonous titleholders, the Mwata Kazembe titleholder, and the growing number of Swahili and Nyamwezi traders.[36] Oral traditions expressed political relationships between these new migrant workers, long-standing owners, traders, and the titleholders of the Eastern Lunda, defining the rules of access to resources, systems of trade and clientage, and hence, when examined closely, an entire political economy.

Changing Patterns: Msiri's Bayeke Networks, 1850s–1880s

By the middle of the nineteenth century, migrants to the Copperbelt area, including miners and traders, began to settle permanently. The first regular settlers were the 'Batushi' reputedly from present-day Tanzania, although

---

35 British Museum (hereafter BM), Snuff box, Copper with brass, Asset #351644001, Reg. #Af1904,0611.12; Knife, Asset #1613039012, Reg. #Af1904,0611.31.a; Luba Charm: Asset #1613057240, Reg. #Af1904,0611.20. (On the knife and the 'charm', the studs here are labelled as copper, even though they are usually brass; I have not been able to inspect the items closely.)
36 Marchal, 'Renseignements historiques', p. 15; for family exploitation, also see 'Procès-Verbale', p. 14.

their exact origins are unclear.[37] Then came the settlement of the Nyamwezi traders who had specialised in the copper trade, of whom Msiri and the Yeke were the most influential. Nyamwezi settlement was part of a broader process of globalised trade and settlement affecting the region. The mid-nineteenth-century Copperbelt was a cosmopolitan, transitory, frontier-like and booming economy. Ivens and Capelo, writing about the end of this period, found Katanga to be 'a refuge for many criminals who abandoned neighbouring lands, such that the chief here is a stranger…from Nyamwezi'.[38] A few years later, the missionary Frederick Stanley Arnot who resided at Msiri's court in the town of Bunkeya from 1886 to 1888 described it as a 'peaceable dwelling of remnants of various tribes under one chief'.[39]

The major political change of this era was a reshaping of older forms of triangulated titleholders through which copper had been previously distributed, and especially the replacement of those at the apex of the triangles. Networks remained; rulers were more transient. The historiography of Msiri's polity, like the Kazembe kingdom, is conventionally oriented towards the persona of the ruler himself, and not the network of relationships in which the polity was entwined. In part, this is because most outside observers, especially those connected with the Congo Free State expeditions, described Msiri as a cruel despot. Those who remained at his court for longer periods, such as Arnot, paint a different portrait, describing many individuals with significant power and authority. Arnot was particularly taken with the 'remarkable' rights of women: 'Women are allowed to attend the court, and to have a voice equally with the men.'[40] Oral traditions, like those of the Kazembe kingdom (in fact some of the narratives seem to be borrowed from the Kazembe kingdom), portray Msiri's rule as rooted in local forms of legitimacy.[41] Copper was one of the principal mechanisms for ensuring that Msiri's polity was entwined with these local networks.

---

37 De Hemptinne, 'Les "Mangeurs"', pp. 377–8; Marchal identifies the 'Baushi', who could be the same 'Tushi' in Marchal, 'Renseignments historiques', p. 11.

38 '*se deve considerar como o valhacouto de quantos criminosos abandonam as terras circumvizinhas, attendendo que o próprio soba é um estranho aqui, oriundo, como se sabe, do Unyamuezi*'. On their 1884–56 expedition, reported in Capelo and Ivens, *De Angola a Contra-costa*, p. 78.

39 Frederick Stanley Arnot *Garanganze or, Mission work in Central Africa* (London: James E. Hawkins, 1889), 236.

40 Arnot, *Garanganze*, p. 241.

41 A point emphasised by the most recent historical account of Msiri, which argues against describing Msiri's polity as 'warlord': Hugues Legros, *Chasseurs d'ivoire: Une histoire du royaume yeke du Shaba (Zaïre)* (Brussels: Editions de l'Université Libre de Bruxelles, 1996).

Oral traditions, first recorded by Arnot, have Msiri gaining his knowledge and experience in Katanga from his father, Kalasa, who was primarily a trader in copper with the Sanga.[42] (A popular version of the oral tradition has Msiri 'following an elephant' to Katanga; this is probably a later emphasis in an oral tradition that valorised Msiri's ivory trade above copper). Msiri then extended his influence by using his guns to aid the Sanga to defeat the Luba. The presence of Msiri further contributed towards the breakdown of the Katanga copper trade with the Luba polities to the immediate north.[43] Msiri's initial alliance with Sanga typified the type of powerbrokering and integration that characterised his polity.[44] With regard to copper production, documentary evidence indicates that Msiri relied on a network of local families to produce copper. For example, Arnot wrote of a type of trade caste involved in the mining of copper, where the 'business is handed down from father to son, and the instructions of the forefathers are followed with the greatest accuracy.'[45] Although based within families, outsiders associated with Msiri's Yeke were incorporated into these castes, making them into more expansive associations.

Early Belgian colonial enquiries portray a different picture of Msiri to Arnot, perhaps because their informants were not as closely aligned with Msiri. (Colonial accounts were also interested in demonstrating Msiri's illegitimacy in Katanga, as they did not want to remunerate Yeke chiefs for mineral rights). Most testimonies claim that Msiri, by insisting on centralisation and control of the copper market, discouraged the egalitarian and associative nature of copper mining, leading to its decline in popularity. In some cases, such as the Kasonta mine of Kasongo, Msiri was said to have prohibited the mining of copper under penalty of death except by those who declared direct allegiance to him.[46]

Msiri and the Yeke are also credited with the introduction of mobile furnaces that were temporary, destroyed after each copper smelting operation.[47] Perhaps such operations were well suited to nineteenth-century warlordism, since they were not re-used and thus did not require major sedentary investments. They could have discouraged the established norms and rituals of copper exploitation, replacing the ties of between copper

42 Arnot, *Garanganze*, p. 231; Legros, *Chasseurs*, p. 40.
43 Wilson, 'Long Distance Trade', p. 586.
44 Legros, *Chasserurs*, pp. 39–57.
45 Arnot, *Garanganze*, p. 238.
46 'Procès-Verbal', p. 12.
47 De Hemptinne, 'Les "Mangeurs"', pp. 379–80.

mining families, societies and titleholders with a type of ad hoc exploitation. The Yeke mobile furnaces relied on extensive labour and energy inputs, such that copper could only be produced in the dry season, once agricultural work was over and there was plentiful wood. The final product of these Yeke mobile furnaces was reputedly not as fine as copper produced by the Sanga. Perhaps the Yeke inability to smelt copper as efficiently as the Sanga and their reliance on the Sanga for finer copper smithing, in addition to the changing trade and other factors detailed below, further contributed to Msiri's abandoning attempts to control the copper trade from the 1880s.

To recap, there are two different emphases in the evidence of the relationship between Msiri's polity and copper production. First, early versions of the oral traditions and Arnot have Msiri relying on and working with local copper producers. Second, however, are the colonial-era sources that indicate Msiri abandoning copper and clamping down on independent production, in favour of ivory.

The incongruous evidence of the relationship of Msiri's polity to copper can be reconciled in part by late nineteenth-century changes in Msiri's approach to copper mining. As he abandoned attempts to control production and trade, autonomous polities, the Sanga in particular, continued small-scale copper production. Thus, while contemporary witnesses such as Arnot describe the trade in copper, it does not appear to have been monopolised by Msiri. This explains why oral informants like Nkuba drew such a stark contrast between a trade in copper for ordinary people and the trade in ivory for the wealthy and powerful. Msiri, never able to control copper production and fearful of providing trading opportunities to his rivals, became intent on having it closed down.

Copper provided the necessity and opportunity for Msiri to root himself in local forms of production, to ally with local leaders, and to rely on local miners and artisans. Motivating Msiri's migration to and settlement in Katanga, copper contributed to the extension of trade and other networks that constituted the Yeke polity, even as it disrupted older flows of copper production, tribute and trade. Msiri was never able to fully control the political economy of copper however. His failure to do so led to an alternative orientation around ivory, along with an entrenchment of some of the despotic and war-like features of the Yeke polity.

Decline:
The Late Nineteenth Century and the Angolan Trade

Independently or in alliance with indigenous small-scale polities, migrants to the nineteenth-century Copperbelt mined, smithed and traded copper. Msiri and his Nyamwezi followers helped to transform the nineteenth-century political economy of copper. At first an agent in the expansion of copper production, in the latter half of his reign Msiri presided over its decline. Around the 1870s, copper mining and production began to decrease, even as copper objects were still valued. Exports of ivory, rubber and beeswax instead of copper, and increased imports of foreign metals, specifically brass, contributed to this decline. By the time the European administrations were formally established in the early 1900s, copper mining had declined or ended, leaving little appreciation of its prior dynamism.

Part of the reason for the declining investment of Msiri in copper production was a reorientation of Msiri's trade from east to west. Trade in copper northwards and eastwards had been disrupted. The Eastern Lunda Mwata Kazembe titleholder had previously received an estimated tribute of 450 kg of in copper from the Sanga per year. The increase in Swahili trade with the Yeke bypassed Kazembe's control, leading to conflict. In one telling and impactful incident in 1868, Mwata Kazembe Muongo confiscated 1,700 kg of copper from the Zanzibari trader Mohammad Bughari, who had purchased it from Msiri. Perhaps this was an attempt by Kazembe to combat the erosion of his Katanga political networks by Msiri's Katanga alliances and the Swahili-Nyamwezi copper trade. This incident, in addition to the usually cited reluctance of the Zanzibari to sell firearms to Msiri, contributed to Msiri's decision to turn away from the eastward trade, and in particular the trade in copper.[48]

Instead, to bypass Kazembe and avoid reliance on Swahili traders, Msiri turned to the west, in particular Ovimbundu caravans financed by Silva Porto. They did not demand copper, in part because cheaper brass, used for similar purposes, was available from Angolan Atlantic ports, as further discussed below. Instead, the Ovimbundu encouraged the collection and sale of rubber, beeswax and ivory.[49] Msiri, initially attracted by the copper fields, thus turned from copper to ivory and other exports. Since copper production wasted local labour inputs compared with other more profitable exports, Msiri discouraged it.[50]

---

48 Legros, *Chasseurs*, p. 115; Macola, *The Kingdom of Kazembe*, p. 141; Bontick, *L'autobiographie*, p. 202, fn. 102; Livingstone, *Last Journals*, pp. 276, 297.
49 According to informants of Marchal, 'Renseignments historiques', p. 13
50 As concluded by Marchal, 'Renseignments historiques', pp. 12–13

Heavy and haphazard exploitation of the richest deposits of the prior decades also contributed to decline. The mines most exploited over the previous decades, which were open-pit and sometimes underground, dug in vertical shafts of 15 to 20 feet, had become dangerous. On at least two recorded occasions, at Kambove and the Sanga mine of Kalabi, they collapsed.[51] At Kalabi, a collapse of the mine in 1882 had closed the mine. The owner of Kalabi, a woman with a royal title *Inamfumo*, was allegedly waiting for a sign, perhaps in a dream, that the mine was safe to be opened once again.[52]

Imported European copper and brass began to replace and undermine the profitability of Katangese copper. With the influx of foreign copper and brass, artisanship – the smithing of copper – was valued above the raw material, confirming earlier trends for the preference of wire over crosses. Copper crosses were still produced, to be sure, but once copper was transformed into wire or bullets, it attained a higher value. Sanga informants claimed that they far preferred to work the copper into wire (*mitako* or *mitaga*) and bullets than to sell it in ingot form. The weight of the ingot was far greater than the equivalent weight of wire of the same value. Copper bullets (*chipolopolo*), which, as Zambian soccer fans know, move at high speed, were the most valued.[53] In other words, people paid for the labour of artisans who could convert copper into forms that were easily used – bullets and wire, in particular. Like iron blacksmithing in this period, coppersmithing and craftmanship were valued above smelting and the production of the metal itself, at least on the Copperbelt.[54]

Copper smithing and craftsmanship could, however, be applied to other, imported copper alloys. In those places that had been significant consumers of Katangese copper, a range of artisanal practices linked to copper alloy artisanry proliferated by the late nineteenth century. The replacement of Katangese copper by imported brass is best appreciated by considering the objects, including insignia of political and religious power, collected in the late nineteenth or early twentieth century, in a vast arc, from Lakes Mweru

---

51 Capelo and Ivens, *De Angola á Contre-costa*, pp. 69–70; de Hemptinne 'Les "Mangeurs"', p. 377; Cornet's report on Kambove in his ms, and in J. Cornet, 'Mines de cuivre du Katanga', *Le Mouvement Geographique* 12, 1 (1895), describes the extent of the deposits and excavations at Kambove.

52 Capelo and Ivens, *De Angola á Contra-costa*, pp. 69–70. The mine collapsed two years prior to their 1884–85 expedition.

53 De Hemptinne 'Les "Mangeurs"', pp. 396–7, 401–2

54 For the argument of the value of blacksmithing above smelting, see Kriger, *Pride of Men*.

and Tanganyika in the east, to Angolan societies around the Kwango river. In this region, the ubiquity of copper is evident. Throughout the Luba region and in related polities to the north and west, which had in the early nineteenth century imported copper from Katanga, late nineteenth-century metal daggers were inlaid, decorated or developed handles with copper. Distinctive styles emerged. For example, in the north of the region, mobile warrior Tetela workshops decorated the handles of the daggers and knifes with pointed or conical copper ends. The function of these pointed ends seems unclear – potentially to attach to a wooden shaft, or as an additional weapon through a back-handed strike. The grips of the handles of these knives were also inlaid with copper wire and studded with brass. Perhaps these knives were meant more as decoration and indicators of power than as functioning weapons.[55] The status element of copper-decorated weaponry was certainly evident for the Songye, immediately east of the Tetela, and with a similar reputation – artists inscribed iron and copper axes with up to 40 faces, perhaps depicting the followers of prominent leaders.[56] Warriors of the Songye of Zappo Zap (Nsapu-Nsapu) coated a stool, presumably for an important man, with copper.[57] Miniature Pende initiation badges, in the form of their renowned masks, often made in ivory or bone, were also moulded in copper.[58]

By the latter half of the nineteenth century brass began to replace copper in the western regions, where authority had passed from the Lunda of Mwaant Yav to Chokwe traders and hunters. As men of the gun, their profession demanded that the Chokwe were masters in metal work. The guns that proliferated through this region were low-quality *lazarinas* or *lazerinos*, flintlock muzzle-loaders, which historian Giacomo Macola argues had a profound impact on warfare and political economy on the Angolan

[55] These include many collected in American Natural History Museum (AMNH); and BM Tetela knife with copper wire handle, Ass# 1613050585, Reg. #Af1909, Ty.782; Tetela knife also with slightly pointed end, but not as sharp Reg. – Ass.# 1613050061 – #Af1907,0528.351.

[56] BM Songye (Zappo-Zap) Ornamental Axe with 40 faces made of iron wood and copper, Ass. # 1613050840, Reg. #Af1907,0528.398; Songye (Nsapo) Asset #34314001, Reg. #Af1909, Ty.976. Also published in C. J. Spring, *African Arms and Armour* (London: British Museum Press, 1993). Also see AMNH collection.

[57] Zappo Zap stool – copper overlaid on wood. BM Asset #1613229315, Reg. #Af1907,0528.402.

[58] Pende initiation badge – mask made of copper, BM Asset #1613047273, Ref. # Af1910,0420.457.

plateau after 1850, coinciding with the rising power of the Chokwe.[59] In addition to marksmanship, Chokwe required expert smithing skills to repair these low-quality guns, and to manufacture bullets. These smithing skills underpinned their craftsmanship in metal, copper, brass and iron. They celebrated their metal-working and the importance of metal to their prosperity by ornamenting themselves and their guns with copper and brass. They inlaid their gunstock with copper and brass wire and studs, to help with grip but also for decoration.[60] The most striking and distinctive element of Chokwe material culture was their *ibenye* or *yipenye* head ornamentation (or diadems) made by flattening brass wire into stylised blades. *Yipenye* were most typically made for the head *(cipenya mutwe)*, but also referred to other forms of Chokwe-made brass pageantry.[61] In his 1904 expedition, Porto adventurer and anthropologist, Fonseca Cardoso photographed a Chokwe chief with an elaborate brass headdress. These *yipenye* became widespread fashion, representing distinction and elegance, worn even by the daughter of the Lunda paramount titleholder, Mwaant Yav.[62] Elites sought Chokwe-fashioned brass ornamentation throughout this region.

The Kuba, who had long traded with the Chokwe, also used Katanga copper, and in the nineteenth century began to value brass. Emil Torday claimed that when brass came from the west, 'it was so rare that it had a value equal to our gold and the king alone was allowed to possess or use it.'[63] Its rarity was linked to it being in high demand by the neighbouring Chokwe, who were also the purveyors of brass and promoted it as a fashionable item to signal elite status across the region. The Kuba, as evidenced by Torday's collections, combined copper and brass, in their varied manufactures: whistles, combs, pipes and razors, were either made or inlaid with copper, in addition to their famous *ikul* knives with copper handles or blades, or both.[64] Copper wire and brass studs were

---

59 Giacomo Macola, *The Gun in Central Africa* (Athens: Ohio University Press, 2016), pp. 53–73.
60 See extensive collection held in National Museum of Ethnology, Lisbon, Portugal.
61 Henrique Augusto Dias de Carvalho, *Ethnographia e Historia Tradicional dos povos da Lunda* (Lisbon: Impresa Nacional, 1890), 340–1; Marie-Louise Bastin, *Statuettes Tshokwe du héros civilisateur 'Tshibinda Ilunga'* (Arnouville: Arts d'Afrique Noire, 1978), pp. 100–1.
62 P. Pogge, *Im Reiche des Muata Jamwo* (Berlin: Verlag von Dietrich Reimer, 1880), p. 195, with an illustration on p. 194.
63 Quoted in Herbert, *Red Gold*, p. 177.
64 Kuba (Bangongo) smoking pipe, copper wire, BM, Asset #1613237540. Reg. Af1907C7.175; Kuba Bangongo razor made of copper, Ass. #1613235461; Kuba whistle with copper wire, Asset #1613243250, Reg. #Af1908, Ty.205; Kuba *ikul* knife. Found in many other collections.

attached to all items to increase decoration and indicate wealth. The prominent polities and traders of the west, from the Chokwe to the Kuba, valued copper, but, as indicated in their material culture, began to replace it with imported European metals, brass in particular.

It is important to nuance the impression left by the art historical record here: gauging by the amount and prominence of nineteenth-century artisanship and use, copper and copper alloy items were first produced and sold by mobile warriors who used them as status items; only then, did the sedentary Lunda and Kuba begin to adopt them. Viewing the relationship of copper to political formation through the production and use of copper by sedentary states misses the key role of mobile associations in the history of copper.

In central Katanga during the 1890s, copper was still widely used and traded among all, even as Msiri did not invest greatly in its actual production. Le Marinel noted plentiful copper around Msiri's settlement, with a copper cross worth three small pieces of cloth (*mouchoirs*). Still, even given the relatively low value that Le Marinel reported, copper adorned precious guns, and a royal execution lance.[65] Bonchamps, on the Stairs expedition that ended Msiri's rule, reports that Msiri wore heavy rings of ivory and copper on his legs.[66] Even as it remained a status item, Msiri concentrated on the production of ivory, rubber and beeswax for export: more profit was to be made from other commodities and westward-oriented trade routes. Copper was still traded to be sure; however, Msiri only insisted on, or could only enforce, his own trade monopoly over ivory.[67] Indeed, so key was ivory to his polity that the Yeke oral tradition came to celebrate Msiri's alleged following of an elephant to Katanga as the founding migration myth. Copper was the trade item of ordinary people; ivory that of the global trader and warlord.

Yet this late-nineteenth-century impression of Msiri's Yeke can be misleading, since the polity was in fact a product of copper-based networks of production and trade. Msiri did not 'follow an elephant' as the myth proclaims, but rather built on the copper-trading relationships of his father. The Yeke allied with local rulers and employed their mining experts and technologies. At least some Yeke were initiated into their mining and

---

65 P. Le Marinel, *Carnets de route dans l'Etat Indépendant du Congo de 1887 à 1910* (Brussels: Progress, 1991), pp. 160, 185.

66 R. de Pont-Jest, 'L'Expedition du Katanga, d'après les notes du Marquis Christian de Bonshamps', *Le Tour du Monde* (1893), pp. 257–72, p. 262.

67 Arnot, *Garangaze*, pp. 234–5.

smithing fraternities. It was only with the collapse of these copper relationships by the late 1880s, when subject peoples near the Yeke heartland,
the Sanga, rebelled against Msiri, that he invested in the arms and ammunition to suppress them. From this period some of the least flattering
portrayals of Msiri as a foreign and illegitimate ivory and slave-trading
despot emerges. These depictions, partly alibis for invasion, justified the
action of King Léopold's mercenaries. In 1891, in the midst of negotiating with Congo Free State agents over guns and ammunition, Omer
Bodson assassinated Msiri.

European colonial regimes succeeded the trader-warlords of Katanga. At
first uninterested in copper, for them as well, indigenous copper mining
represented wasted labour. The first administrator of the only mine still
producing copper in Lukafu, 'Bwana Capitaine' (Commandante Gor),
secured a good portion of the approximate two tons produced in Lukushi
in 1903, and then sent soldiers to ensure the closure of the mine.[68] In the
context of various demands on labour, for hunting, for war, for agriculture,
and, for the collection of tribute by predatory regimes like Msiri's and the
Congo Free State, local leaders could not sustain the labour demands of a
copper-producing economy. Rulers did not deem it profitable for them to
do so: there were more effective ways to capture profit from South-Central
African labour, in the short term at least. Copper's political networks, from
Kazembe through the Yeke to the Chokwe, ended, only to be resurrected
some two decades later.

Conclusion

Nikis and Smith argue that through copper 'there seems to be no doubt
that those political powers [in Katanga] of the nineteenth century strengthened the ties of people in their respective areas of influence.'[69] This chapter
has offered some historical nuance to this argument: copper contributed to
political networks, not necessarily centralised structures. Copper inspired the
migration of workers and traders to Katanga, contributing to a political order
typified first by associations of Katanga locals and migrants. These political
networks invested in certain titleholders, through whom copper tribute
flowed. From *sendwe* titleholders, up the pyramid, through Katanga, and with
Mwata Kazembe at the apex, political formations resembled kingship. But

---

68 Marchal, 'Renseignements historiques', p. 13
69 Nikis and Smith, 'Copper, Trade, and Polities', p. 908.

at the base of these triangles were the copper-producing and trading associations that proved the most durable aspect of copper's political economy. Those at the top of the pyramid were but fleeting elements of copper's political networks.

By the middle of the century, imports of cloth from the east spurred the production of copper. In addition to the currency use of copper crosses and wire, artisans crafted a range of manufactured copper items that signified wealth, power and fashion. As guns became part of this globalised trade, copper bullets were also in demand. With, however, the inability to control local copper production and trade, the increasing globalisation of trade, the influence of Angola traders from the west, along with imports of cheaper brass, the mining of copper declined, and was discouraged by those leaders who prospered through international trade, such as Msiri. Metal-working artisanry and use that had been encouraged by the spread of Katangese copper were now applied to imported European metals, brass in particular, as evidenced by networks of Chokwe brass artisanship. With the declining influence of copper's associations in Katanga, centralised and sometimes violent rule came to predominate.

Across the region and through the nineteenth-century Katangese copper had constituted communities and political networks. Copper contributed to diverse forms of associational life, to the wealth and well-being of many. The political economy of copper in the nineteenth century can be viewed as precursor to the expanding labour arrangements and forms of associational life on the colonial Copperbelt. Nonetheless, it is rarely viewed as an early modern phenomenon, for, by the time the modern and industrial copper mining arose in the early twentieth century, the dynamism of copper mining, production and trade during the nineteenth century appeared part of a distant past, relegated to the study of archaeology, often cast in the idiom of tradition and sedentary kingship, not part of a modern political economy and civil society. This chapter has pointed out the ways in which the history of the nineteenth-century Copperbelt is part of the history of the modern twentieth-century Copperbelt.

7

Of Corporate Welfare Buildings and Private Initiative: Post-Paternalist Ruination and Renovation in a Former Zambian Mine Township

CHRISTIAN STRAUBE

Introduction

'We buried ten people a day', the woman remembered. I was immersed in a conversation with a staff member of Serve Zambia Foundation, a faith-based non-governmental organisation (NGO), in Luanshya's former mine township of Mpatamatu. She painted a ruinous picture of the HIV/AIDS epidemic in Zambia in the early 2000s, one that she linked explicitly to the privatisation of the state-owned Zambia Consolidated Copper Mines (ZCCM). 'Mineworkers never used to save', she added. Her words pointed to a common outsider's critique of the mine's corporate paternalism, and the inertia many believed it generated. Mineworkers had formerly enjoyed comfort and security far beyond that on offer to most Zambians, but they were relatively unprepared for the new conditions they faced with the disappearance of mine company corporate paternalism. When workers were laid off in large numbers, many of Mpatamatu's former mineworkers emigrated in search for a new job. They spread the virus in their new workplaces or brought it back home into their families. The large number of deaths also undermined family structures, leading to a soaring number of child-headed homes. Andrew Kayekesi, the director of the Serve Zambia Foundation, explained to me that in HIV/AIDS work 'you start with one and end up with many'. The combination of the epidemic, unemployment and loss of access to the corporate health facilities posed a devastating situation for the township's population at the time.[1]

Against the background of ZCCM's privatisation and Zambia's HIV/AIDS epidemic, this chapter deals with processes of material and social ruination and renovation in one of Luanshya's former mine townships. Based on the story of the Serve Zambia Foundation, I juxtapose material and social decay with people's private initiative in order to renovate their community. I trace the changing role of the foundation's current headquarters, Mpatamatu's former Section 21 Clinic, in healthcare provision and community formation with the collapse of corporate paternalism. Created as a material manifestation of colonial and corporate paternalist control over mine labourers and their dependants, the Section 21 Clinic also offered mineworkers and their families a level of healthcare provision denied to other Copperbelt residents, and as such became a sign of mineworkers' aspirations and entitlement. Following privatisation, the building of the former Section 21 Clinic became a site of neoliberal abandonment and private initiative.

Based on Stoler and McGranahan's reflections on 'imperial formations' as 'a broader set of practices structured in dominance'[2], Stoler's development of the concept of 'ruination',[3] and Gupta's work on 'renovation' complementing it,[4] I investigate practices of appropriation and reappropriation in the context of Mpatamatu. The establishment of the Copperbelt as an 'extractive space' had been realised through a variety of corporate practices that represented 'polities of dislocation, processes of dispersion, appropriation, and displacement.'[5] These practices were carried out by different agents of the British South Africa Company (BSAC) and were ultimately structured by British colonialism in

---

1   Interview, Serve Zambia Foundation staff member, Mpatamatu, 20 June 2016; interview, Andrew Kayekesi, Mpatamatu, 30 April 2016.
2   Ann Laura Stoler and Carole McGranahan, 'Introduction: Refiguring Imperial Terrains' in Ann Laura Stoler, Carole McGranahan and Peter C. Perdue (eds), *Imperial Formations* (Oxford: James Currey, 2007), pp. 3–44, p. 8.
3   Ann Laura Stoler, 'Imperial Debris: Reflections on Ruins and Ruination', *Cultural Anthropology* 23, 2 (2008), pp. 191–219; 'Introduction "The Rot Remains": From Ruins to Ruination' in Ann Laura Stoler (ed.), *Imperial Debris: On Ruins and Ruination* (Durham NC: Duke University Press, 2013), pp. 1–35; *Duress: Imperial Durabilities in our Times* (Durham NC: Duke University Press 2016), pp. 336–79.
4   Pamila Gupta. *Portuguese Decolonization in the Indian Ocean World: History and Ethnography* (London: Bloomsbury Academic, 2019), pp. 133–5.
5   On 'extractive space', see Tomas Frederiksen, 'Unearthing Rule: Mining, Power and the Political Ecology of Extraction in Colonial Zambia', PhD. Thesis, University of Manchester, 2010, p. 237; Stoler and McGranahan, 'Introduction: Refiguring Imperial Terrains', p. 8.

Southern Africa. This context produced enclosed corporate living environments like Mpatamatu, one of many mine-built townships on the Copperbelt. The trajectory of buildings like Section 21 Clinic reflects the changing
characteristics of such an enclosed living environment. It also illustrates what
this particular material and social environment meant for its residents.

Finally, I show how, amid ruination, private initiative has opened up a
process of local renovation and global reconnection in recent decades. This
process has encompassed the reappropriation of corporate remains, such as
the Section 21 Clinic, resulting in a renewed reference of such buildings
to the township's social context. The transformations in Mpatamatu from
its construction in the late 1950s to my fieldwork in the late 2010s offer
a unique perspective on social change among a mine labour force, on the
industrial history of the Copperbelt in general and the social consequences
of ZCCM's privatisation in particular.

The first part of the chapter is dedicated to the inception of Mpatamatu,
the township's social provisions and the role of former Section 21 Clinic.
I look at the building as a planned health facility within a company town
of a mining corporation. In the second part, I focus on the disintegration
of Mpatamatu as a company town. I consider the consequences of the
separation of the mine's social provisions from its core business of mineral
extraction. Section 21 Clinic became a building left behind, not regarded
as a social investment by the mine anymore but instead as a government
liability. In the final third part, I follow the reappropriation of the building
that was Section 21 Clinic and how it was turned into the headquarters of
the Serve Zambia Foundation. The foundation's story illustrates the renovative practices of people at work, which re-embedded a particular material
building in local social life, reconnected the township with the outside
world through a corporate ruin, and which restructured relationships of
dependence within the former mine township of Mpatamatu.

Colonial and Corporate Control over Bodies

Mpatamatu was initiated by the Roan Antelope Copper Mines (RACM) as
a second mine township for African workers and their dependants in 1958.[6]

---

6   The name 'Mpatamatu' is from Lamba, one of the many Bantu languages spoken
in Zambia: *m-* signifies a location, *-pata* means 'to stick' and *amato* is the plural form
of *ubwato*, 'ship'. The name points to the Mpata Hills west of the township with its
many little seasonal streams, tributaries of the Kafue River on which people travelled
by boat in the past. In the crest (Figure 7.1), Mpatamatu is represented by a man in a

The township was the final corporate extension of Luanshya, a Copperbelt town that was started as a mine camp in the second half of the 1920s. The township was built over a period of twenty years well into the late 1970s. In the beginning, RACM awarded the planning of Mpatamatu to the South African town planning consultants Collings and Schaerer. The first part of the 1957 Development Plan read:

1   The new township, extending westwards from Irwin Shaft and on the southern side of Irwin Shaft and the New [MacLaren] Shaft, is intended to accommodate 3,584 houses for married African employees. The houses are to be single detached units and the prescribed size of a regular plot is 50 feet in frontage and 70 feet deep.

2   The planning must allow division of the residential areas into sections, each section to be in association with its administrative offices, welfare buildings, etc., and each section to have its own water reticulation and electrical systems. Ten sections of 358 houses each are suggested.

3   Provision must be made for Schools, Welfare Halls (i.e. social clubs), Clinics, Sports Fields, Cinema, Beer Halls, Parks, Churches, Trading Sites, and Market, Administration Offices, First Aid Station and Maintenance Workshops.[7]

The first houses in Mpatamatu were occupied in November 1959.[8] In contrast to Luanshya's first African mine township Roan, Mpatamatu was a '"new" company town'.[9] It did not evolve from a mine camp with its makeshift huts for African mineworkers. On the contrary, Mpatamatu was planned in detail on the drawing board. Its location was a direct consequence of the ore extraction underground towards the west, as

boat, hinting at the meaning of the Lamba place name: ZCCM-IH, 11.2.10C Roan-Mpatamatu Mine Township Management Board, 'Invitation Christmas Come-Together Party', 22 December 1978.

7   Zambia Consolidated Copper Mines – Investment Holdings archives (hereafter ZCCM-IH), 21.6.2F, RACM, 'Proposed New African Township: Report on Outline Advisory Development Plan and Detailed Planning of First Portion', April 1957, p. II.

8   In fact, this move was planned for July 1959. However, a handwritten note on the report reads: 'Actual move made in November 1959': ZCCM-IH, 11.2.3D, RACM, 'Social Services at Mpatamatu Township (draft)', 1960, p. 6.

9   See Margaret Crawford, *Building the Workingman's Paradise: The Design of American Company Towns* (London: Verso, 1995), pp. 5, 6–7, 70–75, 151.

Figure 7.1   The coat of arms of the Roan-Mpatamatu mine township. Reproduced by permission, ZCCM-IH archives, Ndola.

depicted on the map in Figure 7.2.[10] The plans by Collings and Schaerer were rooted in the colonial spatial practices of zoning, i.e. the separation of different land uses, and of racial segregation. These practices had already been established within the gold and diamond mining industries of Southern Africa.[11] The self-sustaining character of Mpatamatu was the

10   The plan illustrates the proximity of the African mine townships to the three main shafts and the movement of residential area development with the ore extraction westwards: ZCCM-IH, 12.5.7E, RST Roan Antelope Division, 'Contract CS19 for the Erection of 200 to 325 Houses and Services thereto in Roan and Mpatamatu Townships', June 1964.
11   See Hugh Macmillan, 'Mining, Housing and Welfare in South Africa and Zambia: A Historical View', *Journal of Contemporary African Studies* 30, 4 (2012), pp. 539–50, p. 539; Harri Englund, 'The Village in the City, the City in the Village: Migrants in Lilongwe',

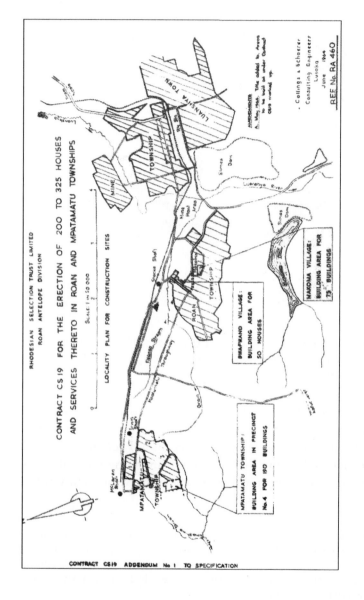

Figure 7.2 1964 'locality plan' showing Mpatamatu's newly constructed Sections 21, 22, 23 and 24 as part of Luanshya's corporate mine townships. Reproduced by permission, ZCCM-IH archives, Ndola.

material realisation of RACM's goal to create an enclosed residential envi-ronment that allowed for the supervision of its African labour force.

The garden-like character of Luanshya's European areas had been already noted before Mpatamatu was built.[12] The city's layout was influenced by the British Garden City movement, however, as Bigon noted on the diffusion of these particular town planning concepts, as an 'anti-social' implementation of the original Howardian idea rooted in the racial residential segregation of colonial Africa.[13] British town-planners promoted the 'garden city' in colonies like Northern Rhodesia especially in the inter-war years, turning colonialism into a 'vehicle' of urban planning models.[14]

On the Copperbelt with its corporate mining settlements, the 'garden city' represented a twofold twin composition: separate government and corporate parts of town with each comprising European and African townships. Following Schumaker,[15] I see a substantial influence of town planning ideas going back to the Garden City movement on Luanshya and more specifically on the plans for Mpatamatu. Figure 7.3 depicts the original 1957 plan for section 21. It includes tree-lined streets, hierarchised roads, alternating house directions, changing street layouts and garden-like playgrounds.[16] Sections 22 and 23 were separated by a park belt. However,

Journal of Southern African Studies 28, 1 (2002), pp. 137–54, p. 140; John Gardiner, 'Some Aspects of the Establishment of Towns in Zambia during the Nineteen Twenties and Thirties', *Zambian Urban Studies* 3 (1970), pp. 1–33, p. 10.

12 Malcolm Watson, malaria expert at the Ross Institute for Tropical Diseases in London, noted that RACM had constructed 'townships laid out like garden cities'. See Malcolm Watson, 'A Conquest of Disease' in Malcom Watson (ed.), *African Highway: The Battle for Health in Central Africa* (London: John Murray, 1953), p. 69.

13 Liora Bigon, 'Garden Cities in Colonial Africa: A Note on Historiography', *Planning Perspectives* 28, 3 (2013), pp. 477–85, pp. 480, 482.

14 Robert Home, 'From Barrack Compounds to the Single-Family House: Planning Worker Housing in Colonial Natal and Northern Rhodesia', *Planning Perspectives* 15, 4 (2000), pp. 327–47, p. 330; A. D. King, 'Exporting Planning: The Colonial and Neo-Colonial Experience' in Gordon E. Cherry (ed.), *Shaping an Urban World* (New York: St Martin's Press, 1980), pp. 203–26, p. 206.

15 Lyn Schumaker, 'The Mosquito Taken at the Beerhall: Malaria Research and Control on Zambia's Copperbelt' in Paul W. Geissler and Catherine Molyneux (eds), *Evidence, Ethos and Experiment* (New York: Berghahn Books, 2011), pp. 403–28, p. 413.

16 This illustrates the self-sustaining character of the township's sections and shows the influence of elements of the Garden City movement in British town planning on Collings and Schaerer's work. Section 21 Clinic was opened in 1959 on the plot originally reserved for a church at the centre of the section: ZCCM-IH, 21.6.2F, drawing number NR.RA2, RACM, 'Proposed New African Township: Report on

these traces of the Garden City movement were only visible in the older sections of Mpatamatu. Budgetary limitations in the 1970s resulted in a rather spartan layout for the township's sections 25, 26 and 27 that were developed later to accommodate labour for the Baluba underground mine.[17]

As the conflict over African unionisation increased in the 1950s, mining companies attempted to prevent the organised mobilisation of the labour force through paternalistic provisions of social welfare.[18] This drew on and extended earlier corporate attempts to use welfare provision to compete with Union Minière du Haut-Katanga (UMHK) in Katanga for experienced mine labour. 'Welfare' is an ambiguous term in this context. The provisions were not acts of charity by the mining companies. They did not represent the materialised Polanyian 'counter-movement' by the colonial government in order to 'check the action of the market'.[19] Rather, these provisions were corporate means of social control. As shown above, point 3 of Collings and Schaerer's development plan explicitly references those social welfare buildings, among them the Section 21 Clinic.

Given this history, in Luanshya, social welfare buildings, except schools and churches, represented a particular type of corporate infrastructure.[20] This infrastructure was planned, constructed and maintained by the mining company. It was preserved in Mpatamatu through many changes in mine ownership, from RACM in colonial days, to the Roan Selection Trust (RST)'s Luanshya Division after Zambia's independence in 1964, and then

---

Outline Advisory Development Plan and Detailed Planning of First Portion', April 1957.

17   The difference becomes quite obvious after a single glance at a map of Mpatamatu, see Open Street Map (OSM), 'Node: Mpatamatu', n.d.: www.openstreetmap.org/node/2567143540 (accessed 2 October 2020). Map data on the township in general and the social welfare buildings in particular was collected by myself during fieldwork and entered into OSM by Erik Falke.

18   See Jane L. Parpart, *Labor and Capital on the African Copperbelt* (Philadelphia: Temple University Press, 1983), pp. 140–43, 152.

19   Karl Polanyi, *The Great Transformation: The Political and Economic Origins of Our Time* (Boston MA: Beacon Press, 2001), pp. 136, 79.

20   My understanding of 'infrastructure' goes back to Larkin's conceptualisation of it as an underlying 'technical system' below (Latin *infra*), see Brian Larkin, *Signal and Noise: Media, Infrastructure, and Urban Culture in Nigeria* (Durham NC: Duke University Press, 2008), p. 5. Moreover, the term allows me to relate it to 'organized practices' in Star and Ruhleder's relational understanding of the term, see Susan L. Star and Karen Ruhleder, 'Steps Toward an Ecology of Infrastructure: Design and Access for Large Information Spaces', *Information Systems Research* 7, 1 (1996), pp. 111–34, p. 113. As such, I use the term to grasp a material network of buildings that was related to corporate practices underlying the social life in a mine township.

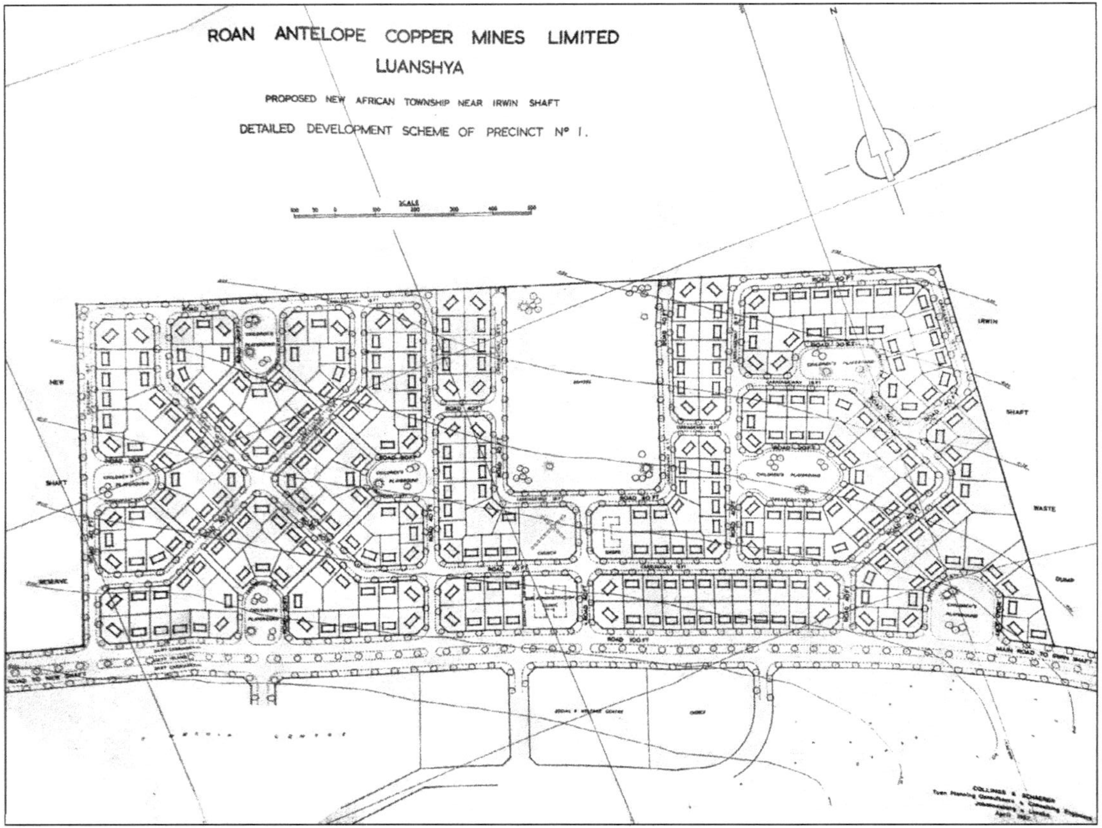

Figure 7.3
1957 plan of
Section 21,
Mpatamatu's
first section.
Reproduced
by permission,
ZCCM-IH
archives, Ndola.

Roan Consolidated Mines (RCM) and ZCCM Luanshya Division after the copper industry's nationalisation in 1969/1970. Four bars, two mine clubs and a sports complex were meant to keep the dominantly male labour force in Mpatamatu occupied after work. Three community centres integrated mineworker's wives and children into the mine structures. Most importantly, first-aid stations and mine clinics monitored the labour force's health and reproduction for the mining company.

The first report of the 'African Welfare Clinic', later Section 21 Clinic, in Mpatamatu that I found in the archives dated to December 1959. It was issued only one month after the first residents had moved into the township. The report registered a total monthly attendance of 158 men, 400 women and 1705 children.[21] Based on Demissie's, Home's and Njoh's understanding of the Foucauldian notion of power translated into built environment,[22] I understand Mpatamatu's social welfare infrastructure as the groundwork of the mine's disciplinary architecture that defined social life in the township. Buildings like Section 21 Clinic provided for 'the controlled insertion of bodies into the machinery of production and the adjustment of phenomena of population to economic processes'.[23] At the same time, the buildings of social welfare represented an aspirational architecture that provided certainty and opportunities. Buildings like Section 21 Clinic were places where mineworkers were born and where they returned for the birth of their children. The quality of the healthcare services was superior to local government clinics. Extended family members living with mine employees could be registered as dependants, expanding corporate health-care far beyond the directly employed household. This particular corporate infrastructure established what Epstein identified as the '"unitary" structure of the mine' during his fieldwork in Luanshya from 1953 to 1954:

> It is important to bear in mind what I may term the 'unitary' structure of the mine. As I have already explained, the mine is a self-contained industrial, residential, and administrative unit. Every employee is housed by the mine, and no African who is a mine employee may live off the

---

21 ZCCM-IH, 12.7.3B, Federation of Rhodesia and Nyasaland Ministry of Health – Northern Rhodesia, 'African Welfare Clinic: Mpatamatu Clinic R.A.C.M. LTD: Report for the Month of December 1959', December 1959.

22 Fassil Demissie, 'In the Shadow of the Gold Mines: Migrancy and Mine Housing in South Africa', *Housing Studies* 13, 4 (1998), pp. 445–69, p. 454; Home, 'From Barrack Compounds to the Single-Family House', p. 327; Ambe J. Njoh, 'Urban Planning as a Tool of Power and Socio-Political Control in Colonial Africa', *Planning Perspectives* 24, 3 (2009), pp. 301–17, p. 302.

23 Michel Foucault, *The Will to Knowledge* (London: Penguin Books, 1998), pp. 140–41.

mine premises. Moreover, until recently, every African was fed by the Company, and the vast majority of the employees continue to draw weekly rations from the Company's Feeding Store. A butchery and a number of other stores enable those who wish to supplement their rations to do so without making a trip to town or the Second Class Trading Area. It is the mine which provides the hospital, and employs the doctors and nurses who care for the sick; and it is the mine, again, which provides for the recreational needs of its employees.[24]

The 'unitary' structure of the mine was a representation of institutionalised corporate paternalism. The mining company did not only employ men as mineworkers but also 'cared for' them after work. It 'cared for' the livelihood of their dependants. The social welfare buildings were one of many 'strategies of inclusion and exclusion'[25] within the fatherly (Latin *paternus*) relationship of the mining company to its labour force. Corporate paternalism on the Copperbelt was built on a shared identity, i.e. being employed by, part of and dependent on the mine. Management and labour force were part of the same 'body' (Latin *corpus*). In biographical interviews with Mpatamatu's residents, it became clear to me, as to Ferguson before, that these 'paternalistic relations of dependence were … central to workers' identities'.[26] I learned how mine employees' identities in Mpatamatu had been informed by a material, social and financial interconnection with the mine before its reprivatisation in 1997.

Boniface Mwanza explained to me how he had not only been a miner under ZCCM's Luanshya Division because he worked as a sampling supervisor. Every major step in his life unfolded within the corporate material provisions: from his birth at Roan Antelope Mine Hospital in 1960 to his consultations as a boy at Mpatamatu's Section 23 Clinic, the housing allocations relative to his pay grade, marital status and family size, to the birth of his first child at the very same Roan Antelope Mine Hospital and the healthcare services provided to his wife and children at Section 25 Clinic. Looking back at this integration of social life and material environment, he recalled: 'The company had a human face.' He told me about the ambulance service available in Mpatamatu and how patient cards were transferred

24 A. L. Epstein, *Politics in an Urban African Community* (Manchester: Manchester University Press, 1958), pp. 123–4.
25 See Günther Schlee, *How Enemies Are Made: Towards a Theory of Ethnic and Religious Conflicts* (New York: Berghahn Books, 2008), pp. 35–42.
26 James Ferguson, 'Declarations of Dependence: Labour, Personhood, and Welfare in Southern Africa', *Journal of the Royal Anthropological Institute* 19 (2013), pp. 223–42, p. 228.

to the nearest clinic from one's mine house. The health facilities followed mineworker families, whenever they were allocated a different house due to changes in work, marital or family status. Boniface Mwanza felt that he and his family were taken care of by the mine.[27]

Most mine employees were men, and mine company policies helped to establish them as successful husbands and fathers, whose families relied on them for access to housing and healthcare. But, as the life of a former typist born in 1964 illustrates, women's employment with the mine could disrupt this gender hierarchy. She had been successful in a secretary course in 1986 and first worked at ZCCM Luanshya Division's General Office before joining the Engineering Department. She was allocated a mine house. When she married, her supervisor made sure her husband was transferred from Nkana to Luanshya Division and not the other way around. 'We were a good team', she remarked. This was an extraordinary move in the male-dominated industry of the time. However, with the birth of her children she retreated to the domestic, albeit still contributing to the household income by tailoring.[28]

Most enduring, however, was the construction of the mineworkers' self-image through the financial dependence on the mine. It generated opportunities that vanished after ZCCM's privatisation. These opportunities were what people missed in general and employees of the new Chinese mine operator in particular. Martin Mulenga, a former accountant at RCM's General Office from 1971 to 1981, first introduced me to what many Zambians consider the economic favouritism towards mineworkers. Mineworkers enjoyed benefits far beyond those available to most Zambians, won through continuous union activism going back to the early days of the mine. Electricity was free, staple food was available at reduced prices, with one 50 kg bag of mealie meal included in the salary.[29] Later, I found its successes to be mirrored in the pay slips I discussed with two of my research participants. 'They were very proud, the miners', the wife noted with a glance at her husband's pay slip. She was a teacher and knew about the tremendous differences in remuneration and privileges.[30] Erik Kazembe, a former mineworker and trade unionist, further unpacked the specificity of the financial interrelationship with the mine for me when we studied the 'deductions' side of the pay slip together: a subsidised rent, a savings

27 Interviews, Boniface Mwanza, Mpatamatu, 28 April and 3 May 2016.
28 Interview, resident of Mpatamatu, Luanshya, 22 September 2016.
29 Interview, Martin Mulenga, Mpatamatu, 13 July 2016.
30 Interview, residents of Mpatamatu, Mpatamatu, 4 August 2016.

scheme, a loan scheme and additional subsidised mealie meal rations on top of the company's free 'mealie meal assistance' mentioned above.[31] These possibilities left their mark and helped construct an identity around mine employees and their entitlements.

The material, social and financial relationships of dependence illustrated above were exclusive to mineworkers and their dependants. African mineworkers, however, did not have access to the same level of service as did their European managers. Both groups were part of the same 'corpus', but in different hierarchical positions marked by job title, remuneration, residence, healthcare services and recreational activities. African mineworkers were simultaneously included based on corporate sameness and excluded based on racial difference. As such, corporate paternalism lived off a hierarchical power difference structuring the entire corporation based on the colour bar.

Until the nationalisation of Zambia's copper industry, substantial promotion opportunities were out of most African mineworkers' reach rendering job positions with major decision-making capacities unattainable.[32] Even without a colour bar, promotion was only available to a few African workers as the number of higher paid, skilled jobs in the industry was low. Furthermore, real-term salaries for unskilled jobs did not rise sufficiently after Zambia's independence in 1964 to meet mineworker expectations. The racial divide going back to the colour bar is still reflected in the Copperbelt's spatial population distribution today. In fact, the colonial order has been revived by companies with an expatriate labour force. Socio-economic differences between Zambians and the migrant workforce from Europe, North America and Asia are mapped onto former colonial definitions of European and African parts of Copperbelt towns.

Section 21 Clinic was at the centre of the mine's paternalist infrastructure in Mpatamatu. It was the primary health facility for residents of sections 21 and 22: sick mineworkers visited the clinic off shift, their wives and children could access care using a mineworker's identification number, pregnant women were looked after and children were born, clinic staff vaccinated township residents and launched public health campaigns against parasites, malaria and tuberculosis. The clinic service

---

31 Interview, Erik Kazembe, Luanshya, 20 September 2016.
32 Michael Burawoy concluded that the process of Zambianisation in the post-independence years of the copper industry remained ineffective: Michael Burawoy, *The Colour of Class on the Copper Mines: From African Advancement to Zambianization* (Manchester: Manchester University Press, 1971), p. 114.

for mineworkers' wives, e.g. nutrition programmes,[33] was integrated with the provisions at the 'women welfare centres'.

Clinics had been among the first corporate welfare buildings in the Copperbelt mine townships. The health of mine labour was crucial for production and its supervision part of employment relations right from the start. After the reprivatisation of Zambia's copper industry and the neoliberal restructuring of the sector, clinics remained among the few social welfare provisions that, although selectively, continued to be run by the mines. They are the relics of corporate paternalism, now termed corporate social responsibility measures, within the mining companies of today.

Corporate Abandonment and Ruination

Against the background of neoliberal reform propagated by the World Bank and the International Monetary Fund (IMF), the Zambian Government was forced to privatise the state-owned company ZCCM from 1997 onwards. [34] The process resulted in a gradual retreat of mining companies from particular material sites and infrastructures that were external to the site of production: from entire townships with their residential houses, roads, water pipes and power supply lines to health, leisure and sports facilities. ZCCM's multinational successor companies refocused on the mines as exclusive sites of mineral extraction. As in many other places on the Copperbelt, the presence of the mine in Mpatamatu went from 'socially thick' to 'socially thin'.[35]

The social welfare infrastructure was abandoned and no longer considered part of the corporation. This was despite the fact that the so-called development agreements, which legalised the transfer of ZCCM's divisions from public into private management, explicitly stated that the successor companies 'assumed ownership, operational control and responsibility for the social assets connected to the mine'.[36] However, investors primarily

---

33 ZCCM-IH, 11.3.5B, 'Community Development Report', March 1970.
34 For details on ZCCM's privatisation process, see John Craig, 'Putting Privatisation into Practice: the Case of Zambia Consolidated Copper Mines Limited', *Journal of Modern African Studies* 39, 3 (2001), pp. 389–410.
35 James Ferguson, *Global Shadows: Africa in the Neoliberal World Order* (Durham NC, Duke University Press, 2006), pp. 35–6.
36 Quoted from the development agreement between the Government of the Republic of Zambia and Roan Antelope Copper Mining Corporation of Zambia (RAMCOZ), see RAID, *Zambia, Deregulation and the Denial of Human Rights: Submission to the Committee on Economic, Social and Cultural Rights* (Oxford, 2000), p. 188, based on Clifford Chance,

sought to generate capital on a short-term basis from copper production. They did not want to continue the mines as sites of social existence and to finance infrastructures unrelated to the production process. Based on Larmer's work in Luanshya and a Rights and Accountability in Development (RAID) report on the consequences of ZCCM's break up,[37] Gewald and Soeters came to the following conclusion concerning the reprivatisation of Luanshya's mine: 'Through the relentless pursuit of profit for investment capital, the liberalization and privatization of the mines has led to the destruction of the social structure of the mines, not only in Luanshya/Baluba but more generally.'[38]

Luanshya and Mpatamatu, the residential township of the majority of Baluba mineworkers, deserve particular attention in this process of 'the destruction of the social structure of the mines'. First, the mine in Luanshya was one of the oldest on the Copperbelt and the first to be sold. It had an extensive social welfare infrastructure. Its reprivatisation, and its management in the following years had an impact on corporate behaviour at other mines. Second, the reprivatisation process was overshadowed by corruption charges. ZCCM's Privatisation Negotiation Team, headed by Francis Kaunda (not related to the former President Kenneth Kaunda), awarded the sale of Luanshya Division to Binani Industries. This company was a scrap metal dealer inexperienced in copper mining. It had not conducted underground studies at the mine in Luanshya. Third, as noted above, the development agreements transferred the ownership, control and responsibility for the social welfare buildings to private transnational corporations and their local subsidiaries. The new neoliberal mode of production with its far-reaching cost-cutting measures reduced the mine's social assets to the status of being 'redundant' in Bauman's terms: 'supernumerary, unneeded, of no use'.[39] Only one year after the sale of ZCCM's Luanshya Division, it was clear that the social welfare buildings' maintenance would be permanently

---

'Development Agreement: The Government of the Republic of Zambia and Roan Antelope Mining Corporation of Zambia plc' (London, 1997), pp. 17–20, courtesy of RAID.

37 See Miles Larmer, 'Reaction and Resistance to Neo-liberalism in Zambia', *Review of African Political Economy* 32, 103 (2005), 29–45; RAID, *Zambia, Deregulation and the Denial of Human Rights*.

38 Jan-Bart Gewald and Sebastiaan Soeters, 'African Miners and Shape-Shifting Capital Flight: The Case of Luanshya/Baluba', in Alistair Fraser and Miles Larmer (eds), *Zambia, Mining, and Neoliberalism: Boom and Bust on the Globalized Copperbelt* (New York: Palgrave Macmillan 2010), pp. 155–83, p. 165.

39 Zygmunt Bauman, *Wasted Lives: Modernity and its Outcasts* (Cambridge: Polity Press, 2008), p. 12.

discontinued. Mpatamatu became the scene of civil unrest culminating in protesters fighting with the local mine police forces in 1998.[40]

Binani Industry's subsidiary Roan Antelope Copper Mining Corporation of Zambia (RAMCOZ) used several clauses in the development agreement to avoid a direct engagement with the social assets connected to the mine. They contracted out the management of the social welfare facilities. This accelerated the abandonment of this particular corporate infrastructure, a practice that had already started under ZCCM,[41] and was continued after RAMCOZ went bankrupt in 2000 and the mine's management was taken over first by a private and then a government receiver. When the mine was resold in 2003, the majority of the mine's social assets remained with RAMCOZ in receivership and were not transferred to the new operator Luanshya Copper Mines (LCM). This legal position downgraded the buildings from an integral part of the mine to a government liability separated from it. Consequently, the buildings were legally detached from the company operating the mine. This separation, as Fraser and Lungu retraced, caused the unitary structure of the Copperbelt mines to collapse:

> ZCCM provided almost everything that held society together in the Copperbelt: jobs, hospitals, schools, housing, and a wide range of social services including HIV-AIDS and malaria awareness and prevention programmes. Towards the end of the ZCCM era, much of this effort was collapsing. The new investors have made little effort to pick up these responsibilities. They are clear that their 'core business' is mining, and that the provision of social infrastructure goes beyond this remit. According to free-market ideology, and the Development Agreements, these goods and services should now be provided either by the local authorities or by market forces.[42]

The break up of ZCCM completely redefined Mpatamatu. From an integrated urban mine township with corporate provisions, a company town directly linked to the extraction of copper and with little involvement by the government, Mpatamatu gradually dissolved into a disconnected settlement. Its inhabitants lost the 'way of life' they had practised under ZCCM and their living environment became marked by what Patience Mususa has described as 'villagisation'. For Mususa, considering villagisation is a way

---

40   RAID, *Zambia, Deregulation and the Denial of Human Rights*, pp. 154, 184.
41   See ZCCM-IH, 12.8.9F, ZCCM, 'Leasing of Mine Taverns', 27 February 1985.
42   Alastair Fraser and John Lungu, *For Whom the Windfalls? Winners & Losers in the Privatisation of Zambia's Copper Mines* (Lusaka: Civil Society Trade Network of Zambia, 2007), p. 4.

of 'thinking about place regardless of how it is *politically* categorised (urban or rural), [focusing] much more on what a place affords its inhabitants, and the affective experiences it generates.'[43] Mpatamatu became a detached part of the municipality of Luanshya, full of abandoned corporate remains, with insufficient government involvement to make up for what the company no longer provided.

For Mpatamatu's unemployed, day labourers, farmers and government workers, practices of subsistence, consumption and existence rooted in rural life regained prominence. Laurence Banda, a former mineworker under RCM, ZCCM and RAMCOZ and a community health worker at Section 26 Clinic at the time of my fieldwork, exclaimed: 'The only hope we have is going into the bush!'[44] Based on my further observations, I would add: 'As well as bringing the bush to Mpatamatu!' The situation was dramatic as these practices happened in a context of a lost urbanity formerly provided by the mine operators: vegetable and maize farming where once groceries were home delivered, water procurement from wells to houses that had once running water, cooking on charcoal with *imbaula* braziers where once electric stoves were used to prepare meals.

Mpatamatu's residents experienced a process of being disconnected from important points of reference: the mines, its labour force, its townships and its global mining community. Ferguson had earlier termed this experience 'abjection' and defined it as a 'process of being thrown aside, expelled, or discarded'.[45] Mineworkers and their families lost access to buildings like Section 21 Clinic. Simultaneously, these buildings lost the people who worked at them, maintained them and used them in their everyday lives. Wisdom Zulu, who had joined the Civil Engineering Department of ZCCM's Luanshya Division in 1991, recalled how he carried out regular maintenance measures at buildings like Section 21 Clinic. This corporate investment in the social welfare

---

43 Patience Mususa, 'There used to be order: Life on the Copperbelt After the Privatisation of the Zambia Consolidated Copper Mines', PhD. Thesis, University of Cape Town, 2014, pp. 31, 38. Devisch first defined 'villagisation' in his work on Kinshasa in the 1970s as 'a process of psychic and social endogenisation of modern city life, thus allowing the migrant to surmount the schizophrenic split between the traditional, rural and "pagan" life as against the new urban, Christian world'. René Devisch, '"Pillaging Jesus": Healing Churches and the Villagisation of Kinshasa', *Africa: Journal of the International African Institute* 66, 4 (1996), pp. 555–86, p. 573.

44 Interview, Laurence Banda, Mpatamatu, 21 September 2016.

45 James Ferguson, *Expectations of Modernity: Myths and Meanings of Urban Life on the Zambian Copperbelt* (Berkeley: University of California Press, 1999), p. 236.

buildings was discontinued with RAMCOZ.[46] The social welfare buildings lost their social role for the mining community and became corporate debris in a township abandoned by the mine.

Stoler conceptualised the 'corrosive process' emanating from a ruinous material site in what she termed 'ruination'. The concept provided a tool to catch the 'material and social afterlife of structures, sensibilities and things' while at the same time shifting the focus 'not on inert remains but on their vital refiguration'.[47] I observed this 'vital refiguration' in manifold ways in Mpatamatu. However, the refiguring practices were very distinct from the material and social ruination around them. They were creative. Stoler has pointed to ruins as 'epicentres' of human actions,[48] however, she still framed their *creative* refiguration under the concept of 'ruination' and a corrosive process.

Based on her study of the reappropriation of leisured spaces in post-colonial Beira (Mozambique), Gupta came to understand people's actions as 'distinct forms of renovation amidst ruination.'[49] Similarly, Mpatamatu's abandoned social welfare buildings represented sites of resourcefulness. Gupta rooted the concept of 'renovation' in the capacity of people to creatively tinker with their material environment and its twofold form of expression by being reviving and restorative. 'Renovation' described a reappropriation of buildings for both new and old usages. In this sense, Gupta's exploration into renovative practices possessed the same multi-temporal dimension that Stoler saw in 'ruination' as a process of abandonment, decay and refiguration.[50] This chapter mainly focuses on Serve Zambia Foundation's headquarters, Section 21 Clinic. The building's current usage represents one of the many ways in which the mine's former social welfare buildings in general and the mine clinics in particular have been reappropriated. Interestingly, the developments at Mpatamatu's four mine clinics (Section 21, Section 23, Section 25 and Section 26 Clinics) represent the three main trajectories of the township's social welfare buildings after the reprivatisation of the mine: (i) continuation as a corporate facility; (ii) takeover by the government; and (iii) reappropriation by private companies and individuals. Therefore, I would like to put the story of Section 21 Clinic into the broader context of Mpatamatu's other three former mine

46   Interview, Wisdom Zulu, Mpatamatu, 18 September 2016.
47   Stoler, 'Imperial Debris', p. 194.
48   Ibid., p. 198.
49   Gupta. *Portuguese Decolonization in the Indian Ocean World*, p. 135.
50   Ibid., pp. 129–30, 133–4.

Figure 7.4   Photo, 'Welcome to half China'. Photograph by the author, 30 September 2016.

clinics. Private initiative, let alone joint community action, was only one of many ways how these buildings were reappropriated after the mine stopped maintaining a social welfare infrastructure.

Section 23 Clinic is now the only mine clinic in Mpatamatu. At the time of my fieldwork, it was managed by China Nonferrous Metal Mining (Group) Corporation's (CNMC) subsidiary CNMC Luanshya Copper Mines (LCM). The Chinese state-owned company had taken over the mine in 2009. While in the past mine health facilities in Mpatamatu were superior to the single government clinic, they were now considered substandard and mine employees preferred the services of the government clinics. In conversations with me about the last remaining corporate health facility of the township, residents frequently noted Section 23 Clinic's dilapidated state. During the time of my fieldwork, LCM's corporate social responsibility programme was invisible in Mpatamatu as possibly indicated by the street writing in Figure 7.4.[51]

---

51 In 2009, Luanshya's mine was taken over by China Nonferrous Metal Mining Corporation (CNMC)'s subsidiary CNMC Luanshya Copper Mines (LCM). The author of the phrase 'Welcome to half China' on the intersection of Kalulu and Kolwe Street between Sections 23 and 24 must have wondered what the Chinese management meant for the township of Mpatamatu.

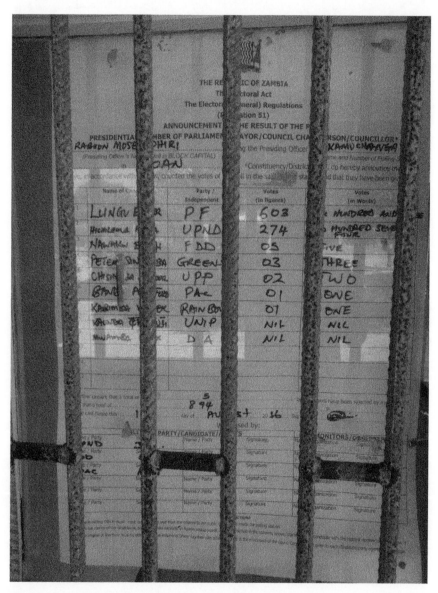

Figure 7.5 Photo of Section 25 clinic as polling station. Photograph by the author, 2 September 2016.

Section 26 Clinic has become the central government health facility for the entire township of Mpatamatu. The Ministry of Health took it over in 2008. The clinic offered 24-hour services including vaccinations, family planning, deliveries, HIV testing, antiretroviral therapy and an outpatient desk. According to a clinic staff member, respiratory tract infections, diarrhoea, malaria and HIV/AIDS were the main health challenges.[52] Section 26 Clinic's importance to the township's inhabitants has increased not only because of the relatively good service quality but also, and importantly, because the share of mine employees among Mpatamatu's residents dropped significantly since the mass retrenchments in the early 2000s. Consequently, more and more people from all sections of Mpatamatu were not entitled to use mine facilities, and thus became reliant on the government clinic for healthcare.

Section 25 Clinic was first rented out by RAMCOZ in receivership from the early 2000s until the early 2010s. In 2015, when it was taken over by the Ministry of Health, the clinic was extended and renovated. It stood idle most of the time during my fieldwork in Mpatamatu in 2016. However, it was used as a polling station during the 2016 presidential elections as depicted in Figure 7.5.[53] Eventually, it reopened as a government clinic in 2018.[54] What becomes clear from the trajectories of these three clinics is that mine company health facilities both declined in quality in the township, and became accessible to far fewer of Mpatamatu's residents, increasing the importance of government healthcare facilities. This development contributed to the changing character of Mpatamatu from a corporate to a municipal township.

---

52 Interview, Section 26 clinic staff member, Mpatamatu, 9 May 2016.
53 The building of Section 25 Clinic was used by the Serve Zambia Foundation for medical services from the early 2000s until 2015. After the takeover of the Ministry of Health, the building was extended and renovated. It stood idle during the largest part of my fieldwork. However, it was used as a polling station during the presidential elections on 11 August 2016, and reopened in 2018.
54 Field notes by author, 11 August 2016. See also United Nations Children's Emergency Fund Eastern and Southern Africa, 'MDGi Hands Over Four Refurbished Copperbelt Health Facilities to Ministry of Health', 5 June 2017, www.unicef.org/zambia/press-releases/mdgi-hands-over-four-refurbished-health-centres-ministry-health-lusaka-and (accessed 21 June 2020).

Local Renovation and Global Reconnection

Section 21 Clinic, Mpatamatu's first and oldest of the four mine clinics, followed the third trajectory: private reappropriation. Following RAMCOZ's bankruptcy, the clinic remained in the hands of the receiver. In 2000, Andrew Kayekesi started to rent the building for the Serve Zambia Foundation. The early years of the NGO, in the late 1990s and early 2000s, were marked by the consequences of ZCCM's privatisation coupled with Zambia's HIV/AIDS epidemic. The foundation, which had started to extend the urban health services of Mpatamatu to surrounding peri-urban and rural areas, quickly found itself at the forefront of the fight against the local ramifications of HIV/AIDS. Section 21 Clinic became the headquarters for this endeavour.

In 1997, when Luanshya's mine was sold to Binani Industries and taken over by RAMCOZ, Andrew Kayekesi was working as a pastor in Mpatamatu. He observed the deteriorating health situation in the township. He was also aware of the consequences this would have for the areas around Mpatamatu. His occupational background was in nursing, so he started 'Mpatamatu Home Based Care' at a time when the central health infrastructure in the township was falling apart. The mine no longer sustained a community around central paternalist provision. Andrew Kayekesi's aim was to overcome the healthcare divide that had been established and maintained by the mine during the colonial and state-owned era. During this period, there were relatively good urban health facilities for mineworkers and their dependants in corporate mine townships like Mpatamatu, but had been little or no health service available in areas close to but outside the mine townships. Andrew Kayekesi started his work in the Mpata Hills west of the township. With a mobile clinic that he manned together with volunteers, and supported by collaborations with regional hospitals, he tried to address rural health challenges and keep up health services in Mpatamatu.

With the HIV/AIDS epidemic spreading, Andrew Kayekesi formally registered his undertaking and founded the Serve Zambia Foundation in 2000. The foundation trained community volunteers in order to enable people to support each other. When more and more parents died and the number of child-headed homes rose, he started a child care programme. He wanted to teach children concrete skills in order to secure their livelihoods in the future. The focus on skill training, long established with mining companies in the Copperbelt and represented by the mine's crafts school in Luanshya, led to the foundation of the Mpatamatu Business and Technical College, an institution affiliated with the Serve Zambia Foundation. The college offered classes in auto mechanics, tailoring, bricklaying, plastering, metal fabrication and computer usage.

From the initiative in skills training, the Serve Zambia Foundation extended its work into household food security. It started to provide families with seeds, fertilisers and small livestock. It started its own farm. The focus on food illustrated how much life for Mpatamatu's residents had changed. They had been urban consumers, who now did not even have the money to buy mealie meal. They had to grow their own crops and bring the maize to a local mill or pound it manually. Subsistence agriculture had always been the back-up strategy for food purchases based on mine wage labour in times of crisis, but its importance to family survival strategies increased dramatically during this period.[55]

Andrew Kayekesi and the Serve Zambia Foundation increasingly took over the provision of services formerly offered by the mine. When the formerly corporate pipes bringing water into Mpatamatu were mismanaged under the private successor company, the foundation drilled bore holes for residents to procure water. From 2009 to 2010, Andrew Kayekesi was the mayor of Luanshya. He witnessed the ongoing dependence of his town's municipal budget on the operation of the mine, and so attempted to work with LCM to improve township facilities. In particular, he considered youth activities to be crucial, and was convinced that when sports was on the decline, the youth was on the decline. Unfortunately, I learned that LCM ceased its financial commitment to Mpatamatu's local football club shortly afterwards, in 2012.[56] Kayekesi's political engagement gradually increased and he ran, unsuccessfully, for the office of the local Member of Parliament in the 2016 presidential elections.

The Serve Zambia Foundation is financed with the help of churches overseas. As Andrew Kayekesi stated, 'NGOs come, NGOs go, but the

---

55 These 'rural' practices had always been part of Copperbelt town life crosscutting the rural-urban divide; see Hortense Powdermaker, *Copper Town: Changing Africa* (New York: Harper & Row, 1962), p. 124; Jane Parpart, 'The Household and the Mine Shaft: Gender and Class Struggle on the Zambian Copperbelt, 1926–64' *Journal of Southern African Studies* 13, 1 (1986), pp. 36–56, p. 48; and Iva Peša, 'Crops and Copper: Agriculture and Urbanism on the Central African Copperbelt, 1950–2000' *Journal of Southern African Studies* 46, 3 (2020), pp. 527–45.

56 Interview, Secretary of Mpatamatu United Football Club, Mpatamatu, 15 June 2016. For more on the relationship between football clubs and Copperbelt mining companies, see Chipande, Chapter 4.

Figure 7.6   Photo of Section 21 clinic. Photograph by the author,
12 July 2016.

church stays'.[57] Mpatamatu was home to several churches. Very similar to
Haynes' field site in Kitwe, the largest congregations belong to groups
established by missionaries: the Catholic and Seventh Day Adventist
churches, and the United Church of Zambia. Other Christian groups
such as the Baptist and Dutch Reformed Church as well as Jehovah's
Witnesses are also present. Moreover, there are more than a dozen Pentecostal groups.[58] This explains why so many of the foundation's projects
addressed church communities. Although they had been present under
ZCCM and before, these communities were relegated to a place under
the corporate community established and maintained by the mine. The
collapse of the corporate community brought forward underlying mechanisms of community building emanating from Christian congregations.

57 Andrew Kayekesi interview.
58 See Naomi Haynes, *Moving By the Spirit: Pentecostal Social Life on the Zambian
Copperbelt* (Oakland: University of California Press, 2017), p. 29. I mapped Mpatamatu's church buildings during fieldwork, see Open Street Map (OSM), 'Node:
Mpatamatu', www.openstreetmap.org/node/2567143540, accessed 2 October
2020.

The Serve Zambia Foundation put Mpatamatu back on the map for people in and outside Luanshya. During one of my many walks across the township, I was asked: 'Are you with Mr Kayekesi?' Foreigners were associated with him, as he confirmed later, because of his many international acquaintances and donors.[59] Back in conversation with the staff member of Serve Zambia Foundation, she introduced me to the foundation's current projects. They were all administered from the building of the former Section 21 Clinic (Figure 7.6).[60]

However, this particular site of renovation was surrounded by ruined materiality. The tarmac of the road leading to the clinic was potholed, street lights broken and dysfunctional. The plot next to the foundation, which seemed to have been never developed, was full of dirt-filled grass, criss-crossed by foot paths. The neighbouring Mpatamatu Primary School, originally founded in 1959 as a 'government school for natives',[61] was in a dire state. No major renovations had taken place since its construction. The former Section 21 Housing Office opposite the clinic stood idle. A housekeeper dozed in front of its door. After ZCCM's privatisation, it first had been rented out and later sold to Bayport Financial Services. After the closure of the underground mine at Baluba in September 2015, the branch office was placed under maintenance.[62] The surrounding former mine houses were marked by shattered walls and patched roofs, showing obvious signs of material decay, mirroring the limited economic means of their now private owners and tenants.

The staff member emphasised that 'the only thing we really do here [i.e. in the sense of a community service] is the computer lab'. It was used by students who were trained at the Mpatamatu Business and Technical College. This assessment was far too humble. In the reception area day-to-day work was coordinated and volunteers instructed. A secretary in Andrew Kayekesi's office communicated with local, national and international partners. Posters on the walls graphically put the foundation into a network ranging from North American to European church organisations. Behind another door a tailoring workshop hid. Two staff members produced clothing for sale and

---

59 Field notes by author, 4 June 2016.
60 The Section 21 Clinic is close to the main road leading into Mpatamatu. At the time of fieldwork, the building was used as the headquarters of the Serve Zambia Foundation. The porch and area in front of the main entrance was used for meetings and group activities.
61 Interview, teacher at Mpatamatu Primary School, Mpatamatu, 9 August 2016.
62 Interview, Bayport Financial Services Luanshya Office Staff, Luanshya, 5 May 2016.

school uniforms to equip children that were supported by the foundation. The porch and area in front of the main entrance was used for meetings and group activities. The plot and building teemed with activity.

In a church networking project, the foundation helped to raise awareness for orphans and vulnerable children, youth and people with HIV/AIDS among other church communities. Its aim was to mobilise communities to address these issues. Many people in Mpatamatu were 'positive', as a nurse put it. The project was funded by the US-American non-denominational megachurch Willow Creek Community Church. In the 'Project Addressing Problems Affecting Child-Headed Homes' supported by the Finland Swedish Baptist Union, the foundation specifically worked with double orphans (both parents deceased). The project involved 350 households in Mpatamatu. It focused on food security and education for the affected children. Foundation staff would go out, visit homes, coordinate with the grandparent generation, offer psycho-social support, and assistance with school fees, books and uniforms. In conversations with different head teachers at Mpatamatu's schools, the Serve Zambia Foundation frequently came up as sponsor of particular students.

The third project 'Expanded Church Response to HIV' dealt further with how church communities could respond to HIV/AIDS. The programme was funded by USAID through the Zambia Family (ZAMFAM) project. Orphans and vulnerable children were the main target group. Among them, sexual abuse cases had been common. Orphans in their desperation, explained the staff member to me, tried to generate an income through the sale of their bodies. Generally, the situation had improved when looking back to the early days of the Serve Zambia Foundation. Awareness campaigns had increased people's understanding of HIV/AIDS. The availability of antiretroviral therapy and T-cell tests in the township made life possible with the virus.[63]

From a building left behind by the mine, Section 21 Clinic became the headquarters of a local NGO with projects funded by international donors. Andrew Kayekesi and Serve Zambia Foundation's staff members and volunteers revived the building with new usages such as the computer lab or a tailoring workshop. At the same time, the foundation restored past uses of the building by offering medical services and using it as the administrative office of home-based care projects in Mpatamatu. The space of the building gave people engaged with the community the possibility to react to the needs of Mpatamatu's residents.

---

63   Serve Zambia Foundation staff member interview.

In view of Mpatamatu's transformation after ZCCM's privatisation, the Serve Zambia Foundation worked to fill the void left behind by the state-owned company. Its work reconnected the building with the community and facilitated a new social role for former Section 21 Clinic. An abandoned material structure was brought back into community service. The private initiative behind the foundation had turned around the direction of social embeddedness of the former corporate social welfare building. From a material manifestation of top-down corporate social control and exclusive healthcare provision in service of an entire bounded community, the building became the headquarters of a small-scale bottom-up renovation project seeking to provide healthcare to the poorest and most marginalised households of Mpatamatu as a whole. As such, the building of former Section 21 Clinic has 'reacted' to the tremendous social and economic changes in the township through the work of the Serve Zambia Foundation.

Conclusion

Mpatamatu existed as a company town for 40 years under the corporate paternalism of the Luanshya mine. During this time, the welfare buildings underlying the social order of the township both provided the means for social control by the mine and manifested a type of dependence that created opportunity for the labour force and its dependants. When the direct connection to the mine through a shared corporate identity collapsed, things fell apart. A holistic system of different types of infrastructure disintegrated, from the residential mine houses to the electricity supplying the bulbs in their rooms. Mpatamatu became diversified. The township on the forefront of copper extraction became the municipal outpost of Luanshya. Water and power supply lines were privatised. The buildings that had made up Mpatamatu's social infrastructure turned into individual corporate remains. They were disconnected and became reconnected in a new way.

The Serve Zambia Foundation took over one of the corporate ruins in Mpatamatu. Its initiative first brought healthcare to homes, decentralising health services in the township. The abandoned Section 21 Clinic gave the foundation the opportunity to centralise its operations and professionalise its work. The foundation adapted the building to its projects and activities. Simultaneously, its focus on health issues revived the previous function of the building within the community. The restructured social embeddedness of Section 21 Clinic both catered to past aspirations under corporate paternalism, to present health issues within the community and to future challenges caused by the reprivatisation of Zambia's copper industry and

HIV/AIDS epidemic.

The local renovation at Section 21 Clinic resulted in a global reconnection of Mpatamatu. The process countered the 'global disconnect' caused by 'abjection',[64] through a different type of incorporation. The work of the Serve Zambia Foundation attracted the attention of other church organisations in Zambia and overseas. Cooperation partners visited the township and brought back a picture of the situation in Mpatamatu. This enabled new financial inflows in forms of donations and a knowledge transfer on faith-based community service.

Andrew Kayekesi's political commitment connected the situation in Mpatamatu with the political decision-making processes in Luanshya and Lusaka. Through its home-based care work, the foundation created new relations of constructive dependence. They offered Mpatamatu's residents new opportunities and a new sense of belonging. In contrast to the times of corporate paternalism, these new relationships of dependence grew out of a bottom-up initiative. The Serve Zambia Foundation had been founded at a time when its staff members and volunteers had to attend to a dramatic number of deaths and far-reaching social decline in the community of Mpatamatu. Built on the material remains of the corporate paternalism that once created and maintained the township, the foundation created something new that integrated a past image of Mpatamatu, the present material environment and the future aspirations of its residents.

---

64   Ferguson, *Expectations of Modernity*, pp. 234–54.

8

From a Colonial to a Mineral Flow Regime: The Mineral Trade and the Inertia of Global Infrastructures in the Copperbelt

HÉLÈNE BLASZKIEWICZ

Introduction

International financial institutions' reports on Africa's international trade and economic development have highlighted how slow and costly it is to move goods across the continent. Numerous World Bank reports, for instance, state that economic and social development in Africa today requires improved conditions for commercial traffic, including transport infrastructures, delays at the border, the quality of logistics services and public corruption, among others.[1] Efficient logistics, in the form of fast and profitable commercial flows on a global scale, seems to have replaced industrial reforms and agricultural progress in the discourses of development,[2] notably after the 2008 financial

---

1   Jean-François Arvis, Gaël Raballand and Jean-François Marteau, *The Cost of Being Landlocked: Logistics Costs and Supply Chain Reliability*, Directions in Development – Trade (Washington DC: World Bank, 2010); Jean-François Arvis, Lauri Ojala, Christina Wiederer, Ben Shepherd, Anasuya Raj, Karlygash Dairabayeva and Tuomas Kiiski, *Connecting to Compete* (Washington DC: World Bank, 2018); Sanjeev Gupta and Yongzheng Yang, 'Unblocking Trade', *Finance and Development (International Monetary Fund)* 43, 4 (2006); Supee Teravaninthorn and Gaël Raballand, 'Transport Prices and Costs in Africa: A Review of the International Corridors' (Washington DC: The International Bank for Reconstruction and Development / World Bank, 2009).
2   Deborah Cowen, *The Deadly Life of Logistics: Mapping Violence in Global Trade* (Minneapolis: University of Minnesota Press, 2014), p. 56; Stefan Ouma and Julian Stenmanns, 'The New Zones of Circulation: On the Production and Securitisation of Maritime Frontiers in West Africa' in Thomas Birtchnell, Satya Savitzky and John Urry (eds), *Cargomobilities: Moving Materials in a Global Age* (London: Routledge, 2015), pp. 87–105, p. 88.

crisis.[3] Logistics has become one of the new modernity tropes impacting the African continent, bringing to the fore the need for fast, easy and secure commercial traffic. But the diagnosis of inefficiency, slowness and frictions usually characterising African logistics does not seem to be true for flows of strategic minerals, like copper and cobalt from the Copperbelt region. Today, it takes less than ten days for a 33-tonne truck filled with copper to travel from a Congolese mine to a South African export port and back to the mine loaded with chemicals used in mineral refining – ten days to travel 6,000 km of roads in diverse conditions and cross three major border posts (Kasumbalesa, Chirundu and Beit Bridge) not once but twice, as well as dense cities like Lubumbashi and Lusaka. The ease with which a copper truck runs through the Copperbelt and crosses borders demonstrates the efficiency of the region's infrastructures and logistics. The Copperbelt territory has been organised to serve the exploitation and exporting of minerals since the era of colonisation. Today, this organisation still benefits these specific commercial flows. The movement of all the other commodities in the region – maize, cement, consumer goods, electrical appliances and frozen fish – have had to adapt to the rhythms and geographies of the mineral trade and endure the dominance of copper convoys in the spaces and temporalities of circulation.[4]

This adaptation highlights how different types of commodities move in different ways in the Copperbelt, depending on their nature and the constellations of actors mobilised around them to animate, control, evaluate or tax them. Some commercial flows, like those of the Copperbelt's strategic minerals on which this chapter will focus, are prioritised. They have access to a series of infrastructures that are material (e.g. roads, one-stop border posts etc.) and immaterial or 'soft'[5] (e.g. laws, contracts, IT systems, standards, etc.) that make them easier and faster. Others that do not have access to such technologies are experiencing more delays and friction. The inequality in the distribution of opportunities for and/or constraints on executing different types of movements enabled me to identify different

---

3   Seth Schindler and Miguel J. Kanai, 'Getting the Territory Right: Infrastructure-Led Development and the Re-Emergence of Spatial Planning Strategies', *Regional Studies*, Online First (2019).

4   Rita Kesselring, 'At an Extractive Pace: Conflicting Temporalities in a Resettlement Process in Solwezi, Zambia', *The Extractive Industries and Society* 5, 2 (2018), pp. 237–44.

5   Cowen, *The Deadly Life of Logistics*, p. 65.

flow regimes in the Copperbelt.[6] Copper, cobalt, their mineral by-products and all the chemicals used to extract and refine them (lime, sulphuric acid, magnesium etc.) are commodities whose movements are commonly organised by a regime emphasising efficiency, speed and fluidity. The specificity of the Copperbelt's mineral flow regime is twofold. First, the infrastructures supporting it date back to the era of colonisation.[7] Second, these infrastructures were established concurrently by public and private actors, and were deeply influenced by the interests of certain key private companies.

This chapter will focus on the effects that such infrastructures have had on the formation of the Copperbelt territory and on the organisation of commercial traffic. Based on a year-long ethnographic fieldwork in the trade and logistics industry in the Copperbelt, mostly in Zambia, this chapter aims to shift the focus away from mining exploitation to the issue of transport and infrastructure. It draws on 91 semi-structured interviews conducted in the trade and policy sectors between 2016 and 2018, as well as a three-month participant observation in a major logistics company active in both Zambia and the Democratic Republic of the Congo (DRC). Studying infrastructures backing the fast and efficient flows of minerals allows me to reflect on two aspects of the globalised mineral trade. First, this chapter will highlight the inertia of infrastructure developments: infrastructures originally developed during colonisation form a kind of dead weight determining present-day commercial movements and how they are managed. Second, the focus on the infrastructures backing the mineral flow regime will enable me to underscore the strength of the ideologies of private companies (such as the British South Africa Company – BSAC) in the Copperbelt's commercial history. Those ideologies have informed the development of colonial infrastructures and have survived to this day. The way infrastructural projects were and continue to be implemented is a symptom of the long-running cooperation between public and private actors in the management of mineral trade.

In this chapter I will demonstrate the historical continuity of the mineral flow regime's modes of management around two types of infrastructural technologies: physical transport infrastructures (in the form of corridors) and administrative technologies (e.g. public-private contracts and legalised

---

6   Hélène Blaszkiewicz, 'Économie politique des circulations de marchandises transfrontalières en Afrique Australe: Les régimes de circulations dans les Copperbelts', PhD Thesis, Université Jean Moulin Lyon 3, 2019.

7   Charis Enns and Brock Bersaglio, 'On the Coloniality of "New" Mega-Infrastructures Projects in East Africa', *Antipode* 52, 1 (2020), pp. 101–23.

monopolies). These two technologies will be the subject of the next two sections and will allow me to reflect on Dara Orenstein's words: 'If scholars of territorial sovereignty have long assumed the nation-state to be a co-pilot in the circulation of commodity capital, then this genealogy (...) helps us appreciate the extent to which the corporation is increasingly in the driver's seat'.[8] I will show that the management of commercial traffic and the influence of private actors that are observable in the infrastructure network enable us to link three historical periods that are usually studied separately in an analysis of Zambian history: colonisation (1890–1964), independence (1964–1990) and liberalisation (1990–). I will focus on the historical conti-nuities of infrastructure development to highlight the uneven geographical development as well as the long-term influence of private actors and values in the management of strategic mineral trade in the Copperbelt region.

Physical Infrastructures and the Uneven Development of Space by the Copperbelt Mineral Trade: The Development Corridor

In technical reports on logistics in Africa, 'development corridors' are one of the solutions of choice for the growth of inland commercial traffic. Corridors are defined as networks of transport infrastructures (e.g. roads, railways or pipelines) linking industrial and/or mining production sites to economic or export hubs – mostly international ports.[9] International experts view development corridors as remedies for the low levels of economic competitiveness, low productivity and lack of social inclusion of African mining economies:[10]

> the global development community has attached a 'win-win' narrative to Africa's corridor agenda, framing development corridors as an effec-tive way of creating conditions that are attractive to investors, while simultaneously driving local, domestic and regional development.[11]

8   Dara Orenstein, 'Warehouses on Wheels', *Environment and Planning D: Society and Space* 36, 4 (2018), pp. 648–65, p. 651.
9   Charis Enns, 'Mobilizing Research on Africa's Development Corridors', *Geoforum* 88 (2018), pp. 105–08.
10   Julia Baxter, Anne-Claire Howard, Tom Mills, Sophie Rickard, Steve Macey, 'A Bumpy Road: Maximising the Value of a Resource Corridor', *The Extractive Industries and Society* 4, 3 (2017), pp. 439–42; Tim Schwanen, 'Geographies of Transport I: Rein-venting a Field?' *Progress in Human Geography* 40, 1 (2016), pp. 126–37.
11   Enns, 'Mobilizing Research on Africa's Development Corridors', p. 105.

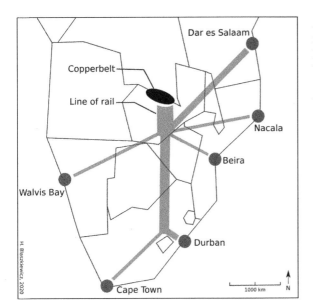

Map 8.1 Schematic map of corridors linking the Copperbelt to international markets. Map drawn by the author.

The international community's enthusiasm for 'development' corridors seems to be rather recent: the aftermath of the 2008 financial crisis put global infrastructures back on the international financial institutions (IFIs)' agenda as they sought to support the return to industrial growth.[12] But corridors, as integrated networks of infrastructures, are not new – especially in the Copperbelt, where the first colonial infrastructure projects took the form of transnational corridors.

Thanks to the two examples of major corridors linking the Copperbelt mines to the export ports of Eastern and Southern Africa (See Map 8.1), this section will show the long history of the corridor and the long-term cooperation of public and private actors that its implementation entails. The North–South corridor and the Great North Road through which the vast majority of Congolese and Zambian copper is exported today originated in the colonial organisation and polarisation of space, and the dynamics of uneven development they produced can still be felt.

12 Morten Ougaard, 'The Transnational State and the Infrastructure Push', *New Political Economy* 23, 1 (2018), pp. 128–44.

The North–South Corridor: Putting the Copperbelt on the Globalised Colonial Map of Southern Africa

Cutting Zambia's territory in half and linking the Congolese and Zambian Copperbelts to ports in South Africa and Mozambique, the North–South corridor is the oldest globalised infrastructure in the region. As 'the presence of huge copper deposits made every inch of this colonial territory valuable',[13] the colonisation of and control over the territory was part of a rush that pitted BSAC against the Congo Free State from 1890.[14] Transport and infrastructures were crucial to this competition. The first phase of exploration and exploitation was made possible by the (ab)use of human porters, as the presence of trypanosomiasis prevented the use of cattle.[15] With the (re)discovery of copper deposits in the Kafue gorge and the beginning of the industrial exploitation of copper (notably in Kansanshi, operational since 1901), railway development soon became a priority for BSAC management, which, through the Rhodesia Railways company, had already controlled the railways through Southern Rhodesia into South Africa and to the port of Beira in Mozambique since 1899. A 198-metre-long bridge across the Zambezi River, the first link to what was then Northern Rhodesia, was completed in September 1905. Trains could reach Broken Hill by 1906, the Bwana Mkubwa mine by 1907 and Elisabethville and Fungurume, on the Congolese side of the border, by 1910–1911 through the Sakania border post. This final link enabled private mining companies (like Anglo American Corporation or the Rhodesian Congo Border Concession Ltd) to exploit copper deposits on both sides of the border. The fast progression of rail in Northern Rhodesia was explained by mineral speculation, but the weak concentration of Zambian copper soon wiped out all profitability for the mining companies. It was the railway track itself that maintained the profitability of the colonial project on the territory.[16]

---

13 John W. Donaldson, 'Pillars and Perspective: Demarcation of the Belgian Congo–Northern Rhodesia Boundary', *Journal of Historical Geography* 34, 3 (2008), pp. 471–93, p. 487.

14 The Congo Free State, covering the large territory of what is now the DRC, operated as a colonial corporate state and was personally ruled by King Léopold II. It became the Belgian Congo, administered by the Belgian government, in 1908.

15 Jan-Bart Gewald, *Forged in the Great War: People, Transport, and Labour, the Establishment of Colonial Rule in Zambia, 1890–1920* (Leiden: African Studies Centre, 2015).

16 Jon Lunn, 'The Political Economy of Primary Railway Construction in the Rhodesias, 1890–1911', *Journal of African History* 33, 2 (1992), pp. 239–54.

Thanks to its infrastructure, Northern Rhodesia ensured an essential and profitable link between two additional productive mining fields: the coal mine of Wankie (today Hwange) in Southern Rhodesia, connected to the railway line since 1903, and the Congolese mines of Katanga, which used Wankie coal in production. Although part of the Belgian colonial empire, Katanga relied entirely on the Rhodesian transport network and investments to exploit its minerals as no export route existed to link Katangese mines to the Atlantic coast until the 1930s.[17] During the first three decades of private colonisation by BSAC, the Northern Rhodesian territory thus played an important role as a space of transit, more than as a space of mineral production. Transport infrastructures not only formed the general frame of the territory but were the only comprehensive exploitation project implemented by the chartered company.

Thus, the North–South corridor and the 'line-of-rail' between Livingstone and Ndola (see Map 8.1 and Chapter 5) established by BSAC had a structuring effect on the Northern Rhodesian (i.e. Zambian) territory's polarities. At the national level, the territorial organisation along the line-of-rail made the land that was situated close to the railway line, where extensive agricultural activities soon took place, very important. However, Africans were excluded from most of this land as British colonial authorities created Native Reserves[18] where Africans would be relocated as soon as 1910. At the time, the whole Copperbelt was looking towards the south, as infrastructures were oriented towards Southern Rhodesia and South Africa. All the copper extracted from the Copperbelt used the Southern route. No competition to Rhodesia Railways' monopoly on transport was allowed, even by road, following an agreement signed in 1936 between the railway provider and major copper companies.[19] This monopoly on copper transport lasted until 1968 when the independent

---

17 Lobito Railway, linking the Copperbelt to the Angolan port of Lobito, was opened in 1927 but BSAC prevented the mining companies using it. In 1928, a new line was opened linking the Katanga mines to the Congo Basin, but the link to Léopoldville/Kinshasa was never finished.

18 Native Reserves were parts of the territory where Africans were to be relocated in order to free the most accessible arable land for settlers and industrial agriculture. Tomas Frederiksen, 'Unearthing Rule: Mining, Power and the Political Ecology of Extraction in Colonial Zambia', PhD Thesis, University of Manchester, 2010; Oliver S. Saasa, *Zambian Policies towards Foreign Investment: The Case of the Mining and Non-Mining Sectors* (Uppsala: Nordiska Afrikainstitutet, 1987), p. 11.

19 R. S. Doganis, 'Zambia's Outlet to the Sea: A Case Study in Colonial Transport Development', *Journal of Transport Economics and Policy* 1, 1 (1967), pp. 46–51, pp. 48–9.

Zambian Government nationalised the company, which became Zambia Railways. Thanks to its prime position on the railway system, the city of Ndola took a central role in the urbanisation of the Copperbelt and was considered a gateway to access the eastern and north-eastern parts of Northern Rhodesia. It became an important city not only linked with mining,[20] but drawing its importance from transport and logistics. This was especially true during the First World War, when troops and military equipment were sent by train from South Africa, offloaded in Ndola and then convoyed to the East African front.[21]

The polarisation effects of the North–South corridor can still be felt in Zambia today, even though, after multiple financial crises and decades of disinvestment, roads gradually started to replace the rails and the original company, BSAC, disappeared in the 1960s. The new road, targeted today by a governmental project to transform it into a dual carriageway,[22] follows the old railway line almost exactly. Just like the road, the new optical fibre network also follows the line-of-rail[23]: in the same way as the railway line, optical fibre started in South Africa and progressed towards the north to reach the Zambian and then the Congolese Copperbelt. This shows the strong inertia of mining geographies regarding infrastructure development: the lines of later projects still stick to those from the colonial era. Indeed, as sources of funding are rare, the new infrastructures have to favour the previous economic organisation of the territory and reinforce it: New roads, for instance, must not harm agricultural, industrial or mining interests and must serve the existent economic centres. Hence, the line-of-rail still attracts most of the country's economic activities (commercial farms, industries). With respect to Ndola, although the Bwana Mkubwa mine closed down in 2010, the city continues to play a pivotal role in the organisation of the territory, and it is still considered the industrial and distribution centre of the Copperbelt.[24] It maintains its position thanks to the concentration of logistics and transport companies in its industrial area, all working closely with the DRC. The origins of these ventures show the globalised nature of the Copperbelt's logistics industry: some are Western (Bolloré Logistics,

20 The city itself was settled some 20 kilometres from the Bwana Mkubwa mine.
21 Brian Siegel, 'Bomas, Missions, and Mines; The Making of Centers on the Zambian Copperbelt', *African Studies Review* 31, 3 (1988), pp. 61–84.
22 At least for the 315 kilometres between Lusaka and Ndola.
23 Liquid Telecom, 'Our Network' [n.d.]: www.liquidtelecom.com/about-us/network-map.html (accessed 24 October 2019).
24 Interview, employee of logistics and transport companies, Ndola, 2017.

Trafigura, DHL), others Southern African (Reload Logistics, Bridge Shipping, Hill and Delamain), or Somali (SomZam Transport, Tigey Transport and many others).

The Great North Road: Reinforcing the Previous Polarisation of Copperbelt Territory

The Great North Road refers to the portion of road linking central Zambia and the Copperbelt to Nakonde, on the border between Zambia and Tanzania, and beyond to the port of Dar es Salaam. During colonisation, this portion of road was seemingly embryonic: It was built by the British in 1915 and used to transport troops and equipment during the First World War, at a time when motor vehicles were rare in this part of Africa.[25] In the 1920s, the Great North Road was also used to transport the African workforce to the mines of Congo, South Africa and, from the 1930s onwards, the Zambian Copperbelt.[26] In the 1950s and 1960s, the Great North Road came to be qualified as a 'Hell Run'[27] by journalists, governments and truckers alike due to its very bad conditions causing accidents and cargo losses.[28] We can conclude that commercial traffic was quite low, or even non-existent, on this stretch during the colonial period.

In 1965, the Great North Road nevertheless attracted international attention when Southern Rhodesia's white supremacist government adopted its Unilateral Declaration of Independence. In that period, the newly independent government of Zambia led by Kenneth Kaunda was actively supporting the black liberation movement to the south. This support led to a diplomatic crisis between the two countries and significant disruptions in the flows of goods using the Southern route, which accounted for

25 Jan-Bart Gewald, Sabine Luning and Klaas van Walraven (eds), *The Speed of Change: Motor Vehicles and People in Africa, 1890–2000* (Leiden: Brill, 2009).

26 Frederiksen, 'Unearthing Rule'.

27 M. B. Gleave, 'The Dar es Salaam Transport Corridor: An Appraisal', *African Affairs* 91, 363 (1992), pp. 249–67, p. 253; Ngila Mwase, 'Zambia, the TAZARA and the Alternative Outlets to the Sea', *Transport Reviews* 7, 3 (1987), pp. 191–206, p. 192; Felix J. Phiri, 'Islam in Post-Colonial Zambia' in Jan-Bart Gewald, Marja Hinfelaar and Giacomo Macola (eds), *One Zambia, Many Histories: Towards a History of Post-Colonial Zambia* (Leiden: Brill, 2008), pp. 164–84, p. 174.

28 See, for instance, the short video clips produced by British Pathé, especially 'Zambia: Hell Run Tarred and Trick Drivers Face Less Risks', in which ZTRS trucks are clearly visible: 12 December 1968, www.britishpathe.com/video/VLVA80VN-LTWBM0EE9DYX332N2KHUK-ZAMBIA-HELL-RUN-TARRED-AND-TRUCK-DRIVERS-FACE-LESS-RISKS/query/Hell+run (accessed 10 March 2020).

nearly 80% of Zambian copper exports before 1965. As a result, the export of Congolese and Zambian copper was put at considerable risk. Zambia also faced a potential fuel shortage as an international fuel blockade was imposed on Southern Rhodesia at the end of 1965 in the port of Beira, thereby cutting Zambia off from its only fuel import route. In 1966, the U.S. Government and the World Bank agreed to finance the paving of the Livingstone–Dar es Salaam road.[29] On the Zambian side, the contract was awarded to three Italian companies: Impregilo, Vianini and Federici.[30] The construction of the road was completed in 1972,[31] just before the complete closure of the border between Southern Rhodesia and Zambia in 1973.

As early as June 1966, a logistics company called ZTRS (Zambia-Tanzania Road Service) was established to handle fuel imports and copper exports on the Great North Road. It was jointly owned by the governments of Zambia (35% of shares) and Tanzania (35% of shares). The remaining shares (30%) were owned by an Italian consortium of companies called Inter-somer (for *Società Mercantile Internazionale*, International Trading Company) comprising the car manufacturer Fiat, the tyre company Pirelli and the trailer specialist Officine Meccaniche U. Piacenza. These companies were joined under the umbrella of the Southern African branch of the investment bank Mediobanca.[32] These Italian companies built special trucks and trailers that could transport both copper and oil and were used on the Great North Road from 1966. At the same time, Mediobanca agreed to finance the 1,710-kilometre TAZAMA (Tanzania–Zambia *Mafuta*, which means oil in Swahili) pipeline linking Dar es Salaam's port refineries to the Indeni refinery, situated 10 kilometres south of Ndola. Both refineries were owned by the Italian petrol company Agip, at least until 2001. Operational from 1968, the TAZAMA pipeline offered a welcome alternative to the Southern route for Zambian fuel imports. The last infrastructure built on this route was TAZARA (Tanzania–Zambia Railway), the railway that was constructed

29 Giulia Scotto and Misato Kimura, 'Highway Africa', Students work, University of Basel, 2017: https://criticalurbanisms.philhist.unibas.ch/files/research-studio/The-Politics-of-Infrastructure.pdf (accessed 12 October 2020).
30 Impregilo had already worked in Zambia and built the Kariba Dam in the 1950s. Many thanks to Michele Vollaro from *Africa e Affari* (Rome) for his precious help on this point.
31 Tonderai Makoni, 'The Economic Appraisal of the Tanzania–Zambia Railway', *African Review* 2, 4 (1972), pp. 599–616.
32 In 1985, ZTRS officially went bankrupt but still existed as part of the Mediobanca portfolio until 2008, with financial stocks in Kwacha: Mediobanca, 'Relazione Semestrale al 31 Dicembre 2008', Annual management report (Milan, 2008).

thanks to Chinese loans and expertise and became fully operational in 1975. By 1977, the reorientation of Zambian trade towards Tanzania was nearly complete: the Great North Road and TAZARA accounted for more than 90% of Zambian copper exports that year.[33] In Figure 8.1, we can see the stark decline of the use of the Southern route (to Beira and Maputo) for copper exports between 1966 and 1976, when TAZARA took the lead. Geographically speaking, the Great North Road rehabilitation in the 1960s opened a new outlet to the sea for Copperbelt strategic minerals. But thanks to this new route, Zambia – in particular, the Zambian Copperbelt – kept its transit position for Congolese copper (whose exports were cut off from the port at Lobito by the Angolan civil war in 1975) and, more generally, for all goods coming from or going to Southern and Eastern DRC.

This short history of infrastructure development on the Great North Road allows us to slightly modify the conventional understanding of 1970s Zambia as a 'socialist' country. Zambia's main trading partners in those years were still Western countries (e.g. Great Britain, European Community and Japan to which Zambia mostly exported copper), while the USSR and China accounted for a very small fraction of Zambia's external trade.[34] Despite the non-aligned political ideologies officially defended by Kenneth Kaunda's 'Humanist' doctrine, Zambia accepted financial help from the West to re-build the Great North Road. Moreover, the relationships that the ruling party (United National Independence Party, UNIP) had with private foreign companies were less tense than most accounts of the 'nationalisation' period would have us believe.[35] This brief history shows the Western private companies' dexterity in creating a monopoly over the strategic oil and copper trade with the backing of the independent government of Zambia. The infrastructure developments on the Great North Road highlight the prevalence of private logics in infrastructures and trade, which stands in stark contrast to Zambia's socialist image at the time.

Although the Southern route was reopened in the 1980s, the Great North Road infrastructures are still in use today. Nonetheless, it does not seem to be a significant part of the mineral flow regime anymore: The traders using the Great North Road do not necessarily prioritise speed and efficiency

33 Gleave, 'The Dar es Salaam Transport Corridor', p. 261.
34 Roel C. Harkema, 'Zambia's Changing Pattern of External Trade', *Journal of Geography* 71, 1 (1972), pp. 19–27.
35 Miles Larmer, 'Historical Perspectives on Zambia's Mining Booms and Busts' in Alastair Fraser and Miles Larmer (eds), *Zambia, Mining, and Neoliberalism: Boom and Bust on the Globalized Copperbelt*, ed. (New York: Palgrave Macmillan, 2010), pp. 31–58.

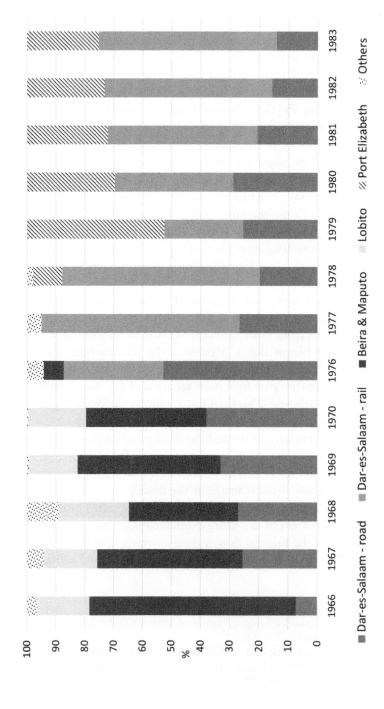

Figure 8.1   Zambian copper export routes. Source: Gleave, 'The Dar Es Salaam Transport Corridor', 1992.

Legend: Dar-es-Salaam - road ■ Dar-es-Salaam - rail ■ Beira & Maputo ■ Lobito ⫽ Port Elizabeth ⁚ Others

in the management of their commercial traffic, as the Nakonde border is well known for its congestion and the port in Dar es Salaam struggles with ageing infrastructure.[36] Most multinational mining and logistics companies now prefer to use the North–South corridor again. However, both the Great North Road and TAZARA are still used to transport small quantities of copper and oil, as well as agricultural imports from Eastern Africa like palm oil and rice, which are usually delivered to the DRC by Chinese and Somali firms that have used this road since the 1970s.

Corridors are now the default form for managing the flow of minerals in the Copperbelt: they materialise the modern utopia of speed and efficiency. Today they are described as 'development' corridors, a way for the IFIs to advertise them as a means of 'greater efficiency, speed and reliability of movement'[37] but also as means to 'ensure equitable distribution of benefits from a specific (mining) project by creating linkages to other parts of the economy'.[38] However, the brief history of two major transport corridors linking the Copperbelt to the international market presented in this section shows that corridors were also part of the colonial agenda to manage the flow of minerals. This aspect has a major impact on today's Copperbelt: the original polarisation of the territory, organised around mining and metal exports, has survived thanks to its infrastructure, and so has the general geography of colonialism, which is characterised by its network of highly developed enclaves linked by corridors[39] on the one hand and vast 'unusable' lands excluded from the flows of goods and capital on the other hand.[40] The schematic presented in Map 8.1 shows the permanence of these long-standing dynamics and the corridor's importance in the region. We see that the present infrastructure reconfigurations altered neither the Copperbelt's central position in the region nor the line-of-rail's position of transit for all corridors, which now link the Copperbelt to no fewer than six international ports. This also means that the influence of private logics of accumulation, which were at the very foundation of the territory's organisation, still matters today and has prevented the engagement

36 Jana Hönke and Ivan Cuesta-Fernandez, 'Mobilising Security and Logistics through an African Port: A Controversies Approach to Infrastructure', *Mobilities* 13, 2 (2018), pp. 246–60.

37 Schwanen, 'Geographies of Transport I', p. 127.

38 Baxter et al., 'A Bumpy Road', p. 439.

39 Lauren Benton, *A Search for Sovereignty: Law and Geography in European Empires, 1400–1900* (Cambridge: Cambridge University Press, 2009).

40 James Ferguson, 'Seeing Like an Oil Company: Space, Security and Global Capital in Neoliberal Africa', *American Anthropologist* 107, 3 (2005), pp. 377–82.

of the administrations in genuine economic diversification programmes, as the focus was always on the mineral trade. Zambian infrastructure projects proved to be a necessary solution for and firmly supported the continuation of the Copperbelt's copper export-based economic system.

However, material infrastructures are not sufficient to enable the fast flow of minerals in the mineral flow regime: several immaterial infrastructures are also needed to make speed possible by coordinating private priorities with public rules. These administrative technologies will be the subject of the second section.

The Administrative Technologies of Trade: Coordinating Private Priorities and Public Rules

As mentioned before, speed and fluidity are the major values governing the Copperbelt's organisation of the flow of strategic minerals. But they cannot be achieved through good material infrastructures alone – they also require coordination between all the actors involved in these systems of movement. Public authorities in charge of controlling and taxing movements and private companies involved in the production and/or the export of minerals may pursue different objectives, which can cause delays in the pace of movement. To prevent conflict and avoid friction, soft infrastructures such as contractualisation rules, IT systems and standards are created at the crossroads between public and private spheres of action. These administrative technologies allow movements to have a regular rhythm and achieve fluidity: They grant 'the integration, standardization and synchronization of customs and trade regulations.'[41]

In the Copperbelt's mineral flow regime, soft infrastructures are generally constructed by the state to enable private accumulation around the fast and efficient flow of minerals. These infrastructures are used to limit stoppages where and when companies need them. Indeed, speed and fluidity paradoxically require stoppages and immobility, as long as they are precisely engineered and do not risk entirely contaminating the logistics chain.[42] For instance, immobility is vitally important to manage the fluctuation of prices on the global market.[43] All trading companies, like the Switzerland-based

---

41 Cowen, *The Deadly Life of Logistics*, p. 65.

42 Julian Stenmanns, 'Logistics from the Margins', *Environment and Planning D: Society and Space* 37, 5 (2019), pp. 850–67.

43 Michael Simpson, 'The Annihilation of Time by Space: Pluri-Temporal Strategies of Capitalist Circulation', *Environment and Planning E: Nature and Space* 2, 1 (2019), pp. 110–28.

Trafigura,[44] store copper and cobalt in the Zambian Copperbelt to sell it at the best price and best time.[45] Immobility and fixity, if controlled by adequate soft infrastructures, can then also form the basis of profitability for private mining, logistics and trading companies.

This section will analyse two examples of administrative infrastructures historically developed by public actors to enable private accumulation thanks to the flow of minerals. Both have long-term territorial consequences. I will first analyse how contractualisation, as a technology of coordination between the public and the private sector, allows the 'spatial fix' of capital.[46] Contractualisation, which is a way of managing social and/or economic relations through contracts, is a commonly used coordination technology between partners collaborating on far-flung commodity chains.[47] Despite being an ontologically private form of organisation, the contract has a long history in the management of territory and trade in colonial Africa,[48] including, more recently, on territorial and planning matters. I will then present a specific form of contractualisation concerning space, time and taxes of movements, namely bonded warehouses. Once again, the long-term perspective of these two technologies will allow highlighting the historical continuity in the management of mineral flows in the Copperbelt through the infrastructures of the mineral flow regime.

Public-Private Contractualisation: The Public Organisation of Territorial Monopolies

Contracts were and still are widely used in the mineral flow regime. The contract has not changed over time – what has changed is the general ideology behind the use of this technology. This subsection will examine

---

44 Gregor Dobler and Rita Kesselring, 'Swiss Extractivism: Switzerland's Role in Zambia's Copper Sector', *Journal of Modern African Studies* 57, 2 (2019), pp. 223–45.
45 Nicky Gregson, Mike Crang and Constantinos N. Antonopoulos, 'Holding Together Logistical Worlds: Friction, Seams and Circulation in the Emerging "Global Warehouse"', *Environment and Planning D: Society and Space* 35, 3 (2017), pp. 381–98; Dara Orenstein, 'Foreign-Trade Zones and the Cultural Logic of Frictionless Production', *Radical History Review* 2011, 109 (2011), pp. 36–61.
46 David Harvey, *Spaces of Neoliberalization: Towards a Theory of Uneven Geographical Development* (Stuttgart: F. Steiner, 2005).
47 Jennifer Bair (ed.), *Frontiers of Commodity Chain Research* (Stanford: Stanford University Press, 2009).
48 Catherine Coquery-Vidrovitch, *Le Congo au temps des grandes compagnies concessionnaires 1889–1930* (Paris: Editions de l'EHESS, 2001).

how public-private contractualisation in the Copperbelt's history allowed for and supported the creation of state-sponsored monopolies.

Cecil Rhodes's BSAC, responsible for the military and commercial conquest of Northern Rhodesia, was a chartered company, meaning it was under contract with the British Colonial Office and officially represented the Crown at the signing of treaties with African authorities. The fact that BSAC acted under a Royal Charter only made the company more powerful in organising its activities: it had no direct competitors in the trade and transport of minerals until 1968. The Company's monopoly on the mineral trade – and later, through Rhodesia Railways, on all rail transport – was hence organised, permitted and supported by the colonial state. From 1924, when the Colonial Office officially took charge of the colonisation process and the organisation of the territory, the monopoly that Rhodesia Railways had over transport was reinforced, as public civil servants had no choice but to rely on the private railway for their administrative activities. During the Second World War, the British state was buying copper at a fixed and advantageous rate from mining companies in Northern Rhodesia to secure its supply to the army. This contract also benefitted Rhodesia Railways by securing it a high level of business even in times of war. This original form of contractualisation in which the development of public-private capitalism in Northern Rhodesia was rooted was subsequently passed on to successive governments.

After Northern Rhodesia became an independent Zambia in 1964, the close relationship between the government and mining companies through contractualisation did not drastically change. Miles Larmer describes the situation as follows:

> an effective alliance between the UNIP government and the international mining companies that would ensure expansion of the industry, with both the companies and the government taking their *carefully negotiated* share of what was assumed would be an ever-increasing cake of mining profits.[49]

The UNIP government's need for funding to achieve the social policies it envisioned required peaceful relationships with investors: the government sought to guarantee the development of new mines in order to secure more contractually negotiated royalties for the state. Based on the 1964 'Seers

---

[49] Larmer, 'Historical Perspectives on Zambia's Mining Booms and Busts', p. 45; emphasis added.

Report',[50] a United Nations economic assessment that framed the economic and social development policies for the newly independent Zambia, the country's first National Development Plans called into question neither the importance of the foreign private sector in mine management nor the setting of copper prices by the London Metal Exchange. The Mulungushi and Matero reforms of 1968–69, often called 'nationalisation reforms', are usually seen as a complete turnaround of the Zambian economic situation in this regard. In practice, the government acquired only 51% of the shares in mining, industrial and financial companies,[51] generously compensating the private companies' losses according to international financial law, as stated in the contract between the independent government and those companies. During the Mulungushi period, the organisation of parastatal companies and public monopolies was justified by the ideology of self-development and Third-Worldist political traditions.

Kaunda's proximity to socialist ideologies, regimes or parties – Angola's Movimento Popular de Libertação de Angola (MPLA), Julius Nyerere's regime in neighbouring Tanzania, South Africa's African National Congress (ANC) – may have suggested that these 'nationalisations' were aimed at socialising the economy. The parapublic sector, through its two major parastatals (the Mining Development Corporation – MINDECO, and the Industrial Development Corporation – INDECO), grew by leaps and bounds, with the financial crisis hitting the Copperbelt in the 1970s and 1980s as private actors that were still engaged in the economy pushed the state to buy more and more shares during these times of difficulty. As a result, the Mulungushi reforms and the so-called nationalisation period of Zambian history can also be understood as the most advanced form of the public-private logic developed during colonisation – the development of monopolistic state capitalism adapted to the discourses of independence and redistribution, and based on contracts.

Parapublic conglomerates eventually unravelled in the 1990s as Zambia adopted liberalisation reforms following severe economic crises and the fall of the UNIP government in 1990. According to the conditions imposed by the International Monetary Fund (IMF) alongside its financial support, the new Movement for Multi-Party Democracy (MMD) government had to

---

50 The official title of the report is the 'Report of the UN/ECA/FAO Economic Survey Mission on the Economic Development of Zambia' and it was written by Dudley Seers.

51 Lise Rakner, *Political and Economic Liberalisation of Zambia, 1991–2001* (Uppsala: Nordic Africa Institute, 2003).

liquidate the public conglomerates. As early as June 1993, it started selling the government's shares in small and medium companies. Between 1995 and 2002, the government sold its shares of the mining conglomerate. The MMD administration was nonetheless reluctant to fully privatise its infrastructures and transport networks: Initially, less than 50% of the shares were offered for sale in the 'National Transport Company', whose subsidiaries included freight transport (e.g. public companies called Contract Haulage and Freight Holdings) and the national airline, Zambia Airways. However, many of these transport companies went bankrupt between 1993 and 1995,[52] paving the way for private competition, particularly in the field of road transport. The latter became increasingly central to the functioning of the Copperbelt economy as the economic crisis of the 1970s and 1980s hit the railway industry hard, jeopardising less profitable flows of goods, such as maize, which were entirely dependent on the low rates of transport by rail.[53] International financial institutions (IFIs) played a key role in legitimising road transport and worked tirelessly to liberalise it in order to lower the costs of freight transport.

The IFIs also endorsed the superiority of the private sector in managing the economy and its logistics component. Hence, contractualisation gained new legitimacy with these new supporters and took the form of public-private partnerships (PPPs). They were and remain very important for the management of infrastructures that the state does not want to privatise in their entirety. They tend to benefit the most financially powerful companies, already well established in the field of infrastructure management. For instance, Zambia Railways, administering the North–South corridor, was subject to a 20-year concession won by a South African consortium in 2003 under the name Railway Systems of Zambia (RSZ). Similarly, the infrastructure at the Kasumbalesa border post was privatised in 2010 on both the Congolese and the Zambian side. The Israeli company that was awarded the contract (Baran Investment Ltd), established two 'single-window facilities'[54] and completely redesigned border infrastructures to reduce crossing time. However, the PPP behind the Kasumbalesa infrastructure is regarded as a

---

52 John Robert Craig, 'State Enterprise and Privatisation in Zambia 1968–1998', PhD Thesis, University of Leeds, 1999; Neo Simutanyi, 'The Politics of Structural Adjustment in Zambia', *Third World Quarterly* 17, 4 (1996), pp. 825–39, p. 837.
53 Interview, manager of an industrial milling company, Mufulira, 2017.
54 Jeroen Cuvelier and Philémon Muamba Mumbunda, 'Réforme douanière néolibérale, fragilité étatique et pluralisme normatif: Le cas du guichet unique à Kasumbalesa', *Politique africaine* 129 (2013), pp. 93–112.

failure from the state's perspective.[55] This infrastructure is now completely privatised, similar to the administration of the US $200 fee imposed on trucks and vehicles crossing the border between the two Copperbelts.

The Kasumbalesa PPP failure is explained inside the administration by the fact that no institutions had managed any PPP contracts before 2012. A 'PPP Unit' was subsequently created but only became fully operational after 2016, when it was put under the direct authority of the State House. Nevertheless, PPPs proved not to be as much of an antidote to capitalism's monopolistic tendencies as this free-market tool was supposed to be. On the contrary, the way they are implemented in Zambia's infrastructure sector reinforces the dominant position of major multinational companies. First, most of the implemented Zambian PPPs are 'unsolicited projects': they are infrastructure projects proposed to the government by major companies that need a specific facility. Because the administration's expertise in this area is limited, it has no other choice but to trust the company regarding the potential for new infra-structure development.[56] Second, the Zambian Development Agency (ZDA), one of the agencies looking into infrastructure development through PPPs, admits that 'non-traditional exports' are not a priority because they are seen as the realm of 'small-scale players'. The Agency only supports 'big players' that 'already know what they want' and 'have already done their homework' about the kind of infrastructures they need.[57] Besides limiting the govern-ment's financial support to a small number of companies, the current PPP framework does not push back against the development of profit-oriented mining infrastructure, and consequently tend to exclude projects that would benefit commodities other than copper.

As the history of public-private relations in the mineral flow regime shows, contractualisation has been one of the preferred administrative tools to manage the relations between those two categories of actors. Contracts that bear the seal of the administration give the companies a particular legiti-macy that can then turn into the consolidation of monopolies. Contracts represent a 100-year-old administrative infrastructure for commercial traffic in which practices and ideologies linked to trade have become sedimented. This section showed the continuity of public-private cooperation over the decades. What has changed are the ideologies legitimising the forms and the recipients of the contracts. In this regard, the period of independence

55 Interview, civil servant working in the Zambian PPP Unit, Lusaka, 2017.
56 Ibid.
57 Interview, civil servant working in the Infrastructure Development Department, ZDA, Lusaka, 2017.

marks nothing more than an ideological reversal of the management of public-private relations in a short period of time. The public-private cooperation built up during colonisation and reinforced during the liberalisation period remains intact.

Bonded Warehouses and Seals: Contractualising Space and Time of Commercial Traffic

Public-private contractualisation also applies to the spaces and times of mineral flows. Bonded warehouses are a case in point. Created by state administrations in the Copperbelt since the time of colonisation, these technologies allow companies to settle and store goods on tax-free state-demarcated parts of the territory. They are zoning technologies: state administrations delineate a portion of their land where common fiscal law does not apply. Goods entering a bonded warehouse are motionless but are still considered as being in transit, which allows the company owning the goods to avoid paying import duties or other taxes. Bonded warehouses are akin to a no-interest credit on import duties by the public administration to private companies:

> A customs bond is an oath that is signed after duties are assessed but before they are paid; it is a promise to fork over duties when the goods are reclaimed from storage, in three days or three years ... if the goods are transferred out of the facility and out of the [country] ... then their owners avoid tariffs altogether.[58]

In a 2018 article, Dara Orenstein runs through the history of bonded warehouses: inspired by the functioning of a free port such as Hamburg or Hong Kong, bonded warehouses are an invention of nineteenth-century US capitalism. It is unclear how they were transplanted to Southern Africa. The first mention of bonded warehouses in the Copperbelt is made in the annual report of 1931 published by the British Colonial Office in Northern Rhodesia. It notes the existence of five bonded warehouses on Northern Rhodesian territory, described as 'major public works' undertaken in the colony.[59] They were situated in Ndola, Mokambo, Livingstone, Fort Jameson (now Chipata) – four major border cities that the office described as 'free warehousing ports'[60] – and Broken Hill (now Kabwe), a

---

58 Orenstein, 'Warehouses on Wheels', p. 650.
59 Colonial Office, 'Annual Report on the Social and Economic Progress of the People of Northern Rhodesia, 1931' (London: His Majesty's Stationery Office, 1932), p. 87.
60 Ibid., p. 27.

mining town in central Zambia located on the line-of-rail. The locations of these five bonded warehouse show the will of Northern Rhodesia's British colonial government to encourage not only mining but also the movement of goods on its territory, as bonded warehouses are 'site[s] of circulation, not of production':[61] Livingstone was the point of entry/exit for goods coming from or going to South Africa on the North–South corridor. Fort Jameson, situated close to the Nyasaland (now Malawi) border, was used as a gateway for commercial traffic going east on an alternative route towards the ports of Nacala and Beira in Northern Mozambique. As for Ndola and Mokambo, they were directly looking at the Congo as the two towns sit on the border splitting the Copperbelt in two. They were strategically set on the trajectory of the roads mentioned in the first part of this chapter: Material and immaterial infrastructures appear to be complementary. Those bonded warehouses were most likely used to store goods to be exported, such as copper, obviously, but also maize and tobacco: Here we see that the infrastructures created for copper can be used for the trade of other goods. The storage of such goods allowed investors to wait for the best time to sell their products according to international market prices. They thus contributed to and exacerbated the commercial specialisation of Northern Rhodesian territory and its polarisation around borders and the line-of-rail.

Bonded warehouses were still in use during the nationalisation period and were aimed at supporting private investments in Zambia. The 1986 Investment Act, for instance, included several incentives for investors such as the 'access to any existing free trade zones' and additional tax breaks for investors.[62] Nowadays, the vast majority of logistics, mining and trading companies in the Copperbelt use bonded warehouses. Bolloré Logistics, Trafigura and Reload Logistics are among the major companies moving Copperbelt minerals across space, and all their storage installations are equipped with bonded warehouse technology. Their proliferation in the Zambian Copperbelt is worth emphasising. Businessmen and -women involved in cross-border economic activities and trade in the Copperbelt always refer to Zambia as a much safer place for people and goods than the DRC. Thus, bonded warehouses contribute to the image and the functioning of Zambia as a 'structured platform'[63] for traders and companies wanting to

---

61 Orenstein, 'Foreign-Trade Zones and the Cultural Logic of Frictionless Production', p. 51.

62 Saasa, *Zambia's Policies towards Foreign Investment*, p. 35.

63 Interview, Congolese trader involved in cross-border trade in the Copperbelt, Kitwe, 2016.

benefit from the riches of the DRC without being based in the country. For instance, Bolloré Logistics has built a 70,000 square metre warehouse in Chingola, including an 18,000 square metre bonded warehouse 'dedicated to the transhipment of copper, cobalt coming from the Katanga region in the DRC, as well as chemicals ... brought to Chingola through the southern and eastern corridors'[64] for the services of a single mining company in the DRC. The installation of this facility is justified by the insecurity in the Congo: close enough to the border but outside the DRC, the Bolloré warehouse constitutes a free-of-charge 'buffer stock'[65] for the mine in case of border closure or political instability.

In Zambia today, the opening of a bonded warehouse is subject to the procurement of an annual 'customs area licence'. Customs officials keep the keys to the bonded space and are entitled to inspect those warehouses anytime to ensure that no goods are leaving them (otherwise, taxes would have to be paid), although unannounced inspections are uncommon. Bonded warehouses are, therefore, delineated spaces where private ownership and public rules combine, and where public and private logics meet and intertwine. However, the bond no longer requires geographical fixity, as the bonded warehouse technology has been expanded to goods in motion. This is what Dara Orenstein calls 'warehouses on wheels': thanks to a unique seal numbered by customs administrations, bundles of copper cathodes can travel, in transit, for several days without paying any duty, as they did not officially or administratively cross the border and enter Zambia. The border itself is moving along with the seal: 'the customs border [is] not so much a riparian line comprised of latitudinal and longitudinal coordinates as a process enacted in a sequence of spatially circumscribed transactions'.[66] The contract between customs administrations and the company managing the movement of copper cathodes allows partners to negotiate when and where the goods will effectively cross the border – if they ever do – and taxes will be due.

This functioning has been further expanded in the form of temporary import/export procedures. They allow a mining company, for example, to import a machine without paying any duty on the basis of a promise that it will be sent back to its country of origin before the end of the

64   Bolloré Logistics, 'Transport et Logistique en Zambie: Focus marché', www.bollore-logistics.com/fr/Pages/FOCUS/Zambia.aspx (accessed 12 March 2020); author's translation from French.
65   Interviews, Bolloré warehouse's managers, Chingola, 2016 and 2017.
66   Orenstein, 'Warehouses on Wheels', p. 654.

365-day period fixed by administrations. This happens frequently between the two sides of the Zambia–Congo border, as the same mining companies (Glencore, First Quantum Minerals) and logistics companies (Bolloré Logistics, Reload, CML) are settled in both countries. Thanks to temporary exports and imports, they can share costly mining equipment between their own subsidiaries. Temporary exports and imports can be extended beyond 365 days with a simple request from a reputable clearing agent, which can pave the way for longer and longer exonerations.[67]

By pretending goods did not enter its territory, thanks to the contracts' administrative technology, the state is depriving itself of the right to tax these movements. Consequently, these types of contracts open profit opportunities to mining and logistics companies that they would not have been able to access without public intervention and rule. It entails close cooperation between customs administrations, which enable, certify and control these zones, and private companies managing copper and cobalt circulations in the Copperbelt. Zones are now presented as the liberal tool par excellence as they represent a way of attracting private investment through loosened fiscal constraints. They are the direct heirs of their colonial counterparts: they mark the deepening of the private accumulation logics developed around the flows of minerals allowed by the state's administrations. Bonded warehouses represent a key infrastructure technology for 'efficient' (i.e. profitable) commercial traffic and are central to the Copperbelt's mineral flow regime. Today, they meet the state's objectives of industrial development and take the form of another liberal zoning technology that has been implemented in the region: special economic zones.

The 'infrastructure-isation'[68] of the Copperbelt started during colonisation, which means the complete organisation of the territory around infrastructures allowing mineral exploitation and exporting is not limited to physical infrastructures. 'Soft' infrastructures were also created and took the form of administrative technologies given the state's importance in their creation and management. Their goal was to coordinate the priorities of the private sector, which was dominant in the first decades of colonisation, with the actions of the state, which created rules to ensure private accumulation. Among those soft infrastructures, contractualisation played

67 Hélène Blaszkiewicz, 'La formalisation inachevée des circulations commerciales africaines par les infrastructures de papier: Cas de l'industrie logistique zambienne', *Politique africaine* 151 (2018), pp. 133–54.
68 Hélène Blaszkiewicz, 'La mise en politique des circulations commerciales transfrontalières en Zambie: infrastructures et moment néolibéral', *Géocarrefour* 91, 3 (2017).

an important role as it allowed monopolies to form and strengthen. In the same way, bonded warehouses as a public technology gave mining and logistics companies control over the rhythms of their movements. Those two administrative technologies work on the question of resolving, through the contractual organisation between actors, all aspects that could constitute obstacles to the fluidity and regularity of traffic – from the organisation of relations with partners and competitors to space and time. This section has also shown the historicity of these two administrative technologies. It underlined the long-term influence of private logics in the organisation of the territory of trade and how public administrations have enabled a certain level of accumulation around flows of minerals.

Conclusion

As a mining hub, the Copperbelt has long been analysed as a copper and cobalt producing region – the centre of African urbanisation, unionisation and the wage-earning economy. As this chapter demonstrates, it is also important to consider the Copperbelt through the prism of the historical links it has forged to the global economy by exporting minerals and through the infrastructures enabling their circulation. This chapter has traced the long history of material and immaterial infrastructures supporting the movement of copper (and, more recently, cobalt). I showed that the technologies governing commercial traffic today date back to the era of colonisation: the territory's polarisation along the line-of-rail and the Zambian Copperbelt cities stems from the design and layout of major export routes drawn during the first decades of the twentieth century. In the same way, the deep cooperation between public and private actors embodied in various contractualisation practices originated in charted companies and the monopolies they had on the territory. These material and immaterial infrastructures enable fast and efficient commercial traffic, prevent undesirable stoppage and maintain the link between the local Copperbelt and the global economy. This chapter also examined the inertia of mineral-related infrastructures. Throughout successive political regimes, the territorial polarisation that emerged during colonisation stayed the same. Infrastructures form a kind of dead weight; they constrain the territory's organisation and the development projects that can be carried out. The Copperbelt territory was organised in the interest of copper exploitation and exporting, but infrastructures cannot adapt to the booms and busts of copper prices:[69] if economic diversification is based on context-specific economic policies, infrastructure diversification can hardly be achieved in a short amount of time. Infrastructures do not change according to political temporalities; only the roles assigned to them can change, and have shifted rapidly: the mineral-related infrastructures that were required to allow the development of the colonial metropolis were then justified as a means to achieve national development and sovereignty after independence. Today, the same infrastructures are legitimised as they represent international connectivity and a vital link to the global markets.[70] The promotion of mining circulations through infrastructure development contributes to the uneven repartition of the advantages linked to fast and efficient movements: from the beginning, the mineral trade has benefitted from this 'arterial'[71] organisation of space. Other types of trade organised according to different rhythms, geographies and sociabilities are deemed illegitimate to use the restricted and saturated infrastructure network and, thus, suffer from more friction and delays.

The emphasis on global mineral flows explains the global position of the Copperbelt despite its landlocked position inside the continent. The territory of the Copperbelt, especially of the Zambian Copperbelt, has developed over more than a century to become a crossroads for regional commercial traffic. A form of capitalism has emerged around the infrastructures designed for the exploitation of mineral wealth, be they Congolese, Zimbabwean, South African or Zambian. It has existed for more than a century and has been maintained even when the economy was nationalised. In this form of capitalism, private and public actors have acted jointly to enable the accumulation of capital. This can explain the success of today's neoliberalisation policies: they only form an additional layer – the latest – of reinvestment in the logics of polarisation and commodification of the Copperbelt territory, organised for the benefit of entities located on the international stage. As in other parts of Africa, the neoliberal organisation of territory in the Copperbelt re-utilises and capitalises on the legacies of

69 Alastair Fraser and Miles Larmer, *Zambia, Mining and Neoliberalism: Boom and Bust on the Globalized Copperbelt* (New York: Palgrave Macmillan, 2010).
70 Tom Goodfellow, 'African Capitalisms, Infrastructure and Urban Real Estate', 17 August 2018: http://roape.net/2018/08/17/african-capitalisms-infrastructure-and-urban-real-estate (accessed 4 November 2019).
71 Frederick Cooper, 'Conflict and Connection: Rethinking Colonial African History', *The American Historical Review* 995 (1994), pp. 1516–45.

colonialism.[72] Material and immaterial infrastructures are interesting media to highlight this continuity as they represent 'the mundane assembly of global circulation'[73] on the field and in history. They show the permanence of private logics in the global connections linking the two sides of the Copperbelt with the global economy. Therefore, public-private collaborations and the infrastructures they built can be understood as the 'carriers' bringing colonial hegemonic transactions into the neoliberal present.[74]

---

[72] Louis Awanyo and Emmanuel Morgan Attua, 'A Paradox of Three Decades of Neoliberal Economic Reforms in Ghana: A Tale of Economic Growth and Uneven Regional Development', *African Geographical Review* 37, 3 (2016), pp. 173–91.
[73] Ouma and Stenmanns, 'The New Zones of Circulation', p. 98.
[74] Jean-François Bayart, 'The Meandering of Colonial Hegemony in French-speaking West Africa', *Politique africaine* 105, 1 (2007), pp. 201–40.

9

Houses Built on Copper: The Environmental Impact of Current Mining Activities on 'Old' and 'New' Zambian Copperbelt Communities

Jennifer Chibamba Chansa

Introduction

Mining inevitably impacts surrounding communities. Some of these impacts are beneficial. Mining investment generates jobs, and local communities often benefit from corporate social responsibility (CSR) strategies implemented by mining companies. However, the benefits reaped by companies far outweigh those of the communities, which suffer from often-irreversible degradation of their environment. This has been the case on the 'old' and 'new' Copperbelt in Zambia, the focus of this chapter, where large-scale mining has had a huge environmental impact.

This chapter highlights the historical neglect of mining-related community concerns in the Zambian mining industry since the development of the 'old' Copperbelt and compares it to the developments on the 'new' Copperbelt. It argues that, despite variations in the 'nature' of mining communities and in the approach of mining companies to environmental protection in each, environmental concerns are a significant challenge in both. The chapter suggests that the continuity in ineffective environmental management, and the complex 'indigenous' nature of the 'new' Copperbelt, means that this region is likely to follow the trajectory of the 'old' Copperbelt if environmental management between the state, mining companies and communities is not improved.

The chapter focuses on communities located closest to mine facilities in the country's most important mining regions, the Copperbelt and

233

the North-Western Province (referred to in this chapter as the 'old' and 'new' Copperbelts respectively). These communities include former mine compounds in the Copperbelt Province as well as indigenous communities affected by new mining activities in the North-Western Province. It draws on research conducted in the 'old' Copperbelt communities of Kankoyo and Butondo in Mufulira and Wusakile and Bwacha in Kitwe. In the 'new' Copperbelt, the Kabwela resettlement site in Solwezi's Kansanshi mine area is included in the study along with the Northern and Southern/Shinengene resettlement sites in Kalumbila. By comparing the two mining regions, the chapter highlights the importance of variations in mine ownership, length of existence and land ownership patterns within the two regions, and their implications for mining investment and environmental management.

Background

African housing on the 'old' Copperbelt dates back to the colonial era. The mine and non-mine townships constructed in the 1930s provided accommodation for those who migrated from villages, mostly in search of employment in the mining industry. This housing was initially meant to address the 'uncontrolled settlement' of Africans. The existing informal settlements were legalised through the Townships Ordinance of 1944.[1] The Copperbelt mines provided housing for their employees in the form of barrack-like hostels or single-family houses. Individual-type huts were constructed for single African mineworkers.[2] These housing facilities were located alarmingly close to mine and refinery facilities, whereas those of white mineworkers were mostly located further away.[3] The proximity and layout of mine compounds also resulted from companies' need to facilitate mine police surveillance of these communities, as well as to limit the distance between mineworkers and their workplaces.[4]

---

1   L. D. Conyngham, 'African Towns in Northern Rhodesia', *Journal of African Administration* 3 (1951), pp. 113–14.
2   R. K. Home, 'From Barrack Compounds to the Single-Family House: Planning Worker Housing in Colonial Natal and Northern Rhodesia', *Planning Perspectives* 15, 4 (2000), pp. 328–30.
3   817 Zambia Consolidated Copper Mines Investments Holdings Archives (hereafter ZCCM-IH), 10.6.9B, Department of Federal Surveys, Street Maps of Kitwe, Chingola and Mufulira.
4   Home, 'From Barrack Compounds', p. 330.

Soon after nationalising the mining industry in 1969, Zambia experienced a major economic crisis that resulted from the oil and copper price crises beginning in the mid-1970s.[5] This had severe consequences for environmental management, as global concerns for natural resource protection were just emerging in the 1970s, and gained momentum in the 1980s.[6] These global developments were important for resource-rich countries like Zambia, in which natural resource exploitation formed the basis of the economy. By the early 1980s, the country was the fifth largest copper producer in the world and held 6% of the world's reserves, necessitating effective mineral resource management and environmental regulation.[7]

The increased international pressure for environmental conservation influenced local legislation, beginning with the enactment of the Natural Resources Act in 1970. Although not specific to the mining industry, the Act marked a significant step towards environmental protection in post-independence Zambia. Soon thereafter, in 1985, the government enacted the National Conservation Strategy.[8] Among the Act's greatest weaknesses was poor implementation due to limited funding availability.[9] Like the National Resources Act before it, the National Conservation Strategy was a 'general' conservation Act with limited benefits for specific industries such as the mining industry.

---

5   M. M. Burdette, 'The Mines, Class Power and Foreign Policy in Zambia', *Journal of Southern African Studies* 10, 2 (1984), pp. 208–9; T. M. Shaw, 'Zambia: Dependence and Underdevelopment', *Canadian Journal of African Studies* 10, 1 (1976), p. 14; M. Ndulo, 'Mining Legislation and Mineral Development in Zambia', *Cornell International Law Journal* 19 (1986), p. 7.

6   For more information on global natural resource conservation efforts during the 1970s and 1980s, see E. Vasseur, 'United Nations Conference on the Human Environment: Stockholm, 5–16 June 1972', *Water Research* 7, 8 (1973), pp. 1227–33 and I. Borowy, *Defining Sustainable Development for our Common Future: A History of the World Commission on Environment and Development (Brundtland Commission)* (London: Routledge, 2013), p. 3.

7   For a detailed understanding of the Act, see Government of the Republic of Zambia, National Conservation Strategy, 1985.

8   Ibid., p. 13.

9   By this time, the Zambian Government could not fund the implementation of the Act. Therefore, the Dutch and Swedish governments provided funding for its implementation while the International Union, comprised of various civil society and government members to promote sustainable natural resources use, provided technical assistance. N. J. Bennett, Robin Roth, Sarah C. Klain, Kai M. A. Chan, et al., 'Mainstreaming the Social Sciences in Conservation', *Conservation Biology* 31, 1 (2017), pp. 56–66.

Environmental and conservation laws enacted between the 1970s and early 1980s were not specific to mining and this undermined environmental management within mining communities. This was compounded by the fact that mining companies focused on the health and safety of workers within the mines rather than in the communities outside the mines. Efforts at addressing the health and safety of workers within the mines included blasting and explosives legislation aimed at preventing blasting-related accidents, factory regulations, as well as first-aid regulations and competitions.[10] The emphasis on accident prevention and mine safety by mining companies was intended to facilitate production. Despite the significance of safety concerns for mineworkers, environmental safety outside the work environment was equally important given its impact on the livelihoods of workers and their families. Furthermore, addressing mining pollution outside the workplace was important given the possibility of the occurrence of unforeseen incidents, such as accidents during the transportation of hazardous substances to offsite locations and subsequent contamination of the areas surrounding these 'outside' locations. In addition to this, mine facilities were often spread out across a town, creating additional safety concerns. In, Kitwe, for example, waste facilities belonging to Nkana Mine are spread out across the town. Uchi and Kitwe tailings facilities are located far from the mine's mineral extraction site, that is situated on the south-western edge of Kitwe, while Nkana East residential area lies between the two waste facilities and is therefore prone to pollution from the two sites.[11] Given the possibility of offsite mine locations, effective management of communities located around mines was necessary.

The Environmental Protection and Pollution Control Act (EPPCA) of 1990 was the final environmental legislation enacted by the United National Independence Party before they were ousted from power by the Movement for Multi-Party Democracy in 1991.[12] Compared with previous laws, the Act had greater impact and enabled the enactment of additional environmental laws, as well as the establishment of the Environmental Council of Zambia

10 For more details on specific health and safety measures, see variously ZCCM-IH, 12.8.5A, Legislation May 1970 to December 1975; National Archives of Zambia (hereafter NAZ), MM1-9-1, Explosives Regulations and ML8-7-27, Mining Regulations.
11 Zambia Consolidated Copper Mines Investments Holdings and Misenge Environmental Technical Services, 'Copperbelt Environment Plan, Nkana Environmental Impact Assessment' (2003), pp. 11–12.
12 For specific provisions of the Act see Government of the Republic of Zambia, 'The Environmental Protection and Pollution Control Act', Chapter 204 of the Laws of Zambia.

(ECZ) and the Ministry of Environment and Natural Resources.[13] The Council was a statutory body tasked with environmental protection and pollution control to improve the health and welfare of both humans and their surroundings.[14] The organisation's mission was to ensure a pollution-free environment in Zambia through the enforcement of the EPPCA. It also undertook research on natural resource and environmental use, disseminated information on natural resources and environmental management and advised the state on environmental management and policy. These functions were performed through the Pollution Control Inspectorate and the Planning and Information Management Unit.[15] In 2011, ECZ transformed into Zambia Environmental Management Agency (ZEMA) through the Environmental Management Act enacted in the same year.[16] The organisation maintained the functions of its predecessor.

Despite the new laws of the early 1990s, the government's ability to effectively implement this legislation was limited by the severe financial constraints of the time, as well as the transition to multi-party democracy and a resultant reduction in state capacity, which negatively influenced policy-making processes.[17] Furthermore, legislation was not specific to mining but addressed general environmental protection. For example, the EPPCA provided for public involvement in environmental management, but did not provide specific guidelines for how this was to be achieved in specific sectors such as mining.[18] This particular omission was disadvantageous for mining communities, as it excluded the most affected members of the public from participating in environmental dialogue.

---

13 Ibid.

14 For more on ECZ see P.T. Sambo, 'The Environmental Management Act (2011): A Basis for the Growth of an Environmental Ethos and Good Environmental Governance in Zambia?' in A. Paterson, *Law, Environment, Africa* (Baden: Nomos Verlagsgesellschaft, 2019), pp. 647–64 and Colin N. Boocock, 'Environmental Impacts of Foreign Direct Investment in the Mining Sector in Sub-Saharan Africa' (Paris: OECD, 2002), pp. 25–6.

15 Interview, Misenge Technical Services employee, Kalulushi, 6 November 2018.

16 Government of the Republic of Zambia, 'The Environmental Management Act of 2011'.

17 M. Larmer, *Rethinking African Politics: A History of Opposition in Zambia* (London: Routledge, 2016), pp. 4–5.

18 For specific provisions of the EPPCA see Government of the Republic of Zambia, 'The Environmental Protection and Pollution Control Act', Chapter 204 of the Laws of Zambia.

As a result of inadequate legislation, economic and political challenges, as well as the government's generally low prioritisation of environmental protection, it was Zambia Consolidated Copper Mines (ZCCM) that spearheaded environmental management within and outside the mines.[19] By the early 1990s, ZCCM had already established environmental management practices on the 'old' Copperbelt. Established several years after the formation of ZCCM, ECZ therefore benefitted from the mining company's environmental strategies.[20] Evidence suggests that environmental monitoring activities were undertaken by ZCCM both within and beyond its premises. For example, ZCCM conducted re-vegetation projects around dam walls and surface dumping several years before the statutory body engaged in environmental monitoring on the 'old' Copperbelt.[21] Other strategies included garden refuse management, capping with topsoil to encourage the growth of vegetation and radiation waste management.[22] In 1994, ZCCM formed a unit called the Group Environmental Services to enhance environmental protection efforts by overseeing environmental monitoring at the various mines.[23]

The disadvantage of the state's limited involvement in environmental regulation was that ZCCM was not held accountable for environmental pollution that was not publicised or considered to be severe. Instead, the government praised the company's environmental achievements despite their own limited participation in the process and subsequent limited knowledge about the extent of pollution. Outlining ZCCM's various achievements in environmental protection in 1985, the government stated:

---

[19] The nationalisation of the Zambian mines was announced in 1969, while ZCCM was formed in 1982 following the merging of Roan Consolidated Copper Mines (RCCM) and Nchanga Consolidated Copper Mines (NCCM): J. Lungu, 'Copper Mining Agreements in Zambia: Renegotiation or Law Reform?' *Review of African Political Economy* 35, 117 (2008), pp. 403–15, p. 404.

[20] Interview, Misenge Environmental Technical Services employee, 25 October 2018; R. Douthwaite, M. Chitalu and C. Lungu, 'Zambia National Environment Situational Analysis Report', Ministry of Tourism, Environment and Natural Resources (2005), p. 1; C. Mulenga, 'Judicial Mandate in Safeguarding Environmental Rights from the Adverse Effects of Mining Activities in Zambia', *Potchefstroomse Elektroniese Regsblad* 22, 1 (2019), p. 8.

[21] D. Limpitlaw and T. Woldai, 'Environmental Impact Assessment of Mining by Integration of Remotely Sensed Data with Historical Data', Proceedings of the Second International Symposium on Mine Environmental Engineering held at Brunei University, London 28–31 July 1998.

[22] Interview, METS employee, Kalulushi, 6 November 2018.

[23] Ibid.

ZCCM operates water quality monitoring programmes in each division and maintains voluntary emission standards. The company is also building special dams to retain mining tailings. In the instance of these dams, for example, ZCCM has shown that conservation can be of direct economic benefit. By containing the copper in routine spill-ages – that would normally have polluted the rivers – the company is also holding onto vast amounts of potential revenue. This helps to sustain an environment external to the mines that might otherwise have become unfit for human life.[24]

However, the extent to which ZCCM was effective in environmental management remains unclear. Given the magnitude of the environmental damage that was later revealed to have existed on the 'old' Copperbelt, it is likely that these positive accounts of effective environmental management are exaggerated, reflecting a nostalgic longing for the nationalised industry.[25] In fact, as the above quote indicates, pollution of rivers by mine waste was considered a 'normal' aspect of the industry. Furthermore, sulphur dioxide pollution was already a significant concern during the early 1990s. In 1992 and 1993, for example, sulphur dioxide results in Mufulira indicated that emissions were higher than the stipulated standards for most of the year. This was especially the case at Clinic 5 in Kankoyo, which provides health services to those living close to the mine smelter.[26] The limited concern despite evidence of severe pollution suggests that mining-induced pollution was considered 'acceptable' to some extent.

Privatisation and Communities: The Consequences for 'Old' Copperbelt Mining Communities

Zambia Consolidated Copper Mines had historically provided a 'cradle to the grave' welfare policy for mine communities, through which employees and their families received housing and social services while in employment

---

24 GRZ, 'National Conservation Strategy', p. 52.

25 For more information on nostalgic longing among Copperbelt residents after priva-tisation, see P. Mususa, 'There Used to Be Order: Life on the Copperbelt After the Privatisation of the Zambia Consolidated Copper Mines', PhD Thesis, University of Cape Town, 2014, pp. 8, 14–15, 30; M. Larmer, 'Permanent Precarity: Capital and Labour in the Central African Copperbelt', *Labour History* 58, 2 (2017), pp. 170–72.

26 ZCCM-IH, 5.14.5B, 5.14.5B Miscellaneous, 1970 to 1995, Sulphur Emissions at Mufulira.

(see Larmer and Taylor, Chapter 12).[27] However, the infrastructure of the mining compounds had severely deteriorated by the time the industry was privatised in the late 1990s. By 1992, for example, the parks and gardens provided by ZCCM were dilapidated and 'non-existent in most of the townships'.[28] Furthermore, water treatment facilities had severely deteriorated. Access to safe water was undermined by high concentrations of suspended solids that resulted from a drought that same year, and the consequent decline of water levels in the streams.[29] To resolve these issues, the company encouraged community engagement in environmental management. This resulted from ZCCM's realisation that its efforts alone were insufficient to ensure environmental safety within mining communities and that community members should be informed about the impact of mining-induced pollution on their environment. It was therefore important for communities to contribute to environmental protection through the rehabilitation of their surroundings by creating green parks and gardens and restoring water treatment facilities.[30] Despite these efforts, the most significant mining-induced environmental challenges on the 'old' Copperbelt remained unresolved, and formed a central part of discussions regarding the privatisation of the industry.[31]

In fact, it was the Zambian Government, despite its own limited involvement in mining-related environmental protection in the decades preceding privatisation, that pointed out the dilapidation of the mine's outside premises, arguing that infrastructure was generally poorly maintained. This was denied by ZCCM, who insisted on the effectiveness of their containment efforts.[32] The extent of pollution on the 'old' Copperbelt by the end of the 1990s highlights the severe impact of poor coordination between the Zambian

27 F. Cronjé, S. Reyneke and C. Chenga, 'Corporate Social Responsibility in the Zambian Mining Sector: An Overview of Three Distinctive Operational Eras', *Koers* 82, 1 (2017), pp. 1–18; Lungu, 'Copper Mining Agreements in Zambia', p. 404; R. Negi, '"You Cannot Make a Camel Drink Water": Capital, Geo-History and Contestations in the Zambian Copperbelt', *Geoforum* 45 (2013), p. 241.
28 ZCCM-IH, 19.4.9E, 'Mine Township Maintenance and Development (Projects), Report on Mine Townships Maintenance and Development' (1992), p. 1.
29 Ibid., pp. 2–3.
30 Ibid., pp. 5–6.
31 For detailed information on the discussions regarding environmental issues during privatisation, see ZCCM-IH, METS, Volume 2.4, 'Nkana Environmental Impact Assessment' (2003), p. 2; 'Project Summary Report' (2005), p. ii.
32 ZCCM-IH, 4.2.3J, 'Privatisation File July 1994 to March 1996, Comments on Strategic Options for the Privatisation of ZCCM Limited', p. 9.

Government and ZCCM on environmental safety on the Copperbelt, as well as its adverse consequences on mining communities.

Following privatisation, ZCCM was reduced to a holding company, Zambian Consolidated Copper Mines Investments Holding (ZCCM-IH), with minority shares in the privatised companies. In 2000, Nkana and Mufulira mines were purchased by the Swiss company Glencore, jointly forming Mopani Copper Mines (MCM) Plc.[33] As part of the privatisation negotiations, the Zambian Government was forced to accept responsibility for the environmental liabilities that had accrued during previous decades of mining. This was reflected in the development agreements (DAs) that were signed between the state and investors.[34] Investors were exempted from both environmental liabilities and penalties on condition that the level of emissions did not exceed previous emission levels under ZCCM.

The DAs also included a stability clause granting investors exemptions of between 15 and 20 years, during which the state could neither alter nor terminate the provisions of the agreements.[35] This adversely affected environmental management within the mining industry, given the extensive length of time granted to investors to operate with limited controls over pollution and the fact that the state and ZCCM-IH bore responsibility for severe environmental liabilities, which have not been fully addressed to date.[36] This means there are still significant environmental challenges for communities on the 'old' Copperbelt, where current concerns encompass both ongoing and historical environmental issues. This highlights that environmental management was not prioritised by the Zambian Government during privatisation. These challenges are examined in the following sections.

33 S. Kangwa, 'Report on the Privatisation of Zambia Consolidated Copper Mines', Copperbelt University (2001), p. 13.

34 J. Lungu, 'Socio-Economic Change and Natural Resource Exploitation: A Case Study of the Zambian Copper Mining Industry', *Development Southern Africa* 25, 5 (2008), p. 544.

35 Cuthbert C. Makondo, Sydney Sichilima, Matthews Silondwa, Richard Sikazwe, Lombe Maiba et al., 'Environmental Management Compliance, Law and Policy Regimes in Developing Countries: A Review of the Zambian Case', *International Journal of Environmental Protection and Policy* 3, 4 (2015), p. 80.

36 In 2002, the Zambian Government founded the Copperbelt Environment Project (CEP). The initial timeframe for the completion of the CEP was 2008. However, when the project finally ended in 2011, some of the environmental liabilities taken on by the government and ZCCM-IH remained unresolved and remain so to date. See, ZCCM-IH METS, 'Copperbelt Environmental Project'; P. Sinkamba, 'Technical and Financial Proposal for Sustainability of the Copperbelt Environment Project in Zambia' (MPhil Dissertation, University of Stellenbosch, 2007).

Figures 9.1 (above) & 9.2 (left)
Water point in Kankoyo. A water point provided to residents in Kankoyo by MCM. Sanitation around the community is a significant challenge. Photographs by the author.

Social Services

On the 'old' Copperbelt, privatisation and the consequent loss of social service provisions also contributed to deterioration among mining communities. During privatisation, the former ZCCM-owned houses were sold off to their sitting tenants. The provision of community services was also removed from mine company responsibility. Instead, this was handed to local municipal councils and the regional commercial utility companies.[37] The resultant services are inadequate and contribute to local grievances. For example, irregular or non-existent refuse collection and inadequate water and sanitation (see Figures 9.1 and 9.2) result from the financial and capacity difficulties faced by local municipal councils. Community services are often supplemented by occasional CSR projects funded by private mine companies, though mining companies tend to exaggerate the positive impact of CSR projects on neighbouring communities. Furthermore, there are often disparities between the CSR strategies of mining companies and the needs of targeted communities.[38] Indeed, few of the CSR initiatives currently employed by MCM within mining communities address environmental rehabilitation. Although the need for environmental rehabilitation is partly fuelled by the mismanagement of urban waste, CSR strategies mostly do not address environmental rehabilitation in communities because Zambian laws do not strictly stipulate that investors must do so.

Nevertheless, the efforts made by MCM do augment otherwise limited government efforts to improve the state of mining communities. For example, to address water and sanitation needs within Kankoyo and Butondo, the company provides several water points within the compounds. The number of such points is, however, insufficient to meet community needs. Furthermore, the commercial utility companies are unable to provide safe running water throughout the day. According to community members, locals therefore rely on the polluted river that runs through part of the mine and the community.[39] Regular water quality tests are conducted by MCM to prevent contamination of public water bodies.[40] Despite these efforts, contamination of public water sources remains an ever-present concern for both the mining company and residents.

---

37 ZCCM-IH, METS, CEP, C'ounterpart Environmental Management Plan 1' (2003), p. 2.

38 A. Hilson, G. Hilson and S. Dauda, 'Corporate Social Responsibility at African Mines: Linking the Past to the Present', *Journal of Environmental Management* 241 (2019), pp. 341–2.

39 Interviews, anonymised, Mufulira, 2 November 2018.

40 Interview, Mopani Copper Mines Environmental Department employee, Mufulira, 8 November 2018.

The challenges in service provision are partly created by the failure of the national government to enact effective legislation to safeguard mining communities, or to maintain adequate service provision to communities. In their defence, Copperbelt municipal councils argue that effective service provision has been hindered by limited support from national leaders. Municipal councils also argue that the mushrooming informal settlements on the Copperbelt have increased pressure on already limited resources. In this regard, politicians reportedly contribute to this problem by permitting the legalisation of informal settlements in order to register additional voters for elections, at the expense of quality service provision.[41] With regards to the severe mining-induced challenges on the Copperbelt, however, officials from Mufulira's Department of Government Planning suggest that, despite the shared social responsibility that mine companies have for these communities, it is difficult to hold them to account due to the provisions of the legally enforceable DAs.[42]

Subsidence

The state of community infrastructure, including the now privately owned houses, has deteriorated significantly since privatisation. In Mufulira, for example, the houses located closest to the mine plant in Kankoyo have developed enormous cracks that reportedly result from mining-related tremors, occurring over several decades (see Figures 9.3 and 9.4). The worst hit homes are mostly located within a section of Kankoyo locally referred to as *Kuma spesho*, translated as 'the special area'. During the colonial era when these houses were constructed, the section housed skilled labourers and their families.[43] In some cases, houses located in *Kuma spesho* have literally collapsed due to long-term exposure to mining-induced tremors.

Today, individual homeowners are legally responsible for house maintenance. However, many residents appear not to agree with this, believing that MCM is partly responsible for their condition and renovation, owing to ongoing mining activities.[44] One Member of Parliament (MP) suggested that the Ministry of Mines and Minerals Development should be involved

---

41 ZCCM-IH, METS,Volume 2.5, Mufulira Environmental Impact Assessment (2003), p. 56.
42 Interview, anonymised, Mufulira, 13 November 2018.
43 Interview, anonymised, Mufulira, 13 November 2018.
44 Interviews, Kankoyo residents, November 2018.

Figures 9.3   Cracked houses in Mufulira. Photographs by the author.

in maintaining former townships alongside local councils in order to bridge the gaps in service provision.[45] This, however, was never implemented and the local municipal councils remained solely responsible for the former mine townships.

The regulation of some historical challenges on the 'old' Copperbelt draws from national legislation that does not directly relate to environmental protection within the mining industry. For example, collapsed houses in one of Mufulira's mining communities benefitted from the Disaster Management Act of 2010. The Act provides strategies for the management of disaster situations, as determined by the Office of the Vice President of Zambia, and the organisation of relief and recovery from disasters. Through the Act's provisions, the Office of the Vice President provided tents to Kankoyo residents whose homes collapsed from extreme mine-induced cracking.[46] Although many have stayed in the tents for longer than planned, this measure has at least prevented victims from becoming homeless.

---

45 National Assembly of Zambia, Parliamentary Debates for the First Session of the Ninth Assembly, 8 February 2001.
46 Interview, anonymised, Mufulira, 2 November 2018.

Figure 9.4   Cracked houses in Mufulira. Photograph by the
author.

Environmental Pollution

Another significant concern for mine communities on the 'old' Copperbelt
is environmental pollution. Mining-induced contamination of air, water and
soil has been a significant concern in the region since the colonial period.
Locals believe the location of African housing close to mining facilities was
deliberate. Long-term residents who previously worked in the mines suggest
that senior employees were aware of the environmental hazard of mining
activities, purposefully situating Africans closer to the mines and whites

further away. Meteorological evidence suggests that Wusakile experienced higher rates of air pollution because of the dominant wind direction from the smelter that blew in a north-east to south-west direction.[47] Likewise, Copperbelt mining communities, such as Kankoyo and Butondo in Mufulira and Bwacha in Kitwe, have been shown to be located within high-risk zones for air pollution.[48] Based on this evidence, it is clear that airborne pollution has been affecting Mufulira and Kitwe residents for many decades.

The privatisation of the mining industry highlighted the severity of pollution due to the exemptions granted to foreign investors, chief among them the exemption from penalties for pollution that did not exceed those emitted under ZCCM mines. One of the most severe environmental concerns on the 'old' Copperbelt is air pollution through the emission of sulphur dioxide into the atmosphere. Historically, air pollution has been of concern in both Kitwe and Mufulira.[49] Air pollution is particularly prevalent in Mufulira, where sulphur dioxide fumes, which locals call *senta*, have had a particularly significant effect. In 2007, Mufulira residents pleaded with MCM to end hazardous *senta* emissions.[50] Local schoolchildren wrote letters to Glencore, requesting that the investor address the problem.[51] This campaign resulted in the construction of a new smelter by Mopani Mine, in the same year, that reportedly captured 50% of the emissions from the smelting process. However, community concern peaked in 2009, when ECZ reported that sulphur dioxide emissions from the mine were up to 70 times in excess of those stipulated by the World Health Organization.[52]

Owing to local complaints and trade union action, pollution claims were investigated by ZEMA and the mining company's mining licence was briefly suspended in 2012, although no severe measures followed.[53] In 2014, MCM

47 ZCCM-IH, METS, ZCCM 'Copperbelt Environmental Project', Volume 2.5, Mufulira EIA, p. 4.
48 Ibid., p. 56.
49 ZCCM-IH, METS, 'Copperbelt Environment Project, Counterpart Environmental Management Plan', p. 38.
50 Mopani Copper Mines Plc., 'Mufulira Mine, Environmental Project Brief for the Smelter Upgrade Project' (2004).
51 Facing Finance, 'Glencore: Severe Health and Environmental Damages', 29 November 2011, www.facing-finance.org/en/database/cases/severe-health-and-environmental-damages-mopani-copper-mines-plcschwere-gesundheits-und-umweltschaeden-mopani-copper-mines-plc (accessed 14 October 2020).
52 Rob Davies, 'Glencore Court Ruling in Zambia May Trigger New Pollution Claims', *The Guardian*, 18 September 2016.
53 Misheck Wangwe and Gift Chanda, 'MUZ Challenges Mopani to End Leaching Mine Pollution', *The Post*, 9 March 2012; Facing Finance, 'Glencore: Severe Health and Environmental Damages'.

constructed a sulphuric acid plant, close to Kankoyo. The plant captures approximately 97% of the sulphur dioxide previously emitted.[54] Representatives from the mine's Environmental Department report a tremendous decrease in the level of sulphur dioxide fumes emitted. However, residents do not share these perceptions and suggest that pollution has in fact worsened because, although they can no longer see the 'acid fumes', they only realise that *senta* has been released into the atmosphere when they experience the stinging sensation in their eyes and choking effect that is associated with it.[55] Reports of respiratory complications, unconsciousness and death have continued despite the construction of the acid plant. Among the most severe cases since the plant was built are the suffocation of seven people in 2014, and the death of a prominent local politician in 2016.[56] The latter case particularly raised public attention. The victim's widower sued Mopani when the post-mortem report indicated that her death was linked to acute respiratory failure resulting from inhalation of toxic fumes. Despite MCM's attempt to cite the environmental indemnity agreements covering its operations, the court dismissed this on the basis that the sulphur dioxide emissions had exceeded legal limits. The deceased's widower received K400,000 (then worth about £30,000) in compensation.[57]

The 'Black Mountains'

Environmental grievances on the 'old' Copperbelt also concern the enormous copper slag heaps known locally as 'black mountains'. Kankoyo and Wusakile are located alarmingly close to these slag dumps, creating additional concerns about pollution. The presence of the dumps has created opportunities for small and large-scale 'miners' to process the slag and extract the remaining copper. In recent years, conflicts have arisen regarding the ownership of these deposits, which were not sold to MCM during privatisation.[58] Local communities have sought access to the slag heaps, resulting in both legal and illegal occupation of these deposits.[59]

---

54 Facing Finance, 'Glencore: Severe Health and Environmental Damages'.
55 Interviews, residents of Kankoyo and Butondo, Mufulira, 2018.
56 Government of the Republic of Zambia, High Court of Zambia Civil Jurisdiction Between Geofrey Elliam Mithi and Mopani Copper Mines Plc., 9 June 2016.
57 Ibid.; Facing Finance, 'Glencore: Severe Health and Environmental Damages'.
58 Kankoyo Community Meeting, 10 November 2018; ZCCM-IH METS, 'Copperbelt Environment Project, Environmental Management Plans' (2003).
59 Interview, anonymised, Kitwe, 15 October 2017.

In recent years, contestations have focused on the Kitwe dump, which is 90% owned by the Nkana Alloy and Smelting Company. However, disputes prevail over ownership of the remaining 10%. In 2013, illegal mining began operating on the premises and in 2018 the contested 10% stake was eventually granted to local small-scale miners known as *Jerabos*.[60] In the same year, however, part of the Kitwe black mountain collapsed, resulting in the death of ten people and injuries to eight more.[61] An additional eight people were injured in the accident. The incident was caused when surface excavators collapsed, blocking the escape of miners who were working underground. The incident was one of the worst in the Zambian mining industry since the Mufulira mine disaster of 1971 and was declared a national disaster.[62] In addition to such a direct threat to the lives of miners, the black mountain has contributed to air, soil and noise pollution and the cracking of houses in nearby Wusakile due to blasting operations.[63] Despite the blatant safety risk posed, the site remains operational.

The situation at the Mufulira 'black mountain' is different, given that 'mining' has not commenced there. However, similar conflicts have arisen concerning its ownership. In 2018, residents from various communities in Mufulira, particularly those located closest to the slag dump, marched to the municipal council offices to seek to determine the dump's 'rightful' beneficiaries. Two weeks later, Kankoyo residents held a community meeting at which they asserted their ownership of the dump.[64] Although the government has yet to decide on this issue, the conflict demonstrates the complexity of community responses to environmental issues on the 'old' Copperbelt. It highlights how residents affected by proximity to mine hazards respond to the perceived injustice of 'outsiders' benefitting from potential resources within their communities. According to Kankoyo residents, the air and soil pollution they experience as a result of the presence of the slag dump gives them the right to exploit the resource, which should not be shared by others, not even with other residents of Mufulira.

---

60 *Lusaka Times*, 'Mining at Kitwe's Black Mountain Resumes', 6 October 2018.

61 National Assembly of Zambia, Statement by the Minister of Mines and Minerals Development, 21 June 2018; *Business Day*, 'Subsistence Miners Die after Black Mountain Mine Dump Collapses in Zambia', 20 June 2018; *Zambia Daily Mail*, 'Black Mountain Accident National Disaster', 23 June 2018.

62 Ibid..

63 Interviews with residents of Wusakile, Kitwe, 2018.

64 Kankoyo Community Meeting, 10 November 2018.

The Impact of Mining on Communities in the 'New' Copperbelt

In the North-Western Province, the context of mine pollution since privatisation differs from that of the 'old' Copperbelt. Although Kansanshi mine has opened and closed several times since it first started operations in the early twentieth century, the recent development of mining in the region did not begin until after the mine was purchased by First Quantum Minerals (FQM) in 2001 (see Kesselring, Chapter 5). Production at Kansanshi mine was underway by 2005.[65] Evidence suggests that prior to privatisation, the Zambian Government was more interested in reaping short-term profits from the mine than in establishing a self-sufficient community, as on the 'old' Copperbelt. When the mine reopened under state ownership in the 1970s, the state was unwilling to invest in the necessary infrastructure for local processing of copper ores, specifically a smelter. The ores mined at Kansanshi were instead transported to smelters located on the 'old' Copperbelt, at Nchanga and Nkana mines.[66] Consequently, mining in the North-Western Province generally developed at a slower pace than the 'old' Copperbelt.[67]

In addition, the lack of infrastructural development and community investment in Solwezi and the limited development of Kansanshi mine during the ZCCM era had negative consequences for local communities, as local residents attest. Consequently, the area remained a labour reserve for migrant labour to the Copperbelt, as it had been during the colonial period.[68] Negi asserts that Solwezi town developed as a small administrative centre, rather than one whose existence focused on mining activities.[69] Solwezi residents were disappointed with the slow development of mining in the area and desired the levels of development associated with the more prosperous 'old' Copperbelt mines. They may however have been unaware of the environmental challenges associated with mining. The expansion of mining in the North-Western Province since the mid-2000s initiated the desired development, but also brought about environmental problems.

---

65 Mining Health Initiative, 'A Mining Health Initiative Case Study: First Quantum Mining Limited, Zambia: Lessons in Government Engagement', 2013, p. 5.
66 R. T. Libby and M. E. Woakes, 'Nationalization and the Displacement of Development Policy in Zambia', *African Studies Review* 23, 1 (1980), pp. 33–50, p. 38.
67 I. Peša, *Roads through Mwinilunga: A History of Social Change in Northwest Zambia* (Leiden: Brill, 2019), pp. 1–2.
68 Negi, '"You cannot make a Camel Drink Water"', p. 241.
69 Ibid., p. 243.

During privatisation, Kansanshi mine was initially sold to Cyprus Amax Minerals Company.[70] This created the prospect of development of the area but, only one year later, Cyprus Amax announced plans to close the mine in order to facilitate exploration works.[71] After two months, the company announced plans to demolish houses and other infrastructure within the mine's licensed area, to facilitate exploration works.[72] The destruction of local infrastructure was alarming for Solwezi residents, particularly those who lost houses and farm plots in the process. Local MPs from both opposition and ruling parties presented the grievances of Solwezi residents to the National Assembly in 2001.[73] According to one of them, Benny Tetamashimba, the destruction of infrastructure had left behind a 'bare' town. Local politicians complained that these developments had placed them in a difficult position with locals, who constantly demanded an explanation for the mining company's actions:

> If you ever reached Kansanshi Mine, you might have seen a lot of houses, a big clinic, a school which had more than a thousand pupils and so on. When the Government sold the mine to Cyprus Amax, the first thing that the people of Solwezi saw were bulldozers to erase all the buildings. Up to today, what is there is grass. This is making all politicians from North Western Province … fail to tell the people what is happening.[74]

By demolishing infrastructure to facilitate mining expansion, Cyprus Amax contributed to the underdevelopment of an already poorly developed region. The mine was however then purchased by FQM in 2001 and production commenced in 2005.[75] Kalumbila Mine, also owned by FQM, began commercial production more recently in 2015. This again raised local expectations. Locals believed that the mine would provide much needed

---

70 In 1999 the Phelps Dodge Corporation bought Cyprus Amax. Kangwa, 'Report on the Privatisation', p. 13; H. I. Torrealday, 'Mineralization and Alteration of the Kansanshi Copper Deposit – Zambia', Master's Thesis, University of Colorado, 2000; M. Hansungule, P. Feeney and R. H. Palmer, 'Report on Land Tenure Insecurity on the Zambian Copperbelt' (Lusaka: Oxfam, 1998), p. 62.

71 Hansungule at al., 'Report on Land Tenure', p. 62.

72 National Assembly of Zambia, Parliamentary Debates for the First Session of the Ninth Assembly, 8 February 2001.

73 Ibid.

74 Ibid.

75 Interview, anonymised, Kalumbila, 18 October 2017; R. Kapesa, J. Mwitwa and D. C. Chikumbi, 'Social Conflict in the Context of the Development of New Mining Concessions in Zambia', *Southern African Peace and Security Studies* 4, 2 (2015), pp. 41–62.

employment that would enable them to improve their socio-economic status, and that the presence of a flourishing mine would facilitate improvements in infrastructure and social service provision, as well as the growth of additional industries to serve the needs of mine employees.[76]

Land Tenure

A striking difference between the 'old' Copperbelt and the North-Western Province is the customary land tenure system that still exists in many parts of the region. This system means that mining companies must first obtain access to land from local customary authorities. Although customary land tenure existed on the 'old' Copperbelt when commercial mines first started operations in the 1920s, customary authorities there were completely ignored by the colonial administration. The indigenous Lamba communities were relatively small and excluded from any claim on mineral rights. In fact, the concerns of customary leaders on the Copperbelt, such as the Lamba Chief Mushili IV, on the underdevelopment of their chiefdoms were only publicly acknowledged during the independence era.[77]

In North-Western Province, interactions between mining investors and customary leaders controlling land access have sometimes proved problematic. For example, in 2010 FQM's Kalumbila Minerals Limited acquired 518 square kilometres of land from the local Lunda Senior Chief Musele.[78] This was in excess of the 250 hectares of customary land that a chief can grant, according to Zambian law. Although the state contested the agreement, FQM officially announced that commercial production was underway in 2016.[79]

Despite strong rural customs in North-Western Province, the new urban areas that have emerged around Kansanshi mine and the newly constructed

76 Interviews, residents of Solwezi and Kalumbila, 2017–18.

77 For a detailed description of relations between Chief Mushili and British colonial authorities, see B. Siegel, 'The "Wild" and "Lazy" Lamba: Ethnic Stereotypes on the Central African Copperbelt', *Anthropology Publications*, Paper 5 (1989), p. 10; B. Siegel, 'Bomas, Missions, and Mines; The Making of Centres on the Zambian Copperbelt', *African Studies Review* 31, 3 (1988), pp. 61–84.

78 'Chipata, Kasama, Solwezi and Mongu to be Transformed into Cities – Lungu', *Lusaka Times*, 2 March 2015.

79 Interview, anonymised, Kalumbila, 18 October 2017; Kapesa et al., 'Social Conflict', pp. 41–62; Mining Watch Canada, 'Agreement between His Royal Highness Senior Chief Musele and Kalumbila Minerals Limited for the Acquisition of Surface Rights within the Chiefdom of Senior Chief Musele for the Trident Project of Approximately 518 Square Kilometres' (2010), https://miningwatch.ca/sites/default/files/fqm-musele-agreement-dated-14-july-2011_1.pdf (accessed 16 June 2019).

Kalumbila town resemble developments on the 'old' Copperbelt during its heyday. The developments at Kalumbila for example include a housing project, and educational, health and recreational facilities.[80] Reflecting this urbanisation, President Edgar Lungu announced in 2015 that Solwezi was one of four Zambian towns that would be given the status of cities.[81] Modern residential areas have emerged across the wider province in proximity to new mines. These include the Kabitaka Hills Housing Project, the Kalumbila town residences, as well as the Golf Estates at Kansanshi and Kalumbila. The settlements include school and health facilities. However, the Golf Estates are up-market residences that also include golf courses, international schools, wildlife viewing and clubhouses with restaurant and sports facilities. Within the Kansanshi mine premises, a second and reportedly more exclusive clubhouse is under construction as of 2020. The dam along which it will be built is only several hundred metres away from the Kabwela resettlement community (see discussion below) and within full view of its residents. Access to the Golf Estate and other mine facilities, including some private schools, is strictly controlled, and therefore most Solwezi residents have not seen these facilities; many are unaware of their existence. On the other hand, the Kabitaka and Kalumbila town houses provide more modest but decent accommodation with a small garden. The houses range from two to four bedroomed houses and it is here that most skilled and semi-skilled mineworkers and contractors reside. Despite these variations in mine housing facilities, most of these facilities are only accessible to a small elite, largely excluding most of the local population who cannot afford them. Interaction between Kabitaka and Kalumbila residents and outsiders is easily facilitated by unrestricted access to the premises. This contrasts sharply with the relationship between the more overtly 'gated' Golf Estates, which are not the subject of this chapter, and the broader Kansanshi and Kalumbila communities discussed here.

Environmental Pollution

On the 'new' Copperbelt, residents cite dust, water and soil pollution as major mining-induced environmental concerns. The wind blows dust from new tailings deposits into their communities, also created by the constant construction of mining facilities. According to locals, mine effluent has also contributed to groundwater pollution. Furthermore, run-off water from the mine dumps is believed to contaminate the soil in surrounding communities.

---

80 Observations based on fieldwork conducted in Kalumbila between 2017 and 2019.
81 'Chipata, Kasama, Solwezi and Mongu', *Lusaka Times*.

According to the Senior Group Leader of Kabwela, Mr Kakonde, this has lowered annual crop yields and made the soil nearly infertile.[82] These claims are generally disputed by mining company officials. In Kalumbila, for example, mine representatives denied the water pollution charges, claiming that, although incidents of accidental water pollution are not uncommon within the industry, the water pollution about which locals have complained is the consequence of the region's soil, as its high iron levels tend to give underground water a reddish appearance. [83]

Kalumbila Mine's denial of mining-induced pollution is consistent with FQM's environmental policy, which claims that the company is committed to pollution prevention, legal compliance, environmental protection, sound environmental mining practices, and responsible management of mining waste and mining products.[84] According to Kalumbila Mine's Environmental Manager Joseph Ngwira, FQM subscribes to internationally accepted guidelines in order to augment in-house and national environmental guidelines, including the Equator Principles and ISO 14001.[85] In line with its environmental policy, FQM has introduced mining processes that are reportedly 'safer' than those previously employed on the 'old' Copperbelt. Examples include the recycling of waste oil in order to reduce hazardous waste. New storage facilities help reduce the use of hydrocarbons. Similarly, enclosing milling and crushing facilities prevents air pollution. Furthermore, the use of electric-powered shovels instead of diesel excavators reduces fossil fuel consumption and resultant carbon emissions.[86] Other sustainable strategies include re-vegetation of eroded mine sites and wildlife conservation within mine premises.[87]

Despite the positive image painted by FQM's environmental policy and its denial of environmental pollution claims by locals, mining companies tend to exaggerate their environmental achievements, just as locals may exaggerate the impact on their communities. Furthermore, the danger mining poses to the environment means that community concerns regarding pollution cannot be entirely dismissed by FQM. In addition, the 'newness' of these mines means that the full effects of mining on the environment may lie in

82 Interview, Mr Kakonde, Solwezi, 15 December 2017.
83 Interviews, Kalumbila Mine representatives.
84 First Quantum Minerals, 'Environmental Policy,' 2011; Interview, J. Ngwira, Kalumbila, 15 October 2017.
85 Ibid.
86 Interview, J. Ngwira, Kalumbila, 15 October 2017.
87 Ibid; interview, anonymised, Kalumbila, 18 October 2017; First Quantum Minerals Limited, Environmental and Safety Data Report (2018), p. 13.

the future. Makondo et al. suggest that environmental, ecological and public health challenges similar to those on the 'old' Copperbelt and in Kabwe can be expected to occur in this region.[88] Lindahl suggests that the newer mines are likely to contribute even more severely to air pollution in the region, given the construction of a new smelter at Kansanshi.[89] In addition, groundwater pollution will largely affect a significant area given the location of the 'new' Copperbelt within both the Zambezi and Kafue River basins.[90]

Despite the pollution concerns that have arisen in the North-Western Province, national regulators downplay the possible environmental damage that may result from these mining activities. A ZEMA official noted:

> Kalumbila is not undertaking any smelting. Therefore, air quality issues are not expected here. At Kalumbila, air pollution could be connected to dust and release from motor vehicle emissions. The most prominent issue is water pollution because the mining process only goes as far as concentration level, after which the slurry is released.[91]

The lack of concern by FQM contrasts with the views of community members who are convinced that pollution is already greater than is officially acknowledged by the mining company. During the same interview, the ZEMA official conceded that in 2016 crops belonging to locals near Kansanshi were affected by sulphur dioxide and that residents demanded compensation from the mine.[92] Despite this, sulphur dioxide pollution continues to be denied by mine representatives.

The disparities between environmental reports produced by government regulators, mining company representatives and the public, highlight a major challenge in environmental regulation, which is that pollution is perceived differently by those who regulate it and those who experience it. Locals tend to exaggerate the effects of mining activities, for example attributing low crop yields to the impact of mining, despite the fact that these are consistent with those obtained before the mines reopened. However, mine management and regulators' denial that pollution has occurred leads to de-prioritisation of environmental protection efforts, despite a clear understanding of the consequences of mining for the environment.

---

88 Makondo et al. 'Environmental Management Compliance', p. 80.
89 J. Lindahl, *Environmental Impacts of Mining in Zambia: Towards better Environmental Management and Sustainable Exploitation of Mineral Resources*, Geological Survey of Sweden Report, 22 (2014), p. 6.
90 Ibid., pp. 10–11; Makondo et al., 'Environmental Management Compliance', p. 80.
91 Interview, anonymised, Ndola, 13 September 2017.
92 Ibid.

Resettlement: The Consequences of 'Houses Built on Copper' on the 'Old' and 'New' Copperbelt

The expansion of mining within the 'new' Copperbelt has resulted in the displacement and resettlement of several communities. Communities are relocated for various reasons. At Kansanshi, locals who began farming on Kansanshi mine premises prior to the reopening of current mining activities were relocated to enable the reintroduction of mining activities. Around Kansanshi, communities have also been resettled to facilitate the extension of mining facilities, for example additional waste facilities and roads.[93] At Kalumbila, communities were resettled to make room for the construction of the greenfield project and housing facilities (see Figures 9.5 and 9.6).

Within the context of extractive industries, displacement is often justified by the supposed benefits of large-scale investment. As Butler asserts,

> foreign-investment led industrial mining is understood to foster economic growth and thus contribute to poverty reduction. For such reason, local population displacements are often deemed a reasonable trade-off, given the economic benefits that are purported to accrue to the nation and the local region.[94]

Despite this assertion, the negative implications of mining investment for relocated communities often outweigh the economic benefits. Around Kansanshi mine, communities were relocated to facilitate the extension of mining facilities such as waste disposal sites. In Kalumbila, the construction of an entirely new mine involved the relocation of indigenous communities to new resettlement sites, creating a sense of loss despite the potentially positive implications of large-scale mining investment.

Resettlement disrupts the social and economic order of communities, creating socio-economic changes that undermine pre-existing livelihoods. Furthermore, relocation may result in feelings of loss and nostalgia for residents' previous communities.[95] Despite this, Askland argues that community

[93] R. Kesselring, 'At an Extractive Pace: Conflicting Temporalities in a Resettlement Process in Solwezi, Zambia', *The Extractive Industries and Society* 5, 2 (2018), pp. 237–44.
[94] P. Butler, 'Colonial Walls: Psychic Strategies in Contemporary Mining-Related Displacement', *Refuge: Canada's Journal on Refugees* 29, 2 (2014), pp. 87–99, p. 91.
[95] Interviews, residents of New Israel, Northern Settlement and Shinengene, Kalumbila, 2017–19.

Figures 9.5 (above) & 9.6 (below)   Northern settlement, Kalumbila.
Photographs by the author.

displacement has the potential to ease experiences of loss and dislocation.[96] Using the example of Wollar, a village in North-Western Australia around which coal mining has gradually expanded since the 1970s, Askland argues that feelings of loss and disruption are common in villagers who reside within affected communities and are daily 'reminded of the uneven battle that has played out in their village and the loss they have endured', whereas those who move away from this region do not experience similar emotions.[97] This analysis is both true and false in the case of the Zambian mining industry. Relocation from affected communities may indeed ease feelings of loss and dislocation. In the case of Kankoyo for example, the relocation of the community would provide relief from the constant effects of continued mining pollution.

On the 'old' Copperbelt, some residents of communities such as Kankoyo are willing to relocate voluntarily. Such residents look to the example of the relocation of Mufulira's Zambia Railways Compound after 2005. This project was funded by the World Bank and Nordic Support Fund to support the Zambian Government in addressing the environmental degradation and social impact of historic mining activities.[98] The Copperbelt Environment Project identified the relocation of the railway operations as a major priority, as it was experiencing severe housing subsidence due to MCM's activities.[99] The community has since been resettled successfully along the Mufulira-Congo Road. In the case of Kankoyo, resettlement plans were initially drawn up several decades ago, when mining expansion after independence led the government to consider relocating the entire town further away from the mining site.[100] However, the project was never implemented. Kankoyo's houses have long passed their original envisaged life span of 50 years, which partly explains their current dilapidation.[101]

Although the relocation of Mufulira's Zambia Railways community seems to be a success story, the same cannot be said for the resettled communities on the 'new' Copperbelt. Prior to the reopening of Kansanshi mine under FQM management, the mine initially occupied a relatively small

96   H. H. Askland, 'A Dying Village: Mining and the Experiential Condition of Displacement', *Extractive Industries and Society* 5, 2 (2018), pp. 230–36, p. 232.
97   Ibid., p. 233.
98   ZCCM-IH, METS, 'Copperbelt Environment Plan, Counterpart Environmental Management Plan', vol. 1 (2003), p. 7.
99   ZCCM-IH, METS, ZCCM Investments Holdings Plc, 'Preparation of Phase 2 of a Consolidated Environmental Management Plan, Project Summary Report' (2005), p. ii.
100 Interviews, Mufulira Municipal Council employees, November 2018.
101 Interview, anonymised, Mufulira, 13 November 2018.

area. According to a senior resident of Mushitala area, Mrs Nkole, and the customary leader of the Kabwela community, Mr Kakonde, several small villages stood on land which now forms part of the mine premises. Locals cultivated various crops including maize, sweet potatoes and groundnuts for subsistence. When the mine reopened under FQM, mining development necessitated the expansion of the mine's territory. These villagers were offered compensation in exchange for their departure, while a minority willingly opted to sell their land to FQM in order to earn some money.[102]

The relocated Kabwela community is located about five kilometres from the mine entrance along its boundary. It provides an excellent case study for the impact of mining on neighbouring communities, owing to its proximity to mine facilities such as dumping and extraction sites. Kabwela community is not an entirely new settlement. It was first established in 1996 as a small village under the current Senior Group Leader's uncle, who held a similar position. The community, comprised of not more than ten residents, was under the jurisdiction of Chief Kapijimpanga. When people were displaced from what is now Kansanshi mine premises, some joined Kabwela community as 'resettled villagers'.[103] For this reason, and given FQM's involvement in service provision at the time of resettlement, the community is considered to be a resettled one. Kabwela now has a population of approximately 1,800 people.[104]

In Kalumbila District, the Northern and Southern/Shinengene settlements were created when FQM acquired customary land for the development of the mining project in 2010.[105] The two settlements are located to the north and south of the mining town centre respectively, and are home to villagers who previously resided on what are now Kalumbila Mine premises. As at Kansanshi mine, FQM constructed a small clinic and school for each resettlement community, as well as providing housing for residents.

Since their establishment however, these communities have been adversely affected by the continued extension of mining facilities. For example, the extension of the Kansanshi mine boundary towards Kabwela community to facilitate the construction of a road and an additional waste dump facility added to the pre-existing displacement and increased the distance that

---

102 Interviews, Mr Kakonde, Solwezi, 15 December 2017 and Mrs Nkole, Solwezi, 12 August 2016.
103 Interview, Mr Kakonde, Solwezi, 15 December 2017.
104 Ibid.
105 Interviews, residents of Kabwela and New Israel resettlement communities, Solwezi, 2017.

Kabwela residents need to travel to access goods and services in Solwezi town.[106] Kabwela residents complained about the insecurity resulting from FQM's boundary expansion to facilitate a new tailings dam, because it occupied part of the land on which Kabwela residents had settled. This created fear within the community that future expansion would push them even further into the outskirts of Solwezi.[107] The community's concerns are valid, given the fast pace at which mining activities are expanding in the region. For example, between 2011 and 2018, the boundary around Kansanshi mine was significantly altered.[108] Specifically, the eastern boundary has been extended further eastwards owing to the establishment of an additional waste facility in 2017.[109]

On the 'new' Copperbelt, other complaints about resettlement sites focus on the long distances to town centres and limited access to goods and services. Except for Kabwela and the Northern Settlement that are situated closer to Solwezi and Kalumbila town centres respectively, the other resettlement communities are located far from health, education and social services. Many residents feel that their previous homes were better located and serviced than these resettlement sites. This example suggests that on the 'new' Copperbelt relocation has created nostalgia for former homes rather than abated feelings of loss and dislocation as suggested by Askland. Mususa refers to a nostalgic memory of the past on the 'old' Copperbelt in the aftermath of privatisation, through which people exaggerate the positive nature of the past.[110] In relation to capital and labour relations on the 'old' Copperbelt, Larmer describes memories as being 'at odds with historical reality' and representing 'a stable and prosperous "Copperbelt" that never existed.'[111] This is certainly applicable to local representations of socio-economic prosperity of former customary settlements on the 'new' Copperbelt. Despite the undeniable impact of large-scale investment on socio-economic organisation, locals tend to present an exaggerated picture of the positive nature of their lives prior to resettlement.

106 Kesselring, 'At an Extractive Pace', pp. 237–44.

107 Interviews, residents of Kabwela Resettlement Community, Solwezi, 2017.

108 For specific maps, see J. Van Alstine, F. Ngosa, J. Manyindo, et al., 'Seeking Benefits and Avoiding Conflicts: A Community-Company Assessment of Copper Mining in Solwezi, Zambia', Report, University of Leeds and London School of Economics, 2011, p. 10; Kesselring, 'At an Extractive Pace', p. 240.

109 Consultation meeting concerning the extension of mining facilities at Kansanshi, August 2017.

110 Mususa, 'There Used to Be Order', pp. 8, 14–15, 30.

111 Larmer, 'Permanent Precarity', pp. 170–72.

Nostalgia may also be used by locals to make claims on the company. For example, residents in Kalumbila expressed concerns about FQM's lack of respect for their culture in relation to the inadequate housing and agricultural provisions offered to them in resettlement locations. The supposed inadequacies of FQM are often presented in comparison to their former homes, where things were done differently. For example, locals complained about the two-bedroomed houses provided for large families in the Kalumbila resettlement sites without consideration for the presence of adult children of both sexes, for whom sharing sleeping quarters is considered culturally inappropriate. They compared this to their 'more appropriate' setup in their former homes, where additional sleeping, leisure and cooking quarters were constructed around the main home to ensure privacy and cultural appropriateness.[112] Although the two-bedroomed houses do indeed tend to be overcrowded for larger families, similar housing was historically provided for African mineworkers on the 'old' Copperbelt. 'Family housing' was only introduced after 1940, following outcries from mineworkers over what they considered to be inadequate housing conditions.[113] The disparities between local and mining company approaches to housing do, however, highlight the challenges in creating an effective and mutually beneficial relationship between companies and indigenous mining communities.

Regarding the limited access to agricultural land, FQM is currently legalising farm plots for residents of resettlement sites, following complaints over the lack of farmland and subsequent encroachment by locals on vacant land that is within FQM's licensed area. Given that some resettled residents were able to continue farming on previously owned land at the time of resettlement, FQM introduced conservation farming. The project adapts traditional farming methods in order to increase the yield from a given plot of land, encouraging sustainable land use and promoting food security.[114] The company planned to provide the initial financing for the project, and then gradually withdraw its support so that it would be self-sustaining in the long term.[115] However, many community members felt 'abandoned' by the mining company when its support was eventually withdrawn.[116] This has again created nostalgia among resettled communities for their former homes, which supposedly facilitated farming activities.

---

112 Interviews, residents of Northern Settlement, Kalumbila, October 2017.
113 Home, 'From Barrack Compounds to the Single-Family House', p. 328.
114 Interview, Anonymised, Kalumbila, 18 October 2017.
115 Ibid.
116 Interview, Senior Group Leader Northern Settlement, Kalumbila, 15 October 2017; Interview, Senior Group Leader, Shinengene, Kalumbila, 20 October 2017.

According to the Kalumbila Trident Foundation CSR Manager, Garth Lappeman, one of the greatest challenges in relocating mining communities is that Zambian legislation lacks clear-cut guidelines for such processes.[117] Therefore, mining companies employ the guidelines provided by the Ministry of Agriculture for crop-related compensation, compensating for relocation from their cultivated land. Drafting a relocation plan is a strenuous process, in which various drafts go back and forth between the company, non-governmental organisations and national government for approval. Although the process supposedly requires the involvement of community members, respondents reported that they were not directly consulted. Negotiations with the mining company are often conducted exclusively by the most senior customary authorities, who do not always represent local grievances effectively.[118] A further complexity arises from the variations in land and agricultural value, which means that relocated families do not receive equal compensation. This raises suspicions among locals about their neighbours' ability to negotiate for better packages and whether these are influenced by possible 'connections' to influential people within the mines or government.[119]

Conclusion

Large-scale mining development presents inevitable consequences for the environment. This is especially the case for neighbouring communities located closest to mining activities. As demonstrated in this chapter, the environmental impact of mining on neighbouring communities is a significant aspect that remains poorly addressed within both the 'old' and 'new' Copperbelt mining regions of Zambia. The history of environmental management in Zambia suggests that the impact of mining on neighbouring communities has generally been neglected since the establishment of the 'old' Copperbelt. The increase in international concern for natural resource protection during the 1970s and 1980s increased government interest in environmental protection, but was limited by an international environmental agenda that was inappropriate for Zambia's economic and political context. Historically, periods of local and international economic decline have hampered the ability of the state and mining companies to effectively invest in mining expansion, let alone environmental protection.

117 Interview, Mr Lappeman, Kalumbila, 18 October 2017.
118 Interviews, residents of Kalumbila, 2017–18.
119 Interviews, residents of Northern and Southern Settlements, Kalumbila, October 2017.

Furthermore, economic transitions such as privatisation were inspired by political and socio-economic factors that overlooked the environmental impact of foreign investment. These factors have ultimately contributed to the decline of mining communities that already existed in the 'old' Copperbelt, as well as predetermined disadvantageous conditions for emerging settlements in the new mining region of the North-Western Province. Facilitated by the poorly negotiated DAs and existing mining and environmental legislation in Zambia, blame is passed back and forth between the state, mining companies and community leaders, while the environmental status of mining communities continues to decline.

This chapter highlights variations in mining communities within the two regions and how they have affected the extent and severity of environmental consequences. In this vein, the chapter argues that despite pollution being a significant challenge in both regions, pollution on the 'new' Copperbelt appears to be less severe owing to the recent nature of mining activities and the consequent limited environmental evidence of pollution. This contrasts to the 'old' Copperbelt, where commercial mining has been undertaken almost continuously since the 1920s. Using the example of the 'old' Copperbelt as a blueprint for the development of environmental concerns, the chapter concludes that, despite the limited evidence of severe pollution on the 'new' Copperbelt, the region is likely to follow in the footsteps of its predecessor if mining communities are not protected. In addition to the existing environmental concerns, the impact of mining on communities on the 'new' Copperbelt is likely to be further shaped by the complexity of state-mining company-community relationships that have emerged in what remains an 'indigenous' society. This is because evidence concerning relations between the three parties suggests differences in approach and understanding of what constitutes effective environmental management for communities adjacent to and affected by mining.

PART 3

PRODUCING AND CONTESTING KNOWLEDGE OF URBAN SOCIETIES

Part 3

10

'The British, the French and even the Russians use these methods': Psychology, Mental Testing and (Trans)Imperial Dynamics of Expertise Production in Late-Colonial Congo

AMANDINE LAURO

Introduction

'Ah this science! Great science! Through which Man sees his humanity.'[1] Thus spoke Stefano Kaoze (1886–1951), a young Congolese apprentice priest, when evoking psychology in what is considered as the first publication by a Congolese author in French. Written in 1910, the article 'The Psychology of Bantu People' is also one of the first attempts at a psychological analysis in colonial Congo. Kaoze became the first Congolese Catholic priest a few years later, and his essay is more theological and philosophical than psychological per se, but it captures perfectly both the ambitions and the impasses of psychological research in the Belgian colony. 'I am at a loss for words to praise this science', Kaoze wrote, while his Belgian preface writer underlined that psychology would 'reveal to us what is going on in the soul of the natives of our colony'.[2] But Kaoze also knew that this faith had its limits: 'What I have

---

1   Stefano Kaoze, 'La psychologie des Bantu', in Maurice Amuri Mpala-Lutebele and Jean-Claude Kangomba (eds), *Stefano Kaoze: Œuvre complète* (Brussels: Archives et Musée de la littérature (MEO), 2018 [1911]), p. 56.
2   Arthur Vermeersch, 'Les sentiments supérieurs chez les Congolais', in Mpala-Lutebele and Kangomba, *Stefano Kaoze*, pp. 47–51, p. 47.

just summarised is in me naturally, in me black [*en moi noir*]. But the terms to express this are European.'[3]

Four decades later, when Kaoze's innovative essay was long forgotten, a group of Belgian psychologists was preoccupied with the same concerns. By the late 1940s, psychological expertise had acquired an overwhelming legitimacy in the Congo, among both colonial scientists and the political milieux. But the possibility of developing effective and culturally appropriate diagnostic tools to assess the 'mentality' and/or the 'intelligence' of Central African people on the basis of Western scientific models remained a highly debated question, further complicated by the (new) challenges raised by urban social change and 'acculturation'. These tensions were certainly not specific to the Belgian empire. As historian Erik Linstrum has shown in his landmark work on psychology in the British Empire, the powerful attraction of psychological techniques in the late-colonial period was inseparable from wider discussions about (in)equality, difference and domination in a context of 'modernisation' plans and developmentalist ambitions.[4] Not surprisingly then, these techniques proved particularly attractive in Haut-Katanga's towns and mining operations.

This chapter explores some of the specific forms and meanings of these discussions – and of the sudden authority of psychological expertise – in late-colonial Congo, including the industrial centres of the Copperbelt. As we shall see, their history is closely connected to the new scientific ambitions towards changing urban society that emerged during the same period, notably in Katanga's mining towns, where the emergence of a supposedly new type of African urban modernity, combined with the need for cutting-edge industrial productivity, necessitated expert assessment and new methods of analysis.[5] This history raises important questions about the ambiguous uses of

---

3   Kaoze, 'La psychologie des Bantu', p. 47. On the early career of Kaoze, see Matthieu Zana Aziza Etambala, 'Kaoze, le "protégé" du roi Albert I: formation, ordination et voyage en Europe', *Annales Aequatoria* 28 (2007), pp. 375–414.
4   Erik Linstrum, 'The Politics of Psychology in the British Empire, 1898–1960', *Past and Present* 215 (2012), pp. 195–233; Erik Linstrum, *Ruling Minds: Psychology in the British Empire* (Cambridge MA: Harvard University Press, 2016).
5   Benjamin Rubbers and Marc Poncelet, 'Sociologie coloniale au Congo belge: Les études sur le Katanga industriel et urbain à la veille de l'Indépendance', *Génèses* 99, 2 (2015), pp. 93–112. See also Miguel Bandeira Jerónimo, 'Restoring Order, Inducing Change: Imagining a "New (Wo)man" in the Belgian Colonial Empire in the 1950s', *Comparativ* 28, 6 (2018), pp. 97–116.

expertise in an empire with a very specific history in the realm of knowledge production. As the few studies devoted to this history have shown,[6] knowledge production in the humanities in the Belgian Congo was, until the late 1940s, almost exclusively in the hands of non-scientists (i.e. of colonial administrators, former magistrates and missionaries). Moreover, in the 1950s, when the landscape of 'colonial sciences' became more 'scientific' and more professionalised, it may be asked if it was completely 'colonial' anymore.

The limits of the analytical category of 'colonial sciences' have been discussed by historians of other empires, an observation that also reveals a history shared across imperial borders.[7] In the Congolese Copperbelt, as in the Belgian empire in general, psychological expertise was clearly built through exchanges and interactions across national and imperial borders, as this chapter demonstrates. There has been, in recent years, a growing interest in conceptualising empire and science as networks connected by various and multidirectional circulations.[8] The role of cross-border exchanges in establishing scholarly collaborations, research agendas and the complex dynamics between science and the politics of empire have attracted renewed attention (especially among historians of the British Empire), either through an imperial framework (flows of exchanges *within* the empire) and, more recently, through an inter-imperial framework (flows of exchanges *between* empires). As this

6   In comparison with other empires, the landscape of colonial sciences in the Belgian empire remains underexplored. See however Marc Poncelet, 'Sciences sociales, colonisation et développement, une histoire sociale du siècle d'africanisme belge', PhD in Sociology, University of Lille I, 1996; Marc Poncelet, *L'invention des sciences coloniales belges* (Paris: Karthala, 2009); Ruben Mantels, *Geleerd in de tropen: Leuven, Congo & de wetenschap, 1885–1960* (Leuven: Leuven University Press, 2007).

7   See for example William Beinart, Karen Brown and Daniel Gilfoyle, 'Experts and Expertise in Colonial Africa Reconsidered: Science and the Interpenetration of Knowledge', *African Affairs* 108, 432 (2009), pp. 413–33; Mark Harrison, 'Science and the British Empire', *Isis* 96, 1 (2005), pp. 56–63; Frederick Cooper, 'Development, Modernization, and the Social Sciences in the Era of Decolonization: The Examples of British and French Africa', *Revue d'histoire des sciences humaines* 10, 1 (2004), pp. 9–38. On the Belgian case, see Myriam Mertens and Guillaume Lachenal, 'The History of "Belgian" Tropical Medicine from a Cross-Border Perspective', *Revue Belge de Philologie et d'Histoire*, 90, 4 (2012), pp. 1249–71.

8   Benedikt Stuchtey, *Science across the European Empires 1800–1950* (London: German Historical Institute, 2005); Brett M. Bennet and Joseph M. Hodge (eds), *Science and Empire: Knowledge and Networks of Science across the British Empire, 1800–1970* (New York: Palgrave, 2011).

chapter underlines, these registers were in no way mutually exclusive, as already suggested by recent historiographical debates about the dynamics of 'imperial globalisation' and the fluid intersections between the international, the imperial and the colonial.[9]

The history of psychological expertise and more precisely of mental testing in the Belgian Congo provides a particularly revealing terrain to analyse these issues. On the one hand, psychology occupied an in-between space in the traditional categorisation of the scientific landscape (social sciences vs 'hard' sciences). On the other hand, the Belgian empire always had a special and complex relationship to internationalism and inter-imperial comparisons. During the scramble for Africa, King Léopold II used strategies of internationalisation to assert the legitimacy of his rule (and to position Brussels as a centre of international expertise on colonial questions)[10]. But the global dimension of the 'red rubber' campaign against the Belgian Congo's atrocities instilled an enduring distrust of international interference in its colonial affairs. As historian Guy Vanthemsche demonstrates, these concerns fed paranoid anxieties among Belgian colonial leaders, that their sovereignty over Congo was threatened, that rival colonial powers and international institutions were sceptical of Belgium's ability to succeed as an imperial power, and that there was an urgent need to demonstrate that Belgium was not only up to the task, but better than the others.[11] The Belgian colonial worldview always remained sensitive about colonial comparisons. Inter-imperial allusions were used to assert the legitimacy of Congo's supposed 'model' colonial practice, deploying discourses of 'bestness' and exemplarity. At the same time, inter-imperial references, while often used to decide between policy options, were publicly played down in favour of the dominant rhetorical process of imperial self-definition that asserted an allegedly 'unique' style of colonial governance built on Belgian expertise and 'know-how'.[12]

---

9   Volker Barth and Roland Cvetkovky (eds), *Imperial Co-operation and Transfer, 1870–1930* (London: Bloomsbury, 2015); Miguel Bandeira Jerónimo and José Pedro Monteiro (eds), *Internationalism, Imperialism and the Formation of the Contemporary World* (New York: Palgrave, 2018).

10   Pierre Singaravélou, 'Les stratégies d'internationalisation de la question coloniale et la construction transnationale d'une science de la colonisation à la fin du XIXe siècle', *Monde(s)*, 1, 1 (2012), pp. 135–57.

11   Guy Vanthemsche, *Belgium and the Congo, 1885–1980* (Cambridge: Cambridge University Press, 2012), pp. 109–111.

12   See for example Amandine Lauro, 'To our Colonial Troops, Greetings from the Far-Away Homeland': Race, Security and (Inter-)Imperial Anxieties in the Discussion

The first part of this chapter explores the ways in which these ambiguities played out in the emergence of psychological expertise in the Congo after the Second World War. The following section analyses the work of leading figures of psychological research conducted in the Congo, notably in industrial contexts and in the psychological laboratory of *Union Minière du Haut-Katanga*. Contrary to previous work on the subject,[13] this analysis is based on new archival material and unexplored sources that enabled investigation not only of the published intellectual work of these figures, but also the conditions of its production (from their sponsorship to the experimental challenges they faced in the field) and the technocratic uses that were made of their results, both in administrative and industrial contexts. The focus on the respective trans-imperial/transnational connections of these scholars also sheds new light on the multi-layered role of psychological expertise in sustaining and reconfiguring racial assumptions and (late) colonial imperial politics, including the intensifying internationalisation of colonial circuits of expertise production, whose Belgian-Congolese resonances are explored in the chapter's final section.

The Multipolar Emergence of Psychological Expertise in Late-Colonial Congo

The new scientific investment by psychologists in Congo-based research in the 1950s was inseparable from the reform of Belgian colonial educational policies initiated in the mid-1940s. While the emphasis had previously been almost exclusively on the development of primary education, 'modernisation' plans associated with developmental colonialism meant that secondary

---

on Colonial Troops in World War One Belgium', *Journal of Belgian History*, 48, 1/2 (2018), pp. 34–55.

13 The history of colonial psychology in the Belgian Congo has already been partly explored by Poncelet, 'Sciences sociales', pp. 688–98; by the world-renowned Belgian artist Vincent Meessen (who created several exhibitions contrasting the work of colonial psychologists André Ombredane and Robert Maistriaux with that of Congolese artist Tshela Tendu in 2013, 2015 and 2017, 'Patterns for (Re)cognition' (Brussels: Snoeck & Bozar, 2017)); and in my own preliminary research published online: see notably Amandine Lauro, 'Sur les traces de la psychologie ethnique – 2/2', 22 June 2017, https://amandinelauro.wordpress.com/2017/06/22/sur-les-traces-de-la-psychologie-ethnique-et-plus-si-affinites-22 (accessed 21 February 2020). More recently and on the exclusive basis of published material, see also Marc Depaepe, 'Tests, Measurements, and Selection in the Belgian Congo during the 1950s: the End of Racist Clichés?' *Paedagogica Historica* 55, 3 (2019), pp. 493–510.

education was expanded. From the mid-1950s, officials finally considered university-level education for Africans.

These changes raised new questions and new demands for expertise about Congolese cognitive abilities, including (alleged) patterns of how intelligence develops and the potential educational adaptations required (of programmes as well as pedagogical methods).[14] As Linstrum has shown for the British Empire, such changes also raised technical challenges, as school places remained insufficient for the number of young people seeking secondary education. 'Rational' tests were therefore required to select the most promising candidates. At the other end of the scale, industrial employers, particularly from Katanga, regularly complained – like their counterparts in Central and Southern Africa – about the lack of qualified Africans for the growing number of skilled jobs, and the impediment this placed on productivity and wider economic development.[15] For companies as well, devising efficient tools of selection and skilling required expert knowledge. The scientific authority of (applied) psychological methods of investigation and, more specifically, of testing prospective workers' aptitudes, appeared an ideal way to optimise logics of selection while avoiding any substantive reflection on the structural consequences of Belgian's limited investment in the education of its Congolese subjects. While these concerns were shared across empires in Africa, the extreme reluctance of Belgian colonial rulers to develop an indigenous educated elite meant that they took a distinct form in the Belgian Congo.

More concretely, the origins of intelligence testing in the Belgian Congo can be found in inter-imperial influences as much as in metropolitan ones. In Belgium as elsewhere in Europe, intelligence testing developed in the early inter-war period. 'Scientific' metrics of intelligence had emerged at the turn of the century on both sides of the Atlantic, but it was only after the First World War that mental testing expanded both in industry and education. Notions of merit, aptitude and efficiency were at the heart of this practice, but eugenicist ideals were also influential.[16] In Belgium, psychometrics were

14   Marc Depaepe, 'Belgian Images of the Psycho pedagogical Potential of the Congolese during the Colonial Era, 1908–1960', *Paedagogica Historica* 45, 6 (2009), pp. 707–25. On the history of colonial education in the Congo, see Charles Tshimanga, *Jeunesse, formation et société au Congo/Kinshasa, 1890–1960* (Paris: L'Harmattan, 2001).

15   Linstrum, 'The Politics of Psychology', pp. 225–6. See also Linstrum, *Ruling Minds*, pp. 146 ff.

16   For example, Adrian Wooldridge, *Measuring the Mind: Education and Psychology in England 1880–1990* (Cambridge: Cambridge University Press, 1994): John Samuel Carson, *The Measure of Merit: Talents, Intelligence and Inequality in the French and American*

first used in industrial contexts and in the surveillance of juvenile delin-
quents and mentally deficient children, before being implemented on a far
greater scale after 1945, notably in educational contexts.[17] Meanwhile, in
the early 1920s, the Minister of Colonies had launched a discussion about
the potential development of 'physio-psychological' tests and laboratories
in the Belgian Congo's emerging industrial centres, especially in Katanga.
Contacts were made with the *Bourse de Travail* (Katanga's parastatal recruitment bureau) but its officers, still struggling to recruit workers, dismissed
the proposal.[18] Nevertheless, the policies of workforce stabilisation pioneered
by *Union Minière* from the 1930s, and their wider implementation across
the colony after the Second World War, fuelled interest both in such testing
and in potential inter-imperial exchanges on the subject.

As Linstrum shows, the Second World War was a turning point in the
development of imperial intelligence testing, in which the British Empire
was the leader.[19] British wartime authorities developed psychological testing
in their quest for effective methods of evaluation and assignment for millions
of new recruits. At the end of the war, Belgian authorities became interested
in this new expertise. When, in 1946, delegates from the Belgian metropolitan army were sent to Britain to investigate its army's new psychotechnical
selection tools, they enquired about their colonial deployment. This Belgian
delegation was apparently warmly welcomed: the British War Office shared
the results of its latest 'confidential' experiments on East African forces.[20]
Delegates came back impressed, and ashamed of having no answer when
their British counterparts asked what had been done in this regard in the
Congo. The Belgian Minister of Colonies expressed great interest in their
report. The appeal of these techniques for the *Force Publique* (the Congolese

---

Republics, 1750–1940 (Princeton: Princeton University Press, 2006). On the more
specific connections between the development of mental testing in colonial empires and
Euro-American eugenic movements, see Linstrum, *Ruling Minds*, pp. 85 and 108–12.

17   Eric Geerkens, *La rationalisation dans l'industrie belge de l'Entre-deux-guerres* (Brussels:
Palais des Académies, 2004); Veerle Massin, 'Measuring Delinquency: The Observation,
Scientific Assessment and Testing of Delinquent Girls in 20th-Century Belgium', *Journal
of Belgian History*, 46, 1 (2016), pp. 105–33; Patrick Sacré, *Historiek van de PMS-Centra:
bijdrage tot de studie van de geschiedenis van de PMS- begeleiding in België* (Brussels: VUB
Press, 1993), Ch. 3.

18   See the epistolary exchanges of October and November 1922 in African Archives
(hereafter AA), MOI (3558).

19   Linstrum, *Ruling Minds*, pp. 120 & foll.

20   AA, FP (2614), 'Selection of the Natives in Africa', report, s.d. (December 1946 –
January 1947?).

colonial army) was strong at a time when 'winds of change seem to blow on the Dark Continent'; the promotion of Congolese non-commissioned officers, requiring new systems of selection and appointment, was envisioned as a potential 'proactive' response to this new context.[21] In Brussels, a search was launched for suitable candidates for a future team of psychometric experts. In the colony however, *Force Publique* commanders were less than excited. They had also sought foreign expertise, but in doing so had favoured other circuits of knowledge circulation, circuits that were less trans-imperial but no less international: they had chosen to go to South Africa.

South Africa already had a solid tradition of scientific, administrative and above all industrial engagement in mental testing procedures. While some South African studies of racial intelligence comparison had already been criticised in international scientific circles in the 1930s, the country's expertise on applied psychometrics was still widely acknowledged.[22] Colonial Belgian medical officers of the *Force Publique* visited the Johannesburg-based South African National Institute for Personnel Research (NIPR) a few months after its establishment in early 1946. It is unclear how the connection was established, but the Belgian delegation returned convinced of the relevance of these techniques, yet apprehensive of the work required, particularly in adapting Western testing methods for use with African people. Their subsequent exchanges with the Ministry of Colonies reveal competing visions of scientific legitimacy in post-war colonial knowledge production. They also reveal the ways in which such competing visions could be nourished and/or justified by different international connections. For the *Force Publique* in Léopoldville, the development of efficient psychotechnical expertise must be anchored in 'colonial sciences' and therefore established by a specialist in 'the mentality of the natives' who would be trained in psychology at a later stage.[23] For some metropolitan administrators however, the appeal of such expertise lay precisely in the fact that it was not specifically 'colonial' but rather 'modern' and global. It thus offered the prospect of a technocratic and efficient government of minds and of people, one that could equally be applied to the reformed methods of colonial planning. They therefore recommended recruiting a Western expert in applied psychology to

---

21 AA, FP (2614), Minister of Defense to Minister of Colonies, 21 December 1946.
22 Saul Dubow, *Scientific Racism in Modern South Africa* (Cambridge: Cambridge University Press, 1995), pp. 197 & foll.; Linstrum, *Ruling Minds*, pp. 106 & foll.
23 AA, FP (2614), Commander in Chief of the *Force Publique* and Governor General to Minister of Colonies, 13 February 1947.

develop such programmes, who could be initiated into colonial specificities at a later stage.[24]

These discussions reveal the growing importance of psychological expertise in the late 1940s, not only among the colonial administration but also among colonial companies. In this context, *Union Minière* was a leading force, with inter-imperial connections of its own. These connections remain difficult to trace, but on the other side of the Copperbelt border, Northern Rhodesian mining companies were pioneers in the use of aptitude testing in industrial areas (well in advance of the Rhodes-Livingstone Institute which only subsidised research on this topic from the 1960s).[25] At a 1949 meeting in Brussels on to the future use of psychological testing by colonial administrators, the *Union Minière* delegate expressed astonishment at the persistent scepticism of some members of the colonial medical aristocracy towards such testing procedures. The UMHK delegate declared that the 'British, the French and even the Russians use these methods', and proceeded to name-drop famous psychology professors from prestigious European and US universities who supported their use; in this way he used Belgium's sensitivity to inter-imperial comparison to defend the legitimacy of psychological testing. As an actor of strategic importance in the Belgian colonial landscape and the global mineral economy, *Union Minière*'s voice was not only well-informed but also influential.

From a larger perspective, psychology also served as a powerful ideological device among Europeans in post-Second World War Congo. In popular publications, colonial writers, ideologues and missionaries talked more than ever about the 'psychology of the native' in a modernist lexicon that often replaced previous references to the 'mentality of the primitive'. This new vocabulary was convenient: it allowed the evocation of the supposedly 'innate' features of the Congolese *état d'esprit* (state of mind) alongside the challenges of 'modernity' and 'acculturation' in the context of intensifying

---

24 AA FP (2614), reports and epistolary exchanges in 1946–47.
25 Lyn Schumaker, *Africanizing Anthropology: Fieldwork, Networks and the Making of Cultural Knowledge in Central Africa* (Durham NC: Duke University Press, 2001), pp. 160–61 and Linstrum, *Ruling Minds*, p. 79. Very little is known about the use of psychometrics by Northern Rhodesian industrial companies before the mid-1960s, notably because this use did not lead to any significant publications before this decade: see e.g. S. H. Irvine, 'Ability Testing in English-Speaking Africa: An Overview of Predictive and Comparative Studies', *Rhodes-Livingstone Journal*, 34 (1963), pp. 44–55. Given the current state of research, a comparison with their Congolese counterparts remains therefore extremely difficult.

urbanisation.[26] These combined preoccupations would offer a breeding ground for the development of research funding opportunities sponsored by the colonial state and companies in the 1950s. While Copperbelt urban centres were not the only focus of this new research, *Union Minière* was particularly invested in the development of this new kind of analysis.

Measuring Congolese Minds: Geographical Biographies, Psychological Experiments and Administrative Uses

Among the leading academic psychologists commissioned to work in the Belgian Congo, scholars André Ombredane (1898–1958) and Robert Maistriaux (1905–1981) led several missions in the 1950s. Their experiences provide a revealing basis for the history of psychological research in late-colonial Congo. They also provide a revealing contrast to the applied psychologists of *Union Minière*'s Centre of Psychology and Pedagogy. My aim is less to investigate their analysis than to explain the context of its production, analysing the two men's professional backgrounds, their field experiments, and the uses made of their work. The contrast between the intellectual, political and geographical itineraries of Ombredane and Maistriaux further reveals the complicated relationship between scientific knowledge and late-colonialism and the ambiguities born of the then ongoing reconfigurations of racial assumptions. Ombredane and Maistriaux, both outsiders in the world of colonial expertise, embraced its dominant paradigms in very different ways. These differences were reflected in their mobilities and in their contrasting international scholarly connections.

André Ombredane: A 'Catechism' for Psychological Research in Central Africa

André Ombredane was born in France at the end of the nineteenth century.[27] His academic journey was characterised by interdisciplinarity

26 As in other contexts, as shown by Linstrum, *Ruling Minds*, pp. 155 & foll. and Megan Vaughan, *Curing Their Ills: Colonial Power and African Illness* (Stanford: Stanford University Press, 1991), Ch. 5. On the specificities of the Belgian-Congolese context, see Bandeira Jerónimo, 'Restoring Order, Inducing Change', pp. 97–116.
27 The following biographical elements are based on the personal file of Ombredane kept in the Archives of the Free University of Brussels (hereafter ULB), as well as on Norbert Laude, 'Hommage à A. Ombredane et E. Dory', *Bulletin des séances de l'ARSOM*, 4, 6 (1958), pp. 1163–5; René Nyssen, 'Notice sur la vie et l'œuvre d'André Ombredane', *Rapport sur l'année académique 1957–1958* (Brussels, 1958), pp. 240–41; Arthur

and cosmopolitanism. He studied philosophy, then medical sciences, and specialised in neuropathology. In parallel to his PhD at Sorbonne University, he acquired a strong clinical experience. In the 1930s, he built a reputation in the field of language disorders and children's '*inadaptation scolaire*' [school misfits]. His left-wing orientation is revealed by his participation in the International Brigades during the Spanish Civil War and by his (co) authoring, just before the Second World War, an essay against the Nazi regime and its racial theories.[28] In 1939, probably because of his politics, Ombredane accepted a position at the University of Rio de Janeiro, where he remained during the war. He used this time to develop expertise in a new field, psychometry and industrial psychology. He then returned to France as a pioneer of intelligence and personality testing. His psychology was experimental and applied, and drew on serious theoretical and methodological influences, including the latest American research. In 1948 he became a Professor at the Free University of Brussels, which was then trying to develop its Department of Psychology. Ombredane's international reputation, and the promise to furnish him with a state-of-the-art laboratory, would aid this effort.

Less than one year after his appointment, Ombredane left for a first mission in the Belgian Congo. Nothing suggests a previous interest in colonial questions. Evidence suggests he was commissioned by the Minister of Colonies to lead a reconnaissance mission: Ombredane was seemingly asked to conduct exploratory research to develop psychotechnical tools for the colony. His fieldwork notebooks and publications show his astonishment with colonial racism and the mediocrity of Belgian 'experts' he met there.[29] In 1951, he was again commissioned by the colonial administration, this time by the new Fund for Native Welfare (*Fonds du Bien-Être Indigène*) to experiment in aptitude and personality testing, in collaboration with Kasai's mining company, *Forminière*.[30] Ombredane led several subsequent missions in the Congo, funded variously by the Fund for Native

Doucy, 'André Ombredane', *Bulletin des séances de l'ARSOM*, 5, 1 (1959), 159–163, and the special issue of the *Bulletin du Centre d'études et recherches psychotechniques*, 8 (1959).

28 André Ombredane and Aurélien Sauvageot, *Mensonges du racisme* (Paris: Civilisation Nouvelle, 1939). On the influence of the testing methods of Ombredane on African psychiatry, see also Alice Bullard, 'The Critical Impact of Frantz Fanon and Henri Collomb: Race, Gender, and Personality Testing of North and West Africans', *Journal of the History of the Behavioral Sciences*, 41, 3 (2005), pp. 225–48.

29 Royal Museum for Central Africa archives (hereafter RMCA) 'Carnets de note André Ombredane', DA.8, in particular notebooks 9, 10 and 11,

30 Forminière was particularly involved in diamond-mining in Kasai.

Welfare,[31] colonial companies, his university, and even by the United Nations Educational, Scientific and Cultural Organization (UNESCO).[32] In 1952 UNESCO included Ombredane in an international team assembled to study 'the psychology of the film experience' in Africa,[33] in the context of the organisation's campaign for the use of cinema in education in 'developing countries'.[34] Meanwhile, Ombredane published his first articles on his Congolese experiences. While his results were consistent with the anti-racist stance of UNESCO, they were probably not those that the colonial administration had expected.

Ombredane's most important article was published in 1951 in *L'Année Psychologique*, the leading French-language cognitive psychology journal. Entitled 'Principles for a Psychological Study of the Blacks in the Belgian Congo', it centred on a provocative statement: most colonial notions regarding Congolese people's intelligence were stereotypes.[35] Ombredane chose to approach the making of these stereotypes from a psychological perspective: he analysed interviews with Europeans introduced to him as *experts* in colonial questions, but whom Ombredane turned into *subjects* of psychological investigation. In what he termed a 'catechism' for psychological research in colonial Africa, Ombredane also insisted that cultural biases were inherent in psychological testing.[36] Even non-verbal tests contained culturally specific visual hints, all the more given that both the context and the very idea of such testing was unfamiliar to those tested. In an original way for the time, for the Belgian Congo and for an applied scientist, Ombredane emphasised the problems arising from the colonial context on the conditions of knowledge production – and even its very possibility.

31 Fonds du Bien-Être Indigène, *Une œuvre de coopération au développement: quinze années d'activité du Fonds du Bien-Etre Indigène au Congo, au Rwanda et au Burundi, 1948–1963* (Brussels FBI, 1964), pp. 130 & foll.
32 ULB archives, A. Ombredane personal file, minutes, meeting of the CEMUBAC – Psychology Section, 9 March 1956.
33 'Enquête filmique au Congo belge par le Docteur Ombredane', *Ouest-France*, 7 March 1956; Francine Robaye, 'Propos inédits du professeur Ombredane sur les niveaux de compréhension du film par les noirs congolais', *Bulletin du Centre d'études et recherches psychotechniques*, 8 (1959), pp. 15–23.
34 Zoë Druick, 'UNESCO, Film, and Education: Mediating Postwar Paradigms of Communication' in Charles R. Acland and Haidee Wasson (eds), *Useful Cinema* (Durham NC: Duke University Press, 2011), pp. 81–102.
35 André Ombredane, 'Principes pour une étude psychologique des Noirs du Congo belge', *L'Année Psychologique* 50 (1949), pp. 521–47.
36 Ombredane, 'Principes', p. 547.

'The more or less brutal and caustic [*grinçante*] acquiescence' demanded by colonial rule and the 'behavioural constraints' it imposed on Congolese people, he declared, necessarily affected their reactions to tests, and scientists should therefore be cautious about their validity.[37] Ombredane also insisted that the differences arising from test subjects' varied level of schooling should not be interpreted in terms of 'intelligence' or 'evolution', but rather as an acquired familiarity with European visual culture and intellectual mechanisms.

Ombredane's work was not however free from primitivist *clichés* or essentialist assumptions about 'African culture'. Many of his assertions, like other late-colonial experts, raised the possibility of arguing 'for cultural difference, without being read as arguing for racial difference'.[38] His work was also based more on observation of than on interaction with his subjects,[39] and he never credited the Congolese testing/research assistants whose anonymous contributions can nevertheless be glimpsed in fieldwork photographs. Nonetheless, after trying various test models, he concluded that 'to go in blind in testing and to compare the results to those of the Whites without giving it second thoughts' would produce 'results which mean nothing'.[40] The political significance of these conclusions was also reflected in his publication strategy: one year later, Ombredane participated in a special issue of the Pan-Africanist and anti-imperialist journal *Présence Africaine*, alongside scholars such as sociologist Georges Balandier and anthropologist Michel Leiris.[41]

André Ombredane's work raises questions about 'science' produced in a colonial context, here commissioned and funded by the colonial state, but whose results did not support the intellectual and political foundations of colonialism, questions that have been at the heart of recent explorations of knowledge production in late-colonial Africa.[42] With regard to Ombredane, the issue arises of the *relevance* of the knowledge he produced for his funders. It is for instance unclear in what ways much of his intellectual work was

37 Ibid., p. 525.
38 Megan Vaughan, 'Introduction', in Sloan Mahone and Megan Vaughan (eds) *Psychiatry and Empire* (Palgrave Macmillan, New York, 2007), p. 9.
39 Gerd Spittler, 'L'anthropologie du travail en Afrique. Traditions allemandes et françaises' in Hélène D'Almeida Topor et al. (eds*), Le travail en Afrique noire: Représentations et pratiques à l'époque contemporaine* (Paris: Karthala, 2003), pp. 17–42, pp. 27–28.
40 Ombredane, 'Principles', p. 547.
41 André Ombredane, 'Les techniques de fortune dans le travail coutumier des Noirs', *Présence Africaine* 13, 1 (1952), pp. 58–68.
42 Similar conclusions have already been made by Linstrum, 'The Politics of Psychology'.

useful for the mining companies that funded his research. Explaining this is not aided by the tendency of many scientists to adopt conflicting positions depending on their audience. Ombredane made many promises to his various funders, while his personal notebooks show that from the start he intended to orient his research in different ways. In his publications and in numerous press interviews, he never openly criticised colonial rule and policies; as Helen Tilley has noted, criticising racial sciences did not necessarily mean criticising racial domination.[43] In his private notebooks however, Ombredane expressed his disdain for the Belgian colonial administration in general and his benefactor in particular: 'Fund for Native Welfare? What welfare? They make constructions that impoverish the customary work of the Blacks and represent for them only forced labour [*corvées*]. Wouldn't it be better to start with providing them with enough food?'[44]

An Industrial Laboratory: Implementing Testing at Union Minière

Ombredane was not the only active participant to doubt the value of psychological testing in Belgian Africa. The staff of the Centre of Psychology and Pedagogy [*Centre de Psychologie et de Pédagogie*] of *Union Minière*, created in 1953, were the first critics of the work they were paid to accomplish. *Union Minière* had developed an interest in psychological testing in the early 1940s, but psychotechnical tools were initially used mainly in the recruitment of its European personnel. In 1952, however, *Union Minière*'s directors invested in an expansion of these techniques, with a double objective in mind. Their aim was to build new tools of expertise for managing their African workers, but also to develop new approaches in the schools provided by the company to its employees' children. The cradle-to-grave paternalist approach of *Union Minière* meant that psychology could be deployed as a resource in the social reproduction of Katangese workers. The company's investment in this new expertise was thus consistent with its wider investment in the making of a productive, skilled and docile workforce, realised through considerable spending on education, social welfare services and housing for its workers and their families (see Larmer and Taylor, Chapter 12). This system, characterised by historians as authoritarian paternalism, went hand-in-hand with the tailoring of work processes through

---

43 Helen Tilley, *Africa as a Living Laboratory* (Chicago: Chicago University Press, 2011), 218.
44 RMCA, 'Carnets de note André Ombredane', DA.8, Notebook 18.

more bureaucratic, 'scientific' management.[45] As a report discussing the creation of the Centre suggested, 'the interest that this knowledge would represent' connected the needs 'for an adapted education and for efficient employment of the Native'.[46] There was also a panoptical dimension to this ambition. The 'coordination of the different activities' of the Centre implied that 'the Native will be followed step by step from his entrance into the schools of *Union Minière* to his retirement'. This was to be implemented through a typically comprehensive bureaucratic surveillance system: 'Once the boy has reached the age of 16, the section of psycho-pedagogy sends to the industrial psychology section the file summarising the results of the psycho-medico-pedagogical tutelage examinations, and the young worker is not a stranger anymore.'[47]

Union Minière's interest in such techniques complemented the preoccupations of the Catholic Church in Katanga. Both church and company were worried about André Ombredane's first research visits, because of his connections with *Union Minière*'s rival *Forminière*,[48] and his affiliation with the non-Catholic Free University of Brussels. This generated concern that his psychological expertise might be infused, as one Catholic professor suggested, 'with a spirit of anti-missionary criticism'.[49] Mission leaders were aware of the growing authority of psychological expertise and its potential influence at a time when their virtual monopoly over colonial education was being questioned.[50] Church leaders were clear that 'we are presently in a phase in which all the educational work of the missionaries is at risk of losing its efficiency and prestige, if we don't try to establish it on a more solid basis'.[51] From the start, *Union Minière* intended the (Catholic) University of Leuven to be a privileged institutional partner of the future

45 See Donatien Dibwe dia Mwembu, *Bana Shaba abandonnés par leur père: structures de l'autorité et histoire sociale de la famille ouvrière au Katanga, 1910–1997* (Paris: L'Harmattan, 2001): John Higginson, *A Working-Class in the Making: Belgian Colonial Labour Policy, Private Enterprise and the African Mineworker, 1907–1951* (Madison: University of Wisconsin Press, 1989).

46 Katholieke Universiteit Leuven (hereafter KUL) Archives, Collection J. Nuttin, 156–7 – 6.005, J. Nuttin and Ch. Mertens, 'Création d'un centre de psychologie et de pédagogie et enseignement indigène à l' Union Minière – Rapport de la mission d'étude accomplie en décembre 1952 au Katanga', February 1953, p. 1.

47 Ibid., p. 21.

48 KUL, Collection J. Nuttin, 154–5 – 6.003, L. Wallef to F. de Hemptinne, 29 September 1952,

49 KUL, Collection J. Nuttin, 155–6 – 6.004, J. Nuttin, note (October 1953).

50 Patrick Boyle, 'School Wars: Church, State, and the Death of the Congo', *Journal of Modern African Studies*, 33, 3 (1995), pp. 451–68.

51 KUL, Collection J. Nuttin, 155–6 – 6.004. J. Nuttin, Confidential Note, n.d. (1953).

Centre.[52] They generously paid two of Leuven's most famous psychology professors (ecclesiastic Joseph Nuttin and psychiatrist Charles Mertens de Wilmars) to plan the Centre and supervise its operations.[53]

The leading role of these Leuven psychologists did not mean that the Centre's connections were limited to Belgium and its empire. By the international standards of the time, the Centre's team was well-qualified: its first director Paul Verhaegen and his colleagues were involved in international networks and published in international journals.[54] At least two of them had received scholarships to study psychology and/or anthropology in the United States. In the context of a growing Americanisation of research, these connections provided important intellectual credentials. While these connections remained Western and Atlantic, they were sometimes wider still, as the case of Maria Leblanc (1926–1959), one of the very few women in the field, illustrates. A young graduate in psychology involved in an international organisation of lay missionaries, Leblanc was studying at the University of Chicago when she was advised by one of her former Leuven professors to apply for a position at the Centre. When she learned her application had been successful, she trained in African studies and took anthropology classes (at the University of Chicago, a world-class university in this field), and arranged discussions with students from African countries to obtain reading recommendations.[55] This was a very different initiation to Africa than was usually provided to new colonial employees at the Belgian *Université Coloniale*, where most professors were former Belgian colonial administrators.

Given this background, the reluctance of some Centre employees to use some of the proposed testing procedures appears more understandable. During the second half of the 1950s, the Centre was closely involved in aptitude/intelligence testing and the professional placement of both adult *Union Minière* employees and their children. Its experts were preoccupied with the cultural biases involved in psychological testing. As their reports reveal, they spent almost two years researching and testing the validity and necessary adaptations of various models. In 1955, while their psychometric toolkit was finally ready, their annual report made clear they were

---

52 Mantels, *Geleerd in de Tropen*, pp. 156–7.
53 See the epistolary exchanges in KUL, Collection J. Nuttin, 156–7 – 6.005.
54 On more details on the published work of Paul Verhaegen, see Depaepe, 'Tests', pp. 497–8.
55 KUL, Collection J. Nuttin, box 156–7 – 6.005, M. Leblanc to J. Nuttin, 1 April and 19 November 1953.

not entirely confident of their choices and that, at least with regards to *Union Minière*'s aim of establishing rational selection for secondary schools, it remained impossible 'to predict the success' of pupils on the basis of testing. They could certainly eliminate the 'duffers and the retards' and select the 'particularly gifted', but going further would mean selecting 'at random'.[56] Their advice to the company was that every Congolese (male) child should be offered a place in general secondary schools while the start of his specialised, professional training should be delayed.[57] Not surprisingly, tensions with the company management emerged in the late 1950s. Several team members criticised the company's utilitarian vision for the Centre,[58] and one even questioned the absence of Congolese psychologists, regrettable given the challenges posed by the necessary 'Africanisation' of testing protocols.[59] This was however one of the only instances where Congolese assistants were mentioned: the staff of the Centre of Psychology and Pedagogy appears to have remained completely white until independence.

Robert Maistriaux: Poor Science, Bureaucratic Triumph

The other major figure of psychology in late-colonial Congo was Robert Maistriaux. Maistriaux's profile is very different from that of Ombredane, from an intellectual and a political point of view, as well as his professional mobility. His biographical trajectory has been far more difficult to reconstruct, primarily because of his lack of scientific posterity: his work was largely forgotten when he died in the early 1980s; significantly, despite his activities in urban Katanga, he was never considered a rival by the UMHK Centre.[60] Maistriaux had no professional training in psychology or even in medical sciences. He graduated in Law and Philosophy in Belgium and started an initially part-time academic career at the *Institut Saint-Louis*, the small Jesuit university of Brussels, in the early 1930s. It was only in the 1950s that he was appointed as a full professor and, as a sign of his colonial

---

56 Belgium State Archives, UMHK archives (hereafter UMHK), I 29, 672, 'Les cancres et les débiles': Trimestrial report of the Centre of Psychology and Pedagogy, September–December 1955
57 UMHK I 29, 672, conclusions of several reports between 1954 and 1958.
58 Jean-Louis Laroche even denounced in 1957 the 'censorship' of his work by the company and the impossibility to develop proper scientific research within the centre: KUL, Collection J. Nuttin, 155–6 – 6.004, J.-L. Laroche to J. Nuttin, 9 January 1957.
59 KUL, Collection J. Nuttin, 155–6 – 6.004, J.-L. Laroche to J. Nuttin, 6 August 1956.
60 KUL, Collection J. Nuttin, 156–7 – 6.005, J. Jadot to J. Nuttin, 14 July 1953.

expertise, started work at the *Institut Universitaire des Territoires d'Oure-Mer* (the renamed *Université Coloniale*), and later at the Royal Military Institute.[61] Maistriaux was a self-proclaimed Catholic intellectual, with a keen interest in the promotion of Christian moral values among the young. It is difficult to assess his engagement with colonialism, but it is likely that his interest in the moral challenges of modern adolescence influenced his turn to psychological sciences.[62] In 1948 Maistriaux published a first essay about personality development in which he revealed himself a fervent disciple of 'characterology', a sub-field of psychology that sought a theory of personality/character classification: echoing some of the epistemological premises of colonial sciences, characterology combined psychological methods with the measurement of bodily characteristics, based on the idea that people's personality 'type' relates to their physical characteristics.[63] This, alongside his expertise on youth and education, and his Catholic background, made Maistriaux, in the 'pillarised' Belgian academic and political context, the mirror image of the secular and liberal Ombredane, and thus a perfect candidate for designing the psychological projects of the colonial administration.[64]

In 1952 and 1953, Maistriaux was appointed and funded by the Minister of Colonies for two three-month missions in the Congo. Their objective was twofold: to provide a general 'scientific' overview of the 'real' level of intelligence of Congolese people, and to devise testing methods to be used as tools of professional selection and educational placement in the colony. That Maistriaux had always been an armchair psychologist, with no clinical or even experimental experience, does not seem to have been a problem for the colonial administration. That he was a complete beginner in colonial issues was, however, an impediment that had to be solved. The authorities therefore supported what may be understood as inter-imperial training visits to the Department of (physical) Anthropology at the *Musée de l'Homme* in Paris and to the French Colonial Health Headquarters in Marseille, where Maistriaux witnessed intelligence testing of West-African

---

61 These biographical elements are based on the personal file of Robert Maistriaux in the Archives of the Université Saint-Louis, on several mentions in the *Revue Saint-Louis* between 1930 and 1981 and on the publications (and their reviews) of Maistriaux.

62 Maistriaux was notably part of an influential group of 'experts' on family issues directed by a Jesuit priest. See Laura Di Spurio, 'La vulgarisation de la notion d'adolescence dans l'Europe de l'après-Seconde Guerre mondiale: échanges et circulations du savoir "psy" entre l'espace francophone européen et l'Italie', *Amnis*, 14 (2015).

63 Robert Maistriaux, *L'étude des caractères* (Tournai/Paris: Casterman, 1949).

64 On the meaning of 'pillarised', see Harry Post, *Pillarization: An Analysis of Dutch and Belgian Society* (Avebury: Gower, 1989).

tirailleurs (French colonial infantry).[65] He also networked with a French research centre founded in the 1930s, the *Institut de Psychologie des Peuples*.[66] This Institute was not exactly a centre of scientific innovation; closely tied to the French colonial milieux, its work continued the French tradition of *psychologie ethnique*, a 'psychology without psychologists' that sought to identify the collective psychological traits of so-called ethnic groups and their racial, environmental and cultural determinants.[67] This discipline was already on the international scientific margins in the inter-war period and by the 1950s the *Institut* was a relic of what was generally regarded as a disreputable tradition of 'applied colonial science'. Maistriaux was virtually the only psychologist working in the 1950s Belgian Congo to refer to their publications. In return, the *Institut's* journal published Maistriaux's first 'colonial' article in 1955: this reported the results of his first investigation in the Congo, in a special issue alongside an article by a self-proclaimed supporter of 'racial psychology' comparing the IQs of the 'black', 'yellow' and 'white' races.[68] Even if Maistriaux's professional itinerary was less cosmopolitan than Ombredane's, his (colonial) career was therefore not without its international connections. They were certainly constructed primarily along inter-imperial (rather than inter-national) lines, but they illustrate the multiple possibilities of scholarly networks and exchanges and the multiple intellectual/political affinities that they could both reflect and produce.[69]

In the Congo, Maistriaux conducted experimental psychological tests in diverse rural and urban locations, notably in Katanga, so as to avoid ethnic and 'environmental' biases. Helped by a colonial official appointed to assist him, Maistriaux did not however share the scruples of Ombredane (or

---

65 Robert Maistriaux, *L'Intelligence noire et son destin* (Brussels: Problèmes d'Afrique centrale, s.d. (1957), pp. 3–11.

66 Frédéric Carbonel, 'Origines et développement de l'Institut Havrais de Sociologie économique et de Psychologie des Peuples', *Les Cahiers Internationaux de Psychologie Sociale* 77, 1 (2008), pp. 69–86.

67 Pierre Singaravélou, 'De la psychologie coloniale à géographie psychologique: Itinéraire, entre science et littérature, d'une discipline éphémère dans l'entre-deux-guerres', *L'Homme et la société* 167/168/169 (2008), pp. 119–48, p. 120.

68 Robert Maistriaux, 'La sous-évolution des Noirs d'Afrique: sa nature, ses causes, ses remèdes', *Revue de Psychologie des Peuples*, 10 (1955), pp. 167 & foll., pp. 997 & foll. George Heuse, 'Race, racisme et antiracisme', *Revue de Psychologie des Peuples*, 10, 4 (1955), pp. 378–81, pp. 368 & foll.

69 Frederick Cooper, 'Development'; Heather Ellis, 'Collaboration and knowledge exchange between scholars in Britain and the Empire, 1830–1914' in Heike Jöns, Peter Meusburger and Michael Heffernan (eds), *Mobilities of Knowledge* (Springer: New York, 2017), pp. 141–55.

even UMHK's team of psychologists) regarding potential cultural biases of tests directly imported from the Western world. Once he had rejected verbal tests and slightly simplified others, he was confident in the relevance of his findings, soon to be known as the '*Batterie Maistriaux*'. This was an assembly of various intelligence/mental aptitude tests (such as the Raven Progressive Matrices, the Kohs Cubes Test or the Golden-Sheerer Stick Test), mostly developed in Western contexts. In order to ensure its validity, Maistriaux made sure to double-check his results once back in Belgium. There, he compared them with tests of a population he considered had 'similar' cognitive abilities as most Congolese subjects: Belgian children considered 'mentally retarded'. Not surprisingly, he concluded that while there was no difference of *nature* between 'Black' and 'White' people, there was a significative difference in *proportion*. While clearly ill at ease with the vocabulary of race, Maistriaux did not avoid discussion of the 'biological conditions' in which the intellectual development of Congolese people occurred. He also attributed the low performance of 'Central African Blacks' in 'all exercises requiring abstract intelligence' to the 'debilitating influence' of their 'environment' (which supposedly provided little intellectual stimulation) and the inner personality traits of 'the Black', referring mainly to his/her 'great emotionality' and 'proverbial idleness'.[70] In short, this work was well suited to the racial premises of colonial domination as well as its new vocabulary: Maistriaux emphasised to his readership that this was not about 'primitive minds' or 'pre-logical thought', but instead about different paths of 'development'.

Even by the standards of the time however, this was poor science[71] and, in a sense, it is precisely this that made Maistriaux's work appealing to the colonial authorities. Maistriaux's confidence in the relevance of psychometric tests and in his own results provided the colonial administration with simple answers to complex questions – and allowed for their straightforward translation into bureaucratic uses. From 1954, the *Batterie Maistriaux* was widely used for the professional selection of African auxiliaries in the administration and the police. The *Batterie* had several 'levels' so that it could be adapted to various contexts and age-groups, and one version became the standard tool of selection for applicants to state-sponsored secondary

---

70 Maistriaux, *L'Intelligence noire*. See also Ch. Didier Gondola, *Tropical Cowboys: Westerns, Violence, and Masculinity in Kinshasa* (Bloomington: Indiana University Press, 2016), pp. 52–3.

71 As already noticed by Mallory Wober, *Psychology in Africa* (London: International African Institute, 1975), p. 57.

education. The Belgian colonial archives contain hundreds of such tests, carried out individually and collectively, and always under the strict surveillance of psychotechnical 'specialists' – at least in theory. For some specific tests, the ways in which the test subjects approached the problems with which they were faced formed part of their evaluation. But here again, 'expertise' proved a relative concept: test evaluations were often approximate, including amateurish comments such as: 'Hesitant, works at random. The pieces do not fit. Close-minded. Poor *coup d'oeil*: gross mistakes!'[72]

From the mid-1950s, most of these tests were planned and implemented by the *Centre Pilote d'Orientation Professionnelle* (Pilot Centre for Vocational Guidance) in Léopoldville, founded in 1956, and by its sub-departments in other provinces. The *Centre Pilote* thus decided the professional fate of thousands of Congolese pupils. It claimed to promote 'more efficiency and justice in the allocation of energies' and asserted that 'one of the biggest hopes of the Congo lays in the ability of Africans to adapt themselves properly to their tasks'.[73] Here again, consistent with *Union Minière*'s approach to workforce management and individual aptitudes,[74] ideals of productivity and efficiency in the context of unprecedented economic development were key. But the challenge was also political. In other contexts, discourses regarding the identification of personal merits of Congolese individuals might have served the prospects of Africanisation. But in a colony so reluctant to train and appoint African elites, they appeared merely as sticking plasters on (de)colonial anxieties. In the face of Congolese social disruption and mounting political claims, they promised to find a suitable place for everybody on the reassuring basis of technocratic certitudes. In short, and as Linstrum has shown for the British Empire, aptitude testing offered 'technical solutions to political problems'.[75] Significantly, the *Centre Pilote* was featured in several colonial propaganda films, two of which are entirely devoted to its activities. The film *Choisis ton avenir* (J.-M. Landier, 1957, 11 min.) praised the *Centre* as a space of social and professional modernity paralleling the colony's economic development and the fantasy '*communauté belgo-congolaise*'.

---

72 AA, GG (7283). Testing Police Academy of Leopoldville, 1957. Traces of the extended use of the *Batterie Maistriaux* can also be found in AA, GG (5398, 6949, 16510, 18059, 18066 and 19067).

73 Emile Lobet, 'L'Orientation professionnelle au Congo belge et au Ruanda-Urundi', *Bulletin des séances de l'ARSOM*, 3, 4 (1957), pp. 800–816, p. 805.

74 For an example of the way in which these discourses were presented to Congolese workers, see 'A chacun sa place', *Mwana Shaba*, March 1957, 3, p. 1.

75 Linstrum, *Ruling Minds*, p. 152.

The film's staging of racial mixing is a model of its kind, as is its failure. The egalitarian principles which are presented as the basis of the *Centre*'s work in Léopoldville (in which white and black children pass tests together under the scrutiny of white and black members of staff) are immediately contradicted by images of rural tests which concern only Congolese boys and manual/low-skilled jobs.[76] There is in fact a bitter irony in the title of the film (*Choisis ton avenir* [Choose your Future]) when, for Congolese children, choice was hardly an option.

Missed Opportunities? New Dynamics of (Scientific) Internationalism in the Decolonising Moment

These contradictions did not prevent Belgian colonial authorities featuring the *Centre*'s work as testimony of the 'civilising' accomplishments of Belgian colonial rule in their reports to various international institutions. In this last section, I explore the potential interference of international institutions in colonial circuits of knowledge production through the example of UNESCO, which in the 1950s was the leading international agency sponsoring psychological research in 'developing countries', before turning to the issue of the Africanisation of the discipline in the light of these dynamics.

UNESCO and Belgian Psychological Expertise

From its establishment in 1945, one of UNESCO's main goals was to promote international scientific collaboration; as such, it contributed to the internationalisation of social sciences in the post-war period. This was also true in the colonial realm, albeit in complex ways. On the one hand, UNESCO fostered new international forums sharing expertise about the challenges of 'modernisation' in 'non-self-governing territories'. In such forums, imperial powers sought to assert and/or defend their intellectual authority on these issues. On the other hand, distrust of UNESCO criticism of colonial policies led the same powers to unite in creating parallel spaces of exchange and re-affirming their legitimacy as 'true' experts on developmentalist issues, especially in Africa.[77]

---

76 As already underlined in Francis Ramirez and Christian Rolot, *Histoire du cinéma colonial au Zaïre, au Rwanda et au Burundi* (Tervuren: RMCA, 1985), pp. 212–3.
77 Jessica Pearson-Patel, 'Promoting Health, Protecting Empire: Inter-Colonial Medical Cooperation in Postwar Africa', *Monde(s)* 7, 1 (2015), pp. 213–30; Damiano Matasci, 'Une "UNESCO africaine"? Le ministère de la France d'Outre-mer, la coopération

The relationship of colonial Belgium with the UN was a complicated one. Belgian leaders saw the UN (and especially its Information Committee for Non-Autonomous Territories) as a threat to their sovereignty over Congo and were reluctant to provide it with information about colonial management, including for 'scientific' purposes. Their hostility was greater than that of French and British imperial authorities, to such an extent that, in 1952, Belgium removed itself from this Committee.[78] As a result, the Belgian Congo remained largely excluded from UN agency programmes.[79] The involvement of Belgian Congo experts in UNESCO's programmes therefore took a mainly non-institutional form, meaning that the participation of Ombredane in UNESCO's visual education surveys was the exception rather than the rule. Ironically, while Belgian colonial scientific institutions never received direct funding from UNESCO (unlike in other empires), those same scientific institutions frequently boasted in their official reports about their researchers being invited by UNESCO.[80] This illustrates their ambivalence surrounding an internationalisation that could provide scientific validation despite fears of its potential anti-colonial stance.

In the late 1950s, this ambivalence was particularly well demonstrated in Belgian official discourses about Congo's educational policies and the ways in which they integrated psychological advances. In this field, as a 1957 Colonial Office press release summarised, Belgium was 'serving as a model for UNESCO'. In rhetoric typical of the 'model colony' discourse, the press release insisted that UNESCO's new educational doctrine in Africa was entirely consistent with what Belgium had been doing in the Congo for decades.[81] Flourishing in the 1950s, UNESCO's projects in 'fundamental education' (programmes promoting instruction in basic literacy skills) provided the main ground for the involvement of psychologists as experts

éducative intercoloniale et la défense de l'Empire, 1947–1957', *Monde(s)*, 13, 1 (2018), pp. 195–21. See also John Kent, *The Internationalization of Colonialism: Britain, France and Black Africa, 1939–1956* (Oxford: Oxford University Press, 1992).

78 Vanthemsche, *Belgium and the Congo*, pp. 138–40.

79 As shown by Paule Bouvier, *L'accession du Congo belge à l'indépendance: Essai d'analyse sociologique* (Brussels: Institut de Sociologie, 1965), pp. 150–51, cited in Poncelet, *Sciences sociales*, p. 524.

80 See for example, Institut pour la recherche scientifique en Afrique centrale, 'Quatrième rapport annuel 1951' (Brussels, 1952).

81 Reproduced in the Belgian newspaper *La Métropole*, 24 September 1957 and mentioned in Chloé Maurel, 'L'UNESCO de 1945 à 1974', PhD thesis, Université Panthéon-Sorbonne – Paris I, 2006, p. 559.

in its missions in the colonial world.[82] The fact that the Belgian empire did not participate in these missions, because of its opposition towards UN interference, might explain why there were not more Belgian psychologists involved in these programmes, despite what was a lucrative new market for international consultancy.

These discourses were also symptomatic of tensions between international and imperial scales of expert knowledge production that did not entirely disappear with decolonisation as, again, the question of psychological expertise in (newly independent) Congo shows. Amid the chaos of the Congo crisis of the early 1960s and in the wake of the UN military intervention, UNESCO launched the Unescongo operation ('*Programme d'urgence de l'UNESCO dans le cadre de l'action des Nations Unies pour le maintien des services éducatifs au Congo*', 1960–1965). The mission aimed not only to recruit replacements for the outflow of Belgian teachers so as to allow the school system to function, but also to provide the country with educational experts. Psycho-pedagogical specialists were needed to advise Congolese authorities on the implementation of 'new' educational policies and, last but not least, to manage the centres of vocational guidance throughout the Congo. While the Unescongo team was critical of colonial educational policies, its programmes were very much in line with late-colonial ideals of 'modernisation', 'development' and technocracy. Despite its somewhat reformed vocabulary ('training for a technological world'[83] was the catch-phrase of the time), the mission's unwavering 'faith ... in the measurability of aptitudes'[84] remained unchanged from the 1950s.

On the ground however, the Unescongo operation was met with criticisms rooted not only in different political interests, but also in conflicting mobilisations of expertise. Indeed, while Unescongo recognised the importance of 'mental decolonisation' (in the words of Joseph Ngalula, Congo's Minister of Education from 1961 to 1963) as a guiding principle of its interventions in schooling programmes, its recommendation for a single, centralised, French-speaking education system was not positively welcomed by all.[85]

---

82 Damiano Matasci, 'Assessing needs, fostering development: UNESCO, illiteracy and the global politics of education (1945–1960)', *Comparative Education*, 53, 1 (2017), pp. 35–53. On UNESCO and psychology, see Linstrum, *Ruling Minds*, pp. 189 & foll.

83 Gary Fullerton, *UNESCO in the Congo* (Paris: UNESCO, 1964), p. 25. See also UNESCO archives Digital Library 0000159568, G. Pasartzis, 'Final Report on Vocational Guidance to UNESCO' (1965).

84 This expression is borrowed from Linstrum, *Ruling Minds*, p. 190.

85 Quoted in Fullerton, *UNESCO in the Congo*, p. 15.

Moïse Tshombe, leader of the Katangese secession, for example, expelled UNESCO's experts in 1961 – a decision obviously reflecting the Katangese state's opposition to the UN's wider role ending the secession.[86] But opposition was also expressed by the powerful, Jesuit-run Bureau for Catholic Education (Bureau de l'enseignement catholique – BEC). For years, BEC had a stranglehold on education policy in the Belgian Congo, promoting schooling in vernacular languages, an adapted-yet-traditional curriculum and a mass education system mostly limited to primary schooling. Not surprisingly, it saw UNESCO as a competitor.[87] With the support of the Catholic Church and of the *Bureau international catholique de l'enfance* (BICE) (the main Francophone Catholic social organisation for childhood issues), BEC's opposition to UNESCO's influence should be understood as a tale of two (competing) internationalisms.

This competition was not new: even before decolonisation, the prospect of dismantling empires had led Western Catholic leaders to develop new international strategies, notably through the expansion of humanitarian organisations, that sought to counter the influence of communist, secular and/or Anglo-Saxon values in key sectors such as education. The 1957 international conference on African Childhood organised by the BICE and held in Yaoundé was intended as a landmark in this strategy.[88] It was attended not only by ecclesiastical authorities and colonial bureaucrats, but also by scientists in general and especially by psychologists, the new disciplinary experts on childhood. One specialist was chosen to present to the conference the results of recent scientific experiments about 'the psychology of the African child' and to advise on future Catholic educational policies in 'detribalised' environments: Belgian psychologist Paul Verhaegen, the director of *Union Minière*'s psychological research centre, who was also, conveniently for Catholic leaders, one of the few international experts of the topic never involved in 'rival' projects funded by UNESCO.[89]

---

86 Mbuyu Mujinga Kimpesa, 'L'opération de l'UNESCO au Congo-Léopoldville et le diagnostic des réalités éducatives congolaises: 1960–64', PhD thesis, University of Geneva, 1983, cited in Maurel, 'L'UNESCO', p. 999.

87 Maurel, 'L'UNESCO', p. 1003–4. See also Roger Verbeek, *Le Congo en question* (Paris: Présence Africaine, 1965), p. 146.

88 Charlotte Walker-Said, 'Science and Charity: Rival Catholic Visions for Humanitarian Practice at the End of Empire', *French Politics, Culture and Society*, 33, 2 (2015), pp. 33–54, pp. 33–4, 41.

89 Paul Verhaegen, 'Contribution à l'étude de la psychologie de l'enfant africain' in BICE (ed.), *L'enfant africain: L'éducation de l'enfant africain en fonction de son milieu de base et de son orientation d'avenir* (Paris: Editions Fleurus, 1960), pp. 107–32.

Paths to Africanisation

On the eve of decolonisation, international actors were not the only newcomers on the stage of psychological expertise in the Congo. Opened in 1954, the University of Lovanium in Léopoldville delivered diplomas to its first African graduates in Pedagogical Sciences in 1958, and the following year extended this programme's scope by offering a joint masters' degree in Psychology and Pedagogy. Most of its first African students were (future) priests in search of a professional training in education. Professors however complained about the lack of attraction of psychological sciences; while the course attracted more students as the 1960s went on, it remained far less popular than medicine, economics or political sciences.[90] In a country which critically needed trained professionals for executive positions, these latter disciplines appeared more relevant than psychology.

The official publications of Lovanium's Department of Psychology and Pedagogy however insisted that psychological expertise 'meets the need of a young Republic' and that psychologists 'face a very big task'. They emphasised the importance given to the Department's 'own typical African identity and personality' and to its 'adapted African programme and training'.[91] These intellectual and political challenges were widely shared in early postcolonial Africa. The decolonisation and the growing internationalisation of African psychology did not mean it had abandoned the ambition of being a 'useful' science in the service of the new authorities' development policies. As a special issue of the International Review of Applied Psychology underlined in 1973, psychologists could play 'a major role in national development' if they focused on a 'clearer understanding of the socio-psychological processes of development' rather than pursuing 'recognition of [their] researches by Western scientists'.[92] As the British psychology professor at Makerere University (Kampala) Mallory Weber emphasised, the political stakes remained important, notably in terms of schooling programmes and vocational aspirations. Indeed, if care was not taken of the psychology of independent Africans, the acceleration of urbanisation and 'modernisation' and its (alleged) corollary, 'unrealistic'

90 Université Lovanium 1961–1962 (Léopoldville, 1963), p. 22 and pp. 98 & foll.; Leo Missine, *L'Institut facultaire de psychologie et de pédagogie: Son organisation et ses recherches* (Léopoldville: Université de Lovanium, 1968).
91 Leo Missine, 'Lovanium University (Congo-Kinshasa) department of psychology and education', *New Africa* (January/February 1967), pp. 18–19.
92 Durganand Sinha, 'Psychology and the Problems of Developing Countries: A General Overview', *International Review of Applied Psychology*, 22, 1 (1973), pp. 5–26, p. 6.

professional and material aspirations, could lead to an escalation of political unrest. Here again, professional guidance and psychology were presented as ideal tools to 'canalise these aspirations towards more realistic goals' so as to avoid political unrest.[93]

In the same article, Weber underlined the extent to which the field of psychology in Eastern Africa remained in the hands of white 'foreigners'.[94] This was also the case in the Congo in the first decade after independence. The academic staff of Lovanium's Department of Psychology and Pedagogy remained predominantly white, with the exception of Michel Karikunzira, a Burundian priest with a PhD degree in Pedagogical Sciences who became Lovanium's first African professor in January 1960.[95] In 1968, he became the Chancellor of the new University of Bujumbura. The role played by the first generation of university-trained Congolese psychologists in the remaking of psychological knowledge remains to be explored.

At independence however, it seems clear that this expertise, despite its influence and visibility, was neither a topic nor a tool of mobilisation for Congolese elites, with one major exception. This exception was Thomas Kanza (1933–2004), the first university graduate in Congolese history. Kanza graduated from the Belgian University of Leuven in 1956, in the discipline of Psychology and Pedagogy. This was not however his first choice: Kanza wanted initially to study law or medicine, but the Belgian authorities discouraged him, apparently believing that psychology was a politically safer science. They should have known better. In 1959, a few months before independence and on the eve of a successful international political career, Kanza published a short satirical essay on 'Colonial Vocation in Africa', in which he used psychological discourses on vocational guidance (with its theories on aptitudes, personality types, educational success, etc.) as metaphors to underline Belgium's illusions about its 'colonial vocation' and the limits of the country's aptitudes in this regard.[96]

---

93 Mallory Wober, 'Some Areas for the Application of Psychological Research in East Africa', *International Review of Applied Psychology*, 22, 1 (1973), pp. 41–52, p. 53.
94 Ibid., p. 50.
95 Mantels, *Geleerd in de Tropen*, p. 267.
96 Thomas Kanza, *Propos d'un Congolais naïf: discours sur la vocation coloniale dans l'Afrique de demain* (Bruxelles: Les Amis de Présence africaine, 1959). On Kanza at the University of Leuven, see Sam Schutter, '1952, Thomas Kanza komt naar Leuven' in Marnix Beyen, M. Boone, B. De Wever, L. Huet, B. Meijns, et al, *Wereldgeschiedenis van Vlaanderen* (Antwerp: Polis, 2018), pp. 469–75.

Conclusion

Five decades after the publication of Stefano Kaoze's 'The Psychology of Bantu People', psychology appeared to be a well-established science in the Belgian Congo. After a late takeover (by comparison with the British Empire), this 'great science' had become in the 1950s a site of vigorous intellectual and political debates forged by (and connected to) international discussions as well as the specificities of late-colonial Belgian-Congolese society – and 'scientific' landscape. Despite the apparent marginalisation of the colony in global scientific forums, the work carried out by scholars in the Congo, most notably in mining towns, provided a compelling body of data and research on the nature of urban 'modern' African society that made it influential in such circles. As a test case of both 'modernisation' and industrial development, the Congolese Copperbelt offered not only a rich laboratory for social scientists, but also a market of expertise, brimming with opportunities for applied psychologists. Their assessment methods and their promise to find (or rather to engineer) a 'suitable' place for every worker appealed to mining compagnies and colonial bureaucrats on both economic and socio-political grounds. In this late-colonial context, the techno-scientific promises of industrial psychology perfectly matched the intertwined ambitions of improving work productivity (through 'scientifically based' hiring practices, training programmes and management methods) and ensuring the docility of an emerging urban working class with mounting social and political aspirations.

While applied psychology certainly suited the new look of late-colonial Belgian 'reformed' paternalism, a closer examination of the bureaucratic characterisation of this knowledge production, and the uses to which it was put, reveals the tensions at play. This can be observed not only in the divergent views of its practitioners about the supposed relationship between race, intelligence and what was perceived as a culture 'in transition' towards 'modernity', but also in the implementation of policies based on models and tests which were still disputed, as illustrated by the disagreements between *Union Minière* and its own research laboratory. In this regard, the multiple dynamics of internationalisation at play, first during the emergence of psychological expertise in the Copperbelt and in the Congo at large, and second in its growth in the late 1950s, did nothing to resolve these tensions. Multiple international connections were built along diverse political affinities and competing visions of psychological expertise. The wide-ranging global interest of the period in the assessment of 'detribalised' environments, enabled by the importance of Haut-Katanga as a primary testing ground of international psychological expertise, ensured this occurred despite the persistent anxieties of Belgian colonial leaders about international circuits of knowledge production and the threatening inter-imperial comparisons that went with them.

11

The Production of Historical Knowledge at the University of Lubumbashi (1956–2018)

Donatien Dibwe dia Mwembu

Introduction

Research is a very important aspect in the life of any university, providing a vital measure of its visibility within the local, provincial, national and international community. The university is an observatory of its environment, its country and its region. Not only does it analyse the facts, but also and above all, it makes available to society the tools and resources for its maintenance and development. In this respect, the University should remain autonomous and respond to the needs expressed by society. It should also be able to anticipate social problems and stay true to its vision. In this context, this quotation from Guy Rocher is highly relevant for Congolese universities in general, and the University of Lubumbashi in particular:

> The university of today, in the context in which it is situated, is facing new and great challenges, which require it to redefine its social and economic role ... A university that continues to be myopic in the face of the changes taking place around it lives in an ivory tower that is in danger of collapsing beneath its feet.[1]

This chapter analyses the impact of Congo and Katanga's history of social, economic and political turbulence on academic activity at the University of Lubumbashi. In particular and since Congolese independence it has focused on the production of knowledge in its Department of Historical Sciences,

---

1   Guy Rocher, 'Redéfinition du Rôle de l'Université' in Fernand Dumont and Yves Martin (eds), *L'éducation 25 ans plus tard! Et après?* (Quebec: Quebec Research Institute, 1990), pp. 181–98, p. 188.

during the university's three phases of existence as the Official University of the Congo (UOC, 1960–71), the National University of Zaire (UNAZA, 1971–81) and finally, the University of Lubumbashi (Unilu, since 1981).

From the University of the Belgian Congo and Ruanda-Urundi to the State University of the Congo (1956–1960)

During the Second World War, cut off from the metropole, Belgian-Congolese authorities wanted to provide Belgian students who had just finished their secondary studies with a curriculum that would allow them to continue university studies in Belgium after the war. In 1944, a commission made up of alumni of Belgian universities (the Free University of Brussels, Louvain, Liège, Ghent and the Polytechnic Faculty of Mons) was made responsible for supervising these future students. In Elisabethville (today Lubumbashi) in 1945, thirteen Belgian candidates, detained in the Belgian Congo by the war, were enrolled in this programme. Teaching was provided by alumni of the Belgian universities. In the west of the Belgian colony, at Kisantu in the province of Kongo Central, a university centre was opened in 1947 for the training of nurses, medical assistants, agronomists and agricultural assistants. In 1951, this university centre, which took the name of Lovanium, was transplanted to Kinshasa, where it later (1954) became the University of Lovanium.[2] As demonstrated in this chapter, it was Lubumbashi which saw the first initiative to set up higher education in the colony.

But the difficulties encountered by these students in Belgium, in particular the government's refusal to grant them the equivalence of their diploma for their studies in Congo, led to the abandonment of this first university experiment in Elisabethville.[3] For Congolese children, the initiative of establishing higher education was prompted by a Belgian senatorial commission sent to the Belgian Congo and Ruanda-Urundi in 1948. The members of this commission recommended that the colonial state should facilitate access to higher education for those Africans who were 'predisposed by talents and training'. It is in this context that Latin

2   Léon de Saint Moulin, 'L'Université au Congo, hier, aujourd'hui et demain', in Isidore Ndaywel è Nziem (ed.), *Les Années UNAZA*, vol. II, *Contribution à l'histoire de l'Université africaine* (Paris: L'Harmattan, 2018), pp. 87–101.
3   Lwamba Bilonda, 'L'Université de Lubumbashi, de 1956 à Nos Jours' in Ndaywel è Nziem (ed.), *L'Université dans le devenir de l'Afrique: Un demi-siècle de Présence au Congo-Zaïre* (Paris: L'Harmattan, 2007); pp. 37–59, p. 37.

humanities courses were commenced in Dungu (Haut-Uele District), Kamponde (Lulua District), Kiniati (Kwilu District) and Mboma Mbanza (Bas-Congo), alongside the establishment of vocational training schools for boys and housekeeping or family training schools for girls.[4] It is important to note here that, until the late 1940s, the well-known 'colonial trinity' – administration, business and religious missions, often presented as the 'pillars' on which the Belgian colonial order was based – was not yet sure of the type of education to be given to Blacks.[5] The general education provided had until this point been limited to middle school level (for the training of assistants, clerks, etc.), teacher training colleges (for the training of primary school teachers) and medical assistants. Later, the Ten-Year Plan for the Economic and Social Development of the Belgian Congo, 1949–1959 (the so-called Van Bilsen Plan) sought to provide for the training of Congolese specialist employees and technicians, in increasing demand as the economy expanded and with the aim of supplementing or replacing high-cost white labour.

It was not until the early 1950s that the colonial government implemented the plan to create a state university, and this was the result of a consensus between the colony's major political, economic and religious actors.[6]. It should be remembered that education in the Belgian Congo was then the monopoly of missionaries, both Catholic and Protestant. After the Second World War, the first official schools were set up for white children. It was only during the 1950s, under Colonial Minister Auguste Buisseret, a liberal, that the desire to put an end to the near-monopoly of the Catholic Church in the field of education for Africans

4   It should be noted that, before the 1950s, the education provided to African children was discriminatory. While boys were trained to become future white workers' helpers in the workplace, girls were trained to become good future housekeepers. 'To give the sons of our workers an education which will later enable them to become good workers by giving them the basic knowledge that their fathers did not have and that the latter only acquired empirically, following a long and arduous apprenticeship. … Girls we want to make good mothers, not to burden them with practically useless knowledge. The education they receive at school must be a preparation for the training they will receive later in the workshops and in the housekeeping schools': Gécamines Lubumbashi, 'Aide-mémoire M.O.I.', fascicule II, Politique M.O.I., annexe 3, 1943.
5   Crawford Young, *Politics in Congo: Decolonisation and Independence* (Princeton: Princeton University Press, 1965), p. 10.
6   Makwanza Batumanisa, 'L'histoire de l'Université de Lubumbashi dans la destinée nationale', in *UNILU, 30ème Anniversaire de l'Université de Lubumbashi* (Lubumbashi: UNILU, 1986), handout file, pp. 23–6.

became a reality. Government schools were created for black children, who sometimes shared benches with European pupils. It was in this same context that the Official University was created in Elisabethville in November 1956. This initiative effectively put an end to the Catholic monopoly of higher education, although Elisabethville coexisted with Lovanium University, established in Léopoldville in 1954 with the help of the Catholic University of Louvain.[7]

Originally envisaged as exclusively for the children of Belgian colonists, the University of Elisabethville was nonetheless 'mixed', in that it accepted Congolese students. During its first academic year in 1956–57, for example, there were eight Congolese among 104 students admitted. This number would steadily grow, while the proportion of European students, especially Belgian students, continued to decline.[8] Throughout the colonial period however, the entire faculty was composed of expatriates from Belgian universities, hired within the framework of technical cooperation. The Africanisation of the teaching staff began only after the country gained independence, first with the hiring of assistants and then, later, of a Congolese academic staff.

The Official University of the Belgian Congo and Ruanda-Urundi had to respond to three concerns of the colonial authorities. First, it was necessary, as noted above, to educate the children of Belgian settlers who lived in Katanga; second, to educate the children of Africans in general and of the Congolese in particular, to meet the demands of the growing economy and, finally, to affirm secularism in order to counterbalance the Catholic Church's monopoly on education. Moreover, the establishment of the official colonial university in a mining-dominated province was indicative of an orientation towards the technical sciences in general and mining technical education in particular, since the colonial companies aspired, inter alia, to replace some European employees with Africans, which would reduce costs. The Official University thus opened its doors with four departments (Sciences, Philosophy and Letters, Engineering, and Educational Sciences). The intention

7   Donatien Dibwe dia Mwembu, 'La formation des élites coloniales: Le cas de la province du Katanga', in Nathalie Tousignant (ed.), *Le manifeste Conscience africaine (1956): Élites congolaises et société coloniale – Regards croisés* (Brussels: Publications des Facultés Universitaires Saint-Louis, 2009), pp. 117–39.

8   After the Congo gained independence, during the 1963–64 academic year there were 327 Congolese as against 104 expatriates, including 53 Belgians, 26 Rwandans, 4 Italians, 3 Rhodesians, 3 Cypriots, 1 French and 1 U.S. American: 431 students in total: Lwamba Bilonda, 'L'Université de Lubumbashi', p. 57.

was then for the colonial university to train and guide the elite among the Congolese populations at the same time as the Europeans, creating the conditions for the existence of a fraternal society across racial lines.[9]

From 1956 to 1960, the only doctoral degree that the Official University of the Belgian Congo and Ruanda-Urundi bestowed was one in history in 1959. Paul Van Vracem, '[t]he happy recipient', notes Ndaywel è Nziem, 'had just defended a doctoral thesis entitled *The border of the Ruzizi-Kivu from 1894 to 1910*'.[10] But the creation of a history department in Congo would have to wait until 1965, at the University of Lovanium (Kinshasa). The first group of Congolese graduates in history obtained their degrees only in the 1970s.

The Official University of the Congo (1960–1971)

With the country's accession to independence in 1960, the University was renamed, as Rwanda and Burundi did not gain international sovereignty until 1962. It became the Official University of the Congo (UOC). However, following the secession of the province of Katanga to become the independent state of Katanga on 11 July 1960, it was renamed the State University in Elisabethville on 14 September 1960. Given its local requirements, the secessionist government of Katanga (in the context where many expatriates had fled the post-independence conflict) sought to ensure the university served as a large technical and vocational training institution that could also deliver results rapidly. Technicians had to be trained to cover immediate needs in various fields, such as geological prospecting, chemistry, metallurgy or botany. Moreover, the presence on the university's governing board of researchers employed by and representatives of companies, in particular *Union Minière du Haut-Katanga*, was an obvious sign of the collaboration between the State University and the leading actors in mining capitalism.

The Katangese secession did not last long. In January 1963, Katanga returned to the Congo and the State University in Elisabethville took the name Official University of the Congo (UOC), which it would keep until 1971. Several foreign, mostly Belgian, professors and researchers left,

---

9   'Histoire d'une vie – Campus de Lubumbashi, 1955–1979. De l'UOC à l'UNAZA' (Lubumbashi, undated), p. 3.
10 Isidore Ndaywel è Nziem, 'De Lovanium au campus de Lubumbashi: Production d'une modernité culturelle congolaise' in Ndaywel è Nziem (ed.), *Les années UNAZA*, pp. 107–27, p. 117.

a situation which disrupted both teaching and research within the university. Very few studies have been devoted to this period. But it should be remembered that the UOC administration during this period oversaw a significant Africanisation of personnel. In the field of history, the period from 1960 to 1970 witnessed the birth, in independent black Africa, of a nationalist historiography which contributed to the rehabilitation of the specific historicity of African societies. Historians of UOC played a significant role in demonstrating what we now take for granted, that Africa has always been in history and has always had a history. We can mention here, by way of illustration, the work of the Africanists, in particular that of Jan Vansina,[11] who opposed the approach of the positivist historians such as Henri Brunschwig.[12] The latter believed that Africa had no history before 1800. Through his research on the Kuba kingdom, Rwanda and Burundi, Jan Vansina also demonstrated that the reconstruction of African history was possible thanks to the use of oral traditions, a source long marginalised because it was perceived as inconsistent, ephemeral and therefore unreliable. The work of the Africanists complemented that of African historians, in particular the revolutionary historian Cheikh Anta Diop[13]. Djibril Tamsir Niane showed, through the publication of his book *Soundjata or the Mandingo Epic* that African history can also be written by the 'griots' who represent the collective memory, the oral tradition worked on and handed down from generation to generation.[14] Other African academics, such as Joseph Ki-Zerbo or Théophile Obenga, sustained their historical research by their nationalist and pan-Africanist convictions.[15] Ambitious collective works written in the 1970s also set out to trace the history of the continent over the long term. They sought to shed light on the way Africans shaped their historic destiny, even under the colonial yoke.[16]

11 Jan Vansina, *De la tradition orale: Essai de méthode historique* (Tervuren: MRAC, 1961).
12 Henri Brunschwig, *Méthodologie de l'histoire et des sciences humaines (Mélanges en l'honneur de Fernand Braudel)* (Toulouse: Privat, 1973), p. 85.
13 Vansina, *De la tradition orale*; Cheikh Anta Diop, *Antériorités des civilisations nègres: Mythe ou vérité historique?* (Paris: Présence Africaine, 1967).
14 Niana Djibril Tamsir, *Soundjata ou l'épopée mandingue* (Paris: Présence Africaine, 1960).
15 Joseph Ki-Zerbo, *Histoire de l'Afrique noire: D'hier à demain* (Paris: Hatier, 1972); Théophile Obenga, *L'Afrique dans l'Antiquité: Egypte pharaonique, Afrique noire* (Paris: Présence Africaine, 1973).
16 Cf. UNESCO, *General History of Africa* (in eight volumes) written by African and Africanist historians; cf. also Ibrahima Baba Kake et Elikia M'Bokolo (eds), *Histoire générale de l'Afrique* (Paris: ABC, 1977); Catherine Coquery-Vidrovitch and Henri Moniot, *L'Afrique noire: De 1800 à nos jours* (Paris: PUF, 1974).

Until the late 1960s, colonial history in the Congo was the story of the actions of Europeans; the Congolese played the role of mere extras.[17] Postcolonial history would take on the task of showing that the African in general, and the Congolese in particular, played a decisive role in the construction of colonial society. Until the early 1970s, more than 90% of Congolese historiography was in the hands of Africanists of various external origins, largely from Western Europe, Eastern Europe and North America. It was these Africanists who, in 1965, created the first Department of History at the University of Lovanium, whose programme was modelled on that of the Belgian universities from which these teachers mainly came. The Congolese research centres were, in a way, offshoots of their European counterparts. The research carried out focused on the precolonial period and was centred on 'tribal' history, written from the narrative sources of the explorers and also from the earliest archival documents.[18]

In 1968, the Department of History was endowed with a bachelor's programme and later, in 1972, a doctoral programme. The main objective was to train the African historian who, according to Bogumil Jewsiewicki, 'must give back to the peoples of this continent their own history, a necessary element of the national consciousness. At the same time, his investigations should make it possible to understand the processes of formation of society and the State today[19]. The year 1970 saw the first Congolese students graduate with a degree in history from the University of Lovanium.

The National University of Zaire, Lubumbashi Campus (1971–1981)

In 1971, under the Mobutu regime, all higher education and university establishments were merged into a single institution called the National University of Zaire (UNAZA), divided into three campuses in Kinshasa,

17 See, by way of illustration, the monographs on large companies such as UMHK, BCK or La Forminière.
18 Jean-Luc Vellut, *Guide de l'étudiant en histoire du Zaïre* (Presses universitaires du Zaïre, 1974), p. 64. See for example: N'Dua Solol, 'Histoire ancienne des populations Luba et Lunda du Plateau de Haut-Lubilashi: des origines au début du XXe siècle (Bena Nsamba, Inimpinim et Tuwidi)', PhD thesis, UNAZA, Campus de Lubumbashi, 1978; Mumbanza mwa Baawele, 'L'histoire des peuples riverains de l'entre-Zaïre-Ubangi: Evaluation sociale et économique, 1780–1930', PhD Thesis, UNAZA, Campus de Lubumbashi, 1981.
19 Bogumil Jewsiewicki, 'Notes sur l'histoire socio-économique du Congo (1880–1960)' in *Etudes d'Histoire africaine*, III (1972), pp. 209–41, p. 209.

Kisangani and Lubumbashi. This reform contributed to the stated objective of the regime to break with Congo's colonial heritage and create a new type of man compatible with the so-called 'authentic' Zairian revolution. The president and his single party, the Popular Movement of the Revolution (MPR), aimed to 'liberate the Zairean people from all mental alienation', thanks to the ideology of 'authentic Zairean nationalism'.[20] This programme did not tolerate pluralism; Mobutu needed intellectuals who were 'truly revolutionary', that is, dedicated, committed and won over to the cause of the political system. This idealised figure contrasted with those who the proponents of the regime presented as 'anarchist intellectuals, driven by an outraged pessimism, who were conspicuous by their inflammatory declarations, demonstrations in the streets, with attitudes which were always assertive.'[21]

The university reform of 1971 was also shaped by the deterioration of relations between the Mobutu regime and the Congolese universities, viewed by the former as places where protesters in the pay of foreign powers were unhelpfully accommodated. The Zairian intellectual – and especially the student – had to be made a responsible man, totally free of any 'neocolonial' influence. This objective seemed particularly pressing in view of the increasing politicisation of Congolese students. In 1961, an assembly of Congolese delegates (but also with members from Belgium, France and the United States of America), identifying themselves as Marxist-Leninists, founded the General Union of Congolese Students (UGEC). The Union opposed successive Congolese governments, which it described as 'the servant of American and Western imperialism'. Moreover, at the end of the symposium on the reform of higher and university education held in Goma in April–May 1969, student representatives demanded co-management of universities, as well as the Africanisation of personnel and programmes.

The government's wholesale rejection of all the symposium's resolutions was an opportunity for the students to express their disapproval on the streets. Demonstrations that took place on 4 June 1969 were violently repressed and led to the death of a significant number of students. The second anniversary of these events gave rise to new demonstrations in 1971, also strongly repressed. Following these, the universities were closed and all students were recruited into the army. Ngoma Binda notes that President

---

20   Kabamba Mbikay, 'Authenticité: condition d'un développement harmonisé', *Jiwe* 1 (1973), pp. 23–37, p. 24.
21   Koli Elombe Motukoa, 'Le portrait de l'intellectuel zaïrois', *ELIMU*, 1 (1973), pp. 76–88, p. 76.

Mobutu also wanted to get rid of supposed dissident elements hostile to his rule by removing them from Kinshasa.[22] The Mobutu political regime now sought to take control of university institutions by politicising them. Indeed, the academic reform of 1971 stipulated that all the decision-making positions had to be occupied by committed MPR militants.

The single party was also working on the indoctrination of Zairian youth. Young people were expected to testify to their 'civic virtues' wherever they were – in the field, on the construction site, in factories, at school, etc. They were expected to know that the success of the revolution greatly depended on their support and that they had to become aware of their responsibility in solving the problems facing the country. In this context, the chief concern of MPR leaders was to provide appropriate political guidance, not only to the student youth, but also to the entire university community. The objective was that everyone would be committed to making UNAZA a pioneering body of the revolution and thus put an end to the instability of the early years of independence.

It is in this context that we must understand the role entrusted to the JMPR (the MPR youth), that of being both the eyes and the ears of the regime. A former member of the student brigade, one of the JMPR branches at the UNAZA Lubumbashi campus, described his role in these terms:

> The student brigade or CADER-UNILU (Corps des Activistes pour la Défense de la Révolution – UNILU) consisted of four platoons: the intervention platoon, the information platoon, the environmental platoon and the mobilisation platoon. The intervention platoon was tasked with the repression of recalcitrant students ... the environmental platoon ensured hygiene in university residences, forcing students to look after their environment ... The mobilisation platoon had a political mission. It was this platoon which was to educate the students to participate in all political demonstrations such as marches, parades, popular rallies, etc. A platoon had at least 16 members or more, and its overall headcount varied between 100 and 120. The brigade presented itself as a police force of the JMPR sub-sectional committee.[23]

The journal *Jiwe*, the ideological organ of the MPR, which was created on the Lubumbashi campus, was a propaganda tool and the champion of the party-state within the university community. The Editorial Board presented it as pursuing

22 Ngoma Binda, 'Faut-il privatiser les universités officielles du Zaïre?' *Zaïre-Afrique*, 288 (1994), pp. 495–505, p. 497.
23 Interview, Jean-Marie Bashizi, 5 March 2019.

a threefold objective: ideological, cultural and scientific. ... *JIWE* takes on the task of holding high the torch of the Revolution, of spreading the ideals of the MPR ... It aims to become the foundation of a new mentality, freed from the after-effects of colonisation, constantly nourished at the sources of our Authenticity. Finally, it aims, through scientific work, to make the scientific heritage of Humanity accessible to all, to ensure the transmission of knowledge, all within the framework of the ideology of the MPR.[24]

The UNAZA years were also marked by various political and economic troubles, such as the two Shaba wars and the policy of Zairianisation. In November 1973, Mobutu launched the policy known as Zairianisation. This was the takeover by the Zaireans of the local subsidiaries of Belgian companies and foreign commercial enterprises, as well as the nationalisation of petroleum product distribution companies. This policy did not achieve its economic objectives and discouraged foreign investors. The departure of foreign traders – particularly Greeks, Portuguese and Indians – plundered by the Mobutu government led to an increase in unemployment. In addition, Gécamines, the country's major source of income, experienced supply difficulties due to the deterioration of Zaïre's economic structure and the closure of the Lobito railway.

The Eighty-Day War or the first Shaba War (8 March to 13 May 1977), was the first attack carried out by Katangese *gendarmes* in exile in Angola against the province of Shaba (Katanga). These rebels were defeated by the Congolese army, supported by Moroccan troops with the logistical assistance of the French army. A year later, the second Shaba War or Six-Day War (12–19 May 1978) saw the same rebels from Zambia and Angola invade the city of Kolwezi.[25] The rebels were driven out by the Zairian army with the support of French paratroopers. Both events led to a sharp fall in Gécamines' copper production.

The UNAZA years were not however altogether bad. Positive achievements were made in the fields of research and teaching, the living conditions of students and the Africanisation of personnel. As a result of bilateral cooperation, the university received financial, technical and academic support from Europe and the United States. Scholarships from the Rockefeller Foundation, for example, were granted to Zairian doctoral students, while

---

24 'Editorial' *Jiwe* I (1973), pp. 1–10, p. 2. The members of the Editorial Committee were all members of the MPR section committee at the Lubumbashi campus of UNAZA.
25 See Eric Kennes and Miles Larmer, *The Katangese Gendarmes and War in Central Africa: Fighting Their Way Home* (Bloomington: Indiana University Press, 2016), pp. 119–45.

American, Belgian, French, German and Polish teaching staff were sent to Zaïre as part of cooperation agreements. These collaborations led to the construction of new infrastructure, such as research laboratories, veterinary clinics or residences for teaching staff.

Nyunda ya Rubango recalls UNAZA's Lubumbashi campus as being characterised by the research carried out there during this period: 'I am still in awe of some spectacular past achievements of the Lubumbashi professors, actions testifying to the influence of the university at national and international level.'[26] In addition, that author cites the various research centres set up during this period, which were the pride of the institution due to the quality and frequency of their academic output.[27] Indeed, during the UNAZA period, the Lubumbashi campus produced 59 doctoral theses, including five in history. It should be noted that, with the merger into UNAZA in 1971, the history departments of the University of Lovanium and UOC were merged into a single department located at Lubumbashi's Faculty of Letters. Here, the history curriculum involved four options: political history, economic and social history, cultural history and the history of the African population.

Indeed, it is important to note that the creation of UNAZA/Lubumbashi marked a turning point in Congolese historiography. It schooled the first class of Congolese history graduates, and its first doctoral degrees were awarded in 1978.[28] Moreover, from 1971, the UNAZA Department of History in Lubumbashi initiated first the Africanisation of its researchers and assistants first (in 1976), and of its teaching staff thereafter (1978). In 1970, the History Department established an organ for the dissemination of academic research, the journal *Etudes d'Histoire Africaine*. In 1973, the Department set up a research centre (the Centre for Studies and Documentary Research on Central Africa (CERDAC) and, alongside *Etudes d'Histoire Africaine*, a CERDAC journal called *Likundoli* ('Awakening'). It is in these

---

26 Nyunda ya Rubango, 'De Lovanium à la Kasapa caserne: mémoires d'un pèlerin métis' in Ndaywel è Nziem (ed.), *L'Université*, pp. 97–124, p. 123.

27 Ibid., p. 123: the author cites research centres, mostly from the Faculty of Letters: CELTA (Centre for Theoretical and Applied Linguistics), CELRIA (Centre for Studies of African-inspired Romance Literature), CIS (International Semiology Centre), CERDAC (Centre for Documentary Studies and Research on Central Africa), CERPHA (Centre for Research in African Philosophy), CEPAC (Centre for Political Studies in Central Africa), etc.

28 The first doctoral thesis in history defended by a Congolese at the Lubumbashi Campus was in 1978. The other four theses were defended in 1980 (2) and in 1981 (2).

research structures that fruitful academic research developed, focusing on the country as a whole, the province of Katanga, the region of the Copperbelt i.e. the mining towns of Lubumbashi, Likasi, Kolwezi, Kipushi, Kambove, Kakanda, etc., and their hinterlands.

With regard to the emergence of a new postcolonial historiography in Africa, it must be recognised that the History Department initially lagged behind. Its alignment to the new postcolonial historiography constituted a challenge, as was emphasised so clearly in 1970 by the rector of UNAZA, Bishop Tshibangu Tshishiku, in the foreword to the first issue of *Etudes d'Histoire Africaine.*

> The history of our continent and our people is being ignored. It is therefore with joy that we welcome all efforts to develop academic awareness of Africa's past … The absence of Congolese contributors in this first collection unfortunately recalls the long delay in undertaking the training of national historians. However, there is every reason to hope that a young and dynamic Congolese historical school, well versed in the sources, will develop rapidly and renew our knowledge of Africa's past.[29]

This delay would indeed be quickly rectified. In 1972, an international symposium on the history of Africa was organised in Lubumbashi, in which eminent researchers such as Cheikh Anta Diop and Théophile Obenga took an active part. The Department of History also had to adapt to the requirements of the regime. Indeed, Ndaywel è Nziem noted in 1979, when he was a professor at UNAZA / Lubumbashi:

> History is a strong factor in mental de-alienation and a powerful lever for national awareness and mobilisation. At this time, when national society finds itself resolutely engaged in the process of integral development, the teaching of history can be an element of raising awareness. However, it must be adapted and be truly in the service of the national cause.[30]

Thus, the pre-UNAZA history programme was strengthened to ensure that the Africanist option of the History Department addressed the concerns of the time. Broadly speaking, before UNAZA, the number of hours of Zairean (Congo) and African history courses constituted only 18.4% of

29 Mgr Tharcisse Tshibangu, cited in Isidore Ndaywel è Nziem, 'De Lovanium au campus de Lubumbashi', pp. 118–19.
30 Ndaywel è Nziem, 'Rapport sur les projets de recherche et de publications en vue de la réunion de la Commission de la Recherche Scientifique de l'UNAZA' (Lubumbashi, 1979), p. 17.

the history students' curriculum. Following the 1976 reform, this rose to 54.4%.[31] In addition, research was initiated at CERDAC on social history. The development of a single-volume history of Zaïre, with a longue durée vision, was a challenge, despite the contribution of Robert Cornevin[32] and another volume of this type that was published by Tshimanga wa Tshibangu in 1974.[33] Further work was undertaken on the development of an encyclopaedic dictionary of Central African history[34]; on biographies of historical personalities of Zaïre, of which a first section including 120 entries was published; and on the development of a history of Zaïre for teaching of the subject in secondary school.[35] Critical re-reading also made it possible to detect prejudices and make corrections to the content of older history textbooks.[36]

The UNAZA Lubumbashi Campus and its Environment

Under Mobutu, the links between UNAZA/Lubumbashi and the local industrial and mining communities were strengthened. The merger of the polytechnic and science faculties concentrated all the mining engineering courses in the copper city of Lubumbashi. The humanities courses trained administrative staff who were then employed by local businesses. The commitment of the University's graduating students gradually increased the rate at which African personnel replaced expatriates in the province's private sector. At Gécamines, for example, the rate of Africanisation of personnel rose from 37.23% in 1971 to 77.71% in 1981.[37]

---

31   Ndaywel è Nziem, 'Programme de formation des historiens africains en faculté des lettres (1963–1976)', *Likundoli: Histoire et devenir*, 1, 4 (1976), pp. 1–56.
32   Robert Cornevin, *Le Zaïre (ex-Congo-Kinshasa)* (Paris: PUF, 1972).
33   Tshimanga wa Tshibangu, *Histoire du Zaïre* (Bukavu: Editions du CERUKI, 1976).
34   Many studies are elaborated in the form of dissertations, theses etc.
35   A first volume was completed and published locally in 1981. See Tshund'Olela Epanya et al., *Histoire du Zaïre* vol. I (Lubumbashi: UNAZA-CERDAC, 1981). This first volume dealt with ancient Zaïre. Volume II was to deal with the colonial and postcolonial period. But it took a long time to see Isidore Ndaywel è Nziem develop and publish a general synthesis of Congo's history: Isidore Ndaywel è Nziem, *Histoire générale du Congo: de l'héritage ancien à la République démocratique du Congo* (Paris: Duculot, 1998).
36   See: Tenda Kikuni, 'Préjugés à dépister dans les manuels d'histoire du cycle d'orientation', *Likundoli* 4, 1–2 (1979), pp. 58–69.
37   Gécamines, Annual reports, 1971–1981.

Nor did the History Department remain isolated from its environment. The 1970s saw the creation of SOHIZA (Society of Historians of Zaïre) and the organisation of several local, national and international symposia and seminars, focusing in particular on issues of national memory. For example, in 1975, a symposium on the elites of Zaïre was held in Lubumbashi, during which the figure of Patrice Emery Lumumba was discussed. Lumumba is a complex historical figure, perceived by some as a liberator, by others as a dictator, a communist or even a murderer.[38] Lumumba, who was controversial in 1960, was transformed into a consensual object of memory under Mobutu. Indeed, the Zairian regime, eager to pass itself off as the political heir to Lumumba, rehabilitated him and turned him into a national hero. His effigy appeared on the twenty makuta bank note, where he was depicted breaking the chains of slavery, while main thoroughfares in Kinshasa and in Lubumbashi came to bear his name. The unified memory of a liberating Lumumba was thus imposed upon the minds of the Congolese people.

The historians of UNAZA/Lubumbashi were also involved in this rehabilitation. They underlined his major role in the national emancipation of the country and presented him as a model to be imitated by the current political elite. During the 1975 symposium, Lumumba was presented as the herald of a unitary nationalism, opposed to tribalism and separatism, in order to better espouse the ideology of the MPR.[39] From this period, Lumumba, once regarded by most Katangese as a communist and the plunderer of Katanga's wealth, came to be remembered as a national hero.

However, in the face of the meteoric rise of Mobutism – the cult of the president's personality, which gained momentum during the 1980s – Lumumba's memory was confiscated and relegated to oblivion. His effigy on the twenty makuta bank note was replaced by that of President Mobutu. 'The historical Lumumba', notes Bogumil Jewsiewicki, 'was returned to the archives and gradually banished from political life and the public space monopolised by the omnipresence of the image of the chief, master of the place, Mobutu himself'.[40]

---

38 Bogumil Jewsiewicki (ed.), *A Congo Chronicle: Patrice Lumumba in Urban Art* (New York: The Museum for African Art, 1999); Matthias de Groof (ed.), *Lumumba in the Arts* (Leuven: Leuven University Press, 2019); Pierre Petit, *Patrice Lumumba: La fabrication d'un héros national et panafricain* (Brussels: Editions de l'Académie, 2016).
39 CERDAC, *Elites et devenir de la société zaïroise, actes des troisièmes journées du Zaïre* (Lubumbashi: CERDAC, 1975), p. 9.
40 Bogumil Jewsiewicki, 'Corps interdits: La représentation christique de Lumumba comme rédempteur du peuple Zaïrois', in *Cahiers d'Etudes africaines*, 141–2 (1996), pp. 113–42, p. 134. After the fall of Mobutu, the memory of Lumumba resurfaced

During the 1980s, that is to say towards the end of the UNAZA years, the living conditions of students and teaching staff began to deteriorate. Subsidies allocated to higher and university education began first to decrease, then disappeared entirely. This led to the growing destitution of teaching staff, who were paid a meagre, starvation wage. Universities throughout Africa similarly entered a period of decline from the 1980s. By way of illustration, we can mention the case of Makerere University in Uganda which, due to both the dictatorship of Idi Amin (1971–79) and the civil war in the south-west, west and central parts of the country (1980–86), experienced a dramatic decline in its academic output. This doubly political situation forced many local researchers into exile and led many expatriate researchers to abandon positions in African universities.[41] Generally speaking, several factors explain this situation. These include the economic crisis and structural adjustment plans that caused the state to withdraw financially from universities almost everywhere. The second major factor was the massification of higher and university education, due mainly to the demographic explosion experienced in African countries.[42] The Democratic Republic of the Congo did not deviate from this reality. However, the abolition of scholarships,[43] the unproductive policy of Zairianisation launched in November 1973, and the neglect of education by Mobutu's government are specific to the DRC. In other words, education in general was not on the list of priorities of the ruling power. 'The university appeared, from the 1970s', notes Julien Kilanga Musinde, 'as a negligible appendage to the priorities defined by the authorities.'[44]

---

with the accession of President Laurent-Désiré Kabila, whose political regime posed as the continuator of Lumumba's politics and thought. Painters reproduced on canvas Lumumba breathing his spirit on Laurent-Désiré Kabila, as in the Old Testament the spirit of the prophet Elijah had entered the prophet Elisha.

41 Henri Médard, 'Histoire populaire et histoire scientifique en Ouganda (1890–2009)' in Nicodème Bugwabari, Alain Cazenave-Piarrot, Olivier Provini and Christian Thibon (eds), *Universités et universitaires en Afrique de l'Est* (Paris: Karthala, 2012), pp. 99–114, p. 108.

42 Hervé Maupeu, 'Les réformes néolibérales des universités est-africaines: eléments d'analyses à partir du cas kényan' in Nicodème Bugwabari, Alain Cazenave-Piarrot, Olivier Provini and Christian Thibon (eds), *Universités et universitaires*, Karthala, pp. 195–212, p. 202; see also Leo Van Audenhove, *Development Co-operation in Higher Education: A Strategic Review of International Donor Policy and Practices* (Brussels: Free University Brussels, 1999), p. 12.

43 Enrolment fees were deducted at source for scholarship students. However, non-scholarship students had to pay their enrolment fees themselves.

44 Julien Kilanga Musinde, *La main de la tradition: l'homme, le destin, l'université* (Lubumbashi: CIRIADA, 2000), p. 14.

The University of Lubumbashi (UNILU), 1981–1989

In 1981, the Mobutu regime abolished the UNAZA structure and implemented a new reform of higher and university education. The mismanagement and extensive bureaucracy of UNAZA seem to have justified this change. It was necessary to return to autonomy at the level of universities and high schools. The three UNAZA campuses became separate autonomous universities, each with its own management committee, but managed by the same board of governors. The UNAZA campus of Lubumbashi became the University of Lubumbashi. Since 1981, this institution has had to deal with the political and economic upheavals experienced by the country as a whole and the province of Katanga in particular.

From 1974 to 1989, there was a major decline in purchasing power and currency depreciation. The exchange rate, which was 2 US dollars for 1 Zaïre on 1 January 1968, moved to 1 Zaïre to 0.34 US dollars at the beginning of 1980. From 30 January 1984 to 31 December 1989, the exchange rate for 1 US dollar rose from 30 to 300 Zaïres. In addition, in September 1989, the main underground mine at Kamoto collapsed, depriving Gécamines of a third of its production. This deteriorating economic situation was worsened by political upheaval. Growing political challenges to Mobutu's reign were marked by a wave of violence. Bloody incidents at the University of Lubumbashi in May 1990 led to the Republic of Zaïre being cut off from credit by the international financial and monetary institutions. In addition, looting orchestrated by the Mobutu government on 21 and 22 October 1991 systematically destroyed the economic fabric of the city of Lubumbashi. Small and medium-sized enterprises had to close their doors and lay off their workers on a massive scale. This situation led to an increase in the unemployment rate and a deterioration in living conditions.

This period of turbulence in the Republic of Zaïre in general, and Katanga in particular, had a profoundly negative impact on the functioning of UNILU and on research. Between 1985 and 1990, the funds paid to the university by the government varied between 3.2% and 14% of the amounts requested, before stopping entirely in 1990.[45] As a result, the research centres, deprived of all funding, saw their collective projects come to a standstill. These gave way to individual research projects, most often carried out on external commission, and therefore not generally addressing local and

---

45 Kilanga Musinde, *La main,* p. 16.

national needs.[46] Moreover, personnel assigned to the research centres were diverted from their original functions to provide teaching, for which they were not hired. How, in this case, could research contribute to the development of society when there was such a mismatch between local, provincial and national needs and the academic output of the Congolese universities in general, and of UNILU in particular.[47]

In addition, UNILU, like other universities in the country, faced the problem of limited access to electronic publications and the acquisition and renewal of scientific and computer equipment. Over time, the quality of higher education graduates deteriorated dangerously, throughout sub-Saharan Africa in general, and the DRC in particular. Many companies, including Gécamines and the rail company Société Nationale des Chemins de Fer du Zaïre (SNCZ), began to express reservations about the quality of the students graduating from universities.[48]

The University of Lubumbashi, 1990s and 2000s

To escape from this quagmire, the academic authorities of the University of Lubumbashi (UNILU) have been developing strategies to make their Alma Mater a real instrument of development through teaching, research and services to society. Like all universities in the world, the missions, functions and roles of higher education and university institutions have evolved and are evolving rapidly.

For nearly seven years (1990–97), Congolese universities operated in a closed environment. The opening up of these institutions of higher and university education in general, and the University of Lubumbashi, in particular, was designed to prevent their descent into hell. This was where the formula of cooperation and partnership between the University of Lubumbashi with foreign universities, especially Belgian universities (both French and Dutch speaking), came into play. This cooperation and partnership helped to begin the tentative opening up of the University from 1998 onwards. It should be

[46] Kakoma Sakatolo Zambeze, *L'Académie congolaise du XXIè Siècle* (Lubumbashi: UNILU, 1999), pp. 4–5.
[47] Kakoma Sakatolo Zambeze, *L'Académie congolaise*, p. 5.
[48] World Bank, *Faire de l'enseignement supérieur le moteur de développement en Afrique subsaharienne* (Washington DC: World Bank, 2008), p. 52; see also Donatien Dibwe dia Mwembu, 'Le rôle social de l'Université de Lubumbashi' in Bogumil Jewsiewicki and Véronique Klauber (eds), *Université de Lubumbashi 1990–2002: société en détresse, pari sur l'avenir* (Paris: L'Harmattan, 2003), pp. 1–120.

noted here that funding and equipment provided by this cooperation and partnership with Belgian universities generally concerned the whole of the University of Lubumbashi. This cooperation and partnership were beneficial to both parties. First, the Belgian universities and UNILU pooled their expertise. Second, the research projects that were developed responded to the concerns of both Congolese and Belgian researchers.

For example, the UNILU project to rehabilitate the Jason Sendwe hospital in Lubumbashi was supported by the Belgian universities, which enabled Belgian medical students interested in tropical diseases to carry out their internships there. Another case is that of the tripartite partnership between UNILU, the University of Liège and South Africa's University of KwaZulu-Natal, whose project was designed in Lubumbashi by representatives of these three institutions. This research partnership focuses on the transformation of urban space and the integration of different social groups, the transformation of family and gender and civil society, social capital and capacity building, especially in the field of education. Its objectives were to maximise the use of the skills, resources and capacities of the three partners, to promote collaboration and the social and mutual commitment of universities and civil society organisations involved in community development, carrying out an annual evaluation meeting following a joint seminar.

Research in history was not neglected in this flourishing of international partnerships. University collaboration led to the creation in 2003 of the Observatoire du Changement Urbain (OCU), a multidisciplinary research centre. Through its empirical studies, OCU aimed to contribute to a better understanding of the transformations affecting Congolese cities, particularly Lubumbashi where the project was based. Its research focuses on different areas of social life: the situation of Lubumbashi households in a precarious economy, encompassing food, education, crime, street children, child labour in mines and quarries, violence and the sexual abuse of women and children. The Observatory is in the process of building a multisectoral and strategic database to serve as an essential resource for researchers and a reliable reference point for planners, policy-makers and stakeholders.

The *Mémoires de Lubumbashi* Project: Linking Historians to the Urban Population

The research carried out in the Department of History is complemented by academic activities organised by the *Mémoires de Lubumbashi* project. The city of Lubumbashi, like other urban centres, has always been a place of meeting and mixing for people of diverse origins, a multicultural space par excellence. Over time, Lubumbashi's residents have changed their behaviours, lifestyles, clothing and eating habits; they have borrowed and at the same time also rejected certain habits. They live in a state of cultural hybridity and have an identity that is both unique and multiple. The urban populations of Lubumbashi are culturally diverse, but all of them participate in the cultural identity of the city.

In the Democratic Republic of the Congo in general, and in Lubumbashi in particular, the collection of life stories began in the 1970s. Bogumil Jewsiewicki initiated the collection of oral histories focusing on the colonial period.[49] Various publications on life stories, autobiographies and religious testimonies were produced during the 1980s. It was, however, in the 1990s that the study of memories of the independence period of the Democratic Republic of the Congo intensified. The fields covered by this research are varied: the first life stories collected were brought together in a book edited by Bogumil Jewsiewicki.[50]

Building on these achievements, the *Mémoires de Lubumbashi* project was created in the year 2000. It was jointly supported by the University of Lubumbashi and the city government, and was financially supported by international cooperation. The project is led by an international multi-disciplinary team composed of historians, archaeologists, sociologists and anthropologists from various academic and research institutions. This project aims to unearth obscure or little-known aspects of everyday urban life, with a view to reconstructing a plural rather than singular understanding of the past past and leading to a comprehensive knowledge of the city. It is from the population that the project gathers individual or collective memories. It thereby seeks to bring the story of the city's inhabitants closer to the inhabitants themselves, giving them the opportunity to know and take ownership of the history of their urban milieu. The project enables the urban population of Lubumbashi to discover the city's cultural heritage and

---

49   Here we cite some of Jewsiewicki's work relating to the collection of oral sources: with Jocelyn Létourneau, *Histoire en Partage: Usages et mises en discours du passé* (Paris: L'Harmattan, 1996); with V.Y. Mudimbe, *History Making in Africa* (Middletown: Wesleyan University Press, 1993); with H. Moniot, *Dialoguer avec le léopard? pratiques, savoirs et actes du peuple face au politique en Afrique* (Paris: L'Harmattan, 1988); with H. Moniot, *Mémoires, histoires, identités*, special issue of *Cahiers d'Études africaines*, 28, 107–109 (1988); and with F. Montal, *Récits de vie et mémoires: vers une anthropologie historique du souvenir* (Paris: L'Harmattan, 1987).

50   Bogumil Jewsiewicki (ed.), *Naître et mourir au Zaïre: un demi-siècle d'histoire au quotidien* (Paris: Karthala, 1993).

to ask themselves a fundamental question, namely, what cultural heritage do they intend to bequeath to posterity and which characterised their past?

As a result of this approach, the urban memories archived and recorded cover all areas of urban daily life. They concern the world of workers, as well as economic, political, social, cultural and religious actors. They are concerned with the spaces occupied by men, women and children, and with diverse institutions and social spaces, such as schools, clinics, maternity wards or markets. They also concern relationships between the different socio-professional strata, for example between employers and workers, or between different communities.

The resultant collections of life stories is a rich, even invaluable source of information for social scientists. In the field of history, Léon Verbeek notes that life stories 'provide an explanation of certain facts and behaviours that written history does not provide'.[51] It should be remembered that the use of oral and pictorial sources enables the historian to associate the population itself with the reconstruction of the past, as both an agent and a holder of the cultural heritage of the past. This approach, already in place at UNILU in the 1970s, was intensified during the 1990s, and this was even more the case following the creation of the 'Memories of Lubumbashi' project in 2000.

The use of oral testimonies in the elaboration of the social history of workers or industrial and urban sociology allows us, among other things, to better understand their relationships in camps or urban centres and their professional relationships in the workplace; to understand their attitudes regarding the behaviour of employers towards them, and to evaluate their active part in efforts to improve their living and working conditions.[52] The collection of memoirs has provided historians of Lubumbashi with an impressive number of 'aides memoires', a variety of media that serve to convey urban oral history. These include photographs, plays performed in popular theatres, popular paintings, popular songs, life stories themselves, as well as the various items kept in homes and representing the heritage of the past.

---

51 Léon Verbeek, 'Histoire et littérature orale', *Cahiers de littérature orale*, 45 (1999), p. 167.
52 In his work *Oral Tradition as History* (Madison: University of Wisconsin Press, 1985), Jan Vansina shows that 'all the questions of methods which arise for urban oral history also arise for the history of rural areas'. See also Donatien Dibwe dia Mwembu, *Faire de l'histoire orale dans une ville africaine: La méthode Jan Vansina appliquée à Lubumbashi (R-D Congo)* (Paris: L'Harmattan, 2008), p. 11.

The study of popular theatre, for example, has significantly contributed to the reconstruction of Lubumbashi's past. It is a form of mass entertainment, produced in vernacular languages, by actors generally without any professional training. It is therefore a popular product, widely available to the public. It speaks of everyday life, of the problems of the moment in reference to those of the past within society or the family.[53] Popular theatre likewise reflects the political, economic, social, cultural and intellectual situation of the country or city and provokes public reflection through its performance. It scrutinises the population's behaviour and in doing so, criticises, informs, trains and moralises. It enables anyone to follow, step by step, the vicissitudes of a society: its past, present and aspirations, its hopes and its fears. It revives and glorifies the past at the same time as it offers an undaunted criticism of the modern mentality. Private life becomes a spectacle and everyone finds themselves in the satirical presentation of everyday life. Performances culminate with a clear ethical message.

This popular theatre is of the same order as popular painting, also known as naïve painting, which is equally the work of untrained painters. Popular painting, as an illustration of the memory of a society at a given moment in its past, provides historians with the feelings, perceptions and representations of the population and makes it possible to analyse these variables. Experience has shown us that as much as there are artists and painters who turn their attention to a given theme of daily life, there are as many memories as well. However, some events in the past leave deeper mark on the collective memory than others, such as instances of punishment of the whip, illustrated in paintings of the 'Belgian colony'; the independence speech of Lumumba which provoked a mood of disbelief and anger among the Belgian colonists; or the Katangese secession.[54] It is also important to mention the *Kalindula* orchestras, led by unemployed young people. They use rudimentary musical equipment, a banjo and a drum. Their songs are

53 Maëline Le Lay, *La parole construit le pays: théâtre, langues et didactisme au Katanga* (Paris: Editions Honoré Champion, 2014): the author deals with popular theatre in Katanga, and the Mufwankolo Group is among the six cases studied; Donatien Dibwe dia Mwembu, 'Le rire, thérapie ultime: le théâtre populaire de Mufwankolo' in Danielle de Lame and Donatien Dibwe dia Mwembu (eds), *Tout passe: instantanés populaires et traces du passé à Lubumbashi* (Paris: L'Harmattan, 2005), p. 279–300; Schicho Walter, *Le Groupe Mufwankolo* (Vienna: Afro-Pub, 1981).
54 Donatien Dibwe dia Mwembu, 'La peine du fouet au Congo Belge (1885–1960)', *Les Cahiers de Tunisie*, 36 (1986), pp. 127–53, pp. 135–6; Jewsiewicki (ed.), *A Congo Chronicle*; Donatien Dibwe dia Mwembu, Marcel Ngandu Mutombo, *Vivre ensemble au Katanga* (Paris: L'Harmattan, 2005).

often social satires. The themes most often discussed are the behaviour of the urban population in the face of death (mourning), the depravity of mores due to precarious living conditions, and the abdication of parents from their responsibilities in the family.

These different popular art forms, that is to say popular painting, popular songs and popular theatre, thus contribute to expressing the collective memory of the population. They deal with the social, cultural, economic and political situation. Popular art therefore constitutes another interpretation of historical facts by non-academic actors, popular 'historians'. It equally provides raw material for academic researchers, a medium for history. The historian uses it in the elaboration of the history that s/he wishes to be more global, more intelligible, alive and richer. As stated, it is this participation of others in the rewriting of history that makes the historian a co-creator of the past.

The Observatory of Urban Change and the *Mémoires de Lubumbashi* project constitute spaces for the promotion of urban culture that have breathed new life into academic research in general and historical research in particular. They bring humanities researchers – especially historians – into contact with the population, who hold the cultural heritage of the past. While OCU provides researchers with an empirical database, resulting from its field surveys, the *Mémoires de Lubumbashi* project provides them with collective and/or individual 'aides memoires' (life stories, photographs, popular art, etc.) which they can utilise to reconstruct the past. Here, history and memory (collective and individual) are brought to the meeting point of research and are invited to walk together. The history of DR Congo is as problematic in its reconstruction as in its interpretation. History and memory help each other. History can be reconstructed through memory, among other things, and memory can be better interpreted and contextualised through history.[55]

Conclusion

This chapter has sought to give a detailed historical overview of the University of Lubumbashi and to attempt, as far possible, to combine it with the deployment of new historiographical horizons. It has shown that from its establishment in 1956 until today, the University of Lubumbashi has been

55 Donatien Dibwe dia Mwembu, 'History and Memory' in John Edward Philips (ed.), *Writing African History* (Rochester NY: University of Rochester Press, 2005), pp. 439–64.

affected in its functioning and in the field of its academic output in general, and its output in history in particular, by the transformations that the DRC and the province of Katanga have undergone.

During the colonial period, from 1956 until 1960 there was no History Department at the University of the Belgian Congo and Ruanda-Urundi, despite the doctoral thesis defended at that institution in 1959. Nationalist history began in 1960, the year of African independence. African historians then sought their cultural identity, to decolonise and de-alienate history and in short, as Achufusi so aptly put it, to 'give a truthful image of history, an image necessary for the historical awareness of the masses in their struggle for national, political, economic, social and cultural independence'.[56]

Shortly after the Congo gained its independence in 1960, the province of Katanga seceded with the support of Belgium. The Official University of the Congo (UOC) was converted into the State University in Elisabethville. However, there was a lack of academic output in history associated with this political event. The first candidatures in history were only inaugurated in 1962–1963 at the Faculty of Letters, at a time when the independent state of Katanga was mainly concerned with the training of indigenous technicians for the development of its various mining, industrial and commercial enterprises. When, in 1963, the Katangese secession came to an end, the reintegration of the province of Katanga into the Democratic Republic of the Congo was marked by the university's return to the identity of the Official University of the Congo

In 1971, the decision by the Mobutu regime to merge the three universities into UNAZA was intended to fulfil the MPR objectives of training responsible Zairian intellectuals to be at the forefront of the authentic Zairian revolution, bearers of a new mentality, free from colonial culture and constantly nourished by African culture. The history departments of the three universities (Lovanium University of Kinshasa, Free University of Kisangani and UOC) were merged into one department within the Faculty of Letters in Lubumbashi. The Africanist character of the Department of History was strengthened through changes to the historical curriculum and by an increase in the number and the volume of courses on Zaïre (Congo) and Africa. The Department of History then initiated the Zairianisation of the research and academic staff.

---

56 M. Achufusi, quoted by Pierre Salmon in Gabriel Thoveron (ed.), *Mélanges Pierre Salmon, Tome I: Méthodologie et politique africaine* (Brussels: Institut de Sociologie de l'Université de Bruxelles, 1993), p. 19.

Academic output in history, which began in the 1970s, generally dealt with the precolonial period (to rehabilitate African history) and more with the colonial period, apparently in view of the availability of archival documents and the fact that knowledge of the past period is necessary in order to claim to solve current problems. The postcolonial period constitutes almost virgin ground to be cleared. One of the pitfalls of this nationalist history is that of a chauvinistic re-reading of the past, of the easy simplification of certain political and social facts of the colonial period, as Bogumil Jewsiewicki notes: 'Any conflict is readily reduced to fundamental and schematic opposition: colonised–coloniser, while the existence of social conflicts between the colonised themselves as well as between the colonisers is too easily forgotten.'[57]

In 1981, the Mobutu regime returned to university autonomy. However, Congolese universities in general, and that of Lubumbashi in particular, experienced lean years because of the deteriorating political, economic and social situation of the country and the province of Katanga. Congolese universities were no longer considered among the priorities of the Mobutu regime. Deprived of public support, they could only implement the policy their means allowed. The descent into hell was inevitable. The centres' research projects were locked away in drawers for lack of funding, and collective research gave way to individual research, generally carried out on external commission, conducted piecemeal and in an unplanned manner, because it was commissioned by various foreign bodies that had no concern for local needs but wanted to satisfy their individual and different needs. The result, generally speaking, as Kakoma Sakatolo Zambeze noted, was a mismatch between the needs of society and teaching and research as practised at the University of Lubumbashi[58].

The decade from 1990 to 2000 was marked by the bloody incidents that took place on the Lubumbashi campus, as well as the looting and destruction of the economic fabric of Katanga's cities and the wider political, military and ethnic conflict of the period. This situation severely disrupted the functioning of the University of Lubumbashi in the core areas of teaching and research. However, the advent of international academic cooperation provided a breath of fresh air for the university. The creation of the OCU research centre and the setting up of the Mémoires of Lubumbashi project were the two mainstays of historical research output in

57 Bogumil Jewsiewicki, 'Contestation Sociale au Zaïre (ex-Congo Belge): Grève administrative de 1920', *Africa-Tervuren*, 22, 2/3 (1976), pp. 57–67, p. 57.
58 Sakatolo Zambeze, *L'Académie Congolaise*, pp. 4–5.

Katanga. Not only did these two centres allow history researchers to come into contact with the population, the holders of the cultural heritage of the past, but also, and above all, gave historians the opportunity to access oral sources, to fill in the gaps in written history and to reconstruct a global, living and far richer urban history. The historian has become the co-recreator of the past.

12

The Decolonisation of Community Development in Haut-Katanga and the Zambian Copperbelt, 1945–1990

MILES LARMER & RACHEL TAYLOR

Introduction

The urban societies of the Central African Copperbelt have been conceptualised as sites of social transformation by academics, states, mining companies and Copperbelt residents alike, who imagined a largely static rural
'tradition' being replaced by urban 'modernity'. In Haut-Katanga, Union
Minière du Haut-Katanga (UMHK) sought to build a stable urban workforce from the 1920s, while across the border in Northern Rhodesia colonial
and company officials were slower in adapting this policy.[1] Nevertheless,
by the 1950s mining companies across the region saw this transformation to urban 'modernity' as necessary, but also dangerous. The loss of the
traditional chiefly authority they believed was key to rural social order
created the danger of a breakdown in traditional morality in the growing
mining towns. They employed social workers – initially Europeans – to
guide workers and their families towards what were considered new and
desirable forms of respectable family life, and away from the perceived
immorality, deviance and delinquency the authorities feared would result
from unguided urbanisation. In the late-colonial period it was increasingly
recognised that effective social intervention would come from 'advanced'
members of African societies themselves, familiar with societal 'custom'

---

1   For inter-war Belgian Congo see Amandine Lauro, 'Maintenir l'ordre dans la
colonie-modèle: Notes sur les désordres urbains et la police des frontières raciales au
Congo Belge (1918–1945)', *Crime, Histoire & Sociétés / Crime, History & Societies*, 15
(2011), pp. 97–121.

but also educated in European languages, domestic styles and academic approaches. This chapter traces the outlines of community development and social intervention in mining communities across the Copperbelt in the second half of the twentieth century. It focuses on the 1960s to the 1980s, a period hitherto neglected by researchers on African social welfare, in which community development programmes were placed in the hands of senior African social workers under the direction of nationalised mining and other state-owned companies.

Social work across the Copperbelt shared some common concerns and themes. On both sides of the border, the need to ensure a productive (male) mineworker was seen as resting on a stable and modernised nuclear family life. Employed by states and mine companies, social workers provided relationship advice, enabled leisure opportunities and combatted 'social ills' such as alcoholism, crime and marriage breakdown. 'Community development' initiatives sought to shape every aspect of family life, from marital relations to household economy, from cleanliness and nutrition to child rearing. Ostensibly technocratic initiatives to manage communities were infused with patriarchal notions of morality in which 'respectable' families were distinguished from those requiring intervention and sanction. There were important differences, however. In Katanga, social work and social welfare programmes were more established, as *Union Minière* had played a pioneering role in training and employing such agents from the 1930s. While UMHK's system of 'authoritarian paternalism' expanded in the post-Second World War period to encompass every aspect of community life, mine companies in Northern Rhodesia only embraced the importance of social work as they belatedly accepted the realities of 'stabilisation' from the 1950s, creating a fragmented system of social intervention compared to that in Haut-Katanga.

Yet social work did not remain simply a colonial imposition. While the first generation of social workers were Europeans, it was increasingly recognised that trained African social workers, sufficiently indigenous to understand custom but educated enough to provide guidance on how to adjust to city life, were crucial to maintain social order. In the context of decolonisation and early independence, companies and states rapidly expanded the training and professionalisation of social workers and community development officers in the booming mine towns of the 1950s and 1960s.

The rapid Africanisation of social work in mining communities raises important questions. How did the role of social work change in post-independence urban societies? How was the burgeoning African social welfare workforce professionalised? We explore these questions through focusing on three main areas central to mining companies' attempts to shape mineworkers' families on both sides of the border: direct intervention into families; women's centres; and children and youth work. As well as tracing changes to social work programmes in this period by use of company and state archival materials, the chapter uses interviews with former community development officers, leisure and sports club officers in both the Zambian and Katangese Copperbelts to explain their own understanding of their role.[2] Using these sources, the chapter investigates the ways in which their understanding of social intervention changed during this period, and explores how the provision of social welfare was influenced by their ideas about the role of companies in managing social change, gender and generational relations, and how they understood the changing role of 'custom' in postcolonial Copperbelt towns. This is not, however, a study of how effective these policies were in delivering social order in these towns, nor does it analyse the general reception of these programmes among urban residents.

We begin by briefly tracing the development of social provision on both sides of the Copperbelt in the early twentieth century, before turning to the justifications given for social welfare provision by companies. We then explore the Africanisation and professionalisation of the community development workforce, which occurred more rapidly than the Africanisation of technical and engineering positions in the mines. The chapter then analyses key areas of social work activity in family life and with youth and women. Brief explanations are provided of the welfare policies of the companies themselves, but the analysis focuses on the ways that social workers and community development officers themselves understood them. We also discuss changing perceptions among social workers of 'customary' practice and how these changed in the postcolonial Copperbelt towns. Finally, the chapter discusses the collapse of social provision with the decline of the international copper price and the mining industry in the 1980s and 1990s. While fragments of company responsibility towards the families of workers and ex-workers remain, social workers today see the collapse of these services as emblematic of economic and social decline, stressing both the benefits brought by company provision and the trauma caused by its sudden disappearance.

2   In this chapter, we draw from interviews with social workers employed by the BCK/ SNCC railway company as well as by UMHK/Gécamines and, in Zambia, the mine companies that were in 1982 consolidated into Zambia Consolidated Copper Mines (ZCCM).

The Origins of African Urban Social Welfare
in the Copperbelt

In 1928, Union Minière du Haut-Katanga (UMHK) decided to build a permanent African labour force living near the mines, rather than relying on migrant labourers.[3] This decision made the family life of its workers a major company concern, as UMHK saw promoting marriage and family residence at the mines as a key way to maintain this permanent workforce. The company initially favoured the recruitment of married workers who would be accompanied by their families, and encouraged their single workers to marry.[4] Quickly, however, company policy shifted to making sure that workers and their families lived in camp in the 'correct' manner, one that would aid worker productivity and development, secure peace and order, and ensure that workers' children were themselves educated to become productive workers, or wives of workers.[5] Its policies and practices were shaped and enabled by the social interventionist policies of the Belgian colonial state, and by the Catholic Church's provision of schools and family services in mine camps.[6]

This was only possible because UMHK already exercised a high level of control over workers themselves. Originally they had to live in company accommodation, dwelling in mine camps presided over by company officials and '*malonda*' (camp policemen), although by the 1950s mineworkers and their families were allowed – and sometimes encouraged – to live elsewhere.[7] All camp residents or visitors needed to be registered. Alongside

---

3   The reasons for this policy are beyond the scope of this chapter. See the introduction to this volume, and the discussion in Donatien Dibwe dia Mwembu, *Bana Shaba abandonees par leur Père: Structures de l'authorite et histoire sociale de la famille ouvriere au Katanga, 1910–1997* (Paris: L'Harmattan, 2001), pp. 12–17.

4   Dibwe, *Bana Shaba*, pp. 55–61.

5   Ibid., pp. 55–87.

6   For the uneasy triumvirate of Belgian colonial social policy, see Guy Vanthemsche, *Belgium and the Congo, 1885–1980* (Cambridge: Cambridge University Press, 2012); for its natalist policy, see Nancy Rose Hunt, '"Le Bebe en Brousse": European Women, African Birth Spacing and Colonial Intervention in Breast Feeding in the Belgian Congo', *International Journal of African Historical Studies*, 21, 3 (1988), pp. 401–32. The specific application of these policies is discussed in Jean-Luc Vellut, 'Les bassins miniers de l'ancien Congo belge': Essai d'histoire économique et sociale (1900–1960)', *Les Cahiers du CEDAF* (Brussels: CEDAF, 1981); Bruce Fetter, *The Creation of Elisabethville 1910–1940* (Stanford: Hoover Institution Press, 1976).

7   For evidence of UMHK encouraging its more senior African workers to live outside of mine accommodation, see 'A chacun sa maison', *Mwana Shaba*, 2, 1957. Jeanette

these controls, UMHK provided services for workers and their families. It provided food rations, family accommodation, hospitals, schools, women's centres and street cleaning from the 1930s onwards. The quality and range of these services steadily expanded and, by the 1950s, came to include leisure centres (*'cercles'*), piped water and electricity.[8] These benefits – or the threat of their removal – could also increase company power over workers and their families. Infractions, such as fights between neighbours, were punished by withholding pay, or the rations of the family members involved.

Union Minière du Haut-Katanga's social policies complemented, and extended, the colony-wide approach to intervention in African family life endorsed by the Belgian colonial state, in collaboration with the Catholic Church. Other large enterprises, particularly the rail company Chemins de fer du Bas-Congo au Katanga (BCK) – later Société Nationale des Chemins de Fer du Congo (SNCC) and then Société Nationale des Chemins de Fer du Zaïre (SNCZ) – took on significant roles in social provision for, and social control over, their workers and their families. The system established by UMHK, and extended in the postcolonial period by its successor company Gécamines, was, while not unique, certainly more pervasive, as the company provided a greater number of services and more generous family provision. Company requirements measured and regulated nearly all aspects of family life. For example, women were required to present their babies for weighing and health checks, primary school attendance was made compulsory, and women were incentivised to carry out domestic activities that they were taught to deliver at company-run classes.

In the Northern Rhodesian Copperbelt, continued hesitancy about worker stabilisation throughout the 1930s and 1940s meant that mine companies in general continued to treat their employees as temporary migrant workers, single men whose families supposedly remained in the village.[9] Mine compa-

---

Kahamba and her husband lived in their own private house in the 1950s before her husband was appointed to a managerial position, and they were approved to move to *La Mission,* the majority-white management housing area. Interview, Jeanette Kahamba, Likasi, 17 July 2019.

8   This did not mean that UMHK workers accepted or were satisfied with the social conditions of the mine camps: Higginson describes a wave of unrest culminating in the 1941 mineworkers' strike: John Higginson, *A Working-Class in the Making: Belgian Colonial Labor Policy, Private Enterprise, and the African Mineworker, 1907–1951* (Madison: University of Wisconsin Press, 1989), pp 181–90.

9   For the 'stabilisation' debate see H. Heisler, 'The Creation of a Stabilized Urban Society: A Turning Point in the Development of Northern Rhodesia/Zambia', *African Affairs,* 70, 279 (1971), pp. 125–45.

nies therefore provided much less for their workers than in Katanga, but also played far less of a role in controlling or shaping workers' family lives. While many women did migrate to mines and some 'married' workers, these marriages were not in forms recognised by the mining companies.[10] Little provision was made for the presence of permanent urban families before mid-century: family housing began to be built in the 1940s, but the provision of social welfare and education began to be taken seriously only in the 1950s. In contrast to the Belgian Congo, where the provision of urban services was understood as a proactive policy of societal management, the provision of social services in Northern Rhodesia began as a largely defensive measure. Urbanisation, it turned out, was unavoidable, and mining companies and government officials alike feared that unplanned urbanisation would adversely affect worker productivity and create social – and ultimately political – unrest.[11] Colonial and company officials in Northern Rhodesia saw UMHK's social provision as a model, but an unachievable one. They believed that socialising workers and their families into urban circumstances was a profound challenge – one they might not be able to meet.

The 1950s was a period of growth in social provision across the Copperbelt that was part of a massive post-Second World War expansion in colonial state intervention encompassing economic growth and urban social welfare and development.[12] Companies and local government embarked on a programme of housing construction, new schools opened under the authority of new African teachers, and social services – run by a network of church, voluntary service, local government and mine companies – expanded rapidly. Underlying these interventions was

---

10 George Chauncey Jr, 'The Locus of Reproduction: Women's Labour in the Zambian Copperbelt, 1927–1953', *Journal of Southern African Studies* 7, 2 (1981), pp. 135–64, p. 137; Jane L. Parpart, 'The Household and the Mine Shaft', *Journal of Southern African Studies*, 13, 1 (1986), pp. 36–56, pp. 40–1; James Ferguson, *Expectations of Modernity: Myths and Meanings of Urban Life on the Zambian Copperbelt* (Berkeley: University of California Press, 1999), pp. 170–7.

11 National Archives of Zambia (hereafter NAZ), MLSS 1/12/5, Northern Rhodesia Council of Social Services 1967–68.

12 D. A. Low and J. M. Lonsdale, 'Introduction: Towards the New Order, 1945–63', in D. A. Low and Alison Smith (eds), *History of East Africa* vol. 3 (Oxford: Clarendon Press, 1976); Monica van Beusekom and Dorothy Hodgson, 'Lessons Learned? Development Experiences in the Late Colonial Period', *Journal of African History*, 41, 1 (2000), pp. 29–33; Frederick Cooper and Randall M. Packard (eds), *International Development and the Social Sciences Essays on the History and Politics of Knowledge* (Berkeley: University of California Press, 1998).

an assumption that transition from rural to urban society necessarily involved the loss of rural patriarchal authority and a consequent decline in customary familial practices, leading to the emergence of an idealised modern nuclear family in which male wage earners were supported by wives who kept their homes and raised their children. The loss of this authority had to be compensated for by informed social intervention to manage this supposed transition, during which custom and modernity would interact in socially disruptive ways. Social science researchers and policy-makers worried about the disruptive effect on 'inter-ethnic' marriages of conflicting customs of their rural societies regarding, for example, the payment of 'bride price', polygamy and the inheritance rights of widows.[13] High urban divorce rates were understood as a manifestation of this social disruption.[14] In UMHK mine camps, polygamy was discouraged by the company's recognition of only one wife and her children as recipients of company rations and housing and, in 1950, was banned outright in Elisabethville's non-mine township.[15]

While Northern Rhodesian companies' provision of social services was belated compared with Katanga, within a few years a territory-wide council was coordinating social service provision by actors including churches, mine companies and European women's groups. Its members worried that the limited opportunities for education and jobs for teenagers was likely to contribute to delinquency and social unrest. A Homecraft Training Scheme served 'a very useful purpose in helping the African woman adapt to the western and urban civilisations'.[16] There was general agreement that '[i]n any scheme the educated Africans must carry the message to their own people. They were essential co-workers.'[17]

---

13 Benjamin Rubbers and Marc Poncelet, 'Sociologie coloniale au Congo belge: Les études sur le Katanga industriel et urbain à la veille de l'Indépendance', *Genèses*, 2, 99 (2015), pp. 93–112, p. 98.

14 Chauncey, 'Locus of Reproduction', p. 162.

15 J. Vannes, 'De l'évolution de la coutume d'Elisabethville', *Bulletin du Centre d'Etude des Problemes Sociaux Indigènes*, 32 (1956), p. 223–68. See also Nancy Rose Hunt, 'Noise over Camouflaged Polygamy, Colonial Morality Taxation, and a Woman-Naming Crisis in Belgian Africa', *Journal of African History*, 32, 2 (1991), pp. 471–94.

16 NAZ, MLSS 1/12/5, Northern Rhodesia Council of Social Services 1967–68 [incorrect dates at source], NRCSS, 'Report of the Chairman to the Sixth Annual General Meeting', 12 September 1960.

17 NAZ, MLSS 1/12/5, Northern Rhodesia Council of Social Services 1967–68 [incorrect dates at source], NRCSS Social Workers' Conference, 25 September 1958, Doctor Donnolly, Medical Officer of Health, Lusaka Municipality.

In efforts to promote monogamous marriage and discourage sex outside marriage, the importance of female African 'welfare assistants' was recognised: the new Oppenheimer College of Social Services would from 1961 train an expanded cadre of professional African social workers.[18] There was in such initiatives a tension between, on the one hand, the need for a cadre of 'advanced' urbanised Africans able to educate and socialise new urban residents; and on the other hand, the belief that urban migrants needed to be kept in touch with their customary culture during transition, and, linked to this, the assumption that educated Africans both understood custom and could manage its declining influence in a developmental way.

By independence, the provision of social welfare services – as a central part of a wider set of interventions ranging from housing to healthcare – shaped the lives of company employees and their families in both Copperbelt regions. A new generation of African social workers inherited the contradictions of late-colonial social welfare policy rooted in the racialised assumptions outlined above. However, they brought to their practice a new set of professional and universalist ideals arising from their social work training coupled with an overriding commitment to the companies' aim of achieving a stable gendered order in its mine townships.

Training and Professionalisation of Social Work after Independence

The early independence period saw the steady replacement of European managers of social welfare provision – some of whom continued to hold senior positions until the 1970s – with a growing cadre of African social workers, themselves part of a much wider system of community services provided to mine and railway employees. In Katanga, nuns and other European women continued to play an important supervisory role in certain areas of social provision, overseeing African staff in women's centres and maternity wards for decades after independence, but they were now accompanied and gradually supplanted by secular African employees and managers.[19] A new generation of educated young Congolese men were appointed

---

18 The college was named after Ernest Oppenheimer, the former head of the Anglo American Corporation, one of the major mining corporations on the Northern Rhodesian Copperbelt.

19 Interview, Charlotte Panga Kelita, Likasi, 16 July 2019; interview, Mme Séraphine, Likasi, 15 July 2019; interview, Mwepu Mudianga, Likasi, 15 July 2019; interview, Marguerite Luse Kibungo, Likasi, 9 August 2019

to the position of *chef de cité* (Town Manager), the senior official responsible for overseeing both mineworkers and their families.[20]

The growing demand for additional social workers meant that many were initially recruited straight from secondary school and learned on the job, while they received further training. In Zambia, many of those who went on to work with adolescents were themselves young men (and later women), often the children of mineworkers who had grown up in mine townships, and were initially identified for their sporting abilities. In Haut-Katanga, professional training schools in nursing and education actively sought out new recruits at secondary schools.[21] These professional training schools, sometimes run by UMHK/Gécamines, then sent students on internships to schools or hospitals, which quickly snapped up the new recruits. As one nurse, who started working at Gécamines in 1978 immediately after her graduation from the Gécamines-run nursing college in Kolwezi, remembered, 'everywhere, there was a need for workers'.[22] Many new social workers moved from education into a specialisation in social work.[23]

By the 1970s, however social welfare officers in Zambia were steadily becoming more professionalised by the increasing provision of training courses: by diploma (one-year) courses in Social Work, Sociology or (in a later period) Pan-African Women's leadership course provided by the church-run Mindolo Ecumenical Foundation (MEF) and the state-controlled Presidential Citizenship College at Mulungushi.[24] Employees in both countries regularly attended a wide range of seminars and other forms of training: senior SNCC social worker Mwepu Mudianga recalled that there was training 'all the time, seminars all the time'.[25] Zambian trainees report instruction by instructors from a range of nationalities, including Western Europeans but also from the Eastern Bloc and the United States. The main Katangese employers seem to have provided much of their training in-house, reflecting their pre-existing capacity in the social sector, while also sending new recruits to state-run professional training schools. Astrid Bilonda, for instance, hired in 1975 after completing secondary school, was sent by Gécamines to the INPP (National Institute for Professional Training) for accelerated training to

20 Interview, Jérôme Kipili Mulungu, Likasi, 4 June 2018.
21 Interview, Matilda Mwinda Kabwe, Likasi, 15 July 2019.
22 Interview, anonymous woman, Likasi, 26 August 2019.
23 Mudianga interview; interview, Nicodème Nguza Yav, Lubumbashi, 23 August 2019.
24 Chishala interview.
25 Mudianga interview.

be a hospital administrator. Throughout her career she was regularly sent for further instruction within Haut-Katanga.[26] UMHK/Gécamines also sent some high-flying workers to attend training courses in Belgium.[27] In both countries, such courses now drew on a characterisation of the socialisation of youth and family dynamics that was consciously universal, and no longer rested on the colonial notion that urban life presented rural African migrants with unique challenges reflecting their racial identity.[28] Trainees returned to their communities equipped with what they felt were the necessary skills to intervene in urban social problems of townships, and empowered by their companies with the capacity to do so.

By the mid-1980s, this ongoing process of professionalisation meant that more aspirant recruits held degrees in relevant areas. A small number of Zambian trainees, such as Leonard Chola, were sponsored for degrees in Public Administration and Sociology, which enabled them to take up the most senior positions overseeing township services.[29] In Katanga, too, a small number of social service employees were hired with degrees, while others pursued degrees alongside their employment, with varying levels of company support, and recognition.[30] The gradual professionalisation of the social welfare cadre, in which younger, more educated Africans were put in charge of older more experienced staff, sometimes led to tension. Josephine Lukwesa's appointment to a senior supervisory role was successfully resisted by older women who insisted that she lacked the life experience required, and she was appointed to a less senior job.[31] In contrast Matilda Mwenda Kabwe, first as a teacher, then as a school head, and then as Gécamines Director of Education for Likasi and Kambove, recalled no difficulties from older (male) staff, who she was careful to treat with respect.[32] Interviewees stressed the validity of

---

26   Interview, Astrid Bilonda, Likasi, 18 July 2019.

27   Interview, Agnès Njamba, Likasi, 16 July 2019.

28   Chishala interview; Joseph Tumba Menzu interview, Mufulira, 11 July 2019; interview, Kilufya Kasongo Apolline, Lubumbashi, 24 August 2019.

29   Interview, Leonard Chola, Kitwe, 4 July 2019.

30   Interview, M. Mukendi [pseudonym], Lubumbashi, 30 July 2019; interview, Eugène Mofya Makumba, Lubumbashi, 23 August 2019; interview, Nicodème Nguza Yav, Lubumbashi, 23 August 2019; Mudianga interview. Ms Mudianga's degree in Sociology, for which she studied while working, was not recognised by her employer (SNCC) because she had not received their permission to study.

31   Interview, Josephine Lukwesa, Mufulira, 8 July 2019.

32   Matilda Mwenda Kabwe interview.

their professional training but equally the need to apply theory in a practical way to individual cases, using counselling and listening skills.[33]

Post-Independence Perceptions of Social Welfare Provision

The Copperbelt region provides a well-known and much documented case of company paternalism (see Peša and Henriet, Chapter 1), in which the older obligations of mine camps to manage the lives of their workers and their families meshed in mid-twentieth-century Africa with statist intervention to create a system in which companies became intimately involved with virtually every aspect of their educational, social and cultural lives.[34] In both Copperbelt regions, the extensive provision of social welfare services is today recalled as evidence that companies were 'caring' for their workers and their families.[35] Most interviewees thought that a company should care for its workers and their families, and that it also had the right to intervene in family life to ensure this. This was presented as a fundamental element of a company's role in the world, and by extension in how society should be structured. As one interviewee put it: 'Gécamines can't abandon social provision, social provision needs Gécamines'.[36]

Equally important was the idea that the companies should promote peace and social harmony by ensuring that township life and that of its workers was not adversely affected by familial disputes. The motivation was, as senior social worker Mark Masumbuko put it, 'to put harmony into the township: the most important thing was that miners, when they came home, they should find a habitable situation. And that was our role.'[37] Masumbuko also linked domestic harmony to broader social peace within mining settlements:

---

33 Menzu interview.
34 For Haut-Katanga: Dibwe dia Mwembu, *Bana Shaba* and Benjamin Rubbers, *Le Paternalisme en question: Les anciens ouvriers de la Gécamines face à la libéralisation du secteur minier Katangais (RD Congo)* (Paris, L'Harmattan, 2013). For the Zambian Copperbelt see Ferguson, *Expectations of Modernity* and Patience Mususa, 'There Used to Be Order: Life on the Copperbelt After the Privatisation of the Zambia Consolidated Copper Mines', PhD thesis, University of Cape Town, 2014.
35 Interview, anonymous man, Mufulira, 11 July 2019.
36 Interview, Brigitte Mukasa Kiwele, Likasi, 17 July 2019.
37 Interview, Mark Masumbuko, Kitwe, 4 July 2019.

> If a miner knocked off, and he didn't find the wife [had] already prepared food, that would arise into talking. Or, if the wife was not at home, without telling the husband … that would create problems. Or the miner himself knocks off, goes for a beer before getting home, he goes home drunk, that would create a problem. So, noise would start, and we would get involved.[38]

Community development worker Victor Chishala likewise asserted: 'A happy marriage will make the breadwinner perform his duties successfully.'[39] Versions of this 'productivity' explanation were articulated by virtually all interviewees in Zambia.

Limited social services were provided by local governments in both Copperbelt regions: in health and education, but also services for youth and women. It was widely recognised, however, that the state lacked the capacity to provide the level of services provided by the mine and other large companies. Mining companies provided all the services the state offered, as well as those the state could not. In Katanga, for instance, Gécamines residential areas had better cleaning and public health services than urban areas served by local councils.[40] As a state-run company, Gécamines also at times supported government social work efforts, for example by providing internships or even jobs for children trained in government social centres.[41]

Social Welfare in Practice I: Family Intervention

In the post-independence Copperbelt, direct social work was part of a much wider network of social provision. In Katanga especially, the 'social' department encompassed schooling and healthcare, as well as the youth and women's centres, leisure centres, company stores, maintenance and sanitation teams and policing that were common to both Copperbelt regions. Mine companies in Zambia did provide clinics and hospitals for their workers and, to a lesser extent, education, but these did not form a direct part of the holistic system of social intervention into family life that had evolved earlier in Katanga (see above).

On both Copperbelts, mining companies employed officials to investigate and attempt to settle intra-family disputes. As a worker's wage and benefits were conceived of as supporting a whole family, a failure of a man to provide that

---

38   Masumbuko interview.
39   Interview, Victor Chishala, Kitwe, 6 July 2019.
40   This was frequently referred to in interviews: see for example Godelieve Ngoie, Likasi, 26 August 2019.
41   Nguza Yav interview.

support was an issue for the company. Mining companies and most workers agreed that being a good worker and a 'good man' – one who supported his family well – were connected. Equally, a wife who, though supported by the company, did not provide for her children, was a source of concern and potential intervention. Interventions were most commonly prompted by a wife's complaint that she was not receiving sufficient money from her husband's pay-packet to feed the family or maintain the household. This could arise because he was drinking too much or keeping another woman, with whom he might have a second family. He might have even 'abandoned' this first family to live with another, often resident outside the company area.

In such a case, the wife of a male mineworker would, in Zambia, visit or telephone the social welfare/community development office, or, in Katanga, go to a social worker or straight to the *chef de cité*.[42] The social worker might invite the husband to a meeting, but if he failed to attend or the case was deemed sufficiently urgent, he was summoned from his workplace (thus revealing the intimate relationship between workplace and community and the single company overseeing both) to address the charges (see Moïse Simba's story, below). In a minority of cases husbands brought complaints about their wives for failing to maintain their households and for themselves drinking too much alcohol.[43] It was also possible for a Personnel Officer, noting an underperforming worker, to contact a Social Welfare Officer to explore if this might be caused by a problem at home. Companies then, while empowering their male employees to act as the heads of their households, might sanction those workers if they failed in their duty to produce stable families and communities and to raise the next generation of company workers.

Social workers aimed to resolve disputes by facilitating discussions between spouses and seeking pledges of good behaviour: husbands were for example urged to give a fixed percentage of their salaries to their wives on pay day.[44] When husband and wife disagreed about the cause of such problems, social workers would sometimes collect evidence from neighbours regarding the situation in the household.[45] Looming over the counselling process were the possible disciplinary implications of non-cooperation. As Joseph Tumba Menzu put it: 'If an employee thinks he will lose his work he will come back. It was just one way of getting the family stable and the

42 Kiwele interview; Nguza Yav interview.
43 Kiwele interview.
44 Ibid.
45 Ibid.

best of an employee.'[46] Interviewees did not see a contradiction in mediating between both parties: Menzu described himself as a 'shock absorber' in managing such conflicts of interests.[47] Social welfare professionals interviewed have, perhaps unsurprisingly, a strong belief in the positive effects of these interventions, not only for the marriage but the workplace and for society as a whole. Chisala for example argued that a husband who stopped spending most of his money away from the home would, in changing his behaviour, ensure that the children would now have school uniforms, enabling their education.[48]

Ultimately, backed by the authority of the company – as employer and landlord – social workers or the *chef de cité* could arrange the payment of part or even all the husband's salary directly to the wife as a way of ensuring the family was properly maintained.[49] The knowledge that one's employer was aware of such marital problems helped discipline male behaviour.[50] Some workers would initially be resistant to 'interference' by company in their marital affairs but equally knew when they began employment that the social work officers were there.[51] One head of social work for Gécamines in Likasi recalled some workers walking off angry at the proposal to dock their pay, but generally they came back a few days later pleading for their jobs.[52]

Social case work included not only cases of adultery but also of spousal abuse, witchcraft accusations and child abduction. Whereas in the colonial era instances of witchcraft might have been regarded as manifestations of a hangover of rural 'tradition', post-independence social workers treated them strictly as family or even legal matters. Cases that started in the social work department might end up in the local magistrates' court but the aim was to resolve them at an earlier stage.[53] In Katanga, social workers often saw their job as preventing divorce or separation, disruptive of the family order, so as to ensure that children were well cared for.[54] A wife's adultery, however,

---

46 Menzu interview.
47 Ibid.
48 Chishala interview.
49 Masumbuko interview.
50 Chola interview.
51 Chishala interview.
52 Kiwele interview.
53 Chishala interview.
54 Kiwele interview.

would often lead to a divorce.[55] As Chishala explained, 'If a mineworker met an accident and the wife committed adultery, then it would be believed that the adultery caused the accident, to the point of ending the marriage.'[56]

Company intervention into the internal workings of individual families reveals the limits of company support of patriarchal control. The nuclear family model on which the system rested assumed that a male worker should not only be able to control his wife, but even had a duty to society to do so. At the same time, married male workers were themselves expected to maintain a happy family home. The involvement of mine companies in family life was not always welcomed by male workers, who at times considered that their employer was interfering with their right to run their family as they saw fit. 'Moïse Simba', for instance, was sanctioned for his 'nonchalance' in responding to his wife's complaint to Gécamines that he had abandoned the marital home. Simba argued that 'this problem between my wife and me will be sorted at the level of the respective families, and not here in the town', an argument rejected by Gécamines officials. Their willingness to intervene in Simba's home life was, however, limited. They were unconcerned that Simba had a second wife, so long as he could live peacefully with, and provide for, his first wife, registered on his company documents. They *were* however concerned that he had allegedly beaten his first wife for complaining to the company, an affront to company authority. They were ultimately pacified by Simba's argument: 'I often corrected my wife because her behaviour is not good.'[57] In addition, in Katanga UMHK/Gécamines demanded that children were cared for – and supervised by the company – in particular ways. Women were obliged to give birth in hospital where their children were weighed, given vaccinations and their mothers given advice. Alongside the provision of food rations, mineworkers' families were provided with free healthcare, primary and, for some students, secondary or vocational schooling. If a mother and baby failed to attend compulsory checks, the woman's husband (or, if the woman worked for Gécamines, she herself) would be called into their supervisor's office, and the worker's pay could be docked for non-attendance.[58]

55 Rubbers, *Le paternalisme en question*, p. 180; interview, Pascal Makombi, Likasi, 6 August 2019.
56 Chishala interview.
57 The names are pseudonyms. GCM Personnel Office, Likasi, Panda, Personnel File 085414/5.
58 Njamba interview.

Social Welfare in Practice II: Children and Youth Work

As indicated above, early-childhood education had been an important focus of missionary and UMHK attention from the 1940s. Most educational theorists at that time argued for of a universalist model – that what children in Katanga needed was the same as children everywhere. They often directed scorn at African mothers' child-raising, but the message was clear that, with the 'right' education, African children could learn and be successful. To this end, *foyers sociaux* offered training for teenage girls and for workers' wives in childcare (see below), as well as housing kindergartens which put these ideas of 'scientific' early years education into practice.

After independence, this universalist mode of teacher training and practice continued in Katanga. One school director, explaining why she felt that Gécamines schools remained superior to other private schools, argued that Gécamines schools would not adopt bad practice simply to receive a child's school fees. If a parent came trying to enrol a too-young child in the school, she would send him or her away, telling them that 'psychologically' the child was too young for formal education.[59] At kindergartens, this universalist mode was even more apparent. As one former teacher explained, the curriculum helped ensure that children learned the skills they needed for formal schooling and day-to-day life. They learned 'how to work together, to not argue, to know to ask forgiveness, and to not hit the others', as well as preparing to learn to read and write.[60] This approach was designed to train a future generation of disciplined company workers, and the company systematically recruited many employees from its own schools.

In Zambia, while school education was generally the preserve of the post-independence state, company intervention focused on adolescent youth. Mine companies, like the Zambian Government, believed that youths needed to be kept busy because otherwise they tended towards mischief of various kinds, vandalism etc. By playing sports and games, attending youth clubs and receiving training, youths learned discipline, an acceptance of authority, and were able to apply this to other areas of their lives. In a context in which, by the 1970s, the number of new jobs in mine companies had stagnated, the provision of skills training enabled mineworkers' children to take up income generation opportunities, for example in carpentry, tailoring, mechanics, plumbing, electrical work or vehicle repair, and obtained employment in

59 Mwinda Kabwe interview.
60 Kilufya Kasongo interview.

other companies or were able to establish small businesses of their own.[61] Some mineworkers' children were hired by the mining companies, as in Katanga, but in Zambia there was a greater effort to train them in areas outside the mines. Efforts were also made to train and motivate young people to engage in farming, with the aim of encouraging them to grow crops in nearby rural areas.[62]

Sports and recreation officers did not simply wait for youth or their parents to approach them. Instead they actively would go into townships to look for and pick up 'roamers', who would otherwise cause a 'nuisance' and vandalise equipment; they then approached the parents with a view to engaging them in sports training. There was a tacit acknowledgement that some youth would not attend school but could find a suitable outlet via sports. Parents would also refer their own badly behaved children to social case workers.[63] Through participation in both sports training and night schools, 'they changed their attitudes'.[64] Moral instruction and socialisation into appropriate behaviour were always an important element of sporting programmes.[65] Some interviewees saw this process of socialisation as analogous to and implicitly replacing the socialisation of youth that would in the past have been provided by elders in rural societies.[66]

In explaining the provision of sports and youth activities, some interviewees articulated versions of the 'productivity' argument, above. They also suggested that they inculcated 'a sense of belonging' between the company and the mine township youth, who might for example protect the company because they regarded it as their own.[67] Similarly, in Katanga, UMHK/ Gécamines sponsored sporting teams and competitions in order to provide entertainment and community for workers and their families. The moral and character-building elements of team sports were less strongly emphasised; instead they were activities that Gécamines supported as the patron of the community.[68]

61 Masumbuko interview.
62 Interview, anonymous man, Mufulira.
63 Chishala interview.
64 Masumbuko interview.
65 Menzu interview.
66 Ibid.
67 Lukwesa interview.
68 Interview, Dieudonné Mupanga, Likasi, 5 August 2019.

Social Welfare in Practice III:
Women's Centres/*foyers sociaux*

Women's centres in both Zambia and Katanga provided forms of post-school education and instruction in what were evidently explicitly gendered forms. In line with the assumption, discussed above, that township residents needed to be taught how to be modern and urban, they were initially designed to train women in domestic tasks – cooking, sewing, knitting, tailoring and raising children. Implicit in the need for training was the sharp difference in the socialisation of young women in town compared with rural areas: in the village, they would learn necessary skills from older female relatives, and the specific skill set required in town – for example, managing a cash-based household budget, or providing meals and a clean domestic environment for a husband working in waged employment – was itself different.[69] One (male) social worker recalled: 'There they would learn to cook, keep the house clean, knitting, a lot of women's activities.'[70] Training women in managing a household budget was equally seen as a key contribution to maintaining family harmony and avoiding marital conflict.[71] The actual acquisition of skills was in some respects secondary to persuading young women to take responsibility for the household.[72]

Yet by the 1970s, and increasingly from the 1980s, these activities developed a dual use, i.e. to generate income. Whereas male wages were initially assumed to be sufficient to raise a family, it was increasingly recognised that women's earnings – usually through some form of trading – were an important source of income to the household and to the woman in particular. Women, interviewees reported, greatly appreciated the skills they gained.[73] Some husbands had to be persuaded to allow their wives to take these courses but in general, the acquisition of such skills was regarded as beneficial to the household.[74] Women who received training in child rearing, cooking and sewing, whether in primary school, as teenagers at '*écoles menagères*',or as adults at '*foyers sociaux*', recall the skills they gained with great pride. Astrid Musambi attended a state '*école menagère*' for three years after primary school in the early 1970s, which she credited for giving

---

69 Masumbuko interview.
70 Ibid.
71 Lukwesa interview; Masumbuko interview.
72 Lukwesa interview.
73 Masumbuko interview.
74 Chishala interview.

her the skills to provide a good home environment for her husband's seven children from his first marriage. She used these skills to decorate the home, arranging artwork and producing embroidery to decorate sofas, tables and beds. Her neighbours paid her to produce similar work. As she explained, 'you make your bed, and if someone sees it, they say "Oh! The cover is perfect!"'[75] She also enrolled her step-daughter, just out of primary school, in a Gécamines *école menagère*, and recalled happily that after three years there 'she [knew] how to knit jumpers, [and] dresses, she start[ed] to sell tablecloths, [with the] *foyer* she knew how to do all the work.'[76] By developing these skills, some women succeeded in developing independent businesses and thereby empowered themselves within the gendered constraints of Copperbelt society.

By the 1980s, domestic skills courses were still being provided, but were now presented mainly as increasing women's opportunities to earn a living in a context of growing economic difficulties, to the extent that their original 'domestic' role had been largely forgotten. Women's centres, some witnesses recall, also provided opportunities for unofficial forms of socialisation and the sharing of advice among women: one asserted that women were taught how to space their children without the use of contraception, which was not widely available.[77] By that time a changing international and local political context meant that 'women's rights' had in Zambia became part of the training courses: this did not mean full equality or that wives should not obey their husbands, but limited efforts were made to help educated women assert their right to paid employment as a positive contribution to the household, and to balance their own health against giving birth to children.[78] On occasion, generational divisions led some older residents to criticise the imposition of what they perceived as 'Western' ideas regarding gender and family relations. Josephine Lukwesa, in her work with the women's programme, challenged older women by drawing an analogy between new ideas about gender and the Western-type school education they commonly desired for their children and grandchildren.[79]

75 Astrid Musumbi interview, Likasi, 6 August 2019.
76 Musumbi interview.
77 Masumbuko interview.
78 Lukwesa interview.
79 Ibid.

Beyond Custom: Building and Maintaining Mining Families

Underlying the need for social intervention in the colonial period had, as we have seen, been the assumption that 'traditional' African family life, supposedly rooted in patriarchy and essentially unchanging rural societies, was radically challenged by urbanisation.[80] Postcolonial social workers however broke from such rigid divisions between 'traditional' and 'modern' life that informed colonial conceptualisations of social intervention. Some however, particularly in Zambia, did discuss the ways in which changed social circumstances affected the ways in which 'custom' was observed. In both Katanga and Zambia, company educators, healthcare staff, youth workers and social workers, did not see their jobs so much as managing a dangerous, but necessary, decline in tradition, or of carefully shepherding new urbanites. Instead, they focused on building strong families and communities, on providing necessary services, and above all on maintaining social order.

Succeeding generations of Copperbelt residents adapted the traditions of marriage and family they learned from their parents, keeping aspects that appealed to them and seemed to still be relevant, and discarding others. In the main, this was done without the direct intervention of social workers or of other company officials. While statistical evidence is not available, research suggests that marriages between members of different 'ethnicities', for instance, became increasingly popular on the Katangese Copperbelt from the 1950 and 1960s, and in Zambia from the late 1970s and 1980s. Élise Matanda, a Gécamines nurse of Katangese origin, remembered her parents' disapproval in the 1970s when she wanted to marry a man from a Kasaian family. Nevertheless, she told them, 'I love him. That's it!' and they got engaged.[81] With the support of her elder sister, a sewing teacher, she persuaded her parents to drop their objections, although they did specify that the Kasaian custom of '*tshibau*' (concerning punishment for adultery) was not to be practised.

Similarly, the Kasaian custom of a '*stage matrimonial*' – a period where a wife would live with her in-laws, and work for them – was maintained or abandoned according to the life circumstances of the couples and families concerned. Élise Matanda, stayed with her Kasaian in-laws for a month after her marriage in their house in Likasi, which was not an easy experience.

---

80 This was common to RLI/CEPSI and late-colonial thinking in both countries.
81 Élise Matanda interview, Likasi, 16 July 2019.

'You wake up at 5am', she recalled, 'you clean the house … yes, it is truly work.'[82] In contrast, Annie Mwenda, an SNCC nurse who also married in the 1970s, moved in with her husband straight away, without a *stage*, as her in-laws were based far away in Kinshasa.[83] As new couples and their extended families negotiated arrangements that worked for them, they were generally left untroubled by social workers, whose interest in marriage was restricted to ensuring that registered wives and children were provided for, and that workers' wives had the skills to maintain a suitable home.[84]

Social workers we interviewed thus recalled little evidence during this period of major problems arising from clashes between different ethnic ideas regarding either marriage or youth socialisation. Concerns remained that family conflict might arise because some wives, newly arrived from the village, struggled with town life because they could not read or write or because they could not fulfil their roles as domestic hosts. These skills were precisely those that could be learned at women's centres.[85] Most social workers were confident that mine township residents could learn about, adjust to and manage potential differences in 'custom' as the influence of the village on their families diminished. Some 'customary' activities, for example the initiation of children into adulthood, now 'was part of life in town. No-one went back.'[86] Any concerns centred not around the customs themselves, or their potential incompatibility with town life, but rather around the necessity of maintaining peace and order in the mine townships. Initiation ceremonies in Zambia, for example, had to be contained in private residences to avoid music and noise disturbing the wider population.[87]

Although post-independence African social workers were far less exercised about 'custom', mine company policies did still try to shape mining communities and families in distinct ways. As in the colonial period, mine and other companies continued to provide housing and other services within an implicit nuclear family framework. In both Zambia and Congo, companies still allowed the registration of only one wife, so if a man was

---

82 Ibid.

83 Annie Mwenda interview, Likasi, 15 July 2019.

84 Mudianga interview. In discussing why they did or did not take a *stage*, no interviewee mentioned company preferences. This silence was matched by contemporary and former social workers, *foyers* workers, and *chefs de cité*, who instead discussed family intervention in terms of distributing a section of a recalcitrant husband's wage to his wife and children, and providing classes in domestic skills.

85 Mudianga interview.

86 Masumbuko interview.

87 Chola interview.

polygamous, 'you marry outside the system of the mines'.[88] In Congo, this meant that a second wife (and, until a change in family law under Mobutu, her children) was not entitled to company-provided medical care, housing or schooling.[89] Nevertheless, social workers interviewed did not regard polygamy as an inherent social problem and, consistent with their general approach, would only intervene if polygamy led to conflict between the wives.[90] In Zambia, there were fewer benefits awarded to workers' families, but official registration was still important for housing allocation, and for benefits in the event of a husband's death.

Social workers and other company officials took a similarly relaxed approach to extended family members. Before independence, companies had restricted how long extended family members could stay with family in mining areas. After independence, these controls were relaxed in both countries, despite occasional memos from Gécamines officials decrying the presence of non-Gécamines kin in company housing.[91] The vast majority of Gécamines workers seem to have hosted and supported extended family. [92] As one nurse explained: 'I haven't been alone in my house since I started working for Gécamines [in 1978].'[93] Social workers and other company officials were no longer concerned with maintaining a strict separation between Gécamines families and their non-Gécamines kin, although which family members were provided for was controlled through an intricate bureaucracy.[94]

---

88   Masumbuko interview.
89   This 1987 change in family law is discussed in Dibwe, *Bana Shaba*, p. 119.
90   Chola interview.
91   One memo informed managerial staff that they could not host people outside their nuclear families in their Gécamines houses, in order to maintain calm and security and avoid theft: GCM Likasi Personnel archives, 'Avis au Personnel de Cadre de Likasi', Likasi, 13 June 1972. However, no interviewees – employees or management – ever mentioned any restrictions on this after independence, and the vast majority of them hosted extended family members for long periods of time. A 1988 report recorded zero permits being granted for temporary hosting of visitors, further suggesting that this supposed rule was completely disregarded in practice: GCM Likasi Personnel archives, Bureau du Personnel Panda, 'Rapport mensuel mois de septembre', Panda, 4 September 1988.
92   For example, Mme Séraphine interview; Charlotte Panga Kelita interview.
93   Anonymous woman interview, Likasi.
94   GCM Personnel Office, Likasi, 'Proces-verbal de la reunion des services administratives du Département du Personnel' Jadotville, 16 April 1967. This documents the company's attempts to computerise the personnel and family records, to clarify family relationships, to keep track of where children were living, to iron out inconsistencies and to provide information on vaccinations to the medical office.

On occasion, orphaned younger siblings or nieces and nephews might be approved as 'charges' of a Gécamines worker, and granted company support, and in some cases Gécamines might pay towards medical care of other resident family members.[95] Otherwise, Gécamines workers had to pay to educate and feed their extended family members.[96] In Zambia, the direct surveillance of households was also significantly reduced in the independence period. The number of residents, or the number of children accessing education, was not limited or closely monitored, and the internal composition of the mineworker's 'family' was not policed as long as conflict did not arise.[97] The lack of services analogous to those provided by Gécamines meant the company had far less concern about classifying who, precisely, were the worker's family.

Decline and Fall: Nostalgia for Company Welfare

In the late 1990s and early 2000s, as the Copperbelt's loss-making mine companies were privatised, social service provision largely collapsed.[98] In both Zambia and Katanga, housing – formerly provided by the mine companies – was distributed to sitting tenants. Workers who did not have company accommodation, instead receiving a housing allowance, were allocated company-owned land, sometimes on former playing fields, to build their own houses. Company oversight of the lived environment declined, with the ending of company-run street cleaning and public hygiene campaigns. In Katanga, the vast majority of the mining workforce was laid off in the early 2000s – a lay off which included teachers, nurses and social workers.[99] Former workers and their families now needed to pay to visit the much diminished (in both quantity and quality) Gécamines hospitals, while in Zambia former workers had recourse only to the

95 For example, Njamba interview. See also, GCM Personnel Office, Likasi, 'Kapinga Ngelula, acces d'un parent aux soins médicaux', 1974. In this case, a worker's widowed mother was granted free medical care.
96 Interview, Stéphanie Matoba, Likasi, 8 August 2019; Mme Séraphine interview; anonymous woman interview, Likasi.
97 Chola interview.
98 For explanations of this financial collapse and privatisation process see Alastair Fraser and John Lungu, *For Whom the Windfalls? Winners and Losers in the Privatisation of Zambia's Copper Mines* (Lusaka: Civil Society Trade Network of Zambia, 2007); and Rubbers, *Le paternalisme en question*, pp. 49–59.
99 For more on the 'Départ voluntaire' and the trauma it caused, see Rubbers, *Le paternalisme en question*, pp. 99–107.

local government welfare services, themselves badly hit by the loss of mine company revenue. Townships that were once the preserve of company employees and their families were now mixed, with houses sold or let to families who had no connection to the company; interviewees universally contrast the order and cleanliness of the past to present-day disorder, crime and unsanitary conditions (see Straube, Chapter 7).[100].

Interviewees typically divide their descriptions of social services into the years before 'the crisis', when, broadly speaking, social welfare provision continued to operate at a high level, and afterwards, when only fragments of provision remained. Some interviewees did, however, volunteer that there were some changes in the 1980s and early 1990s: services, such as sports team membership, were now charged for at a higher level, and the physical infrastructure of hospitals, schools and youth centres began to decline. Similarly, Alick Tembo recalls there were already shortages in sports equipment and transport at this time.[101] Certainly, archival evidence suggests that social service and company welfare provision was already in decline by the 1980s, and it is noteworthy that the memory of this decline is today closely associated with the break up of ZCCM and the 'crisis' of Gécamines associated with the political and military conflicts and redundancies of the 1990s and early 2000s.

Despite the closure of the *foyers* and their SNCC equivalents, there are today in Katanga a few company-supported centres with similar functions. Gécamines, consistent with its continuing role (compared with ZCCM-IH) runs social services centres in many of its former camps, which offer lessons in cooking, knitting, sewing, housekeeping, decoration and household budgeting. These centres are specifically for those who have missed out on education elsewhere, whether teenage mothers or those whose education was disrupted by financial crisis.[102] They also no longer serve just the families of Gécamines workers, but also needy people from the general area. Given the location of the *centres de promotion sociale* in Gécamines camps, and the massive decrease in the Gécamines workforce, many of the 'non-company' attendees had a long family connection with the company. For Brigitte Mukasa Kiwele, the head of social services for Gécamines at Likasi, the purpose of the centres remains to help the advancement of society in

---

100 The popular memory of decline and nostalgia for company paternalism is analysed in Rubbers, *Le paternalisme en question* and Mususa, 'There Used to Be Order'.
101 Tembo interview.
102 Kiwele interview.

general.[103] In Zambia, mine companies continue to provide limited health and recreational services for their much diminished workforce and for some of their retired and retrenched workers, but not for their extended families. At least one privatised mine company, in Mufulira, employs a welfare officer to assist with the domestic problems of its workers, a conscious if small-scale reflection of the past. Some churches have taken over welfare centres and are providing facilities for income generation via activities such as sewing, but at a greatly diminished level. The continuing provision of and appetite for social welfare provision long after the heyday of corporate community development programmes is arguably the greatest evidence of its internalisation and Africanisation by Copperbelt communities.

For most former workers as well as for the social workers we interviewed, the loss of company social services was wrenching; they see today's urban society as less secure and less ordered than in the past, with children and youth struggling, and bringing disruption. In Zambia, former social welfare officers pointed out during interviews that the land on which football pitches and social centres once stood has been sold for housing: 'Our children in the township have nowhere to go.'[104] They believe this has contributed to drinking, vandalism and crime, carried out by young people. The legacy of earlier investment in youth development is however identifiable in small businesses run by their former trainees, now in their middle age.[105] Thus, the current decline enables social workers and community development officers to look back uncritically to a time when they played a vital role in maintaining societal and familial order, in a form entirely unconnected with the colonial origins of these policies.

Certainly, some residents of company areas explicitly argue that company service provision encouraged a dangerous dependency that made it difficult for mineworkers to manage their own affairs when services declined (see Peša and Henriet, Chapter 1). 'It was good, but in some ways it was bad, because Gécamines accustomed us to getting things free', recalled Dieudonné Mupanga, a former Gécamines worker who had spent his whole career in social provision, first as a teacher and then at the canteen, managing the distribution of food and other goods to workers' families.[106] A former housing officer in Zambia likewise argued that the company provision of comprehensive services left employees ill-prepared for managing their own

103 Ibid.
104 Masumbuko interview.
105 Chola interview.
106 Mupanga interview.

affairs when that support was removed.[107] In general however, for the vast majority of social workers the crisis has reinforced their belief and even pride in the system of company oversight and intervention into family and community life for which they were once responsible.

Conclusion

This chapter has argued that the extensive provision of social welfare services in Copperbelt company townships, developing first in Katanga in the 1930s and then expanding rapidly across the region from the late 1940s, rested on a distinctive set of colonial ideas about African society and its supposed transition from rural to urban existence, which, while drawing on wider global notions of company paternalism and developmental intervention, combined these with specific racialised and gendered notions to shape the distinct form of social intervention practised in the late-colonial Copperbelt. This intervention increasingly centred on African social workers who were (by ancestry) informed about rural customary practices regarding familial and marital relations and (by training) able to train Africans into new nuclear family roles.

In the years after political independence, African social workers, trained in universalist forms of social intervention and employed by nationalised companies, rejected the notion that residents of Copperbelt company towns were experiencing any such transition or that 'custom' presented any particular challenge to the communities in which they worked. Rather, they understood social conflict – whether marital disputes, juvenile delinquency or housewives in need of domestic training – as resolvable by intervention, training and socialisation into the appropriate norms necessary for urban living anywhere. While these social interventions were highly gendered and initially continued to turn women into 'housewives' they came to provide opportunities for income generation and independent employment for some women, not least the social workers themselves. What many would see as an authoritarian corporate regime that policed the 'private' lives of workers and their families was justified as evidence of company benevolence, as contributing to what were for them the inherent goods of industrial productivity and social peace. The subsequent drastic decline of social provision on the Copperbelt has only reinforced their belief that their actions were in the interests of the communities they believed they served.

---

107 Interview, anonymous man, Kitwe, 5 July 2019.

13

Reimagining the Copperbelt as a Religious Space

STEPHANIE LÄMMERT

Introduction

A narrative of urban progress, based on the early and formative knowl-edge production of Rhodes-Livingstone Institute (RLI) scholars, has long dominated Copperbelt historiography. For two reasons, religion and spir-ituality have never figured in it centrally. First, the Copperbelt was seen as a difficult mission field by early missionaries who feared negative influences associated with the urban lifestyle. They failed to see the urban apostolate as a fertile ground and instead emphasised its dangers. Second, this view was perpetuated in the secular literature. While RLI scholars did much to debunk the story of urban danger and turned it into the success story of urban modernity, they never saw religion as central to modern urban society. Their emphasis on the flexibility of ethnicity and kinship in the urban environment meant they accepted the nuclear Christian family as the core of the new modern society, and did not see the importance of examining religious expression further.

Subsequent generations of researchers have followed their path[1] – with the exception of missionary-authored publications, which study Christianity from a denominationally narrow angle[2] and the recent boom in the study

---

1 James Ferguson, *Expectations of Modernity: Myths and Meanings of Urban Life on the Zambian Copperbelt*, Berkeley: University of California Press, 1999); Miles Larmer, *Mine-workers in Zambia: Labour and Political Change in Post-Colonial Africa* (London: I.B. Tauris, 2007); Patience Mususa, '"Getting By": Life on the Copperbelt after the Privatisation of the Zambia Consolidated Copper Mines', *Social Dynamics* 46, 2 (2010), pp. 380–94.

2 Hugo F. Hinfelaar, *History of the Catholic Church in Zambia* (Lusaka: Bookworld Publishers, 2004); Michael O'Shea, *Missionaries and Miners: A History of the Beginnings*

of Pentecostalism.[3] Pentecostal churches indeed had an important impact on Copperbelt Christianity. They presented a real threat to mainline churches and, given their emphasis on individualism, the literature has linked their emergence to the rise of the neoliberal order.[4] However, the argument of a total break with the past through conversion, which has characterised the literature on Pentecostal churches, has obscured the openness and interchange as well as continuities of spiritual forms characteristic of Copperbelt spirituality, which serves as this article's main focus.

There are some important exceptions in the historical literature. Walima T. Kalusa's study of Christian funerals on the Copperbelt stands out, as does David Gordon's work on the world of invisible agents. Gordon argues in favour of treating religion and spirituality in Central Africa as an integral part of modernity rather than its obstacle.[5] His study helps us understand that Copperbelt urbanites were both – modern urban class-conscious miners *and* spiritual beings, nationalists *and* believers in a world of invisible agents. Kalusa's focus on mineworkers' appropriation of Christianity as a means to forge urban identity is central to this chapter.[6]

Building on their work, I propose to understand the history of migrant labour and mobility on the Central African Copperbelt through the lens of spirituality and religion. I am arguing that the worship practices on the Copperbelt, characterised as they were by denominational boundary crossing, egalitarianism, strong female initiatives and attempts at popular appropriation, and sometimes possessing a decidedly political agenda, parallel

---

of the Catholic Church in Zambia with Particular Reference to the Copperbelt (Ndola: Ndola Mission Press, 1986); John V. Taylor and Dorothea A. Lehmann, *Christians of the Copperbelt: The Growth of the Church in Northern Rhodesia* (London: SCM Press, 1961).

3   For research on Pentecostalism in Zambia see Austin M. Cheyeka, 'Towards a History of the Charismatic Churches in Post-Colonial Zambia' in Jan-Bart Gewald, Marja Hinfelaar, and Giacomo Macola (eds), *One Zambia, Many Histories. Towards a History of Post-Colonial Zambia* (Leiden: Brill, 2008), pp. 144–63; Naomi Haynes, *Moving by the Spirit: Pentecostal Social Life on the Zambian Copperbelt* (Ewing: University of California Press, 2017); Adriaan van Klinken, 'Pentecostalism, Political Masculinity and Citizenship', *Journal of Religion in Africa* 46, 2–3 (2016), pp. 129–57.

4   For one of the important articles which set the debate on Pentecostalism in Africa, see Birgit Meyer, 'Pentecostalism and Neo-Liberal Capitalism: Faith, Prosperity and Vision in African Pentecostal-Charismatic Churches', *Journal for the Study of Religion* 20, 2 (2007), pp. 5–28.

5   David M. Gordon, *Invisible Agents: Spirits in a Central African History* (Athens: Ohio University Press, 2012), pp. 2, 22, 87.

6   Walima Tuesday Kalusa and Megan Vaughan, *Death, Belief and Politics in Central African History* (Lusaka: Lembani Trust, 2014), p. 92.

histories of mobility and migration and the distinct decentralised political mode of action on the Zambian Copperbelt. It is not within the reach of this chapter to present an exhaustive account of Christianity on the Copperbelt. However, the examples selected, that is the Union Church and the initiatives of Catholic women, are key for our understanding of how religious expression helped fostering a sense of Copperbelt identity, mirroring the mobility of migrants who were used to cross boundaries in order to belong.

The first Copperbelt Christian movement, the so-called Union Church, which was not only non-denominational but also initiated not by missionaries but by African migrant workers with diverse Christian identities, built the foundation for a subsequent Copperbelt spirituality. To Union Church adherents, as for many Catholic women in the second half of the twentieth century, the rejection of denominational exclusiveness was an integral part of their Christian identity, which frequently extended into the social and the political. As they engaged in denominational boundary crossing, Catholic women claimed urban belonging through religious expression. Church involvement gave many women the opportunity to participate in 'respectable' ways in social and political life, opportunities that were rare in the gendered hierarchies of Copperbelt society, which was still influenced by the early missionaries' negative portrayal of women. Copperbelt women took the opportunity to shape the religious space and to bring in their own agenda as they insisted on the mobility and flexibility of religious practices and boundaries. The focus on the Catholic Church and Catholic women in the second part of the chapter owes its existence to the fact that the Catholics eventually turned out to be more successful than other missions. They succeeded precisely because they were able to replicate Copperbelt decentralised political structures in their grassroots approach and pro-poor orientation, and because their Marian tradition reverberated with matrilineal tradition.

In order to understand the development of Christian life between the emergence of the Union Church in the 1920s and the initiatives of Catholic women in the second half of the twentieth century, the chapter explores the influence of early missionaries' narratives concerning gender hierarchies in the urban space as well as the uneasy relationship between industry and missions. It draws on a range of mission, government and mine company publications and archives, among them the little researched archives of the Franciscan friars and the Diocesan archives of the Catholic Church, both in Ndola, as well as the 'informal papers' of the Mindolo Ecumenical Foundation (MEF) in Kitwe.

The Union Church

The first Christian movement on the Zambian Copperbelt, the Union Church, was initiated in the early 1920s not by European missionaries but by African labour migrants. While missionaries in Northern Rhodesia carved out monopolistic rural enclaves,[7] Africans, many of them mineworkers or other labour migrants drawn to the copper towns from across Central and Eastern Africa, organised their own religious life, built churches and ran their own schools in the absence of mission societies. They financed these activities through membership contributions. The Union Church of the Zambian Copperbelt was inaugurated in 1925 with its own board of elders, a number of evangelists, a steady stream of baptisms and with branches in most mine compounds and in the city of Ndola.[8] Their regular meetings were held in Mindolo near Kitwe, to which church elders cycled from Chingola, Mufulira and Ndola for open-air meetings, to discuss the organisation of the young church, or for intertown Christian fellowship. The Union Church thrived via the initiative of local and migrant Christians and the spiritual sagacity of the church elders who felt the need to establish a religious life in the rapidly growing copper towns.[9] The migrants brought their diverse backgrounds with them. Exchanging and mingling with Christians from other denominations, joint worship, regular exchanges and social gatherings, as well as the effort to build churches with one's own hands gave a sense of identity in a broad Christian community instead of a narrow denominational one. This initiative also transcended the religious and helped mineworkers and other labour migrants to socially organise their new lives. Their worship practices and Christian activism brought new structures to urban social life, thus allowing Christian town dwellers to build a sense of identity beyond ethnicity, in the same vein as has been shown for other activities such as the famous Kalela dance and other leisure activities. For the community of cosmopolitan Christian labour migrants, M'Passou finds, 'denominational labels were historical accidents' and they united regardless of their different backgrounds.[10]

---

7   Taylor and Lehmann, *Christians of the Copperbelt*, pp. 13–24.
8   Hugh Cross, *To Africa with Love: A Memoir of Arthur Cross of the United Missions in the Copperbelt of Zambia* (Ottery St Mary: Cross Patch Editions, 2001), p. 36.
9   Denis M'Passou, *Mindolo: A Story of the Ecumenical Movement in Africa* (Lusaka: Baptist Printing Ministry, 1983), pp. 1–5.
10   Ibid., p. 2.

European missionaries, in contrast, deliberately ignored the population of the rapidly growing mine compounds until the landmark Davis commission of enquiry of 1933, 'Modern Industry and the African', called for missionary initiatives to help Africans adjust to the supposed dislocations of urban life. The commission studied the impact of copper mining on Zambian society and the work of the Christian missions in the Copperbelt and was undertaken under the auspices of the International Missionary Council's Department of Social and Industrial Research. Its report praised the 'initiative, leadership and sacrifice of the native Christians' and was impressed by the self-governing and self-supporting structure of the Union Church. It however believed the local church needed to be brought under systematic missionary influence, and recommended that missions co-operate to focus on welfare work and the inclusion of women and children to ease social discontent.[11] It was again African initiative, in the personal form of the Union Church's Elli Chola, whose wide networks and close friendship with London Missionary Society (LMS)'s Mike Moore enabled the merger between the Union Church and Protestant mission societies. The financial security and infrastructural assistance offered through the missions eventually overruled the initial independence of the Union Church, and they appealed for help.[12] Following the recommendation by the Davis commission, the LMS under Mike Moore's lead converted the Union Church into what would become the United Missions to the Copperbelt (UMCB), a union of Protestant churches.

Indeed, Moore and the UMCB's work was only successful because it was built on the foundations of the African Christian pioneers of the Union Church. Soon the Union Church's agenda was determined by the financially more powerful foreign missions. Through the conversion, the Union Church had lost the early ecumenical spirit that was its driving force. The United Missions focused on education: by 1941, they were in charge of all schools in the mine compounds of Chingola, Nkana, Roan and Mufulira.[13] Especially the new urban elite embraced UMCB.[14] However, its moral-

11 Merle J. Davis, *Modern Industry and the African: An Enquiry into the Effect of the Copper Mines of Central Africa upon Native Society and the Work of Christian Missions made under the auspices of the Department of Social and Industrial Research of the International Missionary Council* (London: Macmillan, 1933), p. 295, pp. 385–6.

12 Taylor and Lehmann, *Christians of the Copperbelt*, p. 35.

13 London Missionary Society Collection at SOAS (hereafter SOAS-LMS), CWM/LMS/1941-1950/Box AF 17, 'Fifth Annual Report 1941', pp. 6–7.

14 Jane L. Parpart, '"Where Is Your Mother?": Gender, Urban Marriage, and Colonial Discourse on the Zambian Copperbelt, 1924–1945', *International Journal of African*

ising approach to town life and especially to urban women (see below), was at odds with the Union Church's previous easy juxtaposition of worship approaches and lifestyles.

Denis M'Passou, who headed the research programme of MEF, the Union Church's ultimate successor in the 1980s, identified the Union Church as the cradle of the ecumenical movement in Africa, whose goal is world-wide unity of Christianity across denominational boundaries. This 'purely African initiative in ecumenism', he argues, 'was a spontaneous movement carried out to meet the unique spiritual needs of thousands of people who had found themselves away from their home, their churches and their pastors, and were now living in a new situation.'[15]

The Union Church was not restricted by aspirations of exclusivity. Embracing the coexistence of many spiritual paths and partially shared practices can indeed be said to be the essence of the urban religious experience, paralleling the mobility of the migration processes and the general experience of messiness that characterised rural–urban dynamics and ethnicity in the mining towns. The situation in Haut-Katanga was decidedly different. The Catholic Church, supported by the Belgian colonial state, soon grew into the one exclusive state church.[16] Under the triple alliance between *Union Minière*, the Belgian colonial state and the Catholic Church, the Roman Catholics had successfully eliminated all competition.[17] In contrast, more than a dozen other mission societies from various Christian backgrounds were in operation on the Zambian Copperbelt and there was no state church.

The joint efforts of early African Christians and the members of the Union Church in particular invert our conventional understanding of the primacy of missions in the development of African Christianity. Their initiatives, however, have been obscured by the narratives subsequently created by missions themselves about Copperbelt Christianity, to which this article now turns.

Historical Studies 27, 2 (1994), pp. 241–71, p. 259.

15 M'Passou, *Mindolo*, p. 1.

16 Bruce Fetter, *The Creation of Elisabethville 1910–1940* (Stanford: Hoover Institution Press, 1976), pp. 169–71.

17 Pascale Stacey, 'Missionaries in the Congo: The First 120 Years' in Prem Poddar, Rajeev S. Patke and Lars Jensen (eds), *A Historical Companion to Postcolonial Literatures: Continental Europe and its Empires* (Edinburgh: Edinburgh University Press, 2011), pp. 39–41.

Urban Anxieties: Early Missionaries' Worries

The mission churches were notoriously weak in colonial-era urban and industrial Africa, including the Copperbelt. This institutional weakness reflected missionaries' belief that new urban spaces did not provide the right environment for religious conversion. Instead, it was feared, urban Africans would succumb to the lure of materialism. From a missionary perspective, towns were messy not only because of the 'temptations' they had in store for their adherents, but also because of the competition through other mission societies – contrary to the countryside, where they had successfully carved out exclusive spheres of influence under early colonial rule. Missionary writings of the 1930s reinforced the rural-urban, tradition-modernity divide by depicting Africans as stuck in a temporal order distinct from 'modern time' and unfit to cope with allegedly 'un-African' town life.

As one example, LMS missionary Mabel Shaw painted a wistful picture of the emerging Copperbelt of 1932 as one in which the rural African social order was being broken on the wheels of industry. Shaw referred to an African miner as a 'savage in a powerhouse' who had been 'dragged forward to meet and share in our mechanical civilization'. According to Shaw, he had no means to 'meet the modern world and to understand it', but at the same time he had been cut off from his 'tribal fire'. In her view, they were 'adrift on an alien stream'.[18] Likewise, LMS missionary Mike Moore thought that 'the African' was forcefully 'brought into the twentieth century and his soul left in the middle of the Iron Age'.[19] Such fantastical portrayals highlighted the moral necessity of the missionary and provided a justification of their work and the civilising mission.

In the mid-twentieth century, the colonial government and the mining companies were preoccupied with the question of labour stabilisation.[20] Copperbelt missionaries found themselves drawn into urgent discussions about the dangers of unwanted and uncontrolled permanent settlement of African 'migrant' workers, resulting in so-called 'detribalisation'. All European observers assumed that the 'detribalisation' resulting from labour

---

18 Mabel Shaw, *God's Candlelights: An Educational Venture in Northern Rhodesia* (London: Edinburgh House Press, 1932), pp. 38, 40.
19 Zambia Consolidated Copper Mines Archives (hereafter ZCCM-IH), 10.7.10B, African Churches, 'Co-Operative Work in the African Copper Belt by Rev. RJB Moore of the LMS', 14 November 1937, p. 7.
20 Ferguson, *Expectations of Modernity*, pp. 18–49.

migration would – despite the evidence of earlier initiatives such as the Union Church – destabilise the social order of African society. Very much in line with this reasoning, most missionaries envisioned a rural modernity based on religious education, and practical and vocational training, without competition through other mission societies. They did not see the need for urban missions. The one exception was LMS's Mike Moore. Precisely because he saw the nature of capitalist exploitation in the copper mines so clearly, Moore understood the establishment of urban missions as a Christian and moral obligation in order to stabilise and protect African migrants.[21] Eventually, Moore, who had become too critical of industry and colonial state, was removed from the Copperbelt and transferred to a rural station.[22]

From a missionary perspective, the labour stabilisation discourse was enmeshed with a Christian understanding of the relationship between morality, materialism and sin. Protestant ethics of hard work were combined with the classical view that a society's morality is mirrored through the behaviour of women in general and their sexuality in particular. Accordingly, from a missionary perspective, sinful behaviour was most commonly associated with African women who, LMS missionaries believed, were particularly susceptible to a corrupted lifestyle on the Copperbelt. Mabel Shaw described a typical newly arrived urban woman who

> wore loose wide-legged pyjamas, gay flaunting garments, she carried a sunshade, and walked with her head thrown back, a cigarette in her mouth. A group of young men followed admiringly. A year ago, she would have been one of the crowd of unclad girls who followed by bicycle, shouting and laughing as I passed through the village, a child of the river and the forest.[23]

Shaw's depiction of this urban woman suggests a paradise lost. While the 'child of the river and the forest' is a symbol of innocence, the grown woman has lost her moral standing by succumbing to cigarettes and fashion, taking pleasure in the admiration of men.

In a similar vein, Moore observed that money and 'gay clothes' were enough to persuade a wife to leave her husband and

---

21 Reginald J. B. Moore, *These African Copper Miners: A Study of the Industrial Revolution in Northern Rhodesia, with Principal Reference to the Copper Mining Industry* (London: Livingstone Press, 1948).
22 Sean Morrow, '"On the Side of the Robbed": R. J. B. Moore, Missionary on the Copperbelt, 1933–1941', *Journal of Religion in Africa* 19, 3 (1989), pp. 244–63, p. 253.
23 Shaw, *God's Candlelights*, pp. 39–40.

stay on with another man and then with a third. She is one of many
caught by our materialism. Women, even more than the men, need
guidance in the use of their new leisure and need, too, a new code
of moral behaviour.[24]

This patronising, if not outright misogynous, view reflected the anxiety
felt by missionaries about the independence many women found in the
towns. The 'problem' of Copperbelt women and the 'general paranoia'
which characterised male–female relationships on the Copperbelt has long
been debated. Jane Parpart demonstrated how the image of the immoral
woman was constructed because the new liberties that opened up for
women in the copper towns since the 1920s were perceived as a threat;
economic opportunities that enabled women to challenge male dominance
and to resist formal marriage or even marriage at all.[25] Parpart showed
that the transformation from temporary 'mine marriages' to greater marital
stability from the 1950s, at best in the form of the modern nuclear Christian family, was a joint project of elite Africans, colonial administration,
senior African men and missionaries in an effort to fix gender roles and
limit the economic freedom of unattached Copperbelt women.[26]

Ideas about female respectability changed in the following decades
under British rule and in post-independence Zambia. However, the female
body is still at the heart of crucial debates concerning the morals of the
nation, as the ban on mini-skirts in the 1970s and a later, shrill debate
around ministers wearing mini-skirts in the late 1990s show.[27] In the
1930s, however, missionary concern about urban moral disintegration
in general and women's behaviour in particular was arguably prompted
by some missionaries' own inability to make sense of a rapidly changing
world. Their desire to preserve an alleged rural harmony in Africa stemmed
from the fact that such a scenario was long lost to industrialism in their
native Britain.

24 ZCCM-IH, 10.7.10B, African churches, 'Co-Operative Work in the African Copper
Belt', p. 5.
25 Jane L. Parpart, 'Sexuality and Power on the Zambian Copperbelt, 1926–1964' in
Sharon B. Stichter (ed.), *Patriarchy and Class: African Women in the Home and the Workforce*
(Boulder: Westview Press, 1988), pp. 115–38.
26 Parpart, '"Where Is Your Mother?"', p. 269.
27 Karen Tranberg Hansen, 'Dressing Dangerously: Miniskirts, Gender Relations and
Sexuality in Zambia' in Jean Marie Allman (ed.), *Fashioning Africa. Power and the Politics
of Dress* (Bloomington: Indiana University Press, 2004), pp. 166–85.

The Mining Industry and Christianity

The Union Church's ecumenical vision and open spirituality was replaced by UMCB's more moralising approach to town life, driven by the anxieties of early missionaries. However, mission and church structures on the copper compounds were sites where miners and other labour migrants, many of them women, actively engaged with and shaped their urban environment. Given the negative attitude of many missionaries to the exploitative nature of the copper industry, it is unsurprising that mining companies and missions had uneasy relations. Mining companies feared that the missionaries' critique of urban materialism would encourage criticism of their activities, including from their African employees. As a consequence, the industry was ambiguous about the Christian missions and their contribution to welfare work and education. On the one hand, they encouraged the influence of Christian missions in encouraging hard work and a morally upstanding lifestyle: such values had the potential to maintain high production and social order. In fact, missions were necessary to create a stable and reliable work force by providing welfare services that the industry did not offer before the 1940s as well as by creating a spirit of spiritual belonging for a diverse migrants' society. On the other hand, mining companies worried about some missionaries' critical view of the industry's failure to provide safe working conditions and fair pay. Mine companies therefore did not actively discourage the work of missions in the mine townships, but instead tried to limit their interaction and influence by withholding substantial financial assistance.

This was entirely different in the bordering copper mines of Katanga, where the Roman Catholic Church and *Union Minière* cooperated in education as well as labour recruitment.[28] These differences between the Katangese and the Zambian Copperbelt can be explained by the paternalistic policy in Katanga, which aimed at a stabilisation of the miners and their families, and the cordial relations between the church and the state. Since there was no state church in the Zambian Copperbelt, denominational fluidity and openness was neither encouraged nor impossible. Unlike *Union Minière*, the Anglo American Corporation (AAC) did not regulate where and if their workers worshipped. Thus, the absence of one powerful state church and the lack of a union between churches and industry gave Christians of the Zambian Copperbelt the freedom to live sometimes unorthodox Christian lives that could include idiosyncratic appropriations of Christianity and lead to denominational flexibility.

28 Fetter, *The Creation of Elisabethville*, p. 171.

After initial refusals, Northern Rhodesian mine management reluctantly granted permission to missions to erect churches in mine compounds, although in 1939 church services in Nkana were still held in a hospital because mine management resisted the building of a church.[29] In the early years Copperbelt Christians financed and erected their own churches.[30] It is notable that the sense of belonging and unity joint worship offered to them propelled Copperbelt Christians to use their own financial resources. Following the recommendations of the Davis commission, mining companies offered plots of land and a limited degree of financial support to the mainline churches. *Union Minière*, however, continued to rely mainly on government grants.[31] The cool relationship between mines and churches grew frostier from the mid-1940s when mines introduced their own welfare programmes, and when the colonial government took over responsibility for schooling.[32] Now mine management no longer had to rely on church-provided education, and the last UMCB school was handed to government in 1952.[33]

As a consequence, it became more difficult for the churches to assert their influence on the life on the mines. In the *African Roan Antelope*, a weekly publication provided by the Roan mine in Luanshya for their workers from the late 1950s, religion did not feature prominently. The dominant themes in its educational and advice columns were manners, correct use of the English language, education on cleanliness and workplace safety. When Christianity was evoked, it sought to foster appropriate morals by recourse to Christian values, or to discipline women.

Missions and industry were generally in competition. This becomes clear in an article of 1956 heralding the publication of the Bible in the Bemba language. The article read: 'The whole bible in Chibemba: It is as if one said: "a new mine is now open," because the bible is very like a mine, and all those who go into it well will make the discovery that a great number of valuable things come from it.'[34] The metaphor here is revealing – by comparing the holy book to a mine, a link to the domain of the invisible is established. Copper mining is invisible as the mine's infrastructure lies

29 SOAS-LMS, CWM/LMS/1941–1950, AF 15B, United Church accommodation by Moore, January 1939, p. 1.
30 Cross, *To Africa with Love*, p. 46.
31 SOAS-LMS, CWM/LMS/1941-1950/Box AF 17, 'Fifth Annual Report 1941', pp. 4, 7.
32 Mindolo Ecumenical Foundation archives (hereafter MEF), UMCB II, Minutes 1952–53, 'Christian Co-Operation in the Copperbelt', n.d., p. 1.
33 M'Passou, *Mindolo*, p. 13.
34 ZCCM-IH, 'The African Roan Antelope', 42, September 1956, p. 3.

underneath the surface of the earth, just as the spiritual kingdom is invisible to worldly dwellers. Yet the comparison suggests that both the copper industry and Christianity were powerful precisely because of their respective invisible realms. This power, however, can also be associated with the danger invisibility brings by its very nature – what is invisible cannot be controlled. The imagery of invisibility and its potential connection to danger and power is well known in the region.[35] The article thus can be read as an attempt to suggest equality between the sacred value of the Bible and the worldly wealth of the mine and as a hint at the danger of such powerful invisible worlds. The mines were competing with the church for the souls of the copper town residents; industry and Christian morals were incompatible, and both had a potentially dangerous side.

The theme of dangerous urban women that had so occupied earlier missionaries also reappeared in the magazine. One reader 'would like to point out that a large number of girls lack a sound religious background. They think religion is a secondary way of living.' In addition, 'unwed mothers' should always bear in mind that they were at 'the bottom rung of the ladder.'[36] Discipling women and the attempt to fix gender relations indeed was a theme that had the potential to unite mine management and churches. But it could also bring discord. The Christian elite felt that the church, having blessed their marriages, should be consulted over domestic quarrels, while mine management and the colonial government had installed tribal representatives to control marriages on compounds after 1940.[37] Generally however, the scarcity of religiously themed articles shows both the unease of mine management with the Christian perspective on materialism, as well as their occasional efforts to hijack Christianity for their own ends.

Against the odds, the churches kept providing their services to the mining companies. Following in the footsteps of UMCB, MEF, successor to both the Union Church and UMCB, continued to train students for the expanding mine welfare services.[38] In line with independent Zambia's Mulungushi reforms of 1968, MEF promoted economic justice and contributed to nation-building, for instance training staff for Barclays Bank in

35 Gordon, *Invisible Agents*, p. 77.
36 ZCCM-IH, 'The African Roan Antelope', 140, 24 June 1961, letter, p. 10.
37 Parpart, '"Where Is Your Mother?"', p. 258.
38 MEF, 'MEF Paper Files – M6 – Rhokana Corporation', 1965–68; MEF, 'MEF Paper Files – 13 – Nchanga Mines Correspondence', 1963–68; MEF, 'MEF Paper Files – 11 – Roan/Mpatamatu Correspondence', 1965–68.

order to achieve a quicker Zambianisation of its personnel.[39] The Foundation's interest in nation-building was twofold. They sought to lift Christian ecumenical values from the household to the national level while at the same time they endeavoured to produce more Zambian graduates who would benefit from the economic redistribution.

In addition, MEF offered courses for both mine employees and their wives. Most popular was the Christian home-making course, whose reputation was enhanced by the participation of the president's wife, Betty Kaunda, in the 1950s.[40] The course, MEF claimed, had a positive influence on general work discipline in the mines. 'A miner who reads makes a better leader', argued the director of MEF in 1971:

> many marriages have been helped as a result of wives attending the … Christian home-making courses. We have received reports from husbands employed in the mines saying that after their wives had attended the training here, they had started to live new lives. A miner with a happy home makes a better worker.[41]

From the mid-1970s however, the mines were no longer interested in Mindolo's seminars. This shift happened not only because of the falling copper prices, but also because mine management was not at ease with the new economic drift under the Mulungushi reforms. Anglo American stopped sending their new expatriate recruits to the seminar for newcomers to Zambia because they were 'mainly aimed at the individual who intends to mix very fully with the Zambians and to a certain extent to 'do gooders'.[42] The companies used the pretext of the sharp fall in copper prices in the mid-1970s to end their annual donations to MEF, although private connections between clergy and mine personnel continued and today still generate donations for church projects, albeit not in a systematic or structural way.[43] The annual grants and donations

39 W. Grenville-Grey, 'Mindolo: A Catalyst for Christian Participation in Nation Building in Africa', *International Review of Missions* 58, 229 (1969), pp. 110–17, pp. 113–14.

40 Jonathan Kangwa, 'Christian Mission, Politics, and Socio-Economic Development: The Contribution of Mindolo Ecumenical Foundation', *International Review of Mission* 106, 1 (2017), pp. 167–187, p. 177.

41 ZCCM-IH, 17.5.4B, Mindolo Ecumenical Foundation, 'Letter by MEF Director J. C. Mfula to Mr C. Halliday, Roan Selection Trust', 12 July 1971.

42 ZCCM-IH, 17.5.4B, Mindolo Ecumenical Foundation, 'Letter by JF Drysdale, Personnel Consultant, Nchanga Consolidate Copper Mines Ltd., Anglo American Corporation Ltd. to John?', 22 August 1970.

43 Interview, Fr Ferena Lambe, Ndola, 3 April 2017.

that had been paid by mining companies since the foundation of UMCB were eventually terminated in December 1975.[44]

This interaction at a distance between churches and mining companies was both boon and bane. Ironically, the uneasy stance of the Zambian industry towards religion led to a certain laissez-faire attitude with as little interference as possible, but also with as little support as possible. Faith was more of a private matter that would not be endorsed by the industry. Copperbelt Christians could choose how and where to worship without a patronising state church. This fit with the tradition set up by the Union Church. In addition, it afforded the clergy as well as congregants the possibility to develop an industry- or state-critical stance, as the Catholic Church eventually did (see below).

Pragmatism and a Pro-Poor Orientation: The Roman Catholic Church

Among the mission churches, the Catholic Church proved to be very popular with Copperbelt residents. They managed to tackle the big challenges of Copperbelt society in a less ideological manner, focusing not on the small African elite but on the urban poor. They fostered their Marian tradition, and the devotion to the Virgin Mary surely struck a chord with Copperbelt women and society at large.

The Conventual Franciscans (OFM Conv) were the first Catholics to arrive on the scene. The first Bishop of Ndola, the Italian Franciscan Francis Mazzieri, embraced the chance to proselytise on a large scale in the densely populated and rapidly growing mine townships. He issued a series of measures designed to integrate migrant workers into the urban environment, aimed at providing a 'passport to a good moral sacramental life'.[45] Focusing more on community building than on education or doctrinal orthodoxy, the Franciscan approach was more pragmatic and less moralising. The friars typically put more emphasis on catering to the poor, which attracted the lower working classes and informal inhabitants of the compounds. They were less dedicated to educating their congregants and accepted converts more easily than other congregations as they sought to embrace the structurally less-advantaged population.

---

[44] MEF, DO 280 Box F. Roan Mines, 'Letter by Managing Director Designate Mr. Phiri to MEF Director Mfula', 9 December 1975.
[45] Quoted in O'Shea, *Missionaries and Miners*, p. 280.

This focus on ministering to the poor and converting local communities into strong parishes, ultimately made the Franciscans and by extension the Catholic Church highly influential on the Copperbelt. It is notable that the friars, not usually known for their liberal inclinations but rather as a 'church within the church in Zambia'[46], fostered a particularly participatory, inclusive spirituality. Their non-elitist and pro-poor orientation paralleled the political, social and cultural structures that developed on the Copperbelt. Political culture in the Copperbelt was characterised by strong community mobilisation around trade unions. Such a decentralised mode of action, in which ordinary mineworkers and other Copperbelt residents participated in successful social initiatives, resonated with the comparatively inclusive religious practice promoted by the friars. The downside from church perspective was that due to their non-elitist approach, Catholic adherents were more inclined to transgress denominational boundaries and take their faith 'into their own hands', as we will see below.

After a late start, the Catholic Church gained ground quickly. After developing a critical position towards the colonial state in the 1950s it subsequently distanced itself from its colonial entanglements. This new autonomy from the state helped the Catholic Church to develop a critical stance towards the post-independence state. From the 1970s on and in the 1980s in particular, it became one of the post-independence government's most vocal critics.[47] Similar to developments across the border in the Katangese Catholic Church, the Catholic Church in Zambia was the only formal organisation with the capacity and resources to mobilise large parts of the population without having to rely on government resources.[48] This put them into a position to channel resistance or to act as a mediator, a position they inhabit until today.

46 Interview, Fr Patrick J Gormley, Kitwe, 30 December 2017.
47 Marja Hinfelaar, 'Legitimizing Powers: the Political Role of the Roman Catholic Church, 1972–1991' in Jan-Bart Gewald, Marja Hinfelaar, and Giacomo Macola (eds), *One Zambia, Many histories: Towards a History of Post-Colonial Zambia*, Leiden: Brill, 2008), pp. 129–43; Yvonne Kabombwe, 'A History of the Mission Press in Zambia, 1970–2011', MA Thesis, University of Zambia, 2015.
48 Hinfelaar, 'Legitimizing Powers', p. 131; Stacey, 'Missionaries in the Congo', pp. 40–1.

Mobile Christian Women

For many Copperbelt Christians, devotion to the Virgin Mary provided an easy path to identification with Catholicism as it struck a chord with matrilineal societies in Central Africa, prompting many Copperbelt residents to debate and rework their understanding of Christianity. This conversation transcended the boundaries of Catholic orthodoxy. Besides the challenge this posed to the Catholic Church, the practice of reworking can itself be understood as a way of making sense of and claiming belonging within urban life. Reworking Christianity as inspired by the figure of Mary was most attractive to those who sought a sense of belonging beyond the conventionally gendered hierarchies of the mining industry. By promoting strong women as leaders, such Christian initiatives provided an alternative image to the economically successful yet immoral urban women who populated the missionary accounts, and helped creating role models of 'respectable' and powerful women at the same time. These women too, were sometimes perceived as dangerous, though not because of their sexuality (see below.)

The example of devotion to Mary demonstrates a broader argument about mobility among Copperbelt Christians; at times the Catholic Church successfully accommodated such heterodox enterprises, and at other times felt the need to sever ties with what were labelled 'heretic' movements. The church's reaction depended on the level of threat they felt by the respective offshoot.

In the 1950s, Alice Lenshina's *Lumpa* Church and Emilio Mulolani's *Mutima* Church provide cases that illustrate this argument. *Lumpa* and *Mutima* were both popular on the Copperbelt, and both Lenshina's and Mulolani's teachings should be understood in the context of Central African matrilineal tradition. *Lumpa* was a hybrid movement combining Protestant, Catholic and Watchtower (Jehovah's Witness) elements as well as those from a purification movement called *Bamuchape* from the 1930s which sought to eradicate witchcraft in Zambia. The *Lumpa* Church had a clear pro women agenda. It was initiated by a woman and perceived as a great threat not only by the churches, but also by senior elders and the colonial government.[49] The White Fathers lost nearly 90% of their flock to *Lumpa* in some parts of the Northern Province.[50] *Lumpa* arrived and thrived on the Copperbelt in 1956 amid political turmoil and was suppressed by the

---

49 Gordon, *Invisible Agents*, pp. 95, 99.
50 National Archives of Zambia (hereafter NAZ), NP 3/12-6432-003, 'Lenshina (Lumpa), Intelligence Report', June 1956, p. 55.

state after its clashes with United National Independence Party (UNIP) followers in 1964.[51]

Mutima was a Catholic offshoot, sharing similarities with the *Jamaa* movement in Katanga.[52] Emilio Mulolani, founder of the *Mutima* Church, was a drop-out from a White Fathers seminary, dismissed due to mental health problems.[53] Mulolani's personal history was characterised by abandonment during childhood. Mulolani, son of a Bemba father, was rejected by the Scottish husband of his Bemba mother. A true migrant, he was raised by his grandmother, joined a Catholic seminary in Tanganyika and taught at a school in Malawi before he returned to the Copperbelt to register his church in 1957.[54] His teaching and preaching drew large crowds in rural and urban settings. In particular in the copper towns, he attracted the first members of an indigenous middle class – contrary to the Franciscan mobilisation of the working poor.[55] In all likelihood, his Copperbelt followers were attracted by Mulolani's mobile life and his analysis of the Catholic doctrine that caused deep tensions with Catholic missionaries. *Mutima*'s urban followers saw the reflection of their own mobility and intellectual achievement in their affiliation with the church.

Mary was central in Mulolani's teachings. According to his prophetic revelation, the Virgin Mary had given birth not only to Christ, but also the Godfather and the Holy Spirit. The villages of *Mutima* adherents were called Mary Queen, and both female and male priests celebrated mass. Emilio Mulolani claimed that his church was Catholic, but not Roman Catholic. His male priests, who were allowed to marry, were soon suspected of promiscuity. The movement's free mixing of men and women clergy, and leisure activities such as naked bathing, led to accusations of indecency, and many *Mutima* congregants were brought before the courts for indecent exposure.[56] There were also political allegations, such as that Mulolani's church

---

51 Gordon, *Invisible Agents*, p. 101.

52 Willy de Craemer, *The Jamaa and the Church: A Bantu Catholic Movement in Zaïre* (Oxford: Clarendon Press, 1977); Johannes Fabian, 'Charisma and Cultural Change: The Case of the Jamaa Movement in Katanga (Congo Republic)', *Comparative Studies in Society and History* 11, 2 (1969), pp. 155–73.

53 Hugo F. Hinfelaar, *Bemba-Speaking Women of Zambia in a Century of Religious Change (1892–1992)* (Leiden: Brill, 1994), p. 99.

54 Robert Gary Burlington, '"I Love Mary": Relating Private Motives to Public Meanings at the Genesis of Emilio's Mutima Church', PhD Thesis, Biola University, 2004, pp. 88, 105.

55 Hinfelaar, *Bemba-Speaking Women*, p. 107.

56 Hinfelaar, *History of the Catholic Church in Zambia*, p. 184.

was anti-European and – in the 1970s – that he supported the opposition politician Simon Kapwepwe. Both the *Mutima* church and Kapwepwe's breakaway United Progressive Party (UPP) were banned by the Kaunda government in the 1970s.[57] Such rumours are reminiscent of the rivalry between the *Lumpa* Church and UNIP, demonstrating both the earthly power of Copperbelt churches and the distorting effect of attempts to disconnect its secular politics from the spiritual realm.

Mutima and *Lumpa* both accorded a special role to women. Again, women's significance in leading roles and their high number of female adherents shows that the religious was one of the few realms in which women could play a leading and 'respectable' role at the same time in a society that was shaped by a highly gendered conception of productive and reproductive labour. As noted above, economically successful women on the Copperbelt, especially unattached women, had a bad reputation. In contrast, church involvement in general and *Mutima*'s egalitarian gender concept in particular offered women the opportunity to participate in 'respectable' ways in social and political life and to occupy leading positions.

Another Catholic formation that was rooted in women's action is illustrated by the so-called *BaBuomba* groups. The agenda of *BaBuomba*, groups consisting mostly of women, was to integrate elements of Bemba royal praise song into Catholic ritual. Originally, Bemba society had rested upon a strong tradition of divine kingship. *BaBuomba* groups integrated this idea into Catholic liturgy by weaving royal praise song into it; a practice distinct to migrant workers in Southern and Central Africa as Joel Cabrita records for South Africa.[58] *Ubuomba* literally translates as 'being a royal Musician'.[59] As their approach effectively challenged orthodox Catholic liturgy, women like the *BaBuomba* initiated change in the church and sought to localise worship practices. *BaBuomba* have similarities with *Banacimbusa*, women who traditionally initiated girl children, and acted as midwives. Like the *BaBuomba*, the figure of the *Banacimbusa* was reconceptualised to serve in a new context. 'Traditional' *Banacimbusa* were replaced by or turned into chair-ladies of Catholic lay groups who served also as midwives and godmothers

57 Hinfelaar, *Bemba-Speaking Women of Zambia*, pp. 101–25.

58 Joel Cabrita, 'Politics and Preaching: Chiefly Converts to the Nazaretha Church, Obedient Subjects, and Sermon Performance in South Africa', *Journal of African History* 51, 1 (2010), pp. 21–40.

59 Kapambwe Lumbwe, 'Ubuomba: Negotiating Indigenisation of Liturgical Music in the Catholic Church in Zambia', *Journal for Transdisciplinary Research in Southern Africa* 10, 2 (2014), pp. 151–65, p. 151.

to the christened newborns.[60] Both *BaBuomba and Banacimbusa* were firmly anchored and influential in the parish structures of the Catholic Church.

The growing appeal of *BaBuomba* groups since the 1980s can be understood, aside from the Vatican II changes, as a response to the economic decline Zambia faced at that time. In a world in which people struggled to make a living, *BaBuomba* and *Banacimbusa* groups helped the women involved to feel a sense of purpose and to restore agency.

A greater threat to the Catholic Church emerged in Kitwe in the early 1990s in the form of the 'World Apostolate of Mary' (WAM). This movement considered Mary, not Christ, to be the Saviour, following this line of argument: 'Thus it is that the three persons of the holy trinity made Mary necessary unto themselves in accomplishing the redemption of fallen man. ... Mary is necessary to all mankind for their salvation. Thus we proclaim Virgin Mary as Saviour.'[61] The movement was led, among others, by a woman who claimed to have been visited and instructed by 'Our Lady Mary' during night vigils. The group criticised the 'world full of evil' in which they lived. One of their documents reads: 'Almost everybody in Zambia claims to be a Christian and yet there is so much evil as if the country has never been evangelised before.'[62]

The World Apostolate of Mary's period of popularity coincided with the neoliberal course of the Zambian Government at the time. Emerging in the copper towns, it was a movement that appealed to urban residents and their families. After a brief period of popularity for the freshly elected president Chiluba's neoliberal course, the radical economic liberalisation and privatisation of the mines led in the 1990s to the loss of more than 50% of the jobs in the mining and supply industries, leaving the mining sector devastated.[63] In that context, the 'evil' that WAM referred to, that allegedly surpassed the evil of a pre-evangelisation Zambia, can be read as a metaphor for the people's distress and their attempt to make their voices heard in a situation in which many felt powerless. As mentioned above, recent literature has linked the

60 Thera Rasing, *Passing on the Rites of Passage: Girls' Initiation Rites in the Context of an Urban Roman Catholic Community on the Zambian Copperbelt* (Aldershot: Avebury, 1995), pp. 95–8.
61 Catholic Diocesan Archives of Ndola (hereafter CDN), D4/40, Heretic Groups in Diocese, 'Virgin Mary the Saviour', n.d.
62 CDN, D4/40, Heretic Groups in Diocese, 'Letter by Mr J. G. Chikwanda, Mrs A. M. Chikwanda, Mr K. J. Mumba', n.d.
63 Miles Larmer, '"The Hour Has Come at the Pit": The Mineworkers' Union of Zambia and the Movement for Multi-Party Democracy, 1982–1991', *Journal of Southern African Studies* 32, 2 (2006), pp. 293–312, pp. 302, 331.

salience of the charismatics and the Pentecostal 'gospel of prosperity' to the economic insecurity of the neoliberal order. Like them, WAM also emerged during a time of economic hardship and promised to deal with the 'evil' of the neoliberal order in a new way. It emerged and appealed on the Copperbelt, where other movements that accorded a special role to women had flourished.

Bishop de Jong saw no alternative but excommunication for what he understood to be 'not a Catholic Apostolate, but a dangerous heresy'.[64] The movement challenged Catholic doctrine using a language of sin and corruption that recalled earlier purification movements in the region as well as the early missionary 'urban perils' narrative. This, coupled with the rise of Pentecostalism of the 1990s, explains Bishop de Jong's harsh reaction.

The exponential rise of Pentecostal churches presented a huge challenge for the mainline churches and was met by the Catholic Church with a degree of accommodation, albeit under the condition of guidance by priests. A partial Catholic embrace of the charismatic renewal movement allowed the church to tend to Catholic 'surfers' who were susceptible to the appeal of healing ministries and other churches. Charismatic prayer sessions could be integrated because they neither challenged liturgy (as *BaBuombas* did) nor doctrine (like WAM). But the church sought to appear 'Catholic enough' in other respects; the straightforward rejection of the World Apostolate was one such case, particularly because it brought back painful memories of the Catholic losses to *Lumpa* in the 1950s.

Like *Mutima* and *Lumpa* before them, WAM drew on Bemba matrilineal tradition, with a woman leader promoting the uplift of another woman, Mary, into the Holy Trinity. *Mutima*, *Lumpa*, *BaBuomba*, *Banacimbusa* and WAM were not women's movements in an exclusionist sense. Nonetheless, many of their adherents were motivated by the desire to build a counter-balance to the 'heroic culture of the mining industry'[65] that dominated the mine compounds and later the trade unions, as well as Copperbelt politics. The situation of economic decline in which miners could no longer support their families, presented at the same time, difficult as it was, the opportunity for women to engage in unconventional enterprises to support their families or to reclaim a sense of belonging.

Notably, the movements discussed were all – aside from *Lumpa* with its mixed heritage – Catholic offshoots. One reason is that the Catholic Church

---

64 CDN, D4/40, Heretic Groups in Diocese, 'Letter by Bishop de Jong to Mr J. G. Chikwanda, Mrs A. M. Chikwanda, Mr K. J. Mumba', 1996.
65 John Iliffe, *Honour in African History* (Cambridge: Cambridge University Press, 2005), p. 287.

with its Marian tradition offered a way of celebrating female success that the Protestant churches did not. Other reasons were the grassroots work of the Roman Catholics in the copper towns and the inclusive and pro-poor spirit initiated by the Franciscan friars, which had created a decentralised church. The decentralised small Christian communities made it easier for their adherents to attempt to improve and shape their church. Both *Mutima* and WAM saw themselves as deeply rooted in Catholicism, even as reformers of the Catholic Church, and never as initiatives to create a new church. But their departure from Catholic doctrine was too great to be accommodated by the bishops. However, it was the Catholic Church that lent its imageries to foster women's sense of urban belonging and their presence in liturgy, and gave a face to their aspirations. While this was not an exclusively female world and was not meant to be so, it was a world filled with strong women, a world in which elevating a woman into the Holy Trinity seemed not only possible but advisable. The Catholic Church with its Marian tradition thus attracted those who were critical of 'traditional' gendered hierarchies.

The negative discourse about urban women and their limited choices of either confinement to labour with a bad reputation or marriage drove women to seek respectable forms of public engagement. These were offered by the churches and, ironically, mostly by the most conservative force, the Roman Catholic Church. Participating in church life and community and persevering and shaping their agenda was a way to enhance female respect-ability and offered women opportunities to lay claim to build their society in a moral and practical sense.

Boundary Crossing and Healing Ministries

As elsewhere in Africa, many Copperbelt Christian converts did not use spirituality, prayer, the sacraments and scripture in the way mission-aries had envisaged. Other scholars, most prominently Walima T. Kalusa, have pointed to the creative appropriation of Christianity in Zambia in order to make claims for their own agenda. The Catholic offshoots which centred on the figure of Mary are one example, but there were also constant attempts by Christians to 'surf' between various churches, a process which continues today. The fluid nature of the migrants' spirituality was the greatest challenge from the perspective of individual churches. Moving between churches across weak denominational boundaries, what Lehmann and Taylor called the 'restlessness' and 'general indifference towards dogmatics' of Copperbelt Christians,[66] has long been the norm. It was and is not uncommon for a Copperbelt Catholic to also attend a Pentecostal service or an ecumenical procession, as well as seeking the healing ministries of other denominations outside regular mass. Many Copperbelt residents rather tend to get as many blessings as possible, while the source of the blessing is not a matter of orthodoxy.

Surfing was not a distinctly urban phenomenon, but it was more pronounced in the towns for several reasons. The infrastructure and the mixed social communities of the Copperbelt as well as mission competition have fostered such practices. Copperbelt religious flexibility characterises religious expression and worship and at the same time is manifestation of and reaction to the mobile life lived by Copperbelt urbanites.

The sensual and material aspects of the Catholic faith, represented in the sacraments, in anointing, and in blessing cars and houses, seems to be greatly cherished by many Copperbelt Christians. But sometimes believers wished to express the materiality of their faith in ways that challenged Catholic doctrine. For instance, some members of the Catholic Church challenged the privilege of ordained priests to be the sole administrators of the sacraments. They stole wine and hosts and initiated their own healing sessions, celebrating mass and anointing others.

> We had a case where they would come, steal wine and hosts and go have their own celebration in the compound. ... And then they start anointing others because they feel that, me, I have been given the gift of prayer, I can heal, so bring the oil, I can anoint you, but it's not the priest. They create a lot of confusion. Because there we also have the charismatic movement among the Protestants. ... What I see my brother who is a Protestant doing, I can do it. So we copy things from TV. They see the charismatics on TV, the Nigerians, they are praying, they are jumping and then they fall down, they heal a person, so they would like to do the same. So in that sense there can be confusion if we don't give them guidance.[67]

This example again demonstrates the paralleling of religious and political structures on the Copperbelt. Popular mass mobilisation and participation and the principle of egalitarianism, as practised in trade unions, together with the decentralised and comparatively non-elitist approach of the Franciscan friars, resulted in attempts, albeit unsuccessful, to decentre the privileged role of priests and to democratise church structures.

66 Taylor and Lehmann, *Christians of the Copperbelt*, p. 274.
67 Fr Ferena Lambe interview.

The Catholic Church was however, after the initial Pentecostal challenge, successful at targeting and reintegrating 'lost' adherents. It was easier for the church to embrace lapsed Catholics than those who, like WAM, challenged doctrine from within. They even instituted a sacramental programme for this purpose, consisting of three months' instruction and culminating in a ritual to welcome the returnees.[68] The reintegration programme shows that the Catholic clergy dealt with the less threatening forms of boundary crossing in a lax way, ready to re-embrace a lost flock and sometimes keeping a blind eye to hybrid forms of worship. In that sense, they followed the old tradition of spiritual inclusiveness established by the first African Christians on the Copperbelt and their Union Church.

Urban Belonging and Social Justice

The Catholic Church's popularity and openness created the right environment for the church's politicisation in the 1970s. It was driven by a migrant society's quest for a more egalitarian distribution of the copper wealth, a wealth that they built through their very labour. Contrary to the Pentecostal gospel of prosperity and true to their original pro-poor approach, Catholic adherents voiced egalitarian aspirations not only on a domestic inner church level but also politically. The Catholic Church began to articulate its vision of social justice for the poorer section of labourers and informal residents by the 1970s. While the literature on the politicisation of the church has focused on the clergy, European and Zambian alike, such an orientation was in fact to at least a similar degree based on and influenced by the grievances of ordinary congregants and their vision of social justice.

Several priests promoted the church's new social teaching, thus generating tension with government.[69] Bishop Denis de Jong promoted and supported protests against the eviction of squatters in the 1980s. Mission Press, run by the Franciscans since 1970 and located in Ndola, was famous for its critical stance towards a one-party state which curtailed press freedom; its editors had to endure periodic intimidation by the state. The prominent Bemba magazine *Icengelo* initially focused on evangelical issues, but practically became an anti-government paper in the 1980s after clashing with the Kaunda government first on the issue of scientific socialism, and

---

68 Ibid.
69 Joe Komakoma, *The Social Teaching of the Catholic Bishops and other Christian Leaders in Zambia: Major Pastoral Letters and Statements 1953–2001* (Ndola: Mission Press, 2003).

subsequently growing uneasy with the state's increasing authoritarianism.[70]

Mission Press also launched the popular youth magazine *Speak Out!* in 1984. Thanks to a large section of stories written by young readers and a wealth of letters to the editor, *Speak Out!* provides ample material to foreground ordinary Catholics' ideas of social justice. Aside from evangelistic themes, *Speak Out!* covered topics such as the rights of girl children and people with disabilities, sexualised violence, especially in a situation of high youth unemployment, and of course many features about 'true love', partnership and marriage. The following example takes up the familiar trope about the danger of urban women.

In a passionate letter sent by Lydia B. Chalwe, a student of Luanshya Girls' Secondary School, Lydia made a compelling case for equal education for girls. In this letter, Lydia took up and developed the earlier described debate about urban women as problems. She argued that, against the 'commonly held belief that if the wife has obtained equal educational status with the husband, she becomes pompous and disrespectful towards her husband', an older concept of the girl child existed, according to which she was highly valued. She was usually 'given more attention than the boys in the family'. Lydia's argument was that the way girl children were deprived of their rights in the current situation was a recent development, which was not in accordance with tradition. In her conclusion, she elevated the discussion to the national level, yet she did so in a nice twist; not in order to use the female body as a metaphor for the nation's collective honour, but to show the equality of men and women. She wrote: 'I would like to conclude my arguments by saying that denying girls an education deprives their future husbands, their parents and the nation as a whole of the immense contribution they can make both in the home and outside it.'[71]

The example of Lydia's letter shows that the trope of dangerous women, be they economically and sexually independent as early missionaries and tribal elders had worried, or educated and thus perceived as a threat to the hierarchy of the household, still occupied popular discussions in the late 1980s. Lydia demonstrated her fluency in the debate, challenged it and did so in a Catholic youth magazine which subscribed to the concept of equality before God. By making the argument that a woman could and wanted to make a contribution to her family, her society and her nation, she demonstrated the same aspirations that women engaged in

70 Kabombwe, 'A History of the Mission Press', pp. 4, 11, 85.
71 *Speak Out!*, September–October 1988, pp. 8–9.

BaBuomba groups or leading women in WAM or other religious movements had – she claimed to speak for herself, and to shape her own and her society's agenda. Lydia, too, was one of the Copperbelt women who claimed urban belonging by challenging the gendered hierarchy that she perceived as unjust, doing so through the channels the church provided.

Like Lydia's opinion on equal education, there were many more small contributions in *Speak Out!* that were directed towards a more just world. Taking up everyday life issues, they nonetheless concerned a broader vision of social justice that was influenced by the social teaching of the church and often transcended it. The famous clashes of the clergy with the state were the official face of the church, but they were carried by active and passionate congregants, many of them women.

Conclusion

This chapter has demonstrated that Copperbelt Christians were open to navigate and embrace spiritual messiness, instead of attempting to resolve it. Such spiritual openness is an expression of the history of the mobile Copperbelt, shaped as it was by labour migrants from various places. It was built on the earliest Christian movement on the Copperbelt, the African Union Church.

Seen from the perspective of labour migrants, doctrinal and liturgical transgressions as well as the rearrangements of elements from different traditions make perfect sense in a society that could not be united by claims to a shared rural background or autochthonous identity. Instead urban dwellers were moved by an interest in joint worship, healing ministries, social programmes and visions of social justice. Ultimately, this spiritual openness was a logical initiative by a migrant society to create a spirituality that paralleled their migration histories. While this is not a distinctly urban phenomenon, it found strong expression in the copper towns due to the heterogeneity of its residents.

The Catholic devotion to Mary provided a particularly fertile ground for women who grappled with the question of urban belonging in a society that rested on a highly gendered division of labour. By imagining and proposing a spiritual world of high-ranked women, by being active in the small Christian communities, and by voicing a vision of social justice that promoted women's rights, these women dominated and transformed the everyday practices in their parishes and lay claim to a legitimate urban identity that built upon notions of matrilineal descent and fostered support networks among women in both a spiritual and worldly sense.

Catholicism on the Zambian Copperbelt differed from the Katangese brand, and yet on both sides of the border the Roman Catholics were the most successful church. Catholic success in Katanga was not built on decentralised structures and a pro-poor orientation, but simply on a monopoly sanctioned by the state. The Belgian colonial state endorsed a paternalistic labour policy, into which the Roman Catholics were easily co-opted. In contrast, on the Zambian Copperbelt there was no state church and the relations between the churches and industry were much more distant. There, the Catholic Church attracted adherents through their comparatively egalitarian culture and the opportunity to popular participation and appropriation.

Considering publications such as *Speak Out!* and *Icengelo*, the social teaching of clergy and congregants as well as both the connections and frictions between *Mutima* and *Lumpa* alongside political opposition and activism shows that it does not make sense to disconnect the religious from politics on the Copperbelt. The spiritual and the religious do indeed form a lens through which we can glimpse a central but neglected aspect of Copperbelt society.

Select Bibliography

Ahmed, Sara, *The Cultural Politics of Emotion* (Edinburgh: Edinburgh University Press, 2014)

Akindes, Gerard, 'Football Bars: Urban Sub-Saharan Africa's Trans-local "Stadiums"', *International Journal of the History of Sport*, 28, 15 (2011), pp. 2176–90

Akindes, Gerard, and Peter Alegi, 'From Leopoldville to Liège: A Conversation with Paul Bonga Bonga', in Chuka Onwumechili and Gerard Akindes (eds), *Identity and Nation in African Football: Fans, Community and Clubs* (New York: Palgrave Macmillan, 2014), pp. 254–68

Akyeampong, Emmanuel, and Charles Ambler, 'Leisure in Africa: An Introduction', *International Journal of African Historical Studies*, 31, 1 (2002) pp. 1–16

Alegi, Peter, 'Katanga vs Johannesburg: A History of the First Sub-Saharan African Football Championship, 1949–50', *Kleio*, 3 (1999), pp. 55–74

Alegi, Peter, *African Soccerscapes: How a Continent Changed the World's Game* (Athens: Ohio University Press, 2010)

Alegi, Peter, *Laduma! Soccer, Politics, and Society in South Africa, From its Origins to 2010* (Scottsville: University of KwaZulu-Natal Press, 2010)

Ambler, Charles, 'Alcohol, Racial Segregation and Popular Politics in Northern Rhodesia', *Journal of African History*, 31, 2 (1990), pp. 295–313

Ambler, Charles, 'Popular Film and Colonial Audiences: The Movies in Northern Rhodesia', *American Historical Review*, 106 (2001), pp. 81–105

Appadurai, Arjun (ed.), *The Social Life of Things: Commodities in a Cultural Perspective* (Cambridge: Cambridge University Press, 1988)

Arrighi, Giovanni, and John S. Saul (eds), *Essays on the Political Economy of Africa* (New York: Monthly Review Press, 1973)

Arvis, Jean-François, Gaël Raballand and Jean-François Marteau, *The Cost of Being Landlocked: Logistics Costs and Supply Chain Reliability* (Washington DC: World Bank, 2010)

Arvis, Jean-François, Lauri Ojala, Christina Wiederer, Ben Shepherd, Anasuya Raj, Karlygash Dairabayeva and Tuomas Kiiski, *Connecting to Compete* (Washington DC: World Bank, 2018)

Askland, Hedda Haugen, 'A Dying Village: Mining and the Experiential Condition of Displacement', *Extractive Industries and Society*, 5, 2 (2018), pp. 230–6

Awanyo, Louis, and Emmanuel Morgan Attua, 'A Paradox of Three Decades of Neoliberal Economic Reforms in Ghana: A Tale of Economic Growth and Uneven Regional Development', *African Geographical Review*, 37, 3 (2016), pp. 173–91

Baawele, Mumbanza mwa, 'L'histoire des peuples riverains de *l'entre-Zaïre-Ubangi*: Évaluation sociale et économique, 1780–1930', PhD Thesis, UNAZA, Campus de Lubumbashi, 1981

Bair, Jennifer (ed.), *Frontiers of Commodity Chain Research* (Stanford: Stanford University Press, 2009)

Baldwin, Robert E., *Economic Development and Export Growth: A Study of Northern Rhodesia, 1920–1960* (Berkeley: University of California Press, 1966)

Bancroft, J. Austen, *Mining in Northern Rhodesia: A Chronicle of Mineral Exploration and Mining Development* (Salisbury: British South Africa Company, 1961)

Bandeira Jerónimo, Miguel, and José Pedro Monteiro (eds), *Internationalism, Imperialism and the Formation of the Contemporary World* (New York: Palgrave Macmillan, 2018)

Banjikila, Bakajika, 'Les ouvriers du Haut-Katanga pendant la Deuxième Guerre mondiale', *Revue d'histoire de la Deuxième Guerre mondiale et des conflits contemporains*, 33, 130 (1983), pp. 91–108

Banque Mondiale, *Faire de l'Enseignement supérieur le moteur du développement en Afrique subsaharienne* (Washington DC: World Bank, 2008)

Baptista, P. J., 'Explorações dos Portuguezes no Sertão da África Meridional', *Annaes Maritimos e Coloniaes* III, 5–7, 9–10 (1843)

Barth, Volker, and Roland Cvetkovky (eds), *Imperial Co-operation and Transfer, 1870–1930* (London: Bloomsbury, 2015)

Bastin, Marie-Louise, *Statuettes Tshokwe du héros civilisateur 'Tshibinda Ilunga'* (Arnouville: Arts d'Afrique Noire, 1978)

Bates, Robert H., *Markets and States in Tropical Africa: The Political Basis of Agricultural Policies* (Berkeley: University of California Press, 1981)

Bauman, Zygmunt, *Wasted Lives: Modernity and its Outcasts* (Cambridge: Polity, 2004)

Baxter, Julia, Anne-Claire Howard, Tom Mills, Sophie Rickard and Steve Macey, 'A Bumpy Road: Maximising the Value of a Resource Corridor', *Extractive Industries and Society*, 4, 3 (2017), pp. 439–42

Bayart, Jean-François, 'The Meandering of Colonial Hegemony in French-speaking West Africa', *Politique africaine*, 105, 1 (2007), pp. 201–40

Beez, Jigal, 'Stupid Hares and Margarine: Early Swahili Comics', in John A. Lent (ed.), *Cartooning in Africa* (New York: Hampton Press, 2009), pp. 137–57

Beinart, William, Karen Brown and Daniel Gilfoyle, 'Experts and Expertise in Colonial Africa Reconsidered: Science and the Interpenetration of Knowledge', *African Affairs*, 108, 432 (2009), pp. 413–33

Bennet, Brett M., and Joseph M. Hodge (ed.), *Science and Empire: Knowledge and Networks of Science across the British Empire, 1800–1970* (New York: Palgrave, 2011)

Bennett, Nathan J., Robin Roth, Sarah C. Klain, Kai M. A. Chan, Douglas A. Clark, et al., *Conservation Biology*, 31, 1 (2017), pp. 56–66

Benton, Lauren, *A Search for Sovereignty: Law and Geography in European Empires, 1400–1900* (Cambridge: Cambridge University Press, 2009)

Berger, Elena, *Labour, Race, and Colonial Rule: The Copperbelt from 1924 to Independence* (Oxford: Oxford University Press, 1974)

Bigon, Liora, 'Garden Cities in Colonial Africa: A Note on Historiography', *Planning Perspectives*, 28, 3 (2013), pp. 477–85

Bilonda, Michel Lwamba, 'L'Université de Lubumbashi, de 1956 à Nos Jours', in Isidore Ndaywel è Nziem (ed.), *Les années de l'UNAZA (Université Nationale du Zaïre): Contribution à l'histoire de l'Université Africaine* (Paris: L'Harmattan, 2018), pp. 37–57

Bisson, Michael, 'Pre-Historic Archaeology of North-Western Province, Zambia', in David S. Johnson (ed.), *North-Western Province*, Regional Handbook Series No. 8 (Lusaka: Zambia Geographical Association, 1980), pp. 53–66.

Bisson, Michael, 'Prehistoric Copper Mining in Northwestern Zambia', *Archaeology*, 27, 4 (1974), pp. 242–7

Blaszkiewicz, Hélène, 'Economie politique des circulations de marchandises transfrontalières en Afrique Australe: Les régimes de circulations dans les Copperbelts', PhD Thesis, Université Jean Moulin Lyon 3, 2019

Blaszkiewicz, Hélène, 'La formalisation inachevée des circulations commerciales africaines par les infrastructures de papier: Cas de l'industrie logistique zambienne', *Politique africaine*, 151 (2018), pp. 133–54

Blaszkiewicz, Hélène, 'La mise en politique des circulations commerciales transfrontalières en Zambie: infrastructures et moment néolibéral', *Géocarrefour*, 91, 3 (2017)

Bola n'Teto wa Mujijima, 'Authenticité zaïroise et enseignement national', *Jiwe*, 1 (1973), pp. 15–20

Bond, Mick, *From Northern Rhodesia to Zambia: Recollections of a DO/DC 1962–73* (Lusaka: Gadsden Publishers, 2014)

Bond, Wendy, 'Mporokoso, Chinsali, Bancroft, Mongu, Lusaka, Kitwe', in Tony Schur (ed.), *From the Cam to the Zambezi: Colonial Service and the Path to the New Zambia* (London and New York: Bloomsbury, 2014), pp. 195–212

Bontinck, François (ed.), *L'autobiographie de Hamed ben Mohammed el-Murjebi Tippo Tip, ca. 1840–1905* (Brussels: Académie Royale des Sciences d'Outre-Mer, 1974)

Boonen, Sofie, and Johan Lagae, 'A City Constructed by "des gens d'ailleurs": Urban Development and Migration Policies in Colonial Lubumbashi, 1910–1930', *Comparativ: Zeitschrift für Globalgeschichte und Vergleichende Gesellschaftsforschung*, 4, 25 (2015), pp. 51–69

Borges, Marcelo J., and Susana B. Torres (eds), *Company Towns: Labor, Space, and Power Relations across Time and Continents* (New York: Palgrave Macmillan, 2012)

Borowy, Iris, *Defining Sustainable Development for our Common Future: A History of the World Commission on Environment and Development (Brundtland Commission)* (London: Routledge, 2013)

Bouvier, Paule, *L'accession du Congo belge à l'indépendance: Essai d'analyse sociologique* (Brussels: Institut de Sociologie, 1965)

Boyle, Patrick, 'School Wars: Church, State, and the Death of the Congo', *The Journal of Modern African Studies*, 33, 3 (1995), pp. 451–68

Bradley, Kenneth, *Copper Venture: The Discovery and Development of Roan Antelope and Mufulira* (London: Roan Antelope Copper Mines, 1952)

Bragard, Véronique, 'Belgo-Congolese Transnational Comics Esthetics: Trans-colonial Labor from Mongo Sisse's *Bingo en Belgique* to Cassiau-Haurie and Baruti's *Madame Livingstone: Congo, la Grande Guerre* (2014)', *Literature Compass*, 13, 5 (2016), pp. 332–40

Brausch, Georges, *Belgian Administration in the Congo* (Oxford: Oxford University Press, 1961)

Brigden, J. W., *Trade and Economic Conditions in Southern Rhodesia, Northern Rhodesia and Nyasaland* (London: Department of Overseas Trade, 1933)

Brion, René, and Jean-Louis Moreau, *De la mine à Mars: La genèse d'Umicore* (Tielt: Lanoo, 2006)

Brunschwig, Henri, 'Une histoire de l'Afrique est-elle possible?' in Henri Brunschwig, *Méthodologie de l'histoire et des sciences humaines (Mélanges en l'honneur de Fernand Braudel)* (Toulouse: Privat, 1973), pp. 75–86

Bryceson, Deborah, and Danny MacKinnon, 'Eureka and Beyond: Mining's Impact on African Urbanisation', *Journal of Contemporary African Studies*, 30, 4 (2012), pp. 513–37

Bud, Guy, 'Belgian Africa at War: Europeans in the Belgian Congo and Ruanda-Urundi, 1940–1945', MPhil Thesis, University of Oxford, 2017

Bullard, Alice, 'The Critical Impact of Frantz Fanon and Henri Collomb: Race, Gender, and Personality Testing of North and West Africans', *Journal of the History of the Behavioral Sciences*, 41, 3 (2005), pp. 225–48

Burawoy, Michael, *The Colour of Class on the Copper Mines: From African Advancement to Zambianization* (Manchester: Manchester University Press, 1971)

Burdette, Marcia M., 'The Mines, Class Power and Foreign Policy in Zambia', *Journal of Southern African Studies*, 10, 2 (1984), pp. 198–218

Burlington, R. G., '"I Love Mary": Relating Private Motives to Public Meanings at the Genesis of Emilio's Mutima Church', PhD Thesis, Biola University, 2004

Butler, Larry J., *Copper Empire: Mining and the Colonial State in Northern Rhodesia, c. 1930–64* (Basingstoke: Palgrave Macmillan, 2007)

Butler, Paula, 'Colonial Walls: Psychic Strategies in Contemporary Mining-Related Displacement', *Refuge: Canada's Journal on Refugees*, 29, 2 (2014), pp. 87–99

Cabrita, Joel, 'Politics and Preaching: Chiefly Converts to the Nazaretha Church, Obedient Subjects, and Sermon Performance in South Africa', *Journal of African History*, 51, 1 (2010), pp. 21–40

Capelo, Hermenegildo and Roberto Ivens, *De Angola á contra-costa: Descripcão de uma viagem através do continente africano* (Lisbon: Impresa Nacional, 1886)

Caramento, Alexander, 'Cultivating Backward Linkages to Zambia's Copper Mines: Debating the Design of, and Obstacles to, Local Content', *Extractive Industries and Society*, 7, 2 (2020), pp. 310–20

Carbonel, Frédéric, 'Origines et Développement de l'Institut Havrais de Sociologie économique et de Psychologie des Peuples', *Les Cahiers Internationaux de Psychologie Sociale*, 77, 1 (2008), pp. 69–86

Carson, John Samuel, *The Measure of Merit: Talents, Intelligence and Inequality in the French and American Republics, 1750–1940* (Princeton: Princeton University Press, 2006)

Cassiau-Haurie, Christophe, *Histoire de la BD congolaise* (Paris: Harmattan, 2010)

Chapman, James, *British Comics: A Cultural History* (London: Reaktion Books, 2011)

Chauncey, George, Jr. 'The Locus of Reproduction: Women's Labour in the Zambian Copperbelt, 1927–1953', *Journal of Southern African Studies*, 7, 2 (1981), pp. 135–64

Cheyeka, Austin. M., 'Towards a History of the Charismatic Churches in Post-Colonial Zambia', in Jan-Bart Gewald, Marja Hinfelaar and Giacomo Macola (eds), *One Zambia, Many Histories: Towards a History of Post-Colonial Zambia* (Leiden: Brill, 2008), pp. 144–63

Chipande, Hikabwa D., 'Chipolopolo: A Social and Political History of Football (Soccer) in Zambia', PhD Thesis, Michigan State University, 2015

Chipande, Hikabwa D., 'Copper Mining and Football: Comparing the Game in the Katangese and Rhodesian Copperbelts c. 1930–1980', *Zambia Social Science Journal*, 6 (2016), pp. 28–46

Chipande, Hikabwa D., 'Introduction and Development of Competitive Football in Zambia (1930–1969): A Historical Perspective', Master's Thesis, Norwegian School of Sport Science, 2009

Chipande, Hikabwa D., 'Mining for Goals: Football and Social Change on the Zambian Copperbelt', *Radical History Review*, 125 (2016), pp. 55–73

Chipande, Hikabwa D., 'The Structural Adjustment of Football in Zambia: Politics, Decline and Dispersal, 1991–1994', *International Journal of the History of Sport*, 33, 15 (2016), pp. 1847–65

Choto, Tafadzwa, Manase Kudzai Chiweshe and Nelson Muparamoto, 'Football Fandom, Ethno-Regionalism and Rivalry in Post-colonial Zimbabwe: Case Study of Highlanders and Dynamos', *Soccer and Society*, 20, 1 (2017), pp. 153–67

Clark, P. G. D., 'Kasempa: 1901–1951', *The Northern Rhodesia Journal*, 2, 5 (1954), pp. 62–70

Clyde Mitchell, J., 'Theoretical Orientations in African Urban Studies', in Michael Banton (ed.), *The Social Anthropology of Complex Societies* (London: Routledge, 1966), pp. 37–68

Clyde Mitchell, J., *The Kalela Dance: Aspects of Social Relationships among Urban Africans in Northern Rhodesia* (Manchester: Rhodes-Livingstone Institute, 1956)

Coleman, Francis L., *The Northern Rhodesia Copperbelt, 1899–1962: Technological Development up to the End of the Central African Federation* (Manchester: University of Manchester, 1971)

Conyngham, L. D., 'African Towns in Northern Rhodesia', *Journal of African Administration*, 3 (1951), pp. 113–14

Cooper, Frederick, 'Conflict and Connection: Rethinking Colonial African History', *The American Historical Review*, 99, 5 (1994), pp. 1516–45

Cooper, Frederick, 'Development, Modernization, and the Social Sciences in the Era of Decolonization: The Examples of British and French Africa', *Revue d'histoire des sciences humaines*, 10, 1 (2004), pp. 9–38

Cooper, Frederick, *Africa Since 1940: The Past and Present* (Cambridge: Cambridge University Press, 2002)

Cooper, Frederick, and Randall M. Packard (eds), *International Development and the Social Sciences Essays on the History and Politics of Knowledge* (Berkeley: University of California Press, 1998)

Coquery-Vidrovitch, Catherine, *Le Congo au temps des grandes compagnies concessionnaires 1889–1930* (Paris: Editions de l'EHESS, 2001)

Coquery-Vidrovitch, Catherine, and Henri Moniot, *L'Afrique noire: De 1800 à nos jours* (Paris: PUF, 1974)

Cornet, Jules 'Mines de cuivre du Katanga', *Le Mouvement Geographique* 12, 1 (1895),

Cornevin, Robert, *Le Zaïre (ex-Congo-Kinshasa)* (Paris: PUF, 1972)

Cowen, Deborah, *The Deadly Life of Logistics: Mapping Violence in Global Trade* (Minneapolis: University of Minnesota Press, 2014)

Craig, John, 'Putting Privatisation into Practice: The Case of Zambia Consolidated Copper Mines Limited', *The Journal of Modern African Studies*, 39, 3 (2001), pp. 389–410

Craig, John Robert, 'State Enterprise and Privatisation in Zambia 1968–1998', PhD Thesis, University of Leeds, 1999

Crawford, Margaret, *Building the Workingman's Paradise: The Design of American Company Towns* (London: Verso, 1995)

Crehan, Kate, *The Fractured Community: Landscapes of Power and Gender in Rural Zambia* (Berkeley: University of California Press, 1997)

Cronjé, Freek, Suzanne Reyneke and Charity Chenga, 'Corporate Social Responsibility in the Zambian Mining Sector: An Overview of Three Distinctive Operational Eras', *Koers*, 82, 1 (2017), pp. 1–18

Cross, Hugh G., *To Africa with Love: A Memoir of Arthur Cross of the United Missions in the Copperbelt of Zambia* (Ottery St Mary: Cross Patch Editions, 2001)

Cunningham Bissel, William, 'Engaging Colonial Nostalgia', *Cultural Anthropology*, 20, 2 (2005), pp. 215–48

Cunnison, Ian, 'Perpetual Kinship: A Political Institution of the Luapula Peoples', *Rhodes–Livingstone Journal*, 20 (1956), pp. 28–48

Cuvelier, Jeroen, 'Men, Mines and Masculinities: The Lives and Practices of Artisanal Miners in Lwambo (Katanga Province, DR Congo)', PhD Thesis, University of Ghent, 2011

Cuvelier, Jeroen, and Philémon Muamba Mumbunda, 'Réforme douanière néolibérale, fragilité étatique et pluralisme normatif: Le cas du guichet unique à Kasumbalesa', *Politique africaine*, 129 (2013), pp. 93–112

Daniel, Philip, *Africanisation, Nationalisation and Inequality: Mining Labour and the Copperbelt in Zambian Development* (Cambridge: Cambridge University Press, 1979)

Davis, Merle J., *Modern Industry and the African: An Enquiry into the Effect of the Copper Mines of Central Africa upon Native Society and the Work of Christian Missions* (London: Macmillan, 1933)

de Craemer, Willy, *The Jamaa and the Church: A Bantu Catholic movement in Zaïre* (Oxford: Clarendon Press, 1977)

de Groof, Matthias (ed.), *Lumumba in the Arts* (Leuven: Leuven University Press, 2019).

de Hemptinne, Jean-Félix, 'Les 'Mangeurs de Cuivre' du Katanga', *Bulletin de la Societé Belge d'Études Colonials*, 1, 3 (1926), pp. 371–403 de Lacerda e Almeida, F. J. M., 'Explorações dos Portuguezes no Sertão da África Meridional', *Annaes Maritimos e Coloniaes* 4, 7–11 (1844); 5, 1–3 (1845)

de Maret, Pierre, 'Histoires de Croisettes', in Luc de Heusch (ed.), *Objets–signes d'Afrique* (Tervuren: Musée royal de l'Afrique centrale, 1995), pp. 133–45

de Maret, Pierre, 'L'évolution monetaire du Shaba Centrale entre le 7e et le 18e siecle', *African Economic History* 10 (1981), pp. 117–49

de Maret, Pierre, *Fouilles Archéologiques dans la Vallée du Haut-Lualaba, Zaïre. II: Sanga et Katongo, 1974* (Tervuren: Musée royal de l'Afrique centrale, 1985)

de Maret, Pierre, *Fouilles Archéologiques dans la vallée du Haut-Lualaba, Zaïre. III: Kamilamba, Kikulu, et Malemba Nkulu, 1975* (Tervuren: Musée royal de l'Afrique centrale, 1992)

de Pont-Jest, R., 'L'Expedition du Katanga, d'après les notes du Marquis Christian de Bonshamps', *Le Tour du Monde* (1893)

de Saint Moulin, Léon, 'L'université au Congo, hier, aujourd'hui et demain', in Isidore Ndaywel è Nziem (ed.), *Les années de l'UNAZA (Université Nationale du Zaïre): Contribution à l'histoire de l'Université Africaine* (Paris: L'Harmattan, 2018), pp. 29–36

de Schutter, Sam, '1952, Thomas Kanza komt naar Leuven', in M. Beyen, M. Boone, B. De Wever, L. Huet, B. Meijns, et al. (eds), *Wereldgeschiedenis van Vlaanderen* (Antwerp: Polis, 2018), pp. 469–75

Delisle, Philippe, *Bande dessinée franco-belge et imaginaire colonial, des années 1930 aux années 1980* (Paris: Karthala, 2008)

Demissie, Fassil, 'In the Shadow of the Gold Mines: Migrancy and Mine Housing in South Africa', *Housing Studies*, 13, 4 (1998), pp. 445–69

Depaepe, Marc, 'Belgian images of the Psycho-Pedagogical Potential of the Congolese during the Colonial Era, 1908–1960', *Paedagogica Historica*, 45, 6 (2009), pp. 707–25

Depaepe, Marc, 'Tests, Measurements, and Selection in the Belgian Congo during the 1950s: The End of Racist Clichés?' *Paedagogica Historica*, 55, 3 (2019), pp. 493–510

Devisch, René, "Pillaging Jesus": Healing Churches and the Villagisation of Kinshasa', *Africa: Journal of the International African Institute*, 66, 4 (1996), pp. 555–86

Di Spurio, Laura, 'La vulgarisation de la notion d'adolescence dans l'Europe de l'après-Seconde Guerre mondiale: échanges et circulations du savoir 'psy' entre l'espace francophone européen et l'Italie', *Amnis*, 14 (2015)

Dibwe dia Mwembu, Donatien, 'History and Memory', in John Edward Philips (ed.), *Writing African History* (Rochester NY: University of Rochester Press, 2005), pp. 439–64

Dibwe dia Mwembu, Donatien, 'L'épuration ethnique au Katanga et l'éthique du redressement des torts du passé', *Canadian Journal of African Studies*, 33, 2/3 (1999), pp. 483–99

Dibwe dia Mwembu, Donatien, 'La formation des élites coloniales: Le cas de la province du Katanga', in Nathalie Tousignant (ed.), *Le manifeste Conscience africaine (1956): Élites congolaises et société coloniale – Regards croisés* (Brussels: Publications des Facultés Universitaires Saint-Louis, 2009), pp. 117–39

Dibwe dia Mwembu, Donatien, 'La peine du fouet au Congo belge (1885–1960)', *Les Cahiers de Tunisie*, 36, 135–136 (1986), pp. 127–53

Dibwe dia Mwembu, Donatien, 'La réharmonisation des rapports entre les Katangais et les Kasaïens dans la Province du Katanga (1991–2005)', *Anthropologie et Sociétés*, 30, 1 (2006), pp. 117–34

Dibwe dia Mwembu, Donatien, 'Le rire, thérapie ultime: le théâtre populaire de Mufwankolo', in Danielle de Lame and Donatien Dibwe dia Mwembu (eds), *Tout passe: instantanés populaires et traces du passé à Lubumbashi* (Paris: L'Harmattan, 2005)

Dibwe dia Mwembu, Donatien, 'Le rôle social de l'Université de Lubumbashi', in Bogumil Jewsiewicki and Véronique Klauber (eds), *Université de Lubumbashi 1990–2002: société en détresse, pari sur l'avenir* (Paris: L'Harmattan, 2003), pp. 1–120

Dibwe dia Mwembu, Donatien, 'Les Fonctions des Femmes Africaines dans les Camps de l'Union Minière du Haut-Katanga (1925–1960)', *Zaïre-Afrique*, 272 (1993), pp. 105–18

Dibwe dia Mwembu, Donatien (ed.), *Les identités urbaines en Afrique: Le cas de Lubumbashi, R.D. Congo* (Paris: L'Harmattan, 2009)

Dibwe dia Mwembu, Donatien, and Marcel Ngandu Mutombo, *Vivre ensemble au Katanga* (Paris: L'Harmattan, 2005)

Dibwe dia Mwembu, Donatien, *Bana Shaba abandonnés par leur père: Structures de l'autorité et histoire sociale de la famille ouvrière au Katanga 1910–1997* (Paris: L'Harmattan, 2001)

Dibwe dia Mwembu, Donatien, *Faire de l'histoire orale dans une ville Africaine: La méthode Jan Vansina appliquée à Lubumbashi (R-D. Congo)* (Paris: L'Harmattan, 2008)

Dibwe dia Mwembu, Donatien, *Histoire des conditions de vie des travailleurs de l'Union minière du Haut-Katanga/Gécamines (1910–1999)* (Lubumbashi: Presses Universitaires de Lubumbashi, 2001)

Diop, Cheikh Anta, *Antériorités des civilisations nègres: Mythe ou vérité historique?* (Paris: Présence Africaine, 1967)

Dobler, Gregor, 'Umkämpfter Freiraum: Die Erfindung des Städtischen im Norden Namibias, 1950–1980', *Peripherie*, 36, 141 (2016), pp. 48–68

Dobler, Gregor, and Rita Kesselring, 'Swiss Extractivism: Switzerland's Role in Zambia's Copper Sector', *Journal of Modern African Studies*, 57, 2 (2019), pp. 223–45

Doganis, R. S., 'Zambia's Outlet to the Sea: A Case Study in Colonial Transport Development', *Journal of Transport Economics and Policy*, 1, 1 (1967), pp. 46–51

Domingos, Nuno, *Football and Colonialism: Body and Popular Culture in Urban Mozambique* (Athens: Ohio University Press, 2017)

Donaldson, John W., 'Pillars and Perspective: Demarcation of the Belgian Congo–Northern Rhodesia Boundary', *Journal of Historical Geography*, 34, 3 (2008), pp. 471–93

Doucy, Arthur, 'André Ombredane', *Bulletin des Séances de l'ARSOM*, 5, 1 (1959), pp. 159–63

Druick, Zoë, 'UNESCO, Film, and Education: Mediating Postwar Paradigms of Communication', in Charles R. Acland and Haidee Wasson (eds), *Useful Cinema* (Durham NC: Duke University Press, 2011), pp. 81–102

Dubow, Saul, *Scientific Racism in Modern South Africa* (Cambridge: Cambridge University Press, 1995)

Duga Kugbetolo, 'La responsabilité politique de l'Universitaire Zaïrois', *Jiwe*, 1 (1973), pp. 11–14

Ellis, Heather, 'Collaboration and Knowledge Exchange between Scholars in Britain and the Empire, 1830–1914', in Heike Jöns, Peter Meusburger and Michael Heffernan (eds), *Mobilities of Knowledge* (New York: Springer, 2017), pp. 141–55

Encyclopaedia Africana: Dictionary of African Biography, vol. 2 (*Sierra Leone-Zaire*) (Michigan: Reference Publications, 1979)

Englund, Harri, 'The Village in the City, the City in the Village: Migrants in Lilongwe', *Journal of Southern African Studies*, 28, 1 (2002), pp. 137–54

Enns, Charis, 'Mobilizing Research on Africa's Development Corridors', *Geoforum*, 88 (2018), pp. 105–8

Enns, Charis, and Brock Bersaglio, 'On the Coloniality of "New" Mega-Infrastructure Projects in East Africa', *Antipode*, 52, 1 (2020), pp. 101–23

Epstein, A. L., *Politics in an Urban African Community* (Manchester: Manchester University Press, 1958)

Epstein, Arnold L., *Urbanization and Kinship: The Domestic Domain on the Copperbelt of Zambia, 1950–1956* (London: Academic Press, 1981)

Evans, Alice, '"Women Can Do What Men Can Do": The Causes and Consequences of Growing Flexibility in Gender Divisions of Labour in Kitwe, Zambia', *Journal of Southern African Studies*, 40, 5 (2014), pp. 981–8

Fabian, Johannes, 'Charisma and Cultural Change: The Case of the Jamaa Movement in Katanga (Congo Republic)', *Comparative Studies in Society and History*, 11, 2 (1969), pp. 155–73

Fabian, Johannes, '*Kazi*: Conceptualizations of Labor in a Charismatic Movement among Swahili-Speaking Workers', *Cahiers d'Études africaines*, 50 (1973), pp. 293–325

Fabian, Johannes, *History from Below: The 'Vocabulary of Elisabethville' by André Yav: Text, Translations, and Interpretive Essay* (Amsterdam: John Benjamins Publishing, 1990)

Fabian, Johannes, *Jamaa: A Charismatic Movement in Katanga* (Evanston: Northwestern University Press, 1971)

Fabian, Johannes, *Language and Colonial Power: The Appropriation of Swahili in the Former Belgian Congo 1880–1938* (Cambridge: Cambridge University Press, 1986)

Fabian, Johannes, *Power and Performance: Ethnographic Explorations through Proverbial Wisdom and Theater in Shaba, Zaire* (Madison: University of Wisconsin Press, 1990)

Fabian, Johannes, *Remembering the Present: Painting and Popular History in Zaire* (Berkeley: University of California Press, 1996)

Fair, Laura, 'Kickin' It: Leisure, Politics and Football in Colonial Zanzibar, 1900s–1950s', *Africa*, 67, 2 (1997), pp. 224–51

Fair, Laura, *Pastimes and Politics: Culture, Community, and Identity in Post-colonial Zanzibar, 1890–1945* (Athens: Ohio University Press, 2001)

Ferguson, James, 'Declarations of Dependence: Labour, Personhood, and Welfare in Southern Africa', *Journal of the Royal Anthropological Institute*, 19 (2013), pp. 223–4

Ferguson, James, 'Seeing Like an Oil Company: Space, Security and Global Capital in Neoliberal Africa', *American Anthropologist*, 107, 3 (2005), pp. 377–82

Ferguson, James, *Expectations of Modernity: Myths and Meanings of Urban Life on the Zambian Copperbelt* (Berkeley: University of California Press, 1999).

Ferguson, James, *Global Shadows: Africa in the Neoliberal World Order* (Durham NC: Duke University Press, 2006)

Fetter, Bruce, 'L'Union Minière du Haut-Katanga, 1920–1940: La naissance d'une sous-culture totalitaire', *Cahiers du CEDAF*, 6 (1973), pp. 1–40

Fetter, Bruce, 'The Luluabourg Revolt at Elisabethville', *African Historical Studies*, 2, 2 (1969), pp 269–77.

Fetter, Bruce, *Colonial Rule and Regional Imbalance in Central Africa* (Boulder: Westview Press, 1983)

Fetter, Bruce, *The Creation of Elisabethville, 1910–1940* (Stanford: Hoover Institution Press, 1976)

Findlay, A., 'Kansanshi Mine', in David S. Johnson (ed.), *North-Western Province, Regional Handbook Series No. 8* (Lusaka: Zambia Geographical Association, 1980), pp. 191–200

Fletcher, Marc, 'Reinforcing Divisions and Blurring Boundaries in Johannesburg Football Fandom', in Chuka Onwumechili and Gerard Akindes (eds), *Identity and Nation in African Football: Fans, Community, and Clubs* (New York: Palgrave Macmillan, 2014), pp. 133–51

Foucault, Michel, *The Will to Knowledge* (London: Penguin, 1998)

Fraser, Alastair, 'Introduction', in Alastair Fraser and Miles Larmer (eds), *Zambia, Mining, and Neoliberalism: Boom and Bust on the Globalized Copperbelt* (New York: Palgrave Macmillan, 2010), pp. 1–30

Fraser, Alastair, and John Lungu, *For Whom the Windfalls? Winners and Losers in the Privatisation of Zambia's Copper Mines* (Lusaka: Civil Society Trade Network of Zambia, 2007)

Fraser, Alastair, and Miles Larmer (eds), *Zambia, Mining and Neoliberalism: Boom and Bust on the Globalized Copperbelt* (New York: Palgrave Macmillan, 2010)

Frederiksen, Tomas, 'Political Settlements, the Mining Industry and Corporate Social Responsibility in Developing Countries', *Extractive Industries and Society*, 6, 1 (2019), pp. 162–70

Frederiksen, Tomas, 'Unearthing Rule: Mining, Power and Political Ecology of Extraction in Colonial Zambia', PhD Thesis, University of Manchester, 2010

Fullerton, Gary, *Unesco in the Congo* (Paris: UNESCO, 1964)

Gabilliet, Jean-Paul, *Of Comics and Men: A Cultural History of American Comic Books* (Jackson: University Press of Mississippi, 2010)

Gale, William D., *The Rhodesian Press: The History of the Rhodesian Printing and Publishing Company Ltd* (Salisbury: Rhodesian Printing & Publishing Company, 1962)

Gamitto, A. C. P., *King Kazembe* 2 Vols. (Lisbon: Junta de Investigaç es do Ultramar, 1960 [1937], [1854])

Gann, Lewis H., *A History of Northern Rhodesia: Early Days to 1953* (London: Chatto & Windus, 1964)

Gardiner, John, 'Some Aspects of the Establishment of Towns in Zambia during the Nineteen Twenties and Thirties', *Zambian Urban Studies*, 3 (1970), pp. 1–33

Gérard-Libois, Jules, *Secession au Katanga* (Brussels: CRISP, 1963)

Geerkens, Eric, *La rationalisation dans l'industrie belge de l'Entre-deux-guerres* (Brussels: Palais des Académies, 2004)

Gewald, Jan-Bart, *Forged in the Great War: People, Transport, and Labour, the Establishment of Colonial Rule in Zambia, 1890–1920* (Leiden: African Studies Centre, 2015)

Gewald, Jan-Bart, and Sebastiaan Soeters, 'African Miners and Shape-Shifting Capital Flight: The Case of Luanshya/Baluba', in A. Fraser and M. Larmer (eds), *Zambia, Mining, and Neoliberalism: Boom and Bust on the Globalized Copperbelt* (New York, 2010), pp. 155–83

Gewald, Jan-Bart, Sabine Luning and Klaas van Walraven (eds), *The Speed of Change: Motor Vehicles and People in Africa, 1890–2000* (Leiden: Brill, 2009)

Gleave, M. B., 'The Dar es Salaam Transport Corridor: An Appraisal', *African Affairs*, 91, 363 (1992), pp. 249–67.

Gluckman, Max, 'Anthropological Problems arising from the African Industrial Revolution', in A. Southall (ed.), *Social Change in Modern Africa* (Oxford: Oxford University Press, 1961), pp. 67–82

Goldblatt, David, *The Ball is Round: A Global History of Football* (New York: Riverhead Books, 2008)

Gondola, Ch. Didier, *Tropical Cowboys: Westerns, Violence, and Masculinity in Kinshasa* (Bloomington: Indiana University Press, 2016)

Gordon, David M., 'Slavery and Redemption in the Catholic Missions of the Upper Congo, 1878–1909', *Slavery and Abolition*, 38, 3 (2017), pp. 577–600

Gordon, David M., 'The Abolition of the Slave Trade and the Transformation of the South-Central African Interior', *William and Mary Quarterly*, 66, 4 (2009), pp. 915–38

Gordon, David M., *Invisible Agents: Spirits in a Central African history* (Athens: Ohio University Press, 2012)

Gordon, David M., *Nachituti's Gift: Economy, Society and Environment in Central Africa* (Madison: University of Wisconsin Press, 2006)

Graça, J. R. 'Expidicão ao Muatayanvua: Diaro de Joaquim Rodrigues Graça', *Boletim da Sociedade de Geographia* 9, 8/9 (1890)

Gregson, Nicky, Mike Crang and Constantinos N. Antonopoulos, 'Holding Together Logistical Worlds: Friction, Seams and Circulation in the Emerging "Global Warehouse"', *Environment and Planning D: Society and Space*, 35, 3 (2017), pp. 381–98

Grenville-Grey, Wilfred, 'Mindolo: A Catalyst for Christian Participation in Nation Building in Africa', *International Review of Missions*, 58, 229 (1969), pp. 110–17

Grévisse, Ferdinand, *Le centre extra-coutumier d'Élisabethville: Quelques aspects de la politique indigène du Haut-Katanga industriel* (Brussels: CEPSI, 1951)

Grimstvedt, S., 'The "Swedish Settlement" in the Kasempa District', *The Northern Rhodesia Journal*, 3, 1 (1956), pp. 34–43

Guene, Enid, *Copper, Borders and Nation-Building: The Katangese Factor in Zambian Political and Economic History* (Leiden: African Studies Collection, 2017)

Guene, Enid, 'Copper's Corollaries: Trade and Labour Migration in the Copperbelt (1910–1940)', *Zambia Social Science Journal*, 4, 1 (2013)

Gupta, Pamila, *Portuguese Decolonization in the Indian Ocean World: History and Ethnography* (London: Bloomsbury, 2018)

Gupta, Pamila, 'Ruminations on Renovation in Beira (Mozambique)', *Working Papers of the Priority Programme 1448 of the German Research Foundation* (2018): www.spp1448.de.

Gupta, Sanjeev, and Yongzheng Yang, 'Unblocking Trade', *Finance and Development (International Monetary Fund)*, 43, 4 (2006), pp. 22–5

Haglund, Dan, 'In It for the Long Term? Governance and Learning among Chinese Investors in Zambia's Copper Sector', *China Quarterly*, 199 (2009), pp. 627–46.

Hannerz, Ulf, *Exploring the City: Inquiries Toward an Urban Anthropology* (New York: Columbia University Press, 1983)

Hanretta, Sean, 'Space in the Discourse on the Elisabethville Mining Camps: 1923 to 1938', in Florence Bernault (ed.), *Enfermement, prison et châtiments en Afrique: du 19e siècle à nos jours* (Paris: Karthala, 1999), pp. 305–35

Hansen, Karen Tranberg, 'Dressing Dangerously: Miniskirts, Gender Relations and Sexuality in Zambia', in Jean M. Allman (ed.), *Fashioning Africa: Power and the Politics of Dress* (Bloomington: Indiana University Press, 2004), pp. 166–85

Hansen, Karen Tranberg, *Keeping House in Lusaka* (New York: Columbia University Press, 1997)

Harkema, Roel C., 'Zambia's Changing Pattern of External Trade', *Journal of Geography*, 71, 1 (1972), pp. 19–27

Harvey, David, *Spaces of Neoliberalization: Towards a Theory of Uneven Geographical Development* (Stuttgart: F. Steiner, 2005)

Hastings, Adrian, *A History of African Christianity, 1950–1975* (Cambridge: Cambridge University Press, 1979)

Haynes, Naomi, *Moving by the Spirit: Pentecostal Social Life on the Zambian Copperbelt* (Berkeley: University of California Press, 2017)

Haynes, Naomi, '"Zambia Shall be Saved!" Prosperity Gospel Politics in a Self-Proclaimed Christian Nation', *Nova Religio*, 19, 1 (2015), pp. 5–24

Heisler, Helmuth, 'The Creation of a Stabilized Urban Society: A Turning Point in the Development of Northern Rhodesia/Zambia', *African Affairs*, 70, 279 (1971), pp. 125–45

Henderson, Ian, 'Labour and Politics in Northern Rhodesia, 1900–1953: A Study in the Limits of Colonial Power', PhD Thesis, University of Edinburgh, 1972

Herbert, Eugenia, *Red Gold of Africa: Copper in Precolonial Culture and History* (Madison: University of Wisconsin, 2003)

Heuse, George, 'Race, Racisme et Antiracisme', *Revue de Psychologie des Peuples*, 10, 4 (1955), pp. 378–81

Higginson, John, *A Working Class in the Making: Belgian Colonial Labor Policy, Private Enterprise, and the African Mineworker, 1907–1951* (Madison: University of Wisconsin Press, 1989)

Higginson, John, 'Bringing the Workers Back in: Worker Protest and Popular Intervention in Katanga, 1931–1941', *Canadian Journal of African Studies*, 22, 2 (1988), pp. 199–223

Hilson, Abigail, Gavin Hilson and Suleman Dauda, 'Corporate Social Responsibility at African Mines: Linking the Past to the Present', *Journal of Environmental Management*, 241 (2019), pp. 340–52

Hinfelaar, Hugo F., *Bemba-Speaking Women of Zambia in a Century of Religious Change (1892–1992)* (Leiden: Brill, 1994)

Hinfelaar, Hugo F., *History of the Catholic Church in Zambia* (Lusaka: Bookworld Publishers, 2004)

Hinfelaar, Marja, 'Legitimizing Powers: The Political Role of the Roman Catholic Church, 1972–1991', in Jan-Bart Gewald, Marja Hinfelaar and Giacomo Macola (eds), *One Zambia, Many Histories: Towards a History of Post-Colonial Zambia* (Leiden: Brill, 2008), pp. 129–43

Holleman, J. F., and Simon Biesheuvel, *White Mine Workers in Northern Rhodesia 1959–60* (Leiden: Afrika-Studiecentrum, 1973)

Home, Robert K., 'From Barrack Compounds to the Single-Family House: Planning Worker Housing in Colonial Natal and Northern Rhodesia', *Planning Perspectives*, 15, 4 (2000), pp. 327–47

Hönke, Jana, and Ivan Cuesta-Fernandez, 'Mobilising Security and Logistics through an African Port: A Controversies Approach to Infrastructure', *Mobilities*, 13, 2 (2018), pp. 246–60

Hughes, Matthew, 'Fighting for White Rule in Africa: The Central African Federation, Katanga, and the Congo Crisis, 1958–1965', *International History Review*, 25, 3 (2003), pp. 592–615

Hunt, Nancy Rose, 'Domesticity and Colonialism in Belgian Africa: Usumbura's Foyer Social, 1946–1960', *Signs*, 15, 3 (1990), pp. 447–74

Hunt, Nancy Rose, '"Le Bebe en Brousse": European Women, African Birth Spacing and Colonial Intervention in Breast Feeding in the Belgian Congo', *International Journal of African Historical Studies*, 21, 3 (1988), pp. 401–32

Hunt, Nancy Rose, 'Tintin and the Interruptions of Congolese Comics', in Paul Landau and Deborah S. Griffin (eds), *Images and Empires: Visuality in Colonial and Postcolonial Africa* (Berkeley: University of California Press, 2002), pp. 90–123

Hyslop, Jonathan, 'Workers Called White and Classes Called Poor: The "White Working Class" and "Poor Whites" in Southern Africa 1910–1994', in Duncan Money and Danelle van-Zyl Hermann (eds), *Rethinking White Societies in Southern Africa, 1930s–1990s* (London: Routledge, 2020), pp. 23–41

Iliffe, John, *Honour in African History* (Cambridge: Cambridge University Press, 2005)

International Labour Organisation, 'Interracial Wage Structure in Certain Parts of Africa', *International Labour Review*, 78, 1 (1958), pp. 20–55

Jacobs, Nancy, *Birders of Africa: History of a Network* (New Haven and London: Yale University Press, 2016)

Jacobson, Beth, 'The Social Identity of the Creation of a Sports Fan Identity: A Theoretical Review of the Literature', *Athletic Insight: The Online Journal of Sport Psychology*, 5, 2 (2003), pp. 1–13

Jewsiewicki, Bogumil (ed.), *A Congo Chronicle: Patrice Lumumba in Urban Art* (New York: The Museum for African Art, 1999)

Jewsiewicki, Bogumil, 'Anthropologie Marxiste et Recherche Empirique', *Cahiers d'études africaines*, 26, 101/102 (1986), pp. 265–69

Jewsiewicki, Bogumil, 'Collective Memory and Its Image: Popular Urban Painting in Zaire – A Source of "Present Past"', *History and Anthropology*, 2, 2 (1986), pp. 389–96

Jewsiewicki, Bogumil, 'Contestation sociale au Zaïre (ex–Congo belge): Grève administrative de 1920', *Africa-Tervuren*, 22, 2/3 (1976), pp. 57–67

Jewsiewicki, Bogumil, 'Corps interdits: La représentation christique de Lumumba comme rédempteur du peuple Zaïrois', *Cahiers d'Etudes africaines*, 141/2 (1996), pp. 113–42.

Jewsiewicki, Bogumil, 'Le colonat agricole européen au Congo-Belge, 1910–1960: Questions politiques et économiques', *Journal of African History*, 20, 4 (1979), pp. 559–71

Jewsiewicki, Bogumil (ed.), *Naître et mourir au Zaïre: un demi-siècle d'histoire au quotidien* (Paris: Karthala, 1993)

Jewsiewicki, Bogumil, 'Notes sur l'histoire socio-économique du Congo (1880–1960)', *Etudes d'Histoire africaine*, 3 (1972), pp. 209–41

Jewsiewicki, Bogumil, 'The Great Depression and the Making of the Colonial Economic System in the Belgian Congo', *African Economic History*, 4 (1977), pp. 153–76

Jewsiewicki, Bogumil and Jocelyn Létourneau, *Histoire en partage: Usages et mises en discours du passé* (Paris: L'Harmattan, 1996)

Jewsiewicki, Bogumil and H. Moniot, *Dialoguer avec le léopard? Pratiques, savoirs et actes du peuple face au politique en Afrique* (Paris: L'Harmattan, 1988)

Jewsiewicki, Bogumil and V.Y. Mudimbe, *History Making in Africa* (Middletown: Wesleyan University Press, 1993)

Johnson, David S., 'A Note on the Population of North-Western Province', in David S. Johnson (ed.), *North-Western Province*, Regional Handbook Series No. 8 (Lusaka: Zambia Geographical Association, 1980), pp. 73–86

Kabamba, Mbikay, 'Authenticité: condition d'un développement harmonisé', *Jiwe*, 1 (1973), pp. 23–37

Kabombwe, Y., 'A History of the Mission Press in Zambia, 1970–2011, MA Thesis, University of Zambia, 2015

Kake, Ibrahima Baba, and Elikia M'Bokolo (eds), *Histoire générale de l'Afrique* (Paris: ABC, 1977)

Kalusa, Walima T., and Megan Vaughan, *Death, Belief and Politics in Central African History* (Lusaka: Lembani Trust, 2013)

Kangwa, Jonathan, 'Christian Mission, Politics, and Socio-Economic Development: The Contribution of Mindolo Ecumenical Foundation', *International Review of Mission*, 106, 1 (2017), pp. 167–87

Kanza, Thomas, *Propos d'un Congolais naïf: discours sur la vocation coloniale dans l'Afrique de demain* (Bruxelles: Les Amis de Présence africaine, 1959)

Kaoze, Stefano, 'La psychologie des Bantu', in Maurice Amuri Mpala-Lutebele and Jean-Claude Kangomba (eds), *Stefano Kaoze: Œuvre complète* (Bruxelles, 2018 [1911]), pp. 53–95

Kapesa, Robby, and Thomas McNamara, '"We Are Not Just a Union, We Are a Family": Class, Kinship and Tribe in Zambia's Mining Unions', *Dialectical Anthropology*, 44, 2 (2020), pp. 153–72

Kapesa, Robby, Jacob Mwitwa and D. C. Chikumbi, 'Social Conflict in the Context of Development of New Mining in Zambia', *Southern African Peace and Security Studies*, 4, 2 (2014), pp. 41–62

Kasongo, B. A., and A. G. Tipple, 'An Analysis of Policy towards Squatters in Kitwe, Zambia', *Third World Planning Review*, 12, 2 (1990), pp. 147–65

Katzenellenbogen, S. E., *Railways and the Copper Mines of Katanga* (Oxford: Clarendon Press, 1973)

Katzenellenbogen, Simon, 'The Miner's Frontier, Transport and General Economic Development', in Peter Duignan and L. H. Gann (eds), *Colonialism in Africa 1870–1960*, vol. 4, *The Economics of Colonialism* (Cambridge: Cambridge University Press, 1975), pp. 360–426

Kennes, Erik, and Miles Larmer, *The Katangese Gendarmes and War in Central Africa: Fighting Their Way Home* (Bloomington: Indiana University Press, 2016)

Kent, John, *The Internationalization of Colonialism: Britain, France and Black Africa, 1939–1956* (Oxford: Oxford University Press, 1992)

Kesselring, Rita, 'At an Extractive Pace: Conflicting Temporalities in a Resettlement Process in Solwezi, Zambia', *Extractive Industries and Society*, 5, 2 (2018), pp. 237–44

Kesselring, Rita, 'The Electricity Crisis in Zambia: Blackouts and Social Stratification in New Mining Towns', *Energy Research and Social Science*, 30 (2017), pp. 94–102

Kesselring, Rita, 'The Local State in a New Mining Area in Zambia's North-Western Province', in Jon Schubert, Ulf Engel and Elisio Macamo (eds), *Extractive Industries and Changing State Dynamics in Africa: Beyond the Resource Curse* (London: Routledge, 2018), pp. 129–47

Kikuni, Tenda, 'Préjugés à dépister dans les manuels d'histoire du cycle d'orientation', *Likundoli: Histoire et devenir*, 4, 1–2 (1979), pp. 58–69

Kilanga Musinde, Julien, *La main de la tradition: l'homme, le destin, l'université* (Lubumbashi: CIRIADA, 2000)

King, A. D., 'Exporting Planning: The Colonial and Neo-Colonial Experience', in Gordon E. Cherry (ed.), *Shaping an Urban World* (New York: St Martin's Press, 1980), pp. 203–26

Ki-Zerbo, Joseph, *Histoire de l'Afrique noire: D'hier à demain* (Paris: Hatier, 1972)

Knigge, Andreas C., *Vom Massenblatt ins multimedia Abenteuer* (Hamburg: Rowohlt, 1996)

Koli, Elombe Motukoa, 'Le portrait de l'intellectuel zaïrois', *Jiwe*, 1 (1973), pp. 3–10

Komakoma, Joe, *The Social Teaching of the Catholic Bishops and other Christian Leaders in Zambia: Major Pastoral Letters and Statements 1953–2001* (Ndola: Mission Press, 2003)

Koorts, Lindie, *DF Malan and the Rise of Afrikaner Nationalism* (Cape Town: Tafelberg, 2014)

Kriger, Coleen E., *Pride of Men: Ironworking in Nineteenth-Century West-Central Africa* (Portsmouth NH: Heinemann, 1999)

Kuczynski, Robert, *Demographic Survey of the British Colonial Empire* vol. II (London: Oxford University Press, 1949)

Kudzai Chiweshe, Manase, 'Online Football Fan Identities and Cyber-fandoms in Zimbabwe', in Chuka Onwumechili and Gerard Akindes (eds), *Identity and Nation in African Football: Fans, Community, and Clubs* (New York: Palgrave Macmillan, 2014), pp. 236–53

Kudzai Chiweshe, Manase, 'Till Death do us Part: Football as Part of Everyday Life amongst Dynamos Football Club Fans in Zimbabwe', *African Identities*, 14, 2 (2016), pp. 101–13

Lagae, Johan, 'From "Patrimoine Partagé" to "Whose Heritage"? Critical reflections on colonial built heritage in the city of Lubumbashi, Democratic Republic of the Congo', *Afrika Focus*, 21, 1 (2008), pp. 11–30

Larkin, Brian, *Signal and Noise: Media, Infrastructure, and Urban Culture in Nigeria* (Durham NC: Duke University Press, 2008)

Larmer, Miles, 'At the Crossroads: Mining and Political Change on the Katangese–Zambian Copperbelt', *Oxford Handbooks Online* (2016), DOI: 10.1093/oxfordhb/9780199935369.013.20.

Larmer, Miles, 'Historical Perspectives on Zambia's Mining Booms and Busts', in Alistair Fraser and Miles Larmer (eds), *Zambia, Mining, and Neoliberalism: Boom and Bust on the Globalized Copperbelt* (New York: Palgrave Macmillan, 2010), pp. 31–58

Larmer, Miles, *Mineworkers in Zambia: Labour and Political Change in Post-Colonial Zambia* (London: I.B. Tauris, 2007)

Larmer, Miles, 'Permanent Precarity: Capital and Labour in the Central African Copperbelt', *Labor History*, 58, 2 (2017), pp. 170–84.

Larmer, Miles, 'Reaction and Resistance to Neo-liberalism in Zambia', *Review of African Political Economy*, 32, 103 (2005), pp. 29–45

Larmer, Miles, *Rethinking African Politics: A History of Opposition in Zambia* (Farnham: Ashgate, 2011)

Larmer, Miles, '"The Hour Has Come at the Pit": The Mineworkers' Union of Zambia and the Movement for Multi-Party Democracy, 1982–1991', *Journal of Southern African Studies*, 32, 2 (2006), pp. 293–312

Larmer, Miles, and Giacomo Macola, 'The Origins, Context, and Political Significance of the Mushala Rebellion Against the Zambian One-Party State', *International Journal of African Historical Studies*, 40, 3 (2007), pp. 471–96

Laude, Norbert, 'Hommage à A. Ombredane et E. Dory', *Bulletin des Séances de l'ARSOM*, 4, 6 (1958), pp. 1163–5

Lauro, Amandine, 'Maintenir l'ordre dans la colonie-modèle: Notes sur les désordres urbains et la police des frontières raciales au Congo Belge (1918–1945)', *Crime, Histoire & Sociétés*, 15, 2 (2011), pp. 97–121

Lauro, Amandine, '"To our Colonial Troops, Greetings from the Far-away Homeland": Race, Security and (Inter-)Imperial Anxieties in the Discussion on Colonial Troops in World War One Belgium', *Journal of Belgian History*, 48, 1/2 (2018), pp. 34–55

Le Lay, Maëline, *La parole construit le pays: théâtre, langues et didactisme au katanga* (Paris: Editions Honoré Champion, 2014)

Le Marinel, P., *Carnets de route dans l'Etat Indépendant du Congo de 1887 à 1910* (Brussels: Progress, 1991)

LeCain, Timothy J., *The Matter of History: How Things Create the Past* (Cambridge: Cambridge University Press, 2017)

Legouis, Jacques, 'The Problem of European Settlement in the Belgian Congo', *International Labour Review*, 34, 4 (1936), pp. 483–9

Legros, Hugues, *Chasseurs d'ivoire: Une histoire du royaume yeke du Shaba (Zaïre)* (Brussels: Editions de l'Université Libre de Bruxelles, 1996)

Lent, John A., 'Southern Africa: Hardly A Cartoonist's Eden', in John A. Lent (ed.), *Cartooning in Africa* (New York: Hampton Press, 2009), pp. 219–46

Libby, R. T., and M. E. Woakes, 'Nationalization and the Displacement of Development Policy in Zambia', *African Studies Review*, 23, 1 (1980), pp. 33–50

Lindsay, Lisa A., 'Biography in African History', *History in Africa*, 44 (2017), pp. 11–26

Linstrum, Erik, *Ruling Minds: Psychology in the British Empire* (Cambridge MA: Harvard University Press, 2016)

Linstrum, Erik, 'The Politics of Psychology in the British Empire, 1898–1960', *Past and Present*, 215 (2012), pp. 195–233

Lobet, Emile, 'L'Orientation professionnelle au Congo belge et au Ruanda-Urundi', *Bulletin des Séances de l'ARSOM*, 3, 4 (1957), pp. 800–16

Loffman, Reuben, *Church, State and Colonialism in Southeastern Congo, 1890–1962* (New York: Palgrave Macmillan, 2019)

Low, D. A., and J. M. Lonsdale, 'Introduction: Towards the New Order, 1945–63', in D. A. Low and Alison Smith (eds), *History of East Africa* vol. 3 (Oxford: Clarendon Press, 1976)

Lumbwe, Kapambwe, 'Ubuomba: Negotiating Indigenisation of Liturgical Music in the Catholic Church in Zambia', *Journal for Transdisciplinary Research in Southern Africa*, 10, 2 (2014), pp. 151–65

Lungu, John, 'Copper Mining Agreements in Zambia: Renegotiation or Law Reform?' *Review of African Political Economy*, 35, 117 (2008), pp. 403–15

Lungu, John, 'Socio-Economic change and Natural Resource Exploitation: A Case Study of the Zambian Copper Mining Industry', *Development Southern Africa*, 25, 5 (2008), pp. 543–60

Lunn, Jon, 'The Political Economy of Primary Railway Construction in the Rhodesias, 1890–1911', *The Journal of African History*, 33, 2 (1992), pp. 239–54

Macmillan, Hugh, 'Mining, Housing and Welfare in South Africa and Zambia: An Historical Perspective', *Journal of Contemporary African Studies*, 30, 4 (2012), pp. 539–50

Macmillan, Hugh, 'The Historiography of Transition on the Zambian Copperbelt: Another View', *Journal of Southern African Studies*, 19, 4 (1993), pp. 681–712

Macmillan, Hugh, and Frank Shapiro, *Zion in Africa: The Jews of Zambia* (London: I.B. Tauris, 1999)

Macola, Giacomo, 'Imagining Village Life in Zambian Fiction', *Cambridge Anthropology*, 25, 1 (2005), pp. 1–10

Macola, Giacomo, *The Kingdom of Kazembe: History and Politics in North-Eastern Zambia and Katanga to 1950* (Hamburg: LIT, 2002)

Macola, Giacomo, *The Gun in Central Africa* (Athens: Ohio University Press, 2016)

Maimbolwa, M. M., 'Urban Growth in North-Western Province', in David S. Johnson (ed.), *North-Western Province*, Regional Handbook Series No. 8 (Lusaka: Zambia Geographical Association, 1980), pp. 175–90

Maistriaux, Robert, 'La sous-évolution des Noirs d'Afrique: sa nature, ses causes, ses remèdes', *Revue de Psychologie des Peuples*, 10 (1955), pp. 397–455

Maistriaux, Robert, *L'Étude des Caractères* (Tournai and Paris: Casterman, 1949)

Maistriaux, Robert, *L'Intelligence Noire et son Destin* (Brussels: Éditions de Problèmes d'Afrique centrale, 1957)

Makondo, Cuthbert C., Sydney Sichilima, Matthews Silondwa, Richard Sikazwe, Lombe Maiba, et al., 'Environmental Management Compliance, Law and Policy Regimes in Developing Countries: A Review of the Zambian Case', *International Journal of Environmental Protection and Policy*, 3, 4 (2015), pp. 79–87

Makori, Timothy, 'Abjects retraité, jeunesse piégée: Récits du déclin et d'une temporalité multiple parmi les générations de la "Copperbelt" congolaise', *Politique africaine*, 3, 131 (2013), pp. 51–73

Malambo Kabombwe, Yvonne, 'A History of the Mission Press in Zambia, 1970–2011', Master's Dissertation, University of Zambia, 2015

Mangan, J. A., *The Games Ethic and Imperialism: Aspects of the Diffusion of an Ideal* (New York: Viking, 1985)

Mantels, Ruben, *Geleerd in de tropen: Leuven, Congo & de wetenschap, 1885–1960* (Leuven: Leuven University Press, 2007)

Marchal, R., 'Renseignements historiques relatifs à l'exploitation des cuivre par les indigènes de la région de Luishia', *Bulletin des juridictions indigènes et du droit coutumier congolais* (1936), p. 10.

Martens, George, 'Congolese Trade Unionism: The Colonial Heritage', *Brood en Rozen*, 4, 2 (1999), pp. 128–49

Martin, Phyllis, *Leisure and Society in Colonial Brazzaville* (Cambridge: Cambridge University Press, 1995)

Massin, Veerle, 'Measuring Deliquency: The Observation, Scientific, Assessment and Testing of Delinquent Girls in 20th-century Belgium', *Journal of Belgian History*, 46, 1 (2016), pp. 105–33

Matasci, Damiano, 'Assessing Needs, Fostering Development: UNESCO, Illiteracy and the Global Politics of Education (1945–1960)', *Comparative Education*, 53, 1 (2017), pp. 35–53

Matasci, Damiano, 'Une "UNESCO africaine"? Le ministère de la France d'Outre-mer, la coopération éducative intercoloniale et la défense de l'Empire, 1947–1957', *Monde(s)*, 13, 1 (2018), pp. 195–21

Matitu, Mbaraka, 'Women and the Retailing of Secondhand Clothing in Urban Zambia: A Case Study of Kyawama Market, Solwezi', MA Thesis, University of Basel, 2018

Matongo, Albert B. K., 'Popular Culture in a Colonial Society: Another Look at Mbeni and Kalela Dances on the Copperbelt', in Samuel N. Chipungu (ed.), *Guardians in Their Time: Experiences of Zambians Under Colonial Rule, 1890–1964* (London and New York: Macmillan, 1992), pp. 180–217

Maupeu, Hervé, 'Les réformes néolibérales des universités est-africaines: éléments d'analyses à partir du cas kényan', in Nicodème Bugwabari, Alain Cazenave-Piarrot, Olivier Provini and Christian Thibon (eds), *Universités et universitaires en Afrique de l'Est* (Paris: Karthala, 2012), pp. 195–211

Maurel, Chloé, 'L'UNESCO de 1945 à 1974', PhD in History, Panthéon-Sorbonne – Paris I, 2006

Maxwell, David, '"Delivered from the Spirit of Poverty?" Pentecostalism, Prosperity and Modernity in Zimbabwe', *Journal of Religion in Africa*, 28, 3 (1998), pp. 350–73

Maxwell, David, 'The Creation of Lubaland: Missionary Science and Christian Literacy in the Making of the Luba Katanga in Belgian Congo', *Journal of Eastern African Studies*, 10, 3 (2016), pp. 367–92

Maxwell, James, 'Some Aspects of Native Policy in Northern Rhodesia', *Journal of the Royal African Society*, 29, 117 (1930), pp. 471–7

Médard, Henri, 'Histoire populaire et histoire scientifique en Ouganda (1890–2009)', in Nicodème Bugwabari, Alain Cazenave-Piarrot, Olivier Provini and Christian Thibon (eds), *Universités et universitaires en Afrique de l'Est* (Paris: Karthala, 2012), p. 99–114

Meebelo, Henry S., *African Proletarians and Colonial Capitalism: The Origins, Growth and Struggles of the Zambian Labour Movement to 1964* (Lusaka: Kenneth Kaunda Foundation, 1986)

Meessen, Vincent, *Patterns of (Re)cognition* (Brussels: BOZAR Books, Snoek Publishers, 2017)

Melland, Frank H., *In Witch-Bound Africa: An Account of the Primitive Kaonde Tribe and Their Beliefs* (New York: Barnes & Noble, 1967)

Mertens, Myriam, and Guillaume Lachenal, 'The History of "Belgian" Tropical Medicine from a Cross-Border Perspective', *Revue Belge de Philologie et d'Histoire*, 90, 4 (2012), pp. 1249–71

Missine, Leo, *L'Institut Facultaire de Psychologie et de Pédagogie: Son organisation et ses recherches* (Léopoldville: Université de Lovanium, 1968)

Missine, Leo, 'Lovanium University (Congo-Kinshasa) Department of Psychology and Education', *New Africa* (January/February 1967), pp. 18–19

Money, Duncan, 'Race and Class in the Postwar World: The Southern Africa Labour Congress', *International Labor and Working-Class History*, 94 (2018), pp. 133–55

Money, Duncan, 'The World of European Labour on the Northern Rhodesian Copperbelt, 1940–1945', *International Review of Social History*, 60, 2 (2015), pp. 225–55

Montal, F., *Récits de Vie et Mémoires: vers une anthropologie historique du souvenir* (Paris: L'Harmattan, 1987)

Moore, Henrietta, and Megan Vaughan, *Cutting Down Trees: Gender, Nutrition, and Agricultural Change in the Northern Province of Zambia, 1890–1990* (London: Heinemann, 1993)

Moore, Reginald, and A. Sandilands, *These African Copper Mines: A Study of the Industrial Revolution in Northern Rhodesia, With Principal Reference to the Copper Mining Industry* (London: Livingstone Press, 1948)

Morrow, Sean, '"On the Side of the Robbed": R. J. B. Moore, Missionary on the Copperbelt, 1933–1941', *Journal of Religion in Africa*, 19, 3 (1989), pp. 244–63

Mottoulle, Leopold, 'Medical Aspects of the Protection of Indigenous Workers in Colonies', *International Labour Review*, 41, 4 (1940), pp. 361–70

Motoulle, L., *Politique sociale de l'Union Minière du Haut-Katanga pour sa main-d'œuvre indigène et ses résultats au cours de vingt années d'application* (Brussels: Institut Royal Colonial Belge, 1946)

M'Passou, Denis, *Mindolo: A Story of the Ecumenical Movement in Africa* (Lusaka: Baptist Printing Ministry, 1983)

Mudimbe, Valentin-Yves, 'Et Si Nous Renvoyions à l'Analyse le Concept d'Art Populaire', in Bogumil Jewsiewicki (ed.), *Art Pictural Zaïrois* (Quebec: Septentrion, 1992), pp. 25–8

Mujinga Kimpesa, Mbuyu, 'L'Opération de l'UNESCO au Congo-Léopoldville et le Diagnostic des Réalités Éducatives Congolaises: 1960–64', PhD Thesis, University of Geneva, 1983

Mulenga, Chipasha, 'Judicial Mandate in Safeguarding Environmental Rights from the Adverse Effects of Mining Activities in Zambia', *Potchefstroomse Elektroniese Regsblad*, 22, 1 (2019)

Musambachime, Mwelwa C, *Wealth from the Rocks: Mining and Smelting of Metals in Pre-Colonial Zambia* (Bloomington: Xlibris Corporation, 2016)

Musambachime, Mwelwa C., 'The Ubutwa Society in Eastern Shaba and Northeast Zambia to 1920', *International Journal of African Historical Studies*, 27, 1 (1994), pp. 77–99

Mususa, Patience N., 'There Used to Be Order: Life on the Copperbelt after the Privatisation of the Zambia Consolidated Copper Mines', PhD Thesis, University of Cape Town, 2014

Mususa, Patience, '"Getting By": Life on the Copperbelt after the Privatisation of the Zambia Consolidated Copper Mines', *Social Dynamics*, 36, 2 (2010), pp. 380–94

Mususa, Patience, 'Contesting Illegality: Women in the Informal Copper Business', in Alistair Fraser and Miles Larmer (eds), *Zambia, Mining, and Neoliberalism: Boom and Bust on the Globalized Copperbelt* (New York: Palgrave Macmillan, 2010), pp. 185–208

Mususa, Patience, 'Mining, Welfare and Urbanisation: The Wavering Urban Character of Zambia's Copperbelt', *Journal of Contemporary African Studies*, 30, 4 (2012), pp. 571–87

Mususa, Patience, 'Topping Up: Life Amidst Hardship and Death on the Copperbelt', *African Studies*, 71, 2 (2012), pp. 304–22

Mutale, Emmanuel, *The Management of Urban Development in Zambia* (Burlington: Ashgate, 2004).

Mwabila Malela, Augustin, *Travail et travailleurs au Zaïre: Essai sur la conscience ouvrière du proletariat urbain de Lubumbashi* (Kinshasa: Presses universitaires du Zaïre, 1979)

Myers, Garth, *African Cities: Alternative Visions of Urban Theory and Practice* (London: Zed Books, 2011)

Ndaywel è Nziem, Isidore, 'De Lovanium au campus de Lubumbashi: Production d'une modernité culturelle congolaise', in Isidore Ndaywel è Nziem (ed.),

Les années de l'UNAZA (Université Nationale du Zaïre): Contribution à l'histoire de l'Université africaine (Paris: L'Harmattan, 2018).

Ndaywel è Nziem, Isidore, *Histoire générale du Congo: De l'héritage ancien à la République démocratique du Congo* (Paris: Duculot, 1998)

Ndaywel è Nziem, Isidore, *Nouvelle Histoire du Congo: Des origines à la République démocratique* (Brussels: Le Cri, 2012)

Ndaywel è Nziem, Isidore, 'Programme de formation des historiens africains en faculté des lettres (1963–1976)', *Likundoli: Histoire et devenir*, 1, 4 (1976), pp. 1–56

Ndulo, Muna, 'Mining Legislation and Mineral Development in Zambia', *Cornell International Law Journal*, 19, 1 (1986), pp. 1–35

Negi, Rohit, '"You Cannot make a Camel Drink Water": Capital, Geo-History and Contestations in the Zambian Copperbelt', *Geoforum*, 45 (2013), pp. 240–47

Negi, Rohit, '"Solwezi Mabanga": Ambivalent Developments on Zambia's New Mining Frontier', *Journal of Southern African Studies*, 40, 5 (2014), pp. 999–1013

Negi, Rohit, 'The Mining Boom, Capital and Chiefs in the "New Copperbelt"', in Alastair Fraser and Miles Larmer (eds), *Zambia, Mining, and Neoliberalism: Boom and Bust on the Globalized Copperbelt* (New York: Palgrave Macmillan, 2010), pp. 209–36

Nenquin, Jacques. *Excavations at Sanga, 1957: The Protohistoric Necropolis* (Tervuren: RMCA, 1963)

Ngoma, Binda, 'Faut-il privatiser les universités officielles du Zaïre?', *Zaïre-Afrique*, 288 (1994), pp. 495–505

Niane, Djibril Tamsir, *Soundjata ou l'épopée mandingue* (Paris: Présence Africaine, 1960)

Nikis, Nicolas, and Alexandre L. Smith, 'Copper, Trade and Polities: Exchange Networks in Southern Central Africa in the 2nd Millenium CE', *Journal of Southern African Studies*, 43, 5 (2017), pp. 895–911

Njoh, Ambe J., 'Urban Planning as a Tool of Power and Socio-Political Control in Colonial Africa', *Planning Perspectives*, 24, 3 (2009), pp. 301–17

O'Callaghan, Margaret, *Copperfields: A History of the Impact of the First Decade of a Mining Boom in North Western Province, Zambia, circa 2002–2015* (Canberra: privately published, 2019)

Obenga, Théophile, *L'Afrique sans l'Antiquité: Egypte pharaonique, Afrique noire* (Paris: Présence Africaine, 1973)

Omasombo, Jean (ed.), *Haut-Katanga: Lorsque richesses économiques et pouvoirs politiques forcent une identité régionale*, Monographies des provinces de la RD Congo, Tome 1 (Tervuren: Royal Museum of Central Africa, 2018)

Ombredane, André, 'Les techniques de fortune dans le travail coutumier des Noirs', *Présence Africaine*, 13, 1 (1952), pp. 58–68

Ombredane, André, 'Principes pour une étude psychologique des Noirs du Congo belge', *L'Année Psychologique*, 50 (1949), pp. 521–47

Ombredane, André, and Aurélien Sauvageot, *Mensonges du racisme* (Paris: Civilisation Nouvelle, 1939)

Onwumechili, Chuka, 'Nigeria, Football, and the Return of Lord Lugard', *International Journal of Sport Communication*, 2, 4 (2009), pp. 451–65

Onwumechili, Chuka, and Gerard Akindes, *Identity and Nation in African Football: Fans, Community, and Clubs* (New York: Palgrave Macmillan, 2014)

Orenstein, Dara, 'Foreign-Trade Zones and the Cultural Logic of Frictionless Production', *Radical History Review*, 109 (2011), pp. 36–61

Orenstein, Dara, 'Warehouses on Wheels', *Environment and Planning D: Society and Space*, 36, 4 (2018), pp. 648–65

O'Shea, Michael, *Missionaries and Miners: A History of the Beginnings of the Catholic Church in Zambia with Particular Reference to the Copperbelt* (Ndola: Mission Press, 1986)

Ougaard, Morten, 'The Transnational State and the Infrastructure Push', *New Political Economy*, 23, 1 (2018), pp. 128–44

Ouma, Stefan, and Julian Stenmanns, 'The New Zones of Circulation: On the Production and Securitisation of Maritime Frontiers in West Africa', in Thomas Birtchnell, Satya Savitzky and John Urry (eds), *Cargomobilities: Moving Materials in a Global Age* (London: Routledge, 2015), pp. 87–106

Pannenborg Arnold, *Big Men Playing Football: Money, Politics and Foul Play in the African Game* (Leiden: African Studies Centre, 2012)

Parpart, Jane L., '"Where Is Your Mother?" Gender, Urban Marriage, and Colonial Discourse on the Zambian Copperbelt, 1924–1945', *The International Journal of African Historical Studies*, 27, 2 (1994), pp. 241–71

Parpart, Jane L., 'Sexuality and Power on the Zambian Copperbelt, 1926–1964', in S. B. Stichter (ed.), *Patriarchy and Class: African Women in the Home and the Workforce*, African Modernization and Development Series (Boulder: Westview Press, 1988), pp. 115–38

Parpart, Jane L., 'The Household and the Mine Shaft: Gender and Class Struggles on the Zambian Copperbelt, 1926–1964', *Journal of Southern African Studies*, 2, 1 (1986), pp. 36–56

Parpart, Jane L., *Labor and Capital on the African Copperbelt* (Philadelphia: Temple University Press, 1983)

Pearson-Patel, Jessica, 'Promoting Health, Protecting Empire: Inter-Colonial Medical Cooperation in Postwar Africa', *Monde(s)*, 7, 1 (2015), pp. 213–30

Peemans, Jean-Philippe, 'Capital Accumulation in the Congo under Colonialism: The Role of the State', in P. Duignan and L. H. Gann (eds), *Colonialism in Africa*, vol. 5, *The Economics of Colonialism, 1870–1960* (Cambridge: Cambridge University Press, 1975), pp. 165–212

Perrings, Charles, *Black Mineworkers in Central Africa: Industrial Strategies and the Evolution of an African Proletariat in the Copperbelt, 1911–41* (London: Heinemann, 1979)

Peša, Iva, 'Crops and Copper: Agriculture and Urbanism on the Central African Copperbelt, 1950–2000', *Journal of Southern African Studies*, 46, 3 (2020), pp. 527–45

Peša, Iva, 'From Life Histories to Social History: Narrating Social Change through Multiple Biographies', in Klaas van Walraven (ed.), *The Individual in African History: The Importance of Biography in African Historical Studies* (Leiden: Brill, 2020), pp. 89–113

Peša, Iva, 'Mining, Waste and Environmental Thought on the Central African Copperbelt, 1950–2000', *Environment and History* (2020)

Peša, Iva, *Roads through Mwinilunga: A History of Social change in Northwest Zambia* (Leiden: Brill, 2019)

Petit, Pierre, *Patrice Lumumba: La fabrication d'un héros national et panafricain* (Brussels: Editions de l'Académie, 2016)

Phimister, Ian, 'Proletarians in Paradise: The Historiography and Historical Sociology of White Miners on the Copperbelt', in Jan-Bart Gewald, Marja Hinfelaar and Giacomo Macola (eds), *Living the End of Empire: Politics and Society in Late Colonial Zambia* (Leiden: Brill, 2011), pp. 139–60

Phiri, Felix J., 'Islam in Post-Colonial Zambia', in Jan-Bart Gewald, Marja Hinfelaar and Giacomo Macola (eds), *One Zambia, Many Histories: Towards a History of Post-Colonial Zambia* (Leiden: Brill, 2008), pp. 164–84

Pinto, F. J., 'Explorações dos Portuguezes no Sertão da África Meridional', *Annaes Maritimos e Coloniaes*, 5, 4, 5, 7, 9, 10, 11, 12 (1845)

Pogge, Paul, *Im Reiche des Muata Jamwo* (Berlin: Verlag von Dietrich Reimer, 1880)

Polanyi, Karl, *The Great Transformation: The Political and Economic Origins of Our Time* (Boston MA: Beacon Press, 2001)

Poncelet, Marc, 'Sciences sociales, colonisation et développement, une histoire sociale du siècle d'africanisme belge', PhD Thesis, University of Lille I, 1996

Poncelet, Marc, *L'invention des sciences coloniales belges* (Paris: Karthala, 2008)

Post, Harry, *Pillarization: An Analysis of Dutch and Belgian Society* (Avebury: Gower, 1989)

Pottier, Johan, *Migrants No More: Settlement and Survival in Mambwe District, Zambia* (Manchester: Manchester University Press, 1988).

Potts, Deborah, 'Counter-Urbanization on the Zambian Copperbelt? Interpretations and Implications', *Urban Studies*, 42, 4 (2005), pp. 583–609

Potts, Deborah, 'Debates About African Urbanisation, Migration and Economic Growth: What Can We Learn from Zimbabwe and Zambia?' *Geographical Journal*, 182, 3 (2016), pp. 251–64

Powdermaker, Hortense, *Copper Town: Changing Africa – The Human Situation on the Rhodesian Copperbelt* (New York: Harper & Row, 1962)

Prunier, Gérard, *Africa's World War: Congo, the Rwandan Genocide, and the Making of a Continental Catastrophe* (New York: Oxford University Press, 2011).

Pugliese, Francesca, 'Mining Companies and Gender(ed) Policies: The Women of the Congolese Copperbelt, Past and Present', *Extractive Industries and Society* (2020), https://doi.org/10.1016/j.exis.2020.08.006

Radman, Wolf, 'The Nationalization of Zaire's Copper: From Union Minière to GÉCAMINES', *Africa Today*, 25, 4 (1978), pp. 25–47

Rakner, Lise, *Political and Economic Liberalisation in Zambia, 1991–2001* (Uppsala: Nordic Africa Institute, 2003)

Ramirez, Francis, and Christian Rolot, *Histoire du Cinéma Colonial au Zaïre, au Rwanda et au Burundi* (Tervuren: RMCA, 1985)

Rasing, Thera, *Passing on the Rites of Passage: Girls' Initiation Rites in the Context of an Urban Roman Catholic Community on the Zambian Copperbelt* (Aldershot: Avebury, 1995)

Reid, Richard J., *Warfare in African History* (Cambridge: Cambridge University Press, 2012)

Rights and Accountability in Development (RAID), *Zambia, Deregulation and the Denial of Human Rights: Submission to the Committee on Economic, Social and Cultural Rights* (Oxford, 2000)

Roberts, Andrew, 'Nyamwezi Trade', in Richard Gray and David Birmingham (eds), *Pre-colonial African Trade: Essays on Trade in Central and Eastern Africa before 1900* (London: Oxford University Press, 1970), pp. 47–50

Robinson, Jennifer, *Ordinary Cities: Between Modernity and Development* (London: Routledge, 2006)

Rocher, Guy, 'Redéfinition du Rôle de l'Université', in Fernand Dumont and Yves Martin, *L'éducation 25 ans plus tard! Et après?* (Québec: Quebec Research Institute, 1990), pp. 181–98

Rostow, Walt W., *The Stages of Economic Growth: A Non-Communist Manifesto* (Cambridge: Cambridge University Press, 1960)

Rotberg, Robert I., 'Plymouth Brethren and the Occupation of Katanga, 1886–1907', *Journal of African History*, 5, 2 (1964), pp. 285–97

Rotberg, Robert I., *Christian Missionaries and the Creation of Northern Rhodesia 1880–1924* (Princeton: Princeton University Press, 1965)

Rubango, Nyunda ya, 'De Lovanium à la Kasapa caserne: mémoires d'un pèlerin métis' in Isidore Ndaywel è Nziem (ed.), *L'Université dans le devenir de l'Afrique: Un demi-siècle de présence au Congo-Zaïre* (Paris: L'Harmattan, 2007), pp. 97–124

Rubbers, Benjamin, *Faire fortune en Afrique: Anthropologie des derniers colons du Katanga* (Paris: Karthala, 2013)

Rubbers, Benjamin, *Le paternalisme en question: Les anciens ouvriers de la Gécamines face à la libéralisation du secteur minier katangais (RD Congo)* (Tervuren: Musée royal de l'Afrique centrale / Paris: L'Harmattan, 2013)

Rubbers, Benjamin, 'Mining Towns, Enclaves and Spaces: A Genealogy of Worker Camps in the Congolese Copperbelt', *Geoforum*, 98 (2019), pp. 88–96

Rubbers, Benjamin, 'Towards a Life of Poverty and Uncertainty? The Livelihood Strategies of Gécamines Workers after Retrenchment in the DRC', *Review of African Political Economy*, 44, 152 (2017), pp. 189–203

Rubbers, Benjamin, 'When Women Support the Patriarchal Family: The Dynamics of Marriage in a Gécamines Mining Camp (Katanga Province, DR Congo)', *Journal of Historical Sociology*, 28, 2 (2015), pp. 213–34

Rubbers, Benjamin, and Marc Poncelet, 'Sociologie coloniale au Congo belge: Les études sur le Katanga industriel et urbain à la veille de l'Indépendance', *Genèses*, 2, 99 (2015), pp. 93–112

Ryckbost, Jean, *Essai Sur les Origines et le Développement des Premières Associations Professionnelles Au Congo* (Léopoldville: Universiteum Lovanium, 1962)

Saasa, Oliver S., *Zambian Policies towards Foreign Investment: The Case of the Mining and Non-Mining Sectors* (Uppsala: Nordiska Afrikainstitutet, 1987)

Sacré, Patrick, *Historiek van de PMS-Centra: Bijdrage tot de studie van de geschiedenis van de PMS- begeleiding in België* (Brussels: VUB Press, 1993)

Saint, Lily, 'Not Western: Race, Reading, and the South African Photocomic', *Journal of Southern African Studies*, 36, 4 (2010), pp. 939–58

Sambo, Pamela Towela, 'The Environmental Management Act (2011): A Basis for the Growth of an Environmental Ethos and good Environmental Governance in Zambia? in A. Paterson (ed.), *Law, Environment, Africa: Introducing the Imperatives, Parameters and Trends* (Baden: Nomos Verlagsgesellschaft, 2019), pp. 647–64

Sardanis, Andrew, *Africa, Another Side of the Coin: Northern Rhodesia's Final Years and Zambia's Nationhood* (London and New York: I.B. Tauris, 2011)

Särkkä, Timo, 'The Lure of Katanga Copper: Tanganyika Concessions Limited and the Anatomy of Mining and Mine Exploration 1899–1906', *South African Historical Journal*, 68, 3 (2016), pp. 318–41

Schicho, Walter, *Le Groupe Mufwankolo* (Vienna: Afro-Pub, 1981)

Schindler, Seth, and Miguel J. Kanai, 'Getting the Territory Right: Infrastructure-Led Development and the Re-Emergence of Spatial Planning Strategies', *Regional Studies* (2019)

Schlee, Günther, *How Enemies Are Made: Towards a Theory of Ethnic and Religious Conflicts* (New York: Berghahn Books, 2008)

Schumaker, Lyn, 'Slimes and Death-Dealing Dambos: Water, Industry and the Garden City on Zambia's Copperbelt', *Journal of Southern African Studies*, 34, 4 (2008), pp. 823–40

Schumaker, Lyn, 'The Mosquito Taken at the Beerhall: Malaria Research and Control on Zambia's Copperbelt', in Paul W. Geissler and Catherine Molyneux (eds), *Evidence, Ethos and Experiment* (New York: Berghahn Books, 2011), pp. 403–27

Schumaker, Lyn, *Africanizing Anthropology: Fieldwork, Networks, and the Making of Cultural Knowledge in Central Africa* (Durham NC: Duke University Press, 2001)

Schwanen, Tim, 'Geographies of Transport I: Reinventing a Field?' *Progress in Human Geography*, 40, 1 (2016), pp. 126–37

Shaw, Mabel, *God's Candlelights: An Educational Venture in Northern Rhodesia* (London: Edinburgh University Press, 1932)

Shaw, Timothy M., 'Zambia: Dependence and Underdevelopment', *Canadian Journal of African Studies*, 10, 1 (1976), pp. 3–22

Siegel, Brian, 'Bomas, Missions, and Mines: The Making of Centers on the Zambian Copperbelt', *African Studies Review*, 31, 3 (1988), pp. 61–84

Siegel, Brian, 'The "Wild" and "Lazy" Lamba: Ethnic Stereotypes on the Central African Copperbelt', *Anthropology Publications*, Paper 5 (1989), pp. 1–16

Simpson, Michael, 'The Annihilation of Time by Space: Pluri-Temporal Strategies of Capitalist Circulation', *Environment and Planning E: Nature and Space*, 2, 1 (2019), pp. 110–28

Simutanyi, Neo, 'The Politics of Structural Adjustment in Zambia', *Third World Quarterly*, 17, 4 (1996), pp. 825–39

Singaravélou, Pierre, 'De la psychologie coloniale à la géographie psychologique: Itinéraire, entre science et littérature, d'une discipline éphémère dans l'entre-deux-guerres', *L'Homme et la société*, 167/168/169 (2008), pp. 119–48

Singaravélou, Pierre, 'Les stratégies d'internationalisation de la question coloniale et la construction transnationale d'une science de la colonisation à la fin du XIXe siècle', *Monde(s)*, 1, 1 (2012), pp. 135–57

Sinha, Durganand, 'Psychology and the Problems of Developing Countries: A General Overview', *International Review of Applied Psychology*, 22, 1 (1973), pp. 5–26

Sinkamba, Peter, 'Technical and Financial Proposal for Sustainability of the Copperbelt Environment Project in Zambia', MPhil Dissertation, University of Stellenbosch, 2007

Sitko, Nicholas J., and T. S. Jayne, 'Structural Transformation or Elite Land Capture? The Growth of "Emergent" Farmers in Zambia', *Food Policy*, 48 (2014), pp. 194–202

Sklar, Richard L., *Corporate Power in an African State: The Political Impact of Multinational Mining Companies in Zambia* (Berkeley: University of California Press, 1975)

Slinn, Peter, 'Commercial Concessions and Politics during the Colonial Period: The Role of the British South Africa Company in Northern Rhodesia 1890–1964', *African Affairs*, 70, 281 (1971), pp. 365–84

Solol, N'Dua, 'Histoire ancienne des populations Luba et Lunda du Plateau de Haut-Lubilashi: des origines au début du XXe siècle (Bena Nsamba, Inimpinim et Tuwidi)', PhD Thesis, UNAZA, 1978

Spittler, Gerd, 'L'Anthropologie du Travail en Afrique: Traditions allemandes et françaises', in Hélène D'Almeida Topor, Monique Lakroum and Gerd Spittler (eds*), Le travail en Afrique Noire: Représentations et pratiques à l'époque contemporaine* (Paris: Karthala, 2003), pp. 17–42

Spitulnik, Debra, 'The Language of the City: Town Bemba as Urban Hybridity', *Journal of Linguistic Anthropology*, 8, 1 (1999), pp. 42–45

Spring, C. J., *African Arms and Armour* (London: British Museum Press, 1993)

Stacey, P., 'Missionaries in the Congo: The first 120 Years', in P. Poddar, R. S. Patke and L. Jensen (eds), *A Historical Companion to Postcolonial Literatures: Continental Europe and its Empires* (Edinburgh: Edinburgh University Press, 2011), pp. 39–41

Stanard, Matthew, 'Revisiting Bula Matari and the Congo Crisis: Successes and Anxieties in Belgium's Late Colonial State', *Journal of Imperial and Commonwealth History*, 46, 1 (2018), pp. 144–68

Star, Susan L., and Karen Ruhleder, 'Steps Toward an Ecology of Infrastructure: Design and Access for Large Information Spaces', *Information Systems Research*, 7, 1 (1996), pp. 111–34

Stenmanns, Julian, 'Logistics from the Margins', *Environment and Planning D: Society and Space*, 37, 5 (2019), pp. 850–67

Stoler, Ann Laura, *Duress: Imperial Durabilities in our Times* (Durham NC: Duke University Press, 2016)

Stoler, Ann Laura, 'Introduction, "The Rot Remains": From Ruins to Ruination', in A. L. Stoler (ed.), *Imperial Debris: On Ruins and Ruination* (Durham NC: Duke University Press, 2013), pp. 1–35

Stoler, Ann Laura, and Carole McGranahan, 'Introduction: Refiguring Imperial Terrains', in A. L. Stoler, C. McGranahan and P. C. Perdue (eds), *Imperial Formations* (Oxford: School for Advanced Research Press, 2007), pp. 3–42

Stone, J. C., 'Some Reflections on the History of Administrative Division in Northwest Zambia', in David S. Johnson (ed.), *North-Western Province*, Regional Handbook Series No. 8 (Lusaka: Zambia Geographical Association, 1980), pp. 67–72

Stuchtey, Benedikt, *Science Across the European Empires 1800–1950* (London: German Historical Institute, 2005)

Tambwe, Nyumbaiza, Kasongo Nkulu, Kitaba Kya Ghoanys, Kunkuzya Mwanachilongwe, Kaimbi Mpyana and Kayiba Bukasa (eds), *Le Développement du Katanga Méridional* (Paris: L'Harmattan, 2015)

Taylor, J. V. and D. A. Lehmann, *Christians of the Copperbelt: The Growth of the Church in Northern Rhodesia* (London: SCM Press, 1961)

Tilley, Helen, *Africa as a Living Laboratory* (Chicago: Chicago University Press, 2011)

Torrealday, H. I., 'Mineralization and Alteration of the Kansanshi Copper Deposit – Zambia', Master's Thesis, University of Colorado, 2000

Tshimanga, Charles, *Jeunesse, Formation et Société au Congo/Kinshasa, 1890–1960* (Paris: L'Harmattan, 2001)

Tshund'Olela Epanya, Tshund'Olela Epanya Shamololo, Belepe Bope Mabinch, Muteba Kabemba Nsuya, Tsimba Mabiala, et al, *Histoire du Zaïre* (Lubumbashi: UNAZA-CERDAC, 1981)

UNESCO (eds), *Histoire générale de l'Afrique* (Paris, various years)

Van Audenhove, Leo, *Development Co-operation in Higher Education: A Strategic Review of International Donor Policy and Practices* (Brussels: Belgian Administration for Development Co-operation, 1999)

van Beusekom, Monica, and Dorothy Hodgson, 'Lessons Learned? Development Experiences in the Late Colonial Period', *Journal of African History*, 41, 1 (2000), pp. 29–33

van Klinken, A., 'Pentecostalism, Political Masculinity and Citizenship', *Journal of Religion in Africa*, 46, 2–3 (2016), pp. 129–57

van Zyl-Hermann, Danelle, and Jacob Boersma, 'Introduction: The Politics of Whiteness in Africa', *Africa*, 87, 4 (2017), pp. 651–61

Vannes, J., 'De l'évolution de la coutume d'Elisabethville', *Bulletin du Centre d'Etude des Problèmes Sociaux Indigènes*, 32 (1956), pp. 223–68

Vansina, Jan, *De la tradition orale: Essai de méthode historique* (Tervuren: MRAC, 1961)

Vansina, Jan, *Oral Tradition as History* (Madison: University of Wisconsin Press, 1985)

Vanthemsche, Guy, *Belgium and the Congo, 1885–1980* (Cambridge: Cambridge University Press, 2012)

Vasseur, E., 'United Nations Conference on the Human Environment: Stockholm, 5–16 June 1972', *Water Research*, 7, 8 (1973), pp. 1227–33

Vaughan, Megan, *Curing Their Ills: Colonial Power and African Illness* (Stanford: Stanford University Press, 1991)

Vaughan, Megan, '"Divine Kings": Sex, Death and Anthropology in Inter-War East/Central Africa', *Journal of African History*, 49, 3 (2008), pp. 383–401

Vaughan, Megan, 'Introduction', in Sloan Mahone and Megan Vaughan (eds), *Psychiatry and Empire* (New York: Palgrave Macmillan, 2007), pp. 1–16

Vekemans, Charlotte, and Yves Segers, 'Settler Farming, Agriculture and Development in Katanga (Belgian Congo), 1910–1920', *Historia Agraria*, 81 (2020), pp. 195–226

Vellut, Jean-Luc, *Guide de l'étudiant en histoire du Zaïre* (Kinshasa-Lubumbashi: Presses universitaires du Zaïre, 1974)

Vellut, Jean-Luc, 'La communauté portugaise du Congo belge (1885–1940)', in John Everaert and Eddy Stols (eds), *Flandre et Portugal: Au confluent de deux cultures* (Anvers: Fonds Mercator, 1991), pp. 315–45

Vellut, Jean-Luc, 'Les bassins miniers de l'ancien Congo belge: Essai d'histoire économique et sociale (1900–1960)', *Les Cahiers du CEDAF*, 7 (1981), pp. 1–70

Vellut, Jean-Luc, 'Mining in the Belgian Congo', in D. Birmingham and P. M. Martin (eds), *History of Central Africa* vol. II (London: Longman, 1983), pp. 126–62

Verbeek, Léon, 'Histoire et littérature orale', *Cahiers de littérature orale*, 45 (1999).

Verbeek, Roger, *Le Congo en question* (Paris: Présence Africaine, 1965)

Verhaegen, Paul, 'Contribution à l'étude de la psychologie de l'enfant africain', in BICE (ed.), *L'enfant africain: L'éducation de l'enfant africain en fonction de son milieu de base et de son orientation d'avenir* (Paris: Editions Fleurus, 1960), pp. 107–32

Vermeersch, Arthur, 'Les sentiments supérieurs chez les Congolais', in Maurice Amuri Mpala-Lutebele and Jean-Claude Kangomba (eds), *Stefano Kaoze: Œuvre complète* (Bruxelles: Archives et Musée de la littérature (MEO), 2018), pp. 47–51

Vinckel, Sandrine, 'La violence et le silence: Politiques de réconciliation, relations interpersonnelles et pratiques sociales de coexistence au Katanga, RDC', PhD Thesis, Université Paris I, 2016

wa Tshibangu, Tshimanga, *Histoire du Zaïre* (Bukavu: Editions du CERUKI, 1976)

Walker-Said, Charlotte, 'Science and Charity: Rival Catholic Visions for Humanitarian Practice at the End of Empire', *French Politics, Culture and Society*, 33, 2 (2015), pp. 33–54

Watson, Malcolm, *African Highway: The Battle for Health in Central Africa* (London: John Murray, 1953)

Wele, Patrick, *Kaunda and Mushala Rebellion: The Untold Story* (Lusaka: Multimedia, 1987)

Wilkin, Paul David, *To the Bottom of the Heap: Educational Deprivation and Its Social Implications in the Northwestern Province of Zambia, 1906–1945* (New York, 2016)

Willoughby-Herard, Tiffany, 'South Africa's Poor Whites and Whiteness Studies: Afrikaner Ethnicity, Scientific Racism, and White Misery', *New Political Science* 29, 4 (2007), pp. 479–500

Wilson, Anne, 'Long Distance Trade and the Luba Lomami Empire', *Journal of African History*, 13, 4 (1972), pp. 575–89

Wober, Mallory, 'Some Areas for the Application of Psychological Research in East Africa', *International Review of Applied Psychology*, 22, 1 (1973), pp. 41–52

Wober, Mallory, *Psychology in Africa* (London: International African Institute, 1975)

Wooldridge, Adrian, *Measuring the Mind: Education and Psychology in England 1880–1990* (Cambridge: Cambridge University Press, 1994)

Young, Crawford and Thomas Turner, *The Rise and Decline of the Zairian State* (Madison: University of Wisconsin Press, 1985)

Young, Crawford, *Politics in Congo: Decolonization and Independence* (Princeton: Princeton University Press, 1965)

Yuval-Davis, N., 'Gender and Nation', *Ethnic and Racial Studies*, 16, 4 (1993), pp. 621–32

Zana Aziza Etambala, Matthieu, 'Kaoze, le "protégé" du roi Albert I: Formation, ordination et voyage en Europe', *Annales Aequatoria*, 28 (2007), pp. 375–414

Index

Printed and bound by CPI Group (UK) Ltd, Croydon, CR0 4YY

09/06/2025